Body Sensor Networks

Guang-Zhong Yang (Ed.)

Body Sensor Networks

Foreword by Sir Magdi Yacoub

With 274 Figures, 32 in Full Color

 Springer

Guang-Zhong Yang, PhD
Institute of Biomedical Engineering and Department of Computing,
Imperial College London, UK

British Library Cataloguing in Publication Data
A catalogue record for this book is available from the British Library

Library of Congress Control Number: 2005938358

ISBN-10: 1-84628-272-1
ISBN-13: 978-1-84628-272-0

Printed on acid-free paper

Printed in the United States of America   (MVY)

9 8 7 6 5 4 3 2 1

Springer Science+Business Media
springer.com

Foreword

Advances in science and medicine are closely linked; they are characterised by episodic imaginative leaps, often with dramatic effects on mankind and beyond. The advent of body sensor networks represents such a leap. The reason for this stems from the fact that all branches of modern medicine, ranging from prevention to complex intervention, rely heavily on early, accurate, and complete diagnosis followed by close monitoring of the results. To date, attempts at doing this consisted of intermittent contact with the individual concerned, producing a series of snapshots at personal, biochemical, mechanical, cellular, or molecular levels. This was followed by making a series of assumptions which inevitably resulted in a distortion of the real picture.

Although the human genome project has shown that we are all "equal", it confirmed the fact that each one of us has unique features at many levels, some of which include our susceptibility to disease and a particular response to many external stimuli, medicines, or procedures. This has resulted in the concept of personalised medicines or procedures promised to revolutionise our approach to healthcare. To achieve this, we need accurate individualised information obtained at many levels in a continuous fashion. This needs to be accomplished in a sensitive, respectful, non-invasive manner which does not interfere with human dignity or quality of life, and more importantly it must be affordable and cost-effective.

This book about body sensor networks represents an important step towards achieving these goals, and apart from its great promise to the community, it will stimulate much needed understanding of, and research into, biological functions through collaborative efforts between clinicians, epidemiologists, engineers, chemists, molecular biologists, mathematicians, health economists, and others. It starts with an introduction by the editor, providing a succinct overview of the history of body sensor networks and their utility, and sets the scene for the following chapters which are written by experts in the field dealing with every aspect of the topic from design to human interaction. It ends with a chapter on the future outlook of this rapidly expanding field and highlights the potential opportunities and challenges.

This volume should act as a valuable resource to a very wide spectrum of readers interested in, or inspired by, this multifaceted and exciting topic.

Professor Sir Magdi Yacoub
November 2005
London

Acknowledgments

I would like to express my sincere thanks to all contributing authors to this volume. Without their enthusiasm, support, and flexibility in managing the tight publishing schedule, this book would not have become possible.

I am grateful to members of the pervasive computing team of the Department of Computing, and the Institute of Biomedical Engineering of Imperial College London for all their help throughout the preparation of this book. In particular, I would like to thank Su-Lin Lee, Benny Lo, Surapa Thiemjarus, and Fani Deligianni for all their hard work in providing essential editorial support, as well as being actively involved in the preparation of some of the chapters. My special thanks go to James Kinross and Robert Merrifield for their kind help with the graphical illustrations.

I would also like to thank the editorial staff of Springer, the publisher of this volume. In particular, I am grateful to Helen Callaghan and her colleagues in helping with the editorial matters.

This work would not have been possible without the financial support from the following funding bodies:

- The Department of Trade and Industry, UK
- The Engineering and Physical Sciences Research Council, UK
- The Royal Society
- The Wolfson Foundation

Their generous support has allowed us to establish and promote this exciting field of research – a topic that is so diversified, and yet brings so many challenges and innovations to each of the disciplines involved.

Guang-Zhong Yang
November 2005
London

About the Editor

Guang-Zhong Yang, BSc, PhD, FIEE
Chair in Medical Image Computing, Imperial College London, UK

Guang-Zhong Yang received PhD in Computer Science from Imperial College London and served as a senior and then principal scientist of the Cardiovascular Magnetic Resonance Unit of the Royal Brompton Hospital prior to assuming his current full-time academic post at the Department of Computing, Imperial College London. The department was rated 5* at the last RAE (research quality assessment) and has been placed among the top ten departments worldwide by several academic surveys. Professor Yang's main research interests are focussed on medical imaging, sensing, and robotics. He received a number of major international awards including the I.I. Rabi Award from the International Society for Magnetic Resonance in Medicine (ISMRM) and the Research Merit Award from the Royal Society. He is a Fellow of the IEE, Founding Director of the Royal Society/Wolfson Medical Image Computing Laboratory at Imperial College, co-founder of the Wolfson Surgical Technology Laboratory, Chairman of the Imperial College Imaging Sciences Centre, and Director of Medical Imaging, the Institute of Biomedical Engineering, Imperial College London.

Contents

Contributors

Imperial College London, UK

Costas A. Anastassiou
Omer Aziz
Tony Cass
Timothy G. Constandinou
Sir Ara Darzi
Xiaopeng Hu
Benny Lo
Paul Mitcheson
Danny O'Hare
Bhavik A. Patel
Anna Radomska
Leila Shepherd
Suket Singhal
Surapa Thiemjarus
Chris Toumazou
Guang-Zhong Yang
Eric Yeatman

Philips Research, Aachen, Germany

Javier Espina
Thomas Falck
Oliver Mülhens

University of Glasgow, UK

Jonathan M. Cooper
David R. S. Cumming
Paul A. Hammond
Erik A. Johannessen
Lei Wang

Zarlink Semiconductor, UK

Henry Higgins

List of Acronyms

AAA	Abdominal Aortic Aneurysm
ABM	Analogue Behavioural Modelling
ACL	Asynchronous Connectionless Link
ACLK	Auxiliary Clock
ADA	Active Digital Aura
ADC	Analogue-to-Digital Converter
AES	Advanced Encryption Standard
AF	Application Framework
AIROF	Anodic Iridium Oxide Film
AIS	Artificial Immune System
AM	Active Mode
ANN	Artificial Neural Network
ANS	Autonomic Nervous System
APL	Application Layer
APS	Application Support Sub-Layer
ASIC	Application Specific Integrated Circuit
ATP	Adenosine Triphosphate
AUC	Area Under the ROC Curve
BFFS	Bayesian Framework for Feature Selection
BIS	Biological Immune System
BP	British Petroleum
BPSK	Binary Phase Shift Keying
BSL	Boot Strap Loader
BSN	Body Sensor Network
BSS	Blind Source Separation
BV	Butler-Volmer
CAP	Contention Access Period
CAT	Computed Axial Tomography
CBC-MAC	Cipher Block Chaining Message Authentication Code
CCA	Clear Channel Assessment
CCM	Counter with CBC-MAC
CCP	Cytochrome C Peroxidase
CDRG	Coulomb-Damped Resonant Generator
CEN	European Committee for Standardisation

CEPT	European Conference of Postal and Telecommunications Administrations
CF	Compact Flash
CFP	Contention-Free Period
CFPG	Coulomb-Force Parametric-Generator
ChemFET	Chemically-Sensitive Field-Effect Transistor
CMDS	Classical Multidimensional Scaling
CMOS	Complementary Metal Oxide Semiconductor
COTS	Commercial Off-The-Shelf
CPU	Central Processing Unit
CSMA/CA	Carrier Sense Multiple Access/Collision Avoidance
CSS	Chirp Spread Spectrum
CTR	Counter Mode Encryption
DAA	Detect And Avoid
DAC	Digital-to-Analogue Converter
DAG	Directed Acyclic Graph
DARPA	Defence Advanced Research Projects Agency
DCS	Dynamic Channel Selection
DECT	Digital Enhanced Cordless Telephony
DNA	Deoxyribonucleic Acid
DRC	Design Rule Checking
DRIE	Deep Reactive Ion Etching
DSP	Digital Signal Processor
DSSS	Direct Sequence Spread Spectrum
DUMMBO	Dynamic Ubiquitous Mobile Meeting Board
DVM	Digital Volt Meter
DWT	Discrete Wavelet Transform
ECC	Electronic Communications Committee
ECG	Electrocardiogram
ED	Energy Detection
EEG	Electroencephalogram
EEPROM	Electrically Erasable Programmable Read Only Memory
EIRP	Effective Isotropic Radiated Power
EM	Expectation Maximisation
EMC	Electromagnetic Compatibility
EMG	Electromyogram
EMI	Electromagnetic Interference
EnFET	Enzyme Field-Effect Transistor
ERC	European Radiocommunications Committee (ERC, now ECC)

ERO	European Radiocommunications Office
ERP	Effective Radiated Power
FCC	Federal Communication Commission
FCF	Frame Control Field
FCM	Fuzzy c-Means
FCS	Frame Check Sequence
FEP	Fluorinated Ethylene Plastic
FET	Field-Effect Transistor
FFD	Full Function Device
FFT	Fast Fourier Transform
FG	Factor Graph
FH	Frequency Hopping
FHSS	Frequency Hopping Spread Spectrum
FIFO	First-In, First-Out
FIR	Finite Impulse Response
FP	Fisher Projection
FPGA	Field-Programmable Gate Array
FSCV	Fast Scan Cyclic Voltammetry
FSK	Frequency-Shift Keying
FSM	Finite State Machine
GasFET	Gas-Sensitive Field-Effect Transistor
GDB	GNU Debugger
GDSII	Graphic Design Station II (file format)
GERD	Gastro-Oesophageal Reflux Disease
GH-SOM	Growing Hierarchical Self-Organising Map
GI	Gastrointestinal
GND	Ground
GOD	Glucose Oxidase
GPRS	General Packet Radio Service
GPS	Global Positioning System
GSR	Galvanic Skin Response
GTM	Generative Topographic Mapping
GTS	Guaranteed Time Slot
GUI	Graphical User Interface
HAL	Hardware Adaptation Layer
HCI	Host Controller Interface
HDL	Hardware Description Language
HEC	Hydroxyl Ethyl Cellulose
HIL	Hardware Interface Layer

HL7	Health Level Seven
HMM	Hidden Markov Model
HOMO	Highest Occupied Molecular Orbital
HPL	Hardware Presentation Layer
HT	Hilbert Transform
HUVEC	Human-Umbilical Vein Endothelial Cells

I^2C	Inter Integrated Circuit Bus
IBD	Inflammatory Bowel Disease
IBM	International Business Machine Corporation
ICA	Independent Components Analysis
ICD	Implantable Cardioverter-Defibrillator
ID	Identity
IEEE	Institute of Electrical and Electronics Engineers
IGBT	Insulated Gate Bipolar Transistor
IIR	Infinite Impulse Response
I/O	Input/Output
IR	Infrared
ISE	Ion Selective Electrode
ISFET	Ion-Sensitive Field-Effect Transistor
ISM	Industrial, Scientific, and Medical
ISO	International Standards Organization
ISODATA	Iterative Self-Organising Data Analysis
Isomap	Isometric Mapping
ITO	Indium-Doped Tin Oxide

JDL	Joint Directors of Laboratories
JFET	Junction Field Effect Transistor
JPD	Joint Probability Distribution
JTAG	Joint Test Action Group

KCL	Kirchoff's Current Law
ksps	kilo-samples per second
KVP	Key Value Pair

L2CAP	Logical Link Control and Adaptation Protocol
LALI	Local Activation Long-range Inhibition
LAN	Local Area Network
LEACH	Low-Energy Adaptive Clustering Hierarchy
LED	Light-Emitting Diode
LLE	Local Linear Embedding
LMP	Link Manager Protocol

L-NAME	N^G-Nitro-L-Arginine-Methyl Ester
L-NNA	L-N^W-Nitro-Arginine
LOD	Limit of Detection
LPM	Low-Power Mode
LPU	Local Processing Unit
LQI	Link Quality Indication
LSB	Least Significant Bit
LUMO	Lowest Unoccupied Molecular Orbital
LVS	Layout Versus Schematic
MAC	Medium Access Control
MBOA-SIG	Multiband-OFDM Alliance SIG
MCLK	Master Clock
MCMC	Markov Chain Monte Carlo
MCPS	MAC Common Part Sublayer
MCU	Microcontroller Unit
MDS	Multi-Dimensional Scaling
MEG	Magnetoencephalography
MEMS	Micro Electro-Mechanical System
MetHb	Methaemoglobin
MFR	MAC Footer
MHR	MAC Header
MIB	Medical Information Bus
MIC	Message Integrity Code
MICS	Medical Implant Communications Service
MIPS	Million Instructions Per Second
MISO	Master In, Slave Out
MLME	MAC sub-Layer Management Entity
MMO	Metal Metal Oxide
MORE	Micro-Optical Ring Electrode
MOS	Multithreaded Operating System
MOSFET	Metal Oxide Semiconductor Field-Effect Transistor
MOSI	Master Out, Slave In
MPDU	MAC Protocol Data Unit
MPE	Most Probable Explanation
MRF	Markov Random Field
MRI	Magnetic Resonance Imaging
MSB	Most Significant Bit
MSBN	Multiply Sectioned Bayesian Networks
MSG	Message

MTT	MOS-Triggered Thyristor
NASA	National Aeronautics and Space Administration
NLP	Natural Language Processing
NWK	Network Layer
OFDM	Orthogonal Frequency Division Multiplex
O-QPSK	Offset-Quadrature Phase Shift Keying
OS	Operating System
OSI	Open Systems Interconnection
Palos	Power Aware Lightweight OS
PAN	Personal Area Network
PBP	Periplasmic Binding Protein
PC	Personal Computing
PCA	Principal Components Analysis
PCB	Printed Circuit Board
PCMCIA	Personal Computer Memory Card International Association
PDA	Personal Digital Assistant
PECVD	Plasma Enhanced Chemical Vapour Deposition
PER	Packet Error Rate
PET	Positron Emission Tomography
PHR	PHY Header
PHY	Physical Layer
PID	Proportional Integral Derivative
PIF	Planar Inverted F
PNC	PicoNet Controller
PPDU	PHY Protocol Data Unit
ppm	parts per million
PSDU	PHY Service Data Unit
PT	Project Team
PTFE	Polytetrafluorethylene (Teflon)
PTIO	2-Phenyl-4,4,55,Tetramethyl-Imidazoline-1-Oxyl 3-oxide
PVC	Polyvinyl Chloride
PZT	Lead Zirconate Titanate ($PbZr_xTi_{(1-x)}O_3$)
QCM	Quartz Crystal Microbalance
QoS	Quality of Service
RAM	Random Access Memory
RF	Radio Frequency

RFD	Reduced Function Device
RFID	Radio Frequency Identification
RISC	Reduced Instruction Set Computer
ROC	Receiver Operating Characteristic
ROM	Read Only Memory
RSSI	Received Signal Strength Indicator
RTL	Register Transfer Level
RX	Receive
SAP	Service Access Point
SAR	Specific Absorption Rate
SAW	Surface Acoustic Wave
SBS	Sequential Backward Search
SCL	Signal Wire for Clock
SCLK	Serial Clock
SCO	Synchronous Connection-Oriented link
SDA	Signal Wire for Data
SDL	Specification and Description Language
SDP	Service Discovery Protocol
SFD	Start of Frame Delimiter
SFFS	Sequential Floating Forward Search
SFS	Sequential Forward Search
SHE	Standard Hydrogen Electrode
SIMO	Slave In, Master Out
SHR	Synchronisation Header
SMCLK	Sub-Main Clock
SNEP	Secure Network Encryption Protocol
SNR	Signal-to-Noise Ratio
SoC	System on Chip processor
SoI	Silicon-on-Insulator
SOM	Self-Organising Map
SOMI	Slave Out, Master In
SPI	Serial Peripheral Interface
SPINS	Security Protocols for Sensor Networks
SpO_2	Blood Oxygen Saturation
SPR	Surface Plasmon Resonance
SRAM	Static Random Access Memory
SRD	Short-Range Device
SRF	Self-Resonant Frequency
STE	Slave Transmit Enable
STSOM	Spatio-Temporal Self-Organising Map

SVM	Support Vector Machine
TC	Technical Committee
TCM	Trellis-Coded Modulation
TCNQ	Tetracyanoquinodimethane
TCP	Transmission Control Protocol
TDD	Time Division Duplex
TDMA	Time Division Multiple Access
TEDS	Transducer Electronic Data Sheets
TESLA	Timed, Efficient, Streaming, Loss-tolerant Authentication Protocol
TI	Texas Instruments
TOSSIM	TinyOS Simulator
TTF	Tetrathiafulvalene
TTL	Transistor-Transistor Logic
TX	Transmit
UART	Universal Asynchronous Receiver/Transmitter
UC	University of California
UCLA	University of California, Los Angeles
UHF	Ultra High Frequency
UMTS	Universal Mobile Telecommunication System
URXD	Receive Pin
USART	Universal Synchronous/Asynchronous Receive/Transmit
USB	Universal Serial Bus
USPIO	Ultra-Small Particles of Iron Oxide
UTXD	Transmit Pin
UV	Ultraviolet
UWB	Ultra Wideband
VDRG	Velocity-Damped Resonant Generator
VHF	Very High Frequency
VITAL	Vital Signs Information Representation
VLSI	Very Large-Scale Integration
WiFi	Wireless Fidelity
WLAN	Wireless Local Area Network
WMTS	Wireless Medical Telemetry Service
WPAN	Wireless Personal Area Network
WSN	Wireless Sensor Network
ZDO	ZigBee Device Object

1

Introduction

Omer Aziz, Benny Lo, Ara Darzi, and Guang-Zhong Yang

1.1 Wireless Sensor Networks

Over the past decade, the miniaturisation and cost reduction brought about by the semiconductor industry have made it possible to create computers that are smaller in size than a pin head, powerful enough to carry out the processing required, and affordable enough to be considered disposable. It is thought that this reduction in size and increase in processing capability is likely to continue over the next two decades, with computers becoming even smaller and cheaper year by year [1]. Similarly, advances in wireless communication, sensor design, and energy storage technologies have meant that the concept of a truly pervasive *Wireless Sensor Network* (WSN) is rapidly becoming a reality [2]. Integrated microsensors no more than a few millimetres in size, with onboard processing and wireless data transfer capability are the basic components of such networks already in existence [3, 4]. Thus far, a range of applications have been proposed for the use of WSNs and they are likely to change every aspect of our daily lives.

One of the first applications developed to utilise large-scale pervasive wireless sensor networks was "Smart Dust." This was developed at the *University of California* (UC) at Berkeley and funded by the *Defence Advanced Research Projects Agency* (DARPA). The aim of the project was to produce a self-contained, millimetre-scale sensing and communication platform for massively distributed sensor networks [4]. Primarily meant as a military application, the "Smart Dust" concept involved the use of thousands of tiny wireless sensor "motes" that could be spread over a large battlefield area, allowing enemy movements to be monitored in a covert manner.

In the early stages of the project, the team gained experience by building relatively large motes using *Commercial Off-The-Shelf* (COTS) components. With cooperation from Intel, these motes were created as an open-source hardware and software platform, combining sensors, low power wireless communication, and processing into a single architecture. The motes were also designed to have the ability to "self-organise" (resulting in a self-configuring WSN), and carry out onboard signal processing and distributed inferencing tasks prior to sending relevant information to a central control. Whilst tiny, ubiquitous, low-cost, *Smart Dust* motes have not yet been realised, many reasonably small motes are commercially available. Existing designs have already integrated a range of sensors monitoring a variety of environmental factors including temperature, humidity, barometric pressure, light intensity, tilt and vibration, and magnetic field with short-distance wireless communication.

In addition to its military application, *Smart Dust* may eventually be used in a number of different settings ranging from deploying nodes into the atmosphere for weather condition monitoring, to placing them in environments such as factories to monitor their production output. As an example, Figure 1.1 illustrates two images of optical *Smart Dust* motes currently being developed. It is interesting to note that researchers have also approached *Smart Dust* from a biotechnology perspective to produce motes from chemical compounds rather than electrical circuitry [5].

One of the key developments for WSNs is the small, open source (freely available) energy-efficient software operating system known as the *Tiny Micro-threading Operating System*, or "TinyOS", which has been developed at UC Berkeley. This operating system provides a basic framework and development environment for WSNs, and it functions well under the constraints of power, size, and cost. TinyOS software runs both the hardware and network, making sensor measurements, routing decisions, and controlling power dissipation.

Figure 1.1 A proposed solar-powered mote (left) and its magnified structural field-of-view (right) (*courtesy of Professor K. Pister, University of California at Berkeley*).

Currently, the new applications emerging for WSNs can be categorised into three types as follows: those used for monitoring environments (indoor, outdoor, urban or countryside), monitoring objects (such as machines and buildings) and monitoring the interaction of these objects with environments [6]. For example, companies such as *British Petroleum* (BP) have picked up on the huge potential offered by WSN technology and have recently embarked on a program to develop its large-scale use. One example of this is the setting up of an experimental WSN for monitoring their refinery equipment, in order to measure abnormal vibration and thereby to alert engineers to a potentially malfunctioning piece of equipment before it actually breaks down. BP also aims to use a long-distance WSN to remotely monitor customers' liqueficd pctroleum gas tank fill levels. They intend to use ultrasonic sensors placed at the base of the tanks to detect the fill level, which is then transmitted via a low earth orbit satellite to a control station [2]. As a result, their customers may be alerted to the need to refill their tanks before the fuel actually runs out. Achieving this level of sensor coverage with wired sensors would otherwise be more than simply expensive and difficult to set up, but also almost impossible to maintain.

Another example of proposed WSN use is the "Zebranet" project based at Princeton University. This aims to set up an *ad hoc* WSN with the bandwidth and computational capabilities required to monitor the long-range migration, interspecies interactions, and nocturnal behaviour of zebras in Africa [7]. In this case, it is difficult to imagine how this could be achieved without a WSN.

Whilst WSN technology continues to evolve for the broad range of applications and settings described above, it does not specifically tackle the challenges associated with human body monitoring. The human body consists of a complicated internal environment that responds to and interacts with its external surroundings, but is in a way "separate" and "self contained". Human body monitoring using a network of wireless sensors may be achieved by attaching these sensors to the body surface as well as implanting them into tissues. In essence, the human body environment is not only on a smaller scale, but also requires a different type and frequency of monitoring, with appreciation of different challenges than those faced by WSN. The realisation that proprietary designed WSNs are not ideally suited to monitoring the human body and its internal environment has led to the development of a wireless *Body Sensor Network* (BSN) platform.

Specifically designed for the wireless networking of implantable and wearable body sensors, the BSN architecture aims to set a standard for the development of a common approach towards pervasive monitoring. Figure 1.2 is a diagram illustrating a simplified examplc of such an architecture. It represents a patient with a number of sensors attached to their body, each sensor also being connected to a small processor, wireless transmitter, and battery, and all together forming a "BSN node complex" capable of seamlessly integrating with home, office, and hospital environments. The BSN node ensures the accurate capture of data from the sensor to which it is connected, carries out low level processing of the data, and then wirelessly transmits this information to a *Local Processing Unit* (LPU). The data from all the sensors is in this way collected by the LPU, processed further, and fused before being wirelessly transmitted to a central monitoring server either via a wireless LAN, Bluetooth, or mobile phone (GPRS or 3G) network [8].

Although the challenges faced by BSNs are in many ways similar to WSNs, there are intrinsic differences between the two which require special attention. Some of these differences are illustrated in Table 1.1. The purpose of this chapter is to provide an overview of the development and history of wireless BSNs, highlighting not only the challenges lying ahead but also the direction of its future development.

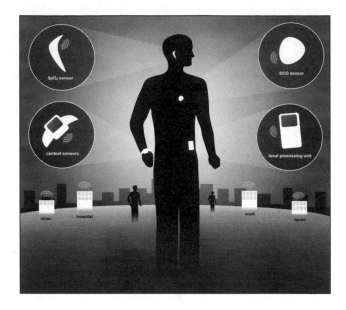

Figure 1.2 Diagrammatic representation of the BSN architecture with wirelessly linked context-aware "on body" (external) sensors and its seamless integration with home, working, and hospital environments. (**See colour insert**.)

1.2 BSN and Healthcare

The observations by Hippocrates, the Greek founder of modern medicine, that audible sounds emanating from the chest were produced by the heart, ultimately led to the development of the stethoscope in 1816. Since then, diagnostic tools have continued to evolve and have revolutionised medical practice, allowing doctors to extract more and more important information about their patients' physiological states. This increased level of sophistication is perfectly illustrated by the stethoscope, which has evolved from a simple tube, into a device has been carefully engineered to accurately relay heart and chest sounds, allowing clinicians to recognise disease processes. The most advanced stethoscopes can also digitally filter and enhance this sound quality. Whilst these diagnostic tools continue to develop, they still offer information that is nothing more than a "snapshot in time". The next great challenge for diagnostic devices lies in their ability to monitor a patient's physical and biochemical parameters continuously, under natural physiological status of the patient, and in any environment. The development of wireless BSNs offers a platform to establish such a health monitoring system, and represents the latest evolution of diagnostic tools. BSN patient monitoring systems will provide information that is likely to be as important, dramatic and revolutionary as those initial observations made by Hippocrates himself.

Table 1.1 Different challenges faced by WSN and BSN.

Challenges	WSN	BSN
Scale	As large as the environment being monitored (metres/kilometres)	As large as human body parts (millimetres/centimetres)
Node Number	Greater number of nodes required for accurate, wide area coverage	Fewer, more accurate sensors nodes required (limited by space)
Node Function	Multiple sensors, each perform dedicated tasks	Single sensors, each perform multiple tasks
Node Accuracy	Large node number compensates for accuracy and allows result validation	Limited node number with each required to be robust and accurate
Node Size	Small size preferable but not a major limitation in many cases	Pervasive monitoring and need for miniaturisation
Dynamics	Exposed to extremes in weather, noise, and asynchrony	Exposed to more predictable environment but motion artefacts is a challenge
Event Detection	Early adverse event detection desirable; failure often reversible	Early adverse events detection vital; human tissue failure irreversible
Variability	Much more likely to have a fixed or static structure	Biological variation and complexity means a more variable structure
Data Protection	Lower level wireless data transfer security required	High level wireless data transfer security required to protect patient information
Power Supply	Accessible and likely to be changed more easily and frequently	Inaccessible and difficult to replace in implantable setting
Power Demand	Likely to be greater as power is more easily supplied	Likely to be lower as energy is more difficult to supply
Energy Scavenging	Solar, and wind power are most likely candidates	Motion (vibration) and thermal (body heat) most likely candidates
Access	Sensors more easily replaceable or even disposable	Implantable sensor replacement difficult and requires biodegradability
Biocompatibility	Not a consideration in most applications	A must for implantable and some external sensors. Likely to increase cost
Context Awareness	Not so important with static sensors where environments are well defined	Very important because body physiology is very sensitive to context change
Wireless Technology	Bluetooth, Zigbee, GPRS, and wireless LAN, and RF already offer solutions	Low power wireless required, with signal detection more challenging
Data Transfer	Loss of data during wireless transfer is likely to be compensated by number of sensors used	Loss of data more significant, and may require additional measures to ensure QoS and real-time data interrogation capabilities

1.2.1 Monitoring Patients with Chronic Disease

The scale of the requirement for patient monitoring in healthcare systems can only be appreciated once the magnitude of human disease processes requiring early diagnosis and treatment is considered. Several examples illustrate this need, but none as dramatically as cardiovascular related illnesses. Abnormalities of heart rhythm (arrhythmias) such as *atrial fibrillation* are commonly encountered in clinical practice, occurring in as many as 4% of the population over the age of 60, increasing with age to almost 9% in octogenarians [9]. Early symptoms of atrial fibrillation include fatigue and palpitations, and often lead to the patient seeking medical advice. *Electrocardiography* (ECG) is eventually performed along with other investigations, and as soon as the diagnosis is made treatment is begun to try and prevent the longer-term complications of tachycardia (rapid heart rate), mediated cardiomyopathy (resulting in heart failure) and stroke.

To prevent stroke, the patient is often placed on anticoagulant (blood thinning) medication placing them at risk of potential bleeding complications from this therapy. All of this results in a two-fold increase in mortality in this elderly patient group, independently of other risk factors [10]. Apart from early detection of this condition using ECG so that prompt treatment can be initiated, regular monitoring is required to ensure control of the heart rate, which results in prevention of much of the associated morbidity and mortality.

BSNs offer the chance to diagnose cardiac arrhythmias earlier than ever in "at risk" groups such as the elderly, as well as the ability to monitor disease progression and patient response to any treatment initiated.

High blood pressure (*hypertension*) is another cardiovascular disease thought to affect approximately 50 million individuals in the United States alone [11]. The diagnosis of this disease is often made in an otherwise asymptomatic patient who has presented to their doctor for other reasons. This condition can, if untreated, result in end-organ failure and significant morbidity; ranging from visual impairment to coronary artery disease, heart failure, and stroke. *Heart failure* in turn affects nearly five million people every year in the United States, and is a contributory factor in approximately 300,000 deaths each year [12]. Early diagnosis of high blood pressure is important for both controlling risk factors such as smoking and high cholesterol, but also for early initiation of antihypertensive treatment. The diagnosis is confirmed using serial blood pressure measurements, and once treatment is commenced this is titrated to the required effect by monitoring the patient's blood pressure over a period of weeks or months. Once a patient has been diagnosed with hypertension, they require regular blood pressure monitoring to ensure adequacy of therapy. Indeed over a patient's life, the pharmacotherapy they receive may be altered many times. One can imagine how labour-intensive blood pressure monitoring in these patients can be, often requiring several visits to clinics. Although home blood pressure testing kits have been made available, the limitations of these devices are their dependence on the operator and patient motivation. Recently, a new category termed "*prehypertension*" has been identified and may lead to even earlier initiation of treatment [13]. BSNs would allow doctors to monitor patients with seemingly high blood pressure during their normal daily lives, correlating this to their other physiology in order to better understand not only the disease process but also to decide what therapy to start the patient on, and to monitor their response to this therapy.

Diabetes mellitus is a well-known chronic progressive disease resulting in several end-organ complications. It is a significant independent risk factor for hypertension, peripheral vascular, coronary artery, and renal disease amongst others. In the United States, the prevalence of diabetes mellitus has increased dramatically over the past four decades, mainly due to the increase in prevalence of obesity [14]. It is estimated that annually 24,000 cases of diabetes induced blindness are diagnosed, and 56,000 limbs are lost from peripheral vascular disease in the United States alone. The diagnosis is often made from measuring fasting blood glucose (which is abnormally raised) either during a routine clinical consultation, or as a result of complications of the condition. Once such acute complication is diabetic keto-acidosis which can be life threatening, and can occur not only in newly diagnosed diabetics, but also in those with poor blood sugar control due to reduce compliance with medication [15]. Once diagnosed, these patients require the regular administration of insulin at several times during the day, with blood glucose "pin-prick" testing used to closely monitor patients' blood sugar in between these injections. This need for repeated drawing of blood is invasive and therefore undesirable for many patients, yet there is at present no clear reliable alternative. As previously mentioned, variable treatment compliance rates (60-80% at best) in these patients are made worse the fact that they are on multiple medications [16]. BSN technology used in the monitoring of this group would allow the networking of wireless implantable and attachable glucose sensors not only to monitor patient glucose levels but also to be used in "closed feedback loop" systems for drug (insulin) delivery, as described later on in this chapter.

Although the three chronic conditions mentioned above illustrate the need for continuous physiological and biochemical monitoring, there other examples of disease processes that would also benefit from such monitoring. Table 1.2 lists some of these processes and the parameters that may be used to monitor them.

1.2.2 Monitoring Hospital Patients

In addition to monitoring patients with chronic diseases, there are two other specific areas where BSN applications offer benefit. The first of these is the hospital setting, where a large number of patients with various acute conditions are treated every year. At present, patients in hospital receive monitoring of various levels of intensity ranging from intermittent (four to six times a day in the case of those suffering with stable conditions), to intensive (every hour), and finally to continuous invasive and non-invasive monitoring such as that seen in the intensive care unit. This monitoring is normally in the form of vital signs measurement (blood pressure, heart rate, ECG, respiratory rate, and temperature), visual appearance (assessing their level of consciousness) and verbal response (asking them how much pain they are in).

Table 1.2 Disease processes and the parameters commonly used to monitor these diseases. Suggested sensor types for measurement of these parameters are listed in brackets. All of these conditions currently place a heavy administrative and financial burden on healthcare systems, which may be reduced if they are reliably detected.

Disease Process	Physiological Parameter (BSN Sensor Type)	Biochemical Parameter (BSN Sensor Type)
Hypertension	Blood pressure (*implantable/ wearable mechanoreceptor*)	Adrenocorticosteroids (*implantable biosensor*)
Ischaemic Heart Disease	Electrocardiogram (ECG), cardiac output (*implantable/ wearable mechanoreceptor*)	Troponin, creatine kinase (*implantable biosensor*)
Cardiac Arrhythmias/ Heart Failure	Heart rate, blood pressure, ECG, cardiac output (*implantable/wearable mechanoreceptor and ECG sensor*)	Troponin, creatine kinase (*implantable biosensor*)
Cancer (Breast, Prostate, Lung, Colon)	Weight loss (body fat sensor) (*implantable/ wearable mechanoreceptor*)	Tumour markers, blood detection (urine, faces, sputum), nutritional albumin (*implantable biosensors*)
Asthma / COPD	Respiration, peak expiratory flow, oxygen saturation (*implantable/ wearable mechanoreceptor*)	Oxygen partial pressure (*implantable/wearable optical sensor, implantable biosensor*)
Parkinson's Disease	Gait, tremor, muscle tone, activity (*wearable EEG, accelerometer, gyroscope*)	Brain dopamine level (*implantable biosensor*)
Alzheimer's Disease	Activity, memory, orientation, cognition (*wearable accelerometer, gyroscope*)	Amyloid deposits (brain) (*implantable biosensor/EEG*)
Stroke	Gait, muscle tone, activity, impaired speech, memory (*wearable EEG, accelerometer, gyroscope*)	
Diabetes	Visual impairment, sensory disturbance (*wearable accelerometer, gyroscope*)	Blood glucose, glycated haemoglobin (HbA1c). (*implantable biosensor*)
Rheumatoid Arthritis	Joint stiffness, reduced function, temperature (*wearable accelerometer, gyroscope, thermistor*)	Rheumatoid factor, inflammatory and autoimmune markers (*implantable biosensor*)
Renal Failure	Urine output (*implantable bladder pressure/volume sensor*)	Urea, creatinine, potassium (*implantable biosensor*)
Vascular Disease (Peripheral vascular and Aneurisms)	Peripheral perfusion, blood pressure, aneurism sac pressure. (*wearable/implantable sensor*)	Haemoglobin level (*implantable biosensor*)
Infectious Diseases	Body temperature (*wearable thermistor*)	Inflammatory markers, white cell count, pathogen metabolites (*implantable biosensor*)
Post-Operative Monitoring	Heart rate, blood pressure, ECG, oxygen saturation, temperature (*implantable /wearable and ECG sensor*)	Haemoglobin, blood glucose, monitoring the operative site. (*implantable biosensor*)

Patients undergoing surgery are a special group whose level of monitoring ranges from very high during and immediately after operation (under general anaesthesia), to intermittent during the post-operative recovery period. Aside from being restrictive and "wired", hospital ward-based patient vital signs monitoring systems tend to be very labour intensive, requiring manual measurement and documentation, and are prone to human error. Automation of this process along with the ability to pervasively monitor patients wherever they are in the hospital (not just at their bedside), is desirable not only to the healthcare provider, but also to the patient. In the post-operative setting, the use of implantable micro-machined wireless sensors to monitor the site of the operation has already begun, with a sensor being used to monitor pressure in the aneurysm sac following endovascular stenting [17]. The next step for any "hospital of the future" would be to adopt a ubiquitous and pervasive in-patient monitoring system enabling carers to predict, diagnose, and react to adverse events earlier than ever before. Furthermore, in order to improve the efficiency of hospital systems, the movements of patients through its wards, clinics, emergency departments and operating theatres may be tracked to try and understand where workflow is being disrupted and may be streamlined. This would help, for example, to maintain optimal capacity to cater for elective (planned) admissions whilst having the ability to admit patients with acute illnesses.

1.2.3 Monitoring Elderly Patients

The second scenario where BSNs may prove invaluable is for the regular and non-intrusive monitoring of "at risk" population groups such as the elderly. With people in industrialised nations living longer than ever before and an increase in average life expectancy of more than 25 years, the size of this group is set to increase, along with its potential demand upon healthcare resources [18].

Identifying ways of monitoring this aging population in their home environment is therefore very important, with one key example of the usefulness of this approach being the vulnerable periods during months of non-temperate weather. There is evidence to suggest that at times of the year when weather conditions are at their extremes (either very cold or very hot), elderly patients are at increased risk of requiring hospital admission [19, 20]. They are at risk because they are not able to seek medical help early enough for simple and treatable conditions, which eventually may lead to significant morbidity. An example of this is an elderly individual who lives alone and acquires a chest infection, which he fails to identify and seek help for until the infection requires hospital admission, or even ventilatory support. This could all be potentially avoided if the infection, or change in patient habits as a result of this infection, was picked up early and antibiotic therapy initiated.

Examples illustrating how people behave differently at the onset of illnesses include a decrease in appetite, a reduction in movement, and propensity to stay indoors. When correlated with physiological vital signs measurement, this system has the potential to clearly identify those most at risk. It is also demonstrates an instance in which a WSN (set up in the patient's home) and a BSN (on the patient's body) may overlap in their applications. It may be, therefore, that monitoring elderly patients in their home environment during non-temperate weather will allow earlier detection of any deterioration in their condition, for which prompt treatment may reduce the need for hospital admission, associated morbidity and even mortality.

The concept of an unobtrusive "home sensor network" to monitor an elderly person's social health (giving feedback not only to that person's carers and family members, but also to the elderly individual themselves) is one that is being developed by several companies such as Intel [21]. Whilst such a sensor network attempts to monitor well-being by identifying the individual and the level of activity they are undertaking, it is easy to see how this network could communicate with a body sensor network relaying physiological data about the individual. Combining these two networks would allow for a much better appreciation of the context in which the sensing is taking place.

1.3 Pervasive Patient Monitoring

In most healthcare systems spiralling costs, inadequate staffing, medical errors, and an inability to get to hospital in time in rural areas is placing a tremendous burden on the provision of care. The concept of "ubiquitous" and "pervasive" human well-being monitoring with regards to physical, physiological, and biochemical parameters in any environment and without restriction of activity [22, 23] has only recently become a reality with the important advances in sensor, miniaturised processor, and wireless data transmission technologies described earlier [24, 25]. Whilst external (attachable) sensors, such as those for measuring vital signs, have continued to improve, it is the area of implantable sensors and more recently biosensors that has generated the greatest interest [26, 27].

Advances in key areas such as power supply miniaturisation, increased battery duration, reduced energy consumption, and power scavenging are eagerly awaited and will be essential to systems that undertake pervasive monitoring, particularly in regard to implantable sensors [28]. *Micro Electro-Mechanical System* (MEMS) technology is another area which has offered the prospect of sophisticated sensing using a miniaturised sensor device [29]. Pervasive healthcare systems utilising large scale BSN and WSN technology will allow access to accurate medical information at any time and place, ultimately improving the quality of the service provided.

With these important advances taking place, clinicians are for the first time able to explore the prospect of not only monitoring patients more closely, but also to do this in an environment where they have never been able to monitor patients before. The chronic conditions of diabetes mellitus and hypertension mentioned previously in this chapter are currently managed on the basis of a series of "snapshots" of information, obtained in a clinical setting which is artificial in comparison to the patient's normal environment.

The long-term management of these conditions would clearly benefit from any technology which could result in a more tailored treatment being offered to the patient. The treatment of atrial fibrillation, which is associated with episodic rather than continuous circulatory abnormalities such as blood pressure surges, paroxysmal arrhythmias or episodes of myocardial ischaemia best illustrates this, as at present much time is wasted in trying to "capture an episode" of these abnormalities. As all of these episodes could be picked up using basic vital signs monitoring but their timing cannot be predicted, a wireless, pervasive, and continuous monitoring system is ideally suited to diagnosing and monitoring the progress of these diseases.

Additionally, better and earlier detection is likely to result in earlier administration of the appropriate treatment, and the prevention of disease-related morbidity. In the more acute hospital setting, the ability to continuously capture data on patient well-being has the potential to facilitate earlier adverse event detection and ultimately treatment. In such a system, the patient would not be required to stay at their bedside for monitoring to take place, increasing their mobility and return to activity in the hospital. In addition to this, a patient's physiological data would be obtained either continuously or at shorter time intervals, picking up said deterioration more quickly. At present, much of the data captured even with the aid of continuous patient monitoring is lost, but in conjunction with an automated pervasive monitoring system all data gathered could be stored for later review and trend analysis.

In order to achieve pervasive monitoring, several research platforms have emerged. The first of these utilises external sensors wearable in clothing, either through integrating them with a textile platform (European Commission "Wealthy" project) [30], or by embedding them into clothes with integrated electronics resulting in "intelligent biomedical clothes" (European Commission "MyHeart" Project[1]). The "MIThril" project based at Massachusetts Institute of Technology Media Lab has been developing a body-worn sensing computation and networking system, integrated in a "tunic" [1]. Proposed wearable applications include "memory glasses" that aim to provide a context-aware memory aid to the wearer.

Targeted to a population of patients with cardiac disease, "CardioNet" is a mobile outpatient telemetry system consisting of a three-lead electrocardiogram connected to a *Personal Digital Assistant* (PDA)-sized processing, display and power unit that aims to provide continuous real-time ECG monitoring, analysis and response for patients with suspected heart rhythm disturbances in their home, work or travelling environment [31]. Aimed at a similar population, Cardionetics is a company that provides an ambulatory ECG monitor (C.Net2000) designed for use by primary care providers, which analyses and classifies cardiac arrhythmias and morphology changes [32]. Finally the "Code Blue" project based at Harvard University has developed a medical sensor network using pulse oximeter, ECG, and motion activity sensor motes based on MicaZ and Telos designs [33]. Figure 1.3 shows some of the devices assembled through the research platforms mentioned in this chapter.

All these strategies share a common aim in providing unobtrusive, pervasive human monitoring irrespective of geographical location. In the case of external sensors, whilst embedding these into a garment does provide a more convenient wearable system, it lacks flexibility for the addition and relocation of sensors as dictated by patient size and shape. With implantable sensors, wiring is impractical and to a large extent can limit sensor placement. A wireless platform specifically designed to network external and implantable sensors on the human body is desirable not only because it allows these various sensors to be networked in a less bulky and intrusive way, but also because it allows the potential to add and remove sensors as required. Wireless sensor networking, data acquisition, data capture, and low power transmission all offer the prospect of flexible body sensor networks that are truly pervasive.

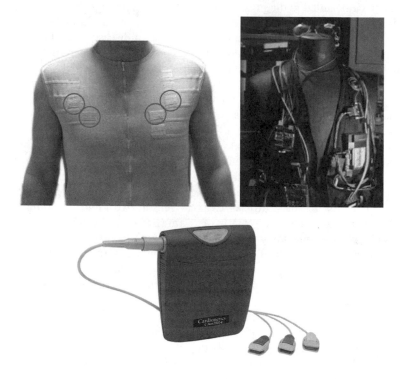

Figure 1.3 (Top left) EC "Wealthy" project sensors embedded in clothing (*courtesy of Rita Paradisao, Smartex Italy*). (Top right) "MIThril" tunic (*courtesy of Professor Alex Pentland, MIT Media Laboratory*). (Bottom) Cardionetics CTS2000 (*reprinted with permission from Cardionetics Ltd., UK*).

The development of implantable sensors offers BSN one of its most exciting components. The European Commission project "Healthy Aims" has been focused on specific sensor applications, namely for hearing aids (cochlear implant), vision aids (retinal implant), detecting raised orbital pressure (glaucoma sensor), and intracranial pressure sensing (implantable pressure sensor) [1]. Other implantable devices include Medtronic's "Reveal Insertable Loop Recorder", which is a fully implantable cardiac monitor used to record the heart's rate and rhythm during instances of unexplained fainting, dizziness, or palpitations. The device provides the clinician with an ECG that can be used to identify or rule out an abnormal heart rhythm as the cause of these symptoms [32]. CardioMEMS is a company that produces an implantable pressure sensor, which has been developed at Georgia Institute of Technology, that can take pressure readings following implantation into an aneurism sac at the time of endovascular repair [17]. This implanted sensor then provides a means of monitoring the status of the repair during the years following. Finally, Given Technologies has developed an endoscopy capsule that transmits images of the small bowel as it travels through the gastrointestinal tract [34]. Figure 1.4 below shows some of the implantable body cavity sensing technologies that may ultimately form part of an implantable wireless BSN.

 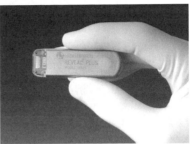

Figure 1.4 (Left) The CardioMEMS Endosure wireless aneurism pressure- sensing device (*courtesy of CardioMEMS Inc. and Professor Mark Allen, Georgia Institute of Technology*). (Right) Medtronic "Reveal Insertable Loop Recorder" (*courtesy of Medtronic Inc.*). (**See colour insert.**)

1.4 Technical Challenges Facing BSN

Although the BSN platform aims to provide the ideal wireless setting for the networking of human body sensors and the setting up of pervasive health monitoring systems, there are a number of technical challenges that lie ahead. These include the need for better sensor design, MEMS integration, biocompatibility, power source miniaturisation, low power wireless transmission, context awareness, secure data transfer, and integration with therapeutic systems, each of which are mentioned briefly below, and covered in more detail throughout this book.

1.4.1 Improved Sensor Design

Advances in biological, chemical, electrical, and mechanical sensor technologies have led to a host of new sensors becoming available for wearable and implantable use. Although the scope of these sensors is very wide, the following examples highlight the potential they offer to pervasive patient monitoring. In the case of patients with diabetes mellitus, trials of implantable glucose sensors are underway in an attempt to rid this patient population of the need for regular invasive blood glucose pinprick testing [35]. In addition, the ability to determine tissue and blood glucose levels using an implantable wireless glucose sensor may also form the sensing part of a "closed feedback loop" system. The other half of this loop would consist of a drug delivery pump which would continuously infuse a variable amount of fast-acting insulin based upon the patient's glucose level [36]. This concept effectively results in the closed feedback loop system acting as an "artificial pancreas", which maintains blood glucose within a closely defined reference range. As a result, diabetics may be able to avoid not only the complications of an acutely uncontrolled blood sugar (hypo- or hyper-glycaemia), but also much of the end-organ damage associated with the condition (retinopathy, cardiac, renal, and peripheral vascular disease).

Reliability is a very important requirement for sensors in closed feedback loop systems such as this, because they ultimately guide treatment delivery. It may be therefore that in this case an implantable biosensor array offers a more accurate result than one isolated sensor [37].

Improvements in sensor manufacturing and nano-engineering techniques, along with parallel advances in MEMS technology offer the potential for producing even smaller implantable and attachable sensors than were previously possible. An example of one such miniaturised nano-engineered sensor currently under development is a fluorescent hydrogel alginate microsphere optical glucose sensor [38]. Physiological sensors benefiting from MEMS technology integration include the microneedle array and the implantable blood pressure sensor [39]. Although much of this technology is still experimental, it is not inconceivable that over the next decade these sensors will guide therapy for chronic conditions such as hypertension and congestive cardiac failure. MEMS devices in particular may prove pivotal in the drug delivery component of any closed feedback loop [40]. In addition, when mass-produced, MEMS technology offers the prospect of delivering efficient and precise sensors for no more than a few dollars. This is well illustrated in the case of accelerometers, which have been used by the automobile industry to efficiently and reliably trigger car airbag releases during simulated accidents.

1.4.2 Biocompatibility

Implantable sensors and stimulators have had to overcome the problems of long-term stability and biocompatibility, with perhaps one of the most successful examples of this being the cardiac pacemaker and the *Implantable Cardioverter-Defibrillator* (ICD) [41]. The scale of implantable ICD use is best demonstrated by the fact that in 2001, a total of 26,151 were implanted at 171 centres in the UK and Ireland [42]. One of the main indications for an ICD is sudden cardiac death, which affects approximately 100,000 people annually in the UK, demonstrating the size of the patient population that may benefit from this device [43]. Other implantable devices currently used in clinical practice include implantable drug delivery systems for chronic pain [44], sacral nerve stimulators for anal incontinence[45], and high frequency brain (thalamic) stimulation for neurological conditions such as Parkinson's disease [46] and refractory epilepsy [47]. Figure 1.5 shows a range of these implantable devices currently in clinical use.

The fact that large groups of the patients already carry implanted devices such as those mentioned above, means that many of the lessons learnt from their use can be extended to any proposed implantable biosensor research. In addition to this, the integration of these already implanted sensors and effectors into a larger wireless BSN is something that deserves consideration. With regards to this last statement, power consumption is obviously an important issue, and until this is addressed it is unlikely that, for example, pacemakers would be used to monitor the cardiovascular status as part of a body sensor network. Interference of these devices with each other, as well as with day-to-day technologies used by patients such as mobile phones, is a concern that has been noted and must be addressed [48]. The concern here is that interference may result in not only sensor malfunction, but also might affect implanted drug delivery systems and stimulators. This supports the call for a new industrial standard for the wireless transmission frequency used in body sensor networks.

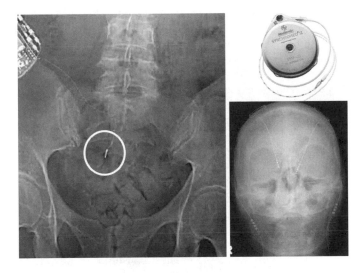

Figure 1.5 (Left) An example of an implantable device (sacral nerve stimulator) in current clinical use. (Bottom right) Deep brain stimulators, (*courtesy of the Radiological Society of North America*). (Above right) Implantable Synchromed® II drug delivery system for chronic pain (*courtesy of Medtronic Inc.*).

1.4.3 Energy Supply and Demand

One of the key considerations for BSNs is power consumption. This is because power consumption determines not only the size of the battery required but also the length of time that the sensors can be left *in situ*. The size of battery used to store the required energy is in most cases the largest single contributor to the size of the sensor apparatus in term of both dimensions and weight. These factors are important not only in the implantable but also the external sensor settings because they determine how "hidden" and "pervasive" the sensors are. Several strategies have been employed to achieve this miniaturisation of the power source. One such strategy is the development of micro-fuel cells that could be used in the case of implantable sensors, reducing the size of the power supply whilst increasing the lifetime of the battery and therefore the sensor. Characteristics that render fuel cells highly attractive for portable power generation include their high energy efficiency and density, combined with the ability to rapidly refuel [49, 50]. Polymer-electrolyte direct methanol [51] and solid-oxide fuel cells [52] are examples of two such technologies that have been suggested as alternatives to Lithium ion batteries in portable settings.

An alternative approach is to use biocatalytic fuel cells consisting of immobilised micro organisms or enzymes acting as catalysts, with glucose as a fuel to produce electricity [53]. This concept of an "enzymatic microbattery" is attractive because it offers the prospect of dramatically reducing the size of the sensor apparatus and is ideally suited to implantable devices to the point that it has even been suggested as a power supply for a proposed "microsurgery robot" [53]. Miniaturising the packaging required to hold a battery's chemical constituents, which currently consists of strong metals such as steel because the battery houses highly corrosive chemicals, is also important. Replacing these chemicals with a substance that is much less corrosive (for example oxygen and water) would therefore require less bulky packaging [54]. Another interesting strategy is the use of acoustic (ultrasound) power transmission into an implantable device, with piezoelectric discs as power transducers [55]. Challenges faced in this case include increasing power storage capability as well as controlling the acoustic beam to achieve maximal efficiency.

Finally, reducing battery consumption through the increased use of power scavenging from on-body sources such as vibration and temperature is a strategy being developed to enhance battery life; especially in the case of implantable sensors [56, 57]. At present, a large proportion of the electrical power consumed by biosensors goes towards the measurement circuit. In a wireless BSN system, the wireless communication link is likely to be the greatest consumer of power. The development of low-power wireless data paths is therefore key to the successful development of wireless BSN systems. Reducing the power consumption of the radio transceiver is crucial to the practical deployment of BSNs [58, 59]. Ultra wideband radio has also been suggested as a mode of short-range wireless communication with relatively high data rates and low power consumption [60]. Self-configuring networks carry the advantage of reducing energy consumption from unnecessary nodes classified as "redundant", thereby increasing the system's lifespan.

1.4.4 System Security and Reliability

Figure 1.6 is a historic photograph showing mass crowding in the healthcare environment. Although this is not representative of the clinical setting in modern hospitals, it highlights the importance of secure and reliable data transfer for BSNs. Security and reliability of the network are two of the crucial elements of the BSN design, as sensitive patient information is being transmitted through the wireless network. Unlike typical wired or wireless network architectures in which the network configuration is mostly static and there is limited constraint on resources, the architecture for BSN is highly dynamic, placing more rigorous constraints on power supply, communication bandwidth, storage and computational resources.

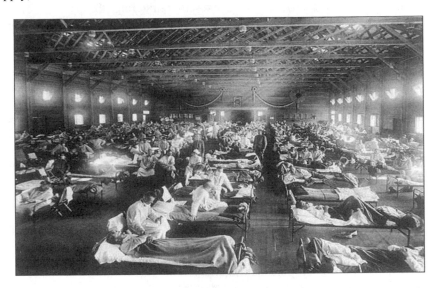

Figure 1.6 A picture from the 1918 influenza epidemic is an extreme example of the number of hospital patients that can be present close proximity (*courtesy of the National Museum of Health and Medicine, Armed Forces Institute of Pathology, Washington, D.C., NCP 1603*).

In terms of security, BSN data must be secured with strong cryptography to protect the patient's privacy. However, strong cryptography requires extensive computation and resources. Considering the limited resources that a BSN node can have, a compromised approach has to be taken to maximise security whilst minimising resource utilisation. Furthermore, the highly dynamic nature of the BSN means that typically static network authentication methods will not be applicable. Even methods proposed for *ad hoc* networks such as the asymmetric cryptography technique would be computationally too expensive for BSN applications [61]. As such, a robust, efficient and lightweight security infrastructure is required for the practical deployment of BSN applications.

The reliability of the network, on the other hand, directly affects the quality of patient monitoring, and in a worst-case scenario, it can be fatal when a life threatening event has gone undetected. However, due to the constraints on communication bandwidth and power consumption, traditional network reliability techniques such as the retransmission mechanism for TCP protocol, may not be practical for BSN applications. With the similar constraints on WSNs, researchers have proposed several methods for improving its reliability. One simple approach is to use limited retransmission where packets are retransmitted for a fixed number of times until the reception of the acknowledgement; however, retransmission often induces significant overhead to the network. Another approach is to form a multi-path network and exploit the multiple routes to avoid disrupted links [62]. It is expected that this will be an area that will attract significant research interest in the coming years, particularly in exploring the autonomic sensing paradigm for developing self-protecting, self-healing, self-optimising, and self-configuring BSNs.

Thus far, most security and network reliability techniques aim to provide maximum security and reliability for generic wireless sensor network applications. However, in the case of BSN, instead of relying solely on the low level network infrastructure, high level context information can also be used to reinforce the security and reliability of the system. An example of this is the use of biometric information for enhancing the inherent security of the network [63]. Furthermore, as multiple sensors are often used in a BSN application to measure or infer the same physiological parameters, the use of intelligent multi-sensor data fusion techniques can significantly enhance the reliability of the system.

Other implications of deploying BSNs include the appreciation of the long-term consequences of their effect on the body, particularly in the case of implantable sensors. This is likely to govern the materials and manufacturing process used to construct BSN nodes, their battery supply, and the type of wireless data transfer used. In the case of WSN, where the effect of large numbers of redundant energy-depleted nodes is likely to be detrimental on the environment [2], these nodes must be re-usable or in some way biodegradable. For BSN, both biodegradability and inertness of materials offer potential solutions, but finding the right material for manufacturing the nodes is likely to pose an important challenge.

1.4.5 Context Awareness

In addition to being able to monitor physiological parameters, research on BSNs has identified the importance of the context (environment) the person being monitored is in when interpreting these parameters. Simple activities such as "sleeping" and "walking" have an effect on not only vital signs such as heart rate and blood pressure, but also on any measure of activity and mobility that is being used. This "context awareness" can also help account for motion artefacts and errors detected by the sensors. Under normal conditions, visual monitoring provides this contextual information most effectively, but in the pervasive healthcare monitoring setting this is not possible. It is therefore important to identify methods of "inferring" context using techniques such as "Naïve Bayesian" classifiers [64] and "hierarchical hidden semi-Markov models"[65] for activity recognition and tracking daily activities. Fusion of data from multiple sensors may provide this contextual information, with selected classifiers designed to yield optimal results based on fusing all sensor readings.

Several types of sensors have been used to develop this context awareness. Accelerometers have been suggested as appropriate candidates for determining activity state (driving, sleeping, exercising) and posture (lying, sitting, standing), although the technical challenge of sensor placement in order to achieve the ideal result is one that is still being addressed [7, 66]. Audio sensors that act by determining either the level of environmental noise, or whether the subject is talking to anyone or not, have also showed potential [67]. Changes in temperature and heat flux may be able to not only determine whether the subject is active or at rest, but also when the subject moves from a warmer indoor to a colder outdoor environment [7]. Skin conductance (affected by sweat gland activity) may be measured using galvanic skin response, with an electrode in contact with the skin surface [68]. Integration of several of these context-sensing modalities is a strategy used by SenseWear™ (Body-Media Inc.), who have produced a device consisting of a multi-sensor array that is worn on the upper arm and includes a two-axis accelerometer, heat flux sensor, galvanic skin response sensor, skin temperature sensor, and near-body ambient sensor [68]. Researchers at MIT has developed a modified ring sensor that uses photoplethysmography to detect a person's pulse rate and blood-oxidation level [69]. They have built "context awareness" into this ring using photocells to detect ambient light, thermistors to detect temperature, and accelerometers to detect motion, all of which may interfere with readings and must therefore be accounted for.

1.4.6 Integrated Therapeutic Systems

Integrating sensors and therapeutic systems and thereby "closing the feedback loop", is likely to play a major part in defining the role for BSN in clinical practice [70]. This is particularly well illustrated in the delivery of pharmacotherapy where currently drugs are administered at doses and frequencies that are based on average sizes, and metabolic rate. When considering the fact that for an individual patient who has an individual size and metabolism, this optimal dosage is likely to vary considerably from the "average", it is clear that individualised dosing is preferable. In addition to this, a patient's drug requirement may temporarily change during an illness, or for example when they are on other medications such as antibiotics. Whilst underdosing in these situations will result in inadequate treatment (for example seizures in patients on anti-epileptic medication), overdosing will result in an increased risk of the patient suffering unwanted side-effects. Drug-delivering medical feedback loops consist of miniaturised sensors that continuously monitor a drug's effect and through medical control algorithms, adjust its delivery from miniaturised drug pumps. The dosage of the drug would therefore be individualised to the patient.

An example of integrated drug-delivering therapeutic systems for fast-acting insulin in diabetics is shown in Figure 1.7 [70]. This proposed system consists of two patches on the skin. One is an implanted sensor-amplifier-transmitter which may be replaced by the user every few days. The other patch would be an insulin-delivering system comprising of a calibrator, *Radio Frequency* (RF) receiver, drug reservoir, pump, battery, and miniature subcutaneously inserted drug inlet. The RF signal from the "sensor" patch would be received by the "insulin delivery" patch and translated through a medical algorithm, to a series of micro-doses of insulin. Like the "sensing" patch, the "insulin delivery" patch would also be replaced by the user every few days.

   The other disease processes (some of which have been mentioned earlier in this
chapter) that would benefit from a similar integrated drug delivery process include
epilepsy, hypertension, ischemic heart disease, and conditions requiring blood anticoagulation. All these disease processes currently require "average dosing" and
their efficacy is currently monitored by measuring the drug level in the patient's
blood, or in the case of hypertensives, their blood pressure when attending their
health clinic. It is important to remember that drug delivery may not be the only
stimulus that is delivered by such integrated feedback systems, with electrical stimuli, for example to brain, nerves, and muscle being other important examples.
Whatever the application, it is clear that the pace at which these integrated feedback
systems develop is dependent largely on the development of suitable components
and medical control algorithms to construct the miniature subsystems.

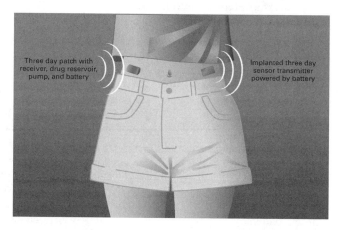

Figure 1.7 (Left) An integrated insulin drug-delivery system consisting of
two communicating skin patches, one monitoring blood subcutaneous glucose, and the other delivering insulin (*courtesy of Professor Adam Heller and
John Wiley & Sons Inc.*).

1.5 Personalised Healthcare

In a population consisting of several vulnerable groups such as those with chronic
disease and the elderly, the need for effective individualised health monitoring and
delivery has resulted in the concept of "personalised healthcare". Such a system is
expected to be 'dynamic' and customised to specifically address the health needs of
individuals. In essence, personalised healthcare systems should take into account an
individual's chronic (long term) and episodic (short term) healthcare needs, and
have clear healthcare objectives. They should also account for the cognitive level of
the patient, and for both social and community factors. BSNs offer perhaps the
greatest chance of developing a personalised healthcare system where treatment
may be tailored to the patient at several levels.

At the monitoring level, this system would have to reliably observe the patient's physiology, activity, and context, detecting adverse changes in their wellbeing early. At the delivery of care level, data processing and decision-making algorithms must prompt the appropriate action to deliver correct therapy. Drug delivery, which as previously mentioned is at present dosed according to population averages, could be tailored exactly to an individual's needs, perhaps by infusion rather than by tablet. The cost-effectiveness of such a personalised healthcare system over existing technology solutions is also important and is likely to drive its development. New bionic technologies such as neuromodulation and neurostimulation devices are likely to enable BSNs to interact with and control a patient's physiological systems themselves. Ultimately, these devices could use information from BSN sensors to control the human body's musculoskeletal system itself. Perhaps one of the most successful examples of a bionic device in clinical use is the cochlear implant, which has had tremendous impact on patients' lives [71].

At the research level, pervasive healthcare systems will allow doctors to learn much more about the disease processes they commonly see in clinical practice. Finally at the information delivery level, giving the patient personalised information (according to their healthcare needs) is likely to help them understand and self-manage their conditions more appropriately [72]. The ultimate aim of all this is the early detection of disease leading to an early intervention, both of which are attributes that may make personalised healthcare-based treatment the next best thing after prevention itself.

In order to deliver truly personalised healthcare, BSN sensors have to become invisible to the patient, thereby avoiding activity restriction or behaviour modification. Whilst sensor miniaturisation and implantability are potential solutions to this, another option being explored is the integration of the sensor into non-clothing items that patients already wear. The ring sensor developed at MIT, for example, can act as an ambulatory telemetric continuous health monitoring device [69]. This wearable biosensor uses advanced photoplethysmographic techniques to acquire data on the patient's heart rate, heart rate variability and oxygen saturation. This ring sensor contains an optical sensor unit, an RF transmitter, and a battery, connected to a microcomputer in the ring itself. This ensures onsite low-level signal processing, data acquisition, filtering, and bidirectional RF communication with a cellular phone which can access a website for data acquisition and clinical diagnosis.

There are, of course, other areas aside from clinical practice where wireless BSN surveillance may be useful in monitoring people and their activity. Professional groups such as fire-fighters and paramedics, who commonly face hazardous situations, as well as policemen and soldiers, may all be monitored with such a system. Fitsense is a company that has developed a system known as "The Body-LAN™". This uses low power wireless body monitoring sensors for a variety of physiological and environmental parameters, which via a proprietary wireless personal area network collect and send data to its users. They can then assess their fitness and performance [73]. Figure 1.8 shows some of these monitoring systems.

One of the challenges of a personalised healthcare system is the wealth of information that the system is going to generate for the healthcare provider above and beyond what is currently available. How this information will be accumulated, stored, and interpreted, and how healthcare systems will respond to adverse events are all questions to be considered. It is important to appreciate that at present whilst much patient information is collected by continuous monitoring, for example during hospital admission, most of this information is lost. Although personalised pervasive healthcare systems will collect a vast amount of information, separating this into "important" and "non-important" is going to require very accurate context sensing. Mining this data and representing it to a user is yet another challenge. Finally, as previously mentioned, reacting to this information is going to require major process automation and structural change to existing healthcare systems.

Figure 1.8 (Left) the first prototype ring sensor with RF transmitter powered by a coin-sized battery (*courtesy of Professor Harry Asada, MIT*). (Right) a FitSense sensor attached to an athlete's shin enabling measurement of stride length, step rate, instantaneous speed, distance, and acceleration (*courtesy of Tom Blackadar, FitSense Inc.*).

1.6 Finding the Ideal Architecture for BSN

The human body houses what is perhaps the most sophisticated and well developed example of a network of body sensors in existence. Innervated by small neurones, the *Autonomic Nervous System* (ANS) comprises of autonomic ganglia and nerves. Also known as the involuntary nervous system, it is concerned primarily with the control of the body's internal environment. It is ironic that in developing a wireless body sensor network to monitor a person's physiological state, we are in essence trying to monitor and act on the reactions of the body's own nerves, sensors, and effectors, to both external and internal environments. Looking towards this advanced sensor network is likely to set the standard for what BSN aims to achieve. The complexity of the human nervous system and its components is clearly much greater than that of any proposed pervasive BSN for patient monitoring. When looking for ideas and solutions to the problems faced by BSN however, the human body may itself hold the key. In order to understand the way in which the autonomic nervous system fulfils the requirement of the ideal body sensor network, we must understand how it overcomes each of the technical challenges mentioned previously in this chapter. We may then be able to translate some of these lessons into design concepts for a truly pervasive patient monitoring system, and look to the challenge of developing feedback loop between wireless sensors as well as effectors. Before doing this, it is important to understand the basic anatomical and functional components that form the ANS.

The ANS controls the human body's internal environment through innervation of the nonskeletal muscle of the heart, blood vessels, bronchial tree, gut, pupils, and secretomotor supply of many glands, namely those in the gastrointestinal tract, its embryological outgrowths, sweat glands, and the adrenal medulla [74]. The higher centres of this system are located in the brain and spinal chord, with peripheral nerve fibres connecting these to both sensor and effector organs. Functionally the ANS can be divided into two groups. The sympathetic nervous system is concerned primarily with stress reactions of the body and when stimulated results in what is commonly termed as the "fight or flight" response. The effect of stimulation of the sympathetic nervous system can in essence be related to a preparation for a stressful situation such as battle. In the eyes, pupils dilate allowing more light onto the retina at the back of the orbit thereby enhancing vision. Peripheral blood vessels constrict resulting in a reduction of heat loss from the skin and a diversion of blood to vital organs. The force of contraction of the heart, along with its rate and oxygen consumption increases, also in an attempt to maintain a good blood pressure and perfusion to vital organs. The diameter of airways in the lung is increased, allowing more oxygen into the lungs and thereby allowing for better oxygenation of blood. The motility and contraction of bowel normally required to digest food is inhibited, and the tone of sphincters increased, slowing the transit of faeces through the alimentary system. In a similar way, bladder contraction is inhibited, and the sphincter controlling the flow of urine out of the bladder stimulated to contract. Blood glucose levels are increased by inhibition of insulin release and increased breakdown of liver glycogen stores into glucose, providing fuel for the increased activity with the body. The adrenal gland is stimulated to secrete hormones such as epinephrine, further stimulating the increased cardiac output. Finally there is an increase in the production of sweat along with an elevation of hairs on the surface of the body. Together all these complex actions prepare the human body for "fight or flight" action.

The opposite of this occurs with stimulation of the parasympathetic system, with for example a reduction in heart rate, conduction, and excitability accompanied by a reduction in pupil size. There is also an increase in gut and bladder motility with sphincter relaxation, resulting in a quicker transit of faeces and urine that with sympathetic stimulation. Although the actions of both systems seem antagonistic, it is important to appreciate that both do work in synergy, with many organs such as the heart, having both a parasympathetic and sympathetic innervation. For these organs, it is the proportion of sympathetic and parasympathetic stimulation they receive that is important in how they behave. Figure 1.9 is a representation of the autonomic system, highlighting important differences between its sympathetic and parasympathetic components.

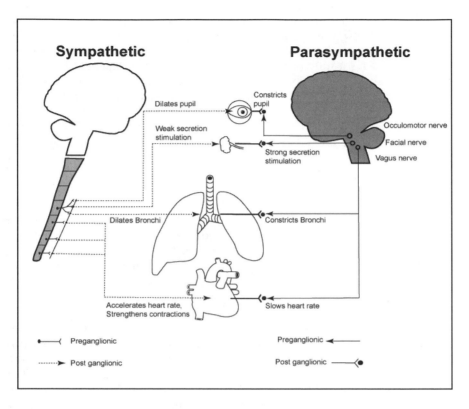

Figure 1.9 A diagrammatic representation of the autonomic nervous system
with both sympathetic (left) and parasympathetic components (right).

Having understood the anatomical makeup of the ANS, one can begin to explore
how it overcomes the challenges faced by the human body sensor network as a
whole. Sensor design, as mentioned previously is a very important part of any such
network, and in the case of the human body, this consists of a range of sensor types
that are both very sensitive and very accurate. For example, chemoreceptors
(chemical receptors) respond to changes in oxygen and carbon dioxide in the blood,
and are located either peripherally (in carotid and aortic bodies) or centrally (in the
brain). Based on the concentration of these solutes the receptors are able to regulate
respiratory rate and cardiac activity, to maintain adequate perfusion of tissues and
vital organs. Alternatively baroreceptors (pressure sensors) found in the aortic arch
and carotid sinus, are sensitive to the rate of blood pressure change as well as to the
steady or mean blood pressure, and are thus able to communicate this information
to higher centres in the brain, thereby regulating the blood pressure by altering both
the heart's output, as well as the diameter of blood vessels. Figure 1.10 shows the
sensor and effector systems used by the human body to detect and regulate changes
in blood pressure.

Other types of mechanical receptors (mechanoreceptors) that the body possesses include "muscle spindles, which are found between skeletal muscle fibres. Arranged in a parallel distribution with these fibres, the spindles respond to the passive stretch of the muscle, but cease to discharge if the muscle contracts isotonically, thus signalling muscle length. They are therefore the receptors responsible for the stretch reflex such as that elicited by tapping at the knee (knee jerk) as shown in Figure 1.10. Similar mechanical receptors also exist within the cardiac musculature that when overstretched due to increased filling of the heart chambers, result in a compensatory increased strength of cardiac contraction.

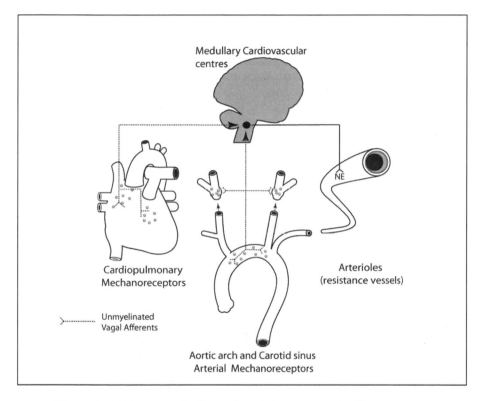

Figure 1.10 Diagrammatic illustration of the sensor and effector systems used by the human body to detect and regulate changes in blood pressure.

Although biocompatibility is not an issue within the body's own sensors because they are self-manufactured, power source miniaturisation is an impressive feature of this system. In general, the body utilises glucose as a substrate using either anaerobic or aerobic respiration to turn this fuel into packets of energy from which is carries in the form of specialised molecules such as *Adenosine Triphosphate* (ATP). Nerves forming the wiring of the system transmit the information in the form of action potentials, with each action potential of approximately 110 millivolts lasting 5-10 milliseconds. The conduction velocity of nerves can be as high as 100 metres per second, making this a very efficient system. Multi-sensory data fusion occurs in the human brain, where each nerve is connected to approximately 10,000 other nerves through special dendritic connections.

Finally, nonvisual context awareness is another important feature of the human nervous system, and is under higher brain centre control. A very good example of this is the body's use of *proprioception* (position sense), particularly with regard to body extremities such as the limbs. To achieve this, the human body uses a number of receptors which signal the position and movement of a limb. These include joint afferents (located in the joints), sensitive to extremes in joint angle, muscle spindles located in the muscle sensitive to position and movement (velocity), Golgi tendon organs located in the muscle tendon sensitive to tension (force), and touch receptors in muscle and overlying skin. Input from all these sensors is processed by the brain and allows the body to know exactly where in space and in what position its different components (limbs) are without the need to look at them (Figure 1.11). Once the input coming into the nervous system is processed, depending on the state of the muscle, commands are sent back to either maintain or change position (Figure 1.12).

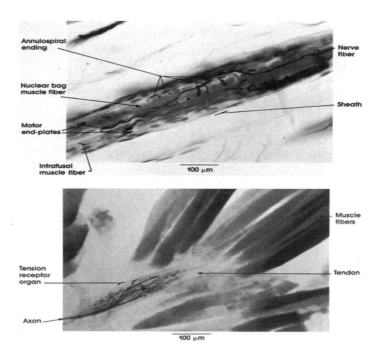

Figure 1.11 Histological slides of the sensors used for context awareness in joint proprioception (*copyrighted material used with permission of the author, the University of Iowa, and Virtual Hospital, http://www.vh.org*).

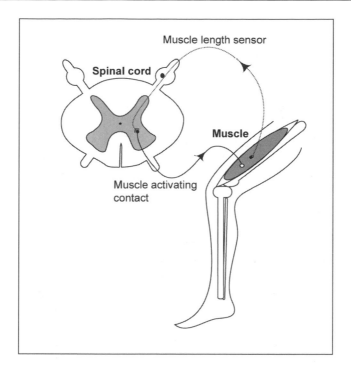

Figure 1.12 Diagrammatic representation reflex arc.

1.7 The Future: Going from "Micro" to "Nano"

Until now, applications for the use of BSNs in clinical practice have focussed around external and implantable sensors that lie relatively static within the body. However, it is the luminal organs such as blood vessels, gastrointestinal tract, urinary tract, ventricles of the brain, spinal canal, lymphatic, and venous systems that offer the greatest opportunity to sense acute disease processes and monitor chronic illnesses quickly and efficiently. These cavities are essentially the "highways" filled with body fluids, inflammatory mediators, cells, and pathogens, forming what are the "battlefields" where disease processes are fought. As the accuracy of our sensors increases and their size decreases, it is in these domains that we would like to have the maximal affect on any disease process. Recent advances in nanotechnology have meant that delivering sensors within these luminal cavities is for the first time a real possibility. Figure 1.13 graphically illustrates the "battle" against disease.

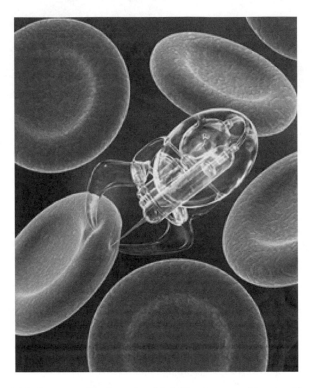

Figure 1.13 Conceptualisation of a MEMS robot attaching itself to a red blood cell (*copyright Coneyl Jay/Science photo library*). (**See colour insert**.)

Miniaturisation of many sensors to the "micro" scale is already taking place. Figure 1.14 shows a conceptual "submarine" type sensor system that may be deployed into the blood stream (either in the arterial or venous system). Nanoscale particles are likely to be the smallest component of sensing systems and may be deployed in a number of ways. For example, nanoscale particles may themselves be coated to form a biomechanical sensing system. An existing example of this is a protein-encapsulated single-walled carbon nanotube sensor that alters its fluorescence depending on exposure to glucose in the surrounding tissues [32]. In fact nanoparticles have even been attached to antigen amyloid-derived diffusible ligands in order to develop a nanoscale optical biosensor for Alzheimer's disease [75]. Finally, nanoparticles may act as sensors themselves. The scenario of injecting nanoscale biosensors into luminal cavities, where the sensor comes in contact with its substrate, binds to it, and is carried to the site of maximal disease activity is no longer unrealistic. Such targeted sensor delivery and binding may allow extremely targeted disease process monitoring, and therapy.

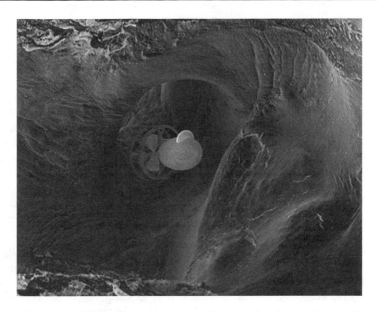

Figure 1.14 Conceptualisation of a MEMS submarine injected into a blood vessel (*copyright microTEC, Germany*). (**See colour insert**.)

An example of nanoscale particles already in use is *Ultra-Small Particles of Iron Oxide* (USPIO) for pathologic tissue characterisation. The long blood circulating time and the progressive macrophage uptake in inflammatory tissues of USPIO particles are properties that can be interrogated by imaging techniques such as *Magnetic Resonance Imaging* (MRI). The USPIO signal alterations observed in ischemic areas of stroke patients can be related to the visualisation of inflammatory macrophage recruitment into human brain infarction, whereas in brain tumours, USPIO particles which do not pass the ruptured blood-brain barrier fairly soon after injection can be used to assess tumour microvascular heterogeneity. Existing research has also shown that USPIO contrast agents can reveal the presence of inflammatory multiple sclerosis lesions. They can also help pick up the spread of rectal cancers to the lymphatic system by increasing the diagnostic accuracy of rectal imaging [76].

Whilst miniaturisation means that deploying microscale sensors is going to become easier, getting the information out of these sensors will be a significant challenge [32]. Optical imaging techniques have been suggested as a solution to the problem of data extraction from such a small sensor, and would allow, for example, dynamic investigation of the signalling processes that go on inside the cell itself.

Finally, self-configuration and self-assembly are both essential requirements of such sensing systems, as we find we are able to place them in increasingly inaccessible locations. Optical technologies such as fluorescence resonance energy transfer may provide on solution to this requirement for self-assembly [77].

1.8 The Scope of the Book

In this chapter, we have highlighted the scope for monitoring human disease processes. Although proprietary designed wireless sensor networks offer some solutions to the problems of health monitoring, it is clear that a specialised BSN platform offers the opportunity to monitor human beings in a way that has not previously been possible. This truly ubiquitous and pervasive patient monitoring system will, in the first instance, allow us to identify these disease processes, and will later on allow us to accurately monitor their progress and devise effective therapeutic measures. The challenges of improving sensor design, biocompatibility, energy supply, power scavenging, secure information transfer, and context awareness must all be overcome before such a system is effective. Closing the feedback loop to deliver targeted therapy, and thus reducing unnecessary drug side-effects is also a real possibility.

The purpose of this book is to address both basic issues and emerging trends concerning biosensor design and interfacing, protein engineering for biosensors, wireless communication, network topology, communication protocols and standards, energy scavenging, bio-inspired sensor processing, multi-sensor fusion, and context-aware and autonomic sensing. Figure 1.15 illustrates the structure of the materials covered.

In Chapter 2, we will introduce the basic concept of electrochemical sensors and biosensors. This chapter covers the basic principles of electrochemical devices based on potentiometry, amperometry and voltammetry. The chapter also outlines the basic instrumentation requirements for these devices and looks at issues surrounding biocompatibility and sensor data handling. In Chapter 3, we will focus on the biological aspects of biosensors in two important regards; the first is the biological molecules involved in the molecular recognition processes that give the biosensors their specificity and sensitivity and the other is concerned with biocompatibility. We will discuss how these proteins can be engineered to improve sensor performance and address the mutual interaction between the sensor and the tissue within which it is located. Although progress has been made in making implantable biosensors reliable and robust for a period of a few days, there are still significant technical issues associated with long-term implantation. This reflects in part the response of the tissue to trauma and the inherent robustness of the biological molecules used in the sensor. This implies that the solution to long-term implantation will come from a combination of factors including minimally invasive implantation, understanding and modulating tissue response to implantation and modifying the properties of the biomolecules.

Chapters 4 and 5 will address wireless communication, network topologies, communication protocols and standards for BSNs. In Chapter 4, we will discuss two types of communication links: the inductive loop and radio frequency communication. The inductive loop is widely used today for transferring small packets of data without requiring an implanted power source. Whilst an RF system does require an implanted battery source, it is capable of transferring larger packets of data within a shorter time period and over greater distances. For this reason, RF-based communication will be the main topic of this chapter. Whilst wireless communication through the air has been extensively documented, communication from implanted devices through the human body is a new area of study. This chapter will discuss body properties and their effect on radio propagation. The human body is an uninviting and often hostile environment for a wireless signal. One of the most important considerations for implanted devices is physical size, meaning in-body communication system designs are restricted to an extremely small antenna that needs to be characterised to enable it to be effectively coupled to the transceiver. A significant portion of this chapter is devoted to antenna measurement and coupling circuit design, as it is critical to the success of an implanted RF system.

Based on the contents described in previous chapters, Chapter 5 illustrates the use of different network topologies for practical deployment of BSNs. Although the initial use of BSNs will only consist of limited sensor nodes, more complex network topology will be adopted as the devices get smaller and more ubiquitous. This will allow more effective use of sensor message hopping, distributed inferencing for improved system robustness and noise resilience with built-in redundancies. Particular emphasis will be made in the chapter touching upon the integration of body sensing with ambient sensing. In such cases, the joining and rejoining of a shifting series of different networks (home, public, and hospital) and the addition or removal of differing sensor nodes under different context requirements can pose significant challenges. A detailed overview of the current and emerging communication protocols and standards for implantable, wearable, and ambient wireless sensing will be provided, and issues concerning standards for overall healthcare system integration with pervasive sensing will also be discussed.

With the increasing miniaturisation and cost reduction of sensors, circuits and wireless communication components come new possibilities for networks of wireless sensors, in wearable and other applications. However, for sensors to be wireless, or untethered, requires not only wireless communication to and from the nodes, but also wireless powering. Batteries, of course, provide this capability in the great majority of portable electronic devices, and thus are the obvious solution for the wireless sensor node application. However, the need for replacement or recharging of batteries introduces a cost and convenience penalty which is already undesirable in larger devices, and is likely to become unacceptable for sensor nodes as their ubiquity grows. As an alternative, sources which scavenge energy from the environment are highly desirable. With the decreasing power demands for sensing, processing, and wireless communication for BSNs due to improved electronic design and miniaturisation, alternatives to battery power based on energy scavenging techniques are becomingly increasingly realistic. In Chapter 6, we will discuss the basic power requirements for BSN nodes and possible architectures, particularly those related to inertial energy scavenging techniques. Issues concerning fabrication, module design, power electronics and system effectiveness will be discussed.

The natural world is analogue and yet the modern microelectronic world to which we are exposed represents real world data using discrete quantities manipulated by logic. The new trend set by BSNs is beginning to see the processing interface move back to using continuous quantities which are more or less in line with the biological processes. This computational paradigm we label "bio-inspired" because of the ability of silicon chip technology to enable use of inherent device physics, allowing us to approach the computational efficiencies of biology. In contrast to the digital approach, where each operation is performed through a network of devices operated in switched fashion, the physics of the elementary device itself, either electrical, chemical or electrochemical, can be exploited to perform the same operation in an analogue way. Therefore both the energy per unit computation and, silicon real-estate are reduced, resulting in significantly increased overall resource efficiency. In Chapter 7 we will first look at the motivation for bio-inspired signal processing and discuss the relative merits of analogue and digital signal processing, and the need for hybrid architectures. The concept of applying bio-inspired design methodologies to CMOS-based biosensors will then be introduced. *Field-Effect Transistor* (FET) based sensors will be presented, including a detailed example of the application of analogue processing techniques to these devices. Finally, future directions and applications for biochemically inspired design will be discussed.

The pursuit for low power, miniaturised, distributed sensing under natural physiological conditions of the patient has also imposed significant challenges on integrating information from what is often heterogeneous, incomplete, and error prone sensor data. For BSNs, the nature of errors can be attributed to a number of sources, but motion artefact, inherent limitation and malfunctions of the sensors, and communication errors are the main causes of concern. In practice, it is desirable to rely on sensors with redundant or complementary data to maximise the information content and reduce both systematic and random errors. This, in essence, is the main drive for multi-sensor fusion described in Chapter 8, which is concerned with the synergistic use of multiple sources of information. In this chapter, we will discuss the basic concept of multi-sensor fusion and the methods related to data, feature and decision levels of data fusion techniques. The key emphasis of the chapter is the introduction of optimal averaging techniques for sensor array data and a feature selection algorithm based on Bayesian theory and receiver operating characteristic analysis.

With BSNs, effective sensor fusion and statistical feature reduction is crucial to the use of wireless sensor networks incorporating both built-in redundancies and tissue heterogeneity. For the monitoring of patients under normal physiological status, the contextual information is important to the capture of clinically relevant episodes. In Chapter 9, we will investigate issues concerning context aware sensing for the practical deployment of BSNs. The key emphasis of this chapter is the introduction of a novel framework, called *Spatio-Temporal Self-Organising Map* (STSOM), by incorporating the spatio-temporal behaviour of self-organising neural networks for reliable context detection. The significance of the contents provided in this chapter is twofold. First, it provides an effective framework for reliably extracting contextual information based on the feature selection framework described in Chapter 8. Secondly, it illustrates the possibility of complete analogue implementation of the framework based on STSOM, such that the sensing architecture can be realistically powered up by the energy scavenging techniques described in Chapter 6.

The use of BSNs can be influenced by a wide range of limitations including processing power, storage, network connectivity, and available power sources. In most cases, it is not possible to guarantee or accurately predict the characteristics of these resources in advance. In particular, wireless network communication is subject to many unpredictable environmental effects, even over short-range connections such as between body and wearable devices. Issues related to *Quality of Service* (QoS), variable resources monitoring, adaptation techniques applied to data including compression, data security, authentication and privacy will need to be addressed. In Chapter 10, we will introduce the basic concepts involved in autonomic sensing and describe a number of other approaches that are inspired by biological systems. The use of the autonomic sensing paradigm for BSNs is relatively new, and in this chapter we will discuss the general issues and new opportunities involved in the development of self-protecting, self-healing, self-optimising, and self-configuring BSNs. The main technical details of the chapter will cover the use of multidimensional scaling for self-discovery of sensor co-locations for automatic configuration of routing structures, and the use of Bayesian belief propagation for efficient, distributed inferencing and fault tolerant sensing.

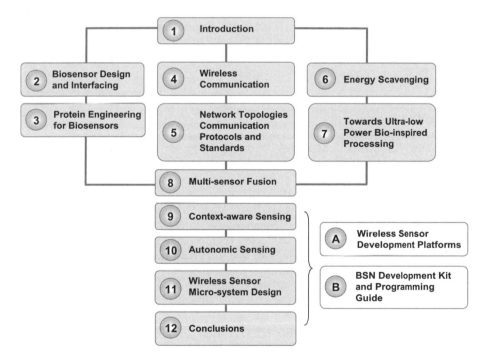

Figure 1.15 The structure of this book and the interdependency of the chapters.

In Chapter 11, we will provide a practical perspective of designing wireless sensor microsystems. Wireless sensor microsystems offer very diverse functionality, and this brings about a range of technical design problems. Design skills include sensors, ASICs, wireless, low power, packaging, software, networking and power sources. These problems become more challenging the smaller the final device must be. In this chapter, we will cover a range of design topics that are of relevance to wireless BSN microsystem designs and the general design principles involved will be elaborated in the context of developing an ingestible lab-in-a-pill device. This offers a particularly challenging case study echoing many of the issues that have been discussed in other chapters. Finally, Chapter 12 concludes the book by summarising the materials presented and highlighting some of the major research and development opportunities lying ahead. To help readers entering into the field and starting up some of the practical experiments involving BSNs, we have provided two appendices outlining the design background and detailed technical and programming issues for the use of the BSN development kit.

The inherent diversity of the materials covered for the effective development of BSNs means it is not essential for the readers to go through the chapters provided in a rigid sequence, and Figure 1.15 outlines the inter-dependency of all the chapters. It is suggested that readers can take an appropriate route depending on your technical background to follow the materials presented, either used as a reference for BSN research and development or as a graduate level text book. A dedicated web site (**http://www.bsn-web.info**) that accompanies the contents of the book has also been created. Interested readers can use this site to find out the latest updates and access BSN related resources, particularly those related to the BSN development kit as described in the appendices of this book.

References

1. Borkar S. Design challenges of technology scaling. IEEE Micro 1999; 19(4):23-29.
2. Bulusu N, Jha S. Wireless sensor network systems: a systems perspective. Artech House Publishers, 2005.
3. Warneke B, Last M, Liebowitz B, Pister KSJ. Smart dust: communicating with a cubic-millimeter computer. Computer 2001; 34(1):44-51.
4. Kahn JM, Katz RH, Pister KSJ. Next century challenges: mobile networking for smart dust. In: Proceedings of the International Conference on Mobile Computing and Networking, Boston, MA, 2000.
5. Link JR, Sailor MJ. Smart dust: self assembling, self-organizing photonic crystals of porous Si. In: Proceedings of the National Academy of Sciences 2003; 100(19):10607-10610.
6. Culler S, Estrin D, Srivastava M. Overview of sensor networks. Computer 2004; 37(8):41-49.
7. Sung M, Pentland A. Minimally-invasive physiological sensing for human-aware interfaces. In: Proceedings of Human-Computer Interaction International 2005.
8. Lo BPL, Yang GZ. Key technical challenges and current implementations of body sensor networks. In: Proceedings of the Second International Workshop on Wearable and Implantable Body Sensor Networks 2005; 1-5.
9. Go AS, Hylek EM, Phillips KA, Chang Y, Henault LE, Selby JV, *et al.* Prevalence of diagnosed atrial fibrillation in adults: national implications for rhythm management and stroke prevention: the AnTicoagulation and Risk Factors in

Atrial fibrillation (ATRIA) study. The Journal of the American Medical Association 2001; 285(18):2370-2375.

10. Benjamin EJ, Wolf PA, D'Agostino RB, Silbershatz H, Kannel WB, Levy D. Impact of atrial fibrillation on the risk of death: the Framingham heart study. Circulation 1998; 98(10):946-952.

11. Chobanian AV, Bakris GL, Black HR, Cushman WC, Green LA, Izzo JL, Jr., *et al.* The seventh report of the Joint National Committee on prevention, detection, evaluation, and treatment of high blood pressure: the JNC 7 report. The Journal of the American Medical Association 2003; 289(19):2560-2572.

12. Hunt SA, Baker DW, Chin MH, Cinquegrani MP, Feldman AM, Francis GS, *et al.* ACC/AHA guidelines for the evaluation and management of chronic heart failure in the adult: executive summary, A report of the American College of Cardiology/American Heart Association task force on practice guidelines (Committee to revise the 1995 guidelines for the evaluation and management of heart failure): developed in collaboration with the International Society for Heart and Lung Transplantation; endorsed by the Heart Failure Society of America. Circulation 2001; 104(24):2996-3007.

13. Qureshi AI, Suri MF, Kirmani JF, Divani AA, Mohammad Y. Is prehypertension a risk factor for cardiovascular diseases? Stroke 2005; 36(9):1859-1863.

14. Brown AS. Lipid management in patients with diabetes mellitus. American Journal of Cardiology 2005; 96(4A):26-32.

15. Maldonado M, D'Amico S, Otiniano M, Balasubramanyam A, Rodriguez L, Cuevas E. Predictors of glycaemic control in indigent patients presenting with diabetic ketoacidosis. Diabetes, Obesity and Metabolism 2005; 7(3):282-289.

16. Rubin RR. Adherence to pharmacologic therapy in patients with type 2 diabetes mellitus. American Journal of Medicine 2005; 118(Supplement 5A):27S-34S.

17. Allen MG. Implantable micromachined wireless pressure sensors: approach and clinical demonstration. In: Proceedings of the Second International Workshop on Wearable and Implantable Body Sensor Networks 2005; 40-43.

18. Butler RN. Population aging and health. British Medical Journal 1997; 315(7115):1082-1084.

19. Aronow WS, Ahn C. Elderly nursing home patients with congestive heart failure after myocardial infarction living in New York City have a higher prevalence of mortality in cold weather and warm weather months. Journals of Gerontology A: Biological Sciences and Medical Sciences 2004; 59(2):146-147.

20. Koken PJ, Piver WT, Ye F, Elixhauser A, Olsen LM, Portier CJ. Temperature, air pollution, and hospitalization for cardiovascular diseases among elderly people in Denver. Environmental Health Perspectives 2003; 111(10):1312-1317.

21. Dishongh T, Rhodes K, Needham B. Room to room location using wearable sensors for tracking social health of elders. In: Proceedings of the Second International Workshop on Wearable and Implantable Body Sensor Networks 2005; 18-20.

22. Chouvarda I, Koutkias V, Malousi A, Maglaveras N. Grid-enabled biosensor networks for pervasive healthcare. Studies in Health Technology and Informatics 2005; 112:90-99.
23. Rubel P, Fayn J, Simon-Chautemps L, Atoui H, Ohlsson M, Telisson D, *et al.* New paradigms in telemedicine: ambient intelligence, wearable, pervasive and personalized. Studies in Health Technology and Informatics 2004; 108:123-132.
24. Wang L, Johannessen EA, Hammond PA, Cui L, Reid SW, Cooper JM, *et al.* A programmable microsystem using system-on-chip for real-time biotelemetry. IEEE Transactions on Biomedical Engineering 2005; 52(7):1251-1260.
25. Jovanov E, Milenkovic A, Otto C, de Groen PC. A wireless body area network of intelligent motion sensors for computer assisted physical rehabilitation. Journal of NeuroEngineering and Rehabilitation 2005; 2(1):6.
26. Vamvakaki V, Fournier D, Chaniotakis NA. Fluorescence detection of enzymatic activity within a liposome based nano-biosensor. Biosensors and Bioelectronics 2005; 21(2):384-388.
27. Suwansa-Ard S, Kanatharana P, Asawatreratanakul P, Limsakul C, Wongkittisuksa B, Thavarungkul P. Semi disposable reactor biosensors for detecting carbamate pesticides in water. Biosensors and Bioelectronics 2005; 21(3):445-454.
28. Shantaram A, Beyenal H, Raajan R, Veluchamy A, Lewandowski Z. Wireless sensors powered by microbial fuel cells. Environmental Science and Technology 2005; 39(13):5037-5042.
29. Arshak A, Arshak K, Waldron D, Morris D, Korostynska O, Jafer E, *et al.* Review of the potential of a wireless MEMS and TFT microsystems for the measurement of pressure in the GI tract. Medical Engineering and Physics 2005; 27(5):347-356.
30. Paradiso R, Loriga G, Taccini N. Wearable system for vital signs monitoring. Studies in Health Technology and Informatics 2004; 108:253-259.
31. Cardionet. http://www.cardionet.com/
32. Vo-Dinh T. Biosensors, nanosensors and biochips: frontiers in environmental and medical diagnostics. In: Proceedings of the First International Symposium on Micro and Nano Technology, Hawaii, 2004; 1-6.
33. Shnayder V, Chen B, Lorincz K, Fulford-Jones TRF, Welsh M. Sensor networks for medical care. Division of Engineering and Applied Sciences, Harvard University, Technical Report, TR-08-05, 2005.
34. Spada C, Spera G, Riccioni M, Biancone L, Petruzziello L, Tringali A, *et al.* A novel diagnostic tool for detecting functional patency of the small bowel: the Given patency capsule. Endoscopy 2005; 37(9):793-800.
35. Garg SK, Schwartz S, Edelman SV. Improved glucose excursions using an implantable real-time continuous glucose sensor in adults with type 1 diabetes. Diabetes Care 2004; 27(3):734-738.
36. Steil GM, Panteleon AE, Rebrin K. Closed-loop insulin delivery-the path to physiological glucose control. Advanced Drug Delivery Reviews 2004; 56(2):125-144.

37. Ward WK, Wood MD, Casey HM, Quinn MJ, Federiuk IF. An implantable subcutaneous glucose sensor array in ketosis-prone rats: closed loop glycemic control. Artificial Organs 2005; 29(2):131-143.

38. Brown JQ, Srivastava R, McShane MJ. Encapsulation of glucose oxidase and an oxygen-quenched fluorophore in polyelectrolyte-coated calcium alginate microspheres as optical glucose sensor systems. Biosensors and Bioelectronics 2005; 21(1):212-216.

39. Najafi N, Ludomirsky A. Initial animal studies of a wireless, batteryless, MEMS implant for cardiovascular applications. Biomedical Microdevices 2004; 6(1):61-65.

40. Richards Grayson AC, Scheidt Shawgo R, Li Y, Cima MJ. Electronic MEMS for triggered delivery. Advanced Drug Delivery Reviews 2004; 56(2):173-184.

41. Trohman RG, Kim MH, Pinski SL. Cardiac pacing: the state of the art. Lancet 2004; 364(9446):1701-1719.

42. National Pacemaker and ICD database. UK and Ireland. Annual Report 2000.

43. Parkes J, Bryant J, Milne R. Implantable cardioverter defibrillators: arrhythmias. A rapid and systematic review. Health Technology Assessment 2000; 4(26):1-69.

44. Turk DC. Clinical effectiveness and cost-effectiveness of treatments for patients with chronic pain. Clinical Journal of Pain 2002; 18(6):355-365.

45. Sheldon R, Kiff ES, Clarke A, Harris ML, Hamdy S. Sacral nerve stimulation reduces corticoanal excitability in patients with faecal incontinence. British Journal of Surgery 2005; 92(11):1423-1431.

46. Benabid AL, Krack PP, Benazzouz A, Limousin P, Koudsie A, Pollak P. Deep brain stimulation of the subthalamic nucleus for Parkinson's disease: methodologic aspects and clinical criteria. Neurology 2000; 55(12 Supplement 6):S40-S44.

47. Chabardes S, Kahane P, Minotti L, Koudsie A, Hirsch E, Benabid AL. Deep brain stimulation in epilepsy with particular reference to the subthalamic nucleus. Epileptic Disorders 2002; 4(Supplement 3):S83-S93.

48. Roscnow JM, Tarkin H, Zias E, Sorbera C, Mogilner A. Simultaneous use of bilateral subthalamic nucleus stimulators and an implantable cardiac defibrillator. Case report. Journal of Neurosurgery 2003; 99(1):167-169.

49. Heinzel A, Hebling C, Muller M, Zedda M, Muller C. Fuel cells for low power applications. Journal of Power Sources 2002; 105:250-255.

50. Dyer CK. Fuel cells for portable applications. Journal of Power Sources 2002; 106:31-34.

51. McGrath KM, Prakash GKS, Olah GA. Direct methanol fuel cells. Journal of Industrial and Engineering Chemistry 2004; 10:1063-1080.

52. Shao Z, Haile SM, Ahn J, Ronney PD, Zhan Z, Barnett SA. A thermally self-sustained micro solid-oxide fuel-cell stack with high power density. Nature 2005; 435(7043):795-798.

53. Sasaki S, Karube I. The development of microfabricated biocatalytic fuel cells. Trends in Biotechnology 1999; 17(2):50-52.

54. Soukharev V, Mano N, Heller A. A four-electron O(2)-electroreduction biocatalyst superior to platinum and a biofuel cell operating at 0.88 V. Journal of the American Chemistry Society 2004; 126(27):8368-8369.
55. Arra S, Heinisuo S, Vanhala J. Acoustic power transmission into an implantable device. In: Proceedings of the Second International Workshop on Wearable and Implantable Body Sensor Networks 2005; 60-64.
56. Guyomar D, Badel A, Lefeuvre E, Richard C. Toward energy harvesting using active materials and conversion improvement by nonlinear processing. IEEE Transactions on Ultrasonics, Ferroelectrics and Frequency Control 2005; 52(4):584-595.
57. Mitcheson PD, Green TC, Yeatman EM, Holms AS. Architectures for vibration-driven micropower generators. IEEE Journal of Microelectromechanical Systems 2004; 13(3):429-440.
58. Otis B, Chee YH, Rabaey J. A 400uW Rx, 1.6mW Tx super-regenerative transceiver for wireless sensor networks. In: Proceedings of the IEEE International Solid Circuits Conference (ISSCC) 2005.
59. Neirynck D, Williams C, Nix AR, Beach MA. Wideband channel characterisation for body and personal area networks. In: Proceedings of the First International Workshop on Body Sensor Networks 2004.
60. Alomainy A, Owadally AS, Hao Y, Parini CG, Nechayev YI, Constantinou CC, *et al.* Body-centric WLANs for future wearable computers. In: Proceedings of the First International Workshop on Wearable and Implantable Body Sensor Networks 2004.
61. Zhou L, Hass ZJ. Securing *ad hoc* networks. IEEE Network Magazine 1999; 13(6).
62. Ganesan D, Govindan R, Shenker S, Estrin D. Highly-resilient, energy-efficient multipath routing in wireless sensor networks. Mobile Computing and Communication Review 2002; 1(2):28-36.
63. Cherukuri S, Venkatasubramanian KK, Gupta SKS. BioSec: a biometric based approach for securing communication in wireless networks of biosensors implanted in the human body. In: Proceedings of International Conference on Parallel Processing Workshops 2003; 432-439.
64. Tapia EM, Intille SS, Larson K. Activity recognition in the home setting using simple and ubiquitous sensors. In: Proceedings of the Second International Conference on Pervasive Computing 2004; 158-175.
65. Kautz H, Etziono O, Fox D, Weld D. Foundations of assisted cognition systems. Department of Computer Science and Engineering, University of Washington, CSE-020AC-01, 2003.
66. Najafi B, Aminian K, Paraschiv-Ionescu A, Loew F, Bula CJ, Robert P. Ambulatory system for human motion analysis using a kinematic sensor: monitoring of daily physical activity in the elderly. IEEE Transactions on Biomedical Engineering 2003; 50(6):711-723.
67. Siuru B. Applying acoustic monitoring to medical diagnostics applications. Sensor Magazine 1997, http://www.sensorsmag.com/articles/0397/acoustic/ index.htm

68. Liden CB, Wolowicz M, Stivoric J, Teller A, Kasabach C, Vishnubhatla S, *et al.* Characterization and implications of the sensors incorporated into the SenseWear armband for energy expenditure and activity detection. http://www.bodybugg.com/pdf/Sensors.pdf

69. Asada HH, Shaltis P, Reisner A, Rhee S, Hutchinson RC. Mobile monitoring with wearable photoplethysmographic biosensors. IEEE Engineering in Medicine and Biology Magazine 2003; 22(3):28-40.

70. Heller A. Drug-delivering integrated therapeutic systems. In: Proceedings of the Second International Workshop on Wearable and Implantable Body Sensor Networks 2005; 6-11.

71. Giorgiou J, Toumazou C. A 126 microWatt cochlear chip for a totally implantable system. IEEE Journal of Solid-State Circuits 2005; 40(2):430-443.

72. Abidi SS, Goh A. A personalised healthcare information delivery system: pushing customised healthcare information over the WWW. Studies in Health Technology and Informatics 2000; 77:663-667.

73. Backadar T. Ambulatory monitoring-embeddable, wearable, 'its all about fashion' studies in wearable electronics. In: Proceedings of the Second International Workshop on Wearable and Implantable Body Sensor Networks 2005; 79-81.

74. Ellis H. Clinical anatomy: a revision andapplied anatomy for clinical students, 10th ed. Blackwell Science Inc., 2002.

75. Haes AJ, Chang L, Klein WL, Van Duyne RP. Detection of a biomarker for Alzheimer's disease from synthetic and clinical samples using a nanoscale optical biosensor. Journal of the American Chemistry Society 2005; 127(7):2264-2271.

76. Koh DM, Brown G, Temple L, Raja A, Toomey P, Bett N, *et al.* Rectal cancer: mesorectal lymph nodes at MR imaging with USPIO versus histopathologic findings--initial observations. Radiology 2004; 231(1):91-99.

77. Medintz IL, Clapp AR, Mattoussi H, Goldman ER, Fisher B, Mauro JM. Self-assembled nanoscale biosensors based on quantum dot FRET donors. Nature Materials 2003; 2(9):630-638.

Biosensor Design and Interfacing

Bhavik A. Patel, Costas A. Anastassiou, and Danny O'Hare

2.1 Introduction

Whilst there have been substantial advances in networking sensors for measuring physical parameters of clinical significance, *e.g.*, for blood pressure and heart rate, progress incorporating sensors into chemical sensor networks has been patchy. This is principally because chemical sensor technology is more lab-based and specialised and there are few examples of widely commercially available devices for developers. The dominant technology is electrochemistry, the study of which is typically confined to senior year chemistry degrees or graduate study in the analytical sciences. Nonetheless, there is reliable, mature technology in the open literature. This chapter is designed to provide a broad background on electrochemical sensors and biosensors, and to outline the major design issues and provide some pointers for the coming technology.

Biosensors are a means of measuring local chemical concentrations. Analytical scientists make a useful classification of the measurement process: there is the *sample* which can be a drop of solution, a blood sample or the whole organism, the *analyte* which is the chemical species of interest and the *matrix* which is the remainder of the sample. The key performance indicators are:

- *Selectivity*: the ability of the sensor to respond only to the analyte.
- *Sensitivity*: the output (typically voltage or current) produced per unit change in concentration.
- *Limit of Detection* (*LOD*): the lowest detectable analyte concentration, commonly defined as the concentration equivalent of three standard deviations of the y-intercept of the calibration working curve.

Stability of the sensitivity and offset are also important factors but frequently depend more on matrix effects such as protein adsorption rather than on intrinsic sensor properties.

Balkanisation of modern technology and science has had many baleful effects. In the case of sensors research, devices have been developed which meet no particular clinical need or have never been tested in real applications. The literature contains thousands of papers per year describing sensors which for various reasons – inadequate LOD, temporal and spatial resolution or poor selectivity – will never be used to solve the problems they purport to address. It is essential that the measurement problem be properly defined in the initial stages of sensor development. This requires multi-disciplinary development teams consisting of clinicians to aid problem definition, analytical scientists and electronic engineers.

The measurement of chemical concentration, frequently seen as obvious, does not *per se* constitute a scientific question. The scientific or clinical problem under examination should be the primary design criterion in any sensors project. There are typically three reasons for measuring concentration:

- *Statutory requirements*: For example, maximum blood alcohol levels for motorists are specified in most countries. The legislation specifies the analytical methods for forensic purposes.

- *Correlation with known clinical states*: Type I diabetes provides the most obvious example. Sensor measurements enable improvements in clinical management by increasing the frequency of measurement and allowing the patient to take measurements away from a formal clinical setting. The biosensor adds value by providing a low cost alternative to direct clinical observation.

- *Fundamental research*: Biological systems are characterised by rapid chemical fluxes. The relationships between the exchange of chemical information within the organism and both normal and pathophysiology require highly localised temporally resolved measurements of concentration. The recent explosion of scientific interest in neurophysiology and the development of devices for directly interfacing neurons with electronics for active prostheses provide strong drivers for the measurement of neurotransmitters in real time. A representative application, the study of aging in neuronal systems, is described later in this chapter.

2.1.1 What Is a Biosensor?

The term "biosensor" strictly refers to chemical sensors where a biological sensing element such as an enzyme or antibody is used to couple the analyte concentration in a sample matrix to a transducer as shown in Figure 2.1.

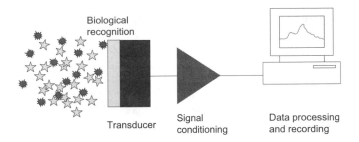

Biological
recognition

Transducer

Signal
conditioning

Data processing
and recording

Figure 2.1 Schematic representation of a biosensor.

However, the term is also more loosely used to describe devices, including signal conditioning and processing elements, which are used to measure chemical concentrations in biological systems, notably living organisms. Whilst it is not helpful to broaden commonly agreed scientific definitions, there is some sense in covering this broader class of devices since they have widespread application in physiological measurement and wide potential application in a clinical setting. For this reason, this chapter will almost exclusively focus on electrochemical sensors, where the transduction event is an electron or ion transfer at the interface of an ionic solution (which could be blood, extracellular fluid or cerebrospinal fluid) and a selective membrane or electrified solid, such as a metal, carbon or organic conductor. Additionally, electrochemical biosensors are those devices which have found the most widespread utility in basic science and established the most commercial success to date.

Electrochemical methods offer unique advantages over other transduction modes such as those based on the interaction of electromagnetic radiation, for example UV/visible spectrometry or magnetic resonance imaging. The principal advantage is that electrochemical events are *kinetic* in origin. That is to say, the resulting electrical signal is a function of the *rate* of a charge transfer or partitioning process. This is in sharp contrast to techniques based on the interaction of electromagnetic radiation with matter where the signal strength is ultimately a function of the number of absorbing species. As a consequence, signal intensity decreases with sample size, a major disadvantage for biological applications where miniaturisation is an important factor in engineering effective measurement. In electrochemical transduction however, the signal is a function of concentration, an intensive property, and one expects the same signal per unit area from a picolitre sample as from an ocean provided the analyte concentration is the same. This enables the investigator to make *a priori* decisions on which is the important length scale for measurement – subcellular machinery (10-100nm) cells (1-100μm), capillaries (10-1000μm) or organs (mm-cm). Successful electrochemical measurements have for many years been undertaken with devices smaller than 0.1 μm offering unparalleled and tuneable spatial resolution. Additional advantages include rapid response times (typically a millisecond or better), ease of miniaturisation, compatibility with CMOS processing and low cost. Miniaturisation and low cost also allows for massive redundancy and signal averaging to provide more durable and robust measurement.

It is however the case that biological tissue is a hostile environment for any measurement device, regardless of the transduction mode. This chapter aims to provide an introduction to electrochemical biosensors, review recent advances and describe representative applications where electrochemical devices have provided important clinical and physiological information. We will also consider the particular problems associated with measurement in the biological milieu (foreign body reactions and sensor fouling) and describe some strategies which have been found to be successful in minimising these difficulties. These issues cannot be adequately addressed without understanding the basic operating principles of these useful and widely-used devices.

2.2 How Do Electrochemical Devices Work?

This section is by no means exhaustive – electrochemistry is composed of a number of complex phenomena and electron transfer at an electrified interface can only be adequately described in terms of electron tunnelling. There is no classical physical model that describes the phenomena. A detailed discussion of the intricacies of quantum mechanics is beyond the scope of this review. However, a basic understanding of the underlying principles greatly aids interpretation of a diverse literature and can inform engineering of successful sensor systems.

There are two predominant modes of operation: *a*) potentiometric where the sensor output voltage can be quantitatively related to the target analyte concentration, and *b*) amperometric or voltammetric where a non-equilibrium voltage is imposed and the resulting current is related to concentration. Potentiometric devices have the following characteristics:

- The system is at equilibrium. No current is passed and the analyte is not consumed.
- Instrumentation is simple. All that is required is a reference electrode and a high impedance voltmeter.
- Selectivity is inherent. The selective element is typically a membrane or oxide coating.
- The response is logarithmic. Typically, there is a 59 mV change in output per decade change in concentration. This leads to a large linear dynamic range but leads to poor sensitivity in electromagnetically noisy environments.
- The practical dynamic range is hard to define since it is determined by deviations from the log-linear response at both ends of the calibration working curve.

Amperometric (current output) and voltammetric (current-voltage output) devices can be characterised as follows:

- A non-equilibrium potential is imposed on the sensor. The resulting current flow under some circumstances is linearly related to concentration (ampcromctry) or the current voltage characteristics can be used to provide both qualitative (identity) and quantitative (concentration) information.
- Selectivity is achieved by potential control and engineering of the electrode surface.
- Non-steady potential programming can be used to provide further selectivity and extend the dynamic range.
- Instrumentation is more complex typically comprising a signal generator, control amplifier, current to voltage conversion, a reference electrode for potential control and a counter electrode to provide the current path.
- The technique is limited to those analytes that undergo electron transfer reaction in the potential range available in water, *i.e.* it must be capable of being reduced at potentials more positive than water reduction to hydrogen or be oxidised at potentials more negative than water oxidation to oxygen. At physiological pH, this potential range is typically -0.9V to +1.2V depending on electrode material.

The selection of potentiometric *versus* amperometric/voltammetric modes of operation is dictated by the nature of the sample and the selectivity and sensitivity required, though there are some useful general rules: *a*) neutral species cannot be directly sensed in the potentiometrc mode, and *b*) those species which cannot be oxidised in the potential range offered by water cannot be directly sensed by amperometry/voltammetry.

2.2.1 Potentiometric Devices

2.2.1.1 Ion Selective Electrodes (ISEs)

The ISEs have their origin in the glass pH electrode though the underlying phenomenon is that which is responsible for cell membrane potentials. At the heart of an ISE is a membrane which shows selective permeability towards the ion of interest. The membrane can be glass, an ionic conducting crystal, an immiscible liquid supported in a porous polymer or a polymer blend containing an ion exchanging or ion binding compound.

Glass and other hydrogen ion selective electrodes are mature technology and were the subject of a review by Bates [1] which nonetheless remains authoritative. Early biological applications of this technology are reviewed by Cater and Silver [2], though special mention must be made of Hinke [3] who produced a 3μm diameter electrode and Thomas [4] who made sub micron device, an astonishing technical achievement. Similar devices were briefly available commercially during the 1980s, though the combination of extreme fragility and high impedance led to their abandonment as commercial products.

ISEs consist of a selective membrane separating the test solution (or experimental subject) and an internal filling solution of known composition. The membrane is supported at the end of an insulating cylinder. The membrane itself can be glass (as for the pH electrode), a solid ionic conductor (such as the Eu(III)-doped LaF_3 single crystal used in the hugely successful fluoride sensor) a PVC membrane with an ion exchanger or ligand dissolved in it or an immiscible liquid held in the end of a pulled glass capillary to produce a sensor capable of operating on the cellular length scale.

ISEs are equilibrium devices. The thermodynamic condition for equilibrium is that the free energy of each chemical species is equal on both sides of the membrane. The free energy for any ion i is the sum of the partial molar free energy, chemical potential μ_i and the electrical potential ϕ scaled by Faraday's constant F and the charge on the ion z (including sign):

$$\mu_i = \left(\frac{\partial G_i}{\partial n_i} \right)_{j,P,T} \tag{2.1}$$

Note that electrochemical potential, $\bar{\mu}_i = \mu_i + zF\phi$.

If we designate the external solution as phase α and the internal filling solution as phase β, the electrochemical potential for the target species i must be equal on each side of the membrane:

$$\mu_i^\circ(\alpha) + RT \ln a_i(\alpha) + zF\phi(\alpha) = \mu_i^\circ(\beta) + RT \ln a_i(\beta) + zF\phi(\beta) \tag{2.2}$$

If we define the electrical potential difference, *i.e.* the voltage we actually measure experimentally, as $E_m = \phi(\beta) - \phi(\alpha)$, simple rearrangement gives:

$$E_m = \varphi(\beta) - \phi(\alpha) = \frac{RT}{zF} \ln \frac{a_i(\alpha)}{a_i(\beta)} \tag{2.3}$$

where a_i is the thermodynamic ion activity. The activity is the thermodynamically effective concentration which is equal to the product of the ion concentration and the ion activity coefficient γ_i. The activity coefficient is a function of the ionic strength and a detailed discussion is beyond the scope of this chapter. However, for the purpose of understanding the operation of an ISE, it is important to note that γ_i is constant, provided the ionic strength is kept constant. This means that any calibration solution must have the same ionic strength as the test solution. This is easily achieved in laboratory-based *ex situ* investigations through the use of ionic strength adjustment buffers. For *in vivo* measurement, the actual concentration detected with an ISE (or indeed any device which depends on membrane potentials such as the ISFET) remains uncertain. However, the change in concentration is likely to be correct since ionic strength is tightly controlled in physiological systems.

The important thing to note about (2.3) is that is shows the origin of the dependence of the membrane potential on the logarithm of the activity (or concentration). It also provides an important design criterion – the internal filling solution of the ISE needs to be of a fixed and known composition.

Practical devices typically contain a silver chloride reference electrode inside the ISE and another silver chloride reference electrode external to the membrane. For practical sensors, the external reference electrode can be packaged with the ISE. The governing equation will therefore contain terms that describe the reference electrode potentials. Since these remain constant under correct operation, the overall equation describing the operation of an ISE can be simplified to:

$$E = K + S \log a_i \qquad (2.4)$$

or

$$E = K' + S \log c_i \qquad (2.5)$$

where K' now includes the ion activity coefficient, under conditions where it is reasonable to assume that it is constant. When converted into base ten logarithms, the ideal slope of calibration (*i.e.* the sensitivity) will be given by:

$$2.303 \frac{RT}{zF} \qquad (2.6)$$

so for a singly charged positive ion, the slope of calibration will be 59mV per decade change in concentration at room temperature.

Limits of detection for ISEs are typically around micromolar. Pioneering research by Pretsch and by Bakker [5] over the last 5-6 years has clearly demonstrated that these limits arose principally from leaching of analyte ions from the selective membrane. By careful design, they have shown that it is possible to extend the LOD by three orders of magnitude down to the nanomolar range. At these ultratrace levels, the approximation that concentration equals activity is of course substantially improved.

2.2.1.2 Metal Metal Oxide (MMOs) pH Electrodes

Measurement of pH is important in the study of tissue metabolism, an indicator of nutritional status and has even been used as a marker of vesicular release in neurophysiology research. Tissue pH will fall if oxygenation falls and the metabolism switches to lactate production. As a consequence, this relatively easy to implement measurement can be a good marker of tissue nutrition or viability and can be an important marker in wound healing.

Glass membrane pH electrodes, though well-established for laboratory use suffer from a number of serious disadvantages in biomedical application: slow response times, high impedance, mechanical fragility, requirement for frequent recalibration and vulnerability to membrane fouling with consequent loss of accuracy and precision. These disadvantages are compounded in biological measurements where rapid transient changes in pH are as of much or greater interest than the steady value.

Alternative techniques include the use of liquid ion exchangers, either in plasticized PVC membranes [6] for intravascular measurements or held by capillary action at the tip of a silanised glass micropipette for intracellular recording [7]. However, both of these approaches retain the key weaknesses of glass electrodes: poor mechanical stability, slow response times and poor stability.

More promising technology is in the form of *Metal-Metal Oxide* (MMO) electrodes, due to their intrinsic mechanical stability, relative ease of miniaturisation and compatibility with CMOS processing, which holds out the possibility of integrated devices. They were the subject of an early review by Ives [8] and their application as pH sensors was reviewed by most recently by Glab [9].

Whereas in glass and liquid membrane electrodes the analytical signal originates in a membrane potential, in metal-metal oxide electrodes the measured electrode potential is due to the equilibrium between a sparingly soluble salt and its saturated solution; in other words potential depends on the thermodynamic solubility product. MMO electrodes are a special case of this kind of electrode since the anion participates in the self-ionisation of the solvent. The potential dependence on pH should therefore be given by:

$$E = E^{\circ}_{M,MO,H^+} - 2.303\frac{RT}{F}pH \qquad (2.7)$$

where E°_{M,MO,H^+} is a constant, lumping together the standard potentials, the solubility product of the metal oxide and the ionization product of water. R is the universal gas constant, T is the absolute temperature and F is Faraday's constant, the charge on one mole of electrons – essentially a scaling factor that converts chemist's units (moles) into electrician's units (volt). The ideal properties of a MMO electrode have been listed by Ives [8] as:

(a) The metal must be sufficiently noble as to resist corrosion.
(b) It must be possible to obtain the metal in a reproducible state.
(c) The oxide must be stable (This is incompatible with (a), though in practice, the oxide must only be scarcely soluble).
(d) It must be possible to obtain the oxide in a reproducible state.
(e) The oxide must be scarcely soluble yet able to participate in the equilibrium reaction sufficiently rapidly to give an adequate current density.

These properties, though scarcely achievable practically ((a) and (e) above are strictly contradictory) are useful guides to experimentation.

No MMO system has been found which is well-behaved for all applications, though antimony electrodes have been widely used for many years in medical applications [10] and have recently seen application as potentiometric sensing tips in scanning electrochemical microscopy [11]. However, there are several serious drawbacks to using antimony electrodes *in vivo*: Ives has noted that they must be used in aerated solutions [8] and that Nernstian or even rectilinear responses can not be relied upon. The solution must not contain oxidising or reducing agents or complexing agents such as citrate, oxalate, tartrate or certain amino acids. There is a response to dissolved oxygen which is caused by localised corrosion for which the cathode reaction is oxygen reduction inevitably leading to sensitivity to stirring.

As a consequence of the shortcomings of the two most widely used pH sensors (glass membrane ISE and the antimony electrode), there has been substantial recent interest in pH sensors based on hydrated iridium oxide. There are several methods for preparing these devices, reviewed by Glab *et al* [9] though they can be conveniently divided into two types: electrochemically generated iridium oxide films (widely known as AIROF – *Anodic Iridium Oxide Film*) and thermally generated iridium oxide which appears to be chemically distinct. These devices are of interest due to their reported stability in a wide range of aqueous solutions, low impedance and fast response [12] and the compatibility of iridium with CMOS processes allowing the prospect of integrated devices. The earliest report is a patent by Perley and Godshalk [13], though intense activity in this area dates from seminal papers describing the fundamental redox chemistry by Burke [14] and the publication of a reliable and well-characterised electrochemical method of preparation of AIROF electrodes by Hitchman [15]. More recently, Ir-based pH sensors have been used as potentiometric probes in scanning electrochemical microscopy [16], in Severinghaus-type CO_2 sensors [17, 18] and mechanistic aspects have been considered in more detail by Hitchman [19]. Biological applications have been thin on the ground but Ir-based devices have been applied to the study of pericellular pH in myocytes during ischaemia [20] and to investigate biofilm formation [21].

There are broadly two methods of preparing iridium oxide pH sensors: *a*) electrolytic generation of the oxide either from iridium metal or direct deposition of a film of hydrated oxide from a solution of iridium (III) hexachloride, and *b*) thermal generation. Reliable protocols for these methods are given below.

Electrolytic Preparation of AIROF Electrodes

Iridium is a dense, brittle and expensive metal, to the extent that it is frequently more convenient to work with small pieces of iridium wire connected to platinum or cheaper material. Iridium wire (0.125mm diameter, 4-5mm in length, 99.99+%) was butt-welded to platinum wire in a natural gas/ O_2 flame. Spot welding is similarly successful but silver-loaded epoxy shows a high fail rate. The wire needs to be insulated everywhere but the sensing surface. This can be accomplished by dip coating in epoxylite resin. Additional mechanical strength can be achieved by embedding in a hypodermic needle using low viscosity epoxy resin. Electrode tips were prepared by sawing on the bevel using a low speed saw (Buehler) followed by polishing on emery paper (1200 grit and 2500 grit) and aqueous alumina slurry (6μm, 1μm and 0.05μm, Buehler) on polishing cloths with ultrasonic cleaning in water between grades. The oxide film was generated by cycling the potential in sulfuric acid (0.5mol dm^{-3}) at 2V s^{-1} for 8000-12,000 cycles between the potentials of hydrogen and oxygen generation finishing with a 10mV s^{-1} scan stopping at the main anodic peak. An iridium rod and Ag|AgCl (3M KCl) served as counter and reference electrode respectively. The reference electrode was connected to the cell using a K_2SO_4 (0.3mol dm^{-3}) salt bridge to minimise chloride ion infiltration. This has been found by the present authors and others to be critical in the preparation of stable films [26]. Cyclic voltammograms were recorded at various intervals to assess the extent of oxide film growth. In all cases, the resulting AIROF electrodes were soaked for 48 hours in deionised water (>15MΩ cm) prior to use. For additional stability in biological measurement, we have found that Nafion coating is very successful and barely affects sensitivity or response time. Nafion films were applied and annealed at 120°C according to the protocol described by Harrison and Moussy [22].

Calibration from pH 3 to 12.1 gave a super-Nernstian response of (69±2)mV per pH unit. Comparison of calibration curves recorded in N_2 and O_2 sparged solutions revealed a maximum perturbation of 0.9mV at pH 7.4. This places an absolute limit on the accuracy of 0.0125pH units if the oxygen concentration is unknown, though this does, of course, represent the worst-case scenario.

Thermally Prepared Iridium Oxide Electrodes

Iridium wire was annealed in a natural gas flame, straightened and carefully cleaned by sonication in acetone followed by rinsing with deionised water. After drying, one end (approximately 2mm) was wetted with NaOH solution (1mol dm^{-3}) and the wire was heated to 800°C in a muffle furnace for thirty minutes. This was repeated until a blue-black coating was clearly visible to the naked eye. This typically took 5-6 applications. The electrode was soaked for three days in deionised water before use. All but the electrode tip (approximately 0.5mm) was insulated using FEP/PTFE dual shrink tubing (Zeuss). Nafion films were applied using the technique described above. Calibration plot in Britton-Robinson buffer over the physiologically-relevant pH range of 6.5 to 8 gave a slope of 59.5mV/pH (r = 0.9999).

Representative Physiological Applications

Tissue culture and tissue engineering are areas of intense research. We have applied both thermally-prepared and AIROF pH sensors to study cultured intervertebral discs and examine the effect of physical loading.

Figure 2.2 shows results from an experiment where an excised L5-S1 porcine intervertebral disc was cultured. pH was monitored in both the bathing solution and in the tissue using the thermally prepared iridium oxide sensors. The sensors showed good stability over the duration of the experiment and were able to track the changes in pH brought about by changes in the pH in the bathing solution.

A major advantage of these devices is the relative ease of miniaturisation, at least down to 100μm. This enables them to be packaged alongside other devices. It is of particular interest to combine pH with the measurement of dissolved oxygen. An iridium wire was co-embedded with a 25μm gold microwire which, when polarised to -950mV served as an oxygen sensor. After anodisation and Nafion coating, the combined sensor was embedded in the intervertebral disc. Figure 2.3 shows how both tissue oxygenation and pH are affected by mechanical loading.

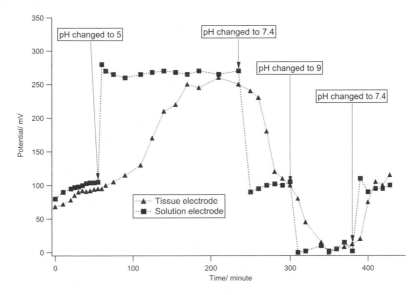

Figure 2.2 The response of a thermally prepared iridium oxide pH sensor in cultured intervertebral disc. Square points show the response of the solution sensor, triangles show the response of the tissue sensor.

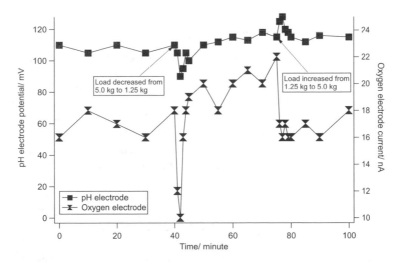

Figure 2.3 Examining the effect of mechanical loading on tissue oxygenation and pH measured using a combined pH/O$_2$ sensor.

In summary, iridium oxide electrodes have demonstrable utility in biology. The AIROF device fabrication is compatible with CMOS processing and the obvious next step is integration with amplification, signal processing, filtering, calibration and temperature compensation. Further miniaturisation may be achievable with templated electrolytic deposition on to, for example, carbon fibres or carbon nano-tubes.

2.2.1.3 Coupling Potentiometry to Biological Receptors

Enzymes are proteins which catalyse chemical reactions. Many enzymes show a high degree of selectivity towards the substrate which can be exploited in sensor design. The key concept is that if we cannot produce a membrane that is selectively conductive for our target analyte, either because it is uncharged or no suitable synthetic ligand or ion exchanger exists, then we can use an enzyme layer on the surface of our potentiometric sensor. The enzyme layer reacts selectively with our target analyte and the reaction produces a detectable chemical species (such as H^+) in direct proportion to our analyte concentration. A widely used example is urease which catalyses the hydrolysis of urea to ammonium and carbon dioxide. The carbon dioxide rapidly hydrolyses to produce bicarbonate and protons. The resulting pH change can be sensed using a pH electrode. Practical devices for this type of biosensor have been reviewed by Kuan and Guilbault [23]. Alternatively, the ammonium can be detected with an ion selective electrode, or the carbon dioxide can be detected using a Severinghaus type gas sensor. The overall reaction scheme is shown below:

$$CO(NH_2)_2 + H_2O \xrightarrow{\quad Urease \quad} 2NH_4^+ + CO_2$$
$$CO_2 + H_2O \rightarrow HCO_3^- + H^+$$

The enzyme layer can be immobilised by trapping behind a semi-permeable membrane or by cross-linking with albumin and glutaraldehyde. A major problem inherent with this design is that the enzyme layer must be permeable to allow the liberated protons to reach the pH sensitive membrane but this inevitably means that the sensor will also be affected by changes in tissue pH, which are likely to accompany any changes in major metabolite concentration. Whilst compensation can be introduced using a similar, but enzymically inactive sensor, this requires excellent reproducibility of both manufacture and performance. The former is relatively easily achieved but receptors of biological provenance are rarely so well-behaved. An additional problem with potentiometric biosensors is their inherent low sensitivity due to the log-linear Nernstian response (*vide supra*). For these reasons, the overwhelming majority of biosensors use electrochemical sensors in the amperometric mode where potential control adds a degree of experimental control of selectivity and the linear relationship between current and concentration provides adequate sensitivity and simplifies the signal processing requirements.

2.2.2 Amperometry and Voltammetry

The fundamental principle of all electrochemical sensors is the transfer of electrons to or from the conduction band of an electronic conductor (usually metal or carbon) to or from a redox active species at the electrode surface. Oxidation involves the loss of electrons from the highest occupied molecular orbital whereas reduction involves electrons being injected into the lowest unoccupied molecular orbital. For some arbitrary pair of compounds where R represents the reduced form and O represents the oxidised form, the reaction can be written as:

$$O + ne^- \Leftrightarrow R$$

though most electrochemical reactions are more complicated and can involve proton transfers and new phase formation (bubbles, electrodeposition). For any redox couple, there is a corresponding electrode potential which is related to the free energy through:

$$\Delta G = -nFE \qquad (2.8)$$

where ΔG is the free energy change, n is the number of moles of electrons, F is Faraday's constant ($96,485.3C \ mol^{-1}$) and E is the electrode potential. Electrode potentials are measured relative to a reference electrode, with the *Standard Hydrogen Electrode* (SHE) being given the arbitrary value of zero volt. Tabulated standard electrode potentials are usually reported relative to this standard. The relationship between equilibrium electrode potential, E_e, and concentration is given by the Nernst equation:

$$E = E^\circ - \frac{RT}{nF} \ln\left(\frac{[R]}{[O]}\right) \qquad (2.9)$$

where E° is the standard electrode potential (the potential where both O and R are in their standard states), and $[R]$ and $[O]$ are the concentrations of the reduced and oxidised forms respectively. (Strictly speaking we should use thermodynamic activities for concentrations, but activity coefficients are generally not known in the physiological situation. However, since the ion activity coefficients are primarily affected by ionic strength, they should at least remain approximately constant).

In voltammetry and amperometry, we impose a non-equilibrium potential to drive the electrode reaction, either as an oxidation or reduction, and the resulting current (amperometry) or current voltage relationship (voltammetry) is recorded. The current voltage relationship is given in Figure 2.4.

The relationship between current and overvoltage ($\eta = E - E_e$) is best understood by considering the processes involved in the electrode reaction. Electron transfer can only take place at the electrode surface. Electron transfer at electrified interfaces with ionic solutions takes place by electron tunnelling and is therefore re-

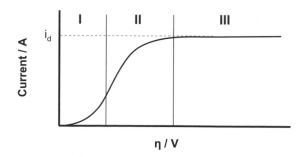

Figure 2.4 Schematic of the voltammetric steady state current-voltage relationship.

stricted to distances of about one bond length. The reactant O must therefore be transported to the electrode surface before electron transfer can take place. Regardless of the electrode system, this mass transport close to the electrode, within the mass transport boundary layer will take place by molecular Brownian diffusion. This can be characterised by a mass transport rate constant whose exact form will depend on electrode geometry and can be evaluated by solutions of Fick's law with appropriate boundary conditions. Solutions exist for most common microelectrode configurations such as microdiscs, fibres and rings [24]. Once at the electrode surface, electron transfer can take place:

$$O_{Surface} + ne^- \rightarrow R_{Surface}$$

Although this is written as a conventional chemical reaction, it is important to note that electrons are one of the reacting species. Therefore, the rate of reaction can be followed either as the rate of change of concentrations of R or O or by the rate of movement of electrons across the electrified interface. When scaled by Faraday's constant, this rate is equivalent to the electrical current flowing in the electrical circuit. The relationship between flux (J, mol s^{-1} m^{-2}) and current i is given by:

$$i = nFAJ \qquad\qquad (2.10)$$

where A is the electrode area.

A key feature of electrochemistry is that the rate of the reaction can be directly and continuously measured from the current. This can be seen clearly in Figure 2.5 below – all of the fluxes must be equal for the current to be sustained.

The rate of electron transfer is characterised by the heterogeneous rate constant k_{het}. This rate constant depends strongly on the overvoltage, given by the empirical Butler-Volmer relationship:

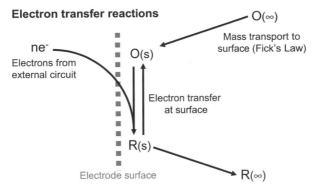

Figure 2.5 Electron-transfer reaction mechanisms.

$$k_{het} = k_{het}^{\circ} \exp\left(-\frac{\alpha n F \eta}{RT}\right) \qquad (2.11)$$

where k_{het}° is the heterogeneous rate constant at the standard electrode potential. α is the symmetry factor, giving the position of the potential energy maximum in the reaction coordinate space. The significance of these variables will be discussed further in 2.6. The key point to note here is the exponential dependence of the rate constant on the overpotential, *i.e.* the rate of reaction and thus the current flowing can easily be altered by many orders of magnitude merely by altering the applied overpotential. There are therefore at least two steps involved in every electrode reaction:

    (*a*) Mass transport which is described by Fick's laws and depends on the concentration gradient at the electrode surface, and

    (*b*) Electron transfer which depends on the overpotential.

The relative rates of these two steps dictate the form of the current-voltage relationship in Figure 2.4. In region I, the electron transfer step is the slowest, rate determining step of the reaction. The observed current in this region depends exponentially on the overpotential. The overall rate of reaction, and therefore the current, is under charge transfer control. In region III, the electron transfer is occurring so rapidly that the slowest step in the overall reaction is mass transport. In region II, the region of mixed control, the rates of electron transfer and mass transport are occurring at broadly comparable rates. Region III is the region of analytical utility and the current is independent of the applied potential, leading to the diffusion limited current i_d. Since electron transfer is so fast, the effective surface concentration of the reacting species is zero and the diffusional flux, and thus the current flow, is directly proportional to bulk concentration. The shape of the current voltage curve is characteristic of the analyte and electrode material and can be used to identify the analyte. However, this identification is largely empirical. We have been developing more rigorous approaches to analyte identification using nonlinear time series analysis.

2.2.2.1 Steady State Techniques

The simplest mode of operation is where the applied potential is held at a value such that the current is diffusion-limited. This is known as amperometry. As soon as the electrode reaction begins, since it is confined to the electrode surface, the region of solution close to the electrode will become depleted, as illustrated in Figure 2.6. This depleted region, known as the Nernst layer, needs to be stabilised against convection arising from density gradients and thermal effects. Three stratagems have been developed:

(a) Impose a well characterised flow regime which overwhelms natural convection.
(b) Place a semipermeable membrane over the electrode thus preventing bulk convection.
(c) Use very small electrodes (microelectrodes or ultramicroelectrodes), such that the Nernst layer is considerably smaller than any hydrodynamic boundary layer caused by natural convection.

Strategy *a*) whilst being of great utility in laboratory based instruments or off-line flow injection analysis is clearly not suitable for most clinical or physiological applications. Strategy *b*) is used in the almost ubiquitous Clark oxygen electrode. The membrane is selected such that its permeability to the analyte is several orders of magnitude lower than the solution. Bulk concentration is thus maintained up to the sensor surface. The membrane offers the additional advantage of preventing fouling of the electrode by surface active matrix components. The use of microelectrode elements is particularly attractive since they can be easily fabricated in the laboratory and can be fabricated using conventional CMOS processes. Insensitivity to flow can usually be achieved in aqueous systems when the characteristic dimension is less than 50μm. Shape is important because the diffusion field must converge. The most practical shapes are discs, made by embedding microwires in insulator; microrings made by vacuum deposition on to an insulating former or microhemispheres by mercury electrodeposition on to iridium microdiscs.

The steady state diffusion limited current i_d at a microdisc electrode is given by:

$$i_d = 4nFcDa \tag{2.12}$$

where c is the bulk concentration, D is the diffusion coefficient and a is the electrode radius. Similar expressions are available for different electrode geometries, though all show a linear relationship with characteristic length (radius for a disc)

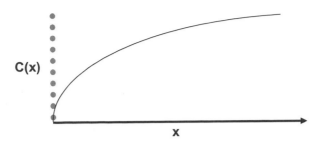

Figure 2.6 The concentration profile close to the electrode surface.

and are linear in concentration and diffusion coefficient. The dependence on diffusion coefficient is clearly a complication in biological systems since this is not generally known. However, it can often be determined directly by chronoamperometry (see below) and in any case, this expression is useful to confirm electrode geometry in well characterised solution.

For a microdisc electrode in the steady state, although the diffusion field asymptotically approaches bulk concentrations only at infinity, in practice, the bulk of the field is confined in a hemisphere six times the radius of the electrode. This allows explicit control of the spatial resolution of the sensor and requires the designer to decide the important length scale, whether cell, capillary or region of tissue, in advance of the experiment. Since microelectrodes can be fabricated down to 100nm, and exceptionally much smaller using nanoparticle templating, this gives electrochemical sensors sub cellular resolution in real time.

Steady state techniques have the fastest response times of all electrochemical techniques. For electrodes without membranes, the response time is essentially instantaneous since it depends primarily on the diffusion characteristics of the test medium. Electron transfer takes place on the femtosecond time scale. It is this combination of excellent temporal resolution and unparalleled and tunable spatial resolution which has allowed direct measurement of single vesicles of neurotransmitters to be quantified in real time, and an example is detailed below. In summary, steady state techniques offer the advantages of simple instrumentation and analytical relationships between the measured current and analyte concentration.

2.2.2.2 A Representative Application: The Measurement of Neurotransmitters in Intact Neuronal Systems

We have an interest in examining the effects of aging on neurotransmitter release. Neurotransmitters are chemical messengers which are released from a pre-synaptic neuron and diffuse across the synapse where another action potential is triggered. There are three types of transmitter: gaseous *e.g.* nitric oxide, amino acids and peptides such as glutamate, or myomodulin and monoamines such as serotonin and noradrenaline. Peptides and monoamines are released through vesicles, subcellular structures originating in the Golgi which fuse with the cell membrane and release their contents. Vesicles contain typically 20,000-50,000 molecules and the release is over in typically 5ms. This presents a challenging measurement requirement –

low concentrations, highly localised release, and a requirement for excellent temporal resolution.

We have measured serotonin release from an identified neuron in the water snail, *Lymnea stagnalis* using carbon fibre microelectrodes fabricated as follows:

- Clean a 7μm carbon fibre by sonication in acetone followed by deionised water.
- Place the fibre inside a pulled glass capillary (where the end as been polished to facilitate insertion). This may be aided by using a capillary filled with ethanol.
- Once placed inside the capillary allow approximately 2mm of the carbon fibre to protrude from the end of the capillary and seal using epoxy resin by capillary action. The resin takes 72 hours to set and cure at room temperature.
- Contact using a silver wire via Woods metal.
- The exposed shanks of the protruding tip are then insulated using electrophoretic paint. To coat the carbon fibre a voltage of 2V was applied for one minute using a platinum coil as the cathode and the carbon fibre electrode as the anode. Following coating, the electrode was removed by micromanuipulator and cured. The anodic paint was then cured after each coating for twenty minutes at 160°C. This process was repeated four more times and the voltage was increased to 3V, 4V, 6V and 8V for each subsequent coating. The carbon fibre was then cut using a scalpel to expose a carbon fibre disc electrode.

The finished sensors and a schematic of their construction are shown in Figure 2.7.

The structure of serotonin is given below in Figure 2.8. When a carbon fibre electrode is polarised to +0.7 V versus an Ag/AgCl electrode, it is oxidised at the hydroxyl group to a quinonoid moiety in a two electron reaction at a rate which is proportional to its concentration.

The serotonin sensors were pressed against the cell surface and spontaneous vesicular release was recorded. Typical responses are shown in Figure 2.9. The individual vesicular events are analysed for peak height, peak area (which can be related to the total number of molecules detected) and the time constant of decay, which is related to re-uptake by the pre-synaptic cell. The resolution of these recordings has been good enough for us to detect changes in neurotransmitter re-uptake kinetics as a function of age.

2.2.2.3 Transient Techniques

Despite the excellent spatial and temporal resolution displayed by steady state voltammetry, there are a number of disadvantages for some applications. Analyte consumption is directly proportional to current. This can be a major disadvantage in

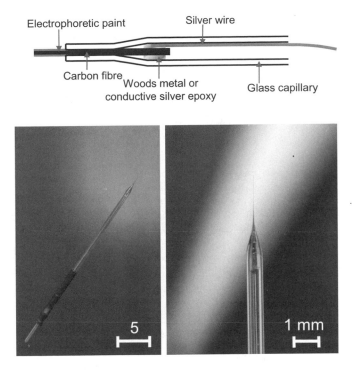

Figure 2.7 Schematic and photographs of serotonin sensors. (**See colour insert.**)

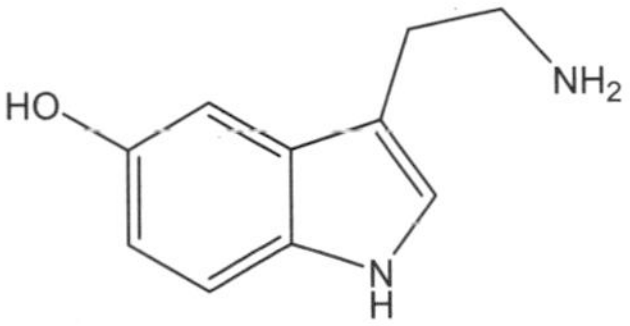

Figure 2.8 The structure of serotonin.

oxygen measurement where the biological problems of greatest interest occur is tissues where oxygen concentration is low. Intermittent operation can provide a solution. The limits of detection and sensitivity of the sensors are frequently limited by noise. When the currents are small, as is necessarily the case in microelectrode measurements (sub-nanoampere currents are typical), the sensitivity may not be adequate. Operating the sensor with a non-steady potential increases the sensitivity by sampling the current when the concentration gradient at the surface is steeper. Operating the sensor in the steady state also raises issues of selectivity. Any molecule which can be electrolysed at or below the applied potential will contribute to

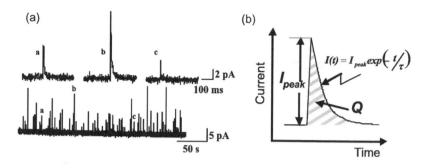

Figure 2.9 Vesicular release of serotonin: (*a*) Sample trace showing spontaneous vesicular release from the cell body of the serotoninergic neuron from *Lymnaea stagnalis*; and (*b*) Schematic of a vesicular event defining peak current (I_{peak}), time constant of decay (which will be expressed as τ from the mathematical equation) and the charge (Q).

the current. This is not necessarily a problem in an anatomically well characterised system, but for many applications, easily oxidisable high concentration components of most biological fluids such as ascorbate (vitamin C) or uric acid present serious problems. Potential programming can be used to confer additional selectivity. Finally, electrode fouling (which we will examine below) can sometimes be overcome by pulsing the electrode potential either to reduce interactions or oxidise any films formed on the electrode surface.

Next, we will consider the most important transient techniques, chronoamperometry, cyclic voltammetry and square wave voltammetry. However, whilst these techniques undoubtedly overcome some problems, they introduce others, most notably capacitive charging.

When a time-varying potential is applied to an electrode, the faradaic current is accompanied by a charging current. This is not simply that due to the leads and instrumentation – the electrical double layer associated with the electrode-electrolyte interface shows capacitor-like behaviour. On the solution side of the interface there is an excess of counter ions to balance the charge on the electrode surface. The dipolar water molecules are also preferentially oriented in the field. When the electrode potential is changed, electrical work must be done to provide the appropriate ion atmosphere and re-orientate the dipoles. This is manifest as a charging current which decays to zero in the steady state. The capacitance of a noble metal electrode is of the order of 20-30μF cm^{-2}. Since capacitance scales with area, this problem is less severe with smaller electrodes. Many of the more sophisticated and sensitive transient techniques have been designed to minimise the influence of double layer charging.

The simplest transient technique is chronamperometry. The electrode potential is instantaneously changed from one at which no electrolysis occurs to one sufficient to generate a diffusion limited current. Intermittent operation decreases analyte consumption.

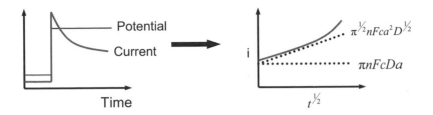

Figure 2.10 Chronoamperometry.

The resulting faradaic current rises instantaneously to infinity (or as fast and as high as the instrumentation will allow) as the surface concentration falls to zero. As the concentration gradient relaxes into the solution, the current decays as $t^{-1/2}$. For a large electrode, the current is given by the Cottrell equation which predicts that the current should approach zero at infinite times. For a disc shaped microelectrode the current asymptotes to $\pi nFcDa$ for short times (where $4Dt/a^2 < 1$) and to $4nFcDa$ for long times [25] as the diffusion to the electrode edge increasingly dominates. The principal advantage of chronomaperometry is that since expressions for slope and intercept on the *i versus* $t^{1/2}$ plot contain both diffusion coefficient and concentration, both of these terms can be obtained from a single experiment. This is a great convenience in biological systems since diffusion coefficient is generally unknown and likely to be different from a calibration solution. Furthermore, the diffusion coefficient is of intrinsic interest and can reflect tissue hydration. We have used this technique to quantify the effects of tissue hydration in the intervertebral disc (which is affected by mechanical loading) on oxygen transport in the tissue [26]. A further potential benefit is that it may be possible to recondition the electrode surface by applying a cleaning pulse between measurements.

However, the early parts of the current transient are distorted by capacitive charging. It is essential to establish the RC time constant for charging in a blank solution and only analyse the current for times longer than 3RC but less than $4Dt/a^2$. This method also does not overcome the principal disadvantage of steady state techniques which is that of unknown selectivity in complex samples. Additionally, the sharp edge of the stimulating voltage can provoke action potentials in neurons. These disadvantages are to some extent overcome by other transient techniques and with modern instrumentation, there is no requirement to use only one technique.

More sophisticated transient techniques are not generally suitable for implementation is sensors, though can be useful for characterising both the sensor and the electrode reaction. Cyclic voltammetry is a particularly useful "first look" technique but, with the exception of neurotransmitter research [27, 28] has not been widely used in biosensing applications due to the relatively high limits of detection. Differential pulse voltammetry and square wave voltammetry both involve modulation of a ramp or staircase respectively with a train of square pulses. By judiciously selecting the sampling period, the effects of double layer capacitance can be substantially reduced. Both of these techniques offer limits of detection down to the nanomolar but are not continuous and are difficult to implement in the clinical setting. The interested reader is referred to standard electrochemistry texts for further details [62]. In practice, AC voltammetry is a promising method that can be easily implemented using computer controlled instrumentation and is amenable to sophisticated signal processing. This is dealt with in some detail in Section 2.4 below.

2.2.2.4 Engineering Electrode Surfaces for Selectivity: Chemically Modified Electrodes and Biosensors

There has been persistent doubt about the ability of electrochemical sensors to perform qualitative analysis *in vivo*. The reason for this is clear – the technique employs a relatively non-specific electroanalytical method in a matrix that is very complex [29]. The following approaches to improve selectivity are discussed: (*a*) voltammetric techniques, (*b*) independent chemical analysis, (*c*) anatomical specificity, (*d*) physiological evidence, and (*e*) pharmacological tests.

(*a*) Each compound will provide a characteristic voltammetric curve. The shape and position of this curve will depend on the chemical structure of the substance and that of the electrode used. In recent years, Wightman's group have developed colour plots of the *Fast-Scan Cyclic Voltammetry* (FSCV) data analysis which have simplified the analysis of results and allowed for the use of time as a third variable for assessment [30]. This data processing has been further advanced with the use of *Principle Component Analysis* (PCA) to analyse unresolved complex signals. The application of these two pattern recognition techniques to electrochemical methods has allowed adrenaline to be resolved from noradrenaline release from chromaffin cells [31].

(*b*) After voltammetric measurements are carried out results are compared to those obtained using microdialysis techniques followed by offline analysis.

(*c*) The chemical composition of many cells, tissue and brain regions are well known. To complement the voltammetric data the specificity of the biological system can be used. Simulation can be used to allow release of specific compounds within a given region.

(*d*) In many biological systems, the mode of operation depends strongly upon a region or network. Using physical lesions, the corresponding loss of cells will diminished the response from the cell that measurements are being obtained from. This can help to confirm that the response that is being measured using the biological preparation can be eliminated.

(*e*) Pharmacological agents on their own can be used as the sole means of carrying out identification of substances. For example during the measurement of vasodilator nitric oxide from *Human Umbilical Vein Endothelial Cells* (HUVEC), the stimulated response can be inhibited using a NOS inhibitor such as N^G-*Nitro-L-Arginine-Methyl Ester Hydrochloride* (L-NAME) or *L–N$^\omega$-Nitro-Arginine* (L-NNA). This will compete with the arginine to prevent the production of citrulline and nitric oxide. However another means of diminishing the response of nitric oxide at the electrode is to use *2-*

Phenyl-4,4,5,5-Tetramethyl-Imidazoline-1-Oxyl 3-Oxide (PTIO), which is able to quench the nitric oxide once it was released.

Clearly, many of the approaches outlined above, whilst appropriate for animal experimentation or during the development, could not be employed in routine monitoring. Additional selectivity, over that achieved by potential control, may be attained by engineering the electrode surface. The major approaches to this are outlined below:

Gas Selective Membranes

If the target analyte is a neutral molecule and the interferent is ionic, then interposing a gas permeable membrane such as PTFE (Teflon) between the test solution and the sensor will prevent the ionic species reaching the working electrode. The condition for this is that the effective pore size must be below two diameters of a water molecule. Ions can go nowhere without their accompanying water molecules that solvate them. A complication with this strategy is that the counter and reference electrode must also be behind the membrane since ions are also the charge carriers between the counter and working electrodes. This principle was first reduced to practice by Leland Clark for what is now universally known as the Clark O_2 electrode. The Clark electrode has been the method of choice for determining blood oxygenation since the late 1950s.

Selective Binding and Catalysis

Should the target analyte be oxidised or reduced at a similar potential to an interfering species, exploiting selective chemistry of the target species can sometimes be successful. A typical example of this is the nitric oxide sensor first reported by Malinski [32] who used a Ni(II)(porphyrin) modified electrode surface to reduce the operating potential for oxidation of NO.

Amperometric Enzyme Electrodes

The key idea is to exploit the extraordinary selectivity of enzymes which evolved over millions of years of natural selection. In these systems, there is no direct oxidation of the target analyte by the electrode. The analyte reacts catalytically with the enzyme to produce a reaction product which is then detected. The so-called "first generation" biosensors operate on this basis, the first reported example of which for the determination of glucose was published by Updike and Hicks in 1967 [33]. This approach was commercialised successfully by Yellow Springs Instruments. The underlying chemistry is shown below:

$$Glucose + O_2 \xrightarrow{\ GOD\ } \delta - gluconolactone + H_2O_2$$

where *GOD* represents the enzyme glucose oxidase from *Aspergilllus niger*. The hydrogen peroxide (H_2O_2) is detected by oxidation on a platinum electrode held at

+0.65V. The enzyme is immobilised by cross linking with glutaraldehyde or by an electropolymerised film [34] or even by simple adsorption. An even simpler strategy can be employed where the working electrode is made of a conducting composite material. With the addition of suitable stabilisers such as polyethlyeneimine or dithiothreitol, enzymes can be incorporated into the bulk of the conducting carbon-epoxy composite to provide a cheap, extrudable or printable biosensor [35]. There are several comprehensive reviews of enzyme immobilisation techniques [36]. An ingenious molecular level assembly has been described by Wilner [37] where the flavin redox centre is first immobilised followed by spontaneous self-assembly of the apoenzyme on to its co-factor.

The major problem with the first generation biosensors is that there are several common interferents which are also oxidised at +0.65V, notably uric acid, ascorbate and acetaminophen. An alternative strategy was adopted for the second generation biosensors where it was recognised that the oxygen in the above reaction is in fact regenerating the enzyme. This is shown schematically below:

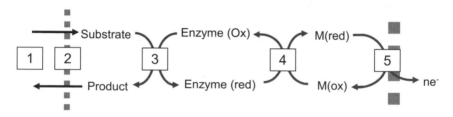

Figure 2.11 Schematic of a second generation biosensor.

In Figure 2.11, the electrode is on the right hand side of the diagram, the test solution on the left. Substrate diffuses from solution (Step 1) through a membrane (where employed) (Step 2) to be oxidised by the enzyme (Step 3). The enzyme must be reduced in this process and needs to be regenerated by oxidation in Step 4 above. The mediator is then regenerated in turn by oxidation at the electrode surface (Step 5). For a concentration sensor, Step 1 or Step 2 needs to be the rate determining step. This ensures that the slope of calibration is not affected if the enzyme denatures slightly or loses activity.

The mediator species can be chosen so that it undergoes fast reversible reaction kinetics at a potential where no other redox species are expected to react. Mediators which have been employed for this purpose include benzoquinone, the ferricyanide ion and various derivatives of the iron(II) compound ferrocene. The ethanolamine derivative of ferrocene is the mediator in the enormously commercially successful biosensor for glucose originally developed by Medisense, the ExacTech system. This concept was originally described by Cass *et al* [38] using dimethyl ferrocene as a mediator. In this device, the enzyme was chemically immobilised on the surface of a screen-printed carbon electrode.

It would obviously be a lot simpler if the enzyme could be persuaded to react directly at the electrode surface. This cannot generally be achieved because the electron conduction path between the electrode surface and the redox centre of the enzyme is too great for there to be an appreciable tunnelling current. Third generation biosensors involve no directly added mediator species. There have been two broadly successful approaches – using electrodes made of low dimensional conducting charge transfer salts of *Tetracyanoquinodimethane* (TCNQ), and redox wired enzymes. The former strategy was first described by Kulys and developed by Albery and others, the most successful compound being the charge transfer salt of TCNQ and *Tetrathiafulvalene* (TTF).

The mechanism was the subject of heated dispute for some time, it being believed that direct electron transfer was occurring. However, Bartlett was able to show that the TTF insinuates its way into the enzyme structure [39] to enable electronic conduction. A detailed mechanism for electrodes made from these materials has more recently been published by Lennox [40] showing that the mechanism is best understood as a form of heterogeneous mediation, where the mediator species is not soluble in water, but is soluble in the hydrophobic regions of the enzyme. Electrodes based on this technology have been used successfully for long-term studies of the glucose metabolism in rats' brains over ten days [41].

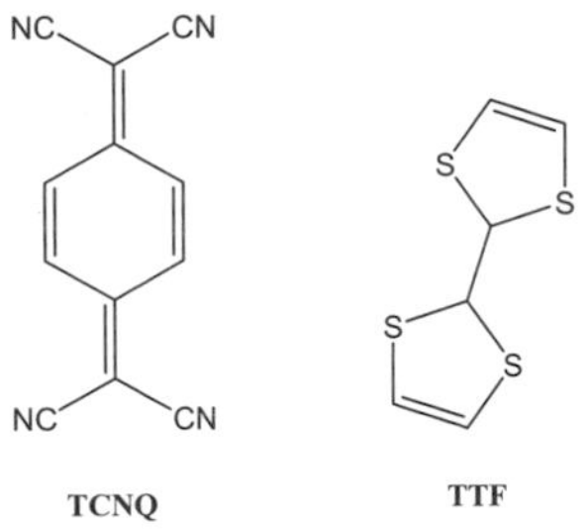

Figure 2.12 The structure of TCNQ and TTF.

Wired enzymes tackle the problem more directly. Reactive sites in the protein structure are identified (or created by protein engineering) and reacted with redox active groups such as ferrocene derivatives, an approach now of some commercial significance and originally pioneered by Adam Heller's group [42]. This technology is now being applied with some success to power generation in biofuel cells by Heller [43].

2.3 Instrumentation

2.3.1 Potentiometry

Potentiometric devices require only a high impedance high resolution voltmeter. There are many commercially available devices, indeed most high-end DVMs have adequate performance for many applications. Glass membrane electrodes and PVC membrane ISEs require input impedance in the range of $1G\Omega$. ISFETs and metal-metal oxide sensors can be made using CMOS compatible processes and it is likely in the future that these devices will be commercially produced with the requisite signal conditioning circuitry integrated with the sensor.

2.3.2 Amperometry and Voltammetry

Steady state amperometry requires a stable voltage source which can respond rapidly to a current load that may vary by many orders of magnitude. Most readout devices (chart recorders, oscilloscopes, analogue-to-digital converters) require the signal to be in the form of a voltage, so some sort of current to voltage conversion is required. In the case of low currents, it may be possible to use a simple two electrode set-up where the counter electrode also serves as a reference electrode. However, passing any current through the reference electrode can reduce sensor lifetime and if an array of electrodes is to be used, the combined sensor current could cause significant current flow and introduce hysteresis into the system. In these cases, a three electrode set up is required. In this case, the electrode potential with respect to the reference electrode is maintained by a control amplifier and a third electrode is introduced to provide a current path. This is shown schematically in Figure 2.13 below.

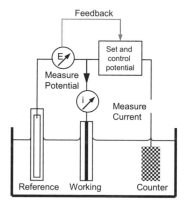

Figure 2.13 Schematic of the functions required of instrumentation for voltammetry and potentiometry.

The functions outlined in Figure 2.13 can be implemented using simple operational amplifier circuits. Usually the working electrode (sensor) is held at ground or virtual ground. The potential is applied through a control amplifier to which the reference electrode and counter electrode are connected. A simple circuit for achieving this function, based on the voltage follower circuit is shown in Figure 2.14.

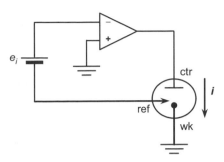

Figure 2.14 A potentiostat control amplifier based on the voltage follower circuit.

Whilst this circuit fulfils the essential functions of the potentiostat in that the reference electrode passes no current, it is not easily adapted for transient techniques where the voltage offset may need to be modulated with a pulse train or an AC voltage perturbation. In order to implement this useful function, an op-amp adder circuit can be used:

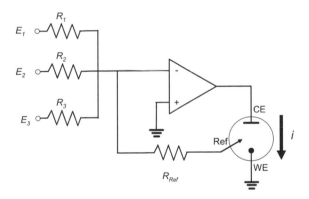

Figure 2.15 An adder type potentiostat.

In the circuit shown in Figure 2.15, the voltage applied to the electrochemical cell (or complete sensor) is given by the sum of the inputs to the three resistors (R_1, R_2, R_3), if they are of equal value. A disadvantage is that the reference electrode is now loaded by the resistor, R_{ref}. This can easily be overcome by imposing a voltage follower into that limb of the circuit. The complete control amplifier function can now be implemented using a monolithic dual op-amp chip.

Current to voltage conversion is commonly achieved in two ways: *a*) passing the current through a high precision measuring resistor and then using standard voltage amplifier circuits to provide adequate gain for interfacing to a chart recorder or analogue-to-digital conversion, and *b*) a current follower. This second circuit has the advantage of holding the working electrode at virtual earth. The measuring resistor approach has the advantage of speed and low noise, but the working electrode takes a variable potential above ground. The current follower circuit maintains the working electrode at virtual earth which reduces the capacitance of the working electrode lead (the central conductor and the shield will be at the same potential) and minimises leakage currents, a major consideration when the current can be as low as picoamperes.

More recently [44], a new approach to current to voltage conversion has been employed in patch clamp amplifiers for neurophysiology. Developed by Axon, the input stage is a current integrator, thus reducing the effect of random noise. Clearly, the integrator needs to be reset periodically and the complete circuit is considerably more sophisticated and, unlike the circuits outlined above, are beyond the means of most laboratories to implement in homemade devices.

Electromagnetic pick-up, principally 50Hz or 60Hz mains noise, is the major limitation on both sensitivity and limit of detection. Regardless of the circuit design, great care needs to be taken over earthing and connections. It is essential to have only a single earth point with all shields connected in a star formation. Miniaturisation of circuits and using on-board connectors and sockets reduces the length of interconnects and their inevitable antenna effect.

2.3.3 Reference and Counter Electrodes

Counter electrodes are most commonly made from inert noble metal wire or gauze, usually platinum. However, stainless steel (306SL grade) has been used with some success in brain voltammetry experiments. Whilst the working electrode performance should be independent of the counter electrode reaction, and this is easy to achieve "in the pot", the nature and location of the counter electrode merits careful consideration in physiological application. The counter electrode is there simply to provide a current path, but no sustained current can flow without electrolysis. When the working electrode is held at a positive potential, the counter electrode reaction is likely to be hydrogen generation, leading to a local rise in tissue pH in the vicinity of the counter electrode. Similarly, when the working electrode is held at a negative potential and passing a reduction current, the counter electrode reaction will cause a decrease in the local pH. It is generally acceptable to place the counter electrode some distance away from the working electrode since the resulting uneven potential field is unlikely to be important and in any case, with microelectrode sensors, the field variation will not be sensed at the working electrode.

The agreed international reference electrode is the SHE which has arbitrarily been assigned a potential of 0V. Any hydrogen electrode is temperamental and difficult to set up and these days are rarely seen outside the undergraduate physical chemistry laboratory. Fortunately, several suitable alternatives exist, the most practical of which is the silver-silver chloride electrode consisting of a silver wire on which has been deposited a thin film of silver chloride, either by anodisation or sputtering. The potential drop between the hook-up wire and the test solution is fixed, provided the chloride ion concentration remains unaltered. This is extremely convenient in physiological applications since chloride ion concentrations are tightly regulated. Since performance depends on the chemical composition of the surface, reference electrodes are particularly prone to contamination by adsorption of surface active tissue components. We have had some success with a design which uses an immobilised salt bridge solution to separate the silver chloride from the experimental subject [26] the construction of which is summarised below:

- Carefully straighten about 5cm of 125µm diameter silver wire (99.995+).
- Clean the wire by sequential sonication in chloroform, acetone and deionised water.
- Chloridise about 2cm of the wire by making it the anode in a cell using a silver or platinum counter electrode in 0.1M HCl. The current density should be 0.4mA cm^{-2}.
- The electrode should then be soaked in deionised water for at least twenty-four hours.
- Place the wire carefully inside about 4cm of fine bore plastic tubing so that the chloridised end is just within the tubing.
- Dip the assembly into a hot solution of NaCl (3mol dm^{-3}) and 3% (w/w) agar and allow to fill by capillary action. Allow to cool until the solution has gelled. Glue the silver wire to the top of the tubing to provide strain relief.
- Further mechanical stability can be achieved by gluing the assembly into hypodermic tubing.
- Test the finished electrode against a reliable standard reference electrode. The potential should be within a few millivolts of +0.197V *vs* SHE.

Similar strategies can be adopted for integrated sensors where the reference electrode can be constructed by chloridising a silver plated pin or pad close to the working electrode surface. Additional information about circuits and sensor ancillaries, complete with recipes, has been published by Cass [45].

2.4 Photoelectrochemistry and Spectroelectrochemistry

A new type of electrochemical device, the *Micro-Optical Ring Electrode*, or MORE was introduced in 1996 [46]. It consists of a fibre optic light guide on which a thin film of gold has been deposited as shown in Figure 2.16. The gold is anchored by chemical bonding to thiol terminated silyl groups to obviate the need for a chromium underlayer. The idea is to provide intimate relationship between a light source and the electrode surface which can, unlike optically transparent electrodes, be readily renewed by conventional lapping processes. There are some redox reactions which take place more rapidly if the reactant is in a photoexcited state.

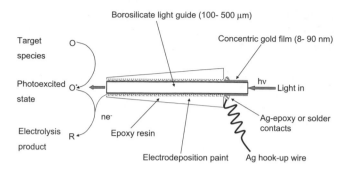

Figure 2.16 A schematic of the MORE device.

If the electrode potential is poised between the energy of *Highest Occupied Molecular Orbital* (HOMO) and the *Lowest Unoccupied Molecular Orbital* (LUMO), the molecule can undergo neither oxidation nor reduction since the HOMO is full and the LUMO is of a higher energy. Once the molecule become photoexcited, promotion of an electron to the LUMO creates a vacancy in the former HOMO and an electron which can be removed from the former LUMO as seen in Figure 2.17.

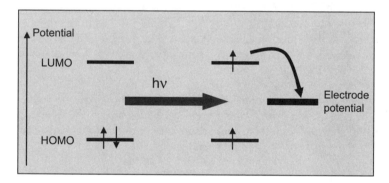

Figure 2.17 How photochemical generation of an excited triplet state can allow electrochemistry to take place.

Proof of this principle was established in the oxidation of the dye, methylene blue. The advantage of this type of approach is twofold: *a*) previously inaccessible analytes may become redox active under illumination; and *b*) a background signal can be recorded in the dark before and after measurement to allow correction for drifting background current. An application for blood cyanide determination is currently under development in our laboratories. Cyanide in blood is bound to *Methaemoglobin* (MetHb) in red cells and not available for analysis. However, the MetHb-CN complex is photolabile and can be decomposed by light in the blue-near UV region. The liberated cyanide can then be determined by oxidation [47]. The complete device is shown in Figure 2.18.

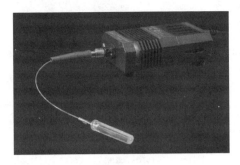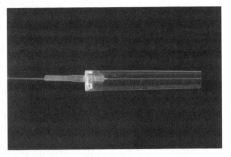

Figure 2.18 The MORE electrode complete with light source. (**See colour insert.**)

Heineman at the University of Cincinnati has also combined light with electrochemistry but in the opposite sense – to use the electrochemistry to modulate a spectroscopic signal [48]. The device is built on a microscope slide-sized light guide coated with an optically transparent electrode made of *Indium-doped Tin Oxide* (ITO). This in turn is coated with a thin film which selectively absorbs the compound of interest. The evanescent wave of light passing through the light guide by total internal reflection penetrates the electrode and goes into the film. Light emerging at the distal end of the light guide will show selective wavelength dependent intensity where it has interacted with the analyte. If the analyte undergoes electron transfer and the reduced and oxidised forms show different spectra in the UV/vis spectrum, then the spectrum can be "chopped" by modulating the electrode potential. If light detection is then accomplished via a lock-in amplifier, limits of detection are dramatically lowered, in principle as low as 10^{-11}mol dm^{-3} for favourable cases such as ruthenium tris(bipyridyl) and demonstrably down to sub micromolar concentrations in real solutions from nuclear waste. This entirely novel approach combining electrochemistry with spectroscopy offers selectivity from three sources: *a*) selective adsorption into the film; *b*) potential control from the ITO electrode; and *c*) wavelength from the spectroscopy. This additional control augurs well for application in complex media such as biological systems.

2.5 Biocompatibility

The attractions of electrochemical methods applied to clinical and biomedical measurement problems include continuous or repeated measurements of high temporal or spatial resolution together with minimal invasion or tissue damage. However, problems can arise from the perspective of both sensor and subject. These are dealt with in turn, along with some strategies for overcoming them.

2.5.1 Sensor Fouling

Measurements over long periods of time are generally compromised by the instability of the sensor. There is typically a fall in sensor current over time due to adsorption of surface active tissue components. The role of surface topology has assumed a greater significance in recent years and been the subject of a recent review [49]. These processes may influence both the reactivity of the electrode (leading to loss of selectivity) and transport to the electrode surface. Membranes may overcome some of these problems but they introduce an additional process step into the sensor manufacture (and thus reduce reliability) and create the additional problem of membrane fouling where the membrane permeability falls as proteins and other tissue macromolecules adsorb on the membrane. Some membranes may release plasticisers into the tissue and there is always some doubt about membrane integrity on inserting the sensor into dense or tough tissue. There is no universal answer to these problems and there is a surprising dearth of hard information in the literature. We have shown [26] that for oxygen measurement on gold, the electrode reaction mechanism is not affected by adsorption of tissue components but that the effective electrode radius needs to be measured after exposure to tissue, as the electrode surface area is substantially affected. For enzyme biosensors for glucose and lactate, we have successfully used very thin films of the biocompatible modifier, polycarboxybetaine to reduce the effects electrode fouling. This was demonstrated to be very effective in measurements in intervertebral discs [35]. Similar to the idea of using a membrane is the microdialysis electrode [50] where the sensor is encapsulated inside a microdialysis electrode. These have been used successfully to measure glutamate in brains and are commercially available from Sycopel Ltd.

Novel electrode materials may however provide another solution. Boron-doped diamond films made by chemical vapour deposition or plasma assisted chemical vapour deposition combine the many attractive properties – the chemical inertness, hardness and high thermal conductivity – of the native diamond with semiconductor or metallic conductivity. Those properties relevant to sensor design have been recently reviewed [51]. Swain's group has been working on producing novel boron-doped diamond microelectrodes for biological measurements. Diamond is attractive for electroanalytical measurements in biological environments because of its *a*) hard and lubricious nature which enables easy penetration into tissue with minimal peripheral damage; *b*) low and stable background current over a wide potential range as well as superb chemical and microstructural stability; *c*) low surface oxygen content (when H-terminated) which leads to minimal change in the background current with variation in solution pH; and *d*) chemical inertness and a nonpolar, hydrophobic surface which renders it resistant to corrosion and molecular adsorption (*i.e.*, fouling). It has also been claimed that diamond film electrodes show good biocompatibility [52] though it is probably too early to know if this is generally applicable.

Another development from novel materials which shows promise for sensor development is the use of nanostructured templated materials plated from lyotropic phases of surfactant solutions. This area has been pioneered by Bartlett and Attard [53]. Nanostructured materials can have fascinating electrical, magnetic and optical properties and can be prepared in the open laboratory without any of the capital expense and personnel commitments of clean room operation. For the purposes of biocompatibility however, the key property is a huge surface area, the vast bulk of which is confined to nanometer-sized pores and thus inaccessible to the surface active macromolecules responsible for much electrode fouling. The materials produced in this way so far include platinum and palladium.

Finally, even if changes in sensor material, shape and surface texture do not provide a complete answer, there are gains to be had from using signal processing. Given the relative ease and low cost of microfabrication, it is relatively straightforward to build sensor arrays where the individually-addressable sensor elements are essentially sampling the same extracellular fluid or region of tissue. Given the multiple modes of sensor fouling and failure, it is unlikely that each sensor element will fail at exactly the same time. By using statistical tools such as principle component regression, outlying data points can be identified and eliminated before taking the mean or median value given by remaining, presumably functioning sensor elements. In this way, prolongation of sensor lifetime is virtually guaranteed with no advance in material science or sensor design.

2.5.2 Tissue Damage

Although the idea of tissue damage and occlusion of capillaries was first discussed by Silver [54] and Albanese [55] several decades ago, there has been remarkably little published on the invasiveness of electrode techniques. Two factors are involved, mechanical and chemical disruption. The physical size of the sensor may be much bigger than the active area of the electrode causing distortion of the tissue and occlusion of blood vessels. It is almost impossible to avoid some aspects of these phenomena. We investigated the invasiveness of microelectrode measurements when measuring tissue perfusion and oxygenation in electrically stimulated skeletal muscle [56]. One important insight was the realisation that the sensor should be blunt and rounded rather than sharp, so that muscle fibres were nudged aside rather than sliced. We excised tissue after the electrode measurements were complete and stained and sectioned the tissue. The tissue slices were then examined by an independent histologist, blind to the origin of the tissue and scored for extravasated neutrophils, bleeding and fibre damage. There was no significant difference between the tissue where the electrode was placed and control sections. This surprising result indicates that tissue measurements are rather less invasive than had been hitherto suspected. Figure 2.19 shows an H & E stained section of rabbit tibialis anterior which had been subject to full tetanic contractions on a 10% duty cycle for over three hours. The electrode defect is at the centre of the picture, the red blobs being individual muscle cells. Tissue damage is clearly confined to one or two cells distal from the electrode tip.

2.6 Novel Approaches to Handling Sensor Data

Though there have been tremendous advances in computing power in the last two decades, these have not thus far been translated into significant advances in the processing of data for electrochemical sensors. In fact, computers have largely been used to emulate the traditional signal generator and X-Y chart recorder approaches of half a century ago. Consequently it is not unusual to record 50,000 pairs of data points in a cyclic voltammetry experiment only to use two or three of these in the analysis, such as peak and half-peak potential and current. The analysis of this data then proceeds using the diagnostics developed by Nicholson and Shain in 1964 [57]. More process-intensive, but based on the same necessarily simplified models, finite difference modelling is used to test the similarity of the experimental data to predictions based on model reaction schemes. A major barrier is the nonlinear nature of electrochemical signals which strictly precludes the use of Fourier transform approaches. Whilst *ad hoc* modelling has undoubtedly been useful, it seems timely to apply some of the tools developed in other branches of engineering for time series analysis into electrochemistry. We have begun this process by applying the Hilbert transform to the study of immobilised redox species at the surface of electrodes and are currently extending this work to include freely diffusing species. The aim of this work is to be able to deduce the thermodynamic ($E°$) kinetic (α, k_0) and mass transport (D, concentration) parameters of electrochemically interrogated species. The combination of the physico-chemical parameters ought to enable unambiguous identification and move electrochemistry away from a correlation-based approach to qualitative analysis and by altering the time scale of the experiment (by, for example chirping the frequency) resolve redox active species that would otherwise overlap. A major advantage that is already manifested is that the capacitance can be removed as an offset rather than through background subtraction [58].

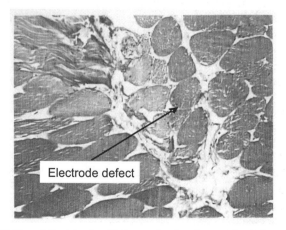

Electrode defect

Figure 2.19 H and E stained rabbit muscle showing minimal tissue damage from an electrode.

In order to apply these techniques, we will however need to consider the underlying theory of electron transfer in more detail. Electrochemical dynamics can quantitatively be described through the *Butler-Volmer* (BV) kinetic equation. The BV kinetic equation for a simple one-electron electrochemical reaction (2.13), is given by (2.14):

$$O + e \Leftrightarrow R \tag{2.13}$$

$$i_{far} = \frac{\partial \vartheta}{\partial \tau} = \kappa_0 \exp\{(1-\alpha)\xi\}(1-\theta) - \kappa_0 \exp\{-\alpha\xi\}\theta \tag{2.14}$$

where $i_{far} = I_{far}/\hat{i}$ is the faradaic current response, $\theta = C_{\mathrm{Red}}/C_{total}$ the concentration of the reduced species on the electrode surface, $\kappa_0 = k_0\hat{t}$ the kinetic constant of the electrochemical reaction, $\xi = (E - E_0)/\hat{E}$ the voltage and α the electron transfer coefficient indicating the symmetry between the locally quasi-linearised Gibbs free energy parabolas of the reactant and the product on the reaction-coordinate [59]. All expressions have been normalised with respect to the following characteristic properties:

$$\hat{E} = RT/F, \quad \hat{t} = \hat{E}/v, \quad \hat{I} = FA\Gamma/\hat{t} \tag{2.15}$$

with R (8.314C V mol^{-1} K^{-1}) being the universal gas constant, T (298K) the absolute temperature, F (96485.3C mol^{-1}) the Faraday's constant and v (V s^{-1}) the DC scan rate. Equation (2.14) is often used to describe processes where the electrochemical species is immobilised on the electrode surface with surface area A (m^2) and species surface concentration Γ (mol m^{-2}) [60, 61].

In voltammetric experiments the investigator has the freedom to select the voltage perturbation to interrogate the electrochemical system under investigation. The selection of the voltage profile depends exclusively on the phenomena to be studied. In the past, a plethora of different waveforms has been utilised, such as potential-step, sawtooth, DC ramp, sinusoid or combinations of the previous [57]. One of the most significant questions to be asked when choosing the voltage perturbation is: what is the characteristic time-scale, in other words time-constant, of the phenomena we would like to investigate? For decades, the main focus of voltammetric methodologies was studying quasi-stationary phenomena in the macroscale. Rapid advances in miniaturisation which made the manufacturing of cheap micro- and nanometre sensors possible have recently turned the focus towards exploration of transient phenomena occurring in the microscale [62, 63]. When interrogating fast electrochemical phenomena the characteristic time of the perturbation has to be short to provide the necessary time resolution to analyse such events. Voltammetric methods like *Fast Scan Cyclic Voltammetry* (FSCV) or large-amplitude/high-frequency AC voltammetry have proven useful towards gaining insight in various systems where the analytes under investigation are present in low concentrations, acting within an active matrix or to simply measure their electrochemical behaviour [64-67]. The challenge with such short characteristic time perturbation methodologies lies in the interpretation of the current response signal.

Many applications of fast voltammetric sensing are related to developing methods that allow the determination of kinetic and thermodynamic parameters through the use of the BV kinetic equation. As seen in (2.14), faradaic phenomena involve exponentially time dependent parameters and thus are highly nonlinear. Additionally, other contributions like the capacitance response i_{cap} caused by the re-organisation of the double-layer at the electrode interphase, described through (2.16), become substantial and have to be taken into account.

$$i_{cap} = C_{dl} A \, \hat{\imath} \, \hat{I} \frac{\partial \xi}{\partial \tau} \tag{2.16}$$

In (2.16), C_{dl} (C V^{-1} m^{-2}) is the double layer capacitance. Often, it is realistic to assume that the overall current response of an electrochemical process i will be $i = i_{far} + i_{cap}$. Characteristic waveforms and current responses are shown in Figure 2.20.

In order to develop a method to determine the kinetic parameters k_0, α and the thermodynamic parameter E_0 from the current output the effect of capacitance, i_{cap}, has to be suppressed. To do so, empirical methods like baseline subtraction have been applied where the contribution of i_{cap} is simply subtracted from the data-set [68]. This reduces the robustness of the estimations when i_{cap} is significantly larger than i_{far}. A more recent approach has been the application of AC voltammetry, where the waveform is a superposition of a DC ramp and a high-frequency harmonic oscillation, in combination with Fourier techniques like the *Fast Fourier Transform* (FFT). If i_{cap} is adequately described through (2.16) then it should manifest itself only, or predominantly, on the fundamental harmonic in the Fourier space [69, 70]. On the other hand, using tools developed for periodic, stationary and linear data-sets, such as the FFT, becomes problematic when they are applied to data obtained from highly nonlinear processes like the faradaic events described through (2.14).

In general, a nonlinear process does not obey the principle of superposition, nor does it have the property of frequency-preservation [71]. A nonstationary signal processing technique that has emerged as an alternative tool for the analysis of nonlinear phenomena is the *Hilbert Transform* (HT) [72]:

$$z(\tau) = i(\tau) + H\left[i(\tau)\right] = \sqrt{i^2(\tau) + H^2\left[i(\tau)\right]} \exp\left\{j\theta(\tau)\right\} \tag{2.17}$$

where $z(\tau)$ is the analytic signal as defined by Gabor [73], $i(\tau)$ is the current output, j is the imaginary number and H[$i(\tau)$] is the HT of $i(\tau)$. The right hand side in (2.17) is the same expression in polar coordinates and defines the instantaneous amplitude $a(\tau)$ and instantaneous frequency $f(\tau)$ with:

$$a(\tau) = \sqrt{i^2(\tau) + H^2\left[i(\tau)\right]} \tag{2.18}$$

$$f(\tau) = \frac{1}{2\pi} \frac{\partial\theta(\tau)}{\partial\tau} \tag{2.19}$$

Kiss and co-workers [74] applied the HT analysis to voltammetric time-series of a population of electrochemical oscillators in order to measure emerging coherence. Anastassiou and co-workers were the first to combine large-amplitude/high-frequency AC voltammetry with the Hilbert transform and pattern formation to deduce kinetic and thermodynamic parameters [58].

Their analysis was based on the influence of the different parameters on the pattern of $a(\tau)$. The main advantage though of the HT was shown to be the minimisation of the capacitance influence to an offset. In both $a(\tau)$ and $f(\tau)$ characteristic envelopes are formed from a large number of spikes. In Figure 2.21, $a(\tau)$ of a typical AC voltammetry output simulation is shown as well as the influence of α and k_0 on the resulting patterns. E_0 (in other literature defined as midway-potential $E_{1/2}$) is determined through the location of the envelope peaks with respect to the DC ramp. Moreover, α is determined from the ratio between the envelope heights whereas k_0 is estimated from the separation between the two characteristic envelopes. This analysis additionally provides a method to assess if the voltage perturbation is adequate to accurately determine the characteristic properties of the process. Depending on the value of k_0, the AC frequency of the voltage perturbation has to be increased or not. Experimental datasets with the blue copper protein azurin immobilised on a paraffin-impregnated carbon electrode which could not be fully interpreted by other methodologies were interpreted using the HT-methodology and the determined parameters were in agreement with the open literature.

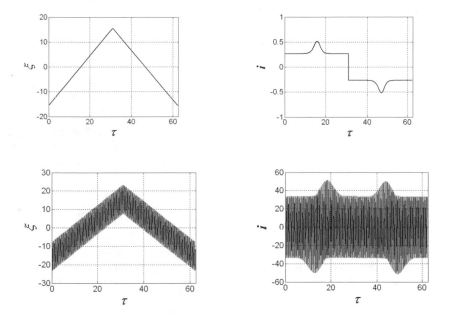

Figure 2.20 The first row shows the voltage perturbation ξ, on the left, and the calculated current response i, on the right, when applying CV (scan rate v = 1V s^{-1}). The faradaic events (i_{far}) are predominantly observed in the vicinity of $\xi = 0$ and the influence of capacitance (i_{cap}) is seen at the offset. The second row shows the voltage perturbation ξ and the current response i for AC voltammetry that uses the excitation waveform from CV superimposed with a fast harmonic oscillation (oscillation amplitude E_{ampl} = 0.2V and oscillation frequency f^* = 100Hz). i_{far} as well as i_{cap} contributions are now observed through the envelope of the oscillations of i. The kinetic and thermodynamic parameters for both simulations are: k_0 = 100 s^{-1}, α = 0.40 and E_0 = 0V.

In many cases, for instance in solutions, the species to be detected or analysed are moving freely in the vicinity of the electrode. The effect of mass transport has to be included in the analysis so as to extract information on kinetic, thermodynamic and mass-transport parameters in electrochemical reaction-diffusion processes interrogated using large-amplitude/high-frequency AC voltammetry.

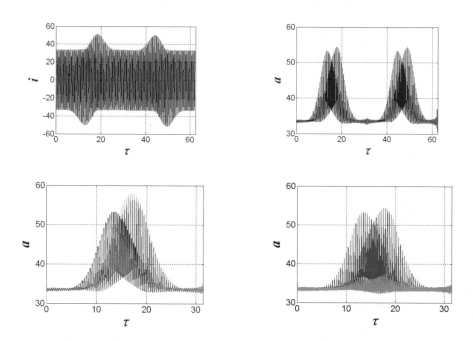

Figure 2.21 In the top right, the instantaneous amplitude a vs τ is shown after applying the HT and defining the analytic signal $z(\tau)$ of the AC voltammetry current response i shown on the left. The effect of i_{cap} is minimised to an offset and we can concentrate on analysing the faradaic events. In the lower row the effect of α and k_0 is shown for three different cases: on the left for $\alpha = 0.40$ (green), $\alpha = 0.45$ (red) and $\alpha = 0.50$ (blue) whereas on the right for $k_0 = 10s^{-1}$ (green), $k_0 = 10^2 s^{-1}$ (green) and $k_0 = 10^3 s^{-1}$ (blue). While the offset remains the same for all calculations (i_{cap} is constant) α is shown to affect the ratio between envelope peak heights and k_0 the envelope peak separation. (**See colour insert**.)

Engblom *et al* [75] and Gavaghan *et al* [76] applied analytical and numerical methods to calculate voltammetric responses in large-amplitude/high-frequency AC voltammetry. In their work, linear diffusion was the governing process and electrochemical reaction appeared as a boundary condition. The authors used FFT for the analysis of the output signal and observed that for high frequencies the kinetic effects manifest themselves in the higher harmonics of the AC spectrum. It has to be mentioned that these attempts much more aimed at showing differences between simulations with different physical parameters and did not include methods to deduce these parameters from the current output. A methodology based on the FFT for developing simple protocols to estimate various parameters of an electrochemical process was recently presented by Sher *et al* [77] A heuristic approach for data analysis was utilised to deduce mechanistic information that can be associated with reversible or quasi-reversible electrode processes. The authors investigated the impact of various parameters on the fundamental and higher harmonics and proposed a strategy of extracting similar information from experimental data through a self-correcting algorithm.

When studying a voltammetric diffusion-reaction process with the boundary condition being (2.14) the same principles regarding nonlinearity and nonstationarity apply as for the surface immobilised case. Therefore, FFT has the same disadvantages and its use on such data-sets can prove problematic. Moreover, one has to keep in mind that diffusion-reaction processes, except of the increase in parameter space due to the spatial coordinate, can illustrate very complex, and under specific conditions even chaotic, dynamics [78, 79]. As shown in Figure 2.22, even if the current response of a simulated diffusion-reaction voltammogram has obvious similarities with the surface adsorbed case the underlying dynamics are totally different.

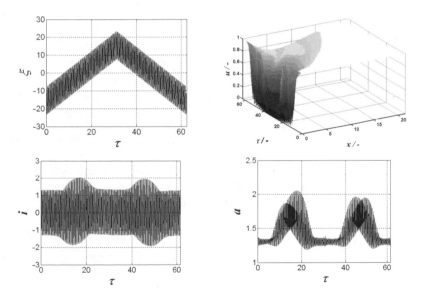

Figure 2.22 In the top left, we show the voltage perturbation and in the top right the simulated spatiotemporal dynamics (normalised quantities). We observe that near $\xi = 0$ there are large variations in concentration u, especially near the electrode surface. We also observe the effect of diffusion: for increasing τ the effect of the u-fluctuations is propagated far from the electrode surface. At the bottom left, the current response $i = i_{far} + i_{cap}$ is shown that is very similar to the surface-confined case shown in Figure 2.20. At the bottom right, the HT-analysis once more minimises capacitance effects and designates kinetic and thermodynamic effects (for the simulation shown $k_0 = 10^{-3}$ ms^{-1}, $\alpha = 0.40$, $E_0 = 0$ V and $D = 10^{-9}$m^{2}s^{-1}). (**See colour insert.**)

The analysis of characteristic patterns that could lead to the determination of the underlying physical parameters using AC voltammetry has recently been attempted [80].

From the previous discussion, it becomes obvious that fast voltammetric sensing is a very vibrant field of research, both from the experimental as well as from the methodology point of view. When considering the voltage perturbation, the relation between waveform characteristics and specific process parameters remains unravelled and extremely empirical. This applies especially for perturbation waveforms that interrogate the process on different time-scales like AC voltammetry. Intuition states that the fast characteristics of the waveform, like the high-frequency harmonic oscillation, should address the rapid kinetic processes whereas the slower characteristic, like the DC ramp, can cater for the slower diffusive process. However, there has not been a strict definition in terms of waveform parameters for designating an algorithm to examine more effectively the underlying processes. Such knowledge would allow new and more versatile voltage perturbation protocols to be designed, for instance waveforms with time-dependent scan rate, amplitude and frequency (chirps).

The interpretation of fast voltammetric methods has also drawn considerable attention in the recent past. However, more effective methods of *a*) suppressing signal contributions from other processes besides the faradaic, and *b*) interpreting the faradaic output especially from more complicated waveforms and kinetic mechanisms are needed. The HT analysis has shown to adequately minimise the effect of capacitance. Other non-faradaic contributions like solution resistance could be addressed via other signal processing methods which are adequate to analyse nonstationary data-sets and could provide even more powerful electroanalytical tools. For instance, methods like the empirical mode decomposition have been applied in the past to monitor nonlinear processes which occur on different time-scales could also provide novel insights in voltammetric datasets [81-83]. Moreover, wavelet transforms or neural network signal processing which have been used for many years for other applications may also provide candidates for the analysis of electrochemical datasets [84, 85].

2.7 Conclusions

As discussed in Chapter 1, the aging population in the developed world presents major challenges to healthcare. Even if it were desirable, it will soon no longer be possible to manage the chronic healthcare needs of an aging population in a hospital setting because there will simply not be sufficient nurses and physicians below the age of retirement. It is vital that we develop sophisticated tools and information management to permit monitoring of patients' vital signs in the home. Aside from the demographic imperative, the ability to make measurements more frequently and in a setting more representative of a patient's normal life will provide benefits for the patient. For example, in the case of type I diabetes, it is well established that better control of blood sugar greatly reduces the risk of long-term cardiovascular complications such as diabetic foot. Chemical sensors and biosensors will have a major part to play in this forthcoming revolution in healthcare.

Electrochemical sensors and biosensors offer unique advantages for biomedical applications. Principal among these is the independence of sensitivity on sample size making them uniquely suited to local measurements of concentration, diffusivity and perfusion. Living systems are characterised by partitioning of solutes and the maintenance of concentration gradients on the sub-cellular length scale. Any analytical technique which cannot resolve to at least the cellular length scale will at best be providing data which is merely correlated with known symptoms. New therapy will require new physiological insights, not merely cheap surrogates of physician's medical history-taking. The next best technology for providing highly spatially resolved clinical information is imaging techniques such as MRI and PET scanning. These methods do provide a near simultaneous image of the tissue, but are capital intensive, necessarily hospital-based and have spatial resolution at best one to two orders of magnitude worse and in any case do not provide detailed or specific chemical information.

Recent progress in autonomous sensors and sensor networks for physical parameters, notably blood pressure and heart rate, have not been matched by progress in biosensor networking. The last two decades have seen enormous advances in chemical sensing and biosensor development, most notably *a*) improved understanding of microelectrode and ultramicroelectrode behaviour for micrometre and sub micrometre spatial resolution; *b*) improved numerical modelling tools which have increased our fundamental understanding of electrode reaction mechanism and kinetics; *c*) new insights and techniques in protein engineering and molecular biology which have enabled the production of new mutant enzymes with improved stability, higher activity and enabled controlled protein immobilisation; and *d*) new biological sensing elements such as catalytic antibodies and aptamers which represent a truly new paradigm in biosensor design and have greatly increased the range of analytes and offered the possibility of hitherto unprecedented selectivity.

Novel materials such as the doped diamond films and nanostructured metal films discussed above show great promise already as sensor materials. Other exciting technology is Macpherson's revolutionary use of carbon nanotubes and nanoparticles to template metal deposition [88] to produce sensor elements which are an order of magnitude smaller than can be achieved by state-of-the-art lithography. Sensors using this technology have already found application as chemically active tips for atomic force microscopy [89]. Other promising technology that may contribute to the production of integrated devices include the use of TFT technology in ion sensing [90], much in the same way as silicon-based MOS is used in ISFETs and ChemFETs.

However, there has been a remarkable dearth of commercial successes based on biosensor technology, particularly for long-term implantation. Any implanted object will cause a foreign body reaction which will lead to deposition of macromolecules and possible inflammation. This is not so critical for passive implants and will barely affect the measurement of indicators such as blood pressure. In chemical sensing, however, key physical events can occur at the sensor surface. There have been advances in biocompatible coatings and improved understanding of the factors affecting tissue-implant interactions but there are nonetheless no generic solutions and we appear to be a long way from long-term implantable biosensors. What can be done, if decades of intensive research has yet to provide an answer? It may well be that in critical applications, active sensors coatings such as the NO releasing, active heparin coated polymers (to prevent clotting) developed by Meyerhoff [91] will be the answer, though new materials and massive redundancy will undoubtedly make a major contribution.

However, recent developments in microfluidics and, more especially in microneedle array technology hold out the possibility of wearable minimally invasive sampling of extracellular fluid. Needle sizes are so small that no red cells are sampled greatly reducing device fouling. Sample volumes are very low (typically picolitre to nanolitre) but this has little effect on the performance of electrochemical biosensors, and other highly sensitive hybrid off-line detector technology such as electrochemiluminescence becomes possible. These strategies will fundamentally alter the way we view biomeasurement. Diagnostics which currently depend on venous blood samples cannot often be justified ethically for all but vital monitoring. With minimally invasive sampling, applications which would currently be regarded as trivial could become real commercial opportunities.

Acknowledgments

The authors would like to thank Dr Martin Arundell for the design and fabrication of the serotonin sensor and the resulting measurements of vesicular release. They would also like to thank Dr Mark Yeoman for additional measurements and helpful discussions. They would like to acknowledge Nick Watkins for the photographs displayed in this chapter.

References

1. Bates RG. Determination of pH: theory and practice, 2nd ed. New York: John Wiley and Sons, 1964.
2. Cater DB, Silver IA. Microelectrodes and electrodes in biology. In: Ives DJG, Janz GJ (eds) Reference Electrodes. New York: Academic Press, 1961.
3. Hinke JAM. Glass microelectrodes for measuring intracellular activities of sodium and potassium. Nature 1959; 184:1257-1258.
4. Ellis D, Thomas RC. Direct measurement of intracellular pH of mammalian cardiac muscle. Journal of Physiology (London) 1976; 262(3):755-771.
5. Bakker E., Pretsch E. Potentiometric Sensors for Trace-Level Analysis Trends in Analytical Chemistry 2005; 24(3): 199-207.
6. Cobbe SM, Poole-Wilson PA. Catheter pH electrodes for continuous intravascular recording. Journal of Medical Engineering and Technology 1980; 4(3):122-124.
7. Ammann D, Lanter F. Steiner RA, Schulthess P and Simon, W. Neutral carrier based hydrogen ion selective microelectrode for extracellular and intracellular studies. Analytical Chemistry 1981; 53:2267-2269.

8. Ives DJG. Oxide, oxygen and sulfide electrodes. In: Ives DJG, Janz GJ (eds) Reference electrodes. New York: Academic Press, 1961.
9. Glab S, Hulanicki A, Edwall G, Ingman F. Metal-metal oxide and metal-oxide electrodes as pH sensors. Critical Reviews in Analytical Chemistry 1989; 21(1):29-47.
10. Haggard HW, Greenberg LA. An antimony electrode for the continuous recording of the acidity of human gastric contents. Science 1941; 93:479-480.
11. Horrocks BR, Mirkin MV, Pierce DT, Bard AJ, Nagy G, Toth K. Scanning electrochemical microscopy: ion selective potentiometric microscopy. Analytical 1993; 65(9):1213-1224.
12. Katsube T, Lauks I, Zemel JN. pH-sensitive sputtered iridium oxide-films. Sensors and Actuators 1982; 2(4):399-410.
13. Perley GA, Godshalk JB. Cell for pH measurements. U.S. Patent no. 2,416,949, 1947.
14. Burke LD, Mulcahy JK, Whelan DP. Preparation of an oxidized iridium electrode and the variation of its potential with pH. Journal of Electroanalytical Chemistry 1984; 163(1-2):117-128.
15. Hitchman ML, Ramanathan S. Evaluation of iridium oxide electrodes formed by potential cycling as pH probes. Analyst 1988; 113(1):35-39.
16. Horrocks BR, Mirkin MV, Pierce DT, Bard AJ, Nagy G, Toth K. Scanning electrochemical microscopy: ion selective potentiometric microscopy. Analytical Chemistry 1993; 65(9):1213-1224.
17. Beyenal H, Davis CC, Lewandowski Z. An improved severinghaus-type carbon dioxide microelectrode for use in biofilms. Sensors and Actuators 2004; B97(2-3):202-210.
18. Suzuki H, Arakawa H, Sasaki S, Karube I. Micromachined severinghaus-type carbon dioxide electrode. Analytical Chemistry 1999; 71(9):1737-1743.
19. Hitchman ML, Ramanthan S. Considerations of the pH-dependance of hydrous oxide-film formed on iridium by voltammetric cycling. Electroanalysis 1992; 4(3):291-297.
20. Marzouk SAM, Ufer S, Buck RP, Johnson TA, Dunlap LA, Cascio WE. Electrodeposited iridium oxide pH electrode for measurement of extracellular myocardial acidosis during acute ischemia. Analytical Chemistry 1998 70(23):5054-5061.
21. VanHoudt P, Lewandowski Z, Little B. Iridium oxide pH microelectrode. Biotechnology and Bioengineering 1992; 40(5):601-608.
22. Moussy F, Harrison DJ. Prevention of the rapid degradation of subcutaneously implanted Ag|AgCl reference electrodes using polymer-coatings. Analytical Chemistry 1994; 66(5):674-679.
23. Kuan SS, Guilbault GG. Ion-selective electrodes and biosensors based on ISEs. In: Turner APF *et al* (eds) Biosensors: Fundamentals and Applications. Oxford University Press 1987.
24. Wightman RM, Wipf DO. Voltammetry at ultramicroelectrodes. Electroanalytical Chemistry 1989; 15:267-353

25. Phillips CG, Jansons KM. The short-time transient of diffusion outside a conducting body. In: Proceedings of the Royal Society of London A: Mathematical and Physical Sciences 1990; 428(1875):431-449.
26. O'Hare D, Parker KP, Winlove CP. Electrochemical method for direct measurement of oxygen concentration and diffusivity in the intervertebral-disk – Electrochemcial characterization and tissue sensor interactions. Journal of Biomedical Engineering 1991; 13(4):304-312
27. Justice JB Jr. (eds) Voltammetry in the neurosciences. Humana Press, 1987.
28. Cahill, PS, Walker QD, Finnegan JM, Mickelson GE, Travis ER, Wightman RM. Microelectrodes for the measurement of catecholamines in biological systems. Analytical Chemistry 1996; 68(18):3180-3186.
29. Wightman RM, Brown DS, Kuhr WG, Wilson RL. Molecular specificity of in *vivo* electrochemical measurements. In: Justice JB Jr. (eds) Voltammetry in the Neurosciences: Principles, Methods and Application. Humana Press, 1987.
30. Michael D, Travis E, Wightman RM. Colour images for fast-scan CV measurements in biological systems. Analytical Chemistry 1998; 70:568A–592A.
31. Heien MLAV, Johnson MA, Wightman RM. Resolving neurotransmitters detected by fast-scan cyclic voltammetry. Analytical Chemistry 2004; 76(19):5697-5704.
32. Malinski T, Taha Z. Nitric-oxide release from a single cell measured *insitu* by a porphrinic-based microsensor. Nature 1992; 358(6388):676-678.
33. Updike JW, Hicks GP. The enzyme electrode. Nature 1967; 214:986-988.
34. Bartlett PN, Caruana DJ. Electrochemical immobilization of enzymes V: Microelectrodes for the detection of glucose based on glucose-oxide immobilized in a poly(phenol) film. Analyst 1992; 117(8):1287-1292.
35. Khurana MK, Winlove CP, O'Hare D. Detection mechanism of metallised carbon epoxy oxidase enzyme based sensors. Electroanalysis 2003; 15:1023-1030.
36. Barker S. Immobilization of biological components of biosensors. In: Turner APF, Karube I, Wilson G (eds) Biosensors: Fundamentals and Applications, Oxford University Press, 1987.
37. Xiao Y, Patolsky F, Katz E, Hainfeld JF, Willner I. "Plugging into enzymes": Nanowiring of redox enzymes by a gold nanoparticle. Science 2003; 299(5614):1877-1881.
38. Cass AEG, Davis G, Francis GD, Hill HAO, Aston WJ, Higgins IJ, *et al.* Ferrocene-mediated enzyme electrode for amperometric determination of glucose. Analytical Chemistry 1984; 56(4):667-671.
39. Bartlett PN, Bradford VQ. Modification of glucose-oxidase by tetrathiafulvalene, JCS Chemical Communications 1990; 16:1135-1136.
40. Zhao S, Korell U, Cuccia L, Lennox RB. Electrochemistry of organic conducting salt electrodes – A unified mechanistic description. Journal of Physical Chemistry 1992; 96(13):5641-5652.
41. Boutelle MG, Stanford C, Fillenz M, Albery WJ, Bartlett PN. An amperometric enzyme electrode for monitoring brain glucose in the freely moving rat. Neuroscience Letters 1986; 72(3):283-288.

42. Ye L, Hammerle M, Olstehoorn AJJ, Schumann W, Schmidt HL, Duine JA, *et al*. High current density "wired" quinoprotein glucose dehydrogenase electrode. Analytical Chemistry 1993; 65(3):238-241.
43. Heller A. Electrical wiring of redox enzymes. Accounts of Chemical Research 1990; 23(5):128-134.
44. Hochstetler SE, Puopolo M, Gustincich S, Raviola E, Wightman RM. Real time amperometric measurements of zeptomole quantities of dopamine released from neurons. Analytical Chemistry 2000; 72:489-496.
45. Cass AEG (eds) Biosensors: a practical approach, 2nd ed. Oxford University Press, 2004.
46. Pennarun GI, Boxall C, O'Hare D. The micro-optical ring electrode: development of a novel electrode for photoelectrochemistry. Analyst 1996; 121:1779-1788.
47. Lindsay A. Development of a photoelectrochemical sensor for the determination of cyanide in the blood of burns victims. PhD Thesis, University of London 2005.
48. Ross SE, Shi YE, Seliskar CJ and Heineman WJ. Spectroelectrochemical sensing:planar waveguides. Electrochimica Acta 2003; 48(20-22):3313-3323.
49. Wisniewski N, Reichert M. Methods for reducing biosensor membrane biofouling. Colloids and Surfaces B: Biointerfaces 2000; 18(3-4):197-219.
50. Albery WJ, Galley PT, Murphy LJ. A dialysis electrode for glycerol, Journal of Electroanalytical Chemistry 1993; 334(1-2):161-166.
51. Compton RG, Foord JS, Marken F. Electroanalysis at diamond-like and doped diamond electrodes. Electroanalysis 2003; 15:1349-1363.
52. Park J, Show Y, Quaiserova V, Galligan JJ, Fink GD and Swain GM. Diamond microelectrodes for use in biological environments. Journal of Electroanalytical Chemistry 2005; 583:56-68.
53. Attard GS, Bartlett PN, Coleman RBN, Elliott JM, Owen JR, Wang JH. Mesoporous platinum films from lyotropic liquid crystalline phases Science 1997; 278:838-840.
54. Silver IA. Problems in investigation of tissue oxygen microenvironment. Advances in Chemistry 1973; 118:343-351.
55. Albanese RA. Use of membrane-covered oxygen cathodes in tissue. Journal of Theoretical 1971; 33(1):91-103.
56. Greenbaum AR, Jarvis JC, O'Hare D, Manek S, Green CJ, Pepper JR, *et al*. Oxygenation and perfusion of rabbit tibialis anterior muscle subjected to different patterns of electrical stimulation. The Journal of Muscle Research and Cell Motility 2000; 21(3):285-291.
57. Bard AJ, Faulkner LR. Electrochemical Methods. Wiley and Sons, 1980.
58. Anastassiou CA, Parker KH, O'Hare D. Determination of Kinetic and Thermodynamic parameters of surface confined species through AC voltammetry and a nonstationary signal processing technique: the Hilbert transform. Analytical Chemistry 2005; 77:3357-3364.
59. Bockris JO'M, Khan SUM. Surface Electrochemistry. New York: Plenum Press 1993.

60. Laviron E. General expression of the linear potential sweep in the case of diffusionless electrochemical systems. Journal of Electroanalytical Chemistry 1979; 101:19-28.

61. Newman JS. Electrochemical Systems. New Jersey: Prentice Hall 1991.

62. Chen K, Hirst J, Camba R, Bonagura CA, Stout CD, Burgess BK, *et al*. Atomically defined mechanism for proton transfer to a buried redox centre in a protein. Nature 2000; 405:814-817.

63. Watkins JJ, Chen J, White HS, Maisonhaute E, Amatore C. Zeptomole voltammetric detection and electron-transfer rate measurements using platinum electrodes of nanometer dimensions. Analytical Chemistry 2003; 75:3962-3917.

64. Wightman RM. Microvoltammetric electrodes, Analytical Chemistry 1981; 53(9):1125A-1134A.

65. Heien MLAV, Khan AS, Ariansen JL, Cheer JF, Phillips PEM, Wassum KM, Wightman RM. Real-time measurement of dopamine fluctuations after cocaine in the brain of behaving rats. In: Proceedings of the National Academy of Sciences 2005; 102(29):10023-10028.

66. Armstrong FA, Heering HA, Hirst J. Reactions of complex metalloproteins studied by protein-film voltammetry, Chemical Society Reviews 1997; 26:169-179.

67. Guo SX, Zhang J, Elton DM, Bond AM. Fourier transform large-amplitude alternating current cyclic voltammetry of surface-bound azurin. Analytical Chemistry 2004; 76:166-177.

68. McNulty DA, MacFie HJH. The effect of different baseline estimators on the limit of quantification in chromatography. Journal of Chemometrics. 1997; 11:1-11.

69. Brazill SA, Bender SE, Hebert NE, Cullison JK, Kristensen EW, Kuhr WG. Sinusoidal voltammetry: a frequency based electrochemical detection technique. Journal of Electroanalytical Chemistry 2002; 531:119-132.

70. Bond AM, Duffy NW, Guo SX, Zhang J, Elton D. Changing the look of voltammetry, Analytical Chemistry 2005; 77(9): 214A-220A.

71. Director SW, Rohrer RA. Introduction to System Theory. McGraw-Hill, 1972.

72. Bendat JS, Piersol AG. Random Data. New York: Wiley and Sons, 2000.

73. Gabor D. Theory of communication. In: Proceedings of IEE 1946; 93:429-457.

74. Kiss IZ, Zhai YM, Hudson JL. Emerging coherence in a population of chemical oscillators. Science 2002; 296:1676-1678.

75. Engblom SO, Myland JC, Oldham KB. Must AC voltammetry employ small signals? Journal of Electroanalytical Chemistry 2000; 480:120-132.

76. Gavaghan DJ, Bond AM. A complete numerical simulation of the techniques of alternating current linear sweep and cyclic voltammetry: analysis of a reversible process by conventional and fast Fourier transform methods. Journal of Electroanalytical Chemistry 2000; 480:133-149.

77. Sher AA, Bond AM, Gavaghan DJ, Harriman K, Feldberg SW, Duffy NW, *et al*. Resistance, capacitance, and electrode kinetic effects in Fourier-transformed large-amplitude sinusoidal voltammetry: emergence of powerful and intuitively

obvious tools for recognition of patterns of behaviour. Analytical Chemistry 2004; 76:6214-6228.

78. Bertram M, Beta C, Pollmann M, Mikhailov AS, Rotermund HH, Ertl G. Pattern formation on the edge of chaos: experiments with CO oxidation on a Pt(110) surface under global delayed feedback. Physical Review E 2003; 67(3):art. no. 036208 part 2.

79. Strogatz SH. Nonlinear dynamics and chaos: with applications to physics, biology, chemistry and engineering. Massachusetts: Perseus Books Publishing, 2000.

80. Anastassiou CA, Ducros N, Parker KH, O'Hare D. Characterisation of AC voltammetric reaction diffusion dynamics: from patterns to physical parameters, Analytical Chemistry, in press.

81. Huang NE, Shen Z, Long SR, Wu MC, Shih HH, Zheng Q, *et al.* The empirical mode decomposition and the Hilbert spectrum for nonlinear and non-stationary time series analysis. In: Proceedings of the Royal Society London 1998; 454:903-995.

82. Huang W, Shen Z, Huang NE, Fung YC. Use of intrinsic modes in biology: examples of indicial response of pulmonary blood pressure to +/- step hypoxia. In: Proceedings of National Academy of Sciences 1998; 95:12766-12771.

83. Huang W, Shen Z, Huang NE, Fung YC. Nonlinear indicial response of complex nonstationary oscillations as pulmonary hypertension responding to step hypoxia. In: Proceedings of National Academy of Sciences 1999; 96:1834-1839.

84. Fu CY, Petrich LI, Daley PF, Burnham AK. Intelligent signal processing for detection system optimization. Analytical Chemistry 2005; 77(13):4051-4057.

85. Zhang XQ, Jin JY. Wavelet derivative: application in multicomponent analysis of electrochemical signals. Electroanalysis 2004; 16(18):1514-1520.

86. Day TM, Unwin PR, Wilson NR, Macpherson JV. Electrochemical templating of metal nanoparticles and nanowires on single-walled carbon nanotube networks. Journal of the American Chemical Society 2005; 127:10639-10647.

87. Burt DP, Wilson NR, Weaver JMR, Dobson PS, Macpherson JV. Nanowire probes for high resolution combined scanning electrochemical microscopy-atomic force microscopy. Nano Letters 2005; 5:639-643.

88. Torsi L, Dodabalapur A. Organic thin-film transistors as plastic analytical sensors. Analytical Chemistry 2005; 380A-387A.

89. Zhou ZR, Meyerhoff ME. Preparation and characterisation of polymeric coatings with combined nitric oxide release and immobilized active heparin. Biomaterials 2005; 26:6506-6517.

3

Protein Engineering for Biosensors

Anna Radomska, Suket Singhal, and Tony Cass

3.1 Introduction

In Chapter 2, we introduced the basic concept of electrochemical sensors and biosensors. In this chapter, we will focus on the biological aspects of biosensors in two important regards; the first being the biological molecules involved in the molecular recognition process that gives the biosensors their specificity and sensitivity as illustrated in Figure 3.1 [1]. We will discuss how these proteins can be engineered to improve sensor performance.

The second aspect is concerned with biocompatibility, which is the mutual interaction between the sensor and the tissue within which it is located. Although progress has been made in making implantable biosensors reliable and robust over a period of days, there are still significant technical issues associated with long-term (weeks to months) implantation. This reflects in part the response of the tissue to trauma and in part the inherent robustness of the biological molecules used in the sensor. This implies that the solution to long-term implantation will come from a combination of factors including minimally invasive implantation, understanding and modulating tissue response to implantation, and modifying the properties of the biomolecules.

Molecular recognition occurring at or near the sensor surface can be transduced through a variety of different physical sensing modalities and this leads to a sensor classification shown below.

- Electrochemical Sensors
  - *Potentiometric*
  - *Amperometric*
  - *Conductimetric*

- Optical Sensors
  - *Optical fibres*

- *Planar Surfaces*
- *Surface Plasmon Resonance*
- *Holographic Grating Sensors*

- Gravimetric Sensors
  - *Quartz Crystal Microbalance*
  - *Surface Acoustic Wave*

- Thermal Sensors

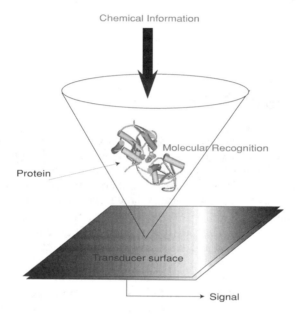

Figure 3.1 Molecular recognition lies at the heart of biosensor function.
(**See colour insert.**)

3.1.1 Electrochemical Sensors

Electrochemistry was the earliest and is still the most widely employed transduction method for use in biosensors and is discussed in more detail in Chapter 2. Its major application has been primarily in monitoring blood glucose levels [2]. Potentiometric sensors are based on the fact that many biochemical reactions, especially those involving hydrolysis, result in the formation of ionically charged products and if the reaction layer where these are generated is separated from a reference solution by a membrane then this change in concentration generates a potential difference. This potential difference is measured against a reference electrode and the change in concentration determined from the Nernst equation:

$$\Delta E = \frac{RT}{nF} \ln \left(\frac{c_{out}}{c_{in}} \right) \tag{3.1}$$

Traditionally, potentiometric sensors have been based on a liquid junction but more recently solid-state devices using *Ion-Selective Field Effect Transistors* (IS-FETs) have also been used. Most work on ISFETs has operated in strong inversion [3] but there are advantages in operating in the unconventional 'weak inversion' region [4] (see Chapter 7).

Amperometric sensors are based on the observation that the application of a potential difference between a pair of electrodes can result in redox reactions at the surface of the electrodes. The resulting current is used to determine the concentration of the redox active species. Originally amperometric sensors used the natural substrates/products (*e.g.* oxygen/hydrogen peroxide) as the detectable species ('first generation sensors'). Subsequent developments have used synthetic electron transfer mediators in ever closer integration with the electrode [5] and with direct electron transfer between protein and electrode [6].

As with potentiometric sensors, conductimetric sensors depend on the change in concentration of charged species. However the measurement is based upon changes in conductivity rather than potential, so the signal is linearly (rather than logarithmically) related to concentration.

3.1.2 Optical Sensors

Optical sensing techniques are broadly divided into either spectroscopic sensors whereby the molecular recognition reaction results in a change in the adsorption or emission of photons at particular wavelengths [7] or integrated optical sensors where the molecular recognition brings about a change in the inherent optical properties of the sensor surface [8].

Optical fibre sensors have been extensively developed as solid phases for fluorescence sensing particularly using antibody-based recognition. Two of the commonest formats are distal tip sensing and evanescent wave sensing. Distal tip sensors immobilise the reagent at the end of the fibre, which is used to transmit both excitation and emission wavelengths. This format lends itself particularly well to multiplexing where a bundle of distal tip sensors can be used to measure many different target analytes [9]. Evanescent wave optical sensors exploit the observation that when light is transmitted through an optical wave guide by total internal reflection it penetrates a short distance (a few hundred nanometres) beyond the surface of the fibre. This means that the light only interacts with molecules within the evanescent field and not with the bulk solution, leading to separation free sandwich or displacement immunoassays [10]. A rather different approach described recently makes use of leaky waveguides to increase the depth penetration of the evanescent field [11].

The scattering or absorption of light by semiconducting, fluorescent or metallic nanoparticles is very sensitive to the size of the particle and this has led to a variety of sensing formats based either on the detection of individual particles or the clustering of particles mediated by molecular interactions [12-15]. In some cases, the measurements are made in solution but solid supports also provide a matrix for such reactions.

Integrated optical sensors detect changes on the optical thickness (refractive index) and the commonest format is *Surface Plasmon Resonance* (SPR). At the interface of two media with different refractive indices, total internal reflection occurs. When the interface is made of a dielectric and a metal, *i.e.*, they have dielectric constants of the opposite sign, then at a certain angle of incidence (known as the resonance angle) the momentum of the photons is transferred to collective motions of electrons in the metal called surface plasmons. The resonance angle depends on the refractive index of the layer covering the metal and hence is sensitive to changes in this, as a consequence of binding reactions [16].

3.1.3 Gravimetric Sensors

Gravimetric Sensors are similar to SPR in that they measure changes in mass loading on the sensor surface through changes in the mechanical properties. The earliest such device to implement this was the *Quartz Crystal Microbalance* (QCM) whose efficacy is based on small shifts in the resonant frequency of a piezoresistive crystal surface [17]. Calibration of the QCM in complex backgrounds can be problematic as the relationship between mass loading and frequency shift depends upon a variety of factors including viscoeleastic coupling to the solution phase. The method has recently found application in the specific detection of microorganisms using antibody-coated crystals [18]. Other gravimetric sensors include *Surface Acoustic Wave* (SAW) [19] and Love Wave [20] and resonant acoustic profiling [21] devices.

Calorimetric Sensors should be in many ways the most generic as the uptake or release of heat is almost the commonest physicochemical change. Advances in microfluidics and MEMS technology has allowed scaling of calorimetric devices to the point where they can take measurements from both small numbers of cells and enzyme reactions [22, 23].

3.1.4 Consuming and Non-Consuming Biosensors

The actual (bio)molecular recognition process is determined by the nature of the biological material and there are a plethora of different combinations of sensors and biological materials. However, virtually all biosensors in the end can be considered to comprise of either a consuming or non-consuming transducer coupled with either a catalytic or affinity reaction in the biomaterial. A common example of a consuming transducer is an amperometric electrode where the oxidation or reduction of a redox active molecule results in a current flowing between the electrode and molecules at its surface. In contrast, a non-consuming transducer is a surface plasmon resonance device where changes in the surface mass are detected. Similarly an example of a catalytic biomaterial is an enzyme whereby the analyte is converted to a more easily detected product whilst an affinity biomaterial simply binds the analyte without a subsequent chemical transformation occurring, as in the case of a DNA strand hybridising with its complement.

This distinction between those biosensors that consume the analyte (either through the biological material or the transducer) and those that do not leads to a further important distinction; non-consuming devices will ultimately reach equilibrium where the signal generated is proportional to the concentration (strictly activity) of the analyte. Where the capacity of the binding agent is much smaller than the amount of analyte present in the sample then the latter is not significantly depleted and the device senses without perturbing the analyte concentration. This is akin to measuring light intensity with a photosensor; photons are adsorbed but there is no appreciable change in the ambient light. In contrast, consuming biosensors act as kinetic devices and the signal is proportional to the rate of the reaction that controls the consumption of analyte.

In both catalytic and affinity based biosensors the first step in the molecular recognition process is the formation of a non-covalent complex between *reagent* (R) and *analyte* (A):

$$R + A \underset{}{\overset{K}{\rightleftharpoons}} R.A \qquad (3.2)$$

In catalytic biosensors the second step is the conversion of this complex to a *product* (P) with regeneration of the reagent:

$$R.A \overset{k}{\longrightarrow} R + P \qquad (3.3)$$

In either case, the formation of the complex shown in (3.2) results in a hyperbolic relationship between the signal and the analyte concentration.

Another theme of this chapter will be the use of optical methods for sensing; although less well developed for implantation they offer a number of potential advantages in terms of sensing formats, fabrication methods and breadth of analytes that can be sensed. Molecular sensing using fluorescent dyes has long been established for simple analytes such as pH, calcium and oxygen and recent advances have extended the range of molecules that can be sensed in this fashion [24]. Given the tremendous diversity of protein scaffolds in ligand binding, the combination of the specificity and affinity of proteins combined with the versatility of fluorescent dyes offers a great many sensing combinations [25].

3.2 Protein Engineering

Proteins have often been referred to as 'molecular machines' [26] and whilst they have many remarkable properties, unlike manmade machines, they have acquired these properties through the process of evolution. This means their 'fitness for purpose' is defined by their physiological function and this does not exactly match the requirements for their use as analytical reagents. Whilst a chemical sensing approach attempts to address these limitations through the use of entirely synthetic receptors, many researchers have chosen to approach the challenge of creating improved reagents through protein engineering [25, 27].

Engineering proteins for defined endpoints usually starts with the DNA containing the gene that codes for the relevant protein. Changes in the nucleotide sequence of the DNA can be made using synthetic DNA fragments containing an altered sequence (mutagenic sequences). Once the DNA sequence of the gene has been changed the altered protein is then expressed in a host organism, most typically the bacterium *E.coli*, and subsequently purified (Figure 3.2). Detailed protocols and examples can be found in the chapter by Gilardi [27].

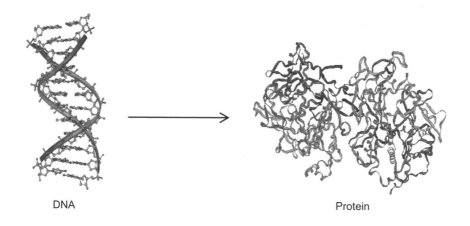

DNA   Protein

Figure 3.2 Protein engineering changes in the sequence of the DNA results in changes in protein sequence and hence protein properties. (**See colour insert**.)

A protein engineering approach to improving the molecular components of biosensors conveniently treats the protein as a collection of modules:

- A *signal transduction module* that converts the molecular recognition reaction into a physicochemical change that can be converted to an electrical signal.
- A *recognition module* that determines the specificity and affinity of the interaction between the protein and the analyte.
- An *immobilisation module* that mediates the interaction between and the attachment to the surface.

There are two broadly complementary approaches to protein engineering, often referred to as "rational" and "evolutionary" design [25, 28, 29]. Rational design is based on classical structure-function relationships and starts with a knowledge of the 3D structure of the protein and an understanding of the relationship between amino acid residues and protein function. This approach uses a combination of inspection of the structure and molecular modelling to identify target residues for alteration.

Evolutionary design starts with the natural protein and then generates a series of random mutations throughout the molecule. This library of variants will be comprised of primarily less or non-functional variants, however there will be a very small proportion of slightly improved variants and if these can be enriched through screening or selection, then over successive 'generations' a significantly improved variant will emerge. Both approaches have strengths and limitations; with rational design there is a straightforward relationship between the desired change in properties and the mutations that need to be made. On the other hand, our understanding of structure function relationships may not be detailed enough to design the most adventitious changes and unexpected consequences may arise from changes in protein sequence. Evolutionary designs can find mutations distant from the site of action that would be difficult to predict but require good screening methods and the 'space' being screened may not be large enough to encompass all the desired mutants.

3.2.1 The Signal Transduction Module

Biosensors are built on the premise that the biomolecular recognition reaction can be transduced into an electrical signal as shown schematically in Figure 3.1. Whilst this has clearly been the case with the 'wild type' of protein, in many instances, there are several ways in which protein engineering can be used to enhance this transduction. In the case of affinity sensors the engineering in of a fluorescent reporter group to signal analyte binding has been a particularly active area of research since the initial descriptions of this approach in 1994 by Gilardi *et al* [30] and Brune *et al* [31]. Both groups used proteins that are members of the *Periplasmic Binding Protein* (PBP) superfamily targeting maltose and phosphate respectively. This protein family is particularly suited to sensing applications as it comprises of around thirty members, highly homologous in terms of structure, with high stability and a common conformational change consequent upon ligand binding. The proteins are bilobal in structure with roughly equally sized N- and C-terminal domains linked by a three or four stranded hinge. In the absence of ligand the two lobes form an open structure which undergoes a closing and twisting upon analyte binding. In this process a number of residues that are solvent exposed in the absence of ligand become solvent shielded. The approach taken to transduce this binding reaction into an optical signal was to introduce environmentally sensitive fluorescent dyes covalently at a unique site in the protein. Gilardi *et al* [30] used a nitrobenzoxadiazole derivative, whilst Brune *et al* [31] used a coumarin. In both cases the dye is quenched by water and so shows an increase in fluorescence on ligand binding.

This environmental sensitivity of fluorescence emission is a consequence of the rate of non-radiative decay of the excited state being sensitive to the local environment. Depending upon the exact nature of the decay mechanism, there may also be wavelength shifts as well as intensity changes (Figure 3.3).

Both groups took advantage of the fact that neither the maltose binding protein nor the phosphate binding protein has cysteine residues and so the introduction of one provides a unique labelling site for thiol reactive dyes. In subsequent papers time-resolved fluorescence spectroscopy and circular dichroism [32] and X-ray crystallography [33, 34] shed further light on the mechanism of the fluorescence change in response to ligand binding. Further work with many other PBPs have shown how generic this approach is [35-40].

Whilst the PBPs have probably been the most intensively studied they are not the only scaffolds for which such an approach has been shown to work. In addition there are antibodies [41], enzymes [42] and lectins [43]. The latter example represents a different approach to site-specific fluorescence labelling where the ligand itself is used to effect the modification.

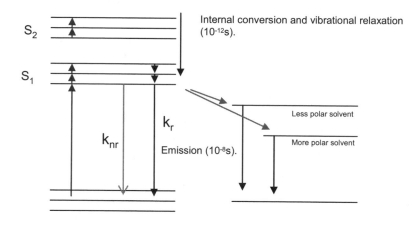

Figure 3.3 Environmental sensitivity of fluorophores.

Periplasmic binding proteins and other proteins have also been labelled site specific with redox active groups [44] however the effect of analyte binding tends to be much smaller than is observed for fluorescence.

Given the widespread use of electrochemical biosensors, the engineering of redox enzymes to improve electrochemical coupling has been pursued on a number of fronts. In most redox enzymes the electron transfer to and from substrates occurs deep within the protein matrix as this then avoids redox reactions with other cellular components and biochemical 'short circuits'. Unfortunately such protection also makes heterogeneous electron transfer slow and therefore artificial electron transfer 'mediators' are used to shuttle electrons between the active site and the electrode. Mediators may be either soluble [5], polymeric [45] or protein bound [46] and there have been several reports of engineering redox proteins to improve their electrical communication with mediators or electrodes. The reaction of mediators with redox enzymes appears to proceed through a typical Michaelis (enzyme/substrate) complex consistent with a specific interaction between the two. Sadeghi *et al* [47] showed that in the case of *Cytochrome C Peroxidase* (CCP), mutations that changed surface residues affected the rate of reaction with ferrocenes differentially, depending on both the ferrocene and the mutation. Some combinations showed overall rates of electron transfer greater than that of wild type CCP with its natural substrate.

Site directed covalent attachment of a mediator can be achieved using the same cysteine mutagenesis and chemical modification approach as described above for fluorescent dyes, and enzymes so modified include cytochrome P450$_{cam}$ and trimethylamine dehydrogenase [48]. A rather different approach was adopted by Chen *et al* [49] who added an oligo(lysine) sequence to the end of glucose oxidase and then modified this with ferrocene mediators. Although glucose oxidase has native lysine residues they are unreactive in the folded form of the enzyme [50] and this engineered form shows an extended linear range and better stability than the wild type with soluble mediators.

Where two (or more) enzymes act sequentially to generate a signal the optimised design of biosensors can be problematic, especially with regard to controlling the loading of the enzymes on the surface. Moreover we know from nature that such sequential reactions often involve close physical association of the enzymes (a process known as substrate channelling) [51]. In designing a biosensor for maltose determination based on the sequential reactions of glucoamylase and glucose oxidase, Zhou *et al* genetically fused the two enzymes together with a resulting improvement in performance [52].

3.2.2 The Recognition Site Module

Altering the analyte recognition site module in proteins effects changes in both specificity and affinity. Changes in specificity can be used to extend or alter the range of molecules that are sensed. This can be particularly valuable when there is no known natural protein that binds to the analyte but an existing scaffold can be modified through alteration of key residues involved in analyte recognition.

Modification of affinity is probably the most straightforward to achieve, particularly where this involves reducing the affinity to sense at higher concentrations. Examples where single mutations can reduce the affinity in a controlled fashion, *i.e.* without loss of specificity, in binding proteins include the maltose binding protein where the replacement of tryptophan residues by alanine was known to reduce the affinity for maltose [53]. Marvin and Hellinga used this knowledge to tune the dynamic range of the fluorescently labelled maltose binding protein [39]. We have used a similar approach with the phosphate binding protein making mutations in the binding pocket and the hinge region as shown in Figure 3.4 [34].

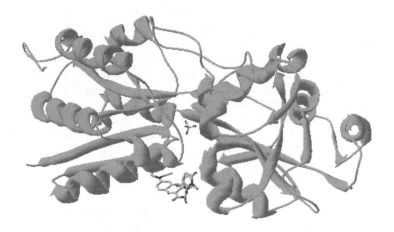

Figure 3.4 Structure of the *E.coli* phosphate binding protein showing the phosphate ligand and the coumarin fluorophore. (**See colour insert.**)

Our aim was to lower the affinity for phosphate from its native value of 100nM to a range more typical of physiological concentrations and as can be seen from Figure 3.5 an approximately three orders of magnitude shift in sensing range was achieved. (S. Oaew and A.E.G. Cass unpublished data).

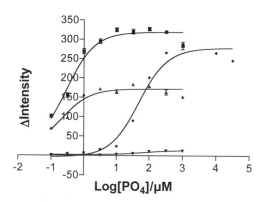

Figure 3.5 Series of phosphate binding curves for different mutants of phosphate binding protein.

Fierke and Thompson have engineered carbonic anhydrase to alter its zinc affinity and kinetics as well as introducing a fluorescent reporter group so that it can be used in imaging zinc concentrations *in vivo* [54] whilst a recombinant urease with extended dynamic range has been immobilised on the gate of an ISFET for urea sensing [55]. We have used evolutionary methods to increase the activity of alkaline phosphates starting from a rationally designed mutant and then further evolving it by error prone PCR and DNA shuffling [56]

Changes in specificity can also be engineered either by relatively small changes in the amino acid residues that interact with the analyte or through wholesale resculpting of the binding site. As an example of the former we have altered the specificity of the phosphate binding protein to increase its affinity for arsenate as compared to the wild type enzyme (Figure 3.6, Oaew and Cass unpublished data).

Fierke, Thompson and co-workers have also altered the specificity of carbonic anhydrase to favour copper and then used this in a distal tip optical fibre format in seawater to detect pM concentrations of copper ions [57].

Engineering of enzymes for sensor applications can be targeted at either the substrate specificity or the inhibitor specificity. As an example of the former, D-amino acid oxidase has had its substrate specificity broadened by evolutionary methods to encompass acidic amino acids [58]. In two interesting papers the acetylcholine esterase of *Drosophila melanogaster* [59] and *Nippostrongylus brasiliensis* [60] were engineered to alter their sensitivity to inhibition by insecticides. By examining the pattern of inhibition the different insecticides could be distinguished. In the case of the *N. brasiliensis* mutants the enzymes could be incorporated into screen-printed electrodes and showed a very long shelf life.

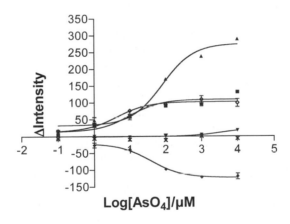

Figure 3.6 Dose-response curves for a series of mutant phosphate binding proteins with arsenate.

More dramatic changes in specificity have been made through introducing new binding sites for quite different analytes. Lipocalins are a robust protein superfamily whose members bind various hydrophobic ligands with greater or lesser specificity [61] and Skerra has engineered these to alter their binding specificity [62] as alternatives to antibodies. Examples include engineering the bilin binding protein to bind fluorescein [63] or phthalates [64]. The main application area for these anticalins has been in drug discovery [62] but they should be well suited to incorporate into biosensors as well.

An even more dramatic change in specificity has been shown with the PBPs where the scaffold is highly versatile [65] and the introduction of metal [38], organophosphate [36] and explosives binding site has been achieved [66].

3.2.3 Immobilisation Module

Biosensors by their very nature require the biorecognition molecules to be at or near the surface and for implantable sensors this immobilisation has to be virtually irreversible (*i.e.* a covalent attachment). Early biosensors typically used rather harsh immobilisation chemistries originating from work on enzyme bioreactors. This was quite effective where the enzymes had high catalytic activity, were stable and where the sensor surface was relatively large. As sensors have become smaller and the biological materials less robust then maintenance of activity is a key issue in determining performance. Indeed work is developing rapidly on nanoscale sensors [12, 13, 67] and issues of detection limit are coming to be discussed [68]. This turn means that greater control over the biomolecule surface interaction is necessary and one approach to this is to use protein engineering to introduce surface binding specific sequences. The related issue of analysing the protein-surface interactions is also of importance and has been reviewed recently [69].

Control of protein immobilisation is in principle achieved by having complementary chemistries on the protein and the surface; the former is through fusion 'tags' and the latter via surface modification. Early work used tags already developed for affinity purification such as the hexa(histidine) sequence that binds to metal chelate surfaces [70, 71]. The histidine tag also immobilises proteins on unmodified gold electrodes [72]. Thiol termination (either N- or C-) has also been used to immobilise proteins to gold electrodes and the resulting device shows improved performance [73]. Cysteine and histidine tagged proteins also bind covalently to electrophilic conducting polymers such as poly(aniline) [74].

Other engineered tags that have been used for controlled immobilisation include the StrepTag (a streptavidin binding sequence) [75]. In the latter case a flexible glycine-serine spacer was used to separate the protein from the tag, minimising steric constraints.

Hydrophobic surfaces can be particularly challenging for protein immobilisation as they have little functionality and immobilisation by adsorption often results in surface induced aggregation [76]. Where such surfaces need to be modified the use of the E12 tag has proven valuable [77] and can be combined with engineering the protein for both immobilisation and signal transduction [78] as shown in Figure 3.7 for the glutamine binding protein (QBP).

In this case also, the inclusion of a flexible linker between the tag and protein improved the performance. In addition to a higher protein loading of this hydrophilic protein on polystyrene, the tag immobilised protein showed essentially no loss of binding or signalling activity compared to the untagged protein in solution as shown in Figure 3.8.

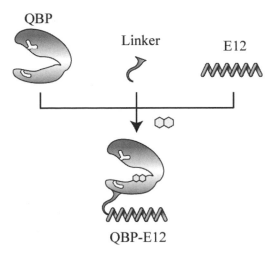

Figure 3.7 Schematic diagram for engineering glutamine binding protein for fluorescence signalling and self assembly on hydrophobic surfaces.

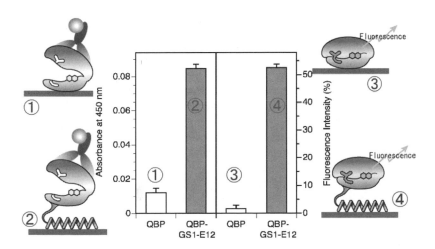

Figure 3.8 The effect of the E12 linker on surface loading and activity of QBP on hydrophobic surfaces. The left hand panel shows the protein loading as assessed from an immunoassay. The engineered protein has about an order of magnitude higher loading. The right hand panel shows that only the E12 immobilised protein is functional as judged from the change in fluorescence.

3.3 Biocompatibility and Implantation

Nanomedicine is a large research area for the application of biosensors due to significant advances in nanotechnology, miniaturisation and other multiple scientific disciplines. The development of nanodevices such as implantable biosensors, which enable the continuous monitoring of biological processes *in vivo* (rapid biochemical changes can be missed by discrete measurements) either intravascularly (in the blood stream) or transcutaneously (across the skin surface), is one of the main goals within this emerging interdisciplinary field. Realtime *in vivo* measurements are seen as a medically desirable diagnostic tool as they are extremely helpful in the revealing and understanding of complex underlying disease mechanisms, therefore ensuring an improvement in the health-related quality of life [79]. Permanent implants are an attractive alternative to conventional screening methods in terms of providing fast, easy and continuous assessment of various physiological parameters for detecting precursors in potentially life threatening events.

In cardiology, for instance, devices inserted in the body can provide early warnings of heart failure, the signs of which can be detected in slight changes in the mix of proteins. Similar applications have been recognised in neurology, where chemical monitoring of brain metabolism (using for example glucose and lactate biosensors) can help in the detection of ischaemic symptoms and to direct the course of therapeutic intervention [2]. Continuous measurements of urea would lead to better monitoring of kidney function and disorders associated with it. Determinations of creatinine play a crucial role in the detection of renal and muscular dysfunction. Monitoring of uric acid, the major product of purine breakdown in humans, offers the opportunity to detect disorders associated with altered purine metabolism (gout, hyperuricaemia or Lesch-Nyhan syndrome). Elevated levels of uric acid are observed in a wide range of conditions such as leukaemia, pneumonia, kidney injury, hypertension and ischaemia, whereas abnormal concentrations of cholesterol are related to hypertension, hyperthyroidism, anemia, and coronary artery disease.

DNA biosensors have enormous applications as a diagnostic tool for inherited diseases and the rapid detection of pathogenic infections [80]. The other potential novel use of sensors, besides *in vivo* monitoring, is in the actual treatment of various diseases. The long-term aim is not only to monitor a wide range of chronic disorders but also to automatically and autonomously treat pharmaceuticals using small drug delivery devices that can be implanted into the patient to manage illness. In managing patients with diabetes the continuously measured level of glucose can control insulin delivery from an inserted reservoir. Implantable glucose biosensors have been proposed as key to developing an automatic insulin injection system, that is an artificial, pancreatic beta cell to maintain a desirable glucose homeostasis [81].

The literature is full of papers on biosensors but only a limited number can fulfil the criteria of *in vivo* application. It should be underlined that performance criteria for *in vivo* biosensors are not only dependent on the specific analyte, but also on the intended application. The main required property for clinically usable sensors is accuracy. Accuracy implies precision, linearity, sensitivity and specificity with appropriate spatial and temporal resolution. It is necessary to achieve an optimum balance among the parameters of interest for a specific application. It is important to note that the development of *in vivo* measurement systems is not straightforward. There are numerous problems, difficult to overcome, which prevent the widespread application of implantable biosensors in clinical practice. These include sterilisation, calibration, long-term stability and biocompatibility of the sensor [2].

Sterilisation is a major prerequisite in optimising the *in vivo* functionality of implantable biosensors for practical clinical use. A useful method of biosensor sterilisation should not only provide microbial verification but also guarantee the functional stability of the sensor. Common approaches for sterilisation (sterilisation by: UV or gamma irradiation, treatment with antiseptic reagents like alcohol or glutaraldehyde, autoclaving or gaseous sterilisation using ethylene oxide) have severe limitations due to their influence on enzyme activity. Biosensors cannot survive reliable thermal sterilisation owing to the destruction of enzyme activity. Likewise gaseous sterilisation using ethylene oxide cannot be recommended due to the toxicity as well as the fate of the adsorption of residues of the active agent. Liquid sterilisation by antiseptics or sterilisation by gamma irradiation is usually employed but not always effective as it additionally causes changes of *in vitro* functionality and polymer structure of the biosensor.

Consequently, methods of antimicrobial treatment have to be specially adapted. As an example, one possible approach is the combined treatment with hydrogen peroxide solution acting over four days with 7kGy gamma irradiation. Effective methods to produce sterile biosensors should be based not only on final product treatment but should also ensure the presence of contamination reducing measures in every manufacturing step [82, 83].

It is commonly known that the assessment of sensor performance is critically dependent on a reliable calibration procedure. For medical applications the output of implanted biosensors has to be related to the actual analyte concentration at the implantation site. Calibration of the device should ideally be done once before insertion ensuring excellent calibration stability following implantation. However it is often not possible to rely on *in vitro* calibrations as the basis for *in vivo* performance owing to drift in the analytical response of the biosensor and/or changes in calibration due to the immunological response of the surrounding tissue [2, 84].

For this reason, one- or two-point *in situ* calibration methods have been developed. In the one-point calibration procedure the output of the implanted device is related to the blood analyte level measured by the conventional *in vitro* test method resulting in an *in vivo* sensitivity coefficient. In the two-point calibration method the plasma analyte level and sensor output reach a new plateau following analyte infusion. In such a case an *in vivo* sensitivity coefficient is obtained from sensor readings during the two steady states. The calculated *in vivo* sensitivity coefficient is then used to determine an apparent analyte concentration from the sensor output and to estimate its variation during changes of blood concentration. However the two-point calibration method is time-consuming and requires linear dependence of the sensor signal on the analyte concentration as well as the induction of blood analyte alteration, so its utility for daily clinical practice is questionable. Use of a one-point calibration technique has been shown to provide more accurate estimates of analyte concentration than the two-point calibration technique. Daily *in situ* one-point recalibrations are suggested to obtain reliable *in vivo* results. However if the number of *in situ* calibrations is excessive there is less value gained from having the sensor implanted in the first place. Furthermore since background signals in the absence of an analyte can change noticeably with time even frequently used one-point calibrations will not ensure measurements accuracy. One solution to obtaining clinically correct readings is to use a second non-enzyme electrode to determine the exact background, but again this method employs two inserted sensors which complicates implant design [84].

Another crucial point in the development of biosensors for *in vivo* use is their long-term stability. Various factors contribute to the failure of implantable biosensor operation. Breakdown of functionality may basically happen in two ways: component-based failures (such as lead detachment or electrical short-circuit) and biocompatibility-based failures (biofouling, hermeticity of encapsulation, electrode passivation, limited life-time of the immobilised enzymes) [85]. Some research advocates enzyme deactivation as the main issue. Immobilisation of enzymes in gels, on membranes or on inert dispersed carriers (usually carbon materials) can significantly increase stability, although the lifetime of the biosensor with immobilised enzymes remains limited. A new approach has been reported where it is possible to extend biosensor life time by *in situ* sensor refilling, that is replacing the deactivated immobilised enzyme with an active enzyme while the electrode remains implanted. The spent immobilised enzyme can be removed from the sensor and the new active enzyme suspension injected via two subcutaneously implanted septa, without surgical intervention [86].

Another major obstacle to the use of implantable biosensors is associated with the unavoidable, progressive changes of their function with time caused by the surrounding biological medium. For all *in vivo* measurements, the inserted device perturbs the environment initiating an inflammatory response in the host [85]. Significant efforts have been made to develop biosensors for intravascular and subcutaneous application. Three different processes can give incorrect analytical results for sensors implanted within the blood stream. Firstly, adsorption of proteins on the surface of the biosensor leads to the adhesion and activation of platelets (highly metabolic cells). This event results in an initiation of thrombus on the surface of the implanted device. The presence of adhered platelets on the sensor surface generates a local surface concentration of analyte species, which is different from the bulk of the blood. Similar analytical errors can be generated by the so called 'wall effect' which is caused by placing the implanted device in a region where it can end up touching the blood vessel wall. Positioning of the sensor near highly metabolically active cells creates localised concentrations of analyte yielding an error pattern identical to that observed by the adhesion and activation of platelets. The third process, which can interfere with sensor readings, is a dramatic fall in blood flow at the implant site due to vasoconstriction around the catheter [84].

Since the idea of implantable sensors is to function within the patient without additional medical supervision, it is the long-term placement of such devices subcutaneously, rather then intravasculary, that represents a more likely approach to clinical success. Subcutaneous tissue is regarded as the most appropriate site of implantation because of good accessibility for surgery and relatively simplified sensor replacement. Naturally implanting sensors subcutaneously does not eliminate biological response issues that can affect analytical performance. Although thrombus formation is no longer a problem there are several other difficulties to overcome [84].

Immunological response in the case of subcutaneous implantation consists of several phases: acute, chronic and fibrotic encapsulation. During the acute response plasma proteins particularly fibrinogen (fouling of the sensor) are firstly adsorbed and then phagocytic cells (neutrophils, monocytes, macrophages) surround the surface of the sensor and attempt to destroy it. This results in a higher consumption of oxygen and accelerates glucose metabolism (the 'respiratory burst') followed by the generation of oxygen-derived free radicals such as H_2O_2, NO, OH. The subsequent phase of acute response is the release of hydrolytic enzymes from lysosomes present in phagocytes, which aim to further degrade the sensor. The acute inflammatory response phase lasts from 24 to 48 hours, after which chronic inflammatory response begins. This reaction continues for 1-2 weeks ultimately resulting in fibrous encapsulation of the implanted material (final stage of wound healing in response to implanted, non-degradable foreign material). The extent and progression of the inflammatory process is dictated by the nature of the implant, specifically size, shape, physical (such as surface structure) and chemical (presence of charge, hydrophobic or hydrophilic nature) properties [86].

The biological reactions described above are tolerable in the case of artificial organs, however in the case of implanted biosensors they are undesirable since their functional characteristic will be changed in an unexpected manner [2, 83]. The consequence of encapsulation is insufficient vascularisation around the inserted biosensor. Due to the absence of dependable flow of blood delivering sample, the implantable device resides in a relatively stagnant environment, therefore diffusion conditions are undefined and the estimation of true analyte level is not possible. This critical problem, which seriously limits not only accuracy of determination but also sensor lifetime, has been known for many years and leads to the biocompatibility issue. According to biocompatibility research on materials and sensors, biocompatibility does not mean that the sensor is inert but that it causes minimal perturbation of surrounding living tissue and likewise the *in vivo* environment does not adversely and significantly influence sensor performance [2, 85, 87].

Partly because of the limitations of biocompatibility (with membrane biofouling playing a leading role in sensor instability), biosensors have proved to be inadequate for providing reliable data for extended time periods of *in vivo* application. However in the past few years novel solutions have been proposed to improve biocompatibility. The following section discusses sensor modifications required to reduce protein adsorption and to increase sensor integration with surrounding tissue by local drug delivery and control of tissue responses such as, for example, angiogenesis.

The need to diagnose and manage the worldwide health problem of diabetes mellitus has resulted in the most widely studied and arguably most successful implantable sensors to date being amperometric glucose sensors. Generally speaking two main analytical transduction methods have found application in the design of implantable chemical sensors: electrochemical and optical techniques, however because of their predominance in the literature, amperometric glucose sensors are discussed most frequently in this section [85].

The reduction of biofouling has predominantly been accomplished by fabrication of outer membranes that serve as a biocompatible interface, which protects the underlying enzyme and electrode from immune system attack [83]. Designing an appropriate biocompatible coating for biosensors is a particularly complicated problem. The chosen material must retard protein adsorption but simultaneously it must be permeable to the analyte and to reaction products. The material must also not cause excessive enzyme deactivation, therefore organic solvents, radicals of decomposing initiators (*e.g.* acetophenones), heat and UV light should be avoided. In addition, the biocompatible material should be free from cytotoxic, irritant, sensitising and carcinogenic effects. Polyurethane, Nafion, cellulose acetate, hydrogels, surfactants, polytetrafluoroethylene, polyvinyl chloride and other chemicals have been used with varying degrees of effectiveness [85]. Kerner and co-workers proposed polyurethane as an outer protective membrane for glucose biosensor and showed the ability to monitor glucose for up to 7h. Poor results was reported owing to loss of sensitivity of the sensor caused by low molecular weight substances from the sample diffusing across the polyurethane biocompatible coating [88]. In a similar study Moussy *et al* demonstrated a needle-type, electrochemical glucose sensor with Nafion as a protective biocompatible coating and found that protein adsorption caused loss of sensitivity and histological analysis showed limited tissue encapsulation after 14 days subcutaneous of implantation in dogs [89]. Ammon *et al* utilised a cellulosic material derived from bacterial source and found that the material showed low adsorption of bovine serum albumin and low complement activation. However the bioprotective layer was secured with on O-ring, a method that cannot be used with miniaturised sensors [90]. Rigby *et al* examined the use of a slow moving stream of phosphate-buffered saline solution over the tip of the sensor as the biointerface in the subcutaneous tissue of rats and found a significant reduction of device fouling by protein adsorption [91]. Kros *et al* compared various sol-gel derived hybrid materials for use as biocompatible coatings (heparin, polyethylene glycol, dextran, Nafion, and polystyrene). They discovered that fibroblast cell proliferation was dramatically diminished on sol-gel coatings that contained dextran or polystyrene [92].

Alternatively a great reduction of inflammatory response *in vivo* is achieved by surface modification to form hydrogels using hydrophilic polymers. The antifouling character in this case is believed to be due to the ability of these polymers to render the surface extremely hydrophilic, so that proteins have difficulty penetrating the surface because of a bound layer of water. Schmidtke and Heller used this phenomenon in their study and demonstrated that subcutaneous glucose electrodes obtained by 'wiring' glucose oxidase to crosslinked poly(4-vinylpyridine) polymer complexed with osmium (II/III)-bis (dipyridine) were less encapsulated [93].

Instead of non-specific binding reduction, another approach can be used when specific functions inducing intended biological responses are introduced. The most obvious issues are the suppression of a defence reaction near the inserted device and the enhancement of neovascularisation around the biosensor.

There are two strategies for providing a better integration of the sensor within the tissue [84, 85]. The first is the application of the controlled release of drugs that prevent inflammation and inhibit fibrosis in favour of the growth of vascularised tissue that would not severely impair delivery of blood analyte to the sensor. The local drug release provides benefits by reducing systemic side effects and improving therapeutic response. There are some potential strategies for delivering low levels of drug around the biosensor. One possible solution is to design the sensor with a small reservoir containing, for example, the anti-fouling agent. The other method is to incorporate a layer that would slowly degrade and thus deliver the medication.

There are two keys to the potential success of this approach. Firstly, the presence of the released immobilised agent within or on the outer layer of the sensor should not perturb the analytical response of the device. Secondly, the loading of the agent within or on the outer surface of the sensor must be adequate to ensure its activity for long-term *in vivo* application. It is commonly known that nitric oxide is a naturally occurring anti-platelet agent, therefore its release chemistry, which mimics a natural physiological process, could provide important conditions for improving the analytical performance of intravascularly inserted sensors [84, 94]. Schoenfish *et al* demonstrated that the adhesion of proteins is limited when the electrochemical oxygen sensor is covered with a polymer that slowly releases physiological levels of NO gas [95]. Subsequently the prospect of using NO release sol-gel outer coatings for glucose sensors has been reported, with biosensors fabricated in the presence of the NO release chemistry [84].

The second technique has the same goal of promoting the growth of vascularised tissue, but accomplishes this by modifying the sensor surface. These modifications can either involve adding certain functional groups to alter the surface chemistry, or by controlling the topography surface through processing, in order to favour the ingrowth of vascularised tissue. It has been suggested that insufficient vascularisation surrounding the inserted biosensors decreases the appropriate analyte concentration at the implant side. However this effect is alleviated after a few days when the foreign body capsule has matured enough to provide ingrowth of tissue bearing a rich supply of capillaries (angiogenesis process) directly to the surface of the biosensor. Improvement of neovascularisation can be achieved be incorporating an angiogenesis factor such as a vascular growth factor or adding a specially structured polytetrafluoroethylene membrane to the sensor surface. The most important requirement of this approach is the maintenance of proper analyte transport through the multi-layer coatings, therefore any additional membrane applied within the biosensors must be extremely thin or sufficiently porous [85, 96].

The concept of initiation and modulation of angiogenesis was used by Updike *et al* in their study. They developed an electrochemical glucose sensor consisting of angiogenic, bioprotective and enzyme layers. The bioprotective membrane reduces the defence mechanism caused by macrophages, whereas the outermost angiogenic layer promotes the development of new blood vessels on the sensor surface. It should be pointed out that at the same time the additional coatings of the biosensor do not affect diffusion of the analyte [97].

The increasing demand and interest in developing implantable sensors has lead to significant progress in the commercial area. Some of the implantable glucose sensors have been successfully tested on animals and have made their way into limited human testing, therefore commercial availability of these devices seems to be moving closer to reality.

Two different concepts of implantable glucose sensors have been proposed: fully implanted and percutaneous (worn through the skin). The fully implanted biosensors are designed for long-term use and need to be inserted by a specialist while the percutaneous needle-like devices are fabricated to operate for a few days and are replaceable by the patient [87].

Several companies have been working independently to develop their own percutanous devices. After a long-term research program, MiniMed (Sylmar, CA, USA) began human trials of an implantable subcutaneous glucose sensor, which resulted in its launch in 2002. Relatively frequent calibration of the sensor is required via periodic *in vitro* tests, and hence the output of the device is not readable by the patient. Access to the obtained information is restricted to the physician [84, 98]. Therasense (Alameda CA, USA) also introduced a subcutaneous needle-type sensor less than 10% of the length of the MiniMed device. The company developed the idea of a 'wired' glucose oxidase sensor proposed by Heller and co-workers. The prototype is wireless, intended for use with a 'pager unit' [84, 98]. A different approach was adopted by Synthetic Blood International who are working on a fully implantable glucose sensor based on materials commonly found in cardiac pacemakers. The device consists of an encased titanium battery, microprocessor and glucose oxidase enzyme system encapsulated in a semipermeable cellophane acetate membrane, which provides continuous, accurate monitoring of blood. Results are displayed as a digital readout in a wearable beeper-sized device, which it is hoped will have an implant life exceeding one year [87]. Several other implantable sensors, from other manufacturers, are in development and are claimed to be close to market.

Finally it should be mentioned that due to the success of intravenous glucose sensors MiniMed have developed a prototype artificial ß-cell system. The sensor itself can be implanted into the superior vena cava via direct jugular access. An implantable intraperitoneal insulin infusion pump is placed in the abdominal wall, and the two are connected by a subcutaneous lead, allowing real-time transmission of sensor data to the insulin pump [98].

In conclusion, biosensors seem to be ideally suited to dealing with the dynamic nature of living systems. Significant advances have been made in the design, electronics, selectivity and sensitivity of biosensors, which enable such devices to perform optimally *in vivo* for extended periods of time; however there are issues that still remain unresolved. The lack of reliable analytical performance of the devices once implanted has prevented widespread use of biosensors in the clinical area. These performance problems appear due to biological response of the host to the implant. Only with a better understanding of the processes involved in sensor deactivation would it be possible to develop adequate strategies to achieve accurate analytical results with inserted biosensors.

It also seems worthwhile to simultaneously investigate the control of tissue reaction to implanted devices. It is now believed that there are reasonable chances for the commercial success of implantable glucose sensors, however there is also great demand for the monitoring of other analytes besides glucose, such as urea, creatinine, lactate or glutamate. Perhaps in the near future a typical doctor's visit will not be needed, as an array of biosensors implanted in the body will act as a constant on-board doctor, detecting disorders at an early stage and indicating the necessary treatment of the disease.

3.4 Conclusions

Many of the issues associated with the extension of biosensor technology from *in vitro* to *in vivo* applications have long been appreciated and solutions to them are slowly developing. Whether the vision of a long-term implantable sensor will ever be realised will depend on advances across a range of disciplines, many of them are discussed in this volume. There is little doubt that a panoply of technologies will need to be combined in new and previously unsuspected ways. There is also little doubt that the rewards of success, in terms of quality and duration of life in the case of many of those suffering from chronic conditions, will be substantial.

References

1. Cooper J, Cass T. Biosensors: a practical approach, 2nd ed. Oxford: Oxford University Press, 2004.
2. Wilson GS, Gifford R. Biosensors for real-time *in vivo* measurements. Biosensors and Bioelectronics 2005; 20(12):2388-2403.
3. Schoning MJ. "Playing around" with field-effect sensors on the basis of EIS structures, LAPS and ISFETs. Sensors 2005; 5(3):126-138.
4. Shepherd L, Toumazou C. Weak Inversion ISFETs for ultra-low power biochemical sensing and real-time analysis. Sensors and Actuators B: Chemical 2005; 107(1):468-473.
5. Forrow NJ, Sanghera GS, Walters SJ. The influence of structure in the reaction of electrochemically generated ferrocenium derivatives with reduced glucose oxidase. Journal of the Chemical Society-Dalton Transactions 2002; (16):3187-3194.
6. Zhang WJ, Li GX. Third-generation biosensors based on the direct electron transfer of proteins. Analytical Sciences 2004; 20(4):603-609.
7. Choi MMF. Progress in enzyme-based biosensors using optical transducers. Microchimica Acta 2004; 148(3-4):107-132.
8. Gauglitz G. Direct optical sensors: principles and selected applications. Analytical and Bioanalytical Chemistry 2005; 381(1):141-155.
9. Monk DJ, Walt DR. Optical fiber-based biosensors. Analytical and Bioanalytical Chemistry 2004; 379(7-8):931-945.
10. Taitt CR, Anderson GP, Ligler FS. Evanescent wave fluorescence biosensors. Biosensors and Bioelectronics 2005; 20(12):2470-2487.

11. Zourob M, Mohr S, Brown BJT, Fielden PR, McDonnell MB, Goddard NJ. An integrated metal clad leaky waveguide sensor for detection of bacteria. Analytical Chemistry 2005; 77(1):232-242.

12. Vaseashta A, Dimova-Malinovska D. Nanostructured and nanoscale devices, sensors and detectors. Science and Technology of Advanced Materials 2005; 6(3-4):312-318.

13. Jain KK. Nanotechnology in clinical laboratory diagnostics. Clinica Chimica Acta 2005; 358(1-2):37-54.

14. Wang J. Nanomaterial-based amplified transduction of biomolecular interactions. Small 2005; 1(11):1036-1043.

15. Nath N, Chilkoti A. Label free colorimetric biosensing using nanoparticles. Journal of Fluorescence 2004; 14(4):377-389.

16. Pattnaik P. Surface plasmon resonance - applications in understanding receptor-ligand interaction. Applied Biochemistry and Biotechnology 2005; 126(2):79-92.

17. Rickert J, Brecht A, Gopel W. Quartz crystal microbalances for quantitative biosensing and characterizing protein multilayers. Biosensors and Bioelectronics 1997; 12(7):567-575.

18. Su XL, Li YB. A self-assembled monolayer-based piezoelectric immunosensor for rapid detection of Escherichia coli O157 : H7. Biosensors and Bioelectronics 2004; 19(6):563-574.

19. Berkenpas E, Bitla S, Millard P, da Cunha MP. Pure shear horizontal SAW biosensor on langasite. IEEE Transactions on Ultrasonics Ferroelectrics and Frequency Control 2004; 51(11):1404-1411.

20. Schlensog MD, Gronewold TMA, Tewes M, Famulok M, Quandt E. A Love-wave biosensor using nucleic acids as ligands. Sensors and Actuators B-Chemical 2004; 101(3):308-315.

21. Godber B, Thompson KSJ, Rehak M, Uludag Y, Kelling S, Sleptsov A, *et al.* Direct quantification of analyte concentration by resonant acoustic profiling. Clinical Chemistry 2005; 51(10):1962-1972.

22. Baier V, Fodisch R, Ihring A, Kessler E, Lerchner J, Wolf G, *et al.* Highly sensitive thermopile heat power sensor for micro-fluid calorimetry of biochemical processes. Sensors and Actuators A: Physical 2005; 123-124:354-359.

23. Johannessen EA, Weaver JMR, Bourova L, Svoboda P, Cobbold PH, Cooper JM. Micromachined nanocalorimetric sensor for ultra-low-volume cell-based assays. Analytical Chemistry 2002; 74(9):2190-2197.

24. Callan JF, de Silva AP, Magri DC. Luminescent sensors and switches in the early 21st century. Tetrahedron 2005; 61(36):8551-8588.

25. Hellinga HW, Marvin JS. Protein engineering and the development of generic biosensors. Trends in Biotechnology 1998; 16(4):183-189.

26. Goodsell DS. Bionanotechnology. Hoboken: Wiley-Liss, 2004.

27. Gilardi G. Protein Engineering for Biosensors. In: Cooper J, Cass T (eds) Biosensors: A Practical Approach. Oxford: Oxford University Press, 2004.

28. Lutz S, Patrick WM. Novel methods for directed evolution of enzymes: quality, not quantity. Current Opinion in Biotechnology 2004; 15(4):291-297.

29. Gilardi G, Fantuzzi A. Manipulating redox systems: application to nanotechnology. Trends in Biotechnology 2001; 19:468-476.
30. Gilardi G, Zhou LQ, Hibbert L, Cass AEG. Engineering the maltose-binding protein for reagentless fluorescence sensing. Analytical Chemistry 1994; 66(21):3840-3847.
31. Brune M, Hunter JL, Corrie JET, Webb MR. Direct, real-time measurement of rapid inorganic phosphate release using a novel fluorescent probe and its applications to actinomyosin subfragment 1 ATPase. Biochemistry 1994; 33:8262-8271.
32. Gilardi G, Mei G, Rosato N, Agro AF, Cass AEG. Spectroscopic properties of an engineered maltose binding protein. Protein Engineering 1997; 10(5):479-486.
33. Brune M, Hunter JL, Howell SA, Martin SR, Hazlett TL, Corrie JET, *et al.* Mechanism of inorganic phosphate interaction with phosphate binding protein from Escherichia coli. Biochemistry 1998; 37(29):10370-10380.
34. Hirshberg M, Henrick K, Haire LL, Vasisht N, Brune M, Corrie JET, *et al.* Crystal structure of phosphate binding protein labeled with a coumarin fluorophore, a probe for inorganic phosphate. Biochemistry 1998; 37(29):10381-10385.
35. Dattelbaum JD, Looger LL, Benson DE, Sali KM, Thompson RB, Hellinga HW. Analysis of allosteric signal transduction mechanisms in an engineered fluorescent maltose biosensor. Protein Science 2005; 14(2):284-291.
36. Allert M, Rizk SS, Looger LL, Hellinga HW. Computational design of receptors for an organophosphate surrogate of the nerve agent soman. Proceedings of the National Academy of Sciences of the United States of America 2004; 101(21):7907-7912.
37. De Lorimier RM, Smith JJ, Dwyer MA, Looger LL, Sali KM, Paavola CD, *et al.* Construction of a fluorescent biosensor family. Protein Science 2002; 11(11):2655-2675.
38. Marvin JS, Hellinga HW. Conversion of a maltose receptor into a zinc biosensor by computational design. Proceedings of the National Academy of Sciences of the United States of America 2001; 98(9):4955-4960.
39. Marvin JS, Corcoran EE, Hattangadi NA, Zhang JV, Gere SA, Hellinga HW. The rational design of allosteric interactions in a monomeric protein and its applications to the construction of biosensors. Proceedings of the National Academy of Sciences of the United States of America 1997; 94(9):4366-4371.
40. Badugu R, Lakowicz JR, Geddes CD. Ophthalmic glucose monitoring using disposable contact lenses - a review. Journal of Fluorescence 2004; 14(5):617-633.
41. Renard M, Bedouelle H. Improving the sensitivity and dynamic range of reagentless fluorescent immunosensors by knowledge-based design. Biochemistry 2004; 43(49):15453-15462.
42. Chan PH, Liu HB, Chen YW, Chan KC, Tsang CW, Leung YC, *et al.* Rational design of a novel fluorescent biosensor for beta-lactam antibiotics from a class A beta-lactamase. Journal of the American Chemical Society 2004; 126(13):4074-4075.

43. Nagase T, Nakata E, Shinkai S, Hamachi I. Construction of artificial signal transducers on a lectin surface by post-photoaffinity-labeling modification for fluorescent saccharide biosensors. Chemistry 2003; 9(15):3660-3669.
44. Benson DE, Conrad DW, de Lorimier RM, Trammell SA, Hellinga HW. Design of bioelectronic interfaces by exploiting hinge-bending motions in proteins. Science 2001; 293(5535):1641-1644.
45. Kase Y, Muguruma H. Amperometric glucose biosensor based on mediated electron transfer between immobilized glucose oxidase and plasma- polymerized thin film of dimethylaminomethylferrocene on sputtered gold electrode. Analytical Sciences 2004; 20(8):1143-1146.
46. Battaglini F, Bartlett PN, Wang JH. Covalent attachment of osmium complexes to glucose oxidase and the application of the resulting modified enzyme in an enzyme switch responsive to glucose. Analytical Chemistry 2000; 72(3):502-509.
47. Sadeghi SJ, G.Gilardi, Cass AEG. Mediated electrochemistry of peroxidases-effects of variations in protein and mediator structures. Biosensors and Bioelectronics 1997; 12(12):1191-1198.
48. Loechel C, Basran A, Basran J, Scrutton NS, Hall EAH. Using trimethylamine dehydrogenase in an enzyme linked amperometric electrode II: rational design engineering of a 'wired' mutant. Analyst 2003; 128(7):889-898.
49. Chen LQ, Zhang XE, Xie WH, Zhou YF, Zhang ZP, Cass AEG. Genetic modification of glucose oxidase for improving performance of an amperometric glucose biosensor. Biosensors and Bioelectronics 2002; 17(10):851-857.
50. Degani Y, Heller A. Direct electrical communication between chemically modified enzymes and metal-electrodes I: electron-transfer from glucose-oxidase to metal-electrodes via electron relays, bound covalently to the enzyme. Journal of Physical Chemistry 1987; 91(6):1285-1289.
51. Easterby JS. The analysis of metabolite channelling in multienzyme complexes and multifunctional proteins. Biochemical Journal 1989; 264(2):605-607.
52. Zhou YF, Zhang XE, Liu H, Zhang ZP, Zhang CG, Cass AEG. Construction of a fusion enzyme system by gene splicing as a new molecular recognition element for a sequence biosensor. Bioconjugate Chemistry 2001; 12(6):924-931.
53. Martineau P, Szmelcman S, Spurlino JC, Quiocho FA, Hofnung M. Genetic approach to the role of tryptophan residues in the activities and fluorescence of a bacterial periplasmic maltose-binding protein. Journal of Molecular Biology 1990; 214(1):337-352.
54. Fierke CA, Thompson RB. Fluorescence-based biosensing of zinc using carbonic anhydrase. Biometals 2001; 14(3-4):205-222.
55. Soldatkin AP, Montoriol J, Sant W, Martelet C, Jaffrezic-Renault N. A novel urea sensitive biosensor with extended dynamic range based on recombinant urease and ISFETs. Biosensors and Bioelectronics 2003; 19(2):131-135.
56. Xu HF, Zhang XE, Zhang ZP, Zhang YM, Cass AEG. Directed evolution of e-coli alkaline phosphatase towards higher catalytic activity. Biocatalysis and Biotransformation 2003; 21(1):41-47.
57. Zeng HH, Thompson RB, Maliwal BP, Fones GR, Moffett JW, Fierke CA. Real-time determination of picomolar free Cu(II) in seawater using a fluores-

cence based fiber optic biosensor. Analytical Chemistry 2003; 75(24):6807-6812.

58. Sacchi S, Rosini E, Molla G, Pilone MS, Pollegioni L. Modulating D-amino acid oxidase substrate specificity: production of an enzyme for analytical determination of all D-amino acids by directed evolution. Protein Engineering Design and Selection 2004; 17(6):517-525.

59. Boublik Y, Saint-Aguet P, Lougarre A, Arnaud M, Villatte F, Estrada-Mondaca S, *et al.* Acetylcholinesterase engineering for detection of insecticide residues. Protein Engineering 2002; 15(1):43-50.

60. Schulze H, Muench SB, Villatte F, Schmid RD, Bachmann TT. Insecticide detection through protein engineering of Nippostrongylus brasiliensis acetylcholinesterase B. Analytical Chemistry 2005; 77(18):5823-5830.

61. Flower DR, North ACT, Sansom CE. The lipocalin protein family: structure and sequence overview. Biochimica et Biophysica Acta-Protein Structure and Molecular Enzymology 2000; 1482(1-2):9-24.

62. Schlehuber S, Skerra A. Lipocalins in drug discovery: from natural ligand-binding proteins to 'anticalins'. Drug Discovery Today 2005; 10(1):23-33.

63. Korndorfer IP, Beste G, Skerra A. Crystallographic analysis of an "anticalin" with tailored specificity for fluorescein reveals high structural plasticity of the lipocalin loop region. Proteins-Structure Function and Genetics 2003; 53(1):121-129.

64. Mercader JV, Skerra A. Generation of anticalins with specificity for a nonsymmetric phthalic acid ester. Analytical Biochemistry 2002; 308(2):269-277.

65. Dwyer MA, Hellinga HW. Periplasmic binding proteins: a versatile superfamily for protein engineering. Current Opinion in Structural Biology 2004; 14(4):495-504.

66. Looger LL, Dwyer MA, Smith JJ, Hellinga HW. Computational design of receptor and sensor proteins with novel functions. Nature 2003; 423(6936):185-190.

67. Stroscio MA, Dutta M. Integrated biological-semiconductor devices. Proceedings of the IEEE 2005; 93(10):1772-1783.

68. Sheehan PE, Whitman LJ. Detection limits for nanoscale biosensors. Nano Letters 2005; 5(4):803-807.

69. Halliwell CM. Nanoanalytical measurement of protein orientation on conductive sensor surfaces. Analyst 2004; 129(12):1166-1170.

70. Davis J, Glidle A, Cass AEG, Zhang JK, Cooper JM. Spectroscopic evaluation of protein affinity binding at polymeric biosensor films. Journal of the American Chemical Society 1999; 121(17):4302-4303.

71. Zhang JK, Cass AEG. A study of his-tagged alkaline phosphatase immobilization on a nanoporous nickel-titanium dioxide film. Analytical Biochemistry 2001; 292(2):307-310.

72. Ferapontova E, Gorton L. Bioelectrocatalytical detection of H2O2 with different forms of horseradish peroxidase directly adsorbed at polycrystalline silver and gold. Electroanalysis 2003; 15(5-6):484-491.

73. Shi JX, Zhang XE, Xie WH, Zhou YF, Zhang ZP, Deng JY, *et al.* Improvement of homogeneity of analytical biodevices by gene manipulation. Analytical Chemistry 2004; 76(3):632-638.

74. Halliwell CM, Simon E, Toh CS, Bartlett PN, Cass AEG. A method for the determination of enzyme mass loading on an electrode surface through radioisotope labelling. Biosensors and Bioelectronics 2002; 17(11-12):965-972.

75. Shao W-H, Zhang X-E, Liu H, Zhang ZP, Cass AEG. An 'anchor-chain' molecular system for orientation control of enzyme immobilization with high recovery of activity. Bioconjugate Chemistry 2000; 11:822-826.

76. Nygren H, Stenberg M. Surface-induced aggregation of ferritin. Kinetics of adsorption to a hydrophobic surface. Biophysical Chemistry 1990; 38:67-75.

77. Sugihara T, Seong GH, Kobatake E, Aizawa M. Genetically synthesized antibody-binding protein self-assembled on hydrophobic matrix. Bioconjugate Chemistry 2000; 11(6):789-794.

78. Wada A, Mie M, Aizawa M, Lahoud P, Cass AEG, Kobatake E. Design and construction of glutamine binding proteins with a self-adhering capability to unmodified hydrophobic surfaces as reagentless fluorescence sensing devices. Journal of the American Chemical Society 2003; 125(52):16228-16234.

79. Haberzettl CA. Nanomedicine: destination or journey? Nanotechnology 2002; 13:R9-R13.

80. Malhotra BD, Chaubey A. Biosensors for clinical diagnostics industry. Sensors and Actuators B 2003; 91:117-127.

81. Renard E. Implanted closed-loop glucose-sensing and insulin delivery: the future for insulin pump therapy. Current Opinion in Pharmacology 2002: 708-716.

82. Woedtke Tv, Jülich W-D, Hartmann V, Stieber M, Abel PU. Sterilisation of enzyme glucose sensors: problems and concepts. Biosensors and Bioelectronics 2002; 17:373-382.

83. Abel PU, Woedtke TV. Biosensors for *in vivo* glucose measurements: can we cross the experimental stage? Biosensors and Bioelectronics 2002; 17:1059-1070.

84. Frost MC, Meyerhoff ME. Implantable chemical sensors for real-time clinical monitoring: progress and challenges. Current Opinion in Chemical Biological 2002; 6:633-641.

85. Wisniewski N, Moussy F, Reichert WM. Characterization of implantable biosensor membrane biofouling. Fresenius' Journal of Analytical Chemistry 2000; 366:611-621

86. Atanasov P, Yang S, Salehi C, Ghindilis AL, Wilkins E, Schade D. Implantation of refillable glucose monitoring-telemetry device. Biosensors and Bioelectronics 1997; 12:669-680.

87. Henry C. Getting under the skin: implantable electrochemical glucose sensors are moving closer to commercialization. Analytical Chemistry 1998; 60:594A-598A.

88. Kerner W, Kiwit M, Linke B, Keck FS, Zier H, Pfeiffer EF. The function of a hydrogen peroxide-detecting electroenzymatic glucose electrode is markedly

impaired in human subcutaneous tissue and plasma. Biosensors and Bioelectronics 1993; 8:473-482.

89. Moussy F, Harrison DJ, O'Brien DW, Rajotte RV. Performance of subcutaneously implanted needle-type glucose sensor employing a novel trilayer coating. Analytical Chemistry 1993; 65:2072-2077.

90. Ammon HP, Ege W, Oppermann M, Gopel W, Eisele S. Improvement in the long-term stability of an amperometric glucose sensor system by introducing a cellulose membrane of bacterial origin. Analytical Chemistry 1995; 67:466-471.

91. Rigby GP, Ahmed S, Horseman G, Vadgama P. *In vitro* glucose monitoring with open microflow – influences of fluid composition and preliminary evaluation in man. Analytica Chimica Acta 1999; 74:23-32.

92. Kros A, Gerritsen M, Sprakel VSL, Sommerdijk NAJM, Jansen JA, Nolte RJM. Silica-based hybrid materials as biocompatible coating for glucose sensors. Sensors and Actuators B 2001; 81:68-75

93. Schmidtke DW, Heller A. Accuracy of the one-point *in vivo* calibration of 'wired' glucose oxidase electrodes implanted in jugular veins of rats in periods if rapid rise and decline of the glucose concentration. Analytical Chemistry 1998; 70:2149-2155.

94. Frost MC, Batchelor MM, Lee Y, Zhang H, Kang Y, Oh B, *et al.* Preparation and characterisation of implantable sensors with nitric oxide realise coating. Microchemical Journal 2003; 74:277-288.

95. Schoenfisch MH, Mowery KA, Rader MV, Baliga N, Wahr JA, Meyerhoff ME. Improving the thromboresitivity of chemical sensors via nitric oxide release: fabrication and *in vivo* evaluation of NO-releasing oxygen-sensing catheters. Analytical Chemistry 2000; 72:1119-1126.

96. Klueh U, Dorsky DI, Kreutzer DL. Enhancement of implantable glucose sensor function *in vivo* using gene transfer-induced neovascularization. Biomaterials 2005; 26:1155-1163.

97. Updike SJ, Shults MC, B.J.Gilligan, R.K.Rhodes. A subcutaneous glucose sensor with improved longevity, dynamic range, and stability of calibration. Diabetes Care 2000; 23:208-214.

98. Newman JD, Turner APF. Home blood glucose biosensors: a commercial perspective. Biosensors and Bioelectronics 2005; 20:2435-2453.

4

Wireless Communication

Henry Higgins

4.1 Introduction

Increasingly, sophisticated implanted medical devices are integrating wireless technology to support an ever-expanding range of therapeutic and diagnostic applications. For example, an implanted heart pacemaker or cardiac defibrillator enabled with a wireless link allows a physician to monitor more easily a patient's response to therapy and adjust device performance as required. With a network of in-body and on-body sensors, muscles can be stimulated to help restore lost limb function. Similarly, a radio-controlled valve in the urinary tract that is operated on-demand by the patient will restore bladder control.

Drug manufacturers are also interested in patient monitoring during treatment to regulate dosages and detect side effects. Introducing a new drug is a costly endeavour with considerable risk, as drugs will be pulled from the market if even a small number of patients have an adverse reaction. By monitoring the internal chemistry, patients susceptible to side effects could be identified earlier in the treatment process and alternative therapies could be considered. This would then benefit the patient, and reduce the risk of a drug being withdrawn that may yet assist others.

Whether it is a pacemaker communicating patient health and performance data to a base station, or a BSN integrating a number of devices, these new applications require a reliable, wireless communication link between implanted devices through the patient's skin to a clinician. The wireless link can be used to interrogate the implant at either irregular intervals, on a regularly scheduled basis or provide near constant communication. A one-way wireless link may be used to obtain patient health or device performance data from the implant, while a two-way link allows external reprogramming of an implanted device.

This chapter will discuss two types of communication links: the inductive loop and *Radio Frequency* (RF) communication. Widely in use today, the inductive loop is useful for transferring small packets of data without requiring an implanted power source (battery). While an RF system does require an implanted battery source, it is capable of transferring larger packets of data within a shorter time period and over greater distances. RF-based communication will be the main topic of this chapter.

While wireless communication through air has been extensively documented, communication from implanted devices through the human body is a new area of study. This chapter will discuss body properties and their effect on radio propagation. The human body is an uninviting and often hostile environment for a wireless signal. One of the most important considerations for implanted devices is physical size, meaning in-body communication system designs are restricted to an extremely small antenna that needs to be characterised to enable it to be effectively coupled to the transceiver. A significant portion of this chapter is devoted to antenna measurement and coupling circuit design, as it is critical to the success of an implanted RF system.

4.2 Inductive Coupling

Before discussing in-body RF communication, it is important to understand inductive coupling. Several applications still use electromagnetic coupling to provide a communication link to implanted devices, with an external coil held very close to the patient that couples to a coil implanted just below the skin surface. The implant is powered by the coupled magnetic field and requires no battery for communication. As well as providing power, this alternating field is also be used to transfer data into the implant. Data is transferred from the implanted device by altering the impedance of the implanted loop that is detected by the external coil and electronics. This type of communication is commonly used to identify animals that have been injected with an electronic tag.

Electromagnetic induction is used when continuous, long-term communication is required, such as for a cochlear implant used to restore hearing. A cochlear implant includes a coil is placed below the skin behind the ear and an external energising coil. Using a magnet in one coil and an iron puck in the other, the coils are kept in alignment without requiring any external support. Power for the implant and encoded sound is transmitted across the small gap. The power source is an external battery that can be changed with ease and the implant can remain in place for many years.

Another application using electromagnetic coupling is in the treatment of an *Abdominal Aortic Aneurysm* (AAA). In this situation, a shaped tube is inserted into the patient through a "keyhole" in the groin and placing it over the affected area. To evaluate the patient's health, a pressure sensor is included that can be interrogated at any time for many years. As a result, major abdominal surgery is replaced with a relatively unobtrusive procedure and the patient can be easily monitored. Electromagnetic coupling is also used to "fine-tune" pacemakers and measure intercranial pressure.

The base band for electromagnetic communication is typically 13.56MHz or 28MHz, with other frequencies also available. Its use is subject to regulation for maximum *Specific Absorption Rate* (SAR); two important standards are ANSI C95.1 and ICNIRP.

Inductive coupling achieves the best power transfer when using large transmit and receive coils, meaning it is impractical when space is an issue or devices are to be implanted deep within the patient. This technique does not support a very high data rate and cannot initiate a communication session from inside of the body [1].

4.3 RF Communication in Body

Compared with inductive coupling, RF communication dramatically increases bandwidth and enables a two-way data link that allows an implant to initiate a communication session. This requires an implanted battery, electronics and suitable antenna. While some in-body communication systems initially used the *Industrial Scientific and Medical* (ISM) [2] bands, the *Medical Implant Communication System* (MICS) [3] band of 403MHz to 405MHz is gaining worldwide acceptance. This band has a power limit of 25µW in air and is split into 300kHz wide channels.

The human body is a medium that poses numerous wireless transmission challenges. Unlike air, the body is composed of varied components that are not predictable and will change as the patient ages, gains or loses weight, or even changes posture. More details on the impact of the changing nature of the human body on wireless communications are discussed by Johansson [4]. While there are simple formulas for designing free-air communications, it is very difficult to calculate performance for an in-body communication system, as each individual is different. To compound the design challenge, the location of the implanted device is also variable. A surgeon fits the implant into the best position to perform its primary function, with little consideration for wireless performance. This means an implanted RF communication system must operate in a wide variety of environments and positions that can change with time.

The typical dielectric constant (ε_r), conductivity (σ) and characteristic impedance (Z_o) properties of muscle and fat are illustrated in Table 4.1. The table demonstrates that these two mediums are very different and properties change with frequency.

Table 4.1 Body electrical properties (*source: FCC and William Scanlon, Queens University Belfast*).

Frequency (MHz)	Muscle			Fat		
	ε_r	$\sigma(\mathrm{Sm^{-1}})$	$Z_o(\Omega)$	ε_r	$\sigma(\mathrm{Sm^{-1}})$	$Z_o(\Omega)$
100	66.2	0.73	31.6	12.7	0.07	92.4
400	58.0	0.82	43.7	11.6	0.08	108
900	56.0	0.97	48.2	11.3	0.11	111

The dielectric constant has an effect on the wavelength of a signal. In air the wavelength can be found from (4.1) where $\varepsilon_r = 1$. However in a different medium the wavelength is reduced as (4.2).

$$\lambda = 300\frac{10^6}{f} \tag{4.1}$$

where λ is the wavelength in air in meters and f is frequency in Hz.

$$\lambda_{medium} = \frac{\lambda}{\sqrt{\varepsilon_r}} \tag{4.2}$$

where λ_{medium} is the wavelength in medium. At 403MHz the wavelength in air is 744mm, but in muscle with $\varepsilon_r = 50$ the $\lambda_{medium} = 105$ mm. This is of considerable help in designing implanted antennas where physical size is an important consideration. The conductivity of muscle is 0.82Sm^{-1} – this is more than air, which is almost zero. The effect of this is similar to surrounding the implant with seawater that will attenuate the signal as it passes through. This results in reduced penetration as shown in Table 4.2.

Table 4.2 Penetration depth of tissue, where penetration depth is where field intensity decreases by e^{-1} (*source: William Scanlon, Queens University Belfast*).

Frequency (MHz)	Muscle (mm)	Fat (mm)
100	75.1	339
400	51.5	229
900	41.6	163

The characteristic impedance (Z_o) is relevant when it changes, such as at the fat-muscle boundary. This will cause part of the signal to be reflected by a term known as reflection co-coefficient Γ, found from (4.3).

$$\Gamma = \frac{Z_o - Z_r}{Z_o + Z_r} \tag{4.3}$$

where Z_o is the impedance of free space (377Ω), and Z_r is the impedance of medium in Ω.

This results in a signal being reflected of magnitude Γ of incident signal power. So for muscle-fat boundary $\Gamma = 80\%$ of the signal is reflected as shown in Figure 4.1. If the signal is incident at the Bragg Angle all of the incident signal will be reflected. This is shown in Figure 4.1.

As an implant does not have an earth (ground), the case or other wires will also radiate. This means that signals will be radiated from the antenna and other structures associated with the implant, as shown in Figure 4.2.

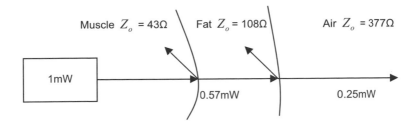

Figure 4.1 Signal reflection at muscle – fat – air boundaries.

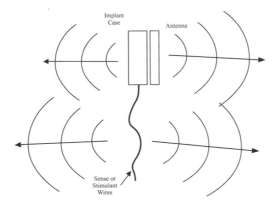

Figure 4.2 Radiation from an implant.

To summarise, a signal travelling through the body will suffer attenuation and reflection from various boundary changes.

4.4 Antenna Design

Of the many books written on the subject of antennas, almost all of them describe operation in air. While some of the principles still hold true for in-body use, as described above, the surrounding medium is very different. A good basic reference is provided by Kraus [5].

A half-wave dipole for 403MHz in air will be 372mm, but in muscle it reduces to 52.6mm. A quarter-wave monopole will be reduced from 186mm in air to 26.3mm in muscle but requires a counterpoise (large conductor at its base, as seen Figure 4.3). The dipole or monopole are resonant antennas requiring a medium of constant ε_r. The first problem is that each body will have a different ε_r that may change as the patient changes weight or the implant moves. This will cause the antenna to be non-resonant and operate with reduced effectiveness. As resonant antennas are also often too large for in-body use, this design is not practical.

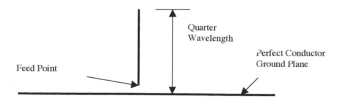

Figure 4.3 Monopole antenna with ground plane.

An in-body antenna needs to tuneable with an intelligent transceiver and routine. This will enable the antenna coupling circuit to be optimised and the best signal strength obtained. Often the size constraints dictate the choice of a non-resonant antenna. A non-resonant antenna will have lower gain and therefore be less sensitive on receive and radiate less of the power generated by the transmitter. This makes design of the antenna coupling circuit even more important.

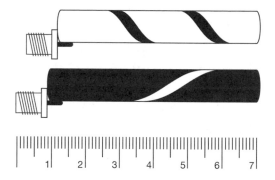

Figure 4.4 Helix antenna copper conductor on a ceramic substrate.

Antenna options are also dictated by the location of the implant. For example, a urethra valve (artificial bladder sphincter) needs to be replaced without surgery at regular intervals. The available diameter is 4mm to 6mm and the length is restricted. This rules out a patch antenna, and it would be difficult to keep a monopole or dipole in place even if they would fit. The best option is to integrate a helical antenna into the shape of the valve implant. The design equations are found in a paper by Krall [6] and two lab versions are shown in Figure 4.4. This type of antenna may also be of use in an oesophagus probe. The conductor could be printed or evaporated on to the surface of the valve.

A patch antenna can be used when the implant is flat and there is no room to deploy a short wire. Patch antennas comprise a flat substrate coated on both sides with conductor. The substrate is typically alumina or similar body-compatible material (biocompatibility will be discussed later), with platinum or platinum/iridium coating both surfaces. The upper surface is the active face and is connected to the transceiver and the back face is typically connected to the implant 0V. The connection to the transceiver needs to pass through the case where the hermetic seal is maintained, requiring a feed-through. The feed-through must have no filter capacitors present; these are common on other devices. The connection to the top (active) surface can be by a hole through the substrate (Figure 4.5) or by a wire connected to the top (Figure 4.6). The back face can be connected to the case with conductive epoxy, if it is attached to 0V, or by wire.

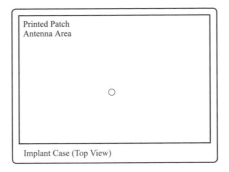

Figure 4.5 Patch with through-hole connection.

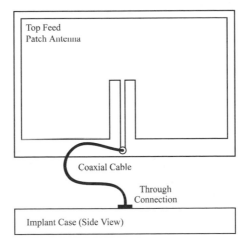

Figure 4.6 Patch with wired top surface connection.

A patch antenna will be electrically larger than its physical size because it will be immersed in a high ε_r medium. It can be made to appear even larger electrically if the substrate is of higher ε_r, such as Titania or Zirconia. Further reading on small antennas can be found in Fujimori [7] and PCB antennas by Lee and Chen [8]. Other antenna reading includes ARRL [9] and Kraus [5].

If an antenna can be mounted on a transmission line (coax or twin wire cable) then a bow tie design can be considered. The bow tie has a wider operating range than a simple linear dipole but is larger. The broadband performance will help when it is in the body medium to reduce the effect of a sharp resonance. A typical bow tie is printed or evaporated onto a flexible substrate, as shown in Figure 4.7.

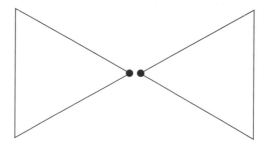

Figure 4.7 Bow-tie antenna.

Another type of design to be considered in the *Planar Inverted F* (PIF) antenna commonly used in small mobile phones. A small phone and an implanted device share many performance challenges. In this case, the antenna is mounted onto the case and encased in a suitable non-conductive material for mechanical stability. This type of antenna is small but found to be effective in some applications.

The off-resonance antennas have low radiation resistance, typically in the order of a few Ohms for a patch. Better radiation is achieved with a higher radiation resistance that typically require a larger structure.

A loop antenna is an option where it can be deployed away from the implant case or other metal. The loop antenna operates mostly with the magnetic field, whereas the dipole, patch, monopole, *etc.* operate mostly with the electric field. The loop antenna delivers comparable performance to that of a dipole, but with a considerably smaller size. Also the magnetic permeability of muscle or fat is very similar to that of air, unlike the dielectric constant that varies considerably as described above. This property enables an antenna to be built and used with much less need for retuning. A loop antenna does need to be mounted away from the case and on a biocompatible structure. Equations (4.4) and (4.5) relate to small and large loops, other equations exist for multi-turn loop designs.

$$R_{rad} = 31200 \left(A / \lambda^2 \right)^2 \qquad (4.4)$$

for $A \le \lambda^2 / 100$, where R_{rad} is radiation resistance and A is the loop area and λ the wavelength in medium.

$$R_{rad} = 3270 \left(A / \lambda^2 \right)^2 \qquad (4.5)$$

for $A > \lambda^2 / 100$.

An important measurement of an antenna performance is the return loss – how much of the signal sent to the antenna is reflected back and how much is radiated.

An ideal value for Γ is 0, with 1 representing total reflection. One feature of a small antenna is that it may have a good return loss but radiate poorly, meaning radiation efficiency must also be measured.

4.5 Antenna Testing

Before designing a matching network for the antenna/transceiver interface it is necessary to measure the impedance of the antenna within a representative medium. Testing an implant antenna in-air has limited use and non-living tissue does not have the same properties as the human body, so a body phantom is used. A mixture of water, sodium chloride, sugar and *Hydroxyl Ethyl Cellulose* (HEC) will mimic muscle or brain tissue [10] for the frequency range 100MHz to GHz (see Table 4.3 below).

Table 4.3 Body tissue recipes.

Ingredient	% By Weight 100MHz to 1GHz	% By Weight 1.5GHz to 2.5GHz
Water	52.4	45.3
Sugar	45.0	54.3
Salt (NaCl)	1.5	0.0
HEC	1.1	0.4

4.5.1 Antenna Impedance and Radiation Resistance Measurement

Knowing the impedance of the antenna is critical for design and operation of the in-body communication system. The example that follows is for a patch but could be adapted for other antenna types.

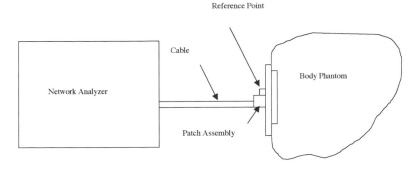

Figure 4.8 Network analyser test set-up for impedance real part >10Ω.

Radiation resistance can be measured with an antenna immersed in body phantom liquid in a Perspex cylinder. This can prove difficult as the liquid may leak into the measurement jig and corrupt the results. As an alternative, a patch, for example, is mounted on a copper plate and pushed against a bag of the phantom (Figure 4.8). If the real part of the impedance is >10Ω then a network analyser can be used, however often the real part is lower, requiring a different method. A way of measuring an antenna with low radiation resistance is described in some detail [5], as it will often be the case that an implanted antenna will be difficult to measure directly on a network analyser.

4.5.2 Quarter Wave Line Impedance Measurement

One alternative to using a network analyser directly is to couple a signal into a quarter wavelength line (or odd integer multiples of quarter wavelength) and measure the signal loss. From this, the change in resonant frequency and the Q (quality factor) can be used to determine the patch impedance.

The resonant line and coupling structure is shown in Figure 4.9. This is a cross-section through the centre of the assembly showing the internal construction. The length of the centre conductor is 0.25λ. The impedance is defined by the diameters of the centre conductor and the outer tube.

The feeds comprise RG402, 50Ω, semi-rigid cable terminated with SMA connectors and clamped in place. The bottom of the centre bar has a split collett to enable the test sample to be attached. The spacers are of PTFE, the rest of the jig is copper.

A reference short circuit plate is also needed to calibrate the line, and this consists of a brass block that contacts the centre conductor and makes good contact to the bottom plate.

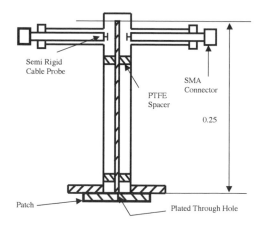

Figure 4.9 Quarter wavelength 400MHz line.

The line is attached to a network analyser, as shown in Figure 4.10, and set to measure the S21 (transmitted signal from Port 1 to Port 2). The S21 measurement will result in a peak in the transmission at the resonant frequency. Further measurements of the peak are used to determine the Q of the antenna. The resonant frequency and Q of the line are measured. Q is defined as

$$Q = \frac{f_{centre}}{B_{3dB}} \tag{4.6}$$

where f_{centre} is centre frequency and B_{3dB} is 3dB bandwidth. With the line impedance, the loss can be derived from

$$\frac{R_{loss}}{Z_o} = \frac{N\pi}{4Q} \tag{4.7}$$

where N is the number of quarter wavelengths, and R_{loss} is the resistance of the line. Having found the losses, the reference short is replaced with a test antenna. Resonant frequency and Q are measured again and the radiation resistance is

$$\frac{R_{measure}}{Z_o} = \frac{N\pi}{4Q} \tag{4.8}$$

and

$$R_{rad} = R_{measure} - R_{loss} \tag{4.9}$$

Once the real part of the impedance is known the imaginary part can be found. This is best done with simulation software using a model of the transmission line created with a load of R_{rad} in parallel, or series, with a capacitor (or inductor as appropriate). The capacitor value is tuned to give the same resonant frequency as measured with the network analyser. It is not necessary to simulate the line feeds, only to measure from the end of the line.

This technique can be adapted for other types of antennas by using a length of semi-rigid coax cut to length or printed transmission line terminated with the reference short and antenna.

Even if an antenna has known impedance, or is resonant at the required frequency, this does not always mean that it will radiate effectively. It is essential to measure the performance using a body phantom with the transceiver in the case and sense or stimulant wires attached. The Wheeler Cap is also useful in measuring antenna efficiency.

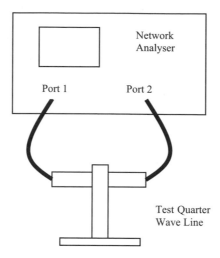

Figure 4.10 Resonant line measurements.

4.6 Matching Network

Once the impedance of the patch is known within a reference liquid, it can be matched to the transceiver. When implanted, a transceiver will be capable of optimisation if it has a built-in variable tuning element. This is typically an array of capacitors that can be switched in or out across an RF terminal. This will enable the implant to be retuned each time it is used to help counter some of the effects of the implant moving or body changes.

A typical transceiver circuit is intended for use in the MICS frequency band of 402MHz to 405MHz. The maximum radiated power allowed in this band is 25μW (-16dBm), but antenna gains in implants are usually very low and more power can be generated at the transmitter to compensate for loss through the body. Additionally, link budgets are also frequently such that the maximum allowed radiated power is required.

The antenna tuning circuits are required to present an optimum load impedance to the transmitter and voltage step-up to the receiver. It should be noted that this does not necessarily lead to a conjugate impedance match.

4.6.1 Transmitter Tuning

A typical transmitter is capable of producing an output signal into the load of 2V peak-peak maximum, with a maximum peak current of about 10mA. Maximum DC to RF conversion efficiency is obtained when using the full voltage swing, as for any particular power output this will require minimum supply current. The tuning circuit is also required to provide a degree of harmonic rejection for regulatory reasons; exactly how much is dependent upon the antenna gain and impedance at the harmonic frequencies. Maximum efficiency is obtained when the output devices are loaded with a purely resistive load, but because of the effects of stray capacity, as well as the provision of internal variable tuning capacity on the output of the transmitter, the actual load presented to the transmitter output pad is required to be inductive.

The efficiency, η, of the tuning network is determined by the ratio of unloaded Q (Q_u) to loaded Q (Q_w), i.e.,

$$\eta = \left(1 - \frac{Q_w}{Q_u}\right)100\% \tag{4.10}$$

The use of too low a value of Q_w should be avoided, however, as the harmonic attenuation of the network will be reduced. Usually, a value of Q_w between 10 and 15 is a reasonable compromise. However, the harmonic attenuation may well be greater than would appear at first sight to be available from such a low value of Q. This is because the impedance presented by the network at the harmonic frequencies may be much lower than at the fundamental frequency, resulting in the harmonic current generating a much lower voltage across the input of the network.

Too high a value of working Q should also be avoided. This is because the increased Q leads to an increase in circulating current within the circuit, and losses are proportional to the square of the circulating current thus doubling the Q increases the actual power lost by four times.

The first step in designing the transmitter-tuning network is to determine the required RF output power, P_o. This is derived from the required radiated power, less the antenna gain and matching circuit losses. Since the latter are unknown at this stage, the process is iterative.

To determine the resistance presented to the transmitter, first establish the maximum voltage swing by

$$R_L = \frac{\left(0.7071V_{pp} / 2\right)^2}{P_o} \tag{4.11}$$

where R_L is load presented to the transmitter. For $2V_{pp}$ (4.11) becomes (4.12).

$$R_L = 0.5 / P_o \tag{4.12}$$

For a maximum available current of 10mA, the lowest value of R_L is 200Ω. A circuit can now be chosen which provides load impedance to the power amplifier of $0.5 / P_o$ Ω in parallel with a tuning capacitance. In many cases, the maximum power will be limited either by the available power supply current or by regulatory limitations on maximum radiated power.

4.6.2 The L Network

The simplest network is the L network shown in Figure 4.11 as it uses only two components. Easing design, the capacitive arm is internal to the device and only an external inductor is required.

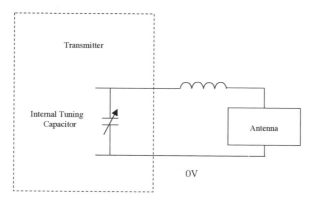

Figure 4.11 L network matching.

There are certain limitations in such an approach. The antenna impedance is constrained in terms of the amount of inductive reactance it can have, and the working Q is given by

$$Q_w = \sqrt{R_L / R_s - 1} \tag{4.13}$$

where R_L is the parallel load resistance presented to the device, and R_s is the sum of the inductor loss resistance and the resistive part of the antenna impedance. R_s must be less than R_L. Note that especially in the case of electrically small antennas, this resistance is not usually the radiation resistance of the antenna as other losses may dominate.

Where the antenna impedance is capacitive, the value of inductance can be increased to resonate the antenna circuit. For the L network, the following equations apply.

$$X'_L = R_{ant} \sqrt{R_L / R_{ant} - 1} \tag{4.14}$$

$$X_C = R_L \sqrt{R_L / R_{ant} - 1} \tag{4.15}$$

The total value of inductive reactance is $X_L = X'_L + X_{ant}$, where X_{ant} is negative for capacitive antenna impedance and positive for an inductive antenna impedance.

The required value of X_C will typically lie between 60 and 390Ω at 403MHz for tuning with the internal capacitor. Lower values of X_C can be accommodated with an external capacitor. The effects of the inductance of the bond wire connecting the IC output pad to the inductance must also be considered. This inductance will be of the order of 1nH/mm. The effect of this should not be ignored.

4.6.3 The π Network

The π network shown in Figure 4.12 has certain advantages in that the Q of the circuit is relatively independent of the impedance transformation required. It is also able to handle antennas with greater inductance than the L network. The Q_w is R_L / X_{C_1}, meaning an external capacitor will be needed, and the tuning range of the internal tuning circuit will be limited, as typically values of X_{C_1} of 20 to 50Ω will be required.

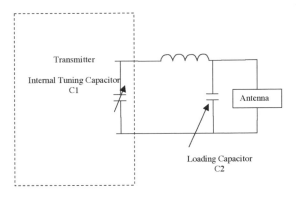

Figure 4.12 The π network.

Equations for the π network are

$$X_{C_1} = R_L / Q_w \tag{4.16}$$

$$X_{C_2} = \left(\frac{R_L R_{ant}}{\left(Q_w^2 + 1\right) - R_L / R_{ant}} \right)^{1/2} \tag{4.17}$$

$$X_L = \frac{Q_w R_L + R_L R_{ant} / X_{C_2}}{Q_w^2 + 1} \tag{4.18}$$

In practice, the value of X_{C_2} is decreased by the amount of parallel capacity of the antenna (in which case the network appears to be an L network), or is increased by the amount of capacity needed to resonate an inductive antenna. When R_{ant} is small, the value of C_2 may become excessively large, thus limiting the application of this circuit. When R_L is high, the working Q may be higher than desirable because of the unavoidable stray capacities across the input to the network. Again, the parasitic inductance of the bond wire from the output pad to the inductor must be accounted for.

4.6.4 The T and π-L Networks

These networks are identical in circuitry. The T network is the 'dual' of the π network, as illustrated in Figure 4.13. It claims to show somewhat greater efficiencies under certain conditions. The design technique is to treat the circuit as consisting of back to back L networks, with a centre 'image' impedance at C_2 chosen to provide suitable Q_w values. This image impedance is higher than the value of R_L and thus is more subject to stray capacity problems. The equations are:

$$X_{L_1} = R_L Q_w + X_{C_{1s}} \tag{4.19}$$

$$X_{L_2} = R_L B \tag{4.20}$$

$$X_{C_2} = \left(A/Q_w + B\right) \tag{4.21}$$

where

$$A = R_L \left(1 + Q_w^2\right) \tag{4.22}$$

and

$$B = \sqrt{\left(A/R_L\right) - 1} \tag{4.23}$$

$X_{C_{1s}}$ is the series equivalent circuit of R_L and X_{C_1}. At a given frequency a parallel circuit of a resistance and a reactance has a parallel equivalent and vice-versa. The series equivalent of a parallel circuit is found in (4.24) and (4.25). The parallel equivalent of a series circuit is shown in (4.26) and (4.27).

$$R_s = \frac{R_p}{1 + \left(R_p/X_p\right)^2} \tag{4.24}$$

$$X_s = R_s R_p / X_p \tag{4.25}$$

$$R_p = R_s \left(1 + \left(X_s/R_s\right)^2\right) \tag{4.26}$$

$$X_p = R_s R_p / X_s \tag{4.27}$$

where R_s = resistance of series equivalent circuit, R_p = resistance of parallel equivalent circuit, X_s = reactance of series equivalent circuit, and X_p = reactance of parallel equivalent circuit. As with the L network, similar limitations to the amount of antenna inductive reactance apply.

As a π-L, the circuit uses a π section to reduce the impedance to an image impedance usually of value $\sqrt{R_L R_{ant}}$. The L section then reduces this to the antenna impedance, and tunes out any antenna reactance. The same problems of allowable antenna reactance apply as in the case of the L network, but as the impedance transformation ratio is reduced the Q_w of the L network is also reduced, allowing an improved efficiency. The extra section also provides increased harmonic rejection as compared with the simple π network.

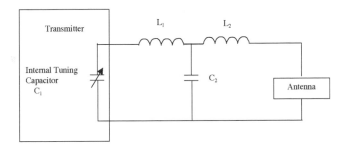

Figure 4.13 The 'T' or 'π-L' network.

4.6.5 Parasitic Effects

The effect of stray capacitance and resistance in inductors also needs to be considered, because operating at close to the *Self-Resonant Frequency* (SRF) of the inductor leads to large changes in Q and apparent inductance. In general, it is recommended that the inductance SRF should be at least three times the operating frequency. Discrepancy between expected and actual harmonic radiation levels when operating with an antenna may often be traced to this cause.

The actual difference in parameters caused by an approach to self-resonance can be found from the following. For an inductor:

$$R_{apparent} = \frac{R_{actual}}{\left(1-\lambda^2\right)^2} \qquad (4.28)$$

where $R_{apparent}$ and R_{actual} refer to the parasitic resistance of the inductor and

$$L_{apparent} = \frac{L_{actual}}{\left(1-\lambda^2\right)^2} \qquad (4.29)$$

where λ is the ratio of actual frequency to self-resonant frequency that is available from the manufacturer.

It should be noted that the networks suggested all have the property of using a series inductor from the output of the device, thus allowing absorption of the stray inductance caused by the bond wire.

4.6.6 Network Choice

The choice of which network to use is dependent upon a number of factors. When one antenna is required for operation at the MICS band and 2.4GHz (wake-up) the 403MHz network must be chosen so that it presents high impedance at 2.4GHz. Similarly, the 2.4GHz tuning system must not have appreciable shunting effect at 403MHz on the antenna. This suggests that an L or T or π-L network has advantages, insofar as the series inductor at the antenna end of the network will present reasonably high impedance to the 2.4GHz wake-up signal.

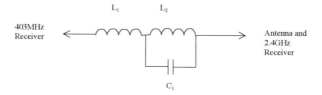

Figure 4.14 Multi-resonant network.

However, this advantage may not be realised in practice if the series inductor has too low an SRF, and thus in the demonstration implementation where an L network is used the inductor has been split into two parts. Connected to the antenna is a small inductor arranged to be parallel resonant at 2.4GHz, and thus presenting high impedance at that frequency. The other inductor in series enables the correct amount of inductance at 403MHz to be achieved, as shown in Figure 4.14.

C_1 and L_2 are resonant at about 2.4GHz. Typical values are about 1.9nH and 2.2pF, resonating at 2.46GHz. L_1 is the remainder of the 403MHz tuning inductance. Without the splitting of the inductance the SRF of this inductor (typically in the order of 10's nH) would have been below 2GHz, and the circuit would therefore have looked like a capacitor at 2.4GHz.

Whichever network is used, there must be DC isolation to ground through the antenna and this may necessitate the addition of a series capacitor. In general, it is desirable that such a capacitor be added at a medium impedance point. At a high impedance point, the effects of parasitic capacity to ground may cause problems, while at very low impedance points the series resistance of a large capacitor may increase losses to an unacceptable value.

4.6.7 Radio Frequency Losses in Components and Layout Issues

In all cases, after the initial values have been established, substitution of more accurate models of inductors (including the available Q and the SRF) are required to establish the circuit efficiency. It may then be necessary to 'fine-tune' the design for a different power output from the transmitter. In general, losses in the capacitors are negligible in comparison with those in inductors, especially for very small chip inductors or printed inductors mounted very close to a ground plane. Microwave type surface mounting chip porcelain or sapphire low loss type capacitors are generally preferred, rather than the lower cost NP0 ceramic types.

Equations (4.28) and (4.29) for the apparent values of inductance and resistance of inductors at frequencies removed from the SRF will allow extrapolation of manufacturers' data where necessary.

Here are a few rules that may be useful when laying out a matching network:

- Remember the track will also influence the performance and should be simulated along with the added components.
- Lay out close inductors at $90°$ to each other. This minimises mutual coupling.
- Take all of the tracking, wiring and feed through into account when designing a matching network.
- As inductor values increase the self-resonance will reduce. A high value inductor may behave like a capacitor at high frequency.
- When building a transceiver be consistent in the choice of component manufacturer and family. A nominal component value may have different parasitics between manufacturers.

4.6.8 Receiver Tuning

The receiver has a very high input impedance, being typically >10kΩ in parallel with a small capacitance. Conjugate matching of the antenna to the receiver is undesirable because half of the received EMF is lost in the antenna internal resistance, while the high input impedance of the receiver allows for a degree of voltage step-up. Additionally, conjugate matching does not give the optimum source resistance for lowest noise. The amount of voltage step is proportional to the working Q of the network, and because of the difficulty of maintaining tuning accuracy as the working Q value increases (always assuming that the Q value is not limited by the unloaded Q values of available components), it is not considered desirable to have too high a voltage step-up. Where the step-up is such that the working Q is dominated by the values of Q in the available components, the losses may well reduce the benefits of attempting to obtain a large step-up.

Link budget calculations are based on *Effective Radiated Power* (ERP) and antenna gains. The resulting power available for the receiver should be considered as being an EMF voltage delivered to the input impedance with a source impedance determined by the step-up ratio, after losses in the components have been taken into account. Thus the voltage available at the receiver input will be

$$E = \left[\left(P_t P_L A_g T_L \right) R_L \right]^{\frac{1}{2}}$$

(4.30)

where E is the available RMS EMF, P_t is the transmitted ERP in watts, P_L is the path loss as a ratio, A_g is the receive antenna gain as a ratio, T_L is the tuning circuit losses as a ratio (which can be derived from (4.10)) and R_L is the resistive part of the load impedance for the transmitter (assuming the use of a tuning circuit common to both receiver and transmitter).

Where receive and transmit use separate antennas, the receiver input tuning can be designed for any desired step-up, bearing in mind the limitations caused by too high a value of Q_w in terms of tuning sensitivity, *etc.* It must be remembered that the various parasitic components, such as bond wires and stray capacities, must be accounted for when evaluating the performance of any particular circuit.

4.6.9 Base Station Antennas

The implanted device and external base station antenna implementations are often very different. In the case of the implant, space considerations may well prevent the use of separate antennas for the frequencies used for communication and 'wake up' (MICS and 2.4GHz respectively). The base unit will have room for larger antennas and preferably separate antennas for 403MHz and 2.45GHz (if used). The 403MHz transmit and receive paths can be split at the antenna with a switch enabling optimisation of both paths separately. The base unit may use external filters in the receive chain to provide maximum rejection of unwanted signals. The loss of such filters (*e.g.* a SAW filter) may be offset by using an external RF amplifier. The gain is not too important as long as it is sufficient to overcome the filter losses; such an amplifier will also need a very low noise figure, and a sufficiently large signal handling range.

The base station could also use more than one antenna to overcome the effect of multi-path fading and polarisation, as detailed by Johansson [4], reducing the signal strength. If space permits, an arrangement of four antennas with suitable switching and software optimisation can be employed. This is shown in Figure 4.15.

4.7 Propagation

The propagation pattern of the antenna, case and any wires for sense or stimulation is required in order to predict the performance of the implant within a body. The Perspex tank filled with a liquid as described above is a useful first representation of a body. This can be done in a lab, or preferably in an anechoic chamber, with care taken to seal the test transceiver from the liquid.

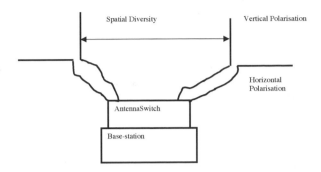

Figure 4.15 Four antennas for spatial and polarisation diversity.

Radiation patterns are made with the body phantom using a self-contained transmitter immersed in the liquid. If the antenna were to be attached to a cable then it would contribute to the radiation pattern. This can be minimised, but not eliminated, with the addition of ferrite beads. The patch attached to an implant case within a body does not have an earth (ground) connection, meaning the case will radiate in anti-phase to the patch. This requires that electronics be self-powered and measured as a whole.

Measurements should be taken with the test device immersed in the liquid and rotated on a horizontal and vertical axis. If vertical rotation is difficult then the 90° points should be measured. Horizontal rotation is straightforward as the test device can be rotated with the tank.

Another important aspect of propagation is polarisation. Human and animal testing has found that the body will cause polarisation of the signal along its long length [4]. This has also been observed with the tank measurements. It has been found that with a vertical tank the polarisation also tends to vertical.

4.8 Materials

An implant case is typically titanium or implant-grade stainless steel. In-body wires are either platinum or platinum/iridium that have conductivity in the order of $9.52MSm^{-1}$ and $5.2MSm^{-1}$ respectively. In comparison, the conductivity of copper, considered one of the best conductors, is $58MSm^{-1}$. At present these are the only two conductors that are used outside of the implant case. Metals such as silver and copper are toxic and blood will erode gold. This low value of electrical conductivity will impede the performance of the antenna, as some energy will be absorbed by the resistance of the metal. Therefore, it is necessary to maximise the thickness of the conductor to minimise the added resistance and losses.

The substrate needs to be non-toxic, mechanically stable and insoluble in blood or other body liquid. Alumina is a material found to be acceptable. Other substrates that have been considered include titania, zirconia and multi-layer substrates. Care must be taken to ensure the suitability of the materials.

The entire implant is often coated in a passive material such as Parylene. Table 4.4 shows Parylene has good water resistant properties compared to other commercially available materials and is acceptable for in-body use. Typical coatings are in the order of a few microns thick and will have no effect on the RF performance of the antenna. Coating cannot be used to isolate a conductor, such as silver from the body, as blood will dissolve most plastics and organic coating and it will become porous.

Table 4.4 Water uptake and other parameters of various polymers, noting these are not all biocompatible [12].

Material	ε_r	Loss Tangent	Water Absorption %
Parylene (C type)	2.9	0.013	0.01
Polyether ketone	3.4	0.005	0.11
Polyether imide	3.2	0.0026	0.25
Polyether ether ketone	3.3	0.0035	0.11

4.9 Environment

The human body may be considered a benign thermal and mechanical environment, with a temperature varying by just $\pm 2°C$ and layers of fat and muscle that will partially absorb shocks. However, regulatory approval for implanted medical devices is extremely stringent. Implant grade components need to work over the full military temperature range and be able to withstand shock and vibration. The assembled implant needs to survive the wide storage temperature range that it may well be exposed to. An implant is also subject to harsh mechanical testing, including a drop test from two metres onto concrete for each of six faces (see EN45502). A layer of silicone may be sufficient to absorb the shock of impact.

4.10 External Transceiver (Base Station)

An in-body communication system relies on a base station that will transmit and receive signals from the implant and relay them to a user interface, such as a personal computer as shown in Figure 4.16. Less rigorous size restrictions on a base station mean larger antennas can be used. The power limit, including any antenna gain, remains at 25µW. The RF environment within a hospital or doctor's office may be even more challenging than inside the human body, meaning adjacent channel signals need to be filtered out using a SAW filter (or similar).

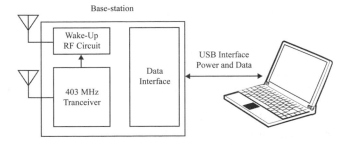

Figure 4.16 Base station and PC.

In the example shown above, the base station has a USB interface that also provides the power to the Base Station that eliminates the need for an additional power supply. Software needs to be written to operate the base station and an easy-to-operate *Graphical User Interface* (GUI) is required. The interface for clinician use would typically show the user identification, download and upload data. For system development a more detailed interface is required.

When designing a base station for use in a sterile hospital environment, care must be taken to avoid corners or rough surfaces that cannot be thoroughly cleaned. Professionals familiar with infection control should be consulted throughout the design.

4.11 Power Considerations

Implants are often designed to consume minimal battery power to extend their useful operating life. For example, a pacemaker may be expected to operate for up to ten years. Adding a radio link to an implant will cause an additional battery drain that needs to be minimised. As a simple rule of thumb, current demand will increase with frequency, transmitter power, receiver sensitivity and processing power. The receiver must be sensitive enough to detect the incoming signal with an acceptable error rate. A high error rate may be corrected by resending the data and error correction, but this increases power consumption. The transmitter must also produce enough power for the base station to receive with a low raw error rate.

Leaving a receiver on to permanently listen for the base station transmission would require a current in the order of 2mA to 3mA – an unacceptable power drain on the battery. The implant needs to detect the base station transmission and start a data exchange session at short notice, on demand, all the while draining minimal battery current. One way to reduce the average current is to switch on a simple receiver for a short time at regular intervals. This is known as the "wake-up" receiver.

The wake-up receiver can use either the MICS band, or the ISM band where more radiated power is permitted. A typical example would be 2.45GHz where in excess of 100mW may be radiated (country dependant). The losses through the body will be greater than for the MICS band, but additional power will compensate and the antenna will be closer to the desired size. It is possible to use the same implant antenna for both MICS and 2.45GHz with care in the matching networks. The wake-up receiver will be switched on at regular intervals for a short period, known as strobe mode. If a signal is detected, the wake-up receiver will switch on and detect if it is a genuine "wake-up" signal. This is a digital code designed to wake up the implant. If this code is not detected the receiver will revert to strobe mode.

Once the code is verified then the remainder of the implant communication system, which typically includes the crystal oscillator, the *Media Access Controller* (MAC) that controls the operation of the part, and the phase lock loop, will power-up. Once the wake-up is complete an acknowledgment is transmitted. An example of a wake-up sequence and power consumption is shown in Figure 4.17. Once the acknowledgment is received a data transfer session can begin.

When a data transfer session has finished, the part reverts to sleep mode with the wake transmitter strobing.

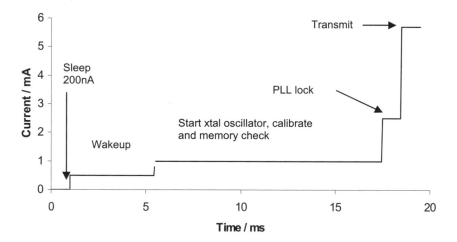

Figure 4.17 Wake-up sequence and current consumption for a typical implant RF transceiver (source: Zarlink Semiconductor).

4.11.1 Battery Challenges

In many applications, an ideal battery is the one that gives a constant voltage for as long as possible and the user changes the battery when the device stops working. In the case of implanted medical devices, this is obviously not possible.

The lithium-iodine cell, most commonly used in pacemakers, has a very different behavior. The battery can be modeled as a voltage of about 2.8V in series with a resistor. The series resistor has a value of about 500Ω at the beginning of the battery life, and increases slowly to end up at 10 to 20kΩ towards the end of the battery life. Assuming a constant average current drain, the resulting battery voltage for the pacemaker electronics starts off at 2.8V and then gradually decreases with time towards 2.0V, when the pacemaker battery should be replaced. It is then quite easy to measure the internal resistance of the battery, and the doctor and patient can be alerted twelve months before the battery needs to be replaced.

Figure 4.18 shows a voltage versus time comparison for a typical watch battery and a lithium-iodine battery used in a pacemaker. Though the patient and the doctor benefit from this battery behavior, it is easy to see the challenges this poses for the designer of an implant system. On top of designing electronics that demand extremely little current, the designer must also cope with a voltage variation over a long operating life of the device.

The other problem for the designer is the presence of a 500Ω resistor in series with the voltage source. If the transceiver draws 5mA during transmit the voltage drop across the resistor will be 5mA × 500Ω = 2.5V which is almost all of the battery voltage. The power source during a data transfer session must be primarily from a capacitor.

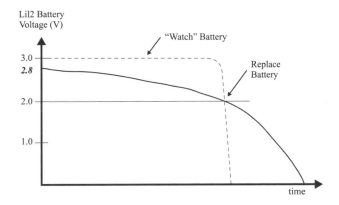

Figure 4.18 Voltage versus time comparison for a typical watch battery and a LiI2 battery used in a pacemaker.

4.12 Defibrillation Pulse

An implant within the chest cavity may need to survive a defibrillation pulse. As well as the external defibrillator, *Implantable Cardioverter-Defibrillators* (ICDs) that deliver a pulse directly to the heart are becoming more common. The pulse can be biphasic with a peak of 800V applied to the heart, and last several milliseconds. A pacemaker, internal heart monitor, ICD or other chest cavity implant, along with an antenna and delicate transmitter and receiver electronics, will need to survive the pulse.

Care must be taken in the design of the matching network to reduce the energy reaching the electronics to within its capability using electrostatic damage protection diodes. Additional protection diodes should be used with care as they will add capacitance and will be part of the matching network. The protection needs to be designed with the knowledge of the transmitter/receiver electronics capability and the expected defibrillation pulse amplitude and duration.

More details can be found in an on line article by the American Heart Association [11].

4.13 Link Budget

The link budget determines if the link will work by taking into account transmit and receive powers, antenna gains, path losses and receiver sensitivity. The signal-to-noise ratio will determine the un-corrected bit error rate for a given range, *i.e.,*

$$S/N(dB) = P_t(dBW) + 204(dBW) - 10\log(B)$$
$$+ G_r(dBi) - P(dB) + G_t(dBi)$$

(4.31)

where $P_t(dBW)$ is the transmit power in *dB* Watts, 204(*dBW*) is thermal noise power for a 1Hz bandwidth, *B* is the bandwidth in Hz, and $G_r(dBi)$ is the receive antenna gain in *dB*, *P* is the path loss in *dB*, this includes the free space (P_f) and body (P_b) losses, where $P = P_f + P_b$, that can be considerable, and G_t is the transmitter antenna gain in *dB*.

The path loss is comprised of losses through the body, which can be in the order of 20dB, and the free space loss is

$$P_f = (\lambda / 4\pi d)^2$$

(4.32)

There may also be losses from multi-path propagation causing fading. From the above it is clear that with a low upper limit on transmit power, significant body losses and a low implant antenna gain, low noise design of the receiver is critical. The reliability of the link will be improved with the addition of error correction and with re-transmission of data that is in error.

4.14 Conclusions

The implant antenna is critical to the operation of the data link, and must be designed as part of the implant to make the best use of the available area. There are several antenna options depending on the given application. Testing to determine antenna characteristics is important to ensure the matching network can be effectively designed. Care should be taken when measuring the impedance of electrically small antennas.

In comparison to strict size limitations on implanted devices, designers should take advantage of the additional space afforded by external base stations for antennas, electronics and filtering. Multiple antennas can be used if there is a polarisation or multi-path fading problem. A very low noise receiver is needed in both the base station and the implant. Error correction can enhance data transfer, but at the cost of longer power-up time and battery drain. The battery will typically not be able to source the peak current used during data transfer, so a large value capacitor will be needed.

Along with wireless performance and power issues, designers must address a multitude of biocompatibility concerns and regulations governing the design of implanted devices and in-body communication systems. The integration of a high data rate transceiver will enhance the operation and capabilities of existing implanted medical devices, and open the door for new techniques that will lead to improved treatments and better quality of life for patients.

References

1. Finkenzeller K. RFID handbook, 2nd ed. John Wiley and Sons, 2003.
2. ISM band. Federal Communications Commission, Title 47 Volume 1; Telecommunications Section, Part 18; Industrial Scientific and Medical Equipment, Sub Part C, Section 18.305.
3. ICS band. Australian Communications Agency Paper, SP 6/03, 2003.
4. Johansson AJ. Wave propagation from medical implants – influence of body shape on propagation pattern. Department of Electroscience, Lund University, Sweden, http://www.tde.lth.se/home/ajn/publications/Houston.pdf
5. Kraus JD. Antennas, 2nd ed. McGraw Hill, 1988.
6. Krall AD, McCorkle JM, Scarzello JF, Syeles AM. The omni microstrip antenna: a new small antenna. IEEE Transactions on Antennas and Propagation 1979; AP27:850-853.
7. Fujimoto K, Henderson A, Hirasawa K, James JR. Small antennas. Baldok, Hertfordshire: Research Studies Press, 1987.
8. Lee FL, Wei C. Microstrip and printed antennas, 1st ed. John Wiley and Sons, 1997.
9. Straw RD, ARRL antenna book, Newington, Connecticut: American Radio Relay League.
10. Wojclk J. Tissue recipe calibration requirements. Spectrum Sciences Institute RF Dosemetry Research Board, Nepean, Ontario, Canada, SSI/DRB-TP-D01-003.
11. Manoharan G, Evans N, Allen D, Anderson J, Adgey J. Comparing the efficacy and safety of a novel monophasic waveform delivered by the passive implantable atrial defibrillator with biphasic waveforms in cardioversion of atrial fibrillation. Circulation 2004; 109:1686-1692.
12. Rostami S. Polymer performance - in a tough world. Bulletin – The Technical Journal for Industrial Members of the Welding Institute 2004; 14-16.

5

Network Topologies, Communication Protocols, and Standards

Javier Espina, Thomas Falck, and Oliver Mülhens

5.1 Network Topologies

Every network has a topology that determines the way that different devices on the network are arranged and how they communicate with each other. Here we distinguish between physical and logical topologies. The former refers to the physical layout of the network, *i.e.* the way devices are physically connected to the network through the actual cables or direct wireless communication links. In contrast, the logical topology of a network refers to the manner that data flows through the network from one node to the other without worrying about the physical interconnection of the devices for transporting a packet from a source to a destination device. The two lower layers of the *Open Systems Interconnection* (OSI) reference model [1], the physical and data link layer, define the physical topology of a network, while the network layer is responsible for the logical topology.

Table 5.1 provides an overview of the most common topologies applicable for wireless sensor networks. Each topology presents its specific set of advantages and disadvantages regarding network characteristics such as latency, robustness, capacity and the complexity of data routing and processing as shown in Table 5.2. The star-mesh hybrid topology seeks to combine the advantages of the star topology with the ones of the mesh topology and additionally provides the highest degree of mobility for star clusters.

The topology is a choice of application design. The application developers have to balance sensor node costs, battery drain, complexity of routing, robustness, scalability, latency, mobility, and spatial coverage to meet the unique characteristics and performance requirements of their application. In the following sections, we will present some typical application scenarios of BSNs to illustrate the usage of the different network topologies.

Table 5.1 Common network topologies.

Point-to-point network

The simplest topology consists of only two devices directly connected with each other.

Star network

All devices are connected to a single central controller often referred to as coordinator or master. The peripheral nodes are called slaves. Slaves can only communicate with the master. Communication between slaves requires passing all data through the master.

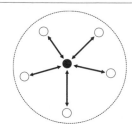

Mesh network

Any device can communicate with other devices as long as they are in range of one another ("peer-to-peer network"). Multi-hop networking protocols enable routing of packets from one device to the other on the network.

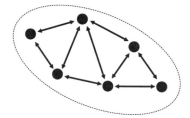

Star-mesh hybrid network

This allows connecting a mesh network with one or more star networks or several star networks with each other. A mixed star and mesh network combines the simplicity of the single-hop star topology with the extendibility and flexibility of the multi-hop mesh topology.

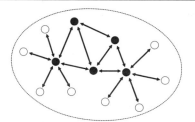

Cluster tree network

The cluster tree topology is a special case of a multi-hop mesh network where there is always only a single path between two devices. The first device starting the network becomes the root of the tree. Another device can join the network as "child" of the root node and in turn allow other devices to join the network through that device. Devices are aware of their "parent" node and any "child" nodes. This hierarchical topology reduces routing complexity.

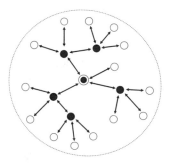

Table 5.2 Advantages and disadvantages of topologies.

Topology	Advantages	Disadvantages
Star	<ul><li>Simplicity</li><li>Simple and cheap slave nodes</li><li>Low power consumption of slave nodes</li><li>Low latency and high bandwidth</li><li>Centralised systems</li></ul>	<ul><li>Dedicated central node</li><li>Limited spatial coverage</li><li>Single point of failure</li><li>Poor scalability, small number of nodes</li><li>Asymmetric power consumption (master consumes much more energy than the slaves)</li><li>Inefficient slave-to-slave communication</li><li>Distributed processing</li></ul>
Mesh	<ul><li>Distributed processing</li><li>Peer-to-peer communication</li><li>Very fault tolerant</li><li>Scalable, many nodes possible</li><li>Large spatial coverage</li><li>Low/medium complexity</li><li>Energy consumption can be balanced among nodes</li></ul>	<ul><li>Nodes used must have same basic functionality, including routing capabilities (may be an overkill in some applications as it increases cost)</li><li>Complexity of routing</li><li>High latency and low bandwidth</li></ul>
Star-mesh hybrid	<ul><li>Low/medium complexity (if nodes can be classified as slaves or masters before deployment)</li><li>Large spatial coverage</li><li>Low latency and high bandwidth between master and its slaves</li><li>Good for local actuation or data aggregation</li><li>High reliability possible</li><li>Scalable, many nodes possible</li><li>Power consumption can be balanced among masters and it is asymmetrical between master and slaves</li><li>Nodes acting as slaves can be relatively inexpensive</li></ul>	<ul><li>High complexity (if all nodes can act as masters)</li><li>High latency and low bandwidth for multi-hop communication</li><li>Power consumption is asymmetrical between master and slaves</li></ul>
Cluster tree	<ul><li>Low power consumption of leaf nodes</li><li>Large spatial coverage area</li><li>Many nodes possible</li><li>Large spatial coverage</li><li>Medium complexity (rerouting is required when a node in the tree dies)</li></ul>	<ul><li>Medium scalability (root of the tree is a bottleneck)</li><li>Low reliability (node failure effects routing)</li><li>High latency and low bandwidth</li><li>Asymmetric power consumption (nodes in the tree backbone consume more)</li><li>Nodes used must have same basic functionality, incl. routing capabilities (may be an overkill in some applications as it increases cost)</li></ul>

5.2 Body Sensor Network Application Scenarios

As mentioned in Chapter 1, wireless sensor networks are an enabling technology for the application domain of unobtrusive medical monitoring. This field includes continuous cable-free monitoring of vital signs in intensive care units [2], remote monitoring of chronically ill patients [3-7], monitoring of patients in mass casualty situations [8], monitoring people in their everyday lives to provide early detection and intervention for various types of disease [9], computer-assisted physical rehabilitation in ambulatory settings [10], and assisted living for the elderly at home [11, 12]. In these scenarios, the sensors range from on-body sensors, to ambient sensors such as positioning devices, to mobile devices such as cellular phones or PDAs. Depending on the application scenario, body sensor networks are employed either in a stand-alone context or in combination with mobile phones or ambient sensor networks.

5.2.1 Stand-Alone Body Sensor Networks

A stand-alone body sensor network consists of small wireless nodes on or in the immediate vicinity of the patient's body, conjointly providing the functionality for sensing and processing required by the application. In the simplest scenario, a central node gathers and records the readings of the biosensors such as ECG, EMG, EEG, SpO_2, blood flow, and blood pressure over a period of time for subsequent offline interpretation and trend analysis by a clinician. The data can be enriched with context information by attaching further sensors including accelerometers and gyro meters to the body. By providing capabilities for local processing of the measurements and user I/O, the patient is alerted in a timely manner when her state of health changes for the worse.

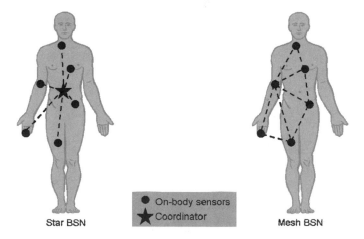

Figure 5.1 Star- *vs* mesh-based body sensor network.

Both star- and mesh-based topologies are applicable to this class of application as depicted in Figure 5.1. The star topology implies a centralised architecture where the intelligence of the system is concentrated on a central node which is superior to the peripheral sensors in terms of resources such as processing, memory, and power. A star network is a common choice. For instance, the UbiMon project [6] takes this approach and utilises a *Personal Digital Assistant* (PDA) as the local processing unit for collecting, displaying and analysing the sensor signals. It is advantageous in situations where a PDA is an inherent part of the system and direct communication between sensors is not required.

In contrast, the BASUMA project [3, 13] pursues the concept of a distributed system with a peer-to-peer network without central controller. As a consequence of shifting the intelligence towards the sensors, the body sensor network consists of smart, self-contained, wireless sensors that communicate with one another. Because peer-to-peer networks are not dependent on any particular component, they are failure-tolerant, *i.e.* even if one component fails the remaining parts of the system continue to operate. This approach is preferable when sensors need to communicate with each other. A non-invasive continuous cuffless blood pressure sensor is a good example for this: by combining the signals from at least one distal pulse wave sensor and a single lead ECG, the pulse wave velocity can be computed that will show a linear relationship with the blood pressure [14].

There remains an interesting challenge to be considered with regards to wireless body sensor networks. If there are no physical wires connecting the sensors into the network, how is a body sensor network to be set up by the user? One proposed solution [15] is to equip all sensors with an IR-receiver and to use a setup pen which emits a unique identifier via IR to limit the scope to a single patient. All sensors receiving the same identifier form a network. The *Active Digital Aura* (ADA) [13] technology takes a similar approach: a tag is worn on the body that capacitively couples a low-frequency RF signal into the body, which is modulated with a unique identifier. Only sensors attached to the body can pick up this identifier and form a network.

5.2.2 Global Healthcare Connectivity

The MobiHealth project [4] and its successor the HealthService24 project [5] developed a health service platform based on a mobile phone which serves as a mobile base station for the wireless sensors worn on the body. It forwards their measurements wirelessly using UMTS or GPRS to a service centre that acts as an intermediary between patients and healthcare providers. It provides three services: collecting and storage of the received data (data repository), forwarding of data to a doctor or medical centre (streaming service), and analysis of the data received and the sending of an alarm or a reminder signal to a predefined destination using SMS (feedback service).

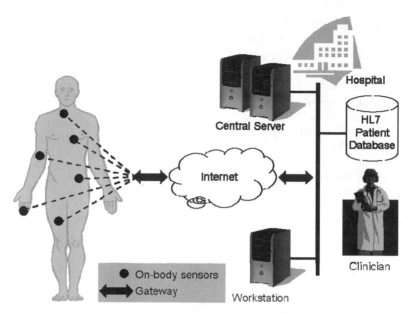

Figure 5.2 Body sensor network connected to hospital network.

The fundamental difference here to the UbiMon [6] and BASUMA [3] projects is that no processing is done locally. Instead of passing only relevant data or alerts to a doctor or a medical centre when detecting a critical event, the concept of MobiHealth is to pipe all sensor readings to a remote data centre where the processing takes place.

Figure 5.2 illustrates the concept of using a mobile phone acting as a gateway for providing connectivity between a body sensor network and a remote medical centre through the Internet, hence enabling the patient to be fully mobile. Alternatives to a mobile phone include a WLAN-enabled PDA or a DECT-based cordless phone for providing access to the Internet via a wireless LAN or DECT infrastructure.

If the body sensor network has a star topology, the gateway is predestined to take over the role of the coordinator. In addition to bridging different communication technologies, the gateway may also translate the lightweight protocols used in the body sensor network to the established medical standards such as HL7 [35] for consumption of the acquired vital signs by clinical information systems.

5.2.3 Pervasive Sensor Networks

We envision in the future pervasive sensor networks combining wearable and ambient sensing. Ambient sensors would be invisibly integrated into the environment. For example MoteTrack [16], a decentralised RF-based localisation system, consists of an ambient radio beacon infrastructure. The location of a mobile wireless node is computed using a received radio signal strength signature from numerous beacon nodes to a database of reference signatures. Other examples of ambient sensors are systems for determining the current activity of a user. Recently, we have demonstrated the new concept of ambient health sensors for measuring medically-relevant parameters outside the hospital with minimal impact on a patient's quality of life [17]. This approach relies on "invisible" ambient health sensors integrated into someone's life, *e.g.* a chair, a bed, or a personal health area, in order to continuously monitor medical condition and fitness. This allows, for example, the determination of the heart rate of a person sitting in a chair without the need for additional body-worn devices.

The ambient sensors are typically part of a stationary wireless sensor network. In contrast, a body sensor network is mobile as it moves with the user. For connecting to the ambient network, a mobile sensor needs to discover an ambient sensor in range and then join the network via the sensor just discovered. When the mobile sensor moves on, it has to regularly repeat this discovery and association procedure to stay connected to the ambient network. Applying this approach to all sensors of a mobile body sensor network would be rather inefficient. A better way is to select only one sensor of the body sensor network to act as a bridge to the ambient sensor network. In this case the bridge sensor alone has to perform these association procedures when the body sensor network is in motion.

Figure 5.3 illustrates this approach for a body sensor network with star and mesh topology, respectively. In a star-based body sensor network, the coordinator acts also as a bridge to the ambient sensor network. The resulting pervasive network has a hybrid star-mesh topology. In a mesh-based body sensor network, one of the sensors has to be selected to take the role of acting as the bridge to the ambient sensor network.

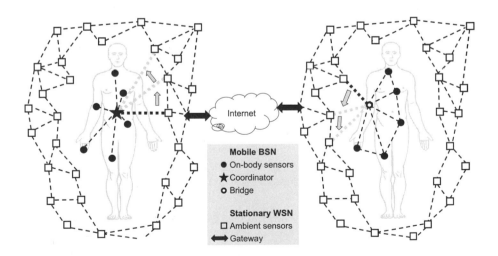

Figure 5.3 Mobile body sensor network connected to ambient sensor network.

5.3 Wireless Personal Area Network Technologies

5.3.1 Overview

The advent of smart wireless sensors that are able to form a body sensor network would not be possible without the availability of appropriate and inexpensive low-power short-range transceivers for low to moderate data rates. These are capable of transmitting real-time data with a latency of typically less than one second within a range of up to five meters. In order to achieve cost-effective, flexible and preferably interoperable solutions, it is almost a necessity to abandon proprietary technological approaches – even though they might be superior for specific applications – and instead choose standardised wireless technology as the basis of a BSN. By means of standards, the short-range wireless communications market has a far better chance to proliferate quickly and hence, costs will be driven down at the same time as the product and feature ranges increase.

Current standardisation efforts affect most of the layers of a communication stack, starting from the *Physical* (PHY) layer, including the *Medium Access Control* (MAC) layer and reaching into higher layers, such as networking or routing layers, and sometimes even the data representation and application layers. Different standardisation bodies may work in a cooperative fashion, as is the case with ZigBee and IEEE 802.15.4, as shown in Figure 5.4.

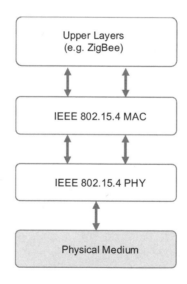

Figure 5.4 Communication protocol stack.

In the following subsections, we present an overview of the current candidate technologies for BSN in the field of wireless short-range connectivity, such as the IEEE 802 family of *Wireless Personal Area Networks* (WPANs) and *Wireless Lo-*

cal Area Networks (WLANs), Bluetooth, and ZigBee. We show that for BSNs, an IEEE 802.15.4-/ZigBee-based system is a favoured approach since other WPAN and WLAN solutions have major drawbacks in this context.

5.3.2 The Wireless Regulatory Environment

Electromagnetic, *i.e.* radio, transmission is always subject to national or international regulation. In Europe, the *Electronic Communications Committee* (ECC) of the *European Conference of Postal and Telecommunications Administrations* (CEPT) is the relevant regulation body, as it brings together the radio and telecommunications regulatory authorities of the 46 CEPT member countries. ECC develops policies on electronic communications in CEPT member countries, and harmonises the efficient use of satellite orbits, numbering resources and the radio spectrum [18]. In the US, the Wireless Telecommunications Bureau of the *Federal Communication Commission* (FCC) regulates the use of the radio spectrum [19].

The portions of the radio spectrum that are most important for BSNs are VHF radio (< 300MHz), UHF radio (*e.g.* 315, 433, 868 – 928MHz), the worldwide 2.4GHz ISM (*Industrial, Scientific and Medical*) band, the worldwide 5GHz band, and, for UWB, the 3 – 10.6GHz band in the US and the EU (currently under study).

In the EU, the spectrum allocations for non-UWB *Short-Range Devices* (SRD) are set forth in ERC Recommendation 70-03 [20]. The ERC Recommendation devises classes of radiated power, channel spacing and duty cycles, and sets the regulatory parameters per field of application. BSNs fall into the category of non-specific SRDs (Annex 1 to ERC/REC 70-03 [20]), whereas WLANs are subject to Annex 3, Wideband Data Transmission Systems, of ERC/REC 70-03 [20]. Another interesting field of applications is treated in Annex 12 to ERC/REC 70-03 [20], Ultra Low Power Active Medical Implants as will be discussed later.

Having a closer look at Annex 1 of non-specific SRDs [20], it becomes obvious that there are stringent restrictions to the important UHF frequency bands from 300 to 3,000MHz. In most cases, either the maximum radiated power is limited to 1 to 10mW, or the band itself is limited to less than 1MHz of bandwidth, or the maximum transmit duty cycle is restricted to 10%, 1% or even 0.1%. There are only two wider bands with few restrictions available, 433.05 – 434.79MHz, and 2,400 – 2,483.5MHz (ISM). It is not surprising that these are the most crowded bands today and their users have to live with interference problems. A quieter band lies from 868 – 868.6MHz and was chosen by IEEE 802.15.4 for systems operating at 1GHz or below. However, it offers a mere 600kHz of bandwidth, and its usage is restricted to a 1% duty cycle. Consequently only occasional data transmissions and very limited data rates are possible in this band.

The wireless industry is hoping for new or relaxed EU radio bands, particularly for an expansion of the limited 868 – 870MHz band down to 863MHz for non-specific SRDs using spread-spectrum techniques with power levels up to 25mW. The ECC prepared a report named "Strategic Plans for the Future Use of the Frequency Bands 862 – 870MHz and 2,400 – 2,483.5MHz for Short Range Devices" in 2002, which is available via the European Radiocommunications Office [18].

Table 5.3 86x MHz SRDs in Europe.

Start of Band [MHz]	Bandwidth [kHz]	Channel Spacing [kHz]	Max. ERP [mW]	Max. Duty Cycle	Application
863.000	2000	(200, 50)	10	-	Microphones, audio
865.000	3000	200	100 (500, 2,000)	-	RFID
868.000	600	-	25	1%	Non-specific
868.600	100	25	10	0.1%	Alarms
868.700	500	-	25	0.1%	Non-specific
869.200	50	25	10	0.1%	Social alarms
869.250	50	25	10	0.1%	Alarms
869.300	100	25	10	-	Non-specific
869.400	250	25	500	10%	Non-specific
869.650	50	25	25	10%	Non-specific
869.700	300	-	5	-	Non-specific

The well-known 2.4GHz ISM band ranges from 2,400 to 2,483.5MHz (83.5MHz bandwidth) in the USA and Europe, and from 2,471 to 2,497MHz (26MHz) in Japan. For wide-band systems in Europe, the maximum radiated power is 100mW EIRP for frequency-hoppers and 10mW/MHz for all other wide-band systems, *e.g.* those employing OFDM or DSSS. For 2.4GHz non-specific SRDs, the output power is limited to 10mW EIRP. There are no restrictions regarding duty cycle or channel spacing.

Except for IEEE 802.11a, which operates in the 5GHz band, and the newer IEEE 802.15 UWB-based proposals, the entire IEEE 802 family of wireless standards rests on the 2.4GHz ISM band: IEEE 802.11 WLANs and IEEE 802.15 WPANs.

Special bands exist for medical applications: these are *Medical Implant Communications Service* (MICS) and *Wireless Medical Telemetry Service* (WMTS). The MICS is an ultra-low power, unlicensed, radio service available worldwide for implanted medical devices, such as cardiac pacemakers and defibrillators. Licensing is not required, but MICS equipment must only be operated by an authorised health care professional [21]. Maximum radiated power in the frequency band from 402-405MHz is 25μW, with 25kHz channel spacing. Therefore, the coverage of MICS is only about 1-2 meters.

The WMTS is available in the US, operating at 608-614MHz, 1,395-1,400MHz and 1,427-1,432MHz. As the name implies, it is used for ambulatory monitoring of a patient's health and gives greater mobility than wired solutions. WMTS permits bi-directional data communications related to medical care, with the exception of voice and video [22]. With respect to BSNs, WMTS has major limitations: it is not available worldwide, home use is prevented, and registration procedures and a human coordinator are required.

Ultra-Wideband (UWB) systems operate at very low radiated power density levels by employing very narrow pulses resulting in very large bandwidths. Originally developed for military purposes, these systems now are poised to enter the consumer market. In 2002, the FCC opened a large band from 3.1 to 10.6GHz with different power levels for UWB. The acceptance of UWB in Europe is still being debated. In March of 2004, the European Commission issued a mandate to CEPT to establish a task group on UWB usage. The resulting maximum generic UWB power limits given in ECC Report 64 were too stringent to facilitate UWB operation throughout Europe. A second mandate was issued in June 2005 to study particular coexistence scenarios and interference mitigation techniques like *Detect And Avoid* (DAA), as mandated in the current draft ECC Decision for the $3.1 - 4.95$GHz range (-70dBm/MHz maximum mean EIRP density).

5.3.3 Wireless Communication Standards

Among the many wireless communication standard activities worldwide, the IEEE 802.11 and IEEE 802.15 family of standards have the largest impact on wireless today. IEEE 802.11 defines different wireless LAN technologies, such as the prominent 2.4GHz, 11Mbit/s IEEE 802.11b, 2.4GHz, 54Mbit/s IEEE 802.11g, and 5GHz, 54Mbit/s IEEE 802.11a. In general, the term WLAN refers to systems with a coverage of 10 to 100 meters that have hundreds of milliwatts at their disposal and often interact with a wired infrastructure (LANs), whereas the term WPAN refers to systems with a coverage of less than 10 meters for highly mobile devices, such as wireless I/O peripherals with very limited power resources.

IEEE 802.15 is the standardisation body that issued three major WPAN technologies so far: IEEE 802.15.1 medium-rate WPAN (derived from the Bluetooth® standard) with up to 720kbit/s peak rate, IEEE P802.15.3 high-rate WPAN supporting hundreds of Mbit/s for multimedia usage, and IEEE 802.15.4 low-rate WPAN, mainly aiming at sensor/actuator networks. Derivatives and expansions of these three are currently under discussion. Finally, IEEE 802.15.2 describes a recommended practice for the coexistence of WPAN and WLAN devices.

As no single technology can suit all needs, it is mainly the IEEE 802.15 WPAN family that best fits the requirements of BSNs, in terms of low power consumption, low complexity, and small form factor.

5.3.4 IEEE 802.15.1: Medium-Rate Wireless Personal Area Networks

Originally developed by the Bluetooth SIG, this medium-rate standard soon became a synonym for short-range wireless communications worldwide. However, it should be pointed out that Bluetooth is mainly meant as a cable replacement with special enhancements for voice data, and not really dedicated to flexible networking scenarios.

After the Bluetooth V1.1 specifications were finalised, the IEEE adopted and converted them into an IEEE Standard, which was officially released in June 2002 [23]. This process not only included the conversion of the specification to IEEE format, but it also encompassed the addition of an IEEE 802 Logical Link Control interface – in order to make Bluetooth a real member of the IEEE 802 family of communication standards – and the addition of SDL (*Specification and Description Language*) material.

Bluetooth supports up to seven simultaneous wireless links at a peak data rate of 720kbit/s over a maximum distance of 10m. Link layer security is supported. Typical transceiver modules measure approximately 25mm×15mm×2mm and consume in the order of 100 to 200mW.

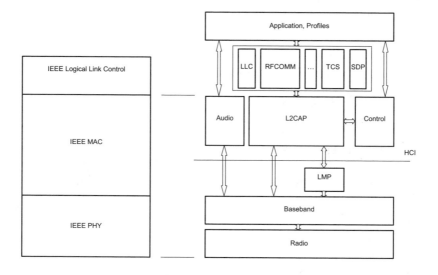

Figure 5.5 IEEE 802.15.1 Bluetooth protocol stack.

The IEEE 802.15.1 Bluetooth Protocol Stack [23] is shown in Figure 5.5. Bluetooth Radio, Baseband, *Link Manager Protocol* (LMP), *Host Controller Interface* (HCI), *Logical Link Control and Adaptation Protocol* (L2CAP), RFCOMM and *Service Discovery Protocol* (SDP) are defined by the specification. Bluetooth Radio deals with channel frequencies and transceiver characteristics. The Baseband handles packet formats and provides a physical link – *Asynchronous ConnectionLess* (ACL) link or *Synchronous Connection-Oriented* (SCO) link – between Bluetooth units. LMP is responsible for link set-up, link control and security aspects. L2CAP provides data services to the upper protocols. It has multiplexing, segmentation and reassembly capabilities and is exclusively supported by the ACL links. RFCOMM is a serial line emulation protocol. Finally, a *Service Discovery Protocol* is also included in the stack.

Bluetooth operates in the 2.45GHz ISM frequency band. This band is split into 79 (USA, Europe) or 23 (Japan) RF channels of 1MHz each, in which a *Gaussian Frequency Shift Keying* (GFSK) modulation scheme is used, very much like in the GSM system. This allows a maximum raw bit rate of 1Mbit/s per RF channel. Bluetooth devices can be classified into three different power classes: Class 1 with a maximum transmitted power of 20dBm; Class 2 with a maximum transmitted power of 4dBm (nominal 0dBm); Class 3 with a maximum output power of 0dBm. This yields a typical radio range of ten meters at 0dBm, and 100 meters at 20dBm. Relevant regulatory rules are set forth in FCC 15.247 (US) and ETSI 300.328 (EU).

IEEE 802.15.1 utilises a spectrum-spreading technique called *Frequency Hopping* (FH). Although a Bluetooth radio transmits in the whole 2.45GHz ISM band, at a certain instant only one of the available 1-MHz RF channels is used. When a frequency hop occurs, the centre transmission frequency switches to that of another channel.

Bluetooth uses a *Frequency-Hopping/Time-Division-Duplex* (FH/TDD) scheme. The physical Bluetooth channel is defined by a pseudo-random frequency-hopping sequence, chosen out of the 79 (23) possible frequencies. Frequency hops occur every 625 microseconds. This makes a nominal rate of 1,600hops/s. The channel is also time-slotted with the same periodicity and the slots are dedicated either to transmit or to receive (TDD scheme). This division in time also allows for multiplexing of different devices when they share the same Bluetooth channel. It should be noted that the newer Bluetooth V1.2 specification adds Adaptive FH, which is able to skip certain frequencies in order to minimise interference.

Despite all the valuable features of Bluetooth, when looking at it from a BSN point of view, a number of severe limitations become obvious. Automatic network formation is not supported, and when the master of an established network moves away, the entire network collapses, which conflicts with the requirements of dynamically changing networks. Starting up a connection is rather slow, *i.e.* up to the order of five seconds. Once a Bluetooth Inquiry (see Figure 5.6) is initiated to look for other Bluetooth devices, it disrupts every on-going communication, such as transmission of an ECG data stream. In addition, a Bluetooth Inquiry will fail if both devices are simultaneously in Inquiry State. Moreover, only single piconets are supported by the Bluetooth PAN profile. The interconnection of several piconets (such as scatternet) is defined but so far not fully specified. Scatternets are therefore proprietary solutions that are rarely used in practice. Finally, efficient multicast or broadcast provisions are missing.

In conclusion, it is evident that Bluetooth offers a vast variety of available and affordable turnkey radio modules. However, Bluetooth is likely to waste too much power and time due to lengthy FH synchronisation procedures. Therefore, weeks of battery life seem unfeasible. In addition, lengthy inquiry procedures interrupt current data transfers. The new Bluetooth V1.2 mitigates some of the above problems, but to a limited degree only.

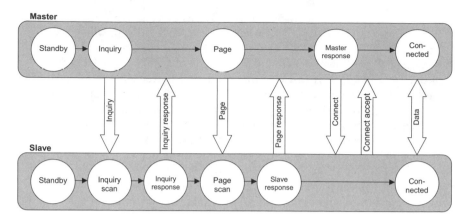

Figure 5.6 Bluetooth connection setup.

5.3.5 IEEE P802.15.3: High-Rate Wireless Personal Area Networks

The intention behind the creation of IEEE P802.15.3 was to enable quick multi-megabyte data transfers within the scope of a WPAN, *e.g.* the transmission of high-quality multimedia files, and even high-definition video transmission (around 20Mbit/s) by means of a low-power and low-cost wireless system. Therefore, new MAC and PHY specifications aiming at high data rates for fixed, portable and moving devices within a personal operating space were created, see [24]. Coexistence with other IEEE 802.15 and IEEE 802.11 devices should also be achieved.

The resulting IEEE P802.15.3 MAC and PHY features [25] are: data rates of 11, 22, 33, 44, and 55Mbit/s over a 2.4GHz ISM radio link, a MAC protocol that supports asynchronous and *Quality-of-Service* (QoS) isochronous data transfers and that is partially based on HiperLAN/2, a security suite and ad-hoc peer-to-peer networking, where wireless devices dynamically become master (Piconet Controller) or slave (Device) according to the existing network structure. Up to 256 active devices can be configured in a piconet (see Figure 5.7) or scatternet configuration. The target network join time is less than one second. *Dynamic Channel Selection* (DCS) helps to ensure low interference levels.

The original physical layer aims at an RF front-end and baseband processors optimised for short-range transmission exhibiting a current drain of less than 100mA (much less than IEEE 802.11) and a small form factor for integration into consumer devices. On top of that, a number of provisions for intelligent power management during idle or scan times is provided through the MAC. As depicted in Figure 5.8, secure and non-secure data frames are supported by the IEEE P802.15.3 MAC layer.

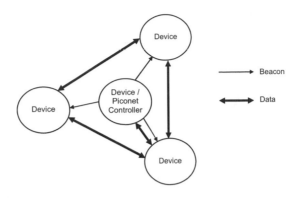

Figure 5.7 IEEE P802.15.3 piconet.

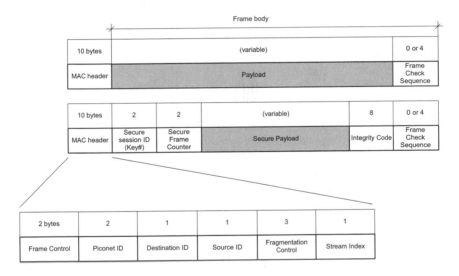

Figure 5.8 Non-secure and secure data frame of IEEE P802.15.3 MAC header.

The current IEEE P802.15.3 PHY layer operates in the 2.4GHz band, occupying 15MHz of RF bandwidth per channel. Hence, three or four non-overlapping channels can be accommodated within the available 83MHz of the 2.4GHz band. Relevant regulatory rules are set forth in FCC 15.249 (US) and ETSI 300.328 (EU).

In contrast to IEEE 802.11 and IEEE 802.15.1, this high-rate WPAN choses a single-carrier PHY in an effort to reduce complexity and power drain. Rather than employing spread-spectrum techniques, the original IEEE P802.15.3 PHY harnesses *Trellis-Coded Modulation* (TCM) with multi-bit symbols at 11MBaud and achieves 11 to 55Mbit/s peak data rate over a range of 10 to 30 meters.

It soon became apparent that these 55Mbit/s were not sufficient to fulfil the ever increasing demands in terms of data rate. After the huge success of IEEE 802.11

WLAN, which by itself became capable of maintaining 54Mbit/s peak data rate (IEEE 802.11a and g), and wired connections like USB 2.0 and IEEE 1394 the market was in quest of a new PHY layer for the existing IEEE P802.15.3 MAC. Data rates from 100 to 500Mbit/s and even more became desirable, for instance to convey multiple video streams at the same time, over a distance of up to ten meters, making IEEE P802.15.3 an ideal USB 2.0 or IEEE 1394 cable replacement.

This led to the inception of the IEEE P802.15.3a Alternate PHY layer [26]. UWB became a promising radio technology at the time when IEEE P802.15.3a was started, particularly owing to the fact that the FCC opened a 3-10GHz 'band' in the US for use by low-power UWB transceivers. In addition to the more traditional pulse-based UWB approaches, Multiband-OFDM as proposed by the *MultiBand-OFDM Alliance* (MBOA) appeared as an alternative solution. Currently, IEEE P802.15.3a has not yet decided between both UWB flavours, and therefore lags behind its expectations.

In summary, IEEE P802.15.3 has been released as a standard for low-power high-rate WPANs featuring a thorough MAC with reservation schemes, powerful sleep modes and even inter-piconet communication support. However, the existing 2.4GHz PHY is quite unlikely to hit the market because of its comparatively low maximum data rate. The alternative PHY layer IEEE P802.15.3a is not yet released, and it is unclear when the situation will change. Moreover, acceptable same-type and different-type coexistence of UWB systems has yet to be proven.

For BSNs, IEEE P802.15.3(a) might in many cases be oversized despite its scalable data rates. While the energy-per-bit figures of IEEE P802.15.3a are at first impressive, the overhead for very small BSN packets might put the overall efficiency in question. It can, however, be very useful when ambient-related information has to be transmitted, *e.g.* originating from a video camera, or if data is transmitted in larger, thus more efficient, bursts.

5.3.6 IEEE 802.15.4: Low-Rate Wireless Personal Area Networks

According to the ZigBee Alliance that builds on top of the IEEE 802.15.4 MAC and PHY standard [27], low-rate WPAN applications address a multi-billion unit market in 2007. Among these are wireless residential, automotive, consumer, and healthcare systems providing a new experience in terms of ease of installation and very large sensor networks. To make this a reality, the underlying technology is required to operate in a license-free band with unrestricted geographic use that has comparatively good RF penetration properties. The IEEE 802.15.4 Working Group defined two physical layers plus a low-complexity MAC layer. The standard was officially released in 2003.

The IEEE 802.15.4 PHY uses *Direct Sequence Spread Spectrum* (DSSS) to fight against the potentially high interference levels in the unlicensed frequency bands used. Two physical layers are defined depending on the frequency band: the 868/915MHz PHY and the 2,450MHz PHY. The following table depicts their characteristics as to maximum data rate and geographical coverage.

Table 5.4 IEEE 802.15.4 frequency bands, data rates, and modulation methods.

Frequency Bands	Coverage	Channels	Data Rate	Data Modulation	Chip Modulation
2.4 GHz	Worldwide	16	250kbit/s	16-ary orthogonal	OQPSK, 2Mchips/s
868 MHz	Europe	1	20kbit/s	BPSK	BPSK, 300kchips/s
915 MHz	Americas	10	40kbit/s	BPSK	BPSK, 600kchips/s

The centre frequencies of the respective channels k can be calculated from the following equations:

$$k = 0: \qquad f_c = 863.3 \text{ MHz}$$
$$k = 1, \ldots, 10: \qquad f_c = 906 + 2(k\text{-}1) \text{ MHz}$$
$$k = 11, \ldots, 26: \qquad f_c = 2405 + 5(k\text{-}11) \text{ MHz}$$

The data rates indicated in Table 5.4 look sufficient for BSNs, which have relatively low bandwidth requirements. Nevertheless, the 20kbit/s and 40kbit/s possible on the 868MHz and 915MHz bands do not enable the more demanding use cases.

As mentioned earlier, the European 868MHz band [20] has currently a duty cycle limitation of 1%, which yields an effective data rate of only 200bit/s. The European radio authorities are planning to extend that band and relax the duty cycle limitations. One of the goals of the standardisation group IEEE 802.15.4b is to enhance the current IEEE 802.15.4 868/915MHz PHY with a higher data rate in the future. The current IEEE 802.15.4b draft [28] introduces two new PHY that enable 100 to 250kbit/s for the 868MHz band and 250kbit/s for the 915MHz band. However, due to the current draft status of IEEE 802.15.4b and eventual changes in radio regulations, the future evolution of the IEEE 802.15.4 868/915MHz band with respect to the achievable data rate still remains uncertain.

Due to the data rate requirements of BSNs, and also to the worldwide availability, the 2,450MHz PHY seems appropriate to enable the envisaged applications. Two drawbacks of the utilization of the 2.4GHz ISM frequency band are the considerable body attenuation and the potentially high interference level. These are discussed later in this chapter.

To allow for very low-cost low-complexity devices, IEEE 802.15.4 defines *Reduced Function Device* (RFD) and *Full Function Device* (FFD). RFDs implement a subset of the IEEE 802.15.4-defined primitives and cannot act as coordinator. FFDs have a full implementation of IEEE 802.15.4 and can adopt any role in the WPAN. An IEEE 802.15.4 radio is capable of performing three different signal power measurements:

- *Link Quality Indication* (LQI): Characterises the strength and/or quality of a received packet. This is useful for the network and application layers (mainly for routing and channel selection).
- *Energy Detection* (ED): Characterises the energy level in the current channel, which can be originated by many radiation sources (IEEE 802.15.4 interferer, interferer using another radio technology, background noise, *etc.*). The network layer uses ED as part of the channel selection mechanism.
- *Clear Channel Assessment* (CCA): Depending on the mode used, CCA assesses if the channel is either free of IEEE 802.15.4-originated transmission (based on IEEE 802.15.4 signal pattern recognition) or free of any interference (based on ED). This functionality is required by the MAC layer for implementing CSMA/CA (*Carrier Sense Multiple Access/Collision Avoidance*).

Although common IEEE 802.15.4 devices are expected to operate with transmit powers between –3dBm (0.5mW) and 10dBm (10mW), 0dBm (1mW) of transmit power is the most typical value. A typical transceiver consumes approximately 60mW when transmitting or receiving. This power consumption is considerably lower than that of a typical Bluetooth transceiver, which consumes around 150mW. IEEE 802.11b transceivers are far more power-hungry, with typical power consumptions between 400mW and 1,500mW.

The IEEE 802.15.4 MAC layer is a simple protocol designed to cater for low-cost, low-power devices but yet flexible enough to enable the delivery of periodic data, intermittent data (such as occasional measurements) and repetitive low-latency data (for instance, real-time ECG streaming). It features a fully handshaked protocol for reliable delivery of data and is able to support extremely low duty cycle (even below 0.1%) operations efficiently.

IEEE 802.15.4 uses four types of MAC frames: beacon frame, data frame, acknowledgement frame, and MAC command frame. The MAC layer optionally supports a superframe structure, the format of which is defined by the coordinator. The superframe is bounded by network beacons, sent periodically by the coordinator of a beacon-enabled network, and is divided into sixteen equally sized slots. The beacons are used to synchronise the attached devices, to identify the WPAN and to describe the structure of the superframes. The superframe can have an active and an inactive portion, during which the coordinator does not interact with its WPAN and may enter a low power (sleep) mode.

For low-latency applications and/or applications requiring fixed data rates, for instance ECG monitoring, the coordinator may dedicate portions of the active superframe to that application. These portions are called *Guaranteed Time Slots* (GTS) and are allocated in the *Contention-Free Period* (CFP), see Figure 5.9. In the rest of the active superframe, known as *Contention Access Period* (CAP), devices use slotted CSMA/CA to access the channel. In non-beacon enabled networks, in which there is no superframe structure or GTS, the channel access mechanism used is always unslotted CSMA/CA.

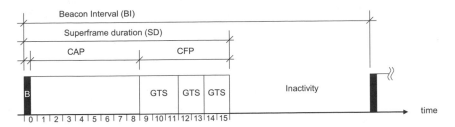

Figure 5.9 Example of the IEEE 802.15.4 superframe structure.

All devices operating in the WPAN shall have unique 64-bit extended addresses, which can be used for communication within the WPAN. Communication with 16-bit addresses is also possible if the coordinator allocates short addresses for its devices during association to the WPAN. Due to this addressing mechanism, IEEE 802.15.4 offers support for over 65,000 devices in a PAN, in contrast to Bluetooth, which supports only up to eight active devices in a network. The number of WPAN members supported by IEEE 802.15.4 is more than sufficient for any envisaged BSN applications.

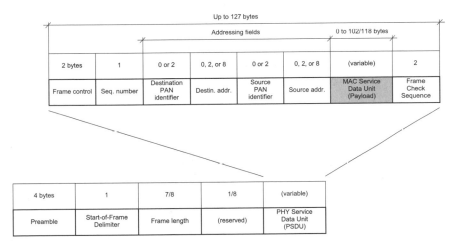

Figure 5.10 General IEEE 802.15.4 MAC and PHY frame formats.

The general MAC frame format is depicted in Figure 5.10 together with the PHY frame format. The maximum payload deliverable by a MAC frame containing data is 102 or 118 bytes, depending on the addressing scheme used and the network topology. In principle, that payload could be directly employed for encapsulating medical data, in case of renouncement to the higher protocol stack layers.

ZigBee, which sits on top of the IEEE 802.15.4 MAC Layer in the protocol stack, must be provided with services that expose the PHY and MAC functionality of IEEE 802.15.4. The interfaces of these services are the *MAC sub-Layer Man-*

agement Entity Service Access Point (MLME-SAP) between ZigBee and MAC layer, and the *MAC Common Part Sub-layer data Service Access Point* (MCPS-SAP). The services offered include data transport, association to a PAN, beacon notification, GTS management, orphan notification, receiver management, scanning for PANs, superframe configuration, synchronisation with the coordinator, and more.

IEEE 802.15.4a [29] is a new Task Group that is going to propose an alternative PHY layer for the low-rate WPAN standard. In March 2005, the baseline specifications for two different PHY technologies emerged, (*a*) UWB Impulse Radio, and (*b*) *Chirp Spread Spectrum* (CSS) in the 2.4GHz ISM band. This alternative PHY baseline will not only provide high aggregate throughput at very low power (aiming at 1mW power consumption), but also better scalability of data rates versus range and even high-precision ranging with sub-meter precision (UWB option only).

Although a wireless BSN is not always a lowest duty cycle application (such as continuous ECG streaming), the ZigBee/IEEE 802.15.4 framework appears to be the most intriguing and suitable protocol suite for it. The IEEE 802.15.4 MAC offers a number of valuable ingredients for BSNs: the MAC is optimised for low power and short messages and includes peer-to-peer network support, guaranteed time slots, *etc.* IEEE 802.15.4 is also likely to be chosen as the radio basis for IEEE P1451.5-based wireless sensors [40]. Highly integrated single-chip IEEE 802.15.4-compliant transceivers are already available from a number of IC manufacturers, yet they are a bit more power hungry than simple FSK transceivers because of DSSS, but they offer better robustness and better interoperability compared with FSK. Of course, the data rate is not sufficient to carry video data in ambient applications, but it could well convey pre-processed data, *e.g.* from a camera system that detects when a person is moving or falling. The IEEE 802.15.4a alternate PHY may add another interesting flavour to BSNs in the not-too-distant future. Worldwide interest in ZigBee-/IEEE 802.15.4-compliant products will inspire global creativity and keep costs down.

5.3.7 ZigBee

The ZigBee wireless technology [30] was developed by the ZigBee Alliance with the ambition of enabling reliable, cost-effective, low power and wirelessly networked monitoring and control products based on an open global standard. The targeted products and applications are medical monitoring, home, industrial and building automation/control, PC peripherals, consumer electronics and toys. ZigBee's primary drivers are simplicity, long battery life, advanced networking capabilities, reliability and low cost. These drivers are shared with IEEE 802.15.4, which is integral part of the ZigBee standard.

ZigBee applications communicate using the PHY and MAC layers specified by the IEEE 802.15.4 standard. As shown in Figure 5.11, ZigBee builds a *Network* (NWK) layer and an *Application* (APL) layer on the IEEE 802.15.4-defined layers. The PHY layer provides the basic communication capabilities of the physical radio. The medium access control layer provides services to enable reliable single-hop communication links between devices. The network layer provides routing and multi-hop functions needed for creating different network topologies. The application layer includes an *Application Support* (APS) sub-layer, the *ZigBee Device Object* (ZDO), and the ZigBee applications defined by the user or designer. Whereas the ZDO is responsible for overall device management, the APS provides servicing to both ZDO and ZigBee applications.

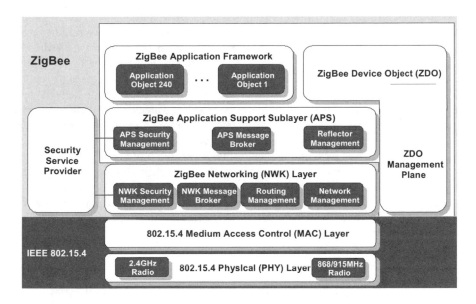

Figure 5.11 ZigBee communication protocol stack.

The ZigBee NWK layer supports star, mesh, and cluster tree topologies. Its responsibilities include mechanisms used to join and leave the network, to apply security to frames and to route frames to their intended destinations. In addition the network layer is responsible for the discovery and maintenance of routes between devices as well as for the discovery of one-hop neighbours. ZigBee defines three device types with respect to their networking capabilities:

- *ZigBee coordinator*: The IEEE 802.15.4 PAN coordinator.
- *ZigBee router*: An IEEE 802.15.4 *Full Function Device* (FFD) that participates in a ZigBee network and is not the ZigBee coordinator but may act as a coordinator within its personal operating space. A ZigBee router is capable of routing messages between devices and supporting device associations.
- *ZigBee end device*: An IEEE 802.15.4 *Reduced* (RFD) or FFD that participates in a ZigBee network and is neither the ZigBee coordinator nor a ZigBee router.

The network layer of the ZigBee coordinator is responsible for starting a network and assigning network addresses to newly associated devices. The underlying medium access layer adopts the ZigBee network address as IEEE 802.15.4 16-bit short address. Network addresses are assigned using a distributed addressing scheme designed to provide every potential parent device (coordinator) with a finite sub-block of network addresses. Addresses are unique to a particular network and are given by a parent to its children (associated devices).

The ZigBee routing algorithm is designed to enable reliable, cost effective, low-power, wirelessly networked monitoring and control products. ZigBee routers must be able to perform hierarchical routing and may, optionally, perform table-driven routing. In hierarchical routing, frames are routed along the hierarchy that is put in place at network formation time and is reflected in the network addresses of source and destination. This routing mechanism is the only possible when the network operates as star or tree network. In table-driven routing, frames are routed according to a routing table, which is set-up and maintained using a request-response route discovery protocol. Table-driven routing overcomes the sub-optimal route problem that occasionally arises with hierarchical routing, yet it is more costly. Devices that have enough memory and processing power to build and maintain routing tables may use table-driven routing.

Neither the ZigBee network layer nor any other ZigBee-defined layer offer a resource reservation functionality though their interfaces. The *Guaranteed Time Slot* (GTS) feature offered by IEEE 802.15.4 remains inaccessible for ZigBee applications.

The ZigBee APL layer consists of the APS sub-layer, the ZDO – containing the ZDO management plane – and the manufacturer-defined application objects, which are embedded in the *Application Framework* (AF). The responsibilities of the APS sub-layer include maintaining tables for binding – the logical connection of devices based on their services and needs – and forwarding messages between bound devices. The responsibilities of the ZDO include defining the role of the device within the network (for instance the ZigBee coordinator or end device), managing the node configuration, initiating and/or responding to binding requests and establishing a secure relationship between network devices. Another responsibility of the ZDO is discovery, which is the ability to determine which other devices are operating in the network. The developer-defined application objects implement the actual applications according to application descriptions specified by ZigBee.

The APS sub-layer enables three addressing modes: direct addressing (normal unicast delivery), indirect addressing and broadcast addressing. Applications that use direct addressing must specify the destination ZigBee address (16- or 64-bit) and the destination endpoint of the APS data unit. On the other hand, applications that use indirect addressing do not have to specify the destination of the APS data unit. The APS can extract the required destination information from the binding table, which is located and managed by the APS of the ZigBee coordinator.

The AF is the environment in which application objects are hosted. An application object sends and receives data over its assigned endpoint, a physical/logical description that enables a single ZigBee device to support up to 240 independent end applications. Endpoints provide ZigBee with a level of sub-addressing additional to network addressing. Applications can be deployed on endpoints 1 to 240. It is a task of the application developer to decide how to deploy applications on endpoints. However, it is required that simple descriptors are created for each used endpoint and that those descriptors are made available for service discovery. Endpoint 0 is used by the ZDO for management purposes. Endpoint 255 is used to address all active endpoints (the broadcast endpoint). Endpoints 241 to 254 are reserved.

ZigBee profiles are an agreement on messages, message formats and processing actions that enable applications residing on separate ZigBee devices to send commands, request data and process commands/requests to create an interoperable, distributed application. A profile defines the following:

- *One or more device description(s)*: A device descriptor is a description of a specific device within an application segment. For instance, the "Switch Remote Control" and the "Light Sensor Monochromatic" are two device descriptions included in the ZigBee application profile "Home Control, Lighting". Each device description is assigned a unique identifier within its profile that is exchanged during the service discovery process carried out by the ZDO.

- *Cluster(s)*: A cluster is a container for one or more attributes, which are, in turn, data entities that represent a physical quantity or state. Each cluster is assigned an 8-bit cluster identifier unique within its specific profile. Equally, each of the attributes contained in a cluster is assigned an attribute identifier. An example of a cluster defined within the "Home Control, Lighting" profile is the "Program Light Sensor Mono-chromatic" cluster, which contains attributes such as "ReportTime" or "MinLevelChange".

- *Service types*: Type of AF data service to be used. It can be either a *Key Value Pair* (KVP) or *Generic Message* (MSG) service.

The ZigBee device profile is a special profile that describes how the ZDO implements its functionality and defines, unlike the rest of ZigBee profiles, capabilities supported by all ZigBee devices. The key to interoperability between ZigBee devices of different vendors is the agreement on a profile. Profile identifiers are unique and assigned by the ZigBee Alliance. ZigBee profiles are administratively classified in three classes: private, published and public. A medical profile for interoperability between body sensors has not been defined as of today.

The ZigBee security services include methods for key establishment, key transport, frame protection and device management. Security is provided at MAC, NWK and APL layers following an open trust model according to which all stack layers and all applications running on a single ZigBee device trust each other. Hence the provided security services cryptographically protect only the interfaces between different devices, and not the interfaces between stack layers. The APS provides services for the establishment and maintenance of security relationships. The ZDO manages the security policies and security configuration of a device.

Security within a ZigBee network is based on 'link' keys and a "network" key. Unicast communication between APL peer entities is secured by means of a 128-bit link key shared by two devices, while broadcast communications are secured by means of a 128-bit network key shared amongst all devices in the network. Ultimately, security between devices depends on the secure initialisation and installation of these keys. For this purpose, ZigBee defines the role of trust centre; the device trusted by devices within a network to distribute keys for the purpose of network and end-to-end application configuration management.

ZigBee defines eight security levels to protect incoming and outgoing frames. Those security levels are applicable to all stack layers involved in security and are based on CCM*, a generic combined encryption and authentication block cipher mode that has been derived from CCM [31] and specified in the IEEE 802.15.4 and ZigBee specifications. CCM* allows the reuse of the same key by the MAC, NWK and APL layers of the ZigBee stack. Furthermore, to simplify interoperability, the security level used by all devices in a given network and by all layers of a device shall be the same.

The use of security is determined by the network designer under consideration of the security requirements of the application to be enabled. The designer should trade off between security level and effective data rate. It is vitally important to provide medical-purpose BSNs with data integrity to ensure that nobody modifies or fakes the output data of BSN sensors. Many applications also require data confidentiality.

5.3.8 Comparison of Technologies

For personal healthcare it is desirable to exploit proven and cheap off-the-shelf radio technology for wireless body sensor networks. Table 5.5 provides an overview of candidate wireless standards that come into consideration. From this, it is obvious that IEEE 802.11b WLAN technology is power hungry to such an extent that users would need to replace the batteries after only a few hours of operation. In this respect the wireless personal area standards IEEE 802.15.1 (Bluetooth) and IEEE 802.15.4 are much better suited for battery-powered body sensor networks.

However, IEEE 802.15.4 scores over IEEE 802.15.1 due to its faster, more flexible and scalable networking features, while it consumes less energy, processing and memory resources. It also supports standard-based security. In addition, IEEE 802.15.4 lays the foundation for ZigBee adding multi-hop networking and an application support layer. ZigBee's multi-hop routing capability enables wireless connectivity of ambient sensors scattered all over the user's home. Defining a medical ZigBee profile could be a promising approach for ensuring interoperability between body-worn wireless medical sensors from different vendors. Therefore, as of today, IEEE 802.15.4 is the standard wireless technology of choice for BSNs.

5.4 Practical Experiences with IEEE 802.15.4

Recently, we have developed a versatile IEEE 802.15.4-based ZigBee-ready wireless sensor node platform for continuous patient monitoring. The platform has been named AquisGrain, in a reference to the words 'Grain', which indicates the small size of the sensor nodes, and 'Aquisgranum', the Latin name of the German city of Aachen, where the platform was developed. The current version of AquisGrain sensor nodes has a board size of 35×36 mm^2 and consists of two main components:

- Atmel Atmega128L 8-bit microcontroller
- Chipcon CC2420 IEEE 802.15.4 radio (2.4GHz ISM frequency band)

Further components are:

- *Battery monitor/ID chip*: Gauges the battery level and uniquely identifies the sensor
- *Step-up/step-down voltage regulator*: Allows for flexibility in the type of battery used to power the node
- *4-Mbit flash memory chip*: Provides local data storage
- *System connector*: Interfaces to the sensing hardware or to an eventual host system
- *λ/4 monopole antenna*

Figure 5.12 depicts the present family of AquisGrain wireless sensor nodes: as a standalone module, as a *Compact Flash* (CF) card, and as an USB stick. The next version of AquisGrain is currently in development. It will be based on the CC2430, which integrates IEEE 802.15.4 radio and 8-bit microcontroller in a single chip. We have used the AquisGrain sensor node platform to perform a practical evaluation of several aspects of IEEE 802.15.4-based BSNs: communication range and link robustness in different environments, power consumption, and coexistence with other wireless technologies.

AquisGrain A1.0 features a typical power consumption of 93mW in active mode and 141µW in sleep mode. These values have been measured at a supply voltage of 3V and transmit power of 0dBm (1mW), which is the maximum transmit power for the radio. The minimum transmit power, -25dBm (3.17µW), leads to a power consumption of 66.3mW in transmit mode. The duty cycle, that is the percentage of time a node is active, has a dramatic impact on the operating lifetime of any sensor node. Let us suppose, as an example, a wireless sensor node with the power consumption of AquisGrain A1.0 at its maximum transmit power and fed with a small 3V lithium coin cell battery with a nominal capacity of 190mAh. Such configuration would allow for an operating lifetime between six hours (for a duty cycle of 100%) and 168 days (for a duty cycle of 0%). The vast majority of envisaged BSN sensors will need to communicate at a low average data rate: from a few

Table 5.5 Overview of wireless standard options for Body Sensor Networks.

	IEEE 802.11b WiFi	IEEE 802.15.1 Bluetooth	IEEE 802.15.4			ZigBee
ISM band	2.4GHz	2.4GHz	2.4GHz	915MHz (US)	868MHz (EU)	
Air interface	Direct-sequence spread spectrum (DSSS)	Frequency-hopping spread spectrum (FHSS)	Direct-sequence spread spectrum (DSSS)			
# Channels/schemes	11 (US), 13 (EU)	10	16	10	1	
Data rate (aggregated)	11Mbit/s (50Mbit/s)	1Mbit/s (10Mbit/s)	250kbit/s (4,000kbit/s)	40kbit/s (400kbit/s)	20kbit/s (20kbit/s)	
Range	100m	10m, 30m, 100m	10-30m			
Network topology	Star, peer-to-peer	Star	Star, peer-to-peer			+ Multi-hop mesh
Network size	32	8	65,535			
Network join time	<3s	<10s	<<1s			
Real-time support	No	No	Guaranteed time slots			No
Protocol complexity	Medium	High	Simple			Low
Stack size	100KB	256KB	24KB			62KB
Security	Authentication, encryption	Authentication, encryption	Authentication, encryption			
Power consumption	400-700mW (Philips BGW200)	200mW (National LMX9820A)	60-70mW (Chipcon CC2420)			

bits/s (for non-streaming sensors with sporadic transmission of measurements or of control/configuration information) up to 10kbits/s (for the most demanding ECG-like streaming sensors). Considering IEEE 802.15.4 sensor nodes operating in the 2.4GHz ISM frequency band, those data rates translate respectively into a 4ppm (0.0004%) duty cycle for the first group of sensors and 4% duty cycle for the second group. Thus, the operating lifetime expected for a typical 2.4GHz IEEE 802.15.4 BSN node – configured as described above – ranges from 168 days (sporadic transmission) to 6.2 days (demanding streaming transmission). Although omitted in the previous considerations, the final operating lifetime of a wireless sensor node also depends on the power consumption of the sensing hardware integrated with the node. Its contribution to the overall operating lifetime depends on the type of sensor used; it can be negligible, comparable or predominant over the contribution of the radio module. In the latter case, it is advisable to spend effort in the development and integration of lower-power sensing modules.

The communication range and link robustness of any 2.4GHz wireless network are strongly dependent on its near environment (for example, the predominance of walls or furniture). For this reason we have performed extensive tests in several indoor environments. Despite the high variance of the measurement results, it can be generalised that AquisGrain A1.0 has a communication range of ten to thirty meters and that, within that range, the link is robust in the first eight to ten meters. Additional tests outdoors have proven that indoor multi-path propagation helps to stabilise the sudden link robustness changes that result from the relative movement amongst sensors.

Figure 5.12 Family of AquisGrain wireless sensor nodes.

In Chapter 4, we discussed how the attenuation that the body causes on RF signals becomes higher with increasing radio frequency. Neirynck *et al* [32] measured the body attenuation on the 2.4GHz ISM band and observed shadowing depths of 30dB to 40dB when the body was obstructing the line-of-sight. Analogue experiments on the 5.2GHz band showed that the attenuation was even 25dB to 30dB higher. The former RF attenuation values are indicative for the expected performance of wireless networks operating at 2.4GHz. Yet RF attenuation is not the only parameter that affects the performance of wireless networks; parameters like modulation technique or spectrum characteristics must also be considered. The packet error rate (observed at application level) better characterises the performance of wireless networks. We have used AquisGrain to determine the packet error rate within an area of 5 meters around a transmitting sensor placed at different places of the body. The following list summarises the results.

- The packet error rate is always far under 1% when the body influence is depreciative.
- The packet error rate is always under 1% when the wireless sensor is attached to the ankle of a person lying in bed and covered with a blanket.
- The packet error rate is always under 4% when the wireless sensor is attached to the left upper arm (blood pressure measurement spot) of a standing person that is periodically moving his trunk and arms.
- The packet error rate is usually under 7% when the wireless sensor is attached to the chest of a standing person whose body is continuously blocking the line-of-sight between transmitter and receiver. Occasionally the packet error rate is considerably higher (up to 26%).

The tests have shown that the influence of the body on IEEE 802.15.4-based BSNs is tolerable. Nevertheless the link becomes weak when the body totally blocks the direct communication path between nodes. Hence it is recommended to use the highest transmit power to minimise such effects. Antenna redundancy (when applicable) and the exploitation of different routes between sensors can further improve the system performance.

The 2.4GHz ISM band is an unlicensed frequency band and therefore prone to radio interference. In view of that, the IEEE 802.15.4 standard dedicates a section to coexistence with other IEEE standards and proposed standards [27, Annex E. The most relevant interference sources identified for IEEE 802.15.4 (2.4GHz) are:

- IEEE 802.11b [33] (WLAN)
- IEEE 802.15.1 [23] (medium-rate WPAN, Bluetooth)
- IEEE P802.15.3 [25] (high-rate WPAN)
- Microwave ovens

The interference level amongst wireless communication systems mainly depends on the transmitted power, channel bandwidth, spectrum spreading mechanism and medium access scheme of each system. Whilst the transmit power of external interferers has an obvious impact on the level of interference induced in a system, the system's own channel bandwidth and spectrum spreading contribute to the robustness against external interference. Medium access schemes that sense the medium before transmitting (such as CSMA/CA) produce less interference than inflexible time-based medium access schemes like TDMA. Table 5.6 summarises these characteristics for IEEE 802.15.4 and its most relevant standards of interference.

Table 5.6 Coexistence-relevant characteristics of wireless communication standards operating at 2.4GHz.

Standards	Typical Transmit Power	Channel Bandwidth	Spectrum Spreading	Medium Access
IEEE 802.15.4	0dBm	2MHz	Direct sequence (DSSS)	CSMA/CA (TDMA optional)
IEEE 802.11b (WLAN)	14-16dBm	22MHz	Direct sequence (DSSS)	CSMA/CA (polling-based TDMA optional)
IEEE 802.15.1 (Bluetooth)	0dBm	1MHz	Frequency Hopping (FHSS)(79 channels)	TDMA
IEEE P802.15.3 Draft 17	8dBm	15MHz	none	CSMA/CA (TDMA optional)

The interference caused by IEEE 802.15.4 on the other systems is relatively low owing to its low transmit power, reduced channel bandwidth and CSMA/CA medium access mechanism. Moreover the typically low duty cycle of IEEE 802.15.4 devices further reduces the interference on other systems. IEEE 802.15.1 (Bluetooth) has a similar transmit power than IEEE 802.15.4 and uses frequency hopping, which reduces 96% the probability of actual mutual interference. Despite Bluetooth's TDMA medium access scheme, the former two facts cater for a relatively grateful coexistence between IEEE 802.15.1 (Bluetooth) and IEEE 802.15.4.

As for the interference of other systems on IEEE 802.15.4, IEEE 802.11b proves to be the most harmful due to its highest transmit power and spectrum bandwidth. The impact of IEEE P802.15.3 on IEEE 802.15.4 is not as big as that of IEEE 802.11b. Moreover, IEEE P802.15.3 is not an established standard yet. Due to the widespread utilisation of IEEE 802.11b and its high interference potential, IEEE 802.11b must be regarded as the most significant source of interference for IEEE 802.15.4-based BSNs. Simulations [27, 34] have shown that channel overlaps between IEEE 802.11b and IEEE 802.15.4 can be very detrimental to IEEE 802.15.4 when the IEEE 802.11b interferer is close enough to the IEEE 802.15.4 receiver.

Practical tests with AquisGrain A1.0 nodes and laptop computers equipped with standard PCMCIA WLAN cards (IEEE 802.11b) have shown that the interference caused by IEEE 802.11b on an IEEE 802.15.4 BSN is, expressed in packet error rate, much lower for non-overlapping channels (in Figure 5.13 IEEE 802.11b Channel 1 and IEEE 802.15.4 Channel 15) than for overlapping channels (in Figure 5.13 IEEE 802.11b Channel 1 and IEEE 802.15.4 Channel 12). Even in case of channel overlap, the measured packet error rate drops noticeably as the offset between the central frequencies of IEEE 802.15.4 and IEEE 802.11b increases. Table 5.7 depicts the main results of the IEEE 802.11b-induced interference experiments. In view of these results, it is recommended to start a BSN preferably on one of the four IEEE 802.15.4 channels that fall in the frequency gaps between IEEE 802.11b channels. This is only possible when the neighbouring IEEE 802.11b WLAN is deployed following the non-overlapping channel scheme shown in Figure 5.13. Independently of the scheme used to deploy the interfering technology, it is always recommended to perform an energy scan of all IEEE 802.15.4 channels before starting the BSN. Thus the BSN can be set up on the channel with the lowest level of interference. Another effective technique to minimise the effect of interferences is to use a dynamic channel selection in which the running BSN continuously scans the channel set to be capable of switching to a better channel whenever it is needed. The procedure used to select the BSN channel – either before starting the network or during operation – is not specified by the IEEE 802.15.4 standard or the ZigBee specification. It is entirely up to the BSN designer how to manage channels to cater for coexistence with other technologies.

5.5 Healthcare System Integration

Standards are the key for ensuring interoperability between wireless medical sensors and for integration of body sensor networks into the healthcare enterprise. In general hospital information systems, standards for the exchange of clinical data and communication between medical devices, collaboration and negotiation protocols are well established.

5.5.1 Existing Interoperability Standards

HL7 (*Health Level Seven*) [35] is a healthcare interoperability standard for the electronic interchange of clinical, financial and administrative information among independent health care oriented computer systems; *i.e.*, hospital information systems, clinical laboratory systems, enterprise systems and pharmacy systems. "Level Seven" refers to the highest level of the *International Standards Organization*'s (ISO) communications model for *Open Systems Interconnection* (OSI) [1] – the application level.

IEEE P1073 [36, 37] standardises the physical (electrical, synchronisation, cable and connector) and transport (network services) characteristics of communication between medical devices for providing plug and play interoperability at the point of care. The IEEE P1073 family of standards – often referred to as *Medical Information Bus* (MIB) – facilitates the efficient exchange of vital signs and medical device data, acquired by patient-connected medical devices, for all health environments. There is also a joint HL7/IEEE P1073 working group identifying and defining interfaces to support interoperability between HL7- and IEEE P1073-based systems.

a) IEEE 802.11b North American non-overlapping channel selection

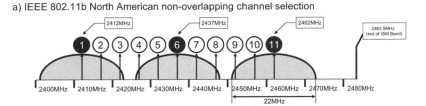

b) IEEE 802.15.4 channels (2.4GHz)

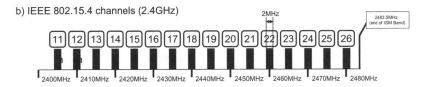

c) Interference-free channel scheme for IEEE 802.11b and IEEE 802.15.4

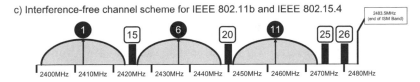

Figure 5.13 IEEE 802.11b (North America) and IEEE 802.15.4 (2.4GHz) channel scheme.

Table 5.7 Relative Packet Error Rate (PER) measured at the IEEE 802.15.4 receiver depending on the offset between the central frequencies of IEEE 802.15.4 and IEEE 802.11b. The PER is normalised to the highest PER measured in every test set-up.

	12MHz Central Frequency Offset (no overlap)	7MHz Central Frequency Offset (overlap)	2mhz Central Frequency Offset (full overlap)
No overlap *vs.* overlap	0.0036	1	n.a.
Overlap *vs.* full overlap	n.a.	0.098	1

The *Technical Committee for Medical Informatics* (TC251) of the European *Committee for Standardisation* (CEN) established a project team (CEN/TC251/PT5-021) to standardise the representation of digitised biomedical signals, measurements, events and alarms. The resulting VITAL (*Vital Signs Information Representation*)/CEN ENV 13734 [38] standard specifies object-oriented models and a nomenclature and coding scheme for the information elements and services required to enable communication from and between medical devices. As illustrated in Figure 5.14 VITAL is directly complementary to IEEE P1073 by defining the higher layers protocols on top of the lower layers that are defined by IEEE P1073.

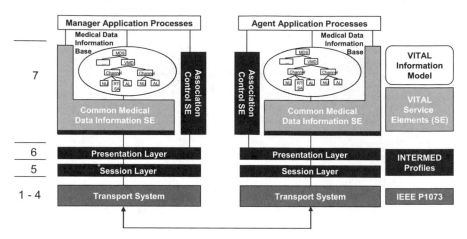

Figure 5.14 IEEE P1073/VITAL architecture.

5.5.2 Wireless Interoperability Standards Under Development

The standardisation of communication processes that has led to the explosion of communications products in the consumer area has yet to take hold in the world of wireless sensors and body sensor networks. Although wireless communication standards such as the IEEE 802.15 family and ZigBee exist, they cover only the "lower" OSI layers (*i.e.* the physical, data link, network, and transport layers) which provide reliable data transport. But additionally, wireless medical devices must be able to understand the format and content of the messages they communicate to each other. Extending the standardisation to the "upper" OSI layers by defining application profiles is required for ensuring that all wireless medical sensors speak the same language. There are only a few ongoing standardisation activities addressing this need and they are all still in their infancy.

IEEE P1073 [36] formed a new RF wireless technologies working group (IEEE P1073.0.1.1) with very broad participation from both technology suppliers and users. This project is targeted at identifying issues related to using current off-the-shelf technologies (for example IEEE 802.11 "WiFi", IEEE 802.15.1/"Bluetooth", and IEEE 802.15.4/"ZigBee") in a shared IT infrastructure where multiple devices and systems from diverse vendors can be integrated to provide safe and effective communication of medical device data. The RF wireless technologies working group has been actively developing a technical report on the use of RF networks for medical device communications [39]. This report outlines specific exercises using detailed case scenarios to estimate the performance, as well as compare and contrast, known technologies operating on body, personal, local, and wide area networks. Considered in these exercises are network architecture and technology, EMI/EMC, quality of service management, co-existence and interface conformance disclosure, service discovery mechanism, security, interface cost, power consumption, and technology configurability. Figure 5.16 provides an overview of the user cases the RF working group is looking at, ranging from clinical, to home, to emergency scenarios.

In September 2005, the ZigBee Alliance [30] Application Framework Working Group issued a call for participation in a new profile task group to develop a new application profile in the area of health monitoring. A medical ZigBee profile will enable plug and play interoperability of wireless ZigBee-enabled medical sensors and devices.

The IEEE P1451.5 [40] project is working on defining wireless communication protocols and data formats for wireless transducers (sensors and actuators) based on the IEEE P1451 family of smart transducer interface standards (see Figure 5.15). The standard will define a *Transducer Electronic Data Sheets* (TEDS), and protocols to access TEDS and transducer data. It will adopt the IEEE 802 family as the basis of the wireless communication protocols.

5.6 Conclusions

Wireless sensor networks are a key technology for pervasive health monitoring. Vital signs such as ECG or SpO_2 are measured by means of body-worn medical sensors or in the future by unobtrusive health sensors that are integrated into the ambient environment. The medical data will be enriched with data from ambient sensors providing additional context information, for example location and activity. The mobile, star- or mesh-based, body sensor networks connect to the ambient multi-hop mesh network resulting in a pervasive wireless hybrid network. Adding a mobile phone or a home gateway to the system, provides global connectivity to distant sites such as hospitals or medical service centres.

Currently there is a lack of application-layer interoperability standards for wireless BSNs and their integration into existing hospital systems. However, some standards development activities, such as the IEEE P1073 wireless technologies working group and the ZigBee medical profile task group, have been initiated to address this issue and they can be potentially used as a foundation for plug and play interoperability of wireless medical sensors.

Concerning wireless connectivity technologies for short-range BSNs, the frequency bands below 1GHz are preferable in terms of body attenuation and low-cost transceiver implementation. However, the available bands are either crowded, as is the case in the 433MHz spectrum range, specialised (such as MICS and WMTS), or not usable on a global basis (for instance, the North American 915MHz ISM band or the European 86xMHz bands). Currently, the worldwide 2.4GHz ISM band appears to be the most promising spectrum for wireless BSNs, although it already accommodates a number of concurrent connectivity standards, such as IEEE 802.15.1 Bluetooth, IEEE 802.11b/g Wireless LANs and IEEE 802.15.4 Wireless PANs – all of which employ spread-spectrum modulation technology for improved interference robustness. For clinical BSNs, IEEE 802.15.4 is recommended, as most medical BSNs do not require data rates in excess of 200kbit/s. IEEE 802.15.4 is also the basis of the ZigBee standard, which enables interoperability throughout all communi-

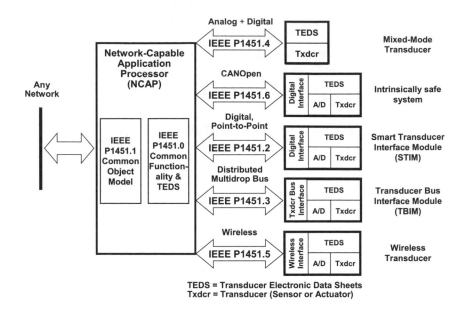

Figure 5.15 The IEEE P1451 family of smart transducer interfaces [40].

cation stack layers and manages even complex star-mesh hybrid network topologies. In comparison, IEEE 802.15.1 Bluetooth exhibits less flexible networking concepts, limited usability for uninterrupted real-time data transfers, and higher average power consumption for maintaining FH synchronisation. IEEE 802.11b/g WLAN, on the other hand, offers a good energy-per-bit ratio, but at a higher complexity, larger form factor, and much higher instantaneous power drain that cannot be coped with in tiny body sensors.

In the not-too-distant future, UWB-modulated systems such as IEEE 802.15.4a low-rate WPANs will provide sub-meter ranging capabilities or even hundreds of Mbit/s throughput (IEEE P802.15.3a), suitable for the transmission of ambient information collected by video cameras and microphones. However, UWB standards and UWB chip sets are still under development, and their usability for BSNs that require days of operation from small power sources and acceptable body attenuation figures has to be proven first.

We have used the wireless node platform AquisGrain to assess the feasibility of 2.4GHz IEEE 802.15.4-based BSN. Whereas the effective communication range and link robustness are strongly affected by the presence of a human body between body sensor nodes, the performance of the BSN remains acceptable within a range of 5 meters around the patient. Additionally, appropriate channel management schemes can cater for a grateful coexistence between IEEE 802.15.4 and the rest of technologies that operate in the 2.4GHz ISM band. In Appendices A and B of this book, a detailed architectural and programming guide of the BSN development kit will be provided.

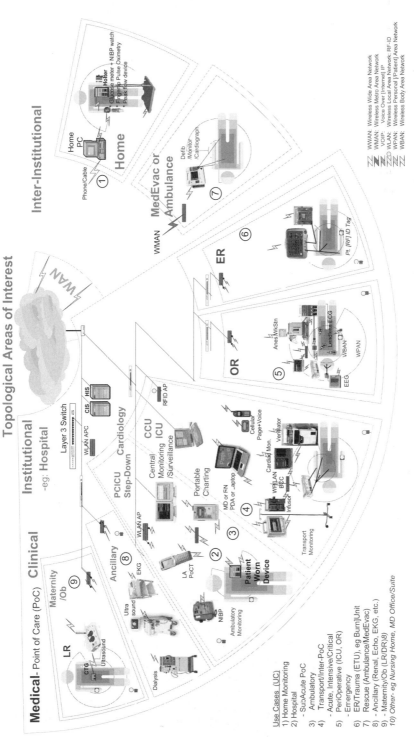

Figure 5.16 Scope of IEEE P1073 RF wireless technologies working group [39].

References

1. ISO/IEC 7498-1, ISO/IEC international standard, Information technology - open systems interconnection - basic reference model: the basic model, 2nd edition, http://standards.iso.org/ittf/PubliclyAvailableStandards/s020269_ISO_IEC_7498-1_1994(E).zip, 1994.
2. Philips Medical Systems. Striving for cableless monitoring. In: Ragil C (eds), Philips Medical Perspective Magazine 2005; 8:24-25.
3. BASUMA project, http://www.basuma.de/
4. MobiHealth project, http://www.mobihealth.org/
5. HealthService24 project, http://www.healthservice24.com/
6. Lo BPL, Yang GZ. Key technical challenges and current implementations of body sensor networks. In: Proceedings of the Second International Workshop on Wearable and Implantable Body Sensor Networks, London, UK, 2005; 1-5.
7. Anliker U, Ward JA, Lukowicz P, Tröster G, Dolveck F, Baer M, *et al.* AMON: a wearable multiparameter medical monitoring and alert system, IEEE Transactions on Information Technology in Biomedicine 2004; 8(4):415-427.
8. Malan D, Fulford-Jones T, Welsh M, Moulton S. Codeblue: an ad hoc sensor network infrastructure for emergency medical care. In: Proceedings of the First International Workshop on Wearable and Implantable Body Sensor Networks, London, UK, 2004; 55-58.
9. MyHeart project, http://www.hitech-projects.com/euprojects/myheart/
10. Jovanov E, Milenkovic A, Otto C, de Groen PC. A wireless body area network of intelligent motion sensors for computer assisted physical rehabilitation. Journal of Neuroengineering and Rehabilitation 2005; 2(1):6.
11. Eklund JM, Hansen TR, Sprinkle J, Sastry S. Information technology for assisted living at home: building a wireless infrastructure for assisted living. In: Proceedings of the Twenty-Seventh Annual International Conference of the IEEE Engineering in Medicine and Biology Society, Shanghai, 2005.
12. Stanford V. Using pervasive computing to deliver elder care. IEEE Pervasive Computing 2002; 1(1):10-13.
13. Wireless connectivity spurs sense and simplicity. Philips Research Password Magazine 2005; 22:20-23.
14. Elter P, Stork W, Müller-Glaser KD, Lutter N. Noninvasive and nonocclusive determination of blood pressure using laser Doppler flowmetry. In: Proceedings of Specialty Fiber Optics for Medical Applications as part of Photonics (West 99 / BIOS 99), San Jose, USA, SPIE 1999; 3596:188-196.
15. Baldus H, Klabunde K, Müsch G. Reliable set-up of medical body-sensor networks. In: Proceedings of the First European Workshop on Wireless Sensor Networks, Berlin, Germany, 2004; Springer LNCS 2920:353-363.
16. Lorincz K, Welsh M. MoteTrack: a robust, decentralized approach to RF-based location tracking. In: Proceedings of the First International Workshop on Location- and Context-Awareness, Oberpfaffenhofen, Germany, 2005; Springer LNCS 3479:63-82.
17. Philips Research. Philips demonstrates new personal healthcare techniques, Press release, http://www.research.philips.com/newscenter/archive/2005/050623-aachen-healthcare.html, June 2005.

18. European Radiocommunications Office, http://www.ero.dk/

19. Federal Communication Commission, http://www.fcc.gov/

20. ERC/REC 70-03, European Radiocommunications Office. ERC recommendation related to the use of short range devices (SRD), http://www.ero.dk/documentation/docs/doc98/official/pdf/REC7003E.PDF, November 2005.

21. Medical implant communications, http://wireless.fcc.gov/services/personal/medicalimplant

22. Wireless medical telemetry service, http://wireless.fcc.gov/services/personal/medtelemetry

23. IEEE 802.15.1™, IEEE standard for information technology – Telecommunications and information exchange between systems – Local and metropolitan area networks – Specific requirements – Part 15.1: wireless medium access control and physical layer specifications for wireless personal area networks, http://standards.ieee.org/getieee802/download/802.15.1-2002.pdf, 2002.

24. IEEE P802.15.3™, Project Authorization Request (PAR), http://grouper.ieee.org/board/nescom/802-15-3.pdf, February 2000.

25. IEEE P802.15.3™, Draft IEEE standard for information technology – Telecommunications and information exchange between systems – Local and metropolitan area networks – Specific requirements – Part 15.3: wireless medium access control and physical layer specifications for high-rate wireless personal area networks, http://standards.ieee.org/getieee802/download/802.15.3-2003.pdf, 2003.

26. IEEE 802.15™ WPAN high rate alternative PHY task group 3a, http://www.ieee802.org/15/pub/TG3a.html

27. IEEE 802.15.4™, IEEE standard for information technology – Telecommunications and information exchange between systems – Local and metropolitan area networks – Specific requirements – Part 15.4: wireless medium access control and physical layer specifications for low-rate wireless personal area networks, http://standards.ieee.org/getieee802/download/802.15.4-2003.pdf, 2003.

28. IEEE 802.15.4b™/D2, Draft revision for IEEE standard for information technology – Telecommunications and information exchange between systems – Local and metropolitan area networks – Specific requirements – Part 15.4b: wireless medium access control and physical layer specifications for low-rate wireless personal area networks. 2005.

29. IEEE 802.15™ WPAN low rate alternative PHY task group 4a, http://www.ieee802.org/15/pub/TG4a.html

30. ZigBee specification version 1.0. ZigBee Alliance, June 2005.

31. Hously R, Whiting D, Ferguson N. Counter with CBC-MAC (CCM), June 2002, http://csrc.nist.gov/encryption/modes/proposedmodes/

32. Neirynck D, Williams C, Nix AR, Beach MA. Wideband channel characterisation for body and personal area networks. In: Proceedings of the First International Workshop on Wearable and Implantable Body Sensor Networks, London, UK, 2004; 41-43.

33. IEEE 802.11b™, IEEE standard for information technology – Telecommunications and information exchange between systems – Local and metropolitan area networks – Specific requirements – Part 11: wireless LAN medium access con-

trol and physical layer specifications, http://standards.ieee.org/getieee802/download/802.11b-1999.pdf, 1999.

34. Golmie N, Cypher D, Rebala O. Performance analysis of low rate wireless technologies for medical applications. Computer Communications 2005; 28(10):1255-1275.

35. Health Level Seven (HL7), http://www.hl7.org/

36. IEEE P1073, IEEE standards on point-of-care medical device communication, http://www.ieee1073.org/

37. Schrenker R, Cooper T. Building the foundation for medical device plug-and-play interoperability. Medical Electronics Manufacturing, Spring 2001; 10-16

38. CEN ENV 13734, 2000, Health informatics – Vital signs information representation, Technical committee for medical informatics (TC251) of the European Committee for Standardisation (CEN).

39. ISO/IEEE 11073-00101, Health informatics – Point-of-care medical device communication – Technical report – Guidelines for the use of RF wireless technologies, http://www.ieee1073.org/standards/11073-00101/11073-00101.html, November 2005.

40. IEEE P1451.5, Wireless transducer interface for sensors and actuators IEEE 1451 working group, http://grouper.ieee.org/groups/1451/5/

Energy Scavenging

Eric Yeatman and Paul Mitcheson

6.1 Introduction

As we have seen in previous chapters, the increasing miniaturisation and cost reduction of sensors, circuits and wireless communication components is creating new possibilities for networks of wireless sensors, in wearable and other applications. However, for sensors to be wireless, or untethered, requires not only wireless communication to and from the nodes, but also wireless powering. Batteries, of course, provide this capability in the great majority of portable electronic devices, and thus are the obvious solution also for wireless sensor node applications. However, their need for replacement or recharging introduces a cost and convenience penalty which is already undesirable in larger devices, and is likely to become unacceptable for sensor nodes as their ubiquity grows. As an alternative, sources which scavenge energy from the environment are therefore highly desirable. With the decreasing power demands for sensing, processing, and wireless communication for BSNs due to improved electronic design and miniaturisation, alternative power sources based on energy scavenging become increasingly realistic.

Where batteries can power a sensor node for its whole expected lifetime without maintenance and without dominating the node cost and weight, the use of existing battery technology is likely to remain the favoured solution in most cases. However, even in such cases energy scavenging methods can have advantages to offer. The materials required in batteries are often toxic or environmentally unfriendly, adding to the burden of both biocompatibility for implanted use and end-of-life disposal. Where a lifetime beyond what a battery can provide is needed, clearly the "eternal" nature of the scavenging supply becomes particularly favourable.

Energy scavenging for the supply of wireless electronics is a relatively young research field. In this chapter, we will review the current state-of-the-art and its future trends after first discussing the likely energy requirements of BSN nodes and the capabilities of batteries. Detailed discussion of implementation will be focused on the general issues of inertial energy scavenging and our recent work in the field.

It should be noted that this chapter is not intended to be a comprehensive survey; for such a purpose, the works of Starner and Paradiso [1], Roundy, Wright and Rabaey [2], and Mitcheson [3] are recommended.

6.1.1 Sensor Node Power Requirements

BSN nodes will require power for three main functions: the sensor itself, any signal conditioning or data processing circuitry, and the wireless data link. For all of these functions, the power requirements depend strongly on the nature of the measurement. For wearable applications, sensor nodes will usually be monitoring environmental conditions or biological functions. The data requirements of many such sensors will be modest, since both the resolution and the required update rate are low. Some examples [4] are summarized in Table 6.1.

Table 6.1 Body sensor data rate requirements.

Signal	Depth	Rate	Data Rate
Heart rate	8 bits	10/min	80 bits/min
Blood pressure	16 bits	1/min	32 bits/min
Temperature	16 bits	1/min	16 bits/min
Blood oxygen	16 bits	1/min	16 bits/min

It is clear that these data rates are negligible (around 1bit/s or less), which implies both a very low clock rate on the circuit, and low transmission power for the wireless uplink.

Ultra-low power wireless communications is a major field in its own right, and has been discussed in detail in Chapter 4. Currently established specifications such as Bluetooth have a power demand well above what is likely to be achievable from energy scavengers of reasonable size. However, they are also over-specified for many BSN applications. Ultimate power limits depend strongly on maximum antenna size, and this has been modelled for a 1m, 100kbit/s link, based on a Colpitts oscillator transmitter in which the antenna coil serves as the inductor in the L-C tank circuit [5, 6]. The results are shown in Figure 6.1, where optimum carrier frequencies are indicated, and for antenna radii of a few *mm*, the required bias currents are in the 4–6μA range. Since the minimum rail voltage for such a circuit is about 1V, this corresponds to 4–6μW. Sub-microwatt transmitter powers are then clearly feasible if a reduced duty cycle is used, and very low duty cycle operation would be possible with the sensor types given in Table 6.1.

Another important aspect of the power usage is the sensors themselves. Both temperature and pressure sensing can be done by measuring the voltage drop of a current through a resistor. In principle, the power needs only to be sufficient to overcome thermal noise ($\approx 10^{-20}$W/Hz at room temperature), and so can be negligible for the very low bandwidths of the application (as low as 1Hz). To reach such theoretical limits would be impractical because of the need for low noise filtering, but the calculation indicates that the sensor elements in many cases need not make a significant contribution to power consumption compared to the other circuitry.

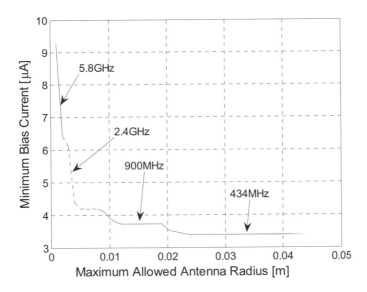

Figure 6.1 Minimum bias current *vs* antenna size for 100kbit/s transmission over 1m, from [6].

Finally, the interface or signal conditioning electronics will also impose power loading. The most straightforward requirement will be for A-D conversion; ADC's have been reported with power consumption levels of 1µW [7], and since this is at sample rates (4ksps) above our requirements, significantly sub-microwatt levels should be achievable. Therefore, total power levels as low as 1µW may well be sufficient for realistic future BSN nodes.

6.1.2 Batteries and Fuel Cells for Sensor Nodes

As stated above, batteries are currently used for powering most wireless devices. Where the power requirements are modest, primary (*i.e.* non-rechargeable) batteries are usually chosen for their higher energy densities, lower leakage rates and low (initial) cost. For BSN applications, a battery lifetime of at least a year will be desirable in many instances. From our previous analysis, a lifetime of one year with a few µW as a likely power requirement corresponds to 32J per µW of average power. Lithium based primary batteries typically provide 1400–3600J/cc [8], so in principle, a lifetime of several years is achievable for a battery well below 1 cc. Thus, although the finite lifetime remains a disadvantage and other issues (such as operating temperature range and toxicity) may reduce their practicality for BSN applications, primary batteries remain a very attractive source for sensor nodes.

Exhaustible sources using fuel are also under investigation for small portable electronics, although mainly for higher power levels. The motivation is the very high specific energy of hydrocarbon fuels, *e.g.*, 17.6kJ/cc for methanol [9]. Converting this energy to electrical form in the conventional way, *i.e.* using a heat engine, is difficult on a micro-scale because of the need to maintain large temperature differences. However, micro-engineered heat engines for this purpose are being investigated [10]. Fuel cells, however, are an attractive alternative, as they require much lower temperatures and have no moving parts. A popular variant for miniaturisation is the direct methanol fuel cell [11]. In these devices, the methanol reacts electrochemically with water at the anode, producing free electrons and protons, the latter being oxidised to water at the cathode after passing through a polymer membrane. Power levels reported were as high as $47mW/cm^2$.

Fuel cells may also provide an attractive type of inexhaustible, energy scavenging source for implantable applications. This can be achieved by using bodily fluids as the fuel source, such as glucose and dissolved oxygen in blood [12]. Power levels are promising, but operating lifetimes are still low.

6.1.3 Ambient Energy Sources

We can move away from finite energy sources by scavenging from the energy types present in the node's environment. There are a variety of such potential sources, and all have been investigated to some degree for energy scavenging applications. The main categories include motion and vibration, air flow, temperature differences, ambient electromagnetic fields and light and infra-red radiation. In the latter case, solar cells provide an excellent solution. This is a relatively mature technology, inexpensive and highly compatible with electronics, and the available power levels can be up to mW per cm^2. However, the drawback is that the sensor must be in a well lit location, correctly oriented and free from obstructions. This creates severe limitations for a BSN application.

Gathering radio frequency radiation suffers much less from these geometric limitations. In the VHF and UHF bands [13], for which miniature antennas can operate with reasonable efficiency, field strengths are from about 10^{-2} to $10^3 V/m$. We can approximate the power density crudely as E^2/Z_0, where $Z_0 = 377\Omega$ is the impedance of free space. For 10 or $1V/m$, for example, this gives 26 or $0.26\mu W/cm^2$. A few V/m thus probably represents the minimum radiation level needed for successful energy scavenging. However, even typical urban environments do not show these levels except in special areas such as in the vicinity of cellular base stations [13]. This suggests that radio frequency scavenging is an approach with limited applicability.

Scavenging thermal energy depends on the presence of temperature differences, for example between the surface of the body and the ambient. The power available is modest; a micro-engineered device reported below $1\mu W/cm^2$ for a ΔT of 10K [14]. In BSN applications, temperature differences of more than a few K are not likely to be available.

The use of air flow is promising for higher power levels, although with correspondingly higher device size; a micro-engineered axial flow turbine with a radius of 6mm has been reported producing 1mW for an air flow of 30l/min [15]. Further miniaturisation may make a breath-powered device feasible.

Scavenging power from vibration or body motion is perhaps the most promising approach for BSNs, and is being pursued by an increasing number of research groups. The main advantages of this approach are that devices based on motion scavenging can function both on and in the body, and are well suited to relatively efficient transduction techniques. It does not require exotic materials and can work in any orientation. We can categorise motion scavenging devices as those that depend on the relative motion between two structures, and those that depend only on the absolute motion of the single structure to which the device is attached. The former can offer substantially higher levels of specific power, but will tend to be larger and have a very limited number of applicable locations. Heel strike devices, which are installed in the shoe and depend on the force between the landing foot and the ground, are the most investigated of these [16]. We can call the latter inertial devices. These are very flexible as regards size and location, and will be the main focus of the rest of the chapter.

6.2 Architectures for Inertial Energy Scavenging

6.2.1 Energy Extraction Mechanisms for Inertial Generators

The basic operating principle of inertial micro-generators can be described with reference to the generic architecture shown in Figure 6.2. The inertia of a proof mass m, which is suspended on a spring suspension with spring constant k, causes the mass to move relative to the generator frame with relative displacement $z(t)$ when the frame, with displacement $y(t)$, experiences acceleration. The maximum and minimum values of $z(t)$ are $\pm Z_l$, as imposed by the finite size of the generator. Energy is converted when work is done against the damping force $f(\dot{z})$, which opposes the relative motion of the proof mass and the frame. As discussed above, inertial generators can be used when only one suitable attachment point is available, as they depend on the absolute motion of the frame rather than relative motion between two anchor points. For micro-generators of the size scale of interest for BSN applications, it can normally be assumed that the loading of the "host" structure by the generator is too small to affect the host's motion. This simplifies the analysis, and means that the available power is effectively infinite, in the sense that it is not a limiting factor on the achievable output of the generator.

In order to generate useful power, the damper must be an implementation of a suitable mechanical to electrical transduction mechanism. Three such mechanisms have been extensively investigated for this application: electromagnetic, electrostatic, and piezoelectric.

Rotating electromagnetic generators have long been in common use, from power levels of a few watts to several hundred megawatts. It is possible to implement the damper of a micro-generator by using the same principle, *i.e.* that described by Faraday's law of induction. This is illustrated in Figure 6.3, where a change of magnetic flux linkage with a coil induces a voltage $v(t)$ in the coil, driving a current $i(t)$ in the circuit. The combined force $f(t)$ on the moving charges in the magnetic field acts to oppose the relative motion which is causing the change in flux linkage, as described by Lenz's law. The mechanical work done against the opposing force is converted to heat in the resistance (external load) of the circuit, and to stored energy in the magnetic field associated with the circuit inductance.

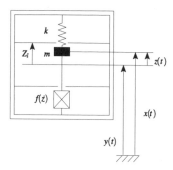

Figure 6.2 Generic architecture of inertial micro-generators.

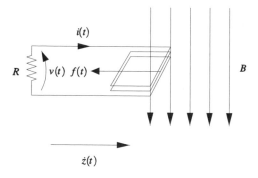

Figure 6.3 Principle of operation of the electromagnetic transducer.

A number of groups have reported micro-generators based on electromagnetic energy scavenging. In a recent work by Glynne-Jones *et al* [17], for example, devices using a coil moving relative to one or two pairs of permanent magnets are described. Although power levels above 100μW are reported, the excitation frequencies (100s of Hz) are much higher than can be expected in BSN applications. A key difficulty is caused by the generated voltages being proportional to the rate of change of flux. Since the achievable flux difference over the range of travel of the coil is very limited in these small geometries, rapid motion is needed to generate significant voltage. At low frequencies, the motion is too slow, so that not only are the generated power levels poor, but the voltages are too low for straightforward rectification.

The second transduction method, electrostatic, involves the use of the force between opposite charges on a pair of electrodes which move relative to each other (*i.e.* one fixed to the frame, and one to the proof mass). Typically, two possible modes of operation are identified: constant charge, and constant voltage. The first involves moving a fixed amount of electric charge through an electric field and thus increases the electrical potential of that charge, as illustrated on the left side of Figure 6.4. For a parallel plate structure with a variable separation and constant overlap, and with a negligible fringing field, the field strength is proportional to the (constant) charge and thus the energy density of the electric field is independent of plate separation. As the electrode separation increases, additional electrical potential energy is stored in the increased volume of the electric field. Alternatively, if the plates are moved relative to each other with a sliding motion at a constant separation, mechanical work is done against the fringing field and there is an increase in stored electrical energy because the electric field strength increases with the reduction in plate overlap. The energy density of the field (proportional to the square of field strength) increases faster than the volume of the field decreases.

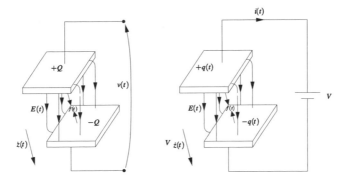

Figure 6.4 Principle of operation of the electrostatic transducer.

The other extreme of operation is constant voltage, illustrated on the right hand side of Figure 6.4. Moving the relative positions of the plates (either due to sliding or normal movement) changes the capacitance between the electrodes under a constant voltage. If the plate separation is increased with a fixed overlap, the electric field strength between the plates falls, causing charge to be pushed off the plates into an external circuit as a current flow $i(t)$. If the plates are moved with constant separation and changing overlap, the field strength stays constant, but current is again forced to flow into the source because the volume of the field decreases. In both cases, the mechanical work done is converted into additional electrical potential energy as an increased charge in the voltage source.

Because of practical implementation constraints, such as non-zero conductance (in the constant charge case) and non-ideal voltage sources (in the constant voltage case), real electrostatic transducers work somewhere between these two extremes, although in many cases very close to one of them, and both types have been reported in the literature for implementations of micro-generators. For constant charge operation, variable gap motion gives a constant force, while for constant voltage devices, a constant force is provided by variable overlap motion. As will be discussed further below, to obtain the highest output power the transduction force should have the maximum value, throughout the proof mass displacement, that does not prevent this displacement. Such power maximisation is not likely to be achieved if the applied force is strongly position-dependent. It should also be noted that electrostatic transducers, unlike electromagnetic ones, normally need the application of an initial "priming" voltage to generate the damping force, and this represents an energy "cost" in the complete cycle. While the priming energy can in principle be small compared to the extracted energy, it does add to the device complexity. Electret designs, employing a buried fixed charge to eliminate the need for cyclic precharging, have been investigated [18].

Both variable overlap and variable gap devices have been reported in the literature. The latter, particularly if micro-engineered, are usually not simple parallel plates, but use the so-called "comb-drive" structure of inter-digitated electrodes, as this allows the two electrodes to be defined in the same level on-chip. Such structures are commonly used in MEMS technology for both electrostatic sensing and actuation. A key difficulty in energy scavenging appears to be in achieving the combination of high capacitance and substantial displacement that is needed to maximise power output. High capacitance values are useful as they allow lower voltages to be used for the same level of force.

Finally, the piezoelectric effect, explained in more detail in [19], is a phenomenon whereby a strain in a material produces an electric field across that material and conversely an applied electric field can produce a mechanical strain. The first of these modes can be used to realise micro-generators. When the material is strained, some of the mechanical work done on the device is stored as elastic strain energy, and some in the electric field brought about by the space charge. Only a small class of materials exhibits strong piezoelectric effects, and of these the most commonly exploited is the ceramic $PbZr_xTi_{(1-x)}O_3$, or *Lead Zirconate Titanate* (PZT). This can be machined as a conventional powder-based ceramic into monolithic pieces, or deposited as a thin film for micro-engineered devices.

Piezoelectric devices offer significant advantages, in particular that relatively high voltages can be obtained with modest strains, and no priming is needed. However, the need for integration of a specialised material, and its associated electrodes, adds significantly to the challenge of fabrication, particularly for very small devices. Furthermore, the geometric possibilities are limited: the material has low maximum strain, so that a high leverage factor is needed to get large proof mass displacement. Most reported devices have used a layered cantilever structure with the proof mass at the free end.

In principle, piezoelectric devices are attractive for BSN applications because they do not depend on rapid motion to achieve substantial voltages. However, there may be a practical limitation in that the piezoelectric material typically has some leakage conductance, which becomes a parasitic path for the generated power of increasing significance as the operating frequency drops.

These transduction methods provide a useful way of classifying devices of inertial energy scavenging. Another useful distinction, particularly for the BSN application regime, is between devices that are mechanically resonant and those that are not. Resonance allows an internal displacement amplitude greater than the source motion amplitude to be achieved, and this can be useful when the source amplitude is slight, as it may well be for high frequency (*e.g.* machine) vibration. However, human body motion amplitude is likely to be greater in most instances than the dimensions of BSN nodes. Body motion also has a complex and widely varying spectral character, which to be effectively exploited by a resonant device is likely to need dynamic tuning of the device's resonant frequency, a capability not yet reported.

Most reported miniature inertial energy scavengers have been resonant; this is partially because in MEMS and other small implementations, support of moving parts by flexure suspensions is more practical than other options such as sliding or rolling bearings. Since the proof mass is thus a mass on a spring, it is inherently a resonant structure. However, it is possible to reduce the suspension stiffness to such a degree that the proof mass is effectively freely moving in the desired direction. On this basis, an alternative, non-resonant device has been described which operates in a non-linear fashion, the proof mass moving rapidly between its end-stops at the peak of the applied acceleration. This device can be called a *parametric generator*, and in the following section we compare its ultimate performance, along with the more widely studied resonant types.

6.2.2 Performance Limits

A comprehensive analytical framework for inertial energy scavengers was recently reported by the present authors and co-workers [20]. This analysis has allowed the different architectures to be compared quantitatively, and has derived the achievable power levels and their dependence on both source and device characteristics. Key practical constraints were also analysed. The results of that study are summarised here.

Two resonant topologies and one parametric generator topology were considered. Of the resonant type, one example is damped by a force which is proportional to velocity, the *Velocity-Damped Resonant Generator* (VDRG), and the other is damped by a constant force, the *Coulomb-Damped Resonant Generator* (CDRG). Of the non-resonant, non-linear generators, only the *Coulomb-Force Parametric-Generator* (CFPG) is considered here, as the velocity-damped parametric generator was found to be ineffective. Variations of VDRGs and CDRGs have been reported previously in the literature. Broadly speaking, the electromagnetic and piezoelectric devices correspond to VDRGs, and the electrostatic devices correspond to CDRGs. In this analysis, the resonant generators were considered to operate in modes in which the proof mass does not strike the end-stop limits, *i.e.* $-Z_l < z(t) < Z_l$, and thus the only forces which act on the mass are the inertial, spring and damping forces, and gravity.

The source motion was assumed to be harmonic, with amplitude Y_0 and frequency ω, from which the maximum acceleration a_{max} can be easily derived as $\omega^2 Y_0$. The fundamental parameters determining the generator output are its proof mass m, resonant frequency (if any) ω_n, and the maximum internal displacement Z_l. From very basic considerations we can derive a maximum power for any energy scavenger driven by harmonic source motion. The damping force by which the energy is extracted cannot exceed the inertial force on the proof mass, ma_{max}, otherwise the mass will not move. If energy is extracted in both directions, and taking the internal motion range as being $2Z_l$, we derive a total energy per cycle of $4Z_lma_{max} = 4Z_lm\,\omega^2Y_0$. To convert this to power is simply a matter of dividing by the excitation period $2\pi/\omega$, giving a maximum power:

$$P_{max} = 2Y_0Z_l\omega^3m/\pi \tag{6.1}$$

If the proof mass motion is also harmonic, as in a resonant device, the maximum power is in fact somewhat less than this, since the acceleration is not a_{max} for the whole journey and so the transduction force must be reduced accordingly. But (6.1) does provide us, on the basis of fundamental considerations, an upper bound on the power of an inertial energy scavenger of any architecture, construction, transduction mechanism or operating mode. It shows the linear dependence on mass and on travel range, and the very strong dependence on frequency, indicating the serious challenge of achieving useful power levels in the low frequency environment of BSNs. In analysis, it was found that for idealised cases of the three architectures considered, the optimal output power can always be derived as a function of the two dimensionless parameters Z_l/Y_0 and ω/ω_n, and can be normalised to a characteristic power $Y_0^2\omega^3m$.

Analysis of the output power of velocity damped generators is a matter of integrating the product of the damping force and the incremental displacement and averaging this over a cycle. Then the optimum power can be found by choosing the damping coefficient to maximise this value. However, if resonant motion is assumed without regard to travel limits, a derivation is obtained which implies infinite power at resonance, although a corresponding infinite internal displacement is implied. A realistic assessment requires that the damping force be optimised only up to the limit imposed by the maximum travel range. Thus, the achievable power of an ideal VDRG takes two forms; firstly, if the damping can be optimised without the displacement constraint being breached:

$$P_{max} = \frac{\omega_c^2Y_0^2\omega^3m}{\sqrt{1-2\omega_c^2+\omega_c^4}} \tag{6.2}$$

and secondly, if the damping is constrained by this limit:

$$P_{max\,c2} = Y_0^2\omega^3m\frac{1}{2\omega_c^2}\left(\frac{Z_l}{Y_0}\right)\sqrt{\omega_c^4\left(\frac{Y_0}{Z_l}\right)^2-(1-\omega_c^2)^2} \tag{6.3}$$

In each case ω_c is the normalised frequency ω/ω_n. It can easily be shown that for operation at resonance ($\omega_c = 1$), (6.3) reduces to:

$$P_{res} = \frac{1}{2}Y_0Z_l\omega^3m \tag{6.4}$$

As anticipated, this is just less than the ultimate limit given by (6.1); a factor $\pi/4$ less in fact.

The Coulomb damped devices do not form linear systems, because the damping force is discontinuous at the boundaries (where the direction changes), and so analytical solutions are not as straightforward to obtain. Nevertheless, closed form solutions to the equations of motion for the CDRG do exist, from which the optimal damping coefficients, and the achievable power levels, can be derived. Just as for the VDRG, the maximum power depends on whether or not the optimal damping is limited by the internal displacement constraint. If not:

$$P_{max} = \frac{\sqrt{2}}{\pi} Y_0^2 \omega^3 m \frac{\omega_c^3}{|(1-\omega_c^2)U|} \left[\frac{1}{(1-\omega_c^2)^2} - \frac{U}{(1-\omega_c^2)} \right]^{\frac{1}{2}} \tag{6.5}$$

although for $\omega_c < 0.72$ this is not valid because the calculated optimal force results in sticking in the motion. For displacement constrained operation:

$$P_{max^{cz}} = \frac{2\omega_c Y_0^2 \omega^3 m}{\pi |U|} \left(\frac{Z_l}{Y_0} \right) \sqrt{ \frac{1}{(1-\omega_c^2)^2} - \frac{1}{\omega_c^4} \left(\frac{Z_l}{Y_0} \right)^2 } \tag{6.6}$$

In both cases the function U is defined as:

$$U = \frac{\sin\left(\dfrac{\pi}{\omega_c} \right)}{\left[1 + \cos\left(\dfrac{\pi}{\omega_c} \right) \right]} \tag{6.7}$$

It can easily be shown that at resonance, (6.6) reduces to (6.4), *i.e.* the optimum power of the CDRG and VDRG are the same if operated at resonance.

The analysis of the CFPG is essentially the same as that used to derive (6.1); the Coulomb (electrostatic) force is constant for the whole travel distance, and so the energy per transit is just the applied force times the travel range. However, a correction is needed to (6.1) because the force applied, in the case of harmonic source motion, cannot be equal to a_{max} since this acceleration is reached only instantaneously at the extremes of the frame displacement. Thus we reduce the damping force to βa_{max}, where β is a dimensionless coefficient, giving:

$$P_{max} = \frac{2\beta}{\pi} Y_0 Z_0 \omega^3 m \tag{6.8}$$

In this general formulation, the displacement limit of the device, Z_l, has been replaced by the actual internal motion amplitude Z_0. Thus, determination of the output power requires not only the optimal value of β, but also the corresponding travel range Z_0, to be determined. For large source displacement amplitudes, however, it can be shown that the optimal β value is that which just allows the full travel range to be traversed, so that $Z_0 = Z_l$. Specifically, this proves to be the case for $Z_l < 0.566Y_0$, *i.e.* the source motion amplitude is more than double the internal displacement limit. This will almost certainly be the case for wearable or implanted devices excited by body or limb motion. It may not be the case for implanted devices driven by cardiac motion.

Having derived expressions for the achievable power levels of the three main device architectures, we can now compare them and determine which is the most effective for a given operating regime. Figure 6.5 shows the result, indicating the operating regions where each architecture is superior and what the maximum power level is, normalised to $Y_0^2\omega^3 m$.

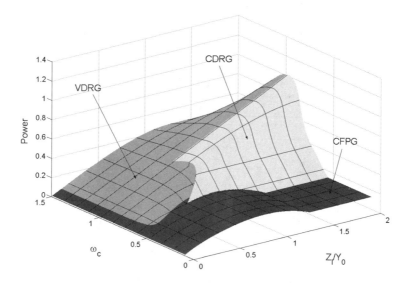

Figure 6.5 Comparison of inertial energy scavenging architectures, with normalised maximum power output. From [20].

Several general conclusions can be drawn from Figure 6.5. For large devices or low source amplitudes ($Z_l/Y_0 > 0.1$), the resonant devices are superior, except where the frequency of operation is more than 2 times below the achievable resonant frequency, in which case the parametric generator is preferred. The CFPG is superior for all cases where the device size is well below the source motion amplitude. As mentioned above, this is likely to be the case for many BSN applications. Furthermore, the CFPG, being non-resonant, can operate effectively over a wide range of source frequencies (as would be expected with BSN) without the need for dynamic tuning. For these reasons, we have investigated MEMS implementations of CFPG devices excited at low frequency, as described in detail in Section 6.3.

All of the analysis above has been looking at harmonic source motion. Clearly body motion is of complex and varying spectral form, and for that reason analysis of the output of inertial energy scavengers with realistic body motion excitation has been carried out [21]. Motion waveforms were captured for three orientation axes, at each of a number of body locations, using accelerometers, and the power output of the various scavenger architectures, for a range of sizes, were simulated and compared using these waveforms. The results are shown in Figure 6.6. As anticipated, the CFPG devices are superior for small devices, particularly for lower body locations where the displacements were greater.

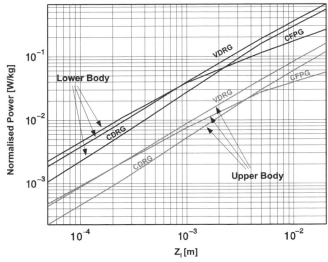

Figure 6.6 Comparison of architecture performance for generators mounted on the upper and lower body. Output power is normalised by the value of proof mass m. After [21].

6.3 Fabrication and Testing

6.3.1 Device Fabrication and Structure

Most reported micro-scale inertial energy scavengers have been mechanically resonant devices. As discussed above, these are not well suited to the low frequencies of human powered applications, and so we have developed a new class of device, the parametric generator [20, 22, 23]. Here we describe its construction and operating principles.

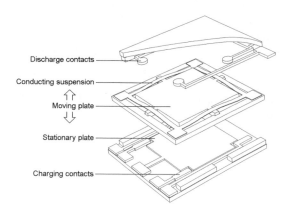

Figure 6.7 Exploded view of the generator construction. From [22].

An exploded view of the device structure is shown in Figure 6.7, with the phases of operation illustrated in Figure 6.8. The structure consists of a moving plate attached to a frame by a low stiffness suspension, a bottom plate containing the counter-electrode and charging studs, and a top plate with the discharge contacts. The operation cycle proceeds as follows:

- At the start of a generation cycle, the capacitor is at its maximum capacitance position, *i.e.* minimum separation (*idle phase*).
- The capacitor is pre-charged to a relatively low voltage which will give the optimal value of β for the current operating conditions (pre-charging or *priming phase*).
- The generator frame is accelerated by the input motion. The proof mass moves along with the frame (*wait phase*) until the magnitude of the frame acceleration is sufficient for the inertial force on the proof-mass to overcome the electrostatic force of attraction between the plates, at which point the proof-mass separates from the frame of the generator and starts to move relative to it. At the point of separation the electrical contact between the moving plate and the charging circuit is broken.
- The relative movement proceeds, and increases the volume of the electric field between the capacitor plates as they separate. Because the charge on the plates remains constant, the energy density of the electric field remains constant and so the electrical potential energy stored increases with the volume of field (*flight phase*).
- The moving plate and proof-mass slow down relative to the generator frame as they approach maximum plate separation. Under optimal conditions for electrical energy generation, the relative velocity tends to zero as the maximum displacement is reached.

- Whilst the plates are separating, the voltage across them increases in proportion to the separation (because the electric field strength is constant).
- The variable capacitor, now at its lowest capacitance and highest voltage, is discharged through power conversion circuitry and the energy is available to drive a load (*conversion phase*).

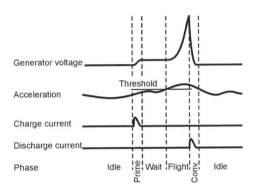

Figure 6.8 Phases of operation of the CFPG.

The device was fabricated using a three-wafer construction. The central wafer contains a silicon proof mass, forming one plate of the variable capacitor, along with a silicon frame and a polyimide suspension, metalised for electrical contact. The proof mass is about 0.12g, and measures ≈ 11×11mm×0.4mm thick. It is separated from the frame by *Deep Reactive Ion Etching* (DRIE), through the whole wafer thickness, after patterning of the suspension. Polyimide is chosen to give the required very low suspension stiffness, as discussed above.

The bottom wafer is glass, to minimise the parasitic capacitance. It includes the fixed electrode of the variable capacitor itself, and the charging studs and spacers for the moving plate and middle wafer, the studs being deposited by electroplating. These set the minimum gap at about 6μm, giving a theoretical starting capacitance of ≈180pF. The measured (static) starting capacitance was ≈150pF, the difference being attributed to wafer bow. The top wafer is also glass, and has studs for discharge. Spacer studs 300μm thick, fabricated from SU8 polymer on the top and bottom wafers, set the layer separation, and thus the proof mass travel distance. The minimum (discharge position) capacitance was measured at 5.5pF. Figure 6.9 shows the completed device.

6.3.2 Device Testing

The device was tested on a low frequency shaker platform, for frequencies in the range 10–100Hz. Reproducible results were not obtained at lower frequencies; this

Figure 6.9 Prototype CFPG fabricated using silicon micromachining. From [22].

is partly because the holding force is not yet sufficient to optimize performance at these frequencies, and also because of limits on the maximum shaker displacement amplitude. Motion was monitored using a linear displacement transducer or an accelerometer, at lower and higher frequencies respectively. Although monitoring of the moving plate voltage during operation is not required in a working device, it was carried out here for diagnostic purposes. The voltage on the moving plate in relation to the acceleration of the generator frame during device operation is shown in Figure 6.10.

As the pre-charge voltage (and thus the holding force) is increased, the release point should occur later in the cycle. Experiments were carried out to verify this, and the behaviour matches the simulations well (Figure 6.11).

Depending on operating frequency and amplitude, output voltages of up to 220V were obtained, corresponding to a net generated power of 120nJ per cycle. This is well above previously reported values for MEMS electrostatic generators [2, 24], which are typically a few nJ/cycle or less.

However, the power obtained remains significantly below theoretically achievable values. We believe an important limitation in this case is the motion of the proof mass in unwanted degrees of freedom; in particular, tilting motion. This reduces the capacitance ratio, by decreasing the charging capacitance if the moving plate is not parallel to the fixed plate and does not contact all the charging studs, and by increasing the discharge capacitance. The dynamic starting capacitance, in

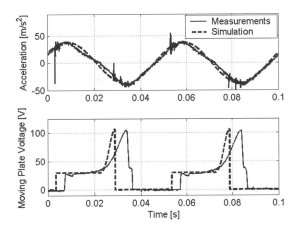

Figure 6.10 Measured acceleration and voltage of moving plate on prototype CFPG, compared to simulation results. From [22].

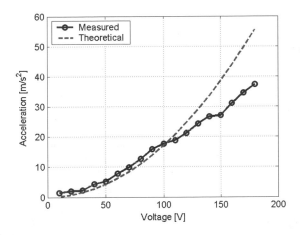

Figure 6.11 CFPG moving plate acceleration at release point *vs* pre-charge voltage. From [22].

particular, was found to deviate significantly from the static value, at only ≈ 50pF. This corresponds to a much greater effective minimum plate separation (assuming parallel plates) of about 21µm. The experimental results provide further evidence that the effective capacitance ratio during operation is below the design value. The maximum inertial force F_i is ma_{max}, and with $m = 0.12$g and a maximum acceleration a_{max} of ≈ 40m/s^2 (Figure 6.10), F_i does not go above ≈ 5mN. The electrostatic holding force is given by:

$$F_e = \frac{1}{2}V^2 \frac{C}{d_{min}}$$
                                                                      (6.9)

Taking the design values of $C = 180\text{pF}$ and minimum plate separation $d_{min} = 6\mu\text{m}$, and the applied priming voltage of 30V (Figure 6.10), we get $F_e - 13.5\text{mN}$, suggesting that the inertial force is never sufficiently strong to release the mass. With the measured effective (dynamic) capacitance of 50pF and an increased minimum plate separation, F_e falls below the maximum inertial force as expected.

Another deviation that can be seen in the experimental results is the late landing of the moving plate on the charging studs, and the slower than predicted transit towards the discharging studs. Viscous air damping provides a likely explanation for these differences.

Future designs will address these issues by better restraining motion in unwanted axes, through a modified suspension, and reducing air damping through perforation of the plates or operation in vacuum. As well as these improvements being made, the starting capacitance should be increased from its current design value, in order to reduce the priming voltage at which the optimum holding force is obtained and to reduce the impact of parasitics on the achievable capacitance ratio.

6.4 Module Design and Simulation

6.4.1 System Modelling

In Section 6.2, we examined results from the modelling of lumped element components (mass-spring-damper systems) arranged into three architectures of generator, in order to determine which architecture attains the highest power density for human powered motion. The CFPG was shown to be superior in this case and a prototype CFPG was constructed. This section discusses the modelling of a capacitive CFPG.

In order to achieve a suitable level of detail in the modelling of a CFPG, it is necessary to consider what components and subsystems, other than the variable capacitor (which provides the Coulomb damping) are required in the implementation and to consider the interactions between these subsystems. A block diagram of a constant charge CFPG system (showing both the mechanical and the required electrical systems), is shown in Figure 6.12. As can be seen from that figure, aside from the mechanical generator itself (the variable capacitor) and the circuitry which precharges and discharges the capacitor, there are a number of other subsystems required for operation of the CFPG. These are:

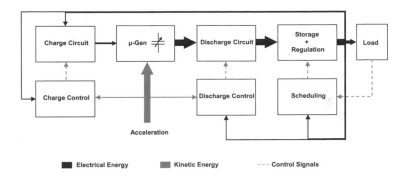

Figure 6.12 Block diagram of a CFPG, showing power flows.

- *Charge control*: It is important that the holding force of the transducer of the CFPG, in this case controlled by the voltage across a parallel plate capacitor, is set to the correct value in order to maximise the generator power density. Circuitry is required for controlling this charging. Because charging always occurs when the variable capacitor is at its minimum separation, the charging can be done through a mechanical contact on the end-stop.

- *Discharge control*: In many operating modes, maximum power is obtained from the CFPG if the moving capacitor plate travels the furthest distance possible (*i.e.* a total distance of $2Z_l$). In this operating mode the capacitor discharge can be self-synchronised with the input motion because the discharge could also occur through mechanical contacts on end-stops. However, under some circumstances, in particular for sinusoidal motion for which the value of Z_l/Y_0 is greater than 1.16, the capacitor must be discharged before it has travelled the full distance of $2Z_l$. Consequently, discharge control circuitry, which includes a controlled semiconductor switch, is required.

- *Storage and regulation*: The load electronics (such as a radio, sensor or ADC) will be designed to run off a specific voltage. If the generator is operated optimally with a changing input motion frequency or amplitude, the output voltage will be variable. Voltage regulation is therefore necessary. In addition, as was shown from Figure 6.10, the raw output of the generator without processing is unsuitable for powering a load. If the micro-generator is powered from human walking motion then there will be periods of inactivity and no generation. If the load electronics must run at times when the generator is not generating, some energy storage facility is required to provide electrical power under these circumstances.

- *Power saving*: As a power saving feature, there is potential for the load to request a value of rail voltage depending upon the required performance of the load at a given point in time. Higher performance from the load may require a higher rail voltage. This will require some interfacing between the power supply and the load.

The complete micro-generator system is clearly a mixed electro-mechanical system. Additionally, because the voltage on the moving plate capacitor is dependent upon the mechanical system (the relative position of the mass and frame), and the mechanical dynamics (in particular the force between the plates) is dependent upon the plate voltage, there is a two way interaction between the electrical and mechanical system. Therefore, the mechanical and electrical sub-systems must be modelled together in a coherent simulation. Simulink is perhaps the most obvious choice of simulation platform; however, as will be demonstrated later in this chapter, accurate semiconductor modelling (in the power electronics) is required.

PSpice [25], a SPICE implementation by OrCAD, contains an *Analogue Behavioural Modelling* (ABM) library which contains ideal mathematical functional blocks and controlled electrical sources. These blocks can be used to realise mathematical functions including differential equations.

The mechanical system of the CFPG can built up in simulation starting from the differential equation of motion of the proof-mass in the CDRG:

$$m\ddot{z} = -kz - F.\mathrm{sgn}(\dot{z}) - m\ddot{y} \qquad (6.10)$$

This system can easily be constructed with two integrators and other blocks from the PSpice ABM library as shown in Figure 6.13 (A sign function block is not a native part of the ABM library but can easily be constructed with, for example, a high gain comparator with an output that saturates at ±1). The CDRG system can then be modified to realise a model of a CFPG, by setting the spring constant very low (to zero in the ideal case) and by adding in the forces acting on the mass when the mass strikes the end stops.

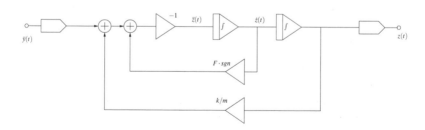

Figure 6.13 SPICE ABM model of CDRG.

A key requirement for achieving a simulation of the CFPG in SPICE is the realisation of a moving plate capacitor model. The standard SPICE capacitor component (known simply as **C** in SPICE syntax) is a 1-port component of fixed capacitance (the value of which is declared in the netlist prior to running the simulation) which implements the first order differential equation $I = C\,dV/dt$.

The CFPG simulation requires a capacitor model with the following characteristics: the device should always obey the equation $I = C\,dV/dt$, but the value of the capacitance needs to be time varying, and able to be controlled from the mechanical part of the simulation (*i.e.* the relative position of the capacitor plates will set the electrical value of the capacitor); the device must provide the normal electrical port to interface with the electrical side of the simulation, and must also provide a mechanical output of the electrostatic force on the capacitor, because the value of this force effects the mechanical dynamics of the model. This mechanical force (calculated from the geometry of the capacitor and the charge of the capacitor plates) would then replace the $F \cdot sgn(\dot{z})$ block shown in Figure 6.13.

Figure 6.14 shows an implementation of a variable parallel plate capacitor in PSpice. The voltage at the output of the electrical port, V_{out}, is given by:

$$V_{out} = V_B(1 + V_A) \tag{6.11}$$

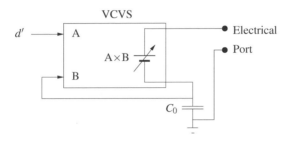

Figure 6.14 Variable parallel plate capacitance SPICE model.

The current through the electrical port is given by:

$$I = C_0 \frac{dV_B}{dt} \tag{6.12}$$

which can be written as:

$$I = \frac{C_0}{1 + V_A} \frac{dV_{out}}{dt} \tag{6.13}$$

This is therefore a realisation of a capacitor whose value can be controlled by altering the value of V_A. The normal force between the plates of a parallel plate capacitor can be calculated as being:

$$F = \frac{1}{2}\varepsilon A \left(\frac{V}{d}\right)^2 \tag{6.14}$$

This equation can be implemented in SPICE by again using the ABM library and feeding the value of F into the rest of the mechanical system of the generator model. The realisation of this component completes the basic electro-mechanical simulation model of the CFPG.

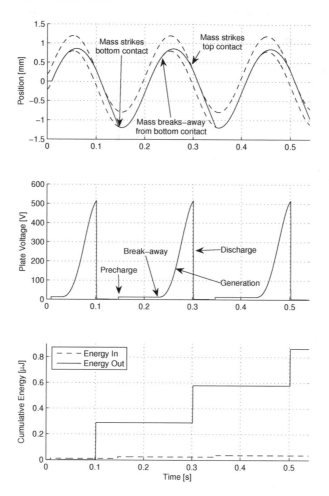

Figure 6.15 Idealised SPICE model with optimal pre-charge.

6.4.2 Integrated Simulation

A simulation result from the PSpice model of the generator mechanics, including the moving plate capacitor, is shown in Figure 6.15. A basic electrical system was set up around this model in order to charge and discharge the capacitor at the correct points in the cycle to generate electrical energy. This involved charging the capacitor at the maximum capacitance and discharging at minimum capacitance into a load resistor. The charging and discharging were done through voltage controlled switches which were activated when the mass struck the end-stop contacts. This mimics the operation of mechanical contacts. Semiconductor switches were not used at this stage of testing.

As can be seen, the moving plate capacitor is charged at low voltage. When the acceleration of the frame is large enough to overcome the holding force between mass and frame, the mass breaks away. This increases the separation of the capacitor electrodes and thus decreases the capacitance. When the capacitance reaches a minimum value, the capacitor is discharged. The corresponding energy flows can be seen in the lower plot of Figure 6.15. A small amount of pre-charge energy is required so that a large discharge energy can be attained. The difference between the two is the generated electrical energy.

As can be seen, the discharge voltage of the capacitor, in this simulation, is around 500V. Whilst the absolute value of this voltage will change depending upon operating conditions and the geometry of the generator, it is safe to assume that it is too high to power the load electronics directly. Suitable power processing, which can down-convert the voltage at the output of the generator, is therefore required.

6.5 Power Electronics and System Effectiveness

6.5.1 Power Electronics Requirements and Trade-Offs

The previous section noted the interaction between the electrical and mechanical systems, and that the output of the CFPG is at a high voltage, with only a very small quantity of charge being present. Power processing electronics are therefore required to down-convert the output of the moving plate capacitor to a voltage suitable for powering the load electronics. The most simple step-down converter topology is the buck design, and this is the topology that has been used in this work. The converter, attached to the moving plate capacitor, is shown in Figure 6.16. The usual configuration of the buck converter uses a diode for freewheeling the current through the inductor when the high-side MOSFET is switched off. In this implementation, the low side diode is replaced by a MOSFET, so that the high-side gate-drive, referenced from the drain, can be charged from a 3V source. The additional diode, in series with the inductor, stops the output discharging when the low-side MOSFET is on to charge the high-side drive. Before being able to correctly specify the component values, the trade-offs in the generator system performance as a function of device parameters must be understood, and this can be estimated by defining the system's effectiveness.

The system effectiveness is defined as a ratio between the useful energy output from the generator and the maximum amount of useful energy, $\hat{W}_{field}$, that could have been generated if the generator had been operating optimally. The useful energy output from the system (which can be used to power a load) is the energy extracted from the down-converter power processing circuitry, E_{out}, less the energy required to pre-charge the capacitor on the next cycle, $E_{pre\text{-}ch}$, and any additional overhead, such as generator control, $E_{o\text{-}head}$. The system effectiveness is therefore:

$$\eta_{system} = \frac{E_{out} - E_{pre\text{-}ch} - E_{o\text{-}head}}{\hat{W}_{field}} \qquad (6.15)$$

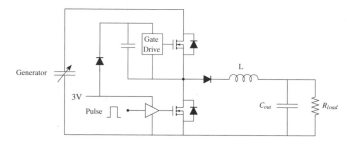

Figure 6.16 Step down converter for electrostatic micro-generator. From [26].

Effectiveness and efficiency ratios can now be defined for the various parts of the generation cycle. In order for the variable capacitor to be able to generate energy, a certain amount of charge must be pre-loaded onto the capacitor before the inertia of the mass causes the plates to separate. The amount of energy stored on the closed capacitor plates, E_{closed}, is a fraction of the energy required from the pre-charge energy, $E_{pre\text{-}ch}$, taken from the generator output. Losses may be due to parasitic capacitance in parallel with the moving plate capacitor and ohmic losses associated with charging the capacitor:

$$\eta_{pre\text{-}ch} = \frac{E_{closed}}{E_{pre\text{-}ch}} \qquad (6.16)$$

When the plates separate, a maximum amount of work, $\hat{W}_{field}$, can be done against the electric field. The limits on $\hat{W}_{field}$ are set by the mechanical operating conditions of the generator, as described in Section 6.2. If the generator has been pre-charged to a non-optimal value, or if charge leaks off the plates during plate separation, only W_{field} work will be done against the field, allowing a mechanical effectiveness to be defined as:

$$\eta_{mech} = \frac{W_{field}}{\hat{W}_{field}} \qquad (6.17)$$

As the plates separate, some charge may leak off the plates through a finite conductance path between the plates, or alternatively be shared with the parasitic capacitance of the power converter attached to the plates. Most of the energy lost from the plates during the plate separation cannot be recovered, meaning that the only available electrical energy (for driving a load) when the plates have reached their full separation, is the energy stored on the variable capacitor itself. This is justified because almost all the charge which leaks off the generator during the plate separation is stored on the junction capacitance of the drain-body diode in the MOSFET. When the MOSFET is turned on to discharge the generator capacitor, this energy is lost as the drain body capacitance is internally short circuited within the MOSFET. This allows a generation efficiency, η_{gen} to be defined as:

$$\eta_{gen} = \frac{E_{open}}{W_{field} + E_{closed}} \tag{6.18}$$

The high voltage on the open generator capacitor then has to be down-converted to low voltage. The efficiency of this down-conversion can then be defined as:

$$\eta_{conv} = \frac{E_{out}}{E_{open}} \tag{6.19}$$

The overall system efficiency can be calculated from these sub-system efficiencies by defining a pre-charge ratio as:

$$\kappa_{pre-ch} = \frac{E_{closed}}{W_{field}} \tag{6.20}$$

and a pre-charge recovery ratio as:

$$\kappa_{roc} = \frac{E_{pre-ch} + E_{o-head}}{E_{out}} \tag{6.21}$$

These quantities give an indication of the electrical energy gain associated with the system, *i.e.* the fraction of the generated energy that has to be initially supplied in an electrical form in order that the generation can take place.

The overall system effectiveness can then be written as:

$$\eta_{system} = \frac{E_{out} - E_{pre-ch} - E_{o-head}}{\hat{W}_{field}} \tag{6.22}$$

$$= \eta_{mech} \times (1 + \kappa_{pre-ch}) \times \eta_{gen} \times \eta_{conv} \times (1 - \kappa_{rec})$$

As can be seen from (6.22), maximising the overall system effectiveness requires maximising several terms and minimising others. The three main system efficiencies, κ_{mech}, κ_{gen} and κ_{conv} should be maximised. κ_{rec} should be minimised and κ_{pre-ch} should be maximised. However, it is not possible to treat the maximisation and minimisation of these terms in isolation because altering the system to have a positive effect on one term may have a negative effect on another.

Parasitic capacitance and conductance in parallel with the moving capacitor will decrease both η_{mech} and η_{gen}. Both of these terms need to be high in order to achieve a high value of η_{system}. This requirement places certain constraints on the power semiconductors, in particular their behaviour in the off-state. They must have very high off-state impedances and very low parasitic capacitances. However, in order that the conversion efficiency, η_{conv}, remains high, the semiconductor devices must also have a low on-state resistance.

Various trade-offs in system effectiveness will now be discussed, for instance:

- Increasing the pre-charge voltage can lead to an increase or decrease in η_{mech}. The pre-charge voltage must be set so that the value of β is correct, as described in Section 6.2. Changes in the frame motion may be beneficial or detrimental to η_{mech} depending upon the limitations on setting the pre-charge voltage. An increased plate flight-time may be necessary to achieve higher values of η_{mech}, but this will reduce η_{gen} due to the increased charge leakage from the plates.

- Increasing the semiconductor cross sectional area will tend to increase η_{conv} until parasitic capacitance begins to dominate, at which point further increases will decrease η_{conv}. Also, increasing the area will decrease η_{gen} as increased charge sharing occurs. Additionally, charge sharing can reduce W_{field}, thus reducing η_{mech}.

- Increasing the inductance of the converter will tend to decrease conduction losses and thus increase η_{conv}. However, increasing the inductance above a certain point may increase the parasitic capacitance (of the inductor) and ultimately cause a reduction in η_{conv}. This increased parasitic capacitance may also decrease η_{gen}.

- Increasing the length of the device drift region (used for voltage blocking) can allow reduced doping of that region, and thus reduces the semiconductor device's capacitance and hence increases η_{gen}. Increasing this length will also increase conduction losses in the devices, but may reduce losses due to reduced capacitances of the diode in the buck converter. If the drift region is increased in length to increase the voltage blocking capability of the device, it is possible that η_{mech} could be increased.

A maximum value of parasitic capacitance and leakage conductance can be found by considering the energy that is actually generated, relative to E_{open}, the energy that would be on the capacitor at maximum plate separation with no loading, as a function of parasitic capacitance and resistance in parallel with the generator. The results are shown in Figure 6.17. The requirements for the semiconductors are unusually strict: to maintain 80% of the generated energy the off-state loading should be more than $10^{12}\Omega$ and less than 1pF. These values are not available with standard discrete MOSFETs (or other switching devices) rated for high voltage blocking.

6.5.2 Semiconductor Device Design

Power semiconductors with the highest possible off-state resistance and lowest parasitic capacitance were designed [26, 27]. The semiconductor device processing steps had to be compatible with MEMS processing (so that in the future a fully integrated generator can be realised) and a thin-layer *Silicon-on-Insulator* (SoI) process was used. Devices designed using this thin-layer SoI process inherently have lower capacitance between their terminals than those made with more traditional process technologies, because the growth of the depletion layer is constrained so that it can only grow in the axis which is useful for voltage blocking.

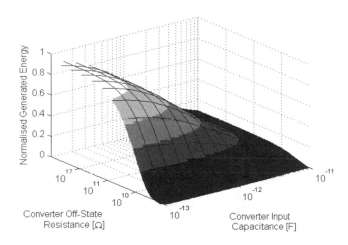

Figure 6.17 Dependence of generator-converted energy as a function of parasitic capacitance and conductance. From [26].

Initially, a MOSFET was designed (Figure 6.18). The long n- region is used to support the high blocking voltages. Although the average currents involved in the micro-generator application are small, the peak currents can be high (due to the high resonant frequency of the variable capacitor and small values of realisable on-chip inductor used in the buck circuit). High voltage MOSFETs suffer from relatively high on-state resistance. One possible improvement to the MOSFET, in order to reduce the on-state impedance, is to add a p+ diffusion to the drain of the MOSFET, creating an IGBT (Figure 6.19). This structure utilises conductivity modulation of the n- region to reduce the on-state losses, and improvements were seen using this device in place of the MOSFET.

A further improvement to the IGBT structure is a thyristor structure. The *MOS-Triggered Thyristor* (MTT) shown in Figure 6.20 realises a lower value of on-state resistance than the IGBT. In the IGBT, the hole current flowing in the emitter p-base material can cause a voltage drop which is sufficient to forward bias the p-base n+ junction, causing electrons to be injected into the device without the need for them to flow through the inverted p-base which forms the channel. This effectively eliminates the high resistance of the pinched off channel, and the device is said to have latched up because it is not possible to turn the device off via the gate. In this application, it is not necessary to switch off the MTT as the current naturally commutates to zero. The MTT is a modification of the IGBT which allows latch-up to occur more easily. Simulations of these custom-designed semiconductors in a finite element device design package showed that the MTT was the superior device in this application.

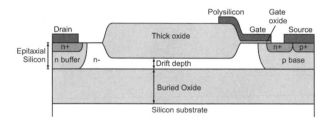

Figure 6.18 SOI MOSFET. From [26].

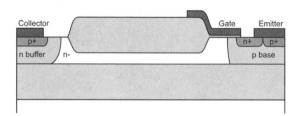

Figure 6.19 SOI IGBT. From [26].

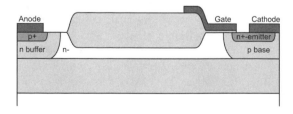

Figure 6.20 SOI MTT. From [26].

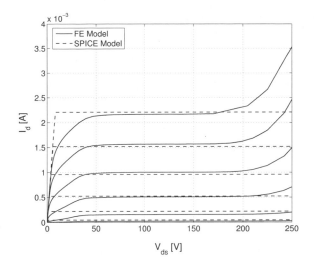

Figure 6.21 Comparison of SPICE MOSFET model to FE results.

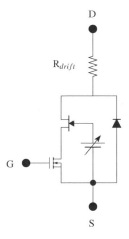

Figure 6.22 Sub-circuit SPICE model of power MOSFET.

6.5.3 Coherent Simulation

As stated previously, the interaction between the electrical and mechanical system of the generator means that a combined simulation is required, and this was achieved in PSpice. In order to accurately model the power electronics, SPICE models of the custom semiconductor devices had to be created. The normal SPICE models do not accurately model some of the effects which occur in power semiconductor devices. As an example, Figure 6.21 shows a best fit SPICE model curve trace of the custom MOSFET device in comparison to the FE simulation result. The discrepancy at the knee of the curve is due to JFET pinch at the drain end of the MOS channel, and is not present in signal MOSFETs. When a sub-circuit SPICE model is used (Figure 6.22) which accounts for this and other effects, the curve fit is significantly better (Figure 6.23).

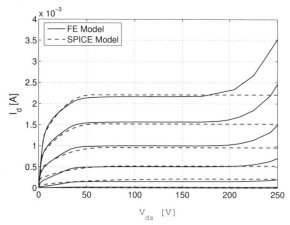

Figure 6.23 SPICE sub-circuit model compared to FE result. From [6].

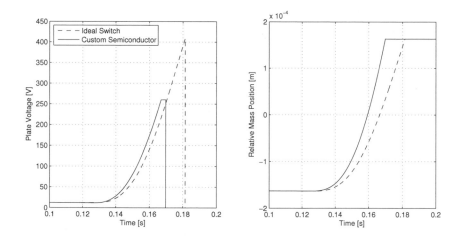

Figure 6.24 Comparison of generator operation with ideal switches and custom MOSFETs.

Once SPICE models of the custom semiconductor devices were achieved, a coherent system simulation, including the generator mechanical system and power electronics (along with detailed semiconductor device effects) could be run. Figure

6.24 shows a comparison between the operation of a CFPG using ideal switches in the power converter compared to using realistic MOSFET models. As can be seen, the generated voltage is less when realistic MOSFET models are used, and the plate flight time is also less (because the attractive force between the electrodes is less as due to charge sharing and leakage).

6.6 Discussion and Conclusions

6.6.1 What Is Achievable in Body-Sensor Energy Scavenging?

We saw in Section 6.2 that for a given source frequency ω and amplitude Y_o, the maximum extractable power from an inertial generator depends only on its proof mass m and internal displacement amplitude Z_l, and is given by

$$P_{max} = \frac{2}{\pi} Y_0 Z_l \omega^3 m \qquad (6.23)$$

We can then define a normalised power $P_n = P/(Y_0 Z_l \omega^3 m)$, which should have a maximum value of $2/\pi = 0.637$. This quantity P_n is a good measure of how close the performance of a specific device comes to the optimum level. Therefore we have calculated P_n for those inertial energy scavengers described in the literature, and the resulting values are plotted in Figure 6.25 as a function of year of publication.

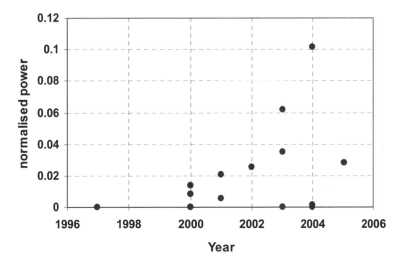

Figure 6.25 Normalised measured power P_n *vs* year of publication for reported inertial devices.

An upwards trend can clearly be seen, although the best values are still well below the theoretical maximum of 0.637. It should also be noted that for most reported devices, not all the parameters needed to calculate P_n are unambiguously given so that estimates were required in these cases, and in a few cases the information provided was insufficient even for an estimate of P_n to be made with any confidence, so these devices are not plotted.

It can also be noted that for a given volume, the performance limiting value $Z_l m$ depends on the fraction of volume taken up by the mass, and on the device shape and its direction of internal motion. Firstly for a given shape and internal direction, allowing the proof mass to occupy half the volume gives the maximum product $Z_l m$, so that if the device is a cube of dimension a, $Z_l m$ will be given by $\rho a^4/8$, or equivalently $\rho V^{4/3}/8$, with ρ the proof mass density and V the device volume. This scaling of power with $V^{4/3}$ indicates that the achievable power density drops as the devices reduce in size, although not rapidly.

Although P_n should not drop with volume, as it is normalised to device size, the same data used for Figure 6.25, but now plotted against device volume (Figure 6.26), show that typically the best P_n values have been achieved for larger devices. This is likely an indication of the technological difficulties encountered at smaller size scales, for example the greater difficulty in achieving high magnetic flux gradients. Again, estimations have been made where the published reports contain insufficient detail.

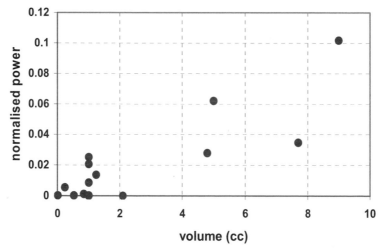

Figure 6.26 Normalised measured power P_n *vs* device volume for reported inertial devices.

For a given volume, half occupied by the proof mass, the internal displacement limit depends on the device shape or aspect ratio. Ideally, one direction would be elongated, so that a long thin cylinder would be an efficient shape from this point of view. However, the volume, independent of shape, is unlikely to be the key constraint. Also, the fabrication technology may well put limits on shape. For example, in MEMS processing or for other planar techniques, one dimension (the out-of-plane one) is typically much shorter than the other two. This constrains the device to a shape like that described in Section 6.3. In such a case, power would clearly be maximised if the travel is in one of the long directions. Again, however, practical constraints may mitigate against this choice. For example, it is difficult to achieve long travel in a lateral (in-plane) suspension without excessive ease of motion in unwanted axes, both out of plane and rotational.

Assuming such limitations are overcome and a planar device is constructed with lateral motion, we can use this format to calculate a maximum specific power for inertial devices in BSN applications [6]. We assume an aspect ratio (out-of-plane to in-plane dimension) of 10, and a proof mass specific gravity of 20 (gold); for the source, we assume a frequency 1Hz and a maximum displacement of 25cm. Then:

$$P \approx 1.7 V^{4/3} \ \mathrm{mW/cm^4} \tag{6.24}$$

For a 0.1cm³ device this gives a maximum power of 80μW; for a cubic millimetre device, only 0.17μW. This suggests 10's of mm³ are likely to be needed for an inertial scavenging device to be of much value for foreseeable body sensor nodes.

6.6.2 Future Prospects and Trends

Inertial energy scavenging continues to attract attention from a large number of researchers, and as shown in Figure 6.25, the performance levels achieved continue to rise. Body-powered applications, however, remain a great challenge because of the low specific power levels at low frequencies, and so substantial progress will be needed in reducing power requirements, particularly for wireless data transmission, before such solutions become feasible. However, such progress is certainly being made, as reported in other chapters.

The body motion that may power energy scavenging will vary substantially with time, and this variation is unlikely to correspond with the varying power demands of the sensor node. Therefore some energy storage is almost certain to be required. While mechanical energy storage based on MEMS is conceivable, there is little sign of such an approach being developed and so secondary batteries are likely to be used. This is also likely to be the case for other, non-inertial forms of energy scavenging. This suggests that if scavenging methods are successfully exploited, they are likely to be supplementary to, rather than a replacement for, battery technologies. The need for integrated power conditioning circuits with energy scavenging also encourages a trend towards intelligent energy modules, possible incorporating several forms of scavenging as well as storage, power conditioning, and power management electronics.

References

1. Paradiso JA, Starner T. Energy scavenging for mobile and wireless electronics. IEEE Pervasive Computing 2005; 4(1):18-27.
2. Roundy S, Wright PK, Rabaey JM. Energy scavenging for wireless sensor networks. Boston, Massachusetts: Kluwer Academic Publishers, 2003.
3. Mitcheson PD. Analysis and optimisation of energy-harvesting microgenerator systems. Imperial College London, London, PhD Thesis, 2005.
4. Balomenos T. User requirements analysis and specifications of health status analysis and hazard avoidance artefacts. DC FET Project ORESTEIA, Deliverable D02, 2001.
5. Yates DC, Holmes AS, Burdett AJ. Optimal transmission frequency for ultralow-power short-range radio links. IEEE Transactions on Circuits and Systems I: Regular Papers 2004; 51(7):1405-1413.
6. Mitcheson PD, Yates DC, Yeatman EM, Green TC, Holmes AS. Modelling for optimisation of self-powered wireless sensor nodes. In: Proceedings of the Second International Conference on Wearable and Implantable Body Sensor Networks, Imperial College London, 2005; 53-57.
7. Sauerbrey J, Schmitt-Landsiedel D, Thewes R. A 0.5-V 1-μW successive approximation ADC. IEEE Journal of Solid-State Circuits 2003; 38(7):1261-1265.
8. Brodd RJ, Bullock KR, Leising RA, Middaugh RL, Miller JR, Takeuchi E. Batteries, 1977 to 2002. Journal of the Electrochemical Society 2004; 151(3):K1-K11.
9. Roundy S, Steingart D, Frechette L, Wright P, Rabaey J. Power sources for wireless sensor networks. In: Proceedings of the First European Workshop on Wireless Sensor Networks 2004; Springer LNCS 2920:1-17.
10. Whalen S, Thompson M, Bahr D, Richards C, Richards R. Design, fabrication and testing of the P-3 micro heat engine. Sensors and Actuators A: Physical 2003; 104(3):290-298.
11. Yen TJ, Fang N, Zhang X, Lu GQ, Wang CY. A micro methanol fuel cell operating at near room temperature. Applied Physics Letters 2003; 83(19):4056-4058.
12. Sato F, Togo M, Islam MK, Matsue T, Kosuge J, Fukasaku N, *et al*. Enzyme-based glucose fuel cell using Vitamin K-3-immobilized polymer as an electron mediator. Electrochemistry Communications 2005; 7(7):643-647.
13. Mantiply ED, Pohl KR, Poppell SW, Murphy JA. Summary of measured radiofrequency electric and magnetic fields (10kHz to 30GHz) in the general and work environment. Bioelectromagnetics 1997; 18(8):563-577.
14. Strasser M, Aigner R, Franosch M, Wachutka G. Miniaturized thermoelectric generators based on poly-Si and poly-SiGe surface micromachining. Sensors and Actuators A: Physical 2002; 97-98:535-542.
15. Holmes AS, Hong G, Pullen KR, Buffard KR. Axial-flow microturbine with electromagnetic generator: design, CFD simulation, and prototype demonstration. In: Proceedings of the Seventeenth IEEE International Conference on Micro Electro Mechanical Systems 2004; 568-571.

16. Shenck NS, Paradiso JA. Energy scavenging with shoe-mounted piezoelectrics. IEEE Micro 2001; 21(3):30-42.
17. Glynne-Jones P, Tudor MJ, Beeby SP, White NM. An electromagnetic, vibration-powered generator for intelligent sensor systems. Sensors and Actuators A: Physical 2004; 110(1-3):344-349.
18. Sterken T, Fiorini P, Baert K, Puers R, Borghs G. An electret-based electrostatic μ-generator. In: Proceedings of the Twelfth International Conference on Transducers, Solid-State Sensors, Actuators and Microsystems 2003; 2:1291-1294.
19. Solymar L, Walsh D. Lectures on the electrical properties of materials. Oxford, UK: Oxford University Press, 1993.
20. Mitcheson PD, Green TC, Yeatman EM, Holmes AS. Architectures for vibration-driven micropower generators. Journal of Microelectromechanical Systems 2004; 13(3):429-440.
21. von Buren T, Mitcheson PD, Green TC, Yeatman EM, Holmes AS, Troster G. Optimization of inertial micropower generators for human walking motion. IEEE Sensors Journal 2005.
22. Miao P, Mitcheson PD, Holmes AS, Yeatman EM, Green TC, Stark BH. MEMS inertial power generators for biomedical applications. In: Proceedings of the Symposium on Design, Test, Integration and Packaging of MEMS/MOEMS, Montreux 2005; 295-298.
23. Mitcheson PD, Miao P, Stark BH, Yeatman EM, Holmes AS, Green TC. MEMS electrostatic micropower generator for low frequency operation. Sensors and Actuators A: Physical 2004; 115(2-3):523-529.
24. Meninger S, Mur-Miranda JO, Amirtharajah R, Chandrakasan A, Lang JH. Vibration-to-electric energy conversion. IEEE Transactions on Very Large Scale Integration (VLSI) Systems 2001; 9(1):64-76.
25. PSpice, OrCAD Inc., http://www.orcad.com
26. Stark BH, Mitcheson PD, Miao P, Green TC, Yeatman EM, Holmes AS. Power processing issues for micro-power electrostatic generators. In: Proceedings of the IEEE Thirty-Fifth Annual Power Electronics Specialists Conference 2004; 6:4156-4162.
27. Stark BH, Green TC. Comparison of SOI power device structures in power converters for high-voltage, low-charge electrostatic microgenerators. IEEE Transactions on Electron Devices 2005; 52(7):1640-1648.

7

Towards Ultra-Low Power Bio-Inspired Processing

Leila Shepherd, Timothy G. Constandinou, and Chris Toumazou

7.1 Introduction

The natural world is analogue and yet the modern microelectronic world with which we interact represents real world data using discrete quantities manipulated by logic. In the human space, we are entering a new wave of body-worn biosensor technology for medical diagnostics and therapy. This new trend is beginning to see the processing interface move back to using continuous quantities which are more or less in line with the biological processes. This computational paradigm we label "bio-inspired" because of the ability of silicon chip technology to enable the use of inherent device physics, allowing us to approach the computational efficiencies of biology. From a conceptual viewpoint, this has led to a number of more specific morphologies including *neuromorphic* and *retinomorphic* processing. These have led scientists to model biological systems such as the cochlea and retina and gain not only superior computational resource efficiency (to conventional hearing aid or camera technology) but also an increased understanding of biological and neurological processes.

We propose to apply a similar approach to "chemically-inspired" microelectronics which would lead to portable ultra low-power micro-systems capable of faster chemical/biochemical discrimination and interrogation of data, integrated monolithically at the sensor end. In contrast to the digital approach, where each operation is performed through a network of devices operated in switched fashion, the physics of the elementary device itself, either electrical, chemical or electro-chemical, can be exploited to perform the same operation in an analogue way. Therefore both the energy per unit computation and silicon real-estate are reduced, resulting in significantly increased overall resource efficiency.

This chapter will first look at the motivation for bio-inspired signal processing and discuss the relative merits of analogue and digital signal processing, and the need for hybrid architectures. The concept of applying bio-inspired design methodologies to *Complementary Metal Oxide Semiconductor* (CMOS)-based biosensors will then be introduced. *Field-Effect Transistor-* (FET-) based sensors will be presented, including a detailed example of the application of analogue processing techniques to these devices. Finally, future directions and applications for biochemically-inspired design will be discussed.

7.2 Bio-Inspired Signal Processing

Although modern microelectronic technologies have surpassed our expectations in virtually all areas, there still remains a vast application space of computational problems either too challenging or complex to be solved with conventional means. These applications often require the transformation of data across the boundary between the real (analogue) world and the digital world. The problem arises whenever a system is sampling and acting on real-world data, for example in recognition or identification tasks. Traditional processing techniques find it prohibitively challenging or at best computationally demanding to identify and process complex structures and relationships in vast quantities of ill-conditioned data (for instance data that is low precision, ambiguous and noisy) [1].

Although great progress has been made in hardware processing techniques (*e.g.* DSP, FPGA) in both computational load and efficiency, the solution to complex recognition tasks still continues to elude us. Furthermore, artificial intelligence, artificial neural networks and fuzzy logic have yet to provide effective and robust solutions for practical sensing applications. However, biological organisms routinely accomplish complex visual tasks such as object recognition and target tracking. For example, a common housefly, with a brain the size of a grain of rice, can outperform our modern multiple gigahertz processors in real-time obstacle avoidance in flight navigation, in addition to countless other perception tasks. Thus fields such as neuromorphic engineering have emerged, aiming to provide a design methodology for tackling such problems using hybrid, distributed processing architectures based on simple primitives. Inspired by biology, modern microelectronic technology is progressing one step closer to finding a workable solution to these problems.

In the context of body-worn sensors for BSN which communicate information over a wireless network, it is vital signs and not necessarily raw data that should be signalled to the user. There is therefore scope for bio-inspired analogue processing to take place local to the sensor, before transmission of data, rather than transmit raw data at high accuracy. In employing this approach, the power saving is twofold: both in reducing the communication bandwidth/duty cycle and therefore the transmit power; and also in excluding the requirement of power-hungry oversampling data converters. Rather than a mere "biosensor" chip, one would have a "biocomputer" chip with the intelligence to extract important features of the data sensed and to discriminate between different scenarios.

7.3 Analogue *vs* Digital Signal Processing

7.3.1 Quantised Data/Time *vs* Continuous Data/Time

Information exists in a three-dimensional media with data encoded in time, amplitude and space. Various techniques of data representation exist for processing this information, with spatial information coded universally by the position of the sensor in the three dimensional medium. For example, in electronics, analogue circuits represent data as continuous voltages and currents, varying both in time and intensity. On the other hand, conventional digital electronics use clocks to synchronise activity – data therefore being represented as discrete voltages quantised in time as well as amplitude. Sampled data techniques also exist such as switched-capacitor [2] and switched-current [3] that use a clock to sample continuous-varying signals and are therefore discrete in time but continuous in amplitude. Such techniques are widely used in signal processing of continuous (analogue) signals, for example in implementing filters for over-sampling data converters.

Exploring this two-dimensional space, *i.e.*, time and amplitude as shown in Figure 7.1, for encoding data, a remaining unexploited representation is continuous-time, discrete-data. This is in fact the principle representation of biology; with spiking neurons conveying no data in the shape or amplitude of the action potential, but rather in the timing. This encoding can easily be achieved using asynchronous digital technology, although it is not widely used in system-level design due to complexity in synthesis.

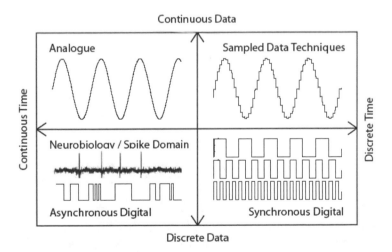

Figure 7.1 Classification of the various data representation techniques in standard microelectronic technologies.

7.3.2 Analogue/Digital Data Representation

A key debate in the low power electronics community is whether analogue or digital signal processing is more computationally efficient. Much work [1, 4-7] has already gone into this by considering factors such as *Signal-to-Noise Ratio* (SNR), power consumption, silicon area, channel utilisation and design time.

The general conclusions from the existing research include [7]:

(a)   Analogue processing can be far more computationally efficient than digital signal processing. This is due to the rich mathematical content in the physics of the devices in comparison to the primitive nature of a digital device (a switch). It follows that to achieve similar functionality with digital logic, many more devices need to be used – in fact this can be several orders of magnitude more devices. Moreover, at high activities this results in significantly higher power consumption. This is because digital logic dissipates both due to continuous sub-threshold "leakage" current (static power) and during switching (dynamic power), whereas analogue devices only have a continuous current supply (static power).

(b)   Digital processing is more tolerant of noise and cumulative offsets. The continuous nature of analogue signals means they cannot be restored at each stage as discrete signals can. Consequently, any noise or circuit-introduced offset accumulates through cascading and can ultimately deteriorate the signal in complex analogue systems. This reduces the accuracy and dynamic range of such a system for a given power budget. If device geometries are increased and more power is dissipated, analogue systems can be made to perform to higher accuracies, however the computational efficiency of digital systems then tends to be superior.

(c)   Quantifying these benefits, it can be shown that the cost (silicon area and power consumption) of analogue computation is exponential with respect to SNR, whereas the cost of digital computation is linear. In addition, the starting overhead (at low SNR) of analogue is low, whereas for digital is high. This sets a trend where the benefits of each method can be divided using SNR alone (see Figure 7.2 [5, 7]). For lower SNRs, analogue techniques can have many orders of magnitude area and power advantage, whereas for higher precision computation digital techniques have the cost advantage.

These conclusions are the result of deriving mathematical expressions to quantify the computational cost based on the fundamental limits of each technique. Although these provide the ultimate theoretical performance of each representation technique, they do not consider implementation issues, with circuit design and wafer processing being far from ideal.

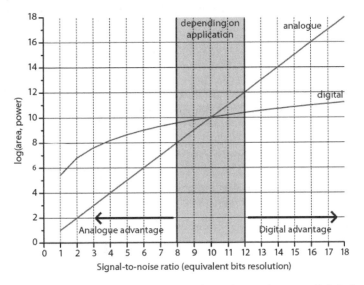

Figure 7.2 The relative cost of computation using analogue or digital signal processing. The crossover between analogue and digital having the advantage is between 50dB to 72dB SNR (8 to 12 bits resolution) depending on application and circuit topology. (**See colour insert.**)

In the subsequent sections, we shall consider qualitative comparisons of various microelectronic representations in performing common computational tasks with implementation issues being considered.

7.3.3 Linear Operations

The most common mathematical computations are in fact linear operations. These include addition, subtraction, multiplication, and division, *etc*. Implementing these computations in different ways can prove beneficial. For example, to add two currents, only a single wire is needed (by Kirchhoff's Current Law), whereas an 8-bit digital implementation would require eight full-adder stages, comprising a total of at least 228 transistors. Similarly, a multiplication can be achieved using a Gilbert (translinear) multiplier circuit [8] employing only eight transistors biased in the "sub-threshold" or "weak inversion" region of operation. Here the equivalent digital solution would be an 8-bit array multiplier requiring an excess of over 2000 transistors. In these examples, silicon area can be saved using analogue techniques, however as always in electronic design, the various trade-offs need to be considered. A qualitative comparison of the most popular techniques used for linear arithmetic computation is illustrated in Table 7.1.

For these comparisons, sampled data techniques have been combined with their respective continuous-time counterparts as these are both based on the same underlying circuit theory. To substantiate this, Furth *et al* [6] have shown these continuous-time and sampled-data techniques to follow similar SNR-to-power-consumption relationships.

Table 7.1 A qualitative comparison of linear computations implemented using different signal representations.

Signal Representation	Topology	Silicon Area	Power	Accuracy	Noise	Speed	Ref.
Addition, Subtraction, Summation							
Current-mode analogue[1]	current addition (KCL)	best	best	good	excellent	good	[9]
Voltage-mode analogue[2]	charge domain (switched-cap)	good	good	good	excellent	good	[10]
Digital[3]	parallel counter, ripple adder	fair	good	excellent	excellent	excellent	[11]
Multiplication, Division							
Current-mode analogue	Gilbert multiplier	excellent	excellent	excellent	good	fair	[8]
Voltage-mode analogue	flipped voltage followers	good	good	good	good	fair	[12]
Digital	array, tree multiplier	poor	fair	excellent	excellent	excellent	[13]
Scaling							
Current-mode analogue	scaled current mirror	excellent	excellent	good	fair	good	-
Voltage-mode analogue	operational amplifier	good	fair	good	good	good	-
Digital	barrel shift and accumulate	fair	good	excellent	excellent	excellent	[14]

[1] *Provide maximum resource efficiency (area and power)* [7]; [2] *Provide good all-round performance;* [3] *Provide highest speed operation and precision* [7].

7.3.4 Non-Linear Operations

In most complex processing tasks, the underlying computation tends to be non-linear. This may comprise of an array or bank of linear functions to achieve the overall non-linear behaviour. A qualitative comparison, as previously presented for linear operations, has been formulated for selected common non-linear functions, shown in Table 7.2.

7.3.5 Hybrid System Organisation

The ultimate goal of using a hybrid approach is to exploit different representation strategies throughout a system – ideally to achieve optimum performance for a given processing task. Most modern applications typically require both analogue and digital techniques to work alongside one another as the bare minimum. Since

Table 7.2 A qualitative comparison of non-linear computations implemented using different signal representation techniques.

Signal Representation	Topology	Silicon Area	Power	Accuracy	Noise	Speed	Ref.
Comparison, Thesholding[1]							
Current-mode analogue	current comparator	excellent	excellent	good	fair	fair	[9]
Voltage-mode analogue	operational amplifier	good	good	good	good	good	-
Digital	subtractor	fair	fair	good	excellent	excellent	[14]
Exponential, Logarithm, Square, Root[2]							
Current-mode analogue	translinear circuits	excellent	excellent	good	good	fair	[15]
Voltage-mode analogue	non-linear V to I	good	fair	good	good	fair	[16]
Digital	root/division algorithm	fair	fair	excellent	excellent	good	[17]
Filtering, Integration, Differentiation, Fourier Transform[3]							
Current-mode analogue	log domain	good	excellent	good	excellent	excellent	[18]
Voltage-mode analogue	charge domain (switched cap)	good	excellent	fair	good	good	[10]
Digital	IIR/FIR filters, FFT	poor	fair	good	excellent	good	[19]

[1]*The direct comparison of continuous signals makes analogue comparators the most easily implementable, whereas digital comparison techniques are typically implemented using subtraction driven combinational logic.*

[2]*Analogue realisations are based on translinear techniques or exploitation of non-linear component response, whereas digital implementations require either ROM-based lookup tables or synthesis of custom arithmetic-logic-unit (ALU) type hardware.*

[3]*Digital implementation provides better reconfigurability, stability to drift/temperature and low frequency operation.*

the real world is analogue, any system requiring a sensor interface requires analogue electronics. On the other hand, as most control systems and communication protocols are digital, any system requiring external interface capability requires digital electronics.

This defines a minimum requirement of one data converter. Therefore, in order to best utilise resources, it would be best to use this data conversion to our advantage by using this as the main conversion stage within a system. By using hybrid processing strategies and shifting the data conversion interface, the required conversion accuracy can be relaxed to specifications that lend themselves to micropower techniques. Using previously mentioned signal representation techniques, there exist several architectures that fulfil these criteria as illustrated in Figure 7.3.

7.4 CMOS-Based Biosensors

CMOS is the dominant semiconductor technology for fabrication of modern microelectronic components such as microprocessors, memories and *Application Specific Integrated Circuits* (ASICs) on a silicon substrate through a defined sequence of material deposition, doping, lithography and etching [20]. CMOS technology has

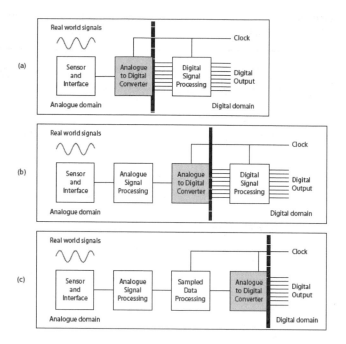

Figure 7.3 Hybrid processing architectures with a single data conversion stage: (*a*) conventional analogue front-end with digital processor and output, (*b*) hybrid analogue/digital processing platform with digital output, and (*c*) hybrid analogue and sampled data processing platform with digital output.

transformed the electronics industry with a seemingly undiminishing[†] ability to integrate more and more uniform devices of ever-decreasing dimensions onto a single silicon wafer. It is no wonder then that a goal of recent miniaturisation trends in electrochemical biosensing has been the fabrication of electrochemical "microsensors" on a CMOS substrate, providing not only low-cost batch fabrication and reproducible sensor characteristics, but also reduced power consumption and rapid sensor response due to reduced device dimensions.

In addition to meeting these key criteria, CMOS-based chemical sensors are amenable to monolithic integration of interface circuitry and thus to the use of the bio-inspired hybrid processing architectures described herein which can potentially extract critical information from noisy signals in an adaptive, intelligent manner.

A key bone of contention is whether or not sensing and processing functions should be combined when this limits one's choice of sensors and materials and can also introduce expensive sensor-specific process steps to standard commercial CMOS fabrication. Of the integrated sensing and electronic functions published so

---

[†] Of course, Moore's 1965 Law predicting the number of transistors per square inch could double every two years (actually more like 18 months) is gradually starting to reach its limits. The latest Intel 'Itanium' processor family uses a minimum feature size of 90nm and has 1.72 billion transistors.

far such as [21] and [22], none have been shown offer higher SNRs than separate sensors and interface electronics, leading to observations by some [23, 24] that integration is not necessarily the most appropriate goal given that the lifetime of sensors can be short. Keeping sensor and processing circuitry separate allows reusable electronic modules and optimised fabrication process for both electronics and sensor. However, the norm for other types of sensors is that integration traditionally results in better SNR. Most high spec sensors, *e.g.*, MEMS microphones, pressure sensors, and even image sensors, have integrated active gain element to massively improve SNR.

For small systems which do not require adaptive or intelligent discrimination, disposable off-chip sensors and reusable electronic modules may well be the most cost effective and high performance solution. However for more complex applications, involving array processing on an array of homo- or heterogeneous sensors, such as bio-inspired learning, adaptivity, feature extraction or redundancy, then large scale integration of sensors and electronic devices is paramount and CMOS technology is the current state-of-the-art for hybrid architectures.

CMOS-based chemical sensors and biosensors comprise a physical transducer and a chemical or biological recognition layer. The reversible change in a physico-chemical property of the recognition layer (such as mass, volume, optical absorption spectrum, conductivity, temperature) upon interaction with a chemical or biological target is converted by a transducer into an electrical signal such as frequency, current or voltage. Electrochemical sensors are a class of sensors with fast response times based on ionic charge transfer between the recognition layer and the target analyte causing changes in electrical potential or conductivity. One of the most popular types of CMOS-based electrochemical sensor is the family of FET-based devices, whose lowest common denominator, the *Ion-Sensitive Field Effect Transistor* (ISFET), will be discussed in more detail in this section.

7.4.1 Ion-Sensitive Field-Effect Transistor (ISFET)

Research into FET-based biochemical sensing began in 1970, when Piet Bergveld proposed a MOSFET without a gate metallisation as an ISFET [25] for measuring ionic flux around a neuron. Accumulation of charge at the exposed insulator (*i.e.*, oxide) surface, is related to the activity (concentration[†]) of ions in the sample solution, and modulates the threshold voltage of the transistor, causing shifts in the current-voltage (I-V) characteristic of the ISFET (Figure 7.4). Being a potentiometric sensor, a reference electrode (such as silver/silver chloride) is required so that the phase boundary potential formed at the oxide-electrolyte interface can be measured with respect to a fixed boundary potential in the bulk of the solution. In transistor terms the reference electrode acts as a remote gate which is capacitively coupled across the electrolyte to the insulator surface.

[†] The term "activity" a_i denotes the effective (active) concentration of the ion, *i.e.*, those ions not engaged in ionic interactions with oppositely charged ions, and is related to concentration c_i by $a_i = f_i c_i$ where f_i is the activity coefficient. In dilute solutions, f_i approaches unity and $a_i \approx c_i$.

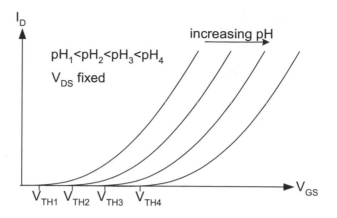

Figure 7.4 pH-ISFET transconductance characteristics.

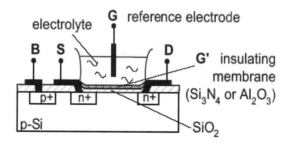

Figure 7.5 Standard pH-ISFET.

In the most common ISFET implementation, the silicon dioxide layer is replaced with a double layer insulator which has better pH-sensitivity and stability to form a pH-ISFET, sensitive primarily to hydrogen ions (Figure 7.5). Examples of the upper layer of these double insulator structures are silicon nitride, aluminium oxide and tantalum oxide. Though an ISFET by definition is a FET without a gate, a goal of recent research has been to fabricate FET-based devices with ion sensitivity using a standard commercial CMOS process. These CMOS-based ISFETs circumvent the fact that the CMOS process requires a polysilicon gate for self-alignment of the source and drain diffusions by using the silicon nitride passivation layer on top of the polysilicon gate as the sensing membrane as shown in Figure 7.6 [21]. Charge accumulation on the passivation layer (typically either silicon dioxide or silicon nitride) is capacitively coupled to the ohmic multiconductor "floating gate" structure of metal layers and polysilicon beneath, thus influencing the inversion within the semiconductor channel and therefore device drain-source current.

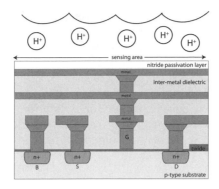

Figure 7.6 A schematic illustration of CMOS ISFET.

7.4.2 ISFET-Based Biosensors

Through modification of the sensing membrane, and/or the addition of further layers of sensitive materials which interact with target species to form ions, ISFETs
can be used to sense ions other than hydrogen, as well as gases, antigens and metabolites such as urea and glucose.

7.4.2.1 ChemFET

Through the deposition of various ionophores (ion-selective channels) on top of the
insulator sensing membrane, ChemFET sensors for key ions such as sodium, potassium and calcium can be created based on the same principle [26-28].

7.4.2.2 GasFET

Gas-sensitive FETs or "GasFETs" can be made by taking an ISFET and surrounding it by a thin film of intermediate electrolyte solution enclosed by a gas-
permeable membrane. This is often achieved by localising the electrolyte solution
to the ISFET surface using a hydrogel, and covering this with a gas-permeable
polyimide layer. Thus the gas of interest diffuses through the membrane and undergoes a chemical reaction with the electrolyte, consuming or forming an ion to be
detected by the underlying ISFET. The local activity of this ion is proportional to
the amount of gas dissolved in the sample, and thus the ISFET response is directly
related to the concentration of sample. One example of this is the Severinghaus
method for the detection of carbon dioxide [29-31].

7.4.2.3 EnFET

Enzyme-FETs or EnFETs use the specific binding capabilities of enzymes as well
as their biocatalytic activity to create FET-based biosensors. Enzymatic action of an
enzyme on its substrate gives rise to the production or consumption of ions which

can be detected by an underlying ISFET or ChemFET if the enzyme is immobilised sufficiently close to its sensing membrane.

The first EnFET was proposed by Janata and Moss in 1976 [32], and was realised in 1980 with a penicillin-sensitive biosensor using the enzyme penicillinase to catalyse the hydrolysis of penicillin – a reaction which produces hydrogen ions [33]. Since then, a wide range of EnFETs have been reported for the detection of glucose, sucrose, maltose, ethanol, lactose, urea and creatinine among others. References to these reports can be found in the review by Schoning and Poghossian [34] and one of the most active research groups in the field of EnFET devices based between Ukraine and the Ecole Centrale de Lyon in France review their own work of the past decade in [35].

EnFET construction involves the attachment of an enzyme or an enzyme-containing layer onto the inorganic gate insulator of the underlying ISFET or ChemFET sensor – a research topic which has generated much investigation. Several methods and protocols have been attempted with varying degrees of success, including physical or chemical adsorption, entrapment within polymeric matrices, covalent binding, cross-linking by bifunctional agents such as glutaraldehyde and mixed physicochemical methods. The simplest and most frequently used methods are the drop-on technique and the spin-coating or dip-coating of a mounted sensor chip into an enzyme solution [34]. To improve often poor adhesion of the enzyme layer, prior surface silinisation of the inorganic gate insulator is often performed.

Specific difficulties associated with EnFETs other than problems of enzyme adhesion are their nonlinear and limited dynamic range. Also, the buffer capacity of the sample solution, which is itself pH-dependent, will often counteract the ion-generating or ion-depletion reaction catalysed by the enzyme in a non-linear manner. This however is not a major concern if the enzyme layer is immobilised close enough to the pH-sensing gate. Another source of non-linearity is the pH-dependency of enzyme kinetics, although this is well modelled and therefore has the potential to be overcome through intelligent local processing.

7.4.3 Towards Biochemically Inspired Processing with ISFETs

Despite some difficulties in terms of reliability and reproducibility, the ISFET and its derivatives have been by far the most popular miniaturised potentiometric sensor over recent decades, and the number of ISFET-related publications between 1999 and 2005 approaches 400. Current research directions in this field are the optimisation of the CMOS-based fabrication process, development of on-chip reference electrodes, drift and temperature compensation techniques, cancellation of interference from other ions and modification of the sensing membrane to sense different ions, metabolites and antigens.

Research thus far has not however strayed from traditional interface techniques of instrumentation amplifiers and op-amps – the main innovation being that these are now being integrated on-chip. Yet ISFETs, being transistor-based, give plenty of scope for exploration of existing knowledge of device physics and circuit techniques that we are familiar with from MOSFET design summarised in Tables 7.1 and 7.2 and their application to devices with a chemical input.

7.4.3.1 Weak Inversion Operation

A first step towards exploiting device characteristics of ISFET-based sensors has been made by operating them in the ultra low power current-mode analogue region known as "weak inversion" or "subthreshold", where in digital terms the transistor would be considered "switched off". The current-mode analogue approach [9] allows operations such as addition, subtraction, multiplication, division, scaling, thresholding, power law operations and filtering to be performed at a fraction of the silicon area and power associated with digital processing, as discussed in Section 7.3.

In the weak inversion region, MOSFET-based transistors are characterised by diffusion of electrons across the channel, rather than drift across an electric field when the device is "switched on" above a given threshold voltage. This operating region is characterised by current levels typically from 1pA to 10nA, and generally powered by low (~1V) power supply voltages, leading readily to the realisation of analogue micropowered designs. Boltzmann diffusion of electrons in weakly-inverted MOSFET devices dictates an exponential voltage to current relationship:

$$I_D = I_0 \frac{W}{L} e^{V_{GS}/nU_T} \tag{7.1}$$

where I_D is the drain current, I_0 is the pre-exponential multiplier, W and L are gate width and length, V_{GS} is the gate-source voltage, n is the subthreshold slope factor and $U_T = kT/q$ is the thermal voltage.

When an ISFET is operated in weak inversion [36], this equation is modified to include the term V_{chem} which accounts for the linear modulation of ISFET threshold voltage by the pH of the solution:

$$I_D = I_0 \frac{W}{L} e^{V_{GS}/nU_T} e^{-V_{chem}/U_T} \tag{7.2}$$

V_{chem} groups various chemical potentials between the reference electrode and the ISFET surface insulator (*e.g.* Si_3N_4) such as liquid junction potentials and work functions and to a first approximation is linearly proportional to pH with a slightly sub-Nernstian sensitivity of 55mV/pH at 298K. This is primarily due to the Boltzmann distribution of hydrogen ions in the electrolyte's diffuse layer, which gives rise to a potential across the electrolyte that varies logarithmically with hydrogen ion concentration and hence linearly with pH.

The dependence of V_{chem} on pH is modelled using a combination of the site-binding theory and the Gouy-Chapman-Stern double-layer theory to model charge distribution across the electrolyte. The ISFET is based on a MOSFET with a remote gate (reference electrode, **G**) exposing a chemically-sensitive insulator (**G'**) to an electrolyte (Figure 7.7) and can be represented by a behavioural macromodel such as that of Martinoia *et al* [37] in which V_{chem} is given by:

$$V_{chem} = \gamma + 2.303\alpha U_T pH \tag{7.3}$$

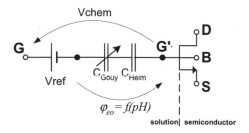

Figure 7.7 ISFET behavioural macromodel.

where γ is a grouping of pH-independent chemical potentials and α varies between 0 and 1 and relates ISFET sensitivity $S = dV/dpH$ to the ideal Nernstian sensitivity $S_N = 2.303 U_T$.

Substituting the sub-Nernstian logarithmic property of the electrolyte (7.3) into the Boltzmann exponential distribution of the ISFET (7.2):

$$I_D = I_0 \exp\left(\frac{V_{GS}}{nU_T}\right) K_{chem} [ionX]^{\alpha/n} \tag{7.4}$$

where $K_{chem} = \exp(-\gamma/nU_T)$ is a pH-independent constant. The operation of the ISFET in weak inversion thus generates a power-law relation between drain current and ion concentration for a fixed gate-source voltage of the form $I_D = k_1 [ion]^{k_2}$ as in (7.4). This is because the exponential current-voltage characteristic of the transistor in weak inversion is countered by the logarithmic voltage-ionic concentration of the Nernst equation. It is the effective cancellation of the same physical phenomenon – diffusion: one ionic, the other electronic.

The advantage of operating in this region is two-fold:

- The lower current bias and voltage levels required to operate the transistor in its weak inversion region results in significantly reduced supply power consumption.
- The exponential transconductance characteristic means that these devices can be used as "translinear elements" in the synthesis of static and dynamic translinear circuits, the current-mode analogue design methodology for realising mathematical operations such as power law manipulations, multiplications, correlations and filtering.

7.4.3.2 Translinear Design Methodology

The *Translinear Principle* was introduced by Barry Gilbert for bipolar transistors in 1975 [15], and is one of the most important circuit theory contributions in the analysis and synthesis of nonlinear circuits. Due to their exponential characteristics, the principle has been extended to MOS transistors in weak inversion [38] for the realization of ultra-low power signal processing circuitry.

The principle has recently been extended to the operation of the ISFET in the weak inversion region to form a *Biochemical Translinear Principle* [39]. The simple "translinear loop" shown in Figure 7.8 has the property that the product of the clockwise currents is equal to the product of the anticlockwise currents, scaled by the ionic concentration ratio of ion B over ion A to a known power:

$$\frac{I_{D4}.I_{D3}}{I_{D1}.I_{D2}} = \frac{K_{chemB}[ionB]^{\alpha/n}}{K_{chemA}[ionA]^{\alpha/n}} \tag{7.5}$$

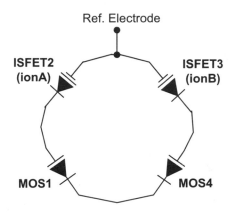

Figure 7.8 A translinear loop for which the ratio of clockwise current densities to anticlockwise current densities is proportional to the concentration ratio of ion B to ion A (to a known power).

This Biochemical Translinear Principle can be manipulated to perform many mathematical operations on biochemical signals. It is immediately apparent from the simple translinear loop shown in Figure 7.8 that if the enzymes urease and creatinase were bound to ISFETs 2 and 3 respectively, then this circuit would calculate in real-time the urea to creatinine concentration ratio to a known power with just four transistors, with no need for digital processing.

A second, purely electronic translinear loop could then be used to raise this concentration ratio to the power of 1. Plasma urea to creatinine ratio is a key biomarker in the signalling of renal failure and gastrointestinal bleeding, and is an example of a useful parameter in the context of real-time monitoring for BSNs.

As well as real-time concentration ratio calculations, translinear circuits are ideally suited to power law manipulations, be it exponents or roots. The circuit in Figure 7.9 performs a squaring function; designed to linearise (7.4). Linear sensor output with respect to concentration of species X as opposed to pX, which is logarithmic, is important for subsequent closed-loop feedback applications on-chip, such as drug or hormone delivery, as the control problem is significantly reduced if the sensor system is linear with respect to the real-world biochemical parameter. This circuit shows how easily the sensor output can be linearised in the current-mode analogue domain using translinear circuits. With the inclusion of capacitors into such circuits, log-domain and dynamic translinear circuits can be synthesised, which is useful in performing frequency-dependent filtering functions on sensed biochemical signals.

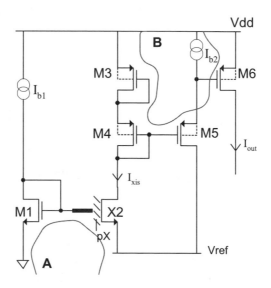

Figure 7.9 I_{out} is linearly proportional to the concentration of the ion species detected by ISFET X2 [39].

Of the operations listed in Tables 7.1 and 7.2, only two (division and squaring) have been demonstrated using the current-mode analogue approach with weak inversion devices. Of the remaining operations, some are trivial using this approach (*e.g.* addition), but there remains much to be explored in terms of applying some of the analogue techniques summarised in these tables, both current- and voltage-mode. For fully optimised, bio-inspired systems, hybrid architectures featuring the interaction between analogue and digital processing should be further investigated.

7.5 Applications of Ultra-Low Power Signal Processing for BSN

In a BSN with limited bandwidth and power constraints, the conventional method of data acquisition and analogue-to-digital data conversion with signal processing taking place after transmission is not optimal. BSNs are a prime candidate for bio-inspired local processing to take place at the sensor front-end before transmission. This processing could include spatial and temporal averaging for drift and failure tolerance, but also trendspotting and adaptivity. The key principle of bio-inspired engineering in this application area is that biology does not often deal in absolute values, but in relative changes from a given norm.

Ultra-low power signal processing is not limited to ISFET-based devices, and design methodologies such as translinear circuit synthesis do not need to be applied directly to the sensor as they were in Section 7.4.3 – indeed, this can only apply to CMOS devices with exponential transconductance properties such as diodes or transistors in weak inversion. The analogue signal processing design methodologies should thus be applied as close to the sensor front-end as possible, thereby building intelligence and adaptivity into the sensor. One example lies in predictive array processing for robustness of sensor output by compensating sensor drift, temperature dependence, sensor failure and interference. Integrated electronics can adaptively change the bias and gain of each sensor in an array individually.

Another direction for on-chip intelligence is the implementation of the Hilbert transform for voltammetric sensors as mentioned in Chapter 2 as an analogue filter bank rather than off-chip digital processing which would give far-reaching instantaneous discrimination capabilities. In optics, interest is developing in the field of integrated optics, which is leading to the development of small chip-sized UV-vis and near-IR spectrometers [40]. A future direction could be the application of expertise from the field of bio-inspired vision chips using hybrid, distributed processing techniques in an embedded photodiode array to facilitate feature extraction [41-43]. Similarly, in ECG sensors, micropower hybrid implementation of low/band pass filters, derivative and template matching functions at the electrode input can extract features such as QRS-wave (heartbeat) complex and detect abnormalities including arrhythmias without the need to continually stream the raw ECG data.

Further scope for bio-inspired design lies in adaptive therapeutics based on neural and metabolic cell modelling. Instead of providing feedback to biological systems using traditional multivariate analysis or PID control, one can use electronic models of excitable cells. It has already been shown that neural models such as the Hodgkin and Huxley model can be realised in silicon with weak inversion analogue devices [44], and this principle can be extended to metabolic cells in the body such as pancreatic beta cells, whose activity is dominated by action potentials generated by cellular sodium, potassium and calcium ion concentrations. Fully integrated CMOS sensors and processing circuitry will have the ability to measure intra- and extra-cellular ion concentration and to then generate the appropriate signalling to neighbouring cells via electrodes or to a biomimetic hormone delivery unit for example. In addition to neural bridge applications, this type of architecture can be useful in therapeutic endocrine control systems for insulin delivery to diabetic patients.

In summary, the biomedical applications which could benefit from the union of CMOS-based sensors with expertise in optimised hybrid electronics are unlimited if one dares to leave the domain of traditional interface techniques. Two current-mode analogue processing implementations have been proposed for CMOS ISFETs and their derivatives, but there remains an extensive toolkit of circuit techniques and mathematical operations to be explored with biosensors in mind, as well as a plethora of CMOS biosensors each with their own signal processing requirements. These biologically-driven intelligent biochemical circuits hold the key to the low power *in situ* diagnostics and therapeutics in future BSN designs.

References

1. Mead CA. Analog VLSI and neural systems. Reading, Massachusetts: Addison-Wesley, 1989.
2. Gregorian R, Temes GC. Analog MOS integrated circuits for signal processing. John Wiley and Sons, 1986.
3. Toumazou C, Hugues JBC, Battersby NC. Switched currents: an analogue technique for digital technology. IEE Publishing, 1993.
4. Hosticka BJ. Performance comparison of analog and digital circuits. Proceedings of the IEEE 1985; 73(1):25-29.
5. Vittoz EA. Future of analog in the VLSI environment. In: Proceedings of the IEEE International Symposium on Circuits and Systems, New Orleans, Louisiana, 1990; 2:1372-1375.
6. Furth PM, Andreou AG. Bit-energy comparison of discrete and continuous signal representations at the circuit level. In: Proceedings of the Fourth Workshop on Physics and Computation 1996.
7. Sarpeshkar R. Efficient precise computation with noisy components: extrapolation from an electronic cochlea to the brain. California Institute of Technology, PhD Thesis, 1997.
8. Gilbert B. A precise four-quadrant multiplier with subnanosecond response. IEEE Journal of Solid-State Circuits 1968; 3(4):365-373.
9. Toumazou C, Lidgey FJ, Haigh DG. Analogue IC design: the current-mode approach. London: Peter Peregrinus Ltd., 1990.
10. Allen PE, Sinencio ES, Sanchez-Sinencio E. Switched capacitor circuits. Kluwer Academic Publishers, 1990.
11. Kinniment DJ, Garside JD, Gao B. A comparison of power consumption in some CMOS adder circuits. In: Proceedings of the International Workshop on Power and Timing Modeling Optimization and Simulation, Oldenburg, Germany, 1995; 119-132.
12. Ramirez-Angulo J, Thoutam S, Lopez-Martin A, Carvajal RJ. Low-voltage CMOS analog four quadrant multiplier based on flipped voltage followers. In: Proceedings of the IEEE International Symposium on Circuits and Systems 2004; 1:681-684.
13. Satyanarayana JH, Parhi KK. A theoretical approach to estimation of bounds on power consumption in digital multipliers. IEEE Transactions on Circuits and Systems II 1997; 44(6):473-481.
14. Weste NHE, Eshraghian K. Principles of CMOS VLSI design: a systems perspective. Addison-Wesley, 1993.
15. Gilbert B. Current-mode circuits from a translinear viewpoint: a tutorial. In: Toumazou C, Lidgey FJ, Haigh DG (eds) Analogue IC Design: the Current-Mode Approach. London: Peter Peregrinus Ltd., 1990; 11-91.

16. Quoc-Hoang D, Trung-Kien N, Sang-Gug L. Ultra low-voltage low-power exponential voltage-mode circuit with tunable output range. In: Proceedings of the IEEE International Symposium on Circuits and Systems, Vancouver, Canada, 2004; 2:729-732.

17. Ercegovac MD, Lang T. Division and square root: digit-recurrence algorithms and implementations. Kluwer Academic Publisher, 1994.

18. Drakakis EM, Payne AJ, Toumazou C. Log-domain filtering and the Bernoulli cell. IEEE Transactions on Circuits and Systems I 1999; 46(5):559-571.

19. Proakis J, Manolakis DG. Digital signal processing: principles, algorithms and applications. Pearson US Imports and PHIPEs, 1995.

20. Hierlemann A, Baltes H. CMOS-based chemical microsensors. Analyst 2003; 128(1):15-28.

21. Bausells J, Carrabina J, Errachid A, Merlos A. Ion-sensitive field-effect transistors fabricated in a commercial CMOS technology. Sensors and Actuators B: Chemical 1999; 57(1-3):56-62.

22. Wong HS, White MH. A CMOS-integrated ISFET-operational amplifier chemical sensor employing differential sensing. IEEE Transactions on Electron Devices 1989; 36(3):479-487.

23. Nam H, Cha GS, Strong TD, Ha J, Sim H, Hower RW, *et al*. Micropotentiometric sensors. Proceedings of the IEEE 2003; 91(6):870-880.

24. Bergveld P. Thirty years of ISFETOLOGY: what happened in the past 30 years and what may happen in the next 30 years. Sensors and Actuators B: Chemical 2003; 88(1):1-20.

25. Bergveld P. Development of an ion-sensitive solid-state device for neurophysiological measurements. IEEE Transactions on Biomedical Engineering 1970; BM17(1):70-71.

26. Sibbald A, Covington AK, Carter RF. Online patient-monitoring system for the simultaneous analysis of blood K^+, Ca^{2+}, Na^+ and pH using a quadruple-function CHEMFET integrated-circuit sensor. Medical and Biological Engineering and Computing 1985; 23(4):329-338.

27. Watanabe K, Tohda K, Sugimoto H, Eitoku F, Inoue H, Suzuki K, *et al*. Ion-sensitive field effect transistor as a monovalent cation detector for ion chromatography and its application to the measurement of Na^+ and K^+ concentrations in serum. Journal of Chromatography 1991; 566(1):109-116.

28. Van der Wal PD, van den Berg A, Derooij NF. Universal approach for the fabrication of $Ca^{(2+)}$-, K^+- and NO_3- - sensitive membrane ISFETs. Sensors and Actuators B: Chemical 1994; 18(1-3):200-207.

29. Tsukada K, Miyahara Y, Shibata Y, Miyagi H. An integrated chemical sensor with multiple ion and gas sensors. Sensors and Actuators B: Chemical 1990; 2(4):291-295.

30. Arquint P, van den Berg A, van der Schoot BH, de Rooij NF, Buhler H, Morf WE, *et al*. Integrated blood-gas sensor for pO_2, pCO_2 and pH. Sensors and Actuators B: Chemical 1993; 13(1-3):340-344.

31. Han JH, Cui DF, Li YT, Cai J, Dong Z, Zhang H, *et al*. A new-type of transcutaneous pCO_2 sensor. Sensors and Actuators B: Chemical 1995; 24(1-3):156-158.

32. Janata J, Moss SD. Chemically sensitive field-effect transistors. Biomedical Engineering 1976; 11(7):241-245.
33. Caras S, Janata J. Field-effect transistor sensitive to penicillin. Analytical Chemistry 1980; 52(12):1935-1937.
34. Schoning MJ, Poghossian A. Recent advances in biologically sensitive field-effect transistors (BioFETs). Analyst 2002; 127(9):1137-1151.
35. Dzyadevych SV, Soldatkin AP, Korpan YI, Arkypova VN, El'skaya AV, Chovelon JM, et al. Biosensors based on enzyme field-effect transistors for determination of some substrates and inhibitors. Analytical and Bioanalytical Chemistry 2003; 377(3):496-506.
36. Shepherd L, Toumazou C. Weak inversion ISFETs for ultra-low power bio-chemical sensing and real-time analysis. Sensors and Actuators B: Chemical 2005; 107(1):468-473.
37. Martinoia S, Massobrio G. A behavioral macromodel of the ISFET in SPICE. Sensors and Actuators B: Chemical 2000; 62(3):182-189.
38. Andreou AG, Boahen KA. Translinear circuits in subthreshold MOS. Analog Integrated Circuits and Signal Processing 1996; 9(2):141-166.
39. Shepherd LM, Toumazou C. A biochemical translinear principle with weak inversion ISFETs. IEEE Transactions on Circuits and Systems I 2005.
40. Diamond D. Principles of chemical and biological sensors. Wiley Interscience, 1998.
41. Moini A. Vision chips. Kluwer Academic Publishers, 1999.
42. Constandinou TG, Georgiou J, Toumazou C. Towards a bio-inspired mixed-signal retinal processor. In: Proceedings of IEEE International Symposium on Circuits and Systems 2004; 5:493-496.
43. Constandinou TG, Georgiou J, Toumazou C. Nano-power mixed-signal tunable edge-detection circuit for pixel-level processing in next generation vision systems. Electronics Letters 2003; 39(25):1774-1775.
44. Toumazou C, Georgiou J, Drakakis EM. Current-mode analogue circuit representation of Hodgkin and Huxley neuron equations. Electronics Letters 1998; 34(14):1376-1377.

8

Multi-Sensor Fusion

Guang-Zhong Yang and Xiaopeng Hu

8.1 Introduction

In previous chapters, we have discussed the issues concerning hardware, communication and network topologies for the practical deployment of *Body Sensor Networks* (BSNs). The pursuit of low power miniaturised distributed sensing under the patient's natural physiological conditions has also imposed significant challenges on integrating information from what is often heterogeneous, incomplete, and error-prone sensor data. For BSN, the nature of errors can be attributed to a number of sources, but motion artefacts, the inherent limitations and possible malfunctions of the sensors, and communication errors are the main causes of concern. In practice, it is desirable to rely on sensors with redundant or complementary data to maximise the information content and reduce both systematic and random errors. This, in essence, is the main drive for multi-sensor fusion, which is concerned with the synergistic use of multiple sources of information.

In cardiac sensing, for example, both ECG and haemodynamic signals, such as the impedance cardiograph or blood pressure, have mutually correlated information of the heart due to the physiological coupling of the mechanical and electrical functions. In situations where the ECG signal is degraded, either due to poor electrode connection or patient movement, joint analysis of additional sensors such as the ventricular pressure, can ensure sustained cardiac rhythm monitoring. This resolves some of the intrinsic ambiguities involved in rhythm disturbance when it is assessed by ECG alone [1]. Whilst the use of multiple identical sensors for error minimisation is relatively intuitive to understand, the reliance on different sensors in terms of both sensing type and location will require the use of general principles of pattern recognition and machine learning. In practice, the use of multiple sensors with information fusion has the following main advantages compared to single sensor systems [2]:

- Improved *Signal-to-Noise Ratio* (SNR)
- Enhanced robustness and reliability in the event of sensor failure
- Extended parameter coverage
- Integration of independent features and prior knowledge
- Increased dimensionality of the measurement

- Improved resolution, precision, confidence, and hypothesis discrimination
- Reduced uncertainty

The origin of sensor fusion can be dated back to 1970s when it was studied extensively for robotics and defence research. To address some of the main issues in data fusion and unify the terminology and procedures involved, a Data Fusion Sub-panel to the *Joint Directors of Laboratories* (JDL) Technical Panel for C3 (command, control, communications) was established by the US Department of Defence in 1986. Under the JDL data fusion framework, five levels of processing have been defined, which include Sub-Object Data Association and Estimation (L0), Object Refinement (L1), Situation Refinement (L2), Significance Estimation or Threat Refinement (L3), and Process Refinement (L4) [3, 4]. The JDL also gave a definition of data fusion, which was subsequently refined as a multilevel, multifaceted process dealing with the automatic detection, association, correlation, estimation, and combination of data and information from single or multiple sources [5]. Although the JDL framework was mainly developed with a strong military emphasis in mind, some of the basic principles provided are still applicable to BSN.

8.1.1 Information Interaction

In general, the nature of information interaction involved in sensor fusion can be classified as *competitive, complementary*, and *cooperative* fusion [6-9]. In competitive fusion, each sensor provides equivalent information about the process being monitored. It typically involves the handling of redundant, but sometimes inconsistent, measurements. The nature of competitive sensing means that it is ideally suited for *in situ* multi-sensor calibration, consistency maximisation, and fault tolerant sensing.

In complementary fusion, on the other hand, sensors do not depend on each other directly as each sensor captures different aspects of the physical process. The measured information is merged to form a more complete picture of the phenomenon. The example given above on combined ECG and haemodynamic sensing is a typical case of complementary fusion. Another form of complementary fusion is the use of a predefined physical model to combine sensor readings to collectively estimate a higher level of measurement indices. For example, arterial compliance, which is related to aging and diseases such as arteriosclerosis, can be quantified from a pressure-volume relationship by measuring the ability of a vessel to distend with increasing transmural pressure.

In cooperative fusion, sensors work together to provide information that is not obtainable by any of the sensors alone. In stereovision, for example, the measured feature disparity in the image pairs permits the estimation of the depth and shape of the object. Due to the compounding effect, the accuracy and reliability of cooperative fusion is sensitive to inaccuracies in all simple sensor components used. For BSN, the main objective of sensor fusion is to combine information from different sensors to capture data with improved reliability, precision, fault tolerance, and inferencing power to a degree that is beyond the capacity of each sensor.

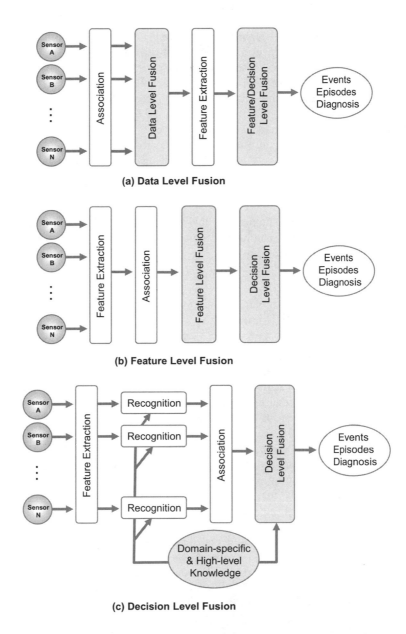

Figure 8.1 Schematic diagrams showing three different fusion architectures at data, feature and decision levels (adapted from DL Hall [3]).

8.1.2 Levels of Processing

From the data processing model point of view, sensor fusion can also be grouped into three different levels of fusion as shown in Figure 8.1, *i.e.*, *direct data fusion*, *feature-level fusion*, and *decision-level fusion* [3].

If the sensors are measuring the same physical parameter with the data derived being commensurate, raw sensor data can be directly combined. Otherwise, the data needs to be fused at the feature or decision level. For feature-level fusion, features are first extracted from the sensor data to form multi-dimensional feature vectors so that general pattern recognition methods can be applied. For decision-level fusion, however, the information used has already been abstracted to a certain level through preliminary sensor or feature level processing such that high-level decision can be made. Popular techniques used for this level of fusion include classical inference, Bayesian inference, and Dempster-Shafer's method. Decision level fusion is also an ideal place to incorporate *a priori* knowledge and high-level domain specific information.

In terms of data communication, the higher levels of data abstraction can have a positive impact on the bandwidth requirement. In a distributed sensor network, feature-level and decision-level fusion allows effective deployment of heterogeneous, independent sensor clusters.

8.2 Direct Data Fusion

In general, sensor replication poses the problem of data integration. For multi-sensor data fusion, it is usually assumed that communication, storage, and processing systems are reliable and the focus is on fusion algorithms that can integrate data from either homogeneous or heterogeneous sources [10]. Direct data fusion is useful for sensor arrays which, unlike the traditional sensor designs, are typically based on the use of poor selective sensors. With sensor fusion, it is possible to overcome some of the inherent limitations of each single element of the ensemble. Another use of direct data fusion for sensor networks is self-calibration. Traditionally, calibration is done during production time and recalibration is necessary periodically for most sensors as factors such as aging, thermal drift, decay and damage can have a detrimental effect on the accuracy of the readings. Frequent recalibration of large scale sensor networks, however, can be problematic in pervasive sensing environments due to the number of sensors involved. Furthermore, MEMS-based sensors such as those used as accelerometers are usually not calibrated after production and the sensors can have a sensitivity and offset bias on each axis. To illustrate the role of direct data fusion, we will outline in this section two examples of direct data fusion for optimal averaging with outlier detection for sensor arrays, and source separation of mixed signals from a set of networked sensors.

8.2.1 Optimal Averaging for Sensor Arrays

In its most basic form, sensor fusion can be implemented as a simple average of all sensor readings. This approach, however, is not robust as any error in the individual measurements is included in the final estimate. As a result, the final signal can deviate significantly from its true value. Weighted averaging reduces the contribution from the worst sensors but do not solve the robustness issue as erroneous sensor measurements are still included in the final estimate. Numerically, the errors involved in sensors can be attributed to systematic errors or so called *bias*, which is an offset of the mean amplitude of the sensor readings from the true value. This bias can be time dependent and affected by external factors such as thermal and chemical drift. Another source of error is random error or noise. This random component can be attributed to hardware noise or other unpredictable transient signals that cause random fluctuations of the readings. In sensor fusion, the statistical distribution of the random error can be modelled with *a priori* knowledge. In the absence of such information, Gaussian distributions are commonly adopted.

By taking into account scaling, bias and random noise errors, the output $x_i(t)$ of the ith sensor in relation to the original signal $s_0(t)$ can be represented as:

$$x_i(t) = \left(1 + \varepsilon_i(t)\right) s_0(t) + b_i(t) + n_i(t) \tag{8.1}$$

where $n_i(t)$ is measurement noise, and $\varepsilon_i(t)$ and $b_i(t)$ are the scale and offset biases, respectively. Given a set of N noisy measurements, the recovery of the true signal for the problem formulated above is ill-posed. It is only solvable with regard to certain constraints or specific objective functions. For example, Unser and Eden [11] have shown that the optimal weighting coefficients for N noisy channels can be determined by maximising a quadratic SNR defined by:

$$\text{SNR} = N \; \frac{\sum_{i=1}^{K}\left(\overline{s}_i - \overline{s}\right)^2}{\frac{1}{N}\sum_{i=1}^{N}\left\|\mathbf{s}_i - \overline{\mathbf{s}}\right\|^2} \tag{8.2}$$

where the temporal signal associated with each sensor is discretised as a K-dimensional vector, *i.e.*, $\mathbf{x}_i$ and $\mathbf{s}_i$ represent the measured and the source signal for sensor i, respectively, and

$$\overline{\mathbf{s}} = \left[\overline{s}_1, \cdots, \overline{s}_K\right]^T \tag{8.3}$$

which represents the ensemble average of $\mathbf{s}_i$ $(i = 1, \cdots, N)$. In the above equations, T denotes vector transpose, and $\|\;\|^2$ is the square norm of a vector. In (8.2), $\overline{s}_i$ represents the cross channel average for sample i, and $\overline{s}$ is the mean signal given by:

$$\overline{s} = \frac{1}{M}\sum_{i=1}^{K}\overline{s}_i \qquad (8.4)$$

The above SNR in fact represents the ratio between the rescaled signal and residual noise energies. In (8.2), the relationship between $\mathbf{s}_i$ and $\mathbf{x}_i$ is given by:

$$\mathbf{s}_i = w_i\left[\mathbf{x}_i - b_i\mathbf{1}\right] \qquad (8.5)$$

where $\mathbf{1}$ is a *K*-dimensional vector of all 1's, and w_i $(i=1,\cdots,N)$ are the optimal coefficients to be sought. By referring to (8.1) and ignoring n_i, it can be seen that the ideal value of w_i is $(1+\varepsilon_i)^{-1}$.

It can be proved that the optimal estimate of the scale and offset biases shown in (8.1) can be derived independently. For any given coefficient $\mathbf{w} = \left[w_1,\cdots,w_N\right]^T$, the optimal value of b_i that maximises (8.2) is given by:

$$b_i = \overline{x}_i \quad (i=1,\cdots,N) \qquad (8.6)$$

i.e., the average of the measured signal values. Furthermore, it can also be shown that the optimal weighting coefficient $\mathbf{w} = \left[w_1,\cdots,w_N\right]^T$ is given by the first generalised eigenvector of the characteristic equation

$$\mathbf{Rw} = \beta\mathbf{Dw} \qquad (8.7)$$

where $\mathbf{R} = \left[r_{ij}\right]$ is the $N \times N$ centred inner product matrix defined by

$$r_{ij} = \mathbf{x}_i^T\mathbf{x}_j - K\overline{x}_i\overline{x}_j \qquad (8.8)$$

and D is the corresponding diagonal matrix

$$\mathbf{D} = \left[d_{ij}\right] \text{ with } \begin{cases} d_{ii} = r_{ii} \\ d_{ij} = 0, \ (i \neq j) \end{cases} \qquad (8.9)$$

To demonstrate the effect of the above optimum averaging scheme, Figure 8.2 shows an example source signal and the corresponding sampled data by five array sensors, each with different scale and offset biases. From this figure, it is evident that signals from channels 1 and 3 are severely corrupted. Direct averaging without discriminating the quality of the data can lead to significant errors. Figure 8.3 gives a comparison of the result with and without the use of the maximum SNR criterion described. It is also interesting to see that after normalising each signal trace with $\left\|\mathbf{x}_i - \overline{x}_i\mathbf{1}\right\|^2$, the associated weights for each channel is 0.12, 0.26, 0.10, 0.26, and

0.26 respectively, *i.e.*, channels 1 and 3 are detected as outliers, thus suggesting the potential use of the method for channel anomaly detection.

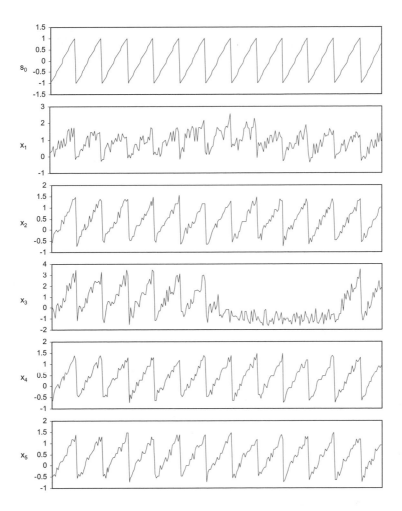

Figure 8.2 An example source signal (top) sampled by an array of five sensors with different scale and offset biases. Each channel is affected by sensor noise but with channels 1 and 3 being most significant.

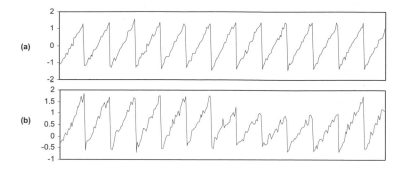

Figure 8.3 The recovered signal with optimal (a) and direct (b) averaging.

8.2.2 Source Recovery

In the previous section, we have assumed that the measured signals are directly at source. For many BSN applications, however, this is not possible. For example, in the case of EEG (*Electroencephalography*) and MEG (*Magnetoencephalography*) measurements, signals associated with the spontaneous activity or evoked potentials are mixed, and each sensor measures a different combination of the source signals. In this case, source separation of mixed signals from a set of sensors is required, and this aspect of direct data fusion has attracted a significant amount of interest in recent years.

The aim of source separation of blindly mixed signals is to recover unobserved signals or sources from temporally and spatially correlated observations. Generally, a *Blind Source Separation* (BSS) problem can be formulated as finding an inverse system that recovers the original signal sources given an observed number of sensor signals $\mathbf{x}(t) = \left[x_1(t), \cdots, x_N(t) \right]^T$ [12]. The mathematical formulation of BSS is typically given in the form of a statistical estimation problem. This model is generative, which means that it describes how the observed data is generated by a process of mixing the source components.

By assuming $\mathbf{s}(t) = \left[s_1(t), \cdots, s_M(t) \right]^T$ as the unknown signal sources mixed according to a vector valued non-linear function $\mathbf{f}$, the observations $\mathbf{x}(t)$ can be represented as a non-linear mixture of $\mathbf{s}(t)$ and additive noise $\mathbf{n}(t)$, *i.e.*,

$$\mathbf{x}(t) = \mathbf{f}\left(\mathbf{s}(t)\right) + \mathbf{n}(t) \tag{8.10}$$

In most applications, it is desirable to separate the original source signals, as well as to provide information about their spatio-temporal distributions. Ideally, BSS algorithms should make minimal assumptions about the underlying process and the nature of the sources. In practice, however, source separation algorithms range from almost blind to highly application specific, where certain characteristics about the sources are available.

For linear mixing models, *Independent Component Analysis* (ICA) is a valuable tool for BSS and it generally conforms to the following main assumptions:

- The sources are linearly mixed, and the standard formulation of ICA requires at least as many sensors as sources.
- The sources are at each time instant mutually independent, and at most one source is normally distributed.
- No sensor noise or only low additive noise signals are permitted. However, noise is an independent source itself and if as many sensor outputs are available as the number of sources, the noise signal can be segregated from the mixtures.
- The mixing is assumed to be instantaneous so there is no time-delay between the sources introduced by the mixing medium.
- The mixing process is assumed to be stationary, which implies that the statistics of the signals do not change over time.

The above assumptions ensure that the ICA model is well-defined, which implies the identifiability, separability and uniqueness of the model [13]. It is important to note that the ICA model can be determined up to a scaling factor and a permutation matrix, and these ambiguities are called fundamental indeterminacy. The identifiability stated above suggests the conditions when it is possible to identify the mixing system up to the fundamental indeterminacy. The linear ICA model is identifiable when either all sources are non-Gaussian or the mixing matrix is of full column rank and at most one source is normal. Separability states that the source signals may be recovered up to some ambiguities, whereas the uniqueness ensures that the distribution of the sources can be determined. This is especially important to consider when source separation involves more sources than observations.

The mathematical formulation of the classical ICA is a simplified form of the BSS problem

$$\mathbf{x}(t) = \mathbf{A}\mathbf{s}(t) \tag{8.11}$$

where A is an $N \times M$ scalar matrix representing the unknown mixing coefficients and it is called transfer or mixing matrix. For most ICA applications, noise is either assumed to be white Gaussian with variance σ^2 or negligible. As stated earlier, noise can also be assumed to be part of the sources. In this case, the noise is assumed to be statistically independent from the other source components. The goal of ICA is to find a linear transformation W of the dependent sensor signals $\mathbf{x}(t)$ that makes the outputs as independent as possible:

$$\hat{\mathbf{s}}(t) = \mathbf{W}\mathbf{x}(t) = \mathbf{W}\mathbf{A}\mathbf{s}(t) \tag{8.12}$$

where $\hat{\mathbf{s}}(t)$ is an estimate of the sources. The sources are exactly recovered when W is the inverse of A up to a permutation and scale change. Since both the sources and the mixing coefficients are unknown, it is impossible to determine either the variances or the order of the independent components.

A common way of solving the ICA problem is to use high-order statistics. A classic result in probability theory is the central limit theorem which states that a sum of two independent random variables with finite variances has a distribution that is closer to Gaussian than any of the two original random variables. Since many real world processes yield distributions with finite variances, this explains the ubiquitous nature of the normal distributions. The above principle suggests that a linear combination of the observed mixture variables is maximally non-Gaussian if it is equal to one of the independent components. Therefore, given a function that measures the non-Gaussianity of a signal, each local maximum is an independent component. ICA estimation can be formulated as the search of directions that are maximally non-Gaussian. In practice, non-Gaussianity can be measured by using kurtosis or negentropy. Kurtosis is a higher-order cumulant based on statistical moments defined as:

$$kurt(\mathbf{x}) = E(\mathbf{x}^4) - 3\left[E(\mathbf{x}^2)\right]^2 \tag{8.13}$$

where E is the expectation. Alternatively, the normalised kurtosis can also be used:

$$\tilde{\kappa}(\mathbf{x}) = \frac{E(\mathbf{x}^4)}{\left[E(\mathbf{x}^2)\right]^2} - 3 \tag{8.14}$$

It can be shown that the kurtosis is zero for a Gaussian distribution. In general, a distribution having zero kurtosis is called mesokurtic, whereas distributions having a positive kurtosis are called super-Gaussian, or leptokurtic in statistics. If the kurtosis is negative, the respective distribution is called sub-Gaussian or platykurtic as the probability densities tend to be flatter than that of the Gaussian.

Prior to ICA estimation, it is usually useful to perform some pre-processing to the measured sensor data to make ICA simpler and better conditioned. One important pre-processing strategy in ICA is to whiten the observed variables, *i.e.*, to transform $\mathbf{x}$ linearly for deriving a new vector $\mathbf{z}$ which is white. This means that the components of $\mathbf{z}$ are uncorrelated and the covariance matrix of $\mathbf{z}$ equals the identity matrix.

In practice, a whitening transformation is always possible and a common method of achieving this is through eigenvalue decomposition of the covariance matrix, *i.e.*,

Table 8.1 Pseudo code segment for the infomax learning algorithm for ICA.

1. *Initialisation*:
   - Remove the mean value;
   - Perform whitening and $\mathbf{z} = Q\mathbf{x} = \mathrm{E}_v \mathrm{D}^{-1/2} \mathrm{E}_v^T \mathbf{x}$;
   - Initialise the separating matrix so that $\hat{V} = \mathrm{I}$.

2. *Initialise optimisation parameters*:
$$\zeta = \hat{V}\mathbf{z}$$

3. *Estimate the sign of normalised Kurtosis*:
$$\tilde{\kappa}(\zeta) = \frac{E(\zeta^4)}{\left[E(\zeta^2)\right]^2} - 3$$

   where $E(\zeta^4)$, $E(\zeta^2)$ are the fourth and second order moments and they are estimated as the mean of the fourth and second power of the random variable, respectively.

4. *Calculate contrast based on the infomax principle*:
$$\hat{V} \leftarrow V + \mu \cdot \left(\mathrm{I} - s \cdot \tanh(\zeta) \cdot \zeta^T - \zeta \cdot \zeta^T\right) \cdot V$$

   where μ is the learning rate and s is the sign calculated according to the estimation of kurtosis above.

5. *Assess convergence criteria, c*:
$$\delta V = \hat{V} - V$$
$$c \leftarrow \delta V \cdot \delta V^T$$

   If convergence criterion has not reached a predefined constant then return to Step 2.

6. *Source separation*:
   - Estimate the mixing matrix as:
$$A = \hat{V}Q^{-1}$$
   - Recover the source components as:
$$\hat{\mathbf{s}} = A^{-1}\mathbf{x} = \hat{V}^T\mathbf{z}$$

$$E\left(\mathbf{xx}^{T}\right) = \mathrm{E}_{v}\mathrm{DE}_{v}^{T} \tag{8.15}$$

where E_{v} is the orthogonal matrix of eigenvectors of $E\left(\mathbf{xx}^{T}\right)$ and

$$D = \mathrm{diag}\left(d_{1}, \cdots, d_{N}\right) \tag{8.16}$$

is the diagonal matrix of the corresponding eigenvalues. Therefore, whitening can be represented as:

$$\mathbf{z} = \mathrm{E}_{v}\mathrm{D}^{-1/2}\,\mathrm{E}_{v}^{T}\,\mathbf{x} = \mathrm{E}_{v}\mathrm{D}^{-1/2}\,\mathrm{E}_{v}^{T}\,\mathrm{A}\,\mathbf{s} \tag{8.17}$$

where $\mathrm{D}^{-1/2} = \mathrm{diag}\left(d_{1}^{-1/2}, \cdots, d_{N}^{-1/2}\right)$. It is easy to prove that $E\left(\mathbf{zz}^{T}\right) = \mathbf{I}$. The effect of whitening is that the new mixing matrix for $\mathbf{s}$ is now orthogonal, and therefore the number of parameters to be estimated for ICA is reduced from N^2 to $N(N-1)/2$.

One popular approach for estimating the ICA model is *Maximum Likelihood* (ML) estimation, which is closely connected to the infomax principle based on maximizing the output entropy, or information, of a neural network with nonlinear outputs. The pseudo-code shown in Table 8.1 outlines the infomax learning algorithm for ICA as suggested by Bell and Sejnowski [14] and further extended by Lee *et al* [15].

To illustrate how ICA can be used for BSN sensing, Figure 8.4 illustrates the epicardial surface motion measured from an *in vivo* experiment showing mixed movement signal along three orthogonal axes. The recovered ICA components are shown in Figure 8.4(b), clearly illustrating the sources of motion due to cardiac, respiratory, and other factors such as noise and jitter.

Since the introduction of the general framework for ICA in the early 80s [16, 17], many new algorithms have been proposed which lead to a range of successful applications in telecommunications, biomedical signal processing, machine learning, speech recognition, and time-series analysis. Some of the important contributions to ICA include the work of Bell and Sejnowski in developing a fast and efficient ICA based on infomax (a principle introduced by Ralph Linsker in 1992), the introduction of natural gradient by Amari and Cardoso, and Lee and Girolami's work on extending infomax ICA for general non-Gaussian signals [18]. Thus far, a number of different approaches have been pursued for blind source separation, which include maximum likelihood, Bussgang methods based on cumulants, projection pursuit and negentropy methods. It is expected that BSN will be served both as an important application base for ICA and as a source of inspiring new algorithms due to the unique features and constraints imposed by BSNs.

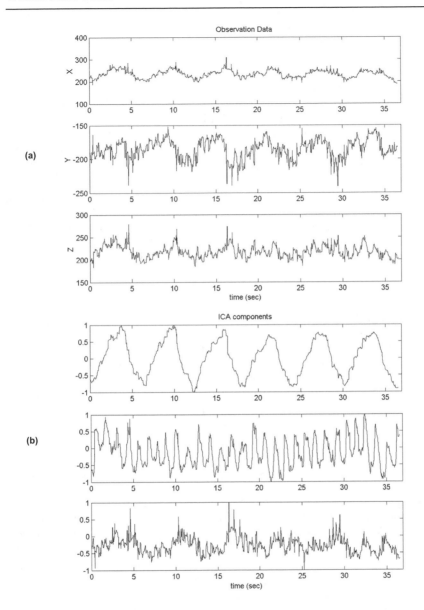

Figure 8.4 (a) The epicardial surface motion measured *in vivo* showing mixed movement signals along three orthogonal axes. (b) The recovered ICA components, illustrating the sources of motion due to respiratory (top), cardiac (middle), and noise jitter (bottom).

8.3 Feature-Level Fusion

Fusion at the feature level is the most important step of sensor fusion and it involves the integration of feature sets corresponding to different sensors. These feature vectors are then fused to form joint feature vectors from which the classification is made. Features are an abstraction of the raw data, and the purpose of feature extraction is to find main characteristics of the data that can accurately and concisely represent the original information whilst maximising the discriminative power of the identification process. The first step towards feature-level data fusion is, therefore, effective feature detection. Once the features are selected, the role of feature-level data fusion is to establish decision boundaries in the feature space that can separate patterns belonging to different classes. For general purpose sensing, there is a wide range of feature extractors that have been developed in the literature. In the following sections, we will provide a brief overview of the main feature detection and classification techniques that are applicable to BSNs.

8.3.1 Feature Detection

In general, signal features can be classified into time-domain, frequency-domain, and hybrid features as summarised in Table 8.2. Time domain features include basic waveform characteristics and signal statistics. Frequency domain features, on the other hand, concentrate on the periodic structures of the signal, which include coefficients such as those derived from Fourier and Chebyshev transforms [19]. For hybrid features, they employ both time and frequency information for complex signals, and a good example of this is the wavelet representation.

Compared to other levels of processing, sensor fusion at the feature level is the most extensively studied yet the most problematic area of research. In terms of BSN, this is also one of the key areas of development. Effective abstraction of the raw sensing data provides important opportunities in using localised processing, such as those described in Chapter 7 for minimising the power and bandwidth utilisation. It also offers the scope of using distributed inferencing for enhancing the reliability and fault tolerance of BSNs for practical deployment. Thus far, the methods developed in this area include deterministic, distance-based, fuzzy logic, neural network, manifold embedding, and probabilistic approaches. Due to the large amount of literature in this area, a comprehensive review of the techniques developed is difficult. In the subsequent sections we will only outline some of the common techniques that are relevant to BSNs. Due to the importance of neural networks for BSNs, particularly the use of *Self-Organising Maps* (SOMs) for context aware sensing and analogue hardware implementation, details concerning this class of techniques will be described in Chapter 9. Similarly, we will dedicate the most part of Chapter 10 to discussing the value of probabilistic approaches in developing autonomic BSNs with distributed inferencing.

Table 8.2 A summary of typical signal features used in general purpose sensing applications as adapted from [20].

Feature types		
Time Domain	Frequency Domain	Hybrid
• Waveform characteristics (*e.g.* slopes, amplitude, envelop, rise time, pulse width, maxima/minima locations, pulse duration, pulse repetition intervals, zero crossing rate) • Waveform statistics (*e.g.* mean, standard deviations, mean/standard deviation of signal derivatives, peak-to-valley ratio, average magnitude difference function), energy, kurtosis, entropy and moments • Chaotic models and fractal features • Ringing, overshoot phenomena, and pulse/ ambient noise floor relationship	• Periodic structures in the frequency domain • Fourier coefficients • Chebyshev coefficients • Spectral peaks • Power spectral density	• Wavelet representation (*e.g.* Gabor wavelet features) • Wigner-ville distributions • Cyclostationary representations

8.3.2 Distance Metrics

As mentioned earlier, the goal of feature-level processing is to choose features that allow pattern vectors belonging to different categories to occupy compact and disjoint regions in the feature space. In this case, the decision boundary can be based either on parametric forms or the use of probability distributions specified or learned through training. Thus far, most feature-based clustering techniques are based on the use of distance metrics for measuring similarity or dissimilarity. Let $\mathbf{u}$ and $\mathbf{v}$ be two nonzero D-dimensional feature vectors, so a true distance metric, $d(\mathbf{u}, \mathbf{v})$, must conform to the following criteria:

$$\begin{cases} d(\mathbf{u}, \mathbf{v}) = 0 \text{ if and only if } \mathbf{u} = \mathbf{v} \\ d(\mathbf{u}, \mathbf{v}) \geq 0 \text{ for all } \mathbf{u} \text{ and } \mathbf{v} \\ d(\mathbf{u}, \mathbf{v}) = d(\mathbf{v}, \mathbf{u}) \\ d(\mathbf{u}, \mathbf{v}) \leq d(\mathbf{u}, \mathbf{u}') + d(\mathbf{u}', \mathbf{v}) \end{cases} \tag{8.18}$$

In practice, distance metrics may not obey all the properties specified above. Examples of widely used distance metrics include L_p distance (Minkowski distance) and Mahalanobis distance and angle between feature vectors. Mathematically, the L_p distance is defined as:

$$d(\mathbf{u}, \mathbf{v}) = \left[\sum_{i=1}^{D} (u_i - v_i)^p \right]^{1/p}$$

(8.19)

where $1 \le p < \infty$. In general, the distance is less affected by outliers when p is small. Due to its geometrical and statistical implications, Euclidean distance (L_2) is the most popular distance metric used in practice. For instance, it corresponds to the total inter-clusters variance when used to construct the objective function in k-Means clustering. The Euclidean distance is translation and rotation invariant but highly dependent on the scale of each feature. The L_1 distance is known as the Manhattan (or city block) distance, and counting the number of disagreements is implicitly a Manhattan metric. It is worth noting that the Manhattan distance is invariant to translation or reflection with respect to a coordinate axis, but not rotation. Finally, the L_∞ distance is also known as Chebyshev distance and it corresponds to the maximum of absolute difference in any single dimension.

The above distance metrics are based on the assumption that features are independent. Mahalanobis distance, on the other hand, uses the correlations between variables to remove several of the limitations in Euclidean metrics. It measures the dissimilarity between two random vectors (**u** and **v**) in the same distribution with the covariance matrix $\Sigma = E\left([\mathbf{u} - E(\mathbf{u})][\mathbf{u} - E(\mathbf{u})]^T\right)$, *i.e.*,

$$d(\mathbf{u}, \mathbf{v}) = \sqrt{(\mathbf{u} - \mathbf{v})^T \Sigma^{-1} (\mathbf{u} - \mathbf{v})}$$

(8.20)

By taking into account the intra-feature correlation, the Mahalanobis distance is scale invariant and it can also provide curved, as well as linear, decision boundaries. However, a robust estimation of the covariance matrix is required, and therefore it is not suitable for high-dimensional feature vectors. In a special case where the covariance matrix is the identity matrix or features are uncorrelated and the variances in all directions are the same, the above equation is the same as the Euclidean distance. Furthermore, if the covariance matrix is diagonal, the measurement becomes normalised Euclidean distance. In pattern recognition, it is also common to use similarity measures based on the angle between two vectors.

8.3.3 Instance-Based Learning

Once the feature set and the similarity measures are defined, pattern classification techniques can be used to fuse the derived sensor data into meaningful events or episodes as shown in Figure 8.1(b). Instance-based learning [21] is one of the simplest non-parametric statistical learning techniques, in which the decision on how to generalise beyond the training data is deferred until a new sample is encountered [22]. The prototype vectors, in this case, are the samples in the training set but the method can also be generalised for cluster-level prototype vectors. A nearest neighbour classifier [23] classifies an unlabelled observation $\mathbf{u}$ by measuring its distances from the labelled training samples $\{(\mathbf{v}_i, c(\mathbf{v}_i))\}_{i=1}^{M}$, where $c(\mathbf{v}_i)$ is the assigned label to $\mathbf{v}_i$, to which the nearest neighbour belongs.

In other words, $\mathbf{u}$ is classified as $c(\mathbf{v}_i) \in \{C_1, C_2, ..., C_K\}$ if

$$d(\mathbf{u}, \mathbf{v}_i) = \min_{1 \leq j \leq N} d(\mathbf{u}, \mathbf{v}_j) \tag{8.21}$$

The decision can also be made based on multiple reference points. In this case, the test sample is classified as belonging to the class with the maximum number of occurrences. The level of confidence in the answer can be measured by using the number of occurrences for each class in the selected set and the distances between the test sample and the selected reference points. This learning technique is known as *k-Nearest Neighbour* (*k*-NN) classifier when a set of reference points is selected based on a predefined value k. When the reference points are selected based on their distances from the test sample by using a window of pre-specified size, the learning technique is known as Parzen window or the kernel density estimation method [24].

8.3.4 Distance-Based Clustering

The purpose of distance-based clustering is to group large sets of data $S = \{\mathbf{u}_i\}_{i=1}^{N}$ into clusters, each of which is represented by its mean (centroid) $\mathcal{C} = \{\mathbf{c}_i\}_{i=1}^{K}$. In general, distance-based clustering utilises *hard* methods where a data point is assigned to a cluster with a probability either 0 or 1, but the idea can be generalised into *soft* methods by the introduction of fuzzy membership functions. In practice, techniques such as *k*-Means [25], ISODATA [26] and agglomerative clustering algorithms [27] are most commonly used for sensor data fusion.

The *k*-Means clustering algorithm is initialised by selecting k initial cluster centres, where k is equal to the final required number of clusters. A common method for selecting the initial points is to assign the centroid of the entire dataset to the first cluster centre and selecting the subsequent centres by the data points farthest form the chosen ones. The *k*-Means training algorithm is an unsupervised iterative optimising process, aiming to minimise the sum of the distance between the data points and the corresponding centroid:

$$J(\mathcal{C}) = \sum_{i=1}^{N} d(\mathbf{u}_i, \mathbf{c}(\mathbf{u}_i)) \tag{8.22}$$

where $\mathbf{c}(\mathbf{u}_i) \in \mathcal{C}$ is the nearest centroid to the data vector $\mathbf{u}_i$. At each step, data points are reallocated to their nearest centroids and the new centroids are recalculated by using the newly assembled clusters. The iteration stops when a stopping criterion is achieved. In other words, when no reassignments occur or the maximum number of iterations is exceeded. This algorithm is insensitive to data ordering and can be parallelised [28], but that is strongly dependent on the cluster initialisation and the predefined value of k.

The *Iterative Self-Organising Data Analysis* (ISODATA) is a partitioning relocation clustering algorithm similar to k-Means. However, it allows merging and splitting of intermediate clusters according to certain parameters, and thus the number of clusters is not fixed to the predefined value k. An example set of parameters that determines the splitting and merging conditions are as follows:

- The minimum distance between two cluster centroids is d_0,
- The minimum number of data points in a cluster is n_0, and
- The maximum standard deviation allowed for each cluster is σ_0.

Two clusters are merged when the distance between their centroids is below d_0. Each cluster with fewer than n_0 samples is discarded and its elements are distributed amongst the remaining clusters. Clusters in which the maximum coordinate-wise standard deviation exceeds σ_0 are split along that coordinate. Extra conditions can also be introduced to constrain the range of the desired number of clusters. A full implementation of the ISODATA algorithm can be founded in [29].

Agglomerative clustering is a type of hierarchical clustering technique. The algorithm is initialised with a set of singleton clusters, each of which is a data point. Clusters are gradually merged based on the distance between clusters until a single big cluster is formed or a stopping criterion is reached. At each level in the hierarchy, clusters are formed from the union of two clusters at the next level down. The distance between clusters can be derived from the distance between individual points. In practice, three common measures of distance between clusters are used and they include single link, complete link and average link metrics. They are equal to the minimum, maximum and average distance from any member of one cluster to any member of the other cluster, respectively, *i.e.*,

$$\begin{cases} d_{\text{single}}\left(C_1,C_2\right) = \min\left\{d\left(\mathbf{u},\mathbf{v}\right) \mid \mathbf{u} \in C_1, \mathbf{v} \in C_2\right\} \\ d_{\text{complete}}\left(C_1,C_2\right) = \max\left\{d\left(\mathbf{u},\mathbf{v}\right) \mid \mathbf{u} \in C_1, \mathbf{v} \in C_2\right\} \\ d_{\text{average}}\left(C_1,C_2\right) = \text{avg}\left\{d\left(\mathbf{u},\mathbf{v}\right) \mid \mathbf{u} \in C_1, \mathbf{v} \in C_2\right\} \end{cases} \qquad (8.23)$$

A single big cluster output from the agglomerative clustering algorithm can be visualised as a tree or a dendrogram. Clusters can be obtained by setting a threshold level across the tree. To test which level in the hierarchy contains the best clusters, the standard measure of within-cluster variance in this case does not apply as the algorithm starts from clusters with no variance at all. Instead, we can use the difference between the level at which it was formed and the level at which it is merged, or compare the average distance within clusters to the average distance between clusters. The disadvantage of this algorithm is decisions made earlier in the process are never revisited. Therefore, if an early agglomeration destroys the structure of a cluster, it will not be detected in the later stages.

As mentioned earlier, feature vectors in the above algorithms are generally partitioned into hard clusters, *i.e.*, each feature vector can be a member of one cluster only. Fuzzy clustering resolves some of the intrinsic problems associated with hard clustering by the introduction of a membership function such that a feature vector can have multiple membership grades to multiple clusters. *Fuzzy c-Means* (FCM) [30] is a clustering technique which allows each data point to be assigned to more than one cluster with different probability or degrees of membership. It is based on an iterative minimisation of the following cost function:

$$ J_m(\mathcal{C}) = \sum_{i=1}^{N} \sum_{j=1}^{K} \lambda_{i,j}^m d\left(\mathbf{u}_i, \mathbf{c}_j\right) \tag{8.24} $$

where m is a weight exponent and $\lambda_{i,j}$ indicates the membership or degree that a data point $\mathbf{u}_i$ belongs to cluster C_j. In a fuzzy set, membership must satisfy the following conditions:

$$ \sum_{j=1}^{K} \lambda_{i,j} = 1, \forall i; \quad \sum_{i=1}^{N} \lambda_{i,j} > 0, \forall j; \quad \lambda_{i,j} \in [0,1], \forall i, j \tag{8.25} $$

At each step, the cluster centres $\mathbf{c}_j$ and the degree of membership $\lambda_{i,j}$ can be updated by:

$$ \lambda_{i,j}^m = \left[\sum_{k=1}^{K} \left(\frac{d\left(\mathbf{u}_i, \mathbf{c}_j\right)}{d\left(\mathbf{u}_i, \mathbf{c}_k\right)} \right)^{\frac{2}{m-1}} \right]^{-1} \tag{8.26} $$

$$ \mathbf{c}_j = \frac{\sum_{i=1}^{N} \lambda_{i,j}^m \mathbf{u}_i}{\sum_{i=1}^{N} \lambda_{i,j}^m} \tag{8.27} $$

A common stopping criterion for this algorithm is when the maximum change between the degree of membership at two consecutive steps is less than a pre-defined threshold ε.

$$ \max_{ij} \left\{ \left| \lambda_{i,j}(t+1) - \lambda_{i,j}(t) \right| \right\} < \varepsilon \tag{8.28} $$

It is also interesting to note that when the degree of membership is constrained to 0 and 1, the FCM becomes the hard k-Means clustering algorithm.

Other techniques for pattern classification include the decision tree method, which is performed by an iterative selection of individual features that are most salient at each node. It therefore implicitly incorporates feature selection during the classification process. The feature selection criteria used include the Fisher's criterion, node purity and the information content. Popular methods in this category include the CART and C4.5 algorithms. Their numerical implementations are both available in the public domain [31, 32]. The main advantage of the method is its speed and the possibility of interpreting the decision rules for each individual feature.

Recently, the use of *Support Vector Machines* (SVMs) has also attracted significant research interest for pattern classification. The original idea of SVM was based on Vapnik's method of finding an optimal hyper-plane for dividing two classes, which does not depend on a probability estimation [33, 34]. This optimal hyper-plane is a linear decision boundary that separates the two classes and leaves the largest margin between the vectors of the two classes. He demonstrated that the optimal hyper-plane is determined by only a small fraction of the data points, the so-called support vectors. In 1995, Cortes and Vapnik extended the method for the case of non-separable classes, and therefore made SVM a general tool for solving general classification problems [35].

Another important approach towards pattern classification is the neural networks method. The most commonly used techniques include feed-forward networks, such as the multi-layer perceptron and radial basis function networks, and SOM or Kohonen Network [36, 37]. The main advantage of the neural networks approach is due to its efficient learning algorithms and the potential for analogue hardware implementation. This is attractive for BSNs, especially for low-power processing requirements. In Chapter 9, we will provide some detailed examples of how the neural networks approach, particularly SOM, can be used for pattern classification required for context aware sensing.

8.4 Dimensionality Reduction

In pattern recognition, dimensionality reduction techniques are commonly used when the sample data is assumed to lie on a manifold, which can be non-linear in most general cases. The intrinsic dimensionality is usually related to the number of independent variables that account for most variability within the data. As only intrinsic features are preserved, dimensionality reduction may lead to a better understanding of the data. Thus far, there are a number of techniques in the literature which address the problem of dimensionality reduction. The most commonly used technique is *Principal Component Analysis* (PCA), which provides a reference system for which the variables with small variance are discarded. Thus, the high-dimensional data is projected to the subspace spanned by the most dominant principal components, leading to an approximation of the original data in a least-squares sense. The linear projections of the data are selected according to the maximal variance subject to the orthogonality constraint.

The main disadvantage of PCA is that it is only able to find linear subspaces, and therefore, cannot deal with data lying in non-linear manifolds. Furthermore, the number of principal components to keep in practice is a complicated issue, although a number of rules of thumb can be applied [38].

Similar to PCA, techniques such as Projection Pursuit can also be used to search for linear projections. It is an unsupervised technique that selects low-dimensional linear orthogonal projections of a high-dimensional point cloud by optimising an objective function called the *projection index*.

Other techniques for dimensionality reduction include *Fisher Projection* (FP) which is based on linear projection of the data to a sub-space where the classes are well-separated. With this technique, however, if the amount of training data is inadequate or the quality of some of the features is poor, then some derived dimensions may be a result of noise rather than the intrinsic differences among feature classes [39].

Although many methods can deal with non-linear dimensionality reduction, most of them rely on local dimensionality reduction. In particular, some locally linear techniques [40, 41] extend PCA to non-linear data by first performing clustering and then applying PCA for each cluster. The main limitation of such techniques is their inability to extract the global structure of the data. Common non-linear techniques leading to a global low-dimensional model of the observations include SOM as mentioned earlier [42] and *Generative Topographic Mapping* (GTM) [43].

8.4.1 Multidimensional Scaling (MDS)

Multidimensional Scaling (MDS) is a technique closely related to PCA, and is based on the definition of a similarity matrix, *i.e.* a matrix whose elements indicate the degree of similarity between the objects under consideration. MDS has been successfully applied to the visualisation of high-dimensional data in low-dimensional spaces and has been used to discover perceptual representations in psychology by analysing the similarity of stimuli to reveal the underlying structure of the data [44, 45]. The similarity matrix may be defined as a metric distance (metric scaling) but can also be provided as rank ordered information (non-metric scaling) in which case the rank order of the dissimilarities must be preserved. A common way to define the similarity matrix is to consider the stimuli as points in a multidimensional space where similarity is inversely related to the Minkowski distance.

In general, methods that explicitly use a metric are preferred since they enable generalisation from a learned embedding to unseen examples. Generalisation in this case becomes an issue of learning an approximation of the function described by the embedding. The use of a global Minkowski metric leads to a linear reconstruction of manifolds, which, by and large, may not be the most appropriate. In particular, if the Euclidean distance is used, MDS is equivalent to PCA and the method is known as *Classical Multidimensional Scaling* (CMDS).

8.4.2 Locally Linear Embedding (LLE)

Locally Linear Embedding (LLE) exploits the local geometry of the neighbouring points in the high-dimensional space in order to map the input data points onto a global coordinate system of lower dimension while the intrinsic relationships between the points are preserved [46]. Each point in the high-dimensional space is approximated by a linear combination of its neighbours and the coefficients for that combination are selected such that the mapping is invariant to scaling, rotation and translation. LLE consists of the following main steps:

1. *Computation of the neighbourhood of each data point* $\mathbf{u}_i$

   The calculations are performed through the selection of the k-nearest neighbours on the basis of the Euclidean metric. However, it is also common to determine a radius, δ, defining a ball that encompasses the neighbourhood of each point.

2. *Computation of the weights* w_{ij} *that best reconstruct each data point* $\mathbf{u}_i$ *from its neighbours*

   The following function is introduced to measure the reconstruction error that needs to be minimised:

$$\varepsilon(w) = \sum_i \left| \mathbf{u}_i - \sum_j w_{ij} \mathbf{u}_j \right|^2 \tag{8.29}$$

   The minimisation is performed subject to two constraints: *a*) each point is reconstructed only using its neighbours ($w_{ij} = 0$ if $\mathbf{u}_j \notin \Omega_i$ where Ω represents the neighbourhood of the point), and *b*) $\forall i$, $\sum_j w_{ij} = 1$ in order to ensure the invariance to translations. The minimisation problem subject to the above constraints can be solved in a closed form. The reconstruction weights characterise intrinsic geometric properties and provide the invariance to rotation, rescaling, and translations of each point and its neighbours.

3. *Computation of the low-dimensional vector* $\mathbf{v}_i$ *corresponding to each data point* $\mathbf{u}_i$ *through the use of the weights* w_{ij} *previously calculated*

   Similarly to the previous step, the coordinates of the vectors are found through the minimisation of a cost function. In this case, however, the weights are fixed and the coordinates must be optimised. Therefore, the cost function now becomes:

$$\Phi(\mathbf{v}) = \sum_i \left| \mathbf{v}_i - \sum_j w_{ij} \mathbf{v}_j \right|^2 \tag{8.30}$$

To ensure the problem is well posed, the cost function is also minimised subject to two constraints: *a*) the **v** coordinates are centred on the origin as the translations of $\mathbf{v}_i$ should not alter the cost function, and *b*) the vectors $\mathbf{v}_i$ have unit covariance, thus avoiding degenerated solutions (*i.e.* $\mathbf{v}_i = 0$). As a consequence of the invariance of the cost function to rotations and homogeneous rescaling, there is no loss of generality in imposing the second condition. The cost function can be rewritten in a quadratic form and the minimisation of the above equation can be performed by solving an $N \times N$ eigenvalue problem.

8.4.3 Isometric Mapping (Isomap)

Alternatively, Tenenbaum *et al* [47] proposed the use of geodesic distance measured on the manifold, defined by the data as the basis to calculate the similarity matrix. Non-linear dimensionality reduction is approached as a problem of discovering a Euclidean feature space embedding a set of observations that attempts to preserve the intrinsic metric structure of the data. It should be noted that an *isometry* $f : M \rightarrow M'$ is an one-one correspondence such that $d'(f(\mathbf{x}), f(\mathbf{y})) = d(\mathbf{x}, \mathbf{y})$ for all $\mathbf{x}, \mathbf{y}$ in *M*. *Isomap* is an isometric feature-mapping procedure that aims to recover low-dimensional non-linear structure and consists of the following three main stages:

1. ***Discrete representation of the manifold*** - Random selection of m points from the *n* observations to serve as nodes of a topology preserving network. The neighbourhood is defined through the selection of *k*-neighbours or a radius *r*. If *m* is too small the distance calculation will be a poor approximation to the true manifold distance, whereas if *m* is too large (relative to *n*) the graph will miss many appropriate links.

2. ***Manifold distance measure*** - This measure starts with the assignment of a weight, w_{ij} , to each link. Such weight is equal to the Euclidean distance between the nodes *i* and *j* in the observation space. The geodesic distance is then considered to be the shortest distance along the path by following the previously calculated weights. Should the data be infinite, the graph-based approximation to manifold distance can be made arbitrarily accurate.

3. ***Isometric Euclidean embedding*** - Classical MDS is used to find a *k*-dimensional embedding that preserves as closely as possible the graph distances.

As an example, Figure 8.5 demonstrates a simple physical exercise sensing experiment where four two-axis accelerometers were placed on the left and right ankles and legs. The activities of the subject during the exercise routine include: 1) *sitting (chair)*, 2) *standing*, 3) *steps*, 4) *sitting (floor)*, 5) *demi-plie*, 6) *galloping left*, 7) *skipping*, 8) *galloping right*, 9) *side kick*, 10) *front kick*, and 11) *walking*.

Although the dimensionality of the original raw signal is eight, the application of the Isomap reveals that the intrinsic dimensionality of this data set is in fact only two. This is evident from the residual variance of the embedded data which decreases rapidly from 0.41 to 0.05, 0.04, and 0.03 within the first four Isomap dimensions.

For pattern recognition, the use of dimensionality reduction is advantageous for many classification tasks, as it avoids the over-fitting issue in many high-dimensional problems due to the practical limit of the training sample size. It also offers a convenient way of visualising the intrinsic structure of the data. For example, it is evident from Figure 8.5 that the separation of the eleven activities involved is good in general, but we may encounter significant challenges when trying to separate activities 6, 7, and 8, (*i.e.*, galloping left, skipping, and galloping right) as with the current sensor placement the distribution of the feature vectors are all mixed together. Another important issue raised by this experiment is that since the intrinsic dimensionality of the sensor data is only two-dimensional, some of the information collected by these sensors is likely to be redundant. With BSNs, this boils down to the question of how to ensure strategic placement of the sensors to guarantee that the information collected provides the most discriminative power in terms of pattern separation. To achieve this, we introduce in the next section the concept of feature selection and explain in detail a new *Bayesian Framework for Feature Selection* (BFFS).

8.5 Feature Selection

In pattern recognition, the aim of feature selection is to reduce the complexity of an induction system by eliminating irrelevant and redundant features. This technique is becoming increasingly important in the field of machine learning for reducing computational cost and storage, and for improving prediction accuracy. Intuitively, a high-dimensional model is more accurate than a low-dimensional one. However, the computational cost of an inference system increases dramatically with its dimensionality, and therefore we have to balance accuracy and overall computational cost.

On the other hand, the accuracy of a high-dimensional model may deteriorate if the model is built upon insufficient training data. In this case, the model would not be able to provide a satisfactory description of the information structures. The amount of training data required to understand the intrinsic structure of an unknown system increases exponentially with its dimensionality. An imprecise description could lead to serious over-fitting problems when learning algorithms are confused by structures brought about by irrelevant features. In a computationally tractable system less informative features, which contribute little to the overall performance, need to be eliminated. Furthermore, the high cost of collecting a vast amount of sampling data requires efficient selection strategies to remove irrelevant and redundant features.

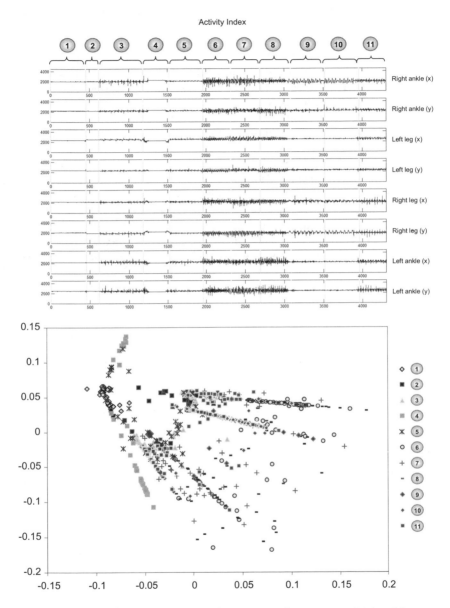

Figure 8.5 Accelerometer readings from an exercise sequence (top) and its corresponding Isomap embedding results (bottom). The residual variance of the embedded data decreases rapidly from 0.41 to 0.05, 0.04, 0.03 within the first four Isomap dimensions. (**See colour insert**.)

In machine learning, feature selection methods can often be divided into two groups [48]: *wrapper* and *filter* approaches based on the relationship between feature selection and induction algorithms. The wrapper approach uses the estimated accuracy of an induction algorithm to evaluate candidate feature subsets [49]. By contrast, the filters learn from data and operate independently of any specific induction algorithm. The filter approach evaluates the suitability of candidate subsets based on their information content with regard to target concepts. The filters are not tuned to the specific interactions between the induction algorithm and the information structures embedded in the training dataset. Given enough features, filter-based methods attempt to eliminate features in a way that can maintain as much information as possible about the underlying structure of the data. This makes the technique particularly useful for BSNs in that only selected sensors with the most informative features are needed.

In this section, we will describe a filter selection algorithm based on Bayesian theory and *Receiver Operating Characteristic* (ROC) analysis for feature selection. We demonstrate that likelihood probability plays an important role in the elimination of both irrelevant and redundant features in the algorithm. The experimental results indicate that the proposed method is fast and efficient, and can be used to improve the performance of the classification process. We also explain its potential application to the understanding of behaviours of human visual search.

8.5.1 Feature Relevance

The techniques for dimensionality reduction have received significant attention in the field of supervised machine learning. Generally speaking, there are two groups of methods: *feature extraction* and *feature selection*. In feature extraction, the given features are transformed into a lower-dimensional space, without much loss of information. One of the feature extraction techniques is PCA as mentioned earlier, which transforms a number of correlated variables into a number of uncorrelated principal components. For feature selection, however, no new feature is created. The dimensionality is reduced by eliminating irrelevant and redundant features. An irrelevant (or redundant) feature provides no (or no new) information about the target concept [50]. In Bayesian inference, the posterior probability is used for a rational observer to make decisions since it summarises the information available. Consequently, the formal definition of relevance can be based on the conditional independence [48, 51].

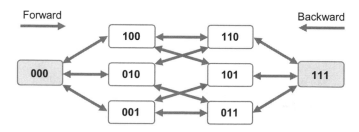

Figure 8.6 The search space for selecting feature subset from three input features. Each state in the space represents a candidate feature subset. For instance, state 101 indicates that the second feature is not included.

Given a set of sensor features $\mathcal{G}^{(1)} = \left\{ \mathcal{G}_i^{(1)}, 1 < i < N_1 \right\}$, event y is conditionally independent of feature set $\mathcal{G}^{(2)} = \left\{ \mathcal{G}_i^{(2)}, 1 < i < N_2 \right\}$ (*i.e.*, given $\mathcal{G}^{(1)}$, $\mathcal{G}^{(2)}$ provides no further information in detecting y) if for any assignment of y

$$P\left(y \middle| \mathcal{G}^{(1)}\right) = P\left(y \middle| \mathcal{G}^{(1)}, \mathcal{G}^{(2)}\right) \text{ when } P\left(\mathcal{G}^{(1)}, \mathcal{G}^{(2)}\right) \neq 0 \qquad (8.31)$$

Optimum selection of feature subset involves two major difficulties: a search strategy to select candidate feature subsets and an evaluation function to assess these candidates. The size of the search space for the candidate subset selection is 2^N, *i.e.* a feature selection method needs to find the best one amongst 2^N candidate subsets, given N features. As an example, Figure 8.6 shows the search space for three features and demonstrates how forward and backward search methods can be used to include/exclude relevant features in the selected feature subset.

Since the size of the search space grows exponentially with the number of input features, an exhaustive search of the space is impractical. As a result, a heuristic search strategy, such as the *greedy search* and the *branch and bound search*, becomes necessary [48, 51-53]. *Forward selection* denotes that the search strategy starts with the empty feature set, while *backward elimination* denotes that the search strategy starts with the full feature set. As an example, Koller and Sahami [51] proposed a sequential greedy backward search algorithm to find 'Markov blankets' of features based on the expected cross-entropy evaluation.

The feature selection methods are divided into two groups (*wrapper* and *filter*) according to how the evaluation function is designed. The filters use the information content (typically measured by interclass distance, statistical dependence, and information-theoretic divergences [54]) of the feature subsets for the evaluation. As a result, the filter approaches are independent of any induction algorithm. Kira and Rendell, in their RELIEF [52] algorithm, formulated a weighting method to evaluate the discriminability of each feature by calculating Near-Hit to measure within-concept spread and Near-Miss to measure between-concept separation, whereas the FOCUS [53] algorithm searches for the minimal feature subset via a systematic consistency test – but this algorithm is sensitive to noise.

On the other hand, the wrappers directly use the predictive accuracy of some induction algorithms to evaluate candidate feature subsets [49]. Statistical techniques such as cross-validation are employed for the purpose of evaluation [55]. Generally speaking, for a given algorithm, wrappers achieve a better accuracy than filters. However, compared to filters, they lack generality and can be computationally demanding. This is because they are directly related to specific induction algorithms, and running these algorithms on a large number of features multiple times can be computationally prohibitive. Other popular feature selection techniques include *Sequential Forward Search* (SFS), *Sequential Backward Search* (SBS), and *Sequential Floating Forward Search* (SFFS) methods [56-58].

Collecting informative training samples from the whole population, and correctly labelling them, are important aspects of feature selection [48]. The cost of labelling can be high, and labelling errors directly affect the performance of feature selection and induction algorithms. In a Bayesian framework, the likelihood probabilities of each class as well as their priors can be estimated independently through controlled experiments. This is useful in practice to avoid direct random sampling from the whole population, which can be a tedious and costly task.

By using the Bayes rule, an assignment of $y = a$, (8.31) can be rewritten as

$$
\frac{P(\mathcal{G}^{(1)} \mid y = a) P(y = a)}{P(\mathcal{G}^{(1)} \mid y = a) P(y = a) + P(\mathcal{G}^{(1)} \mid y \neq a) P(y \neq a)}
$$
$$
= \frac{P(\mathcal{G}^{(1)}, \mathcal{G}^{(2)} \mid y = a) P(y = a)}{P(\mathcal{G}^{(1)}, \mathcal{G}^{(2)} \mid y = a) P(y = a) + P(\mathcal{G}^{(1)}, \mathcal{G}^{(2)} \mid y \neq a) P(y \neq a)}
$$

(8.32)

or

$$
\frac{P(\mathcal{G}^{(1)} \mid y = a)}{P(\mathcal{G}^{(1)} \mid y \neq a)} = \frac{P(\mathcal{G}^{(1)}, \mathcal{G}^{(2)} \mid y = a)}{P(\mathcal{G}^{(1)}, \mathcal{G}^{(2)} \mid y \neq a)}
$$

(8.33)

Consequently, we can obtain an equivalent definition of relevance by using the likelihood ratio, *i.e.*, given a set of features from the sensor network $\mathcal{G}^{(1)} = \{ \mathcal{G}_i^{(1)}, 1 < i < N_1 \}$, event y is conditionally independent of feature set $\mathcal{G}^{(2)} = \{ \mathcal{G}_i^{(2)}, 1 < i < N_2 \}$ if for any assignment of $y = a$ when $P(\mathcal{G}^{(1)}, \mathcal{G}^{(2)}) \neq 0$

$$
L(\mathcal{G}^{(1)} \| y = a, y \neq a) = L(\mathcal{G}^{(1)}, \mathcal{G}^{(2)} \| y = a, y \neq a)
$$

(8.34)

where $L(\mathcal{G} \| y = a, y \neq a)$ is the likelihood ratio:

$$
L(\mathcal{G} \| y = a, y \neq a) = \frac{P(\mathcal{G} \mid y = a)}{P(\mathcal{G} \mid y \neq a)}
$$

(8.35)

Theoretically, Equations (8.31) and (8.34) are equivalent. But (8.31) is based on the posterior probability, whereas (8.34) is based on the likelihood ratio. This modification connects feature selection with the performance assessment of decision making. As will be seen in the following sections, a sufficient performance assessment can be achieved by ROC analysis, in which the likelihood ratio plays an essential role.

8.5.2 Feature Relevance Based on ROC Analysis

With the above definition, we can now examine the relationship between ROC and feature 'irrelevance' to establish the link between feature selection and the performance of decision making. A proper ROC is generated by using the likelihood ratio or its equivalent as the decision variable [59]. Given a pair of likelihoods, the best possible performance of a classifier can be described by the corresponding proper ROC, which can be obtained *via* the Neyman-Pearson ranking procedure by changing the threshold of the likelihood ratio [60]. Given two distributions $P(\mathcal{G} \mid y = a)$ and $P(\mathcal{G} \mid y \neq a)$ as demonstrated in Figure 8.7(a), the hit and false-alarm rates, according to the Neyman-Pearson procedure, are defined as

$$
\begin{cases}
P_h = \int_{L(\mathcal{G}\|y=a, y\neq a) > \beta} P(\mathcal{G} \mid y = a) d\mathcal{G} \\
P_f = \int_{L(\mathcal{G}\|y=a, y\neq a) > \beta} P(\mathcal{G} \mid y \neq a) d\mathcal{G}
\end{cases}
\tag{8.36}
$$

where β is the threshold and $L(\mathcal{G}\|y = a, y \neq a)$ is the likelihood ratio as defined above.

For a given β, a pair of P_h and P_f can be calculated. When β changes from ∞ to 0, P_h and P_f change from 0% to 100%. Therefore, the ROC curve is obtained by changing the threshold of the likelihood ratio. Figure 8.7(b) depicts the ROC curve corresponding to the likelihood distributions shown in Figure 8.7(a). In discrete forms, where only some discrete points of (P_h, P_f) are available, straight-line segments are used to connect these points to form a convex hull. Every point on those straight-line segments is realisable by applying a randomised strategy [59, 61]. When misjudgement costs are taken into consideration, minimal maximal-cost points in the ROC space can only be found on the vertices of the convex hull [62].

In a ROC space, the hit rate is the function of the false-alarm rate. The slope at a point on the ROC curve is equal to the associated likelihood ratio. The *Area Under the ROC Curve* (AUC) is an important measure of discriminability of the two classes described by the two likelihood distributions. The equivalent statistical metric to the AUC is the Wilcoxon statistics, which was originally designed to estimate the probability of the rank of two random variables [63, 64].

Based on the above definition and given two pairs of feature distribution, $P(\mathcal{G}^{(1)} \mid y = a)$, $P(\mathcal{G}^{(1)} \mid y \neq a)$ and $P(\mathcal{G}^{(2)} \mid y = a)$, $P(\mathcal{G}^{(2)} \mid y \neq a)$, we have two corresponding ROC curves obtained from the Neyman-Pearson procedure: $ROC(\mathcal{G}^{(1)}\|y = a, y \neq a)$ and $ROC(\mathcal{G}^{(2)}\|y = a, y \neq a)$. It can be proved that

$$
ROC(\mathcal{G}^{(1)}\|y = a, y \neq a) = ROC(\mathcal{G}^{(1)}, \mathcal{G}^{(2)}\|y = a, y \neq a) \tag{8.37}
$$

if and only if

$$
L(\mathcal{G}^{(1)}\|y = a, y \neq a) = L(\mathcal{G}^{(1)}, \mathcal{G}^{(2)}\|y = a, y \neq a) \tag{8.38}
$$

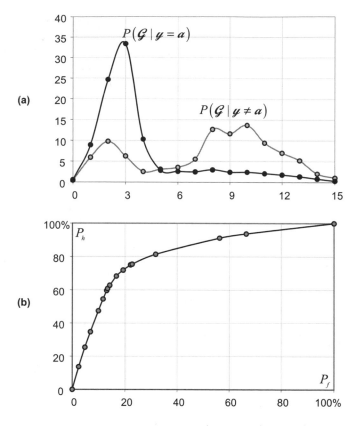

Figure 8.7 Conditional probabilities (a) $P(\mathcal{G} \mid y = a)$ and $P(\mathcal{G} \mid y \neq a)$ and their ROC curve (b). In the ROC space shown in (b), hit rate changes from 0% to 100% when false-alarm rate varies from 0% to 100%.

and that $ROC(\mathcal{G}^{(1)}, \mathcal{G}^{(2)} \| y = a, y \neq a)$ is not under $ROC(\mathcal{G}^{(1)} \| y = a, y \neq a)$ at any point in the ROC space. Based on the above equations, an equivalent definition of feature irrelevance based on ROC can be derived; in other words, given a set of features from the sensor network $\mathcal{G}^{(1)} = \{\mathcal{G}_i^{(1)}, 1 < i < N_1\}$, event y is conditionally independent of feature set $\mathcal{G}^{(2)} = \{\mathcal{G}_i^{(2)}, 1 < i < N_2\}$ if for any assignment of $y = a$

$$ROC(\mathcal{G}^{(1)} \| y = a, y \neq a) = ROC(\mathcal{G}^{(1)}, \mathcal{G}^{(2)} \| y = a, y \neq a) \qquad (8.39)$$

Generally speaking, two ROC curves can be unequal when they have the same AUC. Since $\mathcal{G}^{(1)}$ is a subset of $\{\mathcal{G}^{(1)}, \mathcal{G}^{(2)}\}$ we have:

$$AUC(\mathcal{G}^{(1)} \| y = a, y \neq a) = AUC(\mathcal{G}^{(1)}, \mathcal{G}^{(2)} \| y = a, y \neq a) \qquad (8.40)$$

The above statements point out the effects of feature selection on the performance of decision-making and the overall discriminability of a feature set. It indicates that irrelevant features have no influence on the performance of ideal inference, and the overall discriminability is not affected by irrelevant features. So in summary, the conditional independence of features is determined by their intrinsic discriminability, which can be measured by the AUC.

By using notation $I\left(y,\mathcal{G}^{(2)}\big|\mathcal{G}^{(1)}\right)$ to denote the conditional independence of event y to sensor features $\mathcal{G}^{(2)}$ given $\mathcal{G}^{(1)}$ ($\mathcal{G}^{(1)}$, $\mathcal{G}^{(2)}$ and y are assumed to be disjoint without losing generality), the above framework can be applied to interpret properties of conditional independence. For example, we can obtain the decomposition property:

$$I\left(y,\left(\mathcal{G}^{(2)},\mathcal{G}^{(3)}\right)\big|\mathcal{G}^{(1)}\right)$$

$$\mapsto \begin{cases} AUC\left(\mathcal{G}^{(1)},\mathcal{G}^{(2)}\big\|y=a,y\neq a\right)=AUC\left(\mathcal{G}^{(1)}\big\|y=a,y\neq a\right) \\ AUC\left(\mathcal{G}^{(1)},\mathcal{G}^{(3)}\big\|y=a,y\neq a\right)=AUC\left(\mathcal{G}^{(1)}\big\|y=a,y\neq a\right) \end{cases}$$

$$\mapsto \begin{cases} I\left(y,\mathcal{G}^{(2)}\big|\mathcal{G}^{(1)}\right) \\ I\left(y,\mathcal{G}^{(3)}\big|\mathcal{G}^{(1)}\right) \end{cases}$$

and the contraction property:

$$\begin{cases} I\left(y,\mathcal{G}^{(3)}\big|\left(\mathcal{G}^{(1)},\mathcal{G}^{(2)}\right)\right) \\ I\left(y,\mathcal{G}^{(2)}\big|\mathcal{G}^{(1)}\right) \end{cases}$$

$$\mapsto \begin{cases} AUC\left(\mathcal{G}^{(1)},\mathcal{G}^{(2)},\mathcal{G}^{(3)}\big\|y=a,y\neq a\right)=AUC\left(\mathcal{G}^{(1)},\mathcal{G}^{(2)}\big\|y=a,y\neq a\right) \\ AUC\left(\mathcal{G}^{(1)},\mathcal{G}^{(2)}\big\|y=a,y\neq a\right)=AUC\left(\mathcal{G}^{(1)}\big\|y=a,y\neq a\right) \end{cases}$$

For instance:

$$\begin{cases} I\left(y,\mathcal{G}^{(3)}\big|\left(\mathcal{G}^{(1)},\mathcal{G}^{(2)}\right)\right) \\ I\left(y,\mathcal{G}^{(2)}\big|\mathcal{G}^{(1)}\right) \end{cases}$$

$$\mapsto AUC\left(\mathcal{G}^{(1)},\mathcal{G}^{(2)},\mathcal{G}^{(3)}\big\|y=a,y\neq a\right)=AUC\left(\mathcal{G}^{(1)}\big\|y=a,y\neq a\right)$$

$$\mapsto I\left(y,\left(\mathcal{G}^{(2)},\mathcal{G}^{(3)}\right)\big|\mathcal{G}^{(1)}\right)$$

In the above equations $A\mapsto B$ signifies that B follows from A (in other words, if A, then B).

By applying the contraction and decomposition properties (as described above), we have the following properties for feature selection:

$$
\begin{cases}
I\left(\boldsymbol{y}, \mathcal{G}^{(3)} \middle| \left(\mathcal{G}^{(1)}, \mathcal{G}^{(2)}\right)\right) \\
I\left(\boldsymbol{y}, \mathcal{G}^{(2)} \middle| \mathcal{G}^{(1)}\right)
\end{cases}
\mapsto I\left(\boldsymbol{y}, \left(\mathcal{G}^{(2)}, \mathcal{G}^{(3)}\right) \middle| \mathcal{G}^{(1)}\right)
$$

$$
\mapsto
\begin{cases}
I\left(\boldsymbol{y}, \mathcal{G}^{(3)} \middle| \mathcal{G}^{(1)}\right) \\
I\left(\boldsymbol{y}, \mathcal{G}^{(2)} \middle| \mathcal{G}^{(1)}\right)
\end{cases}
\tag{8.41}
$$

In the above equation, $I\left(\boldsymbol{y}, \mathcal{G}^{(3)} \middle| \left(\mathcal{G}^{(1)}, \mathcal{G}^{(2)}\right)\right)$ and $I\left(\boldsymbol{y}, \mathcal{G}^{(2)} \middle| \mathcal{G}^{(1)}\right)$ represent two steps of elimination; in other words features in $\mathcal{G}^{(3)}$ can be removed when features in $\mathcal{G}^{(1)}$ and $\mathcal{G}^{(2)}$ are given. This can be immediately followed by another elimination of features in $\mathcal{G}^{(2)}$ owing to the existence of features in $\mathcal{G}^{(1)}$. $I\left(\boldsymbol{y}, \mathcal{G}^{(3)} \middle| \mathcal{G}^{(1)}\right)$ indicates that features in $\mathcal{G}^{(3)}$ remain irrelevant after features in $f^{(2)}$ are eliminated. As a result, only truly irrelevant features are removed with each iteration by following the backward elimination process. In general, backward elimination is less susceptible to feature interaction than forward selection.

Because the strong union property $I\left(\boldsymbol{y}, \mathcal{G}^{(2)} \middle| \mathcal{G}^{(1)}\right) \mapsto I\left(\boldsymbol{y}, \mathcal{G}^{(2)} \middle| \mathcal{G}^{(1)}, \mathcal{G}^{(3)}\right)$ does not generally hold for conditional independence, irrelevant features can become relevant if more features are added. Theoretically, this could limit the capacity of low dimensional approximations or forward selection algorithms. In practice, however, the forward selection and approximate algorithms proposed below tend to select features that have large discriminability and provide new information. For example, a forward selection algorithm may be preferable in situations where it is known that only a few of a large set of features are relevant and interaction between features is not expected to be a dominant effect.

With the above theory in place, we can now define the general principle for feature selection for multiple events. We denote that the set of possible events of $\boldsymbol{y}$ is $\{a_i, i = 1 \cdots N\}$ and N is the number of event classes. $AUC\left(\mathcal{G} \middle\| \boldsymbol{y} = a_i, \boldsymbol{y} \neq a_i\right)$ denotes the AUC of $P\left(\mathcal{G} \middle| \boldsymbol{y} = a\right)$ and $P\left(\mathcal{G} \middle| \boldsymbol{y} \neq a\right)$. In this study, the expectation of the AUC is used as an evaluation function:

$$
E_{AUC}\left(\mathcal{G}\right) = E\left(AUC\left(\mathcal{G}\right)\right) = \sum_{i=1}^{N} P\left(\boldsymbol{y} = a_i\right) AUC\left(\mathcal{G} \middle\| \boldsymbol{y} = a_i, \boldsymbol{y} \neq a_i\right) \tag{8.42}
$$

In the above equation, the prior probabilities $P\left(\boldsymbol{y} = a_i\right)$ can either be estimated from data or determined empirically to take misjudgement costs into account. The use of the expected AUC as an evaluation function follows the same principle of sensitivity and specificity. It is not difficult to prove that

$$
E_{AUC}\left(\mathcal{G}^{(1)}, \mathcal{G}^{(2)}\right) = E_{AUC}\left(\mathcal{G}^{(1)}\right)
$$

is equivalent to

$$AUC\left(\mathcal{G}^{(1)},\mathcal{G}^{(2)}\,\middle\|\,y=a_i,y\neq a_i\right)=AUC\left(\mathcal{G}^{(1)}\,\middle\|\,y=a_i,y\neq a_i\right),\{i=1\cdots N\}\,;$$

i.e., features in $\mathcal{G}^{(2)}$ are irrelevant given features in $\mathcal{G}^{(1)}$. $E_{AUC}(\mathcal{G})$ is also a monotonic function that increases with the number of features, and $0.5\leq E_{AUC}(\mathcal{G})\leq 1$. For a binary class, $E_{AUC}(\mathcal{G})=AUC\left(\mathcal{G}\,\middle\|\,y=a_1,y=a_2\right)$ $=AUC\left(\mathcal{G}\,\middle\|\,y=a_2,y=a_1\right)$, *i.e.* the calculation of $E_{AUC}(\mathcal{G})$ is not affected by prior probabilities.

To use likelihood distributions to calculate the expected AUC in multiple-class situations, we need to avoid $P(\mathcal{G}\mid y\neq a_i)$ in (8.42). By using the Bayes rule, one can derive that

$$P\left(\mathcal{G}\mid y\neq a_i\right)=\sum_{\substack{k=1\cdots N \\ k\neq i}} H_{ki}P\left(\mathcal{G}\mid y=a_k\right) \tag{8.43}$$

where

$$H_{ki}=\frac{P\left(\mathcal{G}\mid y=a_k\right)}{\displaystyle\sum_{\substack{j=1\cdots N \\ j\neq i}} P\left(\mathcal{G}\mid y=a_j\right)}\quad\text{for }(i\neq k)$$

By assuming that the decision variable and decision rule for calculating $AUC\left(\mathcal{G}\,\middle\|\,y=a_i,y=a_k\right)$ and $AUC\left(\mathcal{G}\,\middle\|\,y=a_i,y\neq a_i\right)$ are the same [59], we have

$$AUC\left(\mathcal{G}\,\middle\|\,y=a_i,y\neq a_i\right)=\sum_{\substack{k=1\cdots N \\ k\neq i}} H_{ki}AUC\left(\mathcal{G}\,\middle\|\,y=a_i,y=a_k\right) \tag{8.44}$$

where $AUC\left(\mathcal{G}\,\middle\|\,y=a_i,y=a_k\right)$ represents the AUC given two likelihood distributions $P(\mathcal{G}\mid y=a_k)$ and $P(\mathcal{G}\mid y=a_i)$ $i\neq k$. Equation (8.44) can therefore be used for evaluating $AUC\left(\mathcal{G}\,\middle\|\,y=a_i,y\neq a_i\right)$ for multiple-class cases. By substituting (8.44) into (8.42), we have

$$E_{AUC}(\mathcal{G})=\sum_{i=1}^{N}P(y=a_i)\sum_{\substack{k=1\cdots N \\ k\neq i}} H_{ki}AUC\left(\mathcal{G}\,\middle\|\,y=a_i,y=a_k\right) \tag{8.45}$$

8.5.3 Feature Selection Based on ROC Analysis

Since removing or adding an irrelevant feature does not change the expected AUC, both backward and forward greedy selection (filter) algorithms can be designed to use the expected AUC as an evaluation function. A backward elimination approach provides a greedy algorithm for feature selection. It starts with the full feature set and removes one feature at each iteration. A feature $f_j \in \mathcal{G}^{(k)}$ to be removed is determined by using the following equation:

$$f_j = \arg\min_{f_i \in \mathcal{G}^{(k)}} \left(E_{AUC} \left(\mathcal{G}^{(k)} \right) - E_{AUC} \left(\mathcal{G}^{(k)} - \{f_i\} \right) \right) \tag{8.46}$$

where $\mathcal{G}^{(k)}$ is the temporary feature set after k^{th} iteration and $\mathcal{G}^{(k)} - \{f_i\}$ is the set $\mathcal{G}^{(k)}$ with f_i removed.

Estimating the AUC in a high-dimensional space is time-consuming. The accuracy of the estimated likelihood distribution decreases dramatically with the number of features given limited training samples, which in turn introduces ranking error in the AUC estimation [65]. Therefore, an approximation algorithm is necessary to estimate the AUC in a lower-dimensional space. As explained earlier, the decrease of the total AUC after removal of a feature f_i is related to the overlap of the discriminability of the feature with other features. In the approximation algorithm, we attempt to construct a feature subset $\mathcal{H}^{(k)}$ from the current feature set $\mathcal{G}^{(k)}$ and use the degree of discriminability overlap in $\mathcal{H}^{(k)}$ to approximate that in $\mathcal{G}^{(k)}$. Similar methods have been reported in [51, 66]. A heuristic approach is designed to select k_s features from $\mathcal{G}^{(k)}$ that have the largest overlap with feature f_i and we assume that the discriminability overlap of feature f_i with other features in $\mathcal{G}^{(k)}$ is dominated by this subset of features. Tables 8.3 and 8.4 summarise the backward elimination and forward selection algorithms for selecting K features.

As indicated by the fact that the strong union axiom $I\left(y, \mathcal{G}^{(2)} \big| \mathcal{G}^{(1)}\right) \mapsto I\left(y, \mathcal{G}^{(2)} \big| \mathcal{G}^{(1)}, \mathcal{G}^{(3)}\right)$ does not generally hold for conditional independence [67], irrelevant features can become relevant if more information is given. In other words, feature irrelevance in low-dimensional feature space is different from that in high-dimensional feature space. Theoretically, this fact limits the capacities of all low-dimensional approximation algorithms and forward selection algorithms. In general, the proposed algorithm tends to select features that have strong discriminability, and features that provide new information.

To illustrate how the BFFS algorithm works for BSN applications, Figure 8.8 illustrates a laboratory activity sequence as sensed by six two-axes accelerometers placed on the ankles, legs, and wrists. The different activities to be detected include sitting, typing, writing on paper, standing, walking, writing on white board, soldering, and drinking. At a first glance, the placement of the sensors may look rational, as the activities to be differentiated all involve ankles, legs and wrists. Upon further examination, however, it reveals that the intrinsic dimensionality of the data is low as evident from the Isomap embedding result shown in Figure 8.8. The Isomap result also demonstrates the good separation of different activities in the embedded feature space. The question now is if we can reduce the number of sensors without affecting the overall sensitivity and specificity of the classification

Table 8.3 Pseudo-code for BFFS backward elimination algorithm.

(a) Let $\mathcal{G}^{(k)}$ be the full feature set and k be the size of the full feature set;

(b) Calculate the discriminability differential matrix $M(f_i, f_j)$

$$M(f_i, f_j) = E_{AUC}(\{f_i, f_j\}) - E_{AUC}(\{f_i\})$$

for $f_i \in \mathcal{G}^{(k)}, f_j \in \mathcal{G}^{(k)}$ and $f_i \neq f_j$;

(c) If $k=K$, output $\mathcal{G}^{(k)}$;

(d) For $f_i \in \mathcal{G}^{(k)} (i=1 \cdots k)$:

- Select k_s features from $\mathcal{G}^{(k)}$ to construct a feature subset $\mathcal{H}^{(k_i)}$. The criterion of the selection is to find k_s features f_j, for which $M(f_i, f_j)$ is the smallest, where $f_j \in \mathcal{G}^{(k)}$ and $f_i \neq f_j$;

- Calculate $D_{AUC}(f_i) = E_{AUC}(\mathcal{H}^{(k_i)} \cup \{f_i\}) - E_{AUC}(\mathcal{H}^{(k_i)})$;

(e) Select feature f_d with the smallest $D_{AUC}(f_i)$ and set

$$\mathcal{G}^{(k)} = \mathcal{G}^{(k)} - \{f_d\};$$

(f) $k=k-1$; go to (c).

algorithm. By the use of the proposed BFFS algorithm, Table 8.5 illustrates the result of the most discriminative sensor channels as revealed by the backward elimination algorithm. The results in Table 8.5 show that after the incorporation of sensor channels 12, 1, 11, and 2, there is little gain in the AUC by using further sensor channels. In other words, for uniquely separating the eight different activities mentioned above, we only need two accelerometers positioned on the left and right wrists. This result may sound surprising. By careful reasoning, however, the derived sensor placement in fact makes perfect sense. This is because in this problem setting, activities that involve leg and ankle movements are also coupled with unique hand gestures. It is therefore possible in this case to distinguish sitting, standing, and walking from other activities that mainly involve hand motion by the use of wrist sensors only. To demonstrate how the selected sensor channels perform by using different classifiers, Table 8.5 summarises the result of using Naïve Bayes, Pruned C4.5, Instance Based Learning (with $k = 1$ and 3 respectively), and SVM.

Table 8.4 Pseudo-code for BFFS forward feature selection algorithm.

(a)   Let $\mathcal{G}^{(k)}$ be empty and k be zero;

(b)   Calculate the discriminability differential matrix $\mathrm{M}\left(f_i, f_j\right)$

$$\mathrm{M}\left(f_i, f_j\right) = E_{AUC}\left(\{f_i, f_j\}\right) - E_{AUC}\left(\{f_i\}\right)$$

for $f_i \in \mathcal{G}^{(k)}, f_j \in \mathcal{G}^{(k)}$ and $f_i \neq f_j$;

(c)   If $k{=}K$, output $\mathcal{G}^{(k)}$;

(d)   For $f_i \in \mathcal{G}^{(k)} \left(i = 1 \cdots k\right)$:

 • Select k_s features from $\mathcal{G}^{(k)}$ to construct a feature subset $\mathcal{H}^{(k_i)}$. The criterion of the selection is to find k_s features f_j, for which $\mathrm{M}\left(f_i, f_j\right)$ is the smallest, where $f_j \in \mathcal{G}^{(k)}$ and $f_i \neq f_j$;

 • Calculate $\mathrm{D}_{AUC}\left(f_i\right) = E_{AUC}\left(\mathcal{H}^{(k_i)} \cup \{f_i\}\right) - E_{AUC}\left(\mathcal{H}^{(k_i)}\right)$;

(e)   Select feature f_d with the largest $\mathrm{D}_{AUC}\left(f_i\right)$ and set

$$\mathcal{G}^{(k)} = \mathcal{G}^{(k)} \cup \{f_d\};$$

(f) $k{=}k{+}1$; go to (c).

It is evident that through the use of only two accelerometers as determined by BFFS, the performance difference is no more than 3% for all the classifiers concerned. For practical BSN applications, the efficient use of sensor channels plays an important part in the power and communication bandwidth usage. The proposed BFFS algorithm can therefore provide a systematic way of selecting optimal sensing channels for pattern classification.

8.6 Decision-Level Fusion

In previous sections, we have provided detailed explanation of how data- and feature-level sensor fusion techniques can be used for BSN applications. Another important component of multi-sensor fusion as outlined in Figure 8.1 is decision-level fusion. In general, the decision-level fusion is based on a joint declaration of multiple single source results to achieve an improved event or episode detection result. At this level of fusion, it also provides a unique mechanism for incorporating prior knowledge and domain specific information as shown in Figure 8.1. For decision-level sensor fusion, common methods include classical inference, Bayesian inference, and Dempster-Shafer's method [20].

Classical inference seeks to determine the validity of a proposed hypothesis based on empirical probabilities. It computes the joint probability given an assumed hypothesis. In general, classical inference does not take advantage of *a priori* likelihood assessments and can assess only two hypotheses at a time, *i.e.*, a null hypothesis and its alternative. Although the method can be generalised to include multidimensional data from multiple sensors, complexities arise for multivariate data. In terms of hypothesis acceptance or rejection, the method typically uses maximum *a posteriori* or maximum likelihood decision rules. For the former, the method accepts hypothesis H_0 being true if $P(H_0|O)$, *i.e.*, the probability of H_0 given observation O, is greater than $P(H_1|O)$, *i.e.*, the probability of H_1 given O. For the maximum likelihood criterion, it accepts hypothesis H_0 being true if $P(O|H_0) > P(O|H_1)$. Other criteria can also be used, which include minimax, Bayes, and Neyman-Pearson decision rules.

Bayesian inference, on the other hand, uses the likelihood of a hypothesis given a previous likelihood estimate and additional observations. Suppose $H_1, H_2, \cdots, H_N$ represent mutually exclusive and exhaustive hypotheses that can explain the observation O, then we have

$$P(H_i|O) = \frac{P(O|H_i)P(H_i)}{\sum_{k=1}^{N} P(O|H_k)P(H_k)} \tag{8.47}$$

where $P(H_i|O)$ is the *a posteriori* probability of hypothesis H_i being true given evidence O, $P(H_i)$ the *a priori* probability of hypothesis H_i being true, and $P(O|H_i)$ the probability of observing evidence O given that H_i is true. In contrast to the classical inference method, the Bayesian method provides a way of deriving the probability of a hypothesis being true given the observation. This formulation allows the incorporation of *a priori* knowledge about the likelihood of the hypothesis and the ability to use subjective probabilities for *a priori* probabilities for hypotheses when the exact probability density function is not available. In Chapter 10, we will provide more detailed discussion on how to use Bayesian inferencing for BSN applications.

One of the main issues related to Bayesian inferencing is that it requires competing hypotheses being mutually exclusive. In real life, this is not always possible. For humans, we generally do not assign evidence to a set of mutually exclusive and exhaustive hypotheses. Instead, we tend to assign our belief to combinations of hypotheses, or propositions. One important fact to note here is that propositions may include overlapping or even conflicting hypotheses. Based on

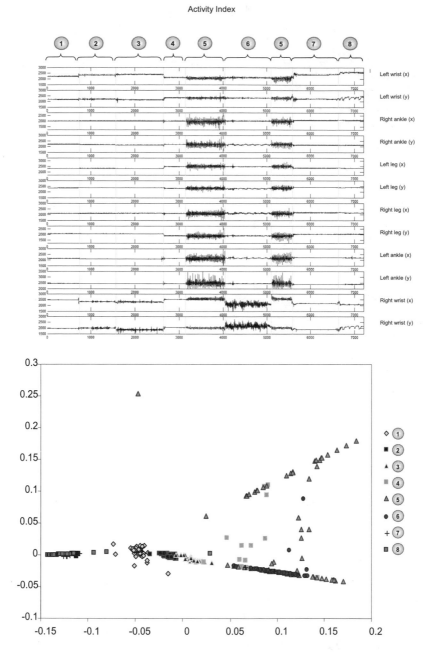

Figure 8.8 Accelerometer readings from an office activity sequence used for feature selection and the corresponding Isomap embedding result showing the separation of different activity classes. (**See colour insert**.)

Table 8.5 Changes of AUC during BFFS backward feature elimination.

AUC	0.89751	0.95948	0.98649	0.99519	0.99823	0.99938	0.99976	0.99991	0.99994	0.99997	0.99997	0.99997
Sensor Channel ID	11	1	12	2	9	7	5	8	6	10	3	4

Table 8.6 Classification accuracy by using different classification techniques with the selection of sensor channels as determined by Table 8.4.

Sensor Channels Used	12	11	10	9	8	7	6	5	4	3	2	1
Naïve Bayes	95.05	95.06	95.16	95.30	95.19	95.13	95.13	95.33	94.25	92.56	91.30	70.28
Pruned C4.5	97.83	97.44	97.69	97.73	97.48	97.30	96.81	96.86	95.84	95.33	94.28	75.17
Instance based learning (k=1)	98.83	98.66	98.72	98.64	98.42	98.03	97.45	97.28	96.19	95.20	92.13	64.31
Instance based learning (k=3)	98.69	98.42	98.44	98.48	98.27	98.05	97.47	97.33	96.47	95.67	93.70	74.83
SVM	92.86	92.61	92.52	92.48	92.03	91.78	91.39	91.41	91.17	89.02	86.48	62.33

this, Shafer and Dempster provided a generalisation of Bayesian theory that could use probability intervals and uncertainty intervals for determining the likelihood of hypotheses based on multiple evidence [68-71]. In Dempster-Shafer's method, evidence is assigned to both single and general propositions and it uses the concept of a probability mass to represent assigned evidence. When the probability masses are assigned only to an exhaustive and mutually exclusive set of elementary propositions, then the Dempster-Shafer's approach is identical to the Bayesian method. The key advantage of the Dempster-Shafer's method is its ability to establish a general level of uncertainty, and thus provides a means of accounting for possible unknown causes of the observed data. For BSN technology, this is clearly an advantage, as many of the observed events may not have well defined causes.

Other techniques for decision level fusion are based on heuristics. For example, the voting sensor fusion method imitates voting as a means for human decision-making. It combines detection and classification declarations from multiple sensors by treating each sensor declaration as a vote, and the voting process may use majority, plurality, or decision-tree rules. Additional methods include ordinal ranking, pair-wise ranking, and Q-sort which have been used extensively in assessing the psychometric process by which a human group achieves consensus [20]. To address some of the drawbacks in conventional rule-based schemes, fuzzy logic has also been used extensively to accommodate imprecise states or variables. In this book, however, we will mainly concentrate on the use of Bayesian Inference for practical applications of BSN technology as it provides the basis for understanding some of the advanced techniques in decision-level sensor fusion, including the generalised evidence processing method as proposed by Thomopoulos for addressing the basic assumptions regarding the assignment of evidence to hypotheses or propositions [2].

8.7 Conclusions

In this chapter, we have presented the basic concept of multi-sensor data fusion and its implementation at data, feature and decision levels. In essence, sensor fusion is analogous to the sensing and cognitive process used by humans to integrate data from different sources. The advantages of effective sensor fusion include improved SNR, enhanced robustness and reliability in the event of sensor failure, extended parameter coverage, improved resolution, precision, confidence, hypothesis discrimination and reduced uncertainty.

In general, sensor replication imposes the problem of data integration. For multi-sensor data fusion, it is usually assumed that communication, storage, and processing systems are reliable and the research focus is placed on different fusion algorithms for integrating data from either homogeneous or heterogeneous data [10]. Research concerning general wireless networks, on the other hand, assumes that the input data is generally in good quality and sources of error are originated from faults in communication and processing systems.

For direct data fusion, we have mainly concentrated on two examples that are useful for sensor arrays and blind source recovery. In general, the use of direct data fusion can be *ad hoc* and it depends on the application requirement one may have. One of the main applications of direct data fusion is for multi-sensor calibration. Calibration in general refers to the process of correcting systematic errors or bias in sensor readings. It has also been used in reference to the procedure by which the raw outputs of the sensors are mapped to standardised units. Traditionally, calibration is done during production time and recalibration is necessary after an interval for most sensors, as factors such as aging, decay and damage can have a detrimental effect on the accuracy of the readings. Frequent recalibration of large-scale sensor networks can be problematic for pervasive sensing environments due to the number of sensors involved. For acceleration sensors, calibration is necessary if they are to be used collaboratively. For example, two orthogonally mounted two-axes accelerometers are often used for providing three-axes acceleration measurement [72, 73]. Furthermore, MEMS-based accelerometers are usually not calibrated after production and the sensors can have a sensitivity and offset bias on each of their axes.

In this chapter, we have dedicated a significant amount of space on feature-level data fusion because this is one of the most important yet difficult levels of sensor fusion. In general, a feature-based classifier consists of two major components that include feature selection and classification. The goal of defining feature is to preserve the class-discriminative information of the data while ignoring information that is irrelevant. Once a feature is identified, it defines a transformation that maps directly sensed data to the feature space, which typically has a lower dimensionality because of the inherent data abstraction involved [74]. For BSNs, effective sensor fusion and statistical feature reduction is crucial to wireless sensor arrays for both built-in redundancies and tissue heterogeneity.

One of the main theoretical components of the chapter is the development of a filter-based algorithm for feature selection based on Bayesian theory. We have demonstrated the relationship between conditional independence and ideal inference performance, which is described by the ROC curve. We have shown that adding and removing an irrelevant feature will not change the associated AUC. This property, together with the monotonic property of the AUC, defines a theoretical framework that is equivalent to the axiomatic system, consisting of decomposition, weak union and contraction properties [67], for probabilistic dependencies. Based on this framework, the proposed algorithm is designed to provide an accurate, robust and fast feature selection method. The algorithm has shown promising strengths in identifying irrelevant features and improving the accuracy of the classifiers. By using both artificial and real-world datasets for accuracy assessment, we also illustrated the roles of prior and likelihood probabilities in the filter selection.

For a specific induction algorithm, wrapper selection usually achieves a better performance than its filter counterparts in terms of accuracy. However, filter selection is usually faster than wrapper selection, and therefore can serve as a pre-processing step for a wrapper-based method. On the other hand, filter selection provides a more accurate description of the intrinsic structure of an information system, since it is not designed to cater for the bias associated with a specific classifier.

In feature selection, we have attempted to reduce the number of selected features and achieve a high value of AUC. This is a dilemma in practice since the AUC is a monotonically increasing function. Given a small training dataset, a high AUC with a large number of selected features could result in over-fitting. Determining the optimal balance is theoretically and practically important. Further investigation is needed to determine the best way to take the factors, such as misclassification cost information and the standard error of the AUC [75], into consideration.

For direct data and feature level fusion, we have omitted in this chapter detailed discussion about the use of neural networks. The use of neural networks is in fact crucial to the practical deployment of BSNs due to its potential for the direct hardware implementation of some of the sensor fusion and classification algorithms. This is useful for implementing low-power processing at the source of the sensing environment in order to provide *in situ* data processing and abstraction.

In the next chapter, we will provide a detailed explanation of the neural networks approach for context-aware sensing and outline the strength of SOMs for effective activity recognition. It is also worth noting that in terms of decision-level sensor fusion, we have only briefly outlined some of the common techniques used without going into extensive details of the techniques. This is because once the data abstraction is reached to this level, the techniques used for BSNs are effectively the same as many other pattern recognition and machine learning techniques, and there is an extensive coverage in the literature of this area. We will however, in Chapter 10, provide a comprehensive analysis of the use of Bayesian inferencing technique for providing an autonomic sensing environment for BSNs.

Finally, for readers that are new to the field of machine learning and pattern recognition, it is important to differentiate the notion of dimensionality reduction and feature selection. For dimensionality reduction, the independent variables that account for most variability within the data are extracted during the processing stage. As only intrinsic features are preserved, dimensionality reduction may lead to better understanding and classification of the data. For feature selection, however, we are mainly concerned with determining the optimum features both in terms of the number of sensing channels used, and the relevant feature extraction algorithms for effective separation of different events or episodes.

For BSN applications, dimensionality reduction is therefore mainly a post-processing step for re-projecting the data onto a low dimensional space that preserves the internal structure of the data whilst revealing its intrinsic pattern separations. Feature selection, however, is generally used for determining which sensors to be used and how they should be placed on the body, given a set of events or episodes to be monitored. The method is therefore mainly used for determining the sensor architecture with minimal power consumption and data bandwidth during practical deployment of BSNs.

References

1. Hernandez A, Carrault G, Mora F, Thoraval L, Passariello G, Schleich JM. Multisensor fusion for atrial and ventricular activity detection in coronary care monitoring. IEEE Transactions on Biomedical Engineering 1999; 46(10):1186-1190.
2. Thomopoulos SCA. Sensor integration and data fusion. Journal of Robotics Systems 1990; 7:337-372.
3. Hall DL. Handbook of multisensor data fusion. Boca Raton: CRC Press, 2001.
4. Esteban J, Starr A, Willetts R, Hannah P, Bryanston-Cross P. A review of data fusion models and architectures: towards engineering guidelines. Neural Computing and Applications 2005.
5. White FE. Data fusion lexicon. Joint Directors of Laboratories, Technical Panel for C3, Data Fusion Sub-Panel Naval Ocean Systems Center, San Diego, 1991.
6. Luo RC, Kay MG. Multisensor integration and fusion in intelligent systems. IEEE Transactions on Systems, Man and Cybernetics 1989; 19(5):901-931.
7. Sadjadi FA. Selected papers on sensor and data fusion. SPIE Milestone, SPIE Optical Engineering Press, 1996.
8. Brooks RR, Iyengar SS. Multi-sensor fusion: fundamentals and applications with software. Upper Saddle River, New Jersey: Prentice Hall, 1998.
9. Luo RC, Yih C-C, Su KL. Multisensor fusion and integration: approaches, applications, and future research directions. IEEE Sensors Journal 2002; 2(2):107-119.
10. Parhami B. Multi-sensor data fusion and reliable multi-channel computation: unifying concepts and techniques. In: Proceedings of the Twenty-Ninth Asilomar Conference on Signals, Systems and Computers, Pacific Grove, California, 1995; 1:745-749.
11. Unser M, Eden M. Weighted averaging of a set of noisy images for maximum signal-to-noise ratio. IEEE Transactions on Acoustics, Speech, and Signal Processing 1990; 38(5):890-895.
12. Cichocki A, Amari S-I. Adaptive blind signal and image processing: learning algorithms and applications. John Wiley, 2002.
13. Eriksson J, Koivunen V. Identifiability, separability, and uniqueness of linear ICA models. IEEE Signal Processing Letters 2004; 11(7):601-604.
14. Bell AJ, Sejnowski TJ. An information maximisation approach to blind separation and blind deconvolution. Neural Computation 1995; 7(6):1004-1034.
15. Lee T-W, Girolami M, Sejnowski TJ. Independent component analysis using an extended infomax algorithm for mixed subgaussian and supergaussian sources. Neural Computation 1999; 11(2):417-441.
16. Herault J, Jutten C. Space or time adaptive signal processing by neural network models. In: Proceedings of Neural Networks for Computing, Snowbird, UT, 1986; 151:207-211.
17. Comon P. Independent component analysis, a new concept? Signal Processing 1994; 36(3):287-314.

18. Hyvarinen A, Karhunen J, Oja E. Independent component analysis. John Wiley and Sons, 2001.

19. Boyd JP. Chebyshev and Fourier spectral methods, 1st ed. Springer-Verlag, 1989.

20. Hall DL, McMullen AHS. Mathematical techniques in multisensor data fusion, 2nd ed. Boston: Artech House, 2004.

21. Aha D, Kibler D, Albert M. Instance based learning algorithms. Machine Learning 1991; 6:37-66.

22. Mitchell T. Machine learning. New York: McGraw Hill, 1997.

23. Cover TM, Hart PE. Nearest neighbour pattern classification. IEEE Transactions on Information Theory 1967; 13(1):21-27.

24. Parzen E. On estimation of a probability density function and mode. The Annals of Mathematical Statistics 1962; 33(3):1065-1076.

25. MacQueen B. Some methods for classification and analysis of multivariate observations. In: Proceedings of the Fifth Berkeley Symposium on Mathematical Statistics and Probability 1967; 1:281-297.

26. Ball GH, Hall DJ. ISODATA, an iterative method of multivariate analysis and pattern classification. In: Proceedings of the International Federation of Information Processing Societies Congress 1965.

27. Gowda KC, Krishna G. Agglomerative clustering using the concept of mutual nearest neighbourhood. Pattern Recognition 1978; 10(2):105-112.

28. Dhillon I, Modha D. A data clustering algorithm on distributed memory multiprocessor. In: Proceedings of the ACM SIGKDD International Conference on Knowledge Discovery and Data Mining, Large-scale Parallel KDD Systems Workshop 1999; 245-260.

29. Friedman M, Kandel A. Introduction to pattern recognition: statistical, structural, neural and fuzzy logic approaches. London: Imperial College Press, 1999.

30. Bezdek JC. Pattern recognition with fuzzy objective function algorithms. New York: Plenum Press, 1981.

31. Breiman L, Friedman JH, Olshen RA, Stone CJ. Classification and regression trees. Belmont, California: Wadsworth International Group, 1984.

32. Quinlan JR. C4.5: Programs for machine learning. San Mateo, California: Morgan Kaufmann Publishers, 1993.

33. Vapnik V. The nature of statistical learning theory. Berlin: Springer-Verlag, 1995.

34. Cristianini N, Shawe-Taylor J. An introduction to support vector machines. Cambridge University Press, 2000.

35. Cortes C, Vapnik V. Support-vector networks. Machine Learning 1995; 20(3):273-297.

36. Jain AK, Mao J, Mohiuddin KM. Artificial neural networks: a tutorial. Computer 1996; 29(3):31-44.

37. Kohonen T. Self-organising maps. Springer Series in Information Sciences, Berlin: Springer-Verlag, 1995.

38. Carreira-Perpinan MA. Continous latent variable models for dimensionality reduction and sequential data reconstruction. University of Sheffield, PhD Thesis, 2001.
39. Duda RO, Hart PE. Pattern classification and scene analysis. New York: Wiley-Interscience, 1973.
40. Hinton GE, Revow M, Dayan P. Recognizing handwritten digits using mixtures of linear models. Advances in Neural Information Processing Systems 1995; 7:1015-1022.
41. Bregler C, Omoundro SM. Nonlinear image interpolation using manifold learning. Advances in Neural Information Processing Systems 1995; 7:973-980.
42. Kohonen T. Self-organization and associative memory, 2nd ed. Berlin: Springer-Verlag, 1987.
43. Bishop CM, Svensen M, Williams CKI. The generative topographic mapping. Neural Computation 1998; 10(1):215-234.
44. Cox TF, Cox MA. Multidimensional scaling, 2nd ed. London: Chapman & Hall, 2001.
45. Steyvers M. Encyclopedia of cognitive science. London: Nature Publishing Group, 2002.
46. Roweis ST, Saul LK. Nonlinear dimensionality reduction by locally linear embedding. Science 2000; 290(5500):2323-2326.
47. Tenenbaum JB, de Silva V, Langford JC. A global geometric framework for nonlinear dimensionality reduction. Science 2000; 290(5500):2319-2323.
48. Blum AL, Langley P. Selection of relevant features and examples in machine learning. Artificial Intelligence 1997; 97(1-2):245-271.
49. Kohavi R, John GH. Wrappers for feature subset selection. Artificial Intelligence 1997; 97(1-2):273-324.
50. John GH, Kohavi R, Pfleger K. Irrelevant features and the subsct selection problem. In: Proceedings of the Eleventh International Conference on Machine Learning, New Brunswick, NJ, 1994; 121-129.
51. Koller D, Sahami M. Towards optimal feature selection. In: Proceedings of the Thirteenth International Conference on Machine Learning, Bari, Italy, 1996; 284-292.
52. Kira K, Rendell LA. The feature selection problem: traditional methods and a new algorithm. In: Proceedings of the Ninth National Conference on Artificial Intelligence, Cambridge, Massachusetts, 1992; 129-134.
53. Almuallim H, Dietterich TG. Learning with many features. In: Proceedings of the Ninth National Conference on Artificial Intelligence, Cambridge, Massachusetts, 1992; 547-552.
54. Dash M, Liu H. Feature selection for classification. Intelligent Data Analysis 1997; 1(3):131-156.
55. Kohavi R. A study of cross-validation and bootstrap for accuracy estimation and model selection. In: Proceedings of the Fourteenth International Joint Conference on Artificial Intelligence, San Mateo, CA, 1995; 1137-1143.
56. Pudil P, Novovicoca J, Kittler J. Floating search methods in feature selection. Pattern Recognition Letters 1994; 15(11):1119-1125.

57. Jain A, Zongker D. Feature selection: evaluation, application, and small sample performance. IEEE Transactions on Pattern Analysis and Machine Intelligence 1997; 19(2):153-158.

58. Pudil P, Novovicova J, Kittler J. Simultaneous learning of decision rules and important attributes for classification problems in image analysis. Image and Vision Computing 1994; 12:193-198.

59. Egan JP. Signal detection theory and ROC analysis. New York: Academic Press, 1975.

60. Van-Trees HL. Detection estimation and modulation theory. New York: Wiley and Sons, 1971.

61. Scott MJJ, Niranjan M, Prager RW. Parcel: feature subset selection in variable cost domains. Department of Engineering, University of Cambridge, England, Technical Report, CUED/F-INFENG/TR, 1998.

62. Srinivasan A. Note on the location of optimal classifiers in n-dimensional ROC space. Oxford University Computing Laboratory, Oxford, England, Technical Report, PRG-TR-2-99, 1999.

63. Wilcoxon F. Individual comparisons by ranking methods. Biometrics 1945; 1:80-83.

64. Hand DJ. Construction and assessment of classification rules. Chichester, England: John Wiley and Sons, 1997.

65. Coetzee F, Lawrence S, Giles CL. Bayesian classification and feature selection from finite data sets. In: Proceedings of the Sixth Conference on Uncertainty in Artificial Intelligence, Stanford, CA, 2000; 89-97.

66. Singh M, Provan GM. Efficient learning of selective Bayesian network classifiers. In: Proceedings of the Thirteenth International Conference on Machine Learning, Bari, Italy, 1996; 453-461.

67. Pearl J. Probabilistic reasoning in intelligent systems: networks of plausible inference. San Mateo, CA: Morgan Kaufmann, 1988.

68. Dempster AP. A generalization of Bayesian inference. Journal of the Royal Statistical Society 1968; 30:205-247.

69. Shafer G. A mathematical theory of evidence. Princeton University Press, 1976.

70. Shafer G. Perspectives on the theory and practice of belief functions. International Journal of Approximate Reasoning 1990; 4(5-6):323-362.

71. Shafer G. Readings in uncertain reasoning. San Mateo, California: Morgan Kaufmann, 1990.

72. Krohn A, Beigl M, Decker C, Kochendorfer U, Robinson P, Zimmer T. Inexpensive and automatic calibration for acceleration sensors. In: Proceedings of the Second International Symposium of Ubiquitous Computing Systems, Tokyo, Japan, 2004; Springer LNCS 3598:245-258.

73. Lukowicz P, Junker H, Troster G. Automatic calibration of body worn acceleration sensors. In: Proceedings of the Second International Pervasive Computing Conference, Vienna, Austria, 2004; 176-181.

74. Liu J, Chang K-C. Feature-based target recognition with a Bayesian network. Optical Engineering 1996; 35(3):701-707.

75. Hanley JA, McNeil BJ. The meaning and use of the area under the receiver operating characteristic (ROC) curve. Diagnostic Radiology 1982; 143:29-36.

Context-Aware Sensing

Surapa Thiemjarus and Guang-Zhong Yang

9.1 Introduction

In recent years, there have been considerable interests in context-aware sensing for pervasive computing. Context can be defined as "*the circumstances in which an event occurs*" and this concept has been successfully used in information processing for over fifty years, particularly for *Natural Language Processing* (NLP) and *Human Computer Interaction* (HCI). The popularity of the context-aware architectures is due to the increasingly ubiquitous nature of the sensors as well as the diversity of the environment under which the sensed signals are collected. To understand the intrinsic characteristics of the sensed signal and determine how BSNs should react to different events, the contextual information is essential to the adaptation of the monitoring device so as to provide more intelligent support to the users.

One of the earliest examples of context-aware computing was the Active Badge from the Olivetti Research Lab in 1992 [1], and the general term "*context-aware computing*" was first introduced by Schilit and Theimer in 1994 [2]. In this work, they described three important aspects of context-awareness: *where you are, who you are with*, and *what resources are nearby*. In other words, they are mainly concerned with location and identity information for context-aware computing. In a mobile distributed computing system named PARCTAB, Schilit *et al* considered four different categories of context-aware applications, which included proximate selection, automatic contextual reconfiguration, commands, and context-triggered action [3]. Proximate selection provides an interface based on the location or capacity of objects, so that located objects are highlighted or made easier to choose from. Reconfiguration, on the other hand, is the process of adding new components, removing existing components or suggesting the connection between components. In the early work of context-aware applications, context triggered actions were simple IF-THEN rules used to specify how the system should adapt to changing environment and user interactions.

Thus far, there has been extensive effort in formally categorising the different features of context-aware applications. Whilst the early taxonomy has aimed at identifying different classes of context-aware applications, Pascoe [4] concentrated on the following considerations:

- *Contextual sensing*: the ability to detect contextual information and present it to the user to augment the user's sensory system;
- *Contextual adaptation*: the ability to execute or modify a service automatically based on the current context;
- *Contextual resource discovery*: allows context-aware applications to locate and exploit relevant resources and services; and
- *Contextual augmentation*: the ability to associate digital data with the user's context in such a way that a user can view the data when he is in the associated context.

It is evident that some of the definitions used above are equivalent to the taxonomy proposed by Schilit *et al.* For example, contextual sensing can be mapped to Schilit's proximity selection, contextual adaptation is similar to context triggered action, and contextual resource discovery can be regarded as automatic contextual reconfiguration. By considering different categorisations of both context and context-aware applications, Dey and Abowd defined context as [5]:

> "*Any information that can be used to characterise the situation of an entity. An entity is a person, place, or object that is considered relevant to the interaction between a user and an application, including the user and applications themselves.*"

In addition to location and identity, activity and time were added to their context categorisation, and context-awareness was defined as:

> "*A system is context-aware if it uses context to provide relevant information and/or services to the user, where relevancy depends on the user's task.*"

From these studies, the main features for context-aware applications can be considered as the presentation of information and services to a user according to the current context, the automatic execution of a service, and the tagging of context to information for later retrieval. The general definition of a context-aware system is therefore related to the issue of whether the system can extract, interpret and use contextual information and adapt its functionality to the current context of use. Table 9.1 illustrates some of the main considerations for designing context-aware systems [6, 7].

For the purpose of BSNs, the main emphasis of a context-aware design is concerned with the interpretation of physical and biochemical signals acquired from both wearable and implantable sensors and their association with the ambient environment. The contextual information is therefore mainly focussed on the user's activity, physiological states, and the physical environment around the user. In this case, the environmental context includes location, proximity, time, social interaction, and connectivity information of the healthcare environment. The user-centred context, on the other hand, includes physical action, cognitive/mental activities, and affective states.

Table 9.1 Considerations of context-aware systems.

Main Considerations

- Identity, *e.g.* user identification
- Spatial information, *e.g.* location, orientation, speed and acceleration
- Temporal information, *e.g.* time of the day, date and season of the year
- Environmental information, *e.g.* temperature, air quality, light or noise levels
- Social interaction, *e.g.* who you are with and people that are nearby
- Resources that are nearby, *e.g.* accessible devices and hosts
- Availability of resources, *e.g.* battery, display, network, and bandwidth
- Physiological measurements, *e.g.* blood pressure, heart rate, respiration rate, tone of voice, and emotions
- Activity, *e.g.* talking, reading, walking and running
- Planned activity, *e.g.* schedules and agenda

The Five W's of Context

- Who – the identity of the user or other people in the environment
- What – human activity and interaction in current systems
- Where – the environment within which the activity is taking place
- When – timestamp of the capture records
- Why – person's affective states and intension

From an information processing point of view, context can be regarded as different levels of details linked to physical and perceptual representations. The description of a user's cognitive activities is generally at an abstract level, whereas the recognition of the physical status of a subject is more descriptive and mainly data-driven. For example, movements are the most elementary primitives for motion recognition, which only require local measurements. Activities, on the other hand, involve sequences of movements and require detailed motion modelling. Finally, action is at the highest level of motion understanding which requires the interpretation of the context (*e.g.* a set of temporal constraints on the relationship between motions) and the interaction of the user with the environment [8].

9.2 Application Scenarios

The above definition outlines the general concepts and considerations for context-aware sensing. The practical application of the method, however, is still in its infancy and some of the early techniques only involve simple measures such as location for contextual interpretation. These systems include a number of office, tourist, and memory aids such as the *Dynamic Ubiquitous Mobile Meeting Board*

(DUMMBO) [9], PARCTAB [3], Cyberguide [10], Forget-Me-Not [11], Remembrance Agent [12], Stick-e Notes [13], and the Olivettit Research Lab's Active Badge [14] mentioned earlier.

Whilst context-awareness in mobile computing is mainly concerned with the adaptation of the application services, its use in BSNs is mainly focussed on how to capture signals under varying physical and environmental conditions. This is because there is a growing need clinically for continuous patient monitoring under their natural physiological state so that transient but life-threatening abnormalities can be reliably detected or predicted. For example, Someren et al [15] illustrated the potential use of motion signal for analysing the effect of medication intake by calculating the average responses during different times of the day for patients with Parkinson's disease. These profiles were then used to evaluate the pharmacological interventions. Bhattacharya et al [16] investigated the heart rate, oxygen uptake and acceleration profiles during exercise to study the relationship between body movement/acceleration and metabolic rates.

The contextual information has also been used to improve the diagnosis accuracy of the acquired physiological signals. This is because similar sensory signals can be interpreted differently depending on the current activities of the patient. For instance, the underlying cause of rapid heartbeats and degenerated ECG can be a result of the vigorous movements of the patient during exercising rather than a genuine cardiac episode. For these reasons, motion signals acquired in situ have been used for recovering biosensor signals corrupted by motion artefacts [17].

Currently, most automatic activity recognition in pervasive sensing is based on the use of motion sensors [18-24], and a record of the daily activities of the patient is used to provide an indication of the general wellbeing of the subject. For patients with disabilities, for example, monitoring tasks that require more effort to accomplish can be used as an objective measure of their functional ability [25, 26]. Tognetti et al [27] demonstrated the use of limb gesture detection for post-stroke rehabilitation. The use of a wearable system for clinical management of individuals undergoing rehabilitation is attractive since it allows the recording of quantitative measurements in settings other than in hospitals or clinics. Existing research has also investigated the value of continuous patient monitoring for exploring the relationship between activity and disease progression, as demonstrated by the studies of Walker et al for rheumatoid arthritis [28] and others in detecting changes of posture and gait in patients with neuromuscular diseases and Parkinson's disease [29-33]. Other sources of information such as acoustics can also be used for activity recognition [34].

Affective states of depression, anxiety and chronic anger have been shown to impede the immune system and they can potentially be used to assess stress, anger and other emotions that can influence health. Teicher [35] studied the correlations between different activity levels and psychiatric disorders. Myrtek and Brügner [36] investigated the perception of daily emotional events by assessing the correlation between physiological parameters such as heart rate, physical activity, and psychological parameters. Picard et al [37] described a recognition framework for detecting a range of emotional states including anger, hate, grief, platonic love, romantic love, joy and reverence based on signals from EMG, blood volume pressure, skin conductance, and Hall-effect respiration sensors. For BSN applications, the emotional states and attention levels are all important contextual information to capture. An example commercial monitoring tool is the SenseWear Armband from BodyMedia [24], which can be worn on the upper arm of the subject to collect data wirelessly from a combination of sensors. Such data includes information about movement, heat flow, skin temperature, ambient temperature, and *Galvanic Skin Response* (GSR).

The use of contextual information has also been used to develop more intelligent healthcare environments. Bardram [38] illustrated the general design principles for context-aware sensing in hospitals and the use of RFID tags for identifying patients and their surrounding clinical team and medical equipment. A context-aware pill container with fingerprint recognition has been proposed to ensure proper dose administration. For introducing context-awareness to BSNs, it is also possible to exploit much of the existing research in pervasive computing, particularly for indoor navigation and tracking [19, 39, 40]. Wearable sensors such as accelerometers, magnetometers, temperature and light sensors have been used extensively for location detection and tracking.

Traditionally, the knowledge of the context of the user is acquired through self-reporting based on diaries or questionnaires. This method is both time-consuming and unreliable, especially for the elderly and subjects with memory impairment. Another method of acquiring contextual information is through clinical observation but it requires specialised equipment and a dedicated laboratory set-up. In addition, measurements made in a clinic may not accurately reflect the patient's behaviour in the normal home environment. With the current advances in sensor and wireless technology, it is now possible to provide ubiquitous monitoring of the subjects under their natural physiological status.

9.3 Preprocessing for Context Sensing

Context recognition can be formulated as a general pattern recognition process which consists of data acquisition, feature extraction, model construction and inference, and performance evaluation. Clustering and high-level inferencing techniques as described in Chapter 8 for multi-sensor fusion can all be applied to context recognition. Before reaching to the recognition stage, a number of signal processing issues related to context detection need to be addressed.

9.3.1 Information Granularity

For context sensing, we are generally more interested in temporal signal variations in the feature space, as the information derived from the instantaneous signal is usually limited. Short time window analysis is the simplest method for segmenting the input sequence. The basic idea is to divide the time-varying signal into meaningful small segments. This can be done by shifting and multiplying a window function of a chosen width, Ω, with the signal. The simplest window function has a rectangular shape but other window functions can also be used to pre-emphasise certain parts of the signal. By the use of a shifting window, the signal can then be divided into a succession of windowed sequences called *frames*, which can be analysed individually. The resolution of the classification process is usually determined by how the feature vectors are constructed. If the window is shifted by a temporal length of $L=1$, a classification label will be assigned to each sample of the original signal. In most studies, L is set to be equal to Ω. In this case, the derived frames do not overlap and some temporal information may be lost. Signals can also be segmented into varying lengths according to their temporal characteristics. This allows the extraction of information from the entire episode of the signal, which tends to provide a more robust result for the classification process. In practice, however, the performance of this approach is highly dependent on the accuracy of the segmentation algorithm, and in many cases the boundary between episodes is difficult to define.

In addition to simple window-based statistics, other signal characteristics such as peak locations, pulse repetition intervals, and zero crossing rates can also be used [41, 42]. In the peak-based feature extraction method, the 'area of activity' is first detected by applying a thresholding scheme on the running variance followed by peak localisation. The drawback of the method is that the peak information is not always available and tracking peaks in multiple dimensions is difficult. A more systematic approach to extracting localised signal features is the use of *Discrete Wavelet Transform* (DWT) and it has been applied successfully to a number of context-aware applications [43]. The choice of appropriate mother wavelets and the corresponding scales for different types of activities, however, remains an active research area.

Recently, Loosli *et al* [44] proposed an interesting online nonparametric signal segmentation technique with one-class *Support Vector Machines* (SVMs) to detect context changes. The technique is based on the concept of change-detection in signal processing [45], and the nonparametric requirement is achieved by the kernel learning method used in SVMs. An one-class SVM is trained by past data to first learn the current state and then examine the subsequent data sequence. A change in signal characteristics is detected when the proportion of misclassification exceeds a given threshold. The method allows decomposition of a multidimensional time series into stationary (or weakly stationary) segments, thus allowing feature extraction to be specific to each context segment and adaptive to context transitions.

9.3.2 Sources of Signal Variations

In context-aware sensing, the acquired signals can be affected by other sources of variations that are detrimental to the classification process. To enhance the overall system sensitivity and specificity, these variations must be carefully considered. Table 9.2 outlines several possible sources of variations that may be encountered by BSN applications.

Table 9.2 Sources of variation for context sensors.

Sources of Variations	
Noise	Sensor noise, node failure, and motion artefact can introduce significant errors to data inferencing results.
Indirect motion	Indirect motion such as those due to car rides, use of wheelchairs or riding an elevator can contribute to movements without actual physical activities [46].
Intra- and inter-subject variability	The difference in anatomy is a major source of subject specific variations. Motion characteristics can have significant inter- and intra-subject variabilities and this must be taken into account when analysing the motion data. Furthermore, the behaviour of individuals can change due to their emotional status and the surrounding environment.
Variation between sensors	Sensors of the same type can be different in terms of characteristic sensitivity, offset, and bias values. These differences can also change over time due to thermal drift [47]. Other subject specific factors such as sensor placement can also introduce sensor variations [46].

In general, the above variations can be handled either during preprocessing or subsequent data classification stages. In preprocessing, blind source separation, such as the ICA algorithm discussed in Chapter 8, can be used to separate the signal components generated by the real sources. In the case of node failure, the missing data can be assigned with the most common values in the training samples or according to a prescribed probability distribution for assigning the missing feature attribute. Finally, systematic sensor variations can be alleviated by effective online/offline sensor calibration.

9.3.3 Data Normalisation

To account for different ranges of the signal collected, direct data normalisation can be applied. The simplest version of data normalisation is to shift the signal baseline to the same mean and then scale it by its variance so that they share the same data range. This allows a proportional influence of all features whilst standardising the dataset at the same time. Translation or phase shift along the time axis is often applied to eliminate signal drift, whereas scaling or time normalisation is applied to cater for signals acquired with different sampling rates. It is worth noting that many of the data normalisation techniques used so far are *ad hoc* and require extensive empirical judgements.

As an example, Picard *et al* used several methods for handling day-to-day variations in their affective sensing framework [37]. These include the use of day matrix, baseline matrix, and day-independent features for the analysis of affective physiological features. For the day matrix, a transform is obtained by applying the Fisher's algorithm to signals appended with a day-dependent vector. The Fisher's algorithm normalises features in the same class so that intraclass difference is minimised whilst interclass differences being maintained. The baseline matrix, on the other hand, is based on the subtraction of the mean of the reference class (baseline) from the respective features of the remaining classes of the same day.

9.4 Context Recognition Techniques

Thus far, most of the context recognition techniques are based on motion sensors and commercially available physiological sensors such as skin conductance, heart rate, and respiratory sensors. Table 9.3 illustrates several examples of the context recognition applications that have been developed in recent years. In this table, we have also listed out the corresponding processing models that have been used. It can be seen that many of the sensor fusion techniques described in Chapter 8 are applicable for this purpose. In this chapter, we will mainly focus on two important approaches for context-aware sensing: *Hidden Markov Models* (HMMs) and *Artificial Neural Networks* (ANNs) – particularly the use of *Self-Organising Maps* (SOMs).

9.4.1 Hidden Markov Models (HMMs)

A HMM consists of a finite set of *states*, and the transition between states is governed by a set of probabilities called *transition probabilities*. In a particular state, an outcome or *observation* can be generated according to the associated probability distribution. It is only the outcome, not the state itself that is visible, hence the name *Hidden Markov Models* because the states are *hidden* from the external world. The basic theory of HMM was published in a series of classic papers by Baum and his colleagues [48] in the late 1960s and since then it has been applied to a wide range of speech processing applications [49, 50]. The key benefit of a HMM is its ability to model temporal statistics of the data by introducing a discrete hidden variable that undergoes a transition from one time step to the next according to a stochastic transition matrix. At each time step, the HMM emits symbols that are dependent on the current state of the hidden variable.

Table 9.3 Examples of recent applications of context-aware sensing and the recognition techniques used.

References	Sensors Used	Context Detection Techniques	Purpose of Study
Krause et al [24]	BodyMedia's Sensewear armband (accelerometers, gyroscope, GSR, heat flux, ambient and skin thermometers)	SOM and 1st order Markov model based on FFT and PCA features; PCA is used for online recalibration	Identification of physiological and activity context
Mantyjarvi et al [51]	Accelerometers	Multilayer perceptron	Walking activity classification (start/stop, level, and walking up/down stairs)
Bao and Intille [18]	Accelerometers	Decision table, instance-based learning, C4.5, and Naïve Bayes using mean, energy, and frequency domain entropy	Activity recognition (20 activities including walking, sitting and relaxing, watching TV, running, stretching, scrubbing, folding laundry, brushing teeth, riding elevator, and eating or drinking, etc)
Lee and Mase [19]	Accelerometers and gyroscope	Three layers of functional blocks (sensing, motion, and location) incorporating fuzzy logic	Activity and location recognition, where activities involved include sitting, standing, walking level, and walking up/down stairs
van Laerhoven and Cakmakci [23]	Accelerometers	SOM for clustering, k-nearest neighbours for classification and Markov chain for modelling context transition	Activity recognition
Loosli et al [44]	EMG, blood volume pressure, skin conductivity and respiration sensors	One class SVM and rupture detection algorithm (SVM is trained based on the data in the past window, when the recognition accuracy drops, context change is detected)	Context change detection
Picard et al [37]	EMG, blood volume pressure, skin conductance sensor, Hall-effect respiration sensor	K-nearest neighbour	Emotion recognition (no emotion, anger, hate, grief, platonic love, romantic love, joy, and reverence)
Patterson et al [52]	GPS	Dynamic Bayesian Network; Bayes particle filter is learned using EM to model the transportation modes as well as location and velocity	Transport behaviour inference (mode estimation and prediction, and location prediction)

Table 9.3 Continued.

References	Sensors Used	Context Detection Techniques	Purpose of Study
Barger et al [53]	The SmartHouse system with motion sensors and switches	Mixture models trained by EM algorithm	Analysis of work and off day behavioural patterns
Noguchi et al [54]	Vivid room	C5.0 decision tree (ID4-based algorithm)	Recognition of human intention (studying, arranging, eating, and resting)
Ravi et al [55]	Accelerometer	Base-level classifier: decision table, decision trees (C4.5), k-nearest neighbours, SVM, Naïve Bayes; meta-level classifiers: boosting, bagging, plurality voting, stacking with ordinary-decision trees and stacking with metadecision trees	Activity recognition (standing, walking, running, climbing up stairs, climbing down stairs, sit-ups, vacuuming, and brushing teeth)
Najafi et al [43]	Accelerometer and gyroscope	A specific rule-based algorithm based on wavelet coefficients	Activity monitoring in the elderly (sleeping posture, sitting, standing, and walking)
Tapia et al [56]	State-change sensors such as reed switches	Multi-class Naïve Bayesian and binary Naïve Bayesian for each activity	Recognition of activities of daily living (such as preparing lunch, toileting, preparing breakfast, bathing, dressing, grooming, preparing a beverage, and watching TV, etc)
Philipose et al [57]	RFID tags	Activities are modelled as a linear sequence of activity stages and then translated into a Dynamic Bayesian Network incorporating a particle filter based inference engine	Modelling activities of daily living (such as oral hygiene, toileting, washing, housework, safe use of appliances, use of heating, care of clothes and linen, taking medication preparing simple snack, and use of telephone, etc)
Chen et al [34]	Microphone	Six-state continuous-density HMMs, each state with two Gaussian mixture components	Bathroom activity recognition
Chambers et al [58]	Accelerometers and video	HMMs	Automatic video annotation

In order to understand HMMs, it is necessary to describe the basic principles of Markov chains. A Markov chain, or first-order Markov model, is a discrete-time stochastic process with a deterministic output function. By describing the evolution of states based on the Markov property (*i.e.* the probability distribution of the current state depends only on the intermediate previous state and the associated action), it provides a compact representation of all possible paths through the state space. A Markov chain can be described with a triple $\Theta = (Q, \mathbf{A}, \boldsymbol{\pi})$, where Q is a finite set of K states, $\mathbf{A}$ is a matrix of $K \times K$ transition probabilities between the states, and $\boldsymbol{\pi} = \{p(\mathbf{q}_i)\}_{i=1}^{K}$ is a prior probability distribution over the states Q indicating the likelihood of a state $\mathbf{q} \in Q$ being the staring point. The prior distribution can sometimes be replaced by the non-emitting (entry and exit) state. In general, the probability of any state sequence $\mathbf{Q}_T = [\mathbf{q}_1, \mathbf{q}_2, ..., \mathbf{q}_T]$ can be defined as:

$$p(\mathbf{Q}_T \mid \Theta) = p(\mathbf{q}_1 \mid \Theta) \prod_{t=2}^{T} p(\mathbf{q}_t \mid \mathbf{q}_{t-1}, \mathbf{q}_{t-2}, ..., \mathbf{q}_1, \Theta) \tag{9.1}$$

Based on the first-order Markov assumption, the joint probability $p(\mathbf{Q}_T \mid \Theta)$ can be redefined as a product of the probability of the first state and the probabilities of subsequent transitions in the sequence, *i.e.*,

$$p(\mathbf{Q}_T \mid \Theta) = p(\mathbf{q}_1 \mid \Theta) \prod_{t=2}^{T} p(\mathbf{q}_t \mid \mathbf{q}_{t-1}, \Theta) \tag{9.2}$$

where $p(\mathbf{q}_1 \mid \Theta)$ is the initial probability of state $\mathbf{q}_1$ and $p(\mathbf{q}_t \mid \mathbf{q}_{t-1}, \Theta)$ is the probability of a transition from state $\mathbf{q}_{t-1}$ to $\mathbf{q}_t$. The maximum likelihood estimation of the transition probabilities is defined as:

$$p(\mathbf{q}_t \mid \mathbf{q}_{t-1}) = \frac{\text{Number of transitions from state } \mathbf{q}_{t-1} \text{ to } \mathbf{q}_t}{\text{Number of transitions from state } \mathbf{q}_{t-1}} \tag{9.3}$$

In context-aware sensing, Markov chains are often used in the supervising layer to extract information about context transitions [23, 24].

The HMM is an extension of the Markov model in which the observation itself is described by a probabilistic output function, but as mentioned earlier, the state sequence in this case is hidden. Each HMM approximates the likelihood that the model generates the observed data based on the assumptions that: *a*) the signal is stationary over a frame; *b*) current observations are statistically independent of the previous outputs (observations); and *c*) transition probabilities are constant (*i.e.* independent of observations or previously visited states). A HMM can be defined as a pentuple $\Theta = (Q, X, \mathbf{A}, \mathbf{B}, \boldsymbol{\pi})$, where Q and X are sets of K (hidden) states and L output symbols, respectively. In this definition, $\mathbf{A}$ represents the state transition probabilities, $\mathbf{B}$ is a $K \times L$ output matrix containing the probabilities of emitting observation $\mathbf{x} \in X$ while in state $\mathbf{q} \in Q$, and $\boldsymbol{\pi}$ represents the initial state distribution vector or indicates the non-emitting states. Given an observation sequence $\mathbf{X}_T = [\mathbf{x}_1, \mathbf{x}_2, ..., \mathbf{x}_T]$ and model Θ, context recognition can be achieved by determining the best state sequence $\mathbf{Q}_T^* \in Q$ which maximises $p(\mathbf{X}_T, \mathbf{Q}_T | \Theta)$, or equivalently:

$$\mathbf{Q}_T^* = \arg\max_{\mathbf{Q}_T \in Q} p(\mathbf{X}_T | \mathbf{Q}_T, \Theta) p(\mathbf{Q}_T | \Theta) \tag{9.4}$$

Since the realisation of $\mathbf{x}_t$ is assumed to be independent of the neighbouring states, the first term of (9.4) can be simplified as multiplications of the output density, *i.e.,*

$$p(\mathbf{X}_T | \mathbf{Q}_T, \Theta) = \prod_{t=1}^{T} p(\mathbf{x}_t | \mathbf{q}_t) \tag{9.5}$$

The second term of (9.4) is used to model the contextual information among states, which can be derived from a first- or higher-order Markov model. The probability of observing a HMM output string $\mathbf{X}_T$ is given by summing the contribution from all the possible state sequences $\mathbf{Q}_T \in Q$ such that

$$p(\mathbf{X}_T | \Theta) = \sum_{\mathbf{Q}_T \in Q} p(\mathbf{q}_1 | \Theta) p(\mathbf{x}_1 | \mathbf{q}_1, \Theta) \prod_{t=2}^{T} p(\mathbf{q}_t | \mathbf{q}_{t-1}, \Theta) p(\mathbf{x}_t | \mathbf{q}_t, \Theta) \tag{9.6}$$

This can be efficiently computed by recursively applying the probabilities of the partial state sequences and observations. The most important criterion used for estimating the HMM parameters is to maximise the likelihood of generating the training data in (9.6). The Viterbi algorithm and Baum-Welch re-estimation method are two of the most commonly used HMM training algorithms. The Viterbi method is a dynamic programming algorithm with which the total likelihood is estimated by the probability of the most likely state sequence $\mathbf{Q}_T^*$, *i.e.,*

$$p(\mathbf{X}_T | \Theta) \approx p(\mathbf{X}_T, \mathbf{Q}_T^* | \Theta) \tag{9.7}$$

From this, each observation vector can be assigned to exactly one emitting state, and the parameters of each output distribution can be estimated independently based the data segment(s) associated with the state. The Baum-Welch re-estimation algorithm, on the other hand, is based on the popular *Expectation Maximisation* (EM) method. At the E-step, soft alignment is made by estimating the probability of state occupation, whereas at the M-step, the transition probabilities and the output distribution parameters are re-estimated by using the probability of state occupation. At each iteration, an increase in likelihood is guaranteed.

A common way to view a HMM is to regard it as a finite state machine as shown in Figure 9.1. A HMM can also be viewed as a simple version of a *Dynamic Bayesian Network* (DBN) with one discrete (unobserved) hidden node and one discrete or continuous observed node per time slice, as illustrated in Figure 9.2.

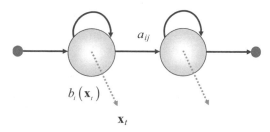

Figure 9.1 A standard HMM as a finite state machine where the shaded nodes denote an emitting state with output probability $b_i(\mathbf{x}_t)$ and the small dark nodes denote nonemitting (entry and exit) states. In this figure, arcs represent state transitions with probability a_{ij}.

This model provides a compact representation of the joint probability distribution and reveals the underlying independence assumptions among variables in the graph.

To model the output probability distribution for each state in a continuous density HMM, it is common to use a Gaussian distribution with diagonal covariance to reduce the number of parameters required. The distribution of the real-world signal, however, can be non-Gaussian. To overcome this problem, the output distribution can be estimated by using a linear mixture of different models such as the popular mixture of Gaussians represented by the following weighted function:

$$b_j\left(\mathbf{x}_t\right) = \sum_{m=1}^{M} \omega_{jm} b_{jm}\left(\mathbf{x}_t\right) = \sum_{m=1}^{M} \omega_{jm} N\left(\mathbf{x}_t; \mathbf{\mu}_{jm}, \mathbf{\Sigma}_{jm}\right) \qquad (9.8)$$

where M is the number of Gaussian components in a state, and ω_{jm} is the component weight or prior that is summed to 1.

Under the Bayesian network representation of HMMs, a general mixture distribution for $b_j\left(\mathbf{x}_t\right) = p\left(\mathbf{x}_t \mid \mathbf{q}_t = j, \Theta\right)$ assumes the existence of a hidden variable ω that determines the active mixture component. It follows that:

$$
\begin{aligned}
p\left(\mathbf{x}_t \mid \mathbf{q}_t = j, \Theta\right) &= \sum_{m=1}^{M} p\left(\mathbf{x}_t, \omega = m \mid \mathbf{q}_t = j, \Theta\right) \\
&= \sum_{m=1}^{M} p\left(\omega = m \mid \mathbf{q}_t = j, \Theta\right) p\left(\mathbf{x}_t \mid \omega = m, \mathbf{q}_t = j, \Theta\right)
\end{aligned} \qquad (9.9)
$$

To illustrate how HMMs can be used for context detection, we present in Figure 9.3 a simple example of activity detection through the use of a sensor glove mounted with an optical bending sensor and two accelerometers sampled at 50Hz [59]. The optical bending sensor was placed across the palm, whereas the two accelerometers were positioned on the back of the index finger and thumb, respectively. The dataset consists of six different activities including *opening the door, turning on/off the tap, opening/closing the cupboard, making coffee, adding milk,* and *drinking coffee.* In this simple example, we used six three-state HMMs with an ergodic fully-connected HMM topology. Baum-Welch re-estimation was used for model training and the output distribution associated with each state is modelled by a simple Gaussian distribution with diagonal covariance matrix so as to keep the number of parameters as small as possible. A total of seven data sets were acquired from the subject; one of which was used for model training and the remaining six were used for evaluating the accuracy of the algorithm.

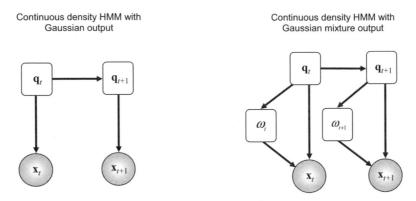

Figure 9.2 Bayesian network representations of HMMs, where circles denote continuous nodes or variables, and squares denote discrete nodes. Unshaded nodes are hidden nodes.

Since the range of each sensor channel can be contrastingly different, the overall mean and standard deviation were used for data normalisation for each dataset so that all data shares the same mean and unit variance. Simple noise filtering was applied to the data, and for each channel we also calculated signal energy over a fixed window size of fifty samples. The raw signal and energy were concatenated to form a ten-dimensional vector for the five sensing channels involved. Figure 9.3 illustrates the six different activity segments captured, and Table 9.4 summarises the overall accuracy of the HMM algorithm for the six test data sets used. In this table, rank *n* accuracy means the correct classification is among the first *n* highest likelihood models.

Albeit being simple, the above example demonstrates some of the advantages of HMMs. The method has a sound statistical grounding and its parameter estimation can take into account different sources of uncertainty. Furthermore, it is modular and can be combined into larger models. In general, HMMs are relatively robust with regards to temporal changes and it is also possible to incorporate high-level domain knowledge. The disadvantages of the method, however, include the relatively strong assumptions made about the data and the amount of training data required due to the large number of parameters involved. Another issue related to HMMs are that their training involves maximising the observed probabilities for examples belonging to a certain class but it does not minimise the probability of observation of instances from other classes. In terms of performance, a HMM involves enumerating of all possible paths through the model. Although the search can be efficiently performed by using the token passing algorithm [60], it can be computationally expensive compared to other techniques. Despite these problems, HMMs remain an attractive technique for context-aware sensing.

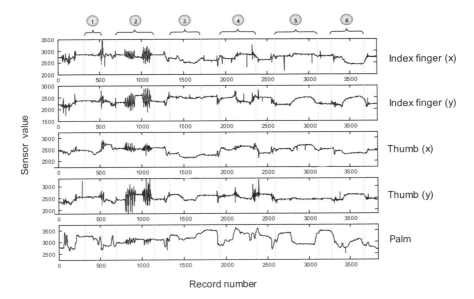

Figure 9.3 Time series plot of a signal sequence obtained from the sensor glove. The six activities marked represent opening the door, turning on/off the tap, opening/closing the cupboard, making coffee, adding milk, and drinking coffee, respectively.

Table 9.4 HMM classification results for the experiment shown in Figure 9.3.

Class	Rank 1 Accuracy	Rank 2 Accuracy	Rank 3 Accuracy
C1	100%	100%	100%
C2	100%	100%	100%
C3	83.33%	83.33%	100%
C4	33.33%	50%	100%
C5	100%	100%	100%
C6	83.33%	100%	100%
Average	83.33%	88.89%	100%

9.4.2 Artificial Neural Networks (ANNs)

For context sensing, the alternative approach of using ANNs offers several important features including nonlinearity (they are suitable for data which is inherently nonlinear), adaptivity (they can be easily retrained to deal with minor changes), evidential response (they can be designed to provide confidence for the decision made), and fault tolerance (their performance degrades gracefully under adverse operating conditions) [61]. Moreover, the relatively small number of operations involved in the combined learning and classification process makes the model particularly suited for a parallel, on-chip analogue implementation [62]. For a BSN, this means some of the processing steps involved can be performed locally on low-power, miniaturised sensor nodes so as to minimise the communication bandwidth required. This is particularly attractive for distributed inferencing.

The underlying mechanism of an ANN is inspired by the neurobiological system of our brain. A neuron consists of a cell body called a soma which contains the nucleus, and a number of short, branching cellular extensions called dendrites. They form the main information receiving network for the neuron. The axon is a much finer, cable-like structure which carries nerve signals away from the neuron to connect with the dendrites and cell bodies of other neurons. The connection point is called a synapse. Neurons have only one axon, but this axon can undergo extensive branching, enabling communication with many target cells. Each neuron can receive, process and transmit electrochemical signals. Synapses can be either chemical or electrical. In an electrical synapse, the membranes of two neurons are continuous at tiny spots called gap-junctions, making the cells electrically contiguous. In the case of chemical synapses, neurotransmitters are released from a presynaptic neuron and dock with receptor proteins on the postsynaptic neuron. Such binding causes the shape of the protein to change and ion channels to open. The firing of a neuron depends on how many inputs it is receiving as well as the nature of each input signal (excitatory or inhibitory) at each synapse. The net result of these inputs determines whether the neuron will become excited, or depolarised, enough to fire an action potential and release neurotransmitter from its axon terminals.

The history of ANNs begins with the model of the biological neuron introduced by McCulloch and Pitts in 1943 [63]. The *McCulloch-Pitts* (MP) neuron is described as a linear threshold computing unit with multiple inputs and a single binary output. Each input x_i is connected to the jth neuron by a directed synaptic connection with weight w_{ij}. The neuron is activated and returns value 1 when the sum of the weighted inputs exceeds a specified threshold θ_j. Otherwise, the output value is 0. Mathematically, the response of an MP neuron can be written as:

$$y_j = f\left(\sum_i w_{ij} x_i(t) - \theta_j\right) \qquad (9.10)$$

where $f(x) = 1$ if $x \geq 0$, otherwise $f(x) = 0$. In 1949, Hebb postulated the first rule for self-organised learning, which states that the effectiveness of a variable synapse between two neurons is increased if the two interconnected neurons are activated at the same time [64]. Based on the McCulloch-Pitts model, the single-layer perceptron was proposed by Rosenblatt in 1958 [65]. The model is considered as the first ANN for supervised learning. A perceptron is a neuron with adjustable weights w_i, for $i = 1, 2, ..., d$, and an externally applied threshold bias w_0. Table 9.5 describes the procedure for learning the weights and threshold for a perceptron.

Table 9.5 The perceptron learning algorithm.

(a) Initialise the weights and threshold to small random values;

(b) For each input vector, $\mathbf{x}(t)$ (t is the time step index):

- Evaluate the output y of the neuron by applying the binary step activation function f to the linear combination of inputs and an externally applied bias;

- Update the weights according to
$$\mathbf{w}(t+1) = \mathbf{w}(t) + \eta (y' - y) \mathbf{x}(t)$$
where the learning rate η is a constant value between 0 and 1, and y' is the desired output.

The perceptron can be considered as the simplest kind of feed-forward neural network. This model can be generalised by simply replacing the activation function f with a more general nonlinear function. However, the perceptron can only deal with linearly separable patterns as long as a monotonic activation function is used. In 1969, Minsky and Papert [66] demonstrated that a single-layer perceptron was incapable of representing a linearly inseparable function such as the "exclusive or" (XOR). The postperceptron era began with the realisation that adding (hidden) layers to the network could yield significant computational versatility. This stimulated a revival of interest in ANNs especially for multilayered feed-forward structures.

One important type of ANN for context-aware sensing is the *Self-Organising Map* (SOM). SOM is a class of unsupervised competitive neural models with an organised geometrical structure of output neurons. It can be considered as a nonlinear projection of a probability density function $p(\mathbf{x})$ of a high dimensional input onto a discrete, usually two-dimensional output space. In addition to the advantages inherent in ANNs, SOM provides an efficient way of data visualisation and clustering.

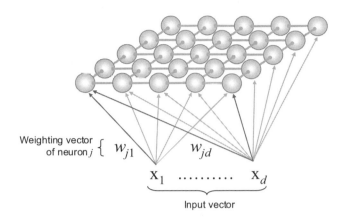

Input vector

Figure 9.4 The basic structure of a standard SOM.

SOM can be viewed as a regular lattice of neurons with different areas of the map tuned to different activity patterns as shown in Figure 9.4. In this figure, the weight vector $\mathbf{w}_j$ associated with each neuron j has an equal dimension to the input vector and is typically initialised with random values. The SOM training algorithm updates the winning node as well as nodes in its topological vicinity. The update rule is formulated so that the node with its weight vector nearest to the input data wins the competition. The most common criterion is based on maximising the inner product $\mathbf{w}_j^T\mathbf{x}$, which is equivalent to minimising the Euclidean distance between the two vectors:

$$i(\mathbf{x}) = \arg\min_j \left\| \mathbf{x} - \mathbf{w}_j \right\|, \, j = 1, 2, \ldots, l \tag{9.11}$$

where $i(\mathbf{x})$ is the winning unit activated by the input vector $\mathbf{x}$ and l is the total number of neurons in the network. The weighting vector of the winning neuron and its neighbours are updated according to the following iterative equation:

$$\begin{aligned}\mathbf{w}_j(t+1) &= \mathbf{w}_j(t) + \Delta \mathbf{w}_j \\ &= \mathbf{w}_j(t) + \eta(t) h_{j,i(\mathbf{x})}(t)(\mathbf{x} - \mathbf{w}_j(t))\end{aligned} \tag{9.12}$$

where $\eta(t)$ is the learning rate and $h_{j,i(\mathbf{x})}(t)$ a neighbourhood function whose value depends on the distance between node j and the wining node $i(\mathbf{x})$. In this way, similar inputs will activate neurons that are close to each other on the SOM map.

A common choice of the neighbourhood function $h_{j,i(\mathbf{x})}(t)$ is a Gaussian function. It has been found that the SOM algorithm converges more quickly with a Gaussian neighbourhood function. The underlying assumptions for the Gaussian neighbourhood function are: *a*) it is symmetric about the winning node; *b*) it decreases monotonically in amplitude with increasing lateral distance $d_{j,i}^2$ and decays to zero as $d_{j,i} \to \infty$ (a necessary condition for convergence); and *c*) it is independent of the location of the winning neuron, *i.e.*, it is translational invariant.

In many applications, the quality of the SOM solutions can be improved by using a time-varying neighbourhood function [67]. A time-varying form of the Gaussian function can be described as:

$$h_{j,i(\mathbf{x})}(t) = \exp\left(\frac{d_{j,i}^2}{2\sigma^2(t)}\right) \qquad (9.13)$$

where t is the time step index used in training and $\sigma(t)$ is the extent of the neighbourhood. Both the learning parameter $\eta(t)$ and the effective width $\sigma(t)$ should be gradually decreasing over time.

In practical implementations, SOM learning often consists of two different phases of the operation, called ordering and converging phases respectively. The ordering phase involves approximately 1000 iterations with the learning rate $\eta(t)$ near unity. It is not crucial whether the learning rate decreases linearly, exponentially or inversely proportional to time n. However, after the ordering phase, $\eta(t)$ should attain a small value (*i.e.* of the order of or less than 0.01), otherwise the map will loose its adaptive behaviour. The exponential decay function

$$\eta(t) = \eta_0 \exp\left(-\frac{t}{\tau_1}\right) \qquad (9.14)$$

provides a way to guarantee the lower bound η_0 of the learning rate, where τ_1 is the time constant. The neighbourhood function $h_{j,i(\mathbf{x})}(t)$ should initially include almost all of the neurons so that the weights will become ordered globally. In the final convergence phase, the number of steps used should be at least 500 times the size of the network in order to achieve a good statistical accuracy [68]. The ordering phase can be omitted if the weight vector is initialised by a linear initialisation scheme. The algorithm in Table 9.6 summarises the main steps involved in the formation of a SOM.

In order to apply a SOM to classification, a class label is assigned to each neuron after convergence. For each neuron that has been activated at least once, it is labelled with the data class that has the highest number of activations for that neuron. For neurons that have not been activated by the training data, they are usually assigned with the label of their nearest neighbours.

Table 9.6 The SOM learning algorithm.

(a) Initialise the weight vector $\mathbf{w}_j$, learning rate and the "effective width" $\sigma(t)$ of the neighbourhood function $h_{j,i(\mathbf{x})}(t)$.

(b) For each input vector, $\mathbf{x}(t)$ (t is the time step index):

- Determine the winning neuron, $i(\mathbf{x})$:

$$i(\mathbf{x}) = \underset{j}{\operatorname{argmin}} \|\mathbf{x} - \mathbf{w}_j\|, \quad j = 1, 2, \ldots, l$$

- Calculate the neighbourhood function:

$$h_{j,i(\mathbf{x})}(t) = \exp\left(\frac{d_{j,i}^2}{2\sigma^2(t)}\right)$$

where $d_{j,i}$ is the distance between weight vectors of node i and j.

- Update the weight vectors of the winning neuron and its neighbours,

$$\mathbf{w}_j(t+1) = \mathbf{w}_j(t) + \eta(t)h_{j,i(\mathbf{x})}(t)(\mathbf{x} - \mathbf{w}_j(t))$$

- Reduce the "effective width" $\sigma(t)$ (ordering phase) and the learning rate $\eta(t)$.

(c) Repeat step (b) until the convergence condition is satisfied, and reuse the input data if necessary.

9.5 Spatio-Temporal Self-Organising Maps (STSOMs)

Due to its simplicity, SOM-based architectures have been used in a range of context-aware applications [23, 41, 69-71]. The conventional SOM, however, has a number of limitations. First, it is based on the matching of a snapshot of the input attributes (or features) with the neurons, and its accuracy is influenced by feature variations. In many context-aware applications, each activity can consist of a series of submovements and the resulting activation pattern in this case is no longer restricted to a local cluster of neurons. It tends to span across a large area of the map and overlaps with neuron activations introduced by other activities. These overlaps in neuron excitation can adversely affect the overall recognition accuracy.

Although it is possible to use methods such as the short-term memory model [72] to convert the temporal variation to stable feature vectors, they can significantly increase the dimensionality of the input vector and are not effective when the sub-movements involved have a large temporal variation and poor repeatability. This problem is also compounded by the fact that activities involved in most context-aware applications can have a mixture of stable and dynamic signal features, and it is practically difficult to find low-level feature representations that are effective for both cases. To overcome these problems, existing research has been concentrated on improved feature extraction and selection methods for deriving stable feature vectors suitable for all the activities involved. The SOM in this case is mainly used as a simple classifier at the final stage of the processing steps.

Another problem associated with SOMs is the fact that the neuron activation pattern of the trained map can be highly dependent on the distribution of the training data [73]. If a particular region of the input space contains more frequently occurring stimuli, it will be represented by a larger area of the SOM, and therefore introducing a bias depending on the number of records per class in the training data. Due to the compounding effect of mixing dynamic and static excitations mentioned above, the class discriminability is difficult to control and interclass misclassification (confusion) is inevitable.

To address the two issues mentioned above, we will describe in this section a technique called *Spatio-Temporal Self-Organising Map* (STSOM) for integrating temporal excitation pattern and adaptive class-separation into a hierarchical SOM model. The key idea of the method is to rely on class-specific neuron activation patterns and the introduction of an additional temporal layer of the SOM to provide improved class separation. It also incorporates a divide-and-conquer multi-resolution classification scheme to adaptively to remove inter-class overlaps.

9.5.1 The Basic Structure of the STSOM

The prerequisite of a STSOM is the introduction of both static and dynamic classes of neuron activation. It is worth noting that this should not be confused with the static and dynamic activities mentioned in context-aware sensing. An activity that is dynamic in the physical space can be associated with a static neuron activation given appropriate feature representation. For example, a fixed frequency sinusoidal movement can be turned into a static representation when Fourier features are used. In a STSOM, we consider classes that continuously activate (or in other words, the activation is fixated onto) the same neurons of the map as static classes. Other classes that involve activation patterns moving across the map are called dynamic classes.

To illustrate the basic concept of STSOM, let's consider a synthetic dataset shown in Figure 9.5 that involves eight different activities captured by two sensor channels. A standard SOM with 10×10 neurons was constructed by using the training and node labelling schemes mentioned above. The resultant trained map is represented by its U-matrix and the node labels shown in Figures 9.6(a) and 9.6(b) respectively. The U-matrix is a visualisation method for SOM, which represents the average distances amongst neighbouring weight vectors [74]. A smaller distance among neighbours implies a higher map resolution due to the large number of support in the training data. In Figure 9.6(a), the darker (blue) shades indicate smaller average distances among neighbours and brighter (orange) shades are associated with larger distances. From the U-matrix, it is evident that four static neuron activation classes corresponding to C1-C4 are formed. Activations associated with C5-C8, however, are scattered across the entire map.

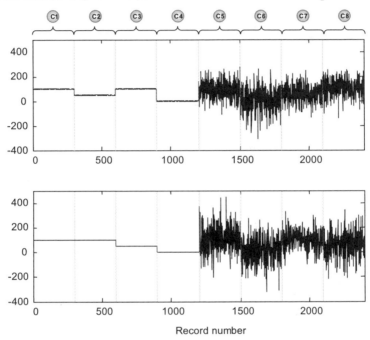

Figure 9.5 A 2D synthetic dataset consists of eight classes.

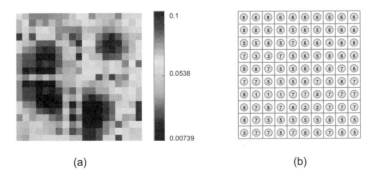

(a)   (b)

Figure 9.6 Two visualisation schemes for the standard SOM: (*a*) the U-matrix representation and (*b*) class label for each neuron. (**See colour insert.**)

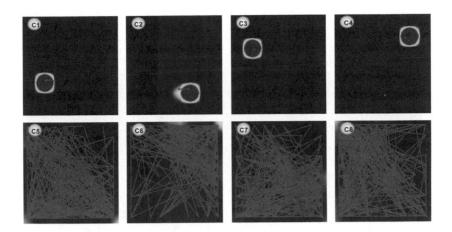

Figure 9.7 Class-specific activation plots of the static map output. (**See colour insert.**)

The images in Figure 9.7 illustrate the class-specific activation plots of the standard SOM superimposed by the node activation trajectories. During classification, a SOM determines the predicted class from the label of the neuron with its weighting vector that is the closest to the input feature vector. It is evident from Figure 9.7 that it is difficult for the standard SOM to differentiate classes C5-C8. In this particular example, the classification accuracy for C5-C8 was in fact as low as 38%-64%.

The key concept of the STSOM is to use the temporal characteristic of the neuron activation to partition the data space. As can be seen from Figure 9.7, the static and dynamic classes can be distinguished by observing the neuron activation patterns. In this example, we use the normalised index entropy to measure the dynamics of the activation by using the following equation:

$$\text{Entropy}(\mathbf{p}) = \alpha \sum_{i}^{N} -p_i \log_2(p_i) \tag{9.15}$$

where N is the number of neurons activated within a fixed time window, p_i is the probability that node i is activated, and α is a normalisation constant. After applying (9.15), the corresponding result for Figure 9.7 is shown in Figure 9.8 where a time window of 10 sampling points is used. This provides a good separation of static and dynamic neuron activation classes, and by pruning out dynamic activations, a revised static labelling shown in Figure 9.9 can be achieved.

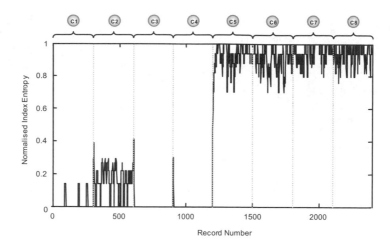

Figure 9.8 The normalised index entropy of the node activation produced by the synthetic dataset in Figure 9.5.

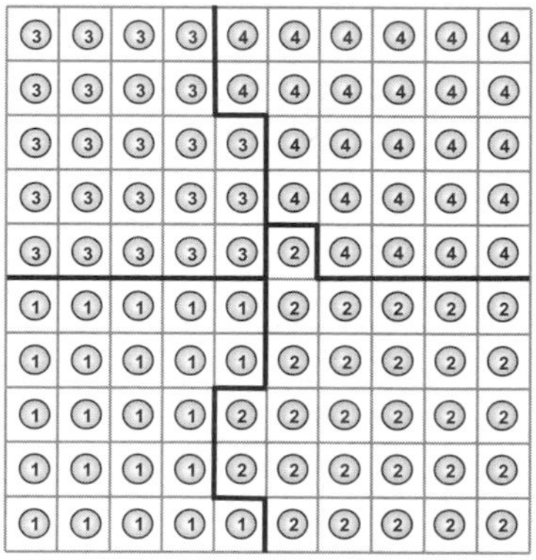

Figure 9.9 Revised static labelling of the STSOM after pruning out dynamic activations.

Since the *static map* is trained with both static and dynamic data, it spans the entire data space. For data corresponding to the index entropy higher than a specified threshold, a second layer of the STSOM called the *dynamic map* is used to extract the temporal signature of the neuron activation produced by the static map. The input to the dynamic map for this experiment consists of the moving average of the positive area ($APA(t)$) and negative area ($ANA(t)$) with regard to the centre of each axis of the static map. That is,

$$APA(t) = \begin{cases} \dfrac{1}{\Omega} \displaystyle\sum_{\tau=t-\Omega+1}^{t} c(\tau) - \dfrac{D+1}{2}, & if \quad c(\tau) > \dfrac{D+1}{2} \\ 0 & otherwise \end{cases}$$ (9.16)

$$ANA(t) = \begin{cases} \dfrac{1}{\Omega} \displaystyle\sum_{\tau=t-\Omega+1}^{t} \dfrac{D+1}{2} - c(\tau), & if \quad c(\tau) < \dfrac{D+1}{2} \\ 0 & otherwise \end{cases}$$ (9.17)

where Ω is the size of the shifted window, and D and $c(\tau)$ are the map dimension and the coordinate of the activated node along a given axis, respectively. These features, in fact, reflect the average position of the activated node trajectory with regard to each quadrant of the map. It is also possible to use other temporal features to provide a good separation for the dynamic classes of interest. In this experiment, the dynamic map consists of 25 neurons and the corresponding result after applying (9.16) and (9.17) is shown in Figure 9.10. In Figure 9.11, we also provide the class-specific activation plots of the dynamic map for C5-C8. It is evident from these maps that a good classification result for these classes is possible.

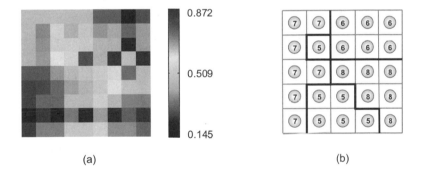

(a)   (b)

Figure 9.10 (*a*) The U-Matrix and (*b*) node labels of the dynamic map.
(**See colour insert**.)

A detailed quantitative comparison of class-specific recognition accuracy between the standard SOM and the proposed STSOM is shown in Figure 9.12. It can be seen that significant improvements have been achieved for the dynamic classes (C5-C8) whilst the recognition accuracy for the static classes (C1-C4) being maintained. In this example, the overall recognition accuracy of the training set by using the standard SOM with 100 neurons is 75.12%, whereas the overall recognition accuracy for the STSOM has improved to 95.63% by using a total of 125 neurons.

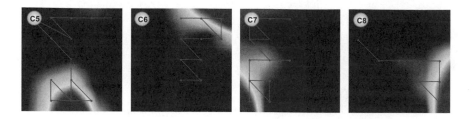

Figure 9.11 Class-specific activation plots of the dynamic map output.
(**See colour insert.**)

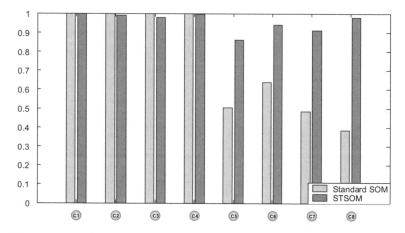

Figure 9.12 The comparison of the class-specific recognition accuracy between the standard SOM and the STSOM.

9.5.2 The Use of Multi-Resolution for Improved Class Separation

Before putting the above STSOM framework to practical use, it is necessary to examine the class separation of both the static and dynamic maps. Due to the compounding effect of mixing dynamic and static excitations mentioned earlier, the class discriminability between static classes can be limited for a STSOM, particularly when the map size is relatively small. To demonstrate this, Figure 9.13 illustrates a dataset used to train a STSOM with sixteen neurons for the static layer. The corresponding class-specific activation is shown in Figure 9.14, where classes C2 and C3 are mapped onto the same area.

This problem is similar to that encountered in a standard SOM and can be solved by expanding the map resolution. A less expensive strategy, however, is to perform an adaptive local expansion to avoid the reconstruction of a larger map from scratch. Existing strategies developed for this purpose include the *Growing*

Hierarchical Self-Organising Map (GH-SOM) [75] as illustrated in Figure 9.15. It incorporates the concept of grid growing proposed by Fritzke [76] to adaptively insert a new row or column of neurons between units with the largest deviation between the weighting and input vectors. The weighting vectors of the nodes are then initialised with the average of their neighbours. The method also allows an expansion of each node with high quantisation error with a multi-layer SOM.

Another approach is proposed by van Laerhoven [71], which uses *k*-means sub-clusters to expand each neuron to avoid the overwriting of prototype vectors on the map. The problem with these methods is that the expansion of the nodes does not directly take into account the class information, and therefore the classification accuracy may not necessarily be improved.

In the proposed STSOM, the expansion of the problematic nodes is only performed when there is a reasonable level of support by data from different classes. This is important as it avoids the expansion of nodes corresponding to transitions of the dynamic classes. To illustrate the effect of node expansion, Figure 9.16 demonstrates the class-specific activation plot of SOM with twenty-five neurons for classes C2 and C3 from the example shown in Figure 9.14. It is evident that by increasing the map dimensionality, the activation map for these two classes starts to separate. Instead of increasing the resolution of the entire map, we can also selectively increase the resolution of the problematic area as shown in Figure 9.17, which demonstrates a much improved class separation compared to that of Figure 9.16. It should be noted that the activation map for a given class may not be limited to a single or several connected neurons. The expansion scheme mentioned above is class-specific, *i.e.,* when a node is expanded, all other nodes belonging to the same class of the current node should also be expanded.

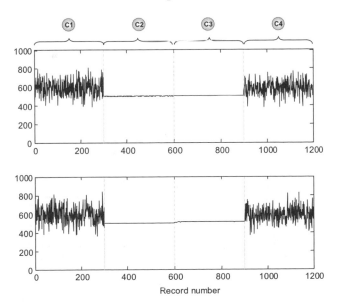

Figure 9.13 A 2D synthetic dataset consists of four classes.

Figure 9.14 A demonstration of errors due to overlaps between static classes. (**See colour insert**.)

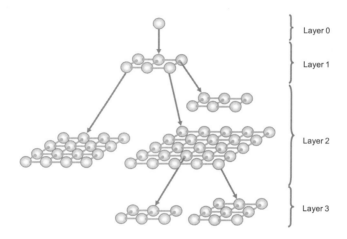

Layer 0

Layer 1

Layer 2

Layer 3

Figure 9.15 Node expansion within a multi-layer SOM through using the GH-SOM architecture.

Figure 9.16 Class separation for C2 and C3 of Figure 9.14 by increasing the map size from 16 to 25 neurons. (**See colour insert**.)

Figure 9.17 The activation plot of node expansion with sixteen neurons to achieve a clear class separation. (**See colour insert.**)

9.5.3 STSOM Algorithm Design

By introducing the basic idea of STSOM and how to use the multi-resolution concept for improved class separation, we are now ready to take a step-by-step tour of the STSOM algorithm. To help with the explanation, we will use a synthetic dataset shown in Figure 9.18 to highlight the major steps involved. In this dataset, the data for classes C1 and C4 are generated by adding different levels of Gaussian noise to a constant vector of (500, 580). The data for classes C2 and C5 are generated by a constant vector of (500, 400) plus small Gaussian noise and sin waves with amplitudes of (1000, 1500) along the two orthogonal axes. The main difference between the raw signal of these two classes is the frequencies used (3Hz for C2 and 2Hz for C5). Finally, the data for classes C3 and C6 are generated by adding a small Gaussian noise to the constant vectors (500, 500) and (501, 501), respectively. We will be using this example to provide a step-by-step guide to the proposed STSOM design.

The first step of the algorithm is to generate a static map based on the feature vectors of the original signal. The details of feature extraction and optimum feature selection are provided in Chapter 8 of this book. Once the static map is generated, a *confusion matrix* is constructed based on this map alone. A confusion matrix contains information about the actual and predicted classifications obtained from the classification system. The diagonal elements of the matrix represent the number of correct classifications, *i.e.*, cases in which the classifier returns the same predicted class as the actual class. The off-diagonal elements represent the number of misclassifications and can be used as an indication of class overlap. Table 9.7 illustrates the derived confusion matrix for the data shown in Figure 9.18 when the static map size is selected to be 36.

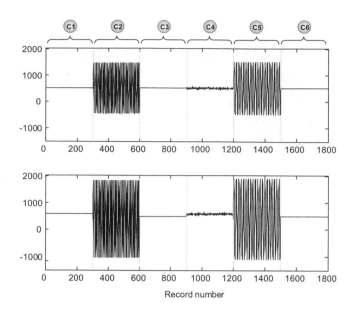

Figure 9.18 A 2D synthetic dataset consists of six classes, generated by constants plus Gaussian noises and sinusoidal waves.

The next step of the STSOM algorithm is to identify class overlap to form a set of combined-classes. One method of achieving this is to use hierarchical clustering which treats each row as a singleton cluster and then successively merges clusters to form a *dendrogram* [77]. In our method, the distance measure is based on the off-diagonal element of the confusion matrix between class pairs. Since the confusion matrix is asymmetric, single linkage hierarchical clustering is used. With this method, we merge in each step the two clusters whose two closest members have the smallest distance. Sub-groups representing the combined-classes can be formed by applying a threshold to the output dendrogram at the point where between-cluster distances increase sharply. Table 9.8 shows the re-ordered confusion matrix when these subgroups are formed by applying the above hierarchical clustering algorithm, illustrating the class overlap within the static map of the STSOM. It can be seen that the result in Table 9.8 corresponds well with the neuron activation map shown in Figure 9.19. For this dataset, there are three different types of class-overlap, *i.e.*, static-static (C3-C6), static-dynamic (C1-C4), and dynamic-dynamic (C2-C5).

The subsequent steps of the STSOM algorithm are to use the strategies described in 9.5.1 and 9.5.2 to separate these overlaps, either by introducing the dynamic map of the STSOM or through adaptive node expansion. To separate static from dynamic activation (*i.e.*, overlap between C1 and C4), the normalised index entropy as described in 9.5.1 can be used. This will upgrade activation associated with C4 to the dynamic map, leaving C1 unambiguously classified. If a dynamic class is overlapped with more than one static class, adaptive node expansion as described in 9.5.2 can be applied to the remaining static classes after the dynamic class is filtered out.

Table 9.7 The confusion matrix for the classification of the synthetic dataset in Figure 9.18 with a static map of 36 neurons.

	C1	C2	C3	C4	C5	C6
C1	300	0	0	131	0	0
C2	0	180	0	0	60	0
C3	0	0	300	0	0	300
C4	0	0	0	169	0	0
C5	0	120	0	0	240	0
C6	0	0	0	0	0	0

Table 9.8 The re-organised confusion matrix for the classification of the synthetic dataset in Figure 9.18 with a static map of 36 neurons.

	C1	C4	C2	C5	C3	C6
C1	300	131	0	0	0	0
C4	0	169	0	0	0	0
C2	0	0	180	60	0	0
C5	0	0	120	240	0	0
C3	0	0	0	0	300	300
C6	0	0	0	0	0	0

To resolve overlaps among dynamic activations, the dynamic map of the STSOM is introduced. In the example shown above, we need to consider class overlap between C2 and C5, as well as C4 which has been upgraded from the previous step. Figure 9.20 demonstrates the result of applying a dynamic map with 16 neurons based on the $APA(t)$ and $ANA(t)$ measures of the static map. Yet again, adaptive node expansion can be applied if between-class overlap persists.

The final step in the class separation process is to resolve the static-static overlap (*i.e.*, the class overlap between C3 and C6). This can be achieved by node expansion as described in 9.5.2, and the corresponding result for the above synthetic data with a sixteen neuron expansion is shown in Figure 9.21.

To achieve adequate class separation for the above synthetic data, a total of 68 neurons have been used (36 for the static map, 16 for the dynamic map, and another 16 for the static node expansion). To assess the value of the proposed STSOM framework, we have compared the achieved classification accuracy with that of a standard SOM. It has been found that the overall accuracy increased from 66.06% to 95.89%, and for a standard SOM to achieve a similar accuracy, the map resolution needs to be increased to at least 20×20, *i.e.*, 400 neurons. In this case, the SOM accuracy is 92.33%, which is still a touch poorer than that of the STSOM. To allow a detailed assessment of the above result, Figure 9.22 illustrates the class-specific activation plots for the standard SOM with 400 neurons, and Tables 9.9 and 9.10 provide the derived confusion matrices for the SOM and STSOM, respectively. Finally, summaries of the STSOM learning and inferencing algorithms are provided in Tables 9.11 and 9.12.

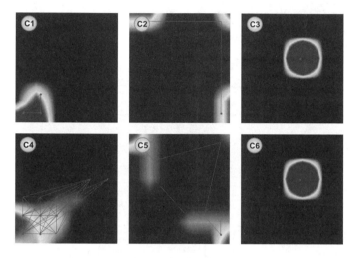

Figure 9.19 Illustration of three types of overlap in the static map with 36 neurons for the test data shown in Figure 9.18. The overlap occurs between static and dynamic classes (C1-C4), two dynamic classes (C2-C5) and two static classes (C3-C6), respectively. (**See colour insert**.)

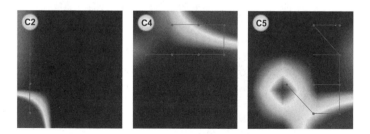

Figure 9.20 Class-specific activation plots for the dynamic map of the test data shown in Figure 9.18. (**See colour insert**.)

Figure 9.21 Class-specific activation plots after node expansion for C3 and C6 of Figure 9.19. (**See colour insert.**)

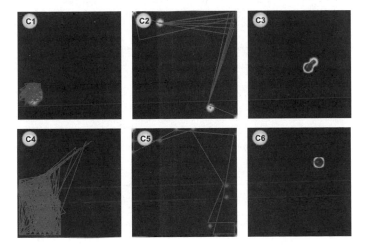

Figure 9.22 Class-specific activation plots of a standard SOM with 400 neurons for the synthetic dataset shown in Figure 9.18. (**See colour insert.**)

Table 9.9 The confusion matrix for the classification of the synthetic dataset in Figure 9.18 by a standard SOM with 400 neurons.

	C1	C2	C3	C4	C5	C6
C1	300	0	0	1	0	0
C2	0	283	0	0	120	0
C3	0	0	300	0	0	0
C4	0	0	0	299	0	0
C5	0	17	0	0	180	0
C6	0	0	0	0	0	300

Table 9.10 The confusion matrix for the classification of the synthetic dataset in Figure 9.18 by using the proposed STSOM a total of 88 neurons.

	C1	C2	C3	C4	C5	C6
C1	296	19	0	3	0	0
C2	0	281	5	14	0	0
C3	0	0	295	0	0	0
C4	4	0	0	269	11	0
C5	0	0	0	14	289	4
C6	0	0	0	0	0	296

9.5.4 STSOM for Context-Aware Sensing

To illustrate the practical value of the STSOM for context-aware sensing, the proposed algorithm is applied to the same experiment described in Figure 8.5 of Chapter 8. It features a simple physical exercise sensing experiment where four two-axis accelerometers are placed on the left and right ankles and legs. The activities of the subject during the exercise routine include 1) *sitting* (*chair*), 2) *standing*, 3) *steps*, 4) *sitting* (*floor*), 5) *demi-plie*, 6) *galloping left*, 7) *skipping*, 8) *galloping right*, 9) *side kick*, 10) *front kick*, and 11) *walking*. From Figure 8.5, it is evident that the decision boundaries for the eleven activities involved are highly complex, particularly for some of the dynamic activities involved. Figure 9.23 reiterates the sensor signals collected for this experiment, showing the moving signal energy calculated for the eight sensory channels involved.

Table 9.11 The STSOM model learning algorithm.

Model learning:

(1) Train the static map with the standard SOM training algorithm.

(2) Assign the class label to each neuron by:
   - *(a) Applying the static map on the training set and keep record of activation frequency of each neuron;*
   - *(b) Pruning out the labels of neurons with activation frequency lower than a specified threshold;*
   - *(c) Assigning a label to an unlabelled node with the label of the nearest labelled neighbour.*

(3) Form sub-clusters of highly confused classes by:
   - *(a) Applying the static map on the training set;*
   - *(b) Calculating the confusion matrix;*
   - *(c) Creating a list of between-class distances and keep only the elements that have values that are greater than a specified threshold;*
   - *(d) Performing single link clustering based on the distance list;*
   - *(e) Representing each independent spanning tree as a sub-cluster of a confused-class.*

(4) If the distance list is empty, relabel the static map by repeating step 2(a) and 2(c), and output the map and terminate. Otherwise, calculate the index entropy of the classes in the confused subclusters.

(5) Extract data samples for dynamic map training
   - *(a) Partition the data of the confused classes using the index entropy calculated over a fixed window Ω_e;*
   - *(b) Based on the number of supporting data decide if a confused class is static or dynamic.*

(6) Perform feature extraction on the outputs of the static map for the samples that correspond to the dynamic classes and use them to construct the dynamic map.

(7) For each subcluster of confused static classes, create a higher layer static map; allocate an integer array to store the class-to-map index.

(8) Keep a record of the labelled maps, entropy threshold, window size, features used, and class-to-map index for model inference.

Table 9.12 The STSOM inferencing algorithm.

Model Inference:

(1) For each input vector, $\mathbf{x}_v(t)$ (t is the time step index), determine the winning neuron, $i_s(t)$ of the static map s.

(2) Calculate the index entropy over a fixed window Ω_e.

(3) If the entropy is higher than a specified threshold,

- Calculate input vector $\mathbf{x}_d(t)$ for the dynamic map d;
- Determine the winning neuron, $i_d(t)$;
- Output the label of the neuron $i_d(t)$.

Otherwise,

(a) Use the label of the neuron $i_s(t)$ and the class-to-map index to determine the appropriate static map:

$$h = \text{class-to-map}\left[\text{label}\left(i_s(t)\right)\right].$$

(b) If map h is the same as map s, output the label of the neuron $i_s(t)$, otherwise

- *Based on the input vector $i_s(t)$, determine the winning neuron, $i_h(t)$ of the static map h;*
- *Output the label of the neuron $i_h(t)$.*

For this experiment, the static map of the STSOM involves one hundred neurons and the total number of neurons we used after the introduction of the dynamic map and node expansion was 164. The input vector consisted of the raw signal and signal energy calculated over a fixed window of fifty samples (2s) for each sensor channel. Figure 9.24 illustrates the class-specific activation plots of the static and dynamic maps of the STSOM for both the training and test data. In order to assess the improvement in model accuracy through the STSOM algorithm, each static map of the STSOM was built from the standard SOM. This enabled a fair comparison since both maps shared the same weight vectors, and so the effect of local minima in different model training was avoided. To compare the performance of the standard SOM and the proposed STSOM, the experiment was repeated fifty times. We compared STSOM using 164 neurons with standard SOMs using 100 and 400 neurons, respectively, and Figure 9.25 illustrates the relative performance observed. It was found that with the standard SOMs the average performance was about 58%, and an increase of the number of neurons from 100 to 400 did not make any noticeable difference. The use of STSOM with a relatively small number of neurons, however, has achieved a marked improvement in performance, especially for classes C1, C3, C6, and C11.

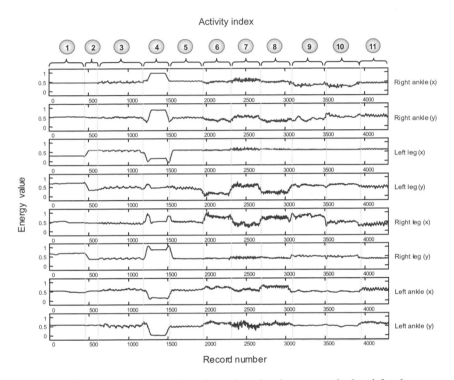

Figure 9.23 A time series plot of moving signal energy calculated for the eight sensory channels involved.

9.6 Conclusions

In this chapter, we have described the use of context awareness for more accurate and intelligent pervasive sensing. The use of contextual information, however, is not new and it has been widely used in many pattern recognition applications including NLP, HCI, image processing, and computer vision. Its use for pervasive sensing, however, has introduced some interesting new challenges. The popularity of context-aware architectures is due to the increasingly ubiquitous nature of the sensors as well as the diversity of the environment under which the sensed signals are collected. For the purpose of BSNs, the main emphasis of a context-aware design is concerned with the interpretation of physical and biochemical signals acquired from both wearable and implantable sensors and their association with the ambient environment. The contextual information is therefore mainly focussed on the user's activity, cognitive/mental activities, physiological and affective states, and the environment context such as location, proximity, time, social interaction, and connectivity to the general healthcare environment.

The use of contextual information is important to the improvement of diagnosis accuracy because in a BSN, similar sensory signals can be interpreted differently depending on the current activities of the patient. To understand the intrinsic characteristics of the sensed signal and determine how BSNs should react to different events, the contextual information is essential to the adaptation of the monitoring device so as to provide more intelligent support to the users.

Our discussion in this chapter has mainly been focussed on the use of HMMs and SOMs for context-aware sensing. The main advantage of the HMM is that it has a sound statistical grounding and its parameter estimation can take into account different sources of uncertainty. Furthermore, it is modular, relatively robust, and can be combined into larger models. It is also possible to incorporate high-level domain knowledge. The disadvantage of the method, however, originates in the relatively strong assumptions about the data and the amount of training data required due to the large number of parameters involved.

The alternative approach of using ANNs, and SOMs in particular, offers the advantages of nonlinearity, adaptivity, evidential response, and fault tolerance. Moreover, the relatively small number of operations involved in the combined learning and classification process makes the model particularly suited for parallel, on-chip analogue implementations. For BSNs, this means some of the processing steps involved can be performed locally on low-power, miniaturised sensor nodes so as to minimise the communication bandwidth required based on effective distributed inferencing.

The main features of the STSOM architecture proposed in this chapter are the introduction of the dynamic layer and an adaptive mechanism for class separation and node expansion. It has been shown that the overall number of the neurons involved in the proposed STSOM is relatively small compared to traditional approaches. This is essential for BSN nodes, which have limited computational and storage resources. For low power analogue implementation, the implications for hardware design are expected to be even greater.

It should be noted that in this chapter, we have paid little attention to signal feature extraction and selection. These are, in fact, essential to the overall performance of context detection techniques. In Chapter 8, we have summarised a number of different approaches for extracting intrinsic signal characteristics. The effective use of these features can greatly enhance the accuracy of the context detection algorithm. Although we have only mentioned in this chapter the use of HMMs and SOMs for context recognition, other techniques such as clustering and high level inferencing techniques as described earlier in the book are equally applicable for this purpose.

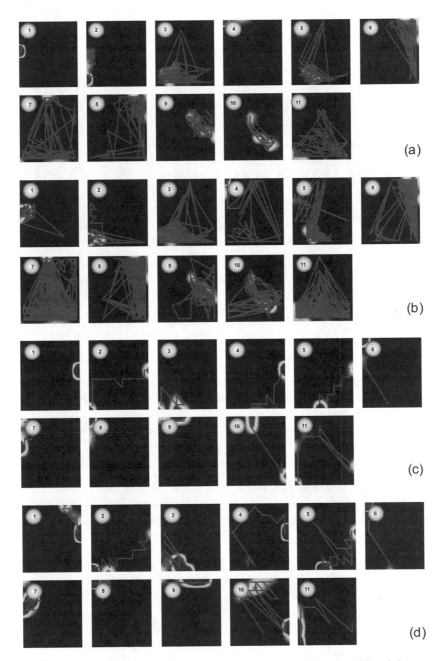

Figure 9.24 Class-specific activation plots of: (*a*) the static map with training data; (*b*) the static map with test data; (*c*) the dynamic map with training data; and (*d*) the dynamic map with test data. (**See colour insert.**)

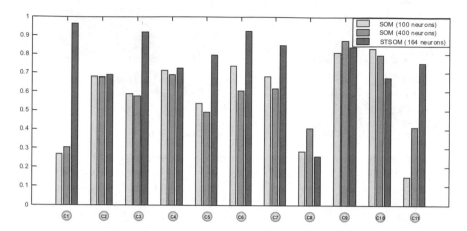

Figure 9.25 A comparison of the recognition accuracy between a standard SOM with 100 neurons, a standard SOM with 400 neurons, and a STSOM with 164 neurons for the experiment shown in Figure 9.23.

References

1. Want R, Hopper A. Active badges and personal interactive computing objects. IEEE Transactions on Consumer Electronics 1992; 38(1):10-20.
2. Schilit B, Adams N, Want R. Context-aware computing applications. In: Proceedings of the Workshop on Mobile Computing Systems and Applications 1994; 85-90.
3. Schilit BN, Adams N, Gold R, Tso MM, Want R. The PARCTAB mobile computing system. In: Proceedings of the Fourth Workshop on Workstation Operating Systems 1993; 34-39.
4. Pascoe J. Adding generic contextual capabilities to wearable computers. In: Proceedings of the Second IEEE International Symposium on Wearable Computers 1998; 92-99.
5. Dey AK, Abowd G. Towards a better understanding of context and context-awareness. In: Proceedings of the CHI 2000 Workshop on "The What, Who, Where, When, and How of Context-Awareness" 2000.
6. Korkea-aho M. Context-aware applications survey. http://users.tkk.fi/~mkorkeaa/doc/context-aware.html, 2000.
7. Abowd GD, Mynatt ED. Charting past, present, and future research in ubiquitous computing. ACM Transactions on Computer-Human Interaction 2000; 7(1):29-58.
8. Bobick AF. Movement, activity and action: the role of knowledge in the perception of motion. Philosophical Transactions of the Royal Society of London B: Biological Sciences 1997; 352(1358):1257-1265.

9. Brotherton JA, Abowd GD, Truong KN. Supporting capture and access interfaces for informal and opportunistic meetings. GVU Center, Georgia Institute of Technology, Technical Report, GIT-GVU-99-06, 1999.

10. Long S, Aust D, Abowd GD, Atkeson CG. Rapid prototyping of mobile context-aware applications: the Cyberguide case study. In: Proceedings of the Second ACM International Conference on Mobile Computing and Networking 1996; 97-107.

11. Lamming M, Flynn M. Forget-me-not: intimate computing in support of human memory. In: Proceedings of FRIEND21: International Symposium on Next Generation Human Interfaces, Meguro Gajoen, Japan, 1994; 125-128.

12. Rhodes BJ. The wearable remembrance agent: a system for augmented memory. In: Proceedings of the First International Symposium on Wearable Computers, Cambridge, Massachusetts, 1997; 123-128.

13. Brown PJ, Bovey JD, Chen X. Context-aware applications: from the laboratory to the marketplace. IEEE Personal Communications 1997; 4(5):58-64.

14. Want R, Hopper, A., Falcao, V., Gibbons, J. The active badge location system. ACM Transactions on Information Systems 1992; 10(1):91-102.

15. van Someren EJ, Vonk BF, Thijssen WA, Speelman JD, Schuurman PR, Mirmiran M, *et al.* A new actigraph for long-term registration of the duration and intensity of tremor and movement. IEEE Transactions on Biomedical Engineering 1998; 45(3):386-395.

16. Bhattacharya A, McCutcheon EP, Shvartz E, Greenleaf JE. Body acceleration distribution and O2 uptake in humans during running and jumping. Journal of Applied Physiology 1980; 49(5):881-887.

17. Asada HH, Jiang H-H, Gibbs P. Active noise cancellation using MEMS accelerometers for motion-tolerant wearable bio-sensors. In: Proceedings of the Twenty-Sixth Annual International Conference of Engineering in Medicine and Biology Society 2004; 1:2157-2160.

18. Bao L, Intille SS. Activity recognition from user-annotated acceleration data. In: Proceedings of the Second International Conference on Pervasive Computing, Vienna, Austria, 2004; 1-17.

19. Lee S-W, Mase K. Activity and location recognition using wearable sensors. IEEE Pervasive Computing 2002; 1(3):24-32.

20. Thiemjarus S, Lo BPL, Yang GZ. Feature selection for wireless sensor networks. In: Proceedings of the First International Workshop on Wearable and Implantable Body Sensor Networks, Imperial College, London, 2004.

21. Thiemjarus S, Lo BPL, Yang GZ. A distributed Bayesian framework for body sensor networks. In: Proceedings of the Second International Workshop on Body Sensor Networks, Imperial College, London, 2005.

22. Thiemjarus S, Lo BPL, Yang GZ. A noise resilient distributed inference framework for body sensor networks. In: Adjunct Proceedings of the Third International Conference on Pervasive Computing, Munich, Germany, 2005; 13-18.

23. van Laerhoven K, Cakmakci O. What shall we teach our pants? In: Proceedings of the Fourth IEEE International Symposium on Wearable Computers 2000.

24. Krause A, Siewiorek DP, Smailagic A, Farringdon J. Unsupervised, dynamic identification of physiological and activity context in wearable computing. In: Proceedings of the Seventh IEEE International Symposium on Wearable Computers 2003; 88-97.
25. Inzitari D, Basile AM. Activities of daily living and global functioning. International Psychogeriatrics 2003; 15(Supplement 1):225-229.
26. Senanarong V, Harnphadungkit K, Prayoonwiwat N, Poungvarin N, Sivasariyanonds N, Printarakul T, *et al.* A new measurement of activities of daily living for Thai elderly with dementia. International Psychogeriatrics 2003; 15(2):135-148.
27. Tognetti A, Lorussi F, Bartalesi R, Quaglini S, Tesconi M, Zupone G, *et al.* Wearable kinesthetic system for capturing and classifying upper limb gesture in post-stroke rehabilitation. Journal of NeuroEngineering and Rehabilitation 2005; 2(1):8.
28. Walker DJ, Heslop PS, Plummer CJ, Essex T, Chandler S. A continuous patient activity monitor: validation and relation to disability. Physiological Measurement 1997; 18(1):49-59.
29. White R, Agouris I, Selbie RD, Kirkpatrick M. The variability of force platform data in normal and cerebral palsy gait. Clinical Biomechanics (Bristol, Avon) 1999; 14(3):185-192.
30. Chang WN, Tsirikos AI, Miller F, Schuyler J, Glutting J. Impact of changing foot progression angle on foot pressure measurement in children with neuromuscular diseases. Gait Posture 2004; 20(1):14-19.
31. Verghese J, Lipton RB, Hall CB, Kuslansky G, Katz MJ, Buschke H. Abnormality of gait as a predictor of non-Alzheimer's dementia. The New England Journal of Medicine 2002; 347(22):1761-1768.
32. Mueller MJ, Salsich GB, Bastian AJ. Differences in the gait characteristics of people with diabetes and transmetatarsal amputation compared with age-matched controls. Gait Posture 1998; 7(3):200-206.
33. Zijlstra W, Rutgers AW, van Weerden TW. Voluntary and involuntary adaptation of gait in Parkinson's disease. Gait Posture 1998; 7(1):53-63.
34. Chen J, Kam AH, Zhang J, Liu N, Shue L. Bathroom activity monitoring based on sound. In: Proceedings of the Third International Conference on Pervasive Computing, Munich, Germany, 2005; 47-61.
35. Teicher MH. Actigraphy and motion analysis: new tools for psychiatry. Harvard Review of Psychiatry 1995; 3(1):18-35.
36. Myrtek M, Brugner G. Perception of emotions in everyday life: studies with patients and normals. Biological Psychology 1996; 42(1-2):147-164.
37. Picard RW, Vyzas E, Healey J. Toward machine emotional intelligence: analysis of affective physiological state. IEEE Transactions on Pattern Analysis and Machine Intelligence 2001; 23(10):1175-1191.
38. Bardram JE. Applications of context-aware computing in hospital work: examples and design principles. In: Proceedings of the 2004 ACM Symposium on Applied Computing, Nicosia, Cyprus, 2004; 1574-1579.

39. Golding AR, Lesh N. Indoor navigation using a diverse set of cheap, wearable sensors. In: Proceedings of the Third IEEE International Symposium on Wearable Computers 1999; 29-36.
40. Wilson D, Atkeson C. The Narrator: a daily activity summarizer using simple sensors in an instrumented environment. In: Adjunct Proceedings of the Fifth International Conference on Ubiquitous Computing, Seattle, Washington, 2003.
41. van Laerhoven K, Kern N, Gellersen HW, Schiele B. Towards a wearable inertial sensor network. In: Proceedings of IEE Eurowearable 2003; 125-130.
42. van Laerhoven K, Gellersen H-W. Spine versus porcupine: a study in distributed wearable activity recognition. In: Proceedings of the Eighth International Symposium on Wearable Computers 2004; 1:142-149.
43. Najafi B, Aminian K, Paraschiv-Ionescu A, Loew F, Bula CJ, Robert P. Ambulatory system for human motion analysis using a kinematic sensor: monitoring of daily physical activity in the elderly. IEEE Transactions on Biomedical Engineering 2003; 50(6):711-723.
44. Loosli G, Lee SG, Canu S. Context changes detection by one-class SVMs. In: Proceedings of Workshop on Machine Learning for User Modeling: Challenges, the Tenth International Conference on User Modelling, Edinburgh, Scotland, 2005.
45. Basseville M, Nikiforov IV. Detection of abrupt changes - theory and application. Prentice-Hall, 1993.
46. Steele BG, Belza B, Cain K, Warms C, Coppersmith J, Howard J. Bodies in motion: monitoring daily activity and exercise with motion sensors in people with chronic pulmonary disease. Journal of Rehabilitation Research and Development 2003; 40(5):45-58.
47. Lukowicz P, Junker H, Tröster G. Automatic calibration of body worn acceleration sensors. In: Proceedings of the Second International Conference on Pervasive Computing, Linz/Vienna, Austria, 2004; 176-181.
48. Baum LE, Pertrie T, Soules G, Weiss N. A maximization technique occurring in the statistical analysis of probabilistic functions of Markov chains. Annals of Mathematical Statistics 1970; 41:164-171.
49. Rabiner L. A tutorial on hidden Markov models and selected applications in speech recognition. Proceedings of the IEEE 1989; 77.
50. Gold B, Morgan N. Speech and audio signal processing: processing and perception of speech and music. New York: John Wiley and Sons, 2000.
51. Mantyjarvi J, Himberg J, Seppanen T. Recognizing human motion with multiple acceleration sensors. In: Proceedings of the IEEE International Conference on Systems, Man, and Cybernetics, Hawaii, USA, 2001; 2:747-752.
52. Patterson D, Fox D, Kautz H, Philipose M. Expressive, tractable and scalable techniques for modeling activities of daily living. In: Proceedings of the Second International Workshop on Ubiquitous Computing for Pervasive Healthcare Applications, Seattle, Washington, USA, 2003.

53. Barger TS, Brown DE, Alwan M. Health-status monitoring through analysis of behavioral patterns. IEEE Transactions on Systems, Man and Cybernetics A, 2005; 35(1):22-27.
54. Noguchi K, Somwong P, Matsubara T, Nakauchi Y. Human intention detection and activity support system for ubiquitous autonomy. In: Proceedings of IEEE International Symposium on Computational Intelligence in Robotics and Automation 2003; 2:906-911.
55. Ravi N, Dandekar N, Mysore P, Littman ML. Activity recognition from accelerometer data. In: Proceedings of the Seventeenth Annual Conference on Innovative Applications of Artificial 2005.
56. Tapia EM, Intille SS, Larson K. Activity recognition in the home setting using simple and ubiquitous sensors. In: Proceedings of the Second International Conference on Pervasive Computing 2004; Springer LNCS 3001:158-175.
57. Philipose M, Fishkin KP, Perkowitz M, Patterson DJ, Fox D, Kautz H, *et al.* Inferring activities from interactions with objects. IEEE Pervasive Computing 2004; 3(4):50-57.
58. Chambers G, Venkatesh S, West G, Bui H. Hierarchical recognition of intentional human gestures for sports video annotation. In: Proceedings of the Sixteenth IEEE Conference on Pattern Recognition 2002; 6.
59. King R, Lo BPL, Yang GZ. Hand gesture recognition with body sensor networks. In: Proceedings of the Second International Workshop on Body Sensor Networks, Imperial College, London, 2005.
60. Young SJ, Rusell NH, Thornton JHS. Token passing: a conceptual model for connected speech recognition. Cambridge University Engineering Department, Technical Report, CUED/F-INFENG/TR38, 1989.
61. Haykin S. Neural networks: a comprehensive foundation, 2nd ed. Upper Saddle River, New Jersey: Prentice Hall, 1994.
62. Macq D, Verleysen M, Jespers P, Legat J-D. Analog implementation of a Kohonen map with on-chip learning. IEEE Transactions on Neural Networks 1993; 4(3):456-461.
63. McCulloch WS, Pitts W. A logical calculus of the ideas immanent in nervous activity. Bulletin Mathematical Biophysics 1943. 5:115-133.
64. Hebb DO. The organization of behavior. New York: John Wiley and Sons, 1949.
65. Rosenblatt F. The perceptron: a probabilistic model for information storage and organization in the brain. Psychological Review 1958; 65(6):386-408.
66. Minsky ML, Papert S. Perceptrons; an introduction to computational geometry. MIT Press, Cambridge, Massachusetts: MIT Press, 1969.
67. Mehrotra K, Mohan CK, Ranka S. Elements of artificial neural networks. Cambridge, Massachusetts: MIT Press, 1997.
68. Kohonen T. The self-organizing map. Proceedings of the IEEE 1990; 78(9):1464-1480.
69. Himberg J, Flanagan JA, Mäntyjärvi J. Towards context awareness using symbol clustering map. In: Proceedings of the Workshop for Self-Organizing Maps, Kitakyushu, Japan, 2003; 249-254.

70. Varsta M, Heikkonen J, Millan JdR. Context learning with the self-organizing map. In: Proceedings of the Workshop on Self-Organizing Maps, Helsinki University of Technology, Finland, 1997.

71. van Laerhoven K. Combining the self-organizing map and k-means clustering or on-line classification of sensor data. In: Proceedings of the International Conference on Artificial Neural Networks 2001; 464-469.

72. Barreto G, Araujo A, Ritter H. Time in self-organizing maps: an overview of models. International Journal of Computer Research, Special Issue on Neural Networks: Past, Present and Future 2001; 10(2):139-179.

73. Yin H, Allinson NM. Towards the optimal Bayes classifier using an extended self-organising map. In: Proceedings of the International Conference on Artificial Neural Networks 1995; 2:45-49.

74. Ultsch A. Self-organizing neural networks for visualization and classification. In: Proceedings of Information and Classification 1993; 307-313.

75. Rauber A, Merkl D, Dittenbach M. The growing hierarchical self-organizing map: exploratory analysis of high-dimensional data. IEEE Transactions on Neural Networks 2002; 13(6):1331-1341.

76. Fritzke B. Growing grid: a self-organizing network with constant neighbourhood range and adaptation strength. Neural Processing Letters 1995; 2(5):9-13.

77. Godbole S, Sarawagi S, Chakrabarti S. Scaling multi-class support vector machines using inter-class confusion. In: Proceedings of the Eighth ACM SIGKDD International Conference on Knowledge Discovery and Data Mining 2002; 513-518.

10

Autonomic Sensing

Guang-Zhong Yang, Benny Lo, and Surapa Thiemjarus

10.1 Introduction

In most engineering problems, our main concern is the exact specification and modelling of the system architecture and its associated responses. In this manner, we can discover whether the analytical solution is tractable and practical. For complex systems, however, this is not always possible and the use of bio-inspired design provides a way of imitating how biological systems adapt to complex, dynamic, and rapidly changing environments. In Chapters 1 and 7, we have already highlighted the importance of bio-inspired design for autonomic sensing and the development of ultra-low power processing for BSNs. Due to the inherent complexities involved in managing a large number of wireless sensors, bio-inspired sensing and networking has attracted significant research interest in recent years.

The use of bio-inspired sensing generally involves the specification of a set of simple rules and how they should be iteratively applied to the population. One well known example of such an approach is *Swarm Intelligence* (SI) developed in artificial intelligence for studying the collective behaviour of decentralised, self-organised systems [1]. SI systems are typically made up of a population of simple agents or devices interacting locally with one another as well as with their environment. Although there is no centralised control dictating how individual devices should behave, local interactions between these devices can lead to the emergence of an effective global behaviour. To provide self-organisation to the sensor network nodes so that they can coordinate themselves autonomously, large-scale spatial patterns (found in the clustering behaviour of ants) using *Local Activation Long-range Inhibition* (LALI) have been investigated [2]. This is an example of how simple mechanisms can lead to an effective collective behaviour with functionality and adaptivity amplified on a global scale in the absence of a rigid central management structure.

Another example of bio-inspired sensing and networking is quorum sensing. Quorum sensing is the ability of bacteria to communicate and coordinate behaviour via signalling molecules. Bacteria use quorum sensing to produce and secrete certain signalling compounds called auto-inducers or pheromones. These bacteria also have a receptor that can specifically detect the inducer. This means that when the inducer binds the receptor, it activates the transcription of certain genes, including those for inducer synthesis. The purpose of quorum sensing is to coordinate certain behaviour or actions between bacteria of the same kind within the local vicinity. When the concentration of the inducer exceeds a threshold due to the clustering of the same bacteria, more inducer is synthesised which causes a positive feedback loop that fully activates the receptor. For example, bacteria such as *Pseudomonas Aeruginosa* can grow within a host harmlessly until they reach a certain concentration. At this point they become aggressive, and in numbers sufficient to overcome the host's immune system and lead to disease [3].

Quorum sensing is a useful concept for sensor networks because the bacterial cells need to be aware of the global cell concentration, and in the same way a sensor needs to know if there are enough sensors to form a cluster for the purpose of monitoring a particular area of the network collectively [3].

In searching for biological inspiration for sensor network design, two biological systems are regarded to be of particular importance to the BSN – the *Autonomic Nervous System* (ANS) and the *Biological Immune System* (BIS). The ANS comprises of autonomic ganglia and nerves and is primarily responsible for the control of the body's internal environment. In Chapter 1, we have explained the basic structure and complexity of the ANS. Having understood the anatomical makeup of the ANS, one can begin to explore how it overcomes the challenges faced by the human body sensor networks as a whole. Some of the major features of the ANS have been summarised as the so-called *self-** properties such as self-management, self-organisation and self-healing. The BIS, on the other hand, provides us with important design considerations for developing sensor networks with effective self-protection mechanisms by exploiting the adaptivity and versatility of the biological system in dealing with bacterial attack and virus infection. In the subsequent sections of this chapter, we will illustrate some of the design principles of autonomic sensing based on the features derived from the ANS and BIS, and highlight some of the computational considerations involved in implementing these concepts.

10.2 Autonomic Sensing

The term *Autonomic Sensing* follows the concept of *Autonomic Computing* coined by IBM in their manifesto in response to the looming crisis of software complexity facing the IT industry. The spiraling cost of managing increasingly complex systems is becoming a significant obstacle that is undermining the future growth and societal benefits of IT technology. As stated by Kephart and Chess of IBM in their article on the vision of autonomic computing [4]:

> *"Computing systems' complexity appears to be approaching the limits of human capability, yet the march toward increased interconnectivity and integration rushes ahead unabated. This march could turn the dream of pervasive computing – trillions of computing devices connected to the Internet – into a nightmare."*

Table 10.1 The eight defining characteristics of an autonomic system (*adapted from http://www.research.ibm.com/autonomic/*).

Characteristics of Autonomic Systems	
Self-management	An autonomic system needs to have detailed knowledge about its components, current status, ultimate capacity, and all connections to other systems to govern itself through effective resource management, utilisation, and sharing.
Self-configuration	An autonomic system can automatically and dynamically configure and reconfigure itself under varying conditions and changing environments.
Self-optimisation	An autonomic system can constantly optimise its performance and resource utilisation by monitoring its constituent components, and fine-tune workflow to achieve predetermined performance and resource utilisation goals.
Self-healing	An autonomic computing system can gracefully recover from routine and extraordinary events that cause component malfunction. It is able to discover problems and establish means of using alternative resources or configuration to maintain system functionality.
Self-protection	An autonomic computing system must be able to exert self-protection by automatically detecting and identifying different types of attacks to maintain overall system security and integrity.
Self-adaptation	An autonomic system must be context-aware and adapt itself for improved interaction and performance under changing working environments and user requirements.
Self-integration	An autonomic system can fully function under heterogeneous infrastructures and be seamlessly and securely integrated with other systems.
Self-scaling	An autonomic system will anticipate the optimised resources required and scale its functionality while keeping its complexity hidden from the user.

The biological connotation of autonomic sensing is not coincidental. It reflects our inspiration by biological systems, which are able to manage complex networks so effectively and gracefully. It also echoes our desire to develop self-management systems that can deal with the present complexity crisis and free us from the system administration nightmare. It has been expected that IT systems, particularly considered within the context of pervasive computing, will become so massive that even the most skilled system integrators will find them too complex to install, configure, optimise, and maintain [4]. All of these considerations have motivated the search for an alternate paradigm based on the strategies used by biological systems to deal with the challenges of scale, complexity, heterogeneity, and uncertainty involved in pervasive sensing.

The overall goal of an autonomic system is to provide self-management in accordance with high-level guidance from the humans. Table 10.1 outlines the eight defining characteristics of an autonomic system advocated by IBM. While the definition of autonomic sensing is likely to evolve as the contributing technologies mature and become established, these eight *self-** properties have highlighted some of the major requirements, as well as challenges, faced by the pervasive sensing community.

In this chapter, we will focus on three of the *self-** properties listed in Table 10.1, *i.e.*, *self-healing*, *self-organisation*, and *self-protection* for improved design of BSNs. It must be pointed out that our aim is not to reverse-engineer biological systems but only to follow some of the design principles so that plausible computational architectures suitable for BSNs can be developed.

10.3 Fault Detection and Self-Healing

Effective fault detection and recovery is one of the major concerns of wireless sensing. Although the basic principles of fault localisation and analysis have been addressed by the control and process engineering communities for many years [5, 6], fault detection and self-healing for BSNs present a number of unique challenges. For a BSN, we need to examine both hard and soft failures by considering the mobile, *ad hoc* nature of the underlying network, the presence of both transient and permanent abnormalities, and the possibility of multiple and correlated failures. The *hard failure* mentioned above includes node failures due to faulty sensors, loss of wireless communication or depleted battery, whereas *soft failure* can be caused by excessive noise artefact due to poor sensor contact and motion. The isolation of these problems is also compounded by the complexity of the BSNs in interacting with the heterogeneous ambient sensing environment.

Figure 10.1 illustrates a typical system architecture for fault diagnosis. Many of the traditional systems take a global approach and assume that only one fault may occur in the system at a given time. In addition, these systems frequently use deterministic models that assume all dependencies and causal relationships are known. More recently, the use of *Finite State Machines* (FSMs) and probabilistic models have gained considerable interest. The latter is particularly relevant to BSNs as it provides an effective means of managing heterogeneous networks with non-deterministic factors. For example, uncertainty about the dependencies amongst the sensor nodes can be represented by assigning probabilities to the links in the dependency or causality graph that can be transformed into a belief network.

Given an evidence set, belief networks can be used for queries including: 1) belief assessment, 2) *Most Probable Explanation* (MPE), 3) maximum *a posteriori* hypothesis, and 4) maximum expected utility [7]. As an example, MPE can be used to find a complete assignment of values to variables in a way that best explains the observed evidence, and therefore its value in fault diagnosis. The main advantage of belief networks is in their ability to handle uncertainties and being able to be implemented in a distributed framework. They are therefore particularly suited for wireless sensor networks, due to their similarity to biological systems in using simple local processing and messaging to form an effective global behaviour with fault detection and self-healing properties.

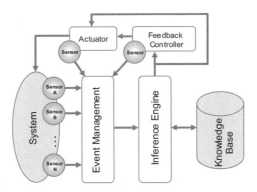

Figure 10.1 Architecture for a typical fault diagnosis system.

10.3.1 Belief Networks

To understand how belief networks work, it is necessary to explain these probabilistic graphical models, which are a marriage of graph theory and probability theory. Qualitatively, their structures are graphs in which the nodes represent random variables and the arcs represent dependencies. Generally, there are two types of graphs: undirected and directed graphs. Undirected graphical models are known as *Markov Random Fields* (MRFs) or Markov networks. Directed graphs, particularly *Directed Acyclic Graphs* (DAGs), are known as Bayesian networks or Belief Networks. The latter have a more complicated notion of dependency by taking into account the directionality of the arcs which connote the causality. Recently, the concept of *Factor Graphs* (FGs) [8, 9] has been developed. An FG is a bipartite graph which subsumes both Bayesian networks and MRFs. All of the independency relationships in a Bayesian network or MRF can be expressed in an FG, so that a single unified belief propagation algorithm can be used for data inferencing.

Quantitatively, probabilistic graphical models provide an economical way to encode a complete *Joint Probability Distribution* (JPD) over a large set of variables. The basic decomposition scheme offered by the probabilistic graphical models relies on the chain rule of probability calculus, *i.e.*,

$$P(x_1,...,x_n) = \prod_{j}^{n} P(x_j \mid x_1,...,x_{j-1}) \qquad (10.1)$$

which permits the decomposition of a joint distribution $P(x_1,...,x_n)$ as a product of n local conditional distributions. Under certain conditional independence assumptions, large distribution functions can be decomposed into several small distributions while the global nature of the problem domain is preserved.

In a Bayesian network, the direction of the arc denotes a direct child-parent relationship between two variables. That is, the arc is directed from a Markovian parent to a child node. The conditional probability of X_i is sensitive only to the Markovian parents when

$$P(x_i \mid x_1,...,x_{i-1}) = P(x_i \mid pa_i) \tag{10.2}$$

In this case, the joint distribution is equivalent to the product decomposition:

$$P(x_1,...,x_n) = \prod_{i=1}^{n} P(x_i \mid pa_i) \tag{10.3}$$

In other words, under the conditional independence assumptions denoted by the network structure, the product of the local conditional distributions of all nodes is equal to their JPD. This is essential to the calculation of JPD because as the number of variables grows, their JPD is not readily accessible. Figure 10.2 illustrates an example Bayesian network, where the JPD of the Bayesian network can be simplified as:

$$P(A,B,C,D,E,F,G) = P(A)P(B)P(C \mid A,B)P(D \mid C)P(E \mid C)$$
$$P(F \mid D,E)P(G \mid E)$$

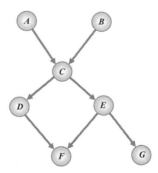

Figure 10.2 An example Bayesian network showing how the JPD can be calculated.

In real-life problems, it is often possible through observation that some consequences are more likely to occur than the other, although not with absolute certainty. By summing over all the possible values of the irrelevant variables (called marginalisation), all possible inference queries can be answered accordingly. In practice, however, more efficient inference methods are used, as the direct method yields exponential time complexity.

Bayesian networks were first introduced during the mid 1980s, largely through the work of Judea Pearl when he developed a belief propagation algorithm for inferencing in a singly-connected network [10, 11]. This algorithm is also commonly called the polytree algorithm. A singly-connected network is a network that contains no closed loops, *i.e.*, there is only one single path between any two nodes in the network. Inferencing in a general Bayesian network has been proven to be NP-Hard [12] but for graphs that are singly-connected, there exist algorithms that can provide exact solutions run in polynomial time.

The inference tasks in Bayesian networks include:

- *Belief updating vs belief revision*: belief updating involves the determination of the probabilities of a set of query variables given the evidence. Belief revision (MAP explanation) consists of determining the most probable instantiations of a set of variables given the evidence [13].

- *Diagnostic vs causal reasoning*: diagnostic reasoning infers the most likely cause from the obtained evidence, while causal or "top-down" reasoning infers how the cause generates effects [14].

Learning in Bayesian networks involves two parts: *structure learning* and *parameter learning*. Murphy [14], for example, classified structure and parameter leaning in Bayesian networks based on the prior knowledge of the network structure and the availability of the data. When the structure of the network is known (*e.g.* from prior knowledge) and the data is fully observed, maximum likelihood estimation can be used. That is, the parameters can be derived from data distribution typically by counting. Due to the potential sparse data involved, small priors are usually added to the calculation of the conditional probabilities.

When the structure is known but the data is partially observed, the probabilities associated with the unobservable or hidden nodes can be learned from optimisation methods based on *Expectation Maximisation* (EM) or gradient descent.

Finally, when the structure is unknown, model selection can be formulated as a search problem. For example, a spanning tree is an objective approach in constructing a Bayesian network structure for observable cases, and the *Maximum Weight Spanning Tree* (MWST) algorithm proposed by Chow and Liu [15] is a well-known algorithm for constructing Bayesian networks with singly-connected structures.

10.3.2 Belief Propagation Through Message Passing

Belief Propagation is a decentralised iterative algorithm that operates by transmitting messages between nearby nodes in the network. Each node acts as a processing unit which can communicate only to its direct neighbours via local message passing. Associated with each node in the network are the conditional probability distributions that quantify the node and its parents.

In local message propagation, when a message is received, the node will pass messages to all of its neighbours, with the exception of the node from which the receiving message originated. The actual mechanism also depends on its instantiation status and how it interconnects with other nodes, as shown in Figure 10.3. The belief propagation can be accomplished in the following three steps (in any order): 1) belief updating, 2) bottom-up propagation, and 3) top-down propagation.

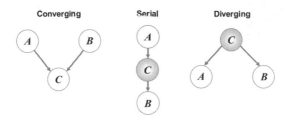

Figure 10.3 Three cases of blocked paths. In the converging case, the path between A and B is blocked when C is not instantiated and has no λ evidence. In serial and diverging cases, the paths are blocked when C is instantiated.

Consider node X in a typical fragment of a singly connected network, as shown in Figure 10.4. Let e be the total evidence available, e^- the evidence connected to X via its children, $\mathbf{Y} = \{Y_1,...,Y_m\}$ and e^+ the evidence connected to X via its parents $\mathbf{U} = \{U_1,...,U_n\}$. The belief distribution of a particular node X is updated based on the evidence received from its child- and parent-nodes. This can be derived as:

$$P'(x) = P(x\,|\,e) = \alpha P(e^-\,|\,x, e^+) P(x\,|\,e^+)$$

$$= \alpha P(e^-_{XY_1},...,e^-_{XY_m}\,|\,x) P(x\,|\,e^+_{U_1 X},...,e^+_{U_n X})$$

$$= \alpha \lambda(x) \pi(x) \tag{10.4}$$

$$= \alpha \left[\prod_{j=1}^{m} \lambda_{Y_j}(x) \right] \left[\sum_{u_1,...,u_n} P(x\,|\,u_1,...u_n) \prod_{i=1}^{n} \pi_X(u_i) \right]$$

where $\alpha = P(e)^{-1}$ is a normalisation constant, $e^-_{XY_j}$ denotes the evidence contained in the subnetwork that connects to node X via link $X \rightarrow Y_j$, and $e^+_{U_i X}$ denotes the evidence contained in the subnetwork that connects to node X via link $U_i \rightarrow X$. The belief update in node X can be performed by inspecting the evidence in the λ messages from its children, $\lambda_{Y_j}(x)$, $j = 1,...,m$, and the evidence in the π messages from its parents, $\pi_X(u_i)$, $i = 1,...,n$. The accumulation of the evidence from child nodes is also known as diagnostic support or λ evidence, $\lambda(x)$. The accumulation of the evidence from the parent-nodes is also known as causal support or π evidence, $\pi(x)$.

During bottom-up belief propagation, each node updates its parents' λ message array. For example, the new $\lambda_X(u_i)$ message from node X for parent U_i is calculated by:

$$\lambda_X(u_i) = \beta \sum_x \lambda(x) \sum_{u_k:k\neq i} P(x \mid u_1,...,u_n) \prod_{k\neq i} \pi_X(u_k)$$ (10.5)

which is the accumulation of evidence in messages from all children and parents of X apart from U_i. The summations indicate marginalisation over all possible values of the variables given bellow the Σ sign.

During top-down belief propagation, each node updates its children's π message array. For example, the new $\pi_{Y_j}(x)$ message from node X to the child Y_j is calculated by:

$$\pi_{Y_j}(x) = P'(x) / \lambda_{Y_j}(x)$$ (10.6)

which is the accumulation of evidence in messages from all children and parents of X apart from Y_j. At the boundary, exceptions are applied. For root nodes, for example, the π evidence is set to be the prior probability. If X has no children and has not been instantiated, all of the elements in the λ evidence vector are set to be 1. Finally, if X is instantiated for x_k, the elements of the λ evidence vector at the kth position is set to 1, but 0 otherwise [13].

In Figure 10.4, $\pi_x(u_1)$ and $\pi_x(u_2)$ are π messages from the parent-nodes U_1 and U_2 to X, $\pi_{Y_1}(x)$ and $\pi_{Y_2}(x)$ are π messages from X to the child-nodes Y_1 and Y_2, $\lambda_{Y_1}(x)$ and $\lambda_{Y_2}(x)$ are λ messages from its child-nodes Y_1 and Y_2 to X, and $\lambda_x(u_1)$ and $\lambda_x(u_2)$ are λ messages from X to the parent-nodes U_1 and U_2. In a multiply-connected network where loops exist, messages may circulate infinitely and not converge. To avoid evidence being counted twice in a multiply-connected network, alternative inference mechanisms have been proposed. A list of currently used inference mechanisms in Bayesian networks can be summarised in Table 10.2, which categorises these techniques into exact (modelling all the dependencies in the data) and approximate inference algorithms as suggested by Guo and Hsu [16].

It has been shown that for all exact inference methods, the time complexity is exponential to the induced width of the graph (*i.e.,* the size of the largest clique in the triangulated moral graph). For networks with many loops and large induced widths, the exact solutions can become intractable. In this case, approximation that trades the complexity of the running time with the accuracy of the results can be used. In addition to the techniques listed in Table 10.2, other approaches are also available. For example, it is possible to use orthogonal transformation of variables; for instance, using the PCA to remap the data so that the correlations between variables are minimised [17]. It is also possible to use the hidden node insertion algorithm to represent the arc between two or more child-nodes of the same parent from which the link matrices associated with the hidden node can be calculated by an error minimisation scheme [18].

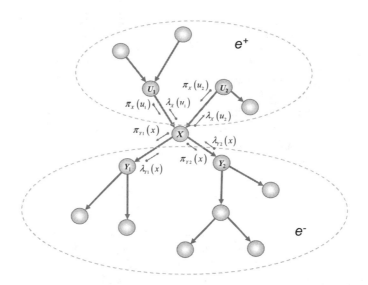

Figure 10.4 A fragment of a singly connected network to illustrate the message passing to/from parents and children of node X.

The use of belief networks with distributed inferencing for WSNs has attracted significant interests in recent years. For instance, to illustrate how a Bayesian network can be used to isolate faulty sensor responses, Figure 10.5 demonstrates one example of how child-parent dependency is used to indicate noise interference before and after Gaussian noise is introduced into a subnet of a BSN [19, 20].

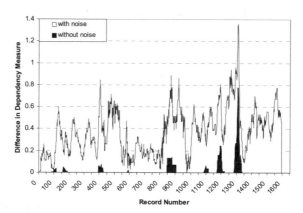

Figure 10.5 Difference in child-parent dependency between a normal BSN node and a node corrupted by Gaussian noise with one standard deviation of the signal.

Table 10.2 A summary of the exact and approximate belief network inference methods.

Exact Inference	Polytree Algorithm	A generalisation of the forwards-backwards algorithm for HMMs, which is only for singly-connected networks. For multiply-connected models this becomes the loopy belief propagation algorithm [13].
	Clustering	The algorithm involves transforming the graph structure into clique tree by node clustering. Local message-passing is used for data inference, and the time complexity of the clique tree propagation algorithm is exponential to the size of the largest clique [21-25].
	Cutset Conditioning	The method is based on breaking the loops in the multiply-connected network by instantiating a selected group of variables called a loop cutset [13].
	Variable Elimination	The key idea of the method is to rewrite the operations in a manner which minimises the number of numerical operations required, typically through iteratively moving all irrelevant terms outside the innermost sum so that the variable associated to the innermost sum can be eliminated by marginalisation [26, 27].
	Arc Reversal	The method is based on applying a sequence of operators to the network that reverses the links using Bayes' rule so that the network is reduced to just the query nodes with the evidence nodes as immediate predecessors [28, 29].
	Symbolic Probabilistic Inference	Treats probabilistic inference as a combinatorial optimisation problem of finding an optimal factoring given a set of probabilistic distributions [30].
	Differential Method	Formulates a Bayesian network as a multivariate polynomial and computes its partial derivatives with respect to each variable so that answers to a very large class of probabilistic queries can be computed in a constant time [31].
Approximate Inference	Stochastic Simulation Algorithm	Uses random instantiations from the Bayesian network and only keeps those that are consistent with the values of the observations. They can be divided into two main categories: importance sampling algorithms [32, 33] and *Markov Chain Monte Carlo* (MCMC) methods [34].
	Model Simplification	Simplifies the model until an exact method become feasible. It includes partial evaluation methods such as the bounded cutset conditioning algorithm (which works by instantiating subsets of the variables and break loops in the graph) [35] and Mini-buckets [36].
	Search Based Method	Assumes the majority of the probability mass is contained in small regions of the probability space, and uses high probability instantiations to approximate the true distribution.
	Loopy Belief Propagation	The use of Pearl's polytree propagation algorithm in a Bayesian network with loops, the marginals are often good approximations to the true marginals found through the junction tree algorithm [37]. Loopy belief propagation is equivalent to using the Bethe approximation in the variational methods [38].
	Variational Methods	A class of inference methods is based on reformulating the belief propagation inference problem as an energy minimisation method. The idea is to approximate the true posterior distribution with a simpler but similar distribution. Searching for the approximate distribution can be performed by minimising the distance, such as the Kullback-Leibler divergence, between the two [39].

To address link and node failures combined with resource constraints and asynchrony, Chu *et al* [40] illustrated the use of FG representation and evolution mechanisms for *Multiple Target Tracking* which is concerned with estimating multiple target trajectories given noisy observations of the target states. The progression of a target entering, moving through, and leaving a sensor field is represented by model evolution, which consists of the following three mechanisms: spawning (hypothesising the existence of new phenomenon), updating (of both distribution and topological changes) and pruning (resolving inconsistencies between expected observations and measured observations by pruning the variable nodes associated with the target from the representation).

A distributed implementation can be derived from this architecture by assigning nodes of the graph to sensors based on the so-called agent assignment algorithm. Such an approach can be particularly useful for integrating BSNs with ambient sensing environments due to the highly mobile nature of the BSNs in entering, traversing through, and leaving the ambient sensing environments.

To enhance the understanding of how network topologies may affect the consensus of the MAP estimation, Alanyali *et al* [41] studied the behaviour of Pearl's belief propagation algorithm in different predefined network topologies. The objective of the work is to identify communication schemes which guarantee each sensor eventually being able to identify a MAP estimate. Other recent research includes the use of *Nonparametric Belief Propagation* combined with Monte Carlo stochastic approximation for self-localisation under noisy sensor measurements [42], and the application of loopy belief propagation for asynchronous, rapidly changing environments troubled with node failures [43]. Recently, Paskin and Guestrin [44, 45] have also developed an inference architecture and *Robust Message Passing* algorithm for probabilistic inferencing in distributed systems. The inference architecture is tailored for distributed implementation and consists of a spanning tree formation, optimised junction tree formation and message passing. Compared to other approaches, the algorithm is more robust when it comes to dealing with node failure and missing messages.

10.4 Routing and Self-Organisation

Routing for WSNs in general is a challenging issue. There are a number of major differences to the routing used in existing communication networks. In their review of routing protocols for WSNs, Akkaya and Younis [46] discussed the following four reasons why routing for a WSN is unique:

- It is not possible to build a global addressing scheme for the deployment of a large number of sensor nodes, and it is impractical to use classical IP-based protocols for sensor networks.

- Unlike typical communication networks, most applications of sensor networks require the flow of sensed data from multiple regions to a particular sink.

- The data involved in sensor networks has significant redundancy, either due to the built-in redundancy for fault-tolerance of the system or due to a cluster of sensors within the local vicinity of the target. This redundancy needs to be exploited by the routing protocols for improved energy and bandwidth utilisation.

- Wireless sensor nodes generally have very limited transmission power, on-board energy, processing capacity, and storage, and thus require careful resource management.

In Chapter 5, we discussed the routing algorithm for ZigBee, which is designed to enable reliable, cost effective, low-power, wireless monitoring and control. A Zig-Bee router can incorporate hierarchical as well as table-driven routing. In hierarchical routing, frames are routed along the hierarchy defined during network formation and are reflected in the network source and destination addresses. This routing mechanism, however, is only possible when the network operates as a star or tree network. In table-driven routing, on the other hand, frames are routed according to a routing table that is set up and maintained using a request-response route discovery protocol. This overcomes the suboptimal route problem that arises in hierarchical routing.

In general, existing routing protocols can be classified as data-centric, hierarchical, and location-based techniques. The use of data-centric protocols is due to the fact that it is not feasible to assign global identifiers to each node in a large scale, randomly deployed sensor network. For this reason, it is difficult to select specific sensor nodes for data query, and data in the sensor network has to be transmitted from all sensor nodes within the same deployment region. The significant redundancy involved means it is necessary to develop routing strategies that can make use of data aggregation during the relaying of the data.

The hierarchical routing protocols, on the other hand, are mainly concerned with the scalability of the sensor networks; they form sensor clusters so that cluster heads can perform effective data aggregation and reduction.

Finally, location-based routing uses the position information as an addressing scheme. This means that a query can be propagated only to a particular region, thus significantly reducing the number of transmissions.

In all of the three routing strategies mentioned above, existing research has directed significant emphasis on low-power, scalable, and fault-tolerant architectures [47-50]. For BSNs, energy-aware routing is of particular interest as power consumption and its balanced usage across the BSN nodes whilst maintaining the overall system performance are major challenges to their practical deployment.

For most routing algorithms, the prerequisite for attaining overall system performance is self-organisation. For hierarchical routing, for example, a number of researchers have investigated hierarchical architectures in which local sensor nodes can be aggregated into clusters in order to reduce the communication bandwidth and power consumption [51]. These clusters are self-organised based on proximity to each other or to a known target. For distributed sensor network organisation, a number of different architectures have been proposed [52].

One effective technique for performing self-organisation of sensors is through *Multi-Dimensional Scaling* (MDS) [53]. MDS refers to a group of techniques for finding a low-dimensional representation of a set of high-dimensional data for which the distances are preserved. The starting point of MDS is a matrix consisting of the pair-wise dissimilarities (or distances as mentioned in Chapter 8) of the entities. In a simple BSN deployment example, let's assume that the RF attenuation model is given by:

$$P_{receive} \propto \frac{P_{send}}{r^{\alpha}} \tag{10.7}$$

where r is the transmission distance between the nodes and α is the RF attenuation exponent. Given the deployment of the sensor nodes with unknown relative sensor locations, a pairwise distance d_{ij}^{*} between nodes i, j can therefore be derived. From these pairwise distance measures, the main idea of MDS is to find a configuration of the nodes in a low dimensional space so that the mapped distance in this low dimensional space d_{ij} is as close as possible to d_{ij}^{*}. When a square-error cost is used, the objective function to be minimised can be written as

$$E = \sum_{i \neq j} \left(d_{ij}^{*} - d_{ij} \right)^{2} \tag{10.8}$$

An effective projection method closely related to MDS is through the use of Sammon's mapping [54] where the errors in distance preservation are normalised with the distance in the original space, *i.e.*,

$$E_{s} = \frac{1}{\sum_{i<j} \left[d_{ij}^{*} \right]} \sum_{i<j} \frac{\left(d_{ij}^{*} - d_{ij} \right)^{2}}{d_{ij}^{*}} \tag{10.9}$$

It can be shown that the problem stated above can be solved iteratively by using the error measure in (10.9). By defining $E_{s}(m)$ and $d_{ij}(m)$ as the mapping error and the mapped low-dimensional distance after the mth-iteration, respectively, the newly estimated coordinates of the sensor nodes at iteration $m+1$ is given by

$$x_{pq}(m+1) = x_{pq}(m) - \alpha \left[\frac{\partial E(m)}{\partial x_{pq}(m)} \right] \left| \frac{\partial^{2} E(m)}{\partial x_{pq}(m)^{2}} \right|^{-1} \tag{10.10}$$

where x_{pq} is the qth coordinate component of sensor p, and α is the step size (referred to as *magic factor* by Sammon).

To demonstrate how this nonlinear mapping can be used for the self-organisation of BSNs, Figure 10.6 illustrates a group of twenty sensors with their pairwise distances given in Figure 10.6(left) based on the signal attenuation model given in (10.7). In this figure, the dark (blue) cells represent short distances whereas bright (orange) cells signify large distances between the sensor nodes. Figure 10.6(right) is the corresponding nonlinear embedded result, showing a near perfect reconstruction of the co-locations of the sensors. To further illustrate the ability of the algorithm to engage in self-organisation in the presence of sensor failures, Figure 10.7 shows the nonlinear mapped result of how the defective sensor (3) is singled out from the sensor cluster, while the relative geometrical configuration of the remaining sensors is kept intact.

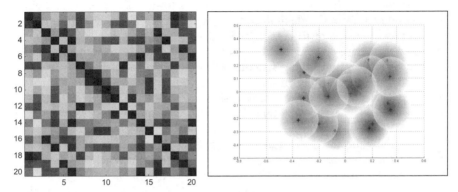

Figure 10.6 Result of nonlinear mapping based on the relative distance measures between the twenty sensors. (Left) The pairwise signal attenuation matrix. (Right) The reconstructed relative spatial configuration of the sensors represented in 2D. (**See colour insert.**)

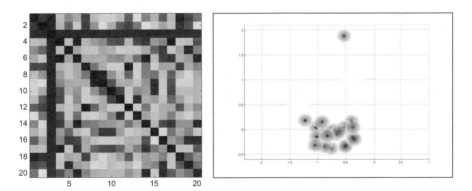

Figure 10.7 Result of nonlinear mapping based on the relative distance measures between the twenty sensors when one of the sensor nodes is faulty, illustrating the ability of the algorithm to single out the defective node (node 3) while the relative geometrical configuration of the other sensors remains intact. (Left) Pair-wise signal attenuation matrix. (Right) The reconstructed relative spatial configuration of the sensors represented in 2D. (**See colour insert.**)

Based on the self-organising capabilities of the sensor nodes, a number of energy-aware routing protocols have recently been proposed. For example, the *Low-*

Energy Adaptive Clustering Hierarchy (LEACH) protocol [55] is one of the popular hierarchical routing algorithms based on the received signal strength, and uses local cluster heads as routers to the sink. With this method, all data processing such as data fusion and aggregation is local to the cluster, and cluster heads change randomly over time in order to balance energy consumption.

Another energy-aware hierarchical routing protocol is PEGASIS [56] which is an improvement on the LEACH protocol: it works by forming chains from sensor nodes such that each node transmits and receives from its neighbours and only one node is selected from the chain to communicate to the sink. Hierarchical PEGASIS is a further extension of PEGASIS and reduces the packet delays. Shah *et al* [57] proposed an energy-aware routing method that extends the directed diffusion method by randomly selecting a single path from multiple alternatives to minimise energy consumption. Other methods include TEEN [58] which is designed to respond to sudden changes in the sensed signals, and APTEEN [59] which is an extension of TEEN devised for capturing periodic data, as well as reacting to time-critical events.

To encapsulate the main features involved in self-organising networks, Subramanian *et al* described self-organising protocols [60] that include *discovery, organisation, maintenance*, and *self-organisation* phases. Yan *et al* [61] also estimated the overall energy consumption of a sensor network by using different energy-aware routing schemes. It has been shown that performing localised data fusion and information passing is the most efficient way of sensor routing. However, as the size of the network grows, the process of aggregating inferences can become computationally intractable. They have therefore proposed the use of *Multiply Sectioned Bayesian Networks* (MSBN) [62, 63] as an efficient partitioning and energy-aware routing scheme [61]. In this regard, the use of bio-inspired local processing algorithms can play a key role in resolving some of the computational complexities involved.

10.5 Security and Self-Protection

For practical deployment of BSNs, another important consideration of the system architecture is security and self-protection. The nature of BSN nodes in handling patient information and coordinating real-time data for both wearable and implantable sensors, can potentially become an ideal target for malicious intervention. It is not difficult to appreciate that the potential impact involved can far exceed the damage caused to desktop computers. For this reason, security and self-protection are an integral part of BSN design.

An analogy is often drawn between biological systems and computer systems. In terms of security, "virus" is a well known term for security attacks on computer systems, as computer viruses share certain characteristics with the real viruses that lead to diseases. In biological systems, infectious disease is caused by a biological agent, called a pathogen. There are four main types of pathogen; including viruses, bacteria, fungi and parasites [64]. A virus is a microscopic parasite [65], which contains only a limited genetic blueprint and is incapable of ordinary reproduction. It can only replicate by hijacking other biological cells and injecting its RNA into the cell, which will then cause the cell to create more virus out of its own tissues. A bacterium, on the other hand, is a cellular organism that can reproduce itself. It attacks the host by releasing toxins which could damage a cell or block the transmission of cellular signals. In a BSN, bacteria can be seen as compromised sensor nodes that attack the sensor network integrity, whereas virus can be regarded as data packets or malicious programs injected into a sensor node with the intent to damage the sensor and thus the network.

An ideal model for such a self-protection system is the human immune system, as it is an extremely effective defence mechanism that is capable of preventing the onset of infection from approximately 10^{16} different molecules [66]. In addition to being able to identify and destroy antigens autonomously, the immune system is able to adapt to virus mutation. From an architectural perspective, the BIS has multiple layers where each layer is independently equipped with different defence mechanisms [64, 67-69] as schematically illustrated in Figure 10.8. They include:

- *Physical barrier*: The first line of defence of the immune system is the skin, and also mucus coating of the gut and airway which physically blocks pathogens from entering the host. In addition, the respiration system also helps in keeping pathogens out of the system by trapping irritants in nasal hairs, coughing and sneezing.

- *Physiological barrier*: The physiological properties of the human body, such as temperature and acidity, actually present a hostile environment for many pathogens.

- *Innate immune system*: This is composed of the build-up of phagocyte cells which can engulf pathogens and the complement system which is made up of several plasma proteins. The plasma proteins normally circulate in an inactive form and are sequentially activated when an antigen is detected in order to eliminate the microorganism. This leads to cytolysis, inflammation, and other immune responses. During an inflammatory response, the body temperature will rise and the blood flow increase, fever being a possible consequence.

- *Adaptive immune system*: This consists of two systems:

    - *Humoral immune system*: the production of antibodies by B-cells in response to antigens.

    - *Cellular immune system*: this recognises and destroys infected cells with T-cells. There are two types of T-cells. The killer T-cells detect infected cells by using T-cell receptors to probe cell surfaces and release granzomes to command the cell to become apoptotic (commit suicide) [70], whereas the helper T-cells activate and control other immune cells where they initiate the production of antibodies by B-cells, control the growth of killer T-cells, and activate macrophages (cells that ingest dangerous material).

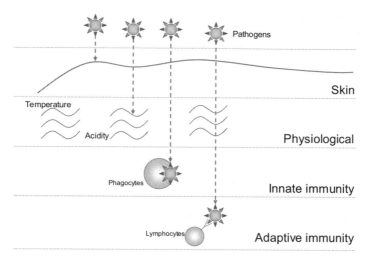

Figure 10.8 The basic architecture of human immune system.

To outline some of the main security considerations for BSNs, we will investigate in this section some of the identifiable threats to BSNs by following a bio-inspired framework. We will also discuss related protocols in the WSNs and draw a parallel between the AIS and the future design of BSNs with effective security and self-protection measures.

10.5.1 Bacterial Attacks

In this chapter, we will use the analogy of bacterial attack to describe attacks that require the subordination of at least one sensor node (or a sensor node emulated by a more powerful device, such as a laptop computer) to overcome the self-protective system and lead to system failure. Thirteen possible bacterial attacks are described in the following section, which include jamming, collision, exhaustion and interrogation, selective forwarding, sinkhole attacks, Sybil attack, wormholes, acknowledgement spoofing, HELLO flood attacks, buffer overflow, network scanning, traffic analysis, and false alarms.

- *Jamming Attack*

    One low level technique to disrupt the service of a wireless network is through the jamming of the frequency band of the wireless device. However, in the case of BSNs, due to the ubiquitous nature of the application and the short range radio design, jamming can only cause localised interruption to the service of the system. In addition, the use of frequency hopping schemes, such as the *Direct Sequence Spread Spectrum* (DSSS), means that the effect of jamming is minimal. Figure 10.9 illustrates an example of a jamming attack where a strong radio signal is transmitted by the attacker and the transmission between sensors A and B is disrupted.

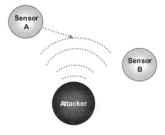

Figure 10.9 Jamming.

- *Collision*

Similarly to the physical layer attack, attackers can jam the data transmission path by corrupting the packets at the link layer [71, 72] . For example, the attacker can disrupt the checksum of a packet causing retransmission, thus leading to collisions in the network. Figure 10.10 shows a collision attack on the network and how the message is corrupted.

Figure 10.10 Collision.

- *Exhaustion and Interrogation*

For certain critical messages, the sensor node has to retransmit the message repeatedly until it reaches the server, if the message itself or the acknowledgement message is corrupted. In most wireless network protocol designs, there are a number of power consuming commands such as network initialisation and time synchronisation. If an attacker continuously broadcasts those commands, the battery power of the sensors will soon be exhausted. This repeated solicitation of energy-draining responses is called interrogation [72].

Figure 10.11 demonstrates a simple interrogation attack on a network caused by sending initialisation commands to the sensor node, with the aim of draining the battery power of the sensors.

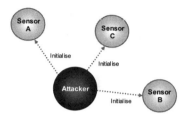

Figure 10.11 Interrogation.

- *Selective Forwarding*

In a multi-hop network, messages are expected to be forwarded to the sink through multiple hops. In a selective forwarding attack, a compromised node may selectively reject certain messages, or may randomly drop messages, thus causing data loss and inducing the use of costly network recovery mechanisms [72]. Figure 10.12 shows an example of a selective forwarding attack where the attacker only forwards packets 2 and 4 and drops packets 1 and 3.

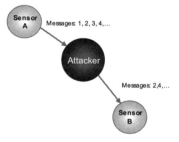

Figure 10.12 Selective forwarding.

- *Sinkhole Attacks*

In a sinkhole attack, an attacker attempts to lure network traffic through a compromised node, and does this by making the compromised node look especially attractive with respect to the routing algorithm [73]. Once the sinkhole is created, the network is opened to other attacks, such as selective forwarding or eavesdropping. Figure 10.13 illustrates a sinkhole attack in the network, where all of the packets from the sensors are routed through the malicious node.

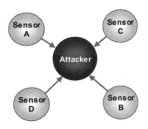

Figure 10.13 Sinkhole attack.

- *Sybil Attacks*

To form a network and create routing tables, every sensor node has to have a unique identity. In a Sybil attack [74], a malicious node creates fake identities, in order that it can appear in multiple places at the same time. It will therefore be more likely to be selected as part of a hop for forwarding messages, thus opening the gate for selective forwarding attacks. Figure 10.14 shows a Sybil attack where multiple identities of a compromised node are sent to neighbouring sensor nodes.

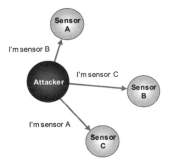

Figure 10.14 Sybil attack.

- *Wormholes*

In a wormhole attack, attackers cooperate to simulate a low-latency communication link [72, 75]. Messages received by one of the attackers will be replayed by the other one, so that the message appears to be forwarded from a nearby hop. As such, the neighbouring sensor nodes will favour the attacker for routing [72], similarly to a sinkhole. In addition, the network will be severely disrupted when the wormhole is removed. An example wormhole attack is illustrated in Figure 10.15, where the compromised nodes simulate a short link between them with a false distance of 1, leading to a sinkhole where all of the traffic is routed through the wormhole nodes.

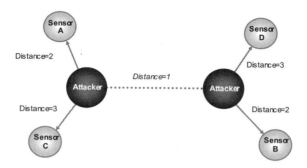

Figure 10.15 Wormhole attack.

- *Acknowledgement Spoofing*

To ensure the integrity of the link and improve the reliability of the data transmission, acknowledgement messages are often required from the receiver. In an acknowledgement spoofing attack, the malicious node spoofs acknowledgement messages aiming to trick the sender into believing that a weak link is strong or a dead node is alive [73]. As typical routing protocols select hops based on the reliability of the link, the attacker can effectively launch a selective forwarding attack by encouraging the target node to transmit packets through those weak links. Figure 10.16 illustrates an example acknowledgement spoofing attack, where an acknowledgement message is sent by the attacker who has overheard the message sent to the dead sensor node C.

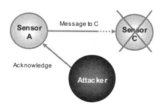

Figure 10.16 Acknowledgement spoofing.

- *HELLO Flood Attacks*

To enable the introduction of new sensors and update the routing table dynamically, many wireless network protocols require the new sensor to broadcast an announcement message, the HELLO message, to notify its neighbours of its request to join the network. In a HELLO flood attack, an adversary broadcasts powerful HELLO messages to many nodes in the network, so that every node thinks the attacker is within a short radio range [73]. This will cause a large number of nodes to attempt to use the attacker as a hop to route messages, thus confusing the entire routing system. The

HELLO attack is depicted in Figure 10.17 as a strong HELLO message is sent to each sensor node to trick them into making the malicious sensor a node for routing.

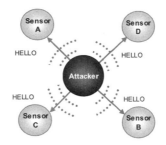

Figure 10.17 HELLO flood attack.

- *Buffer Overflow Attacks*

As limited storage is provided by the sensor hardware, flooding a sensor node with messages will lead to buffer overflow and subsequently crash the sensor node. For example, Figure 10.18 shows a simplified buffer overflow attack on a sensor node.

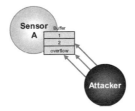

Figure 10.18 Buffer overflow

- *Network Scanning*

Through scanning the network and obtaining the network topology, the attacker can locate a particular sensor node or even the individual wearing the sensors.

- *Traffic Analysis*

As the network traffic pattern is often used to detect and defend attacks on the network; through observing the traffic patterns, the attacker can potentially compromise the security defence of the system.

- *False Alarms*

Being a pervasive monitoring system, BSNs are required to accurately capture abnormal events and transmit alarm messages to the system. By generating numerous false alarm messages, an attacker can effectively undermine the system's ability to detect genuine abnormal events.

10.5.2 Virus Infection

In biological virus infection, the virus hijacks a cell by injecting its genes into the cell. Similarly, an attacker can use a compromised sensor node like a virus and inject malicious data packets or programs into sensor nodes. Unlike bacterial attacks which do not alter the internal properties of the sensors, virus infections damage the system by altering the parameters or programs of the nodes. The following section outlines seven possible virus infections, which include corrupting the routing information, misdirection, time synchronisation corruption, worms, Trojan horse installation, backdoor installation and hoaxes.

- *Corrupting the Routing Information*

  The most direct and effective approach to attacking a network is to corrupt the routing information. By spoofing, altering, or replaying the routing information, attackers can severely damage the sensor network by creating routing loops, attracting or repelling network traffic, and making false partitions in the network [73]. A simple example of corrupting the routing is shown in Figure 10.19, where invalid routing information is sent to sensor nodes.

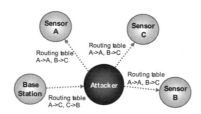

Figure 10.19 Corrupting the routing information.

- *Misdirection*

  In a misdirection attack, an attacker corrupts the message forwarding paths by advertising false routing updates which could isolate sensor nodes or flood a victim. Figure 10.20 shows an example of a misdirection attack where invalid routing updates are sent to Sensor A and cause it to direct the data incorrectly. The message is lost as C is too far away from node D.

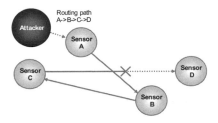

Figure 10.20 Misdirection.

- *Time Synchronisation Corruption*

Due to the high bandwidth requirement and limited battery power available to miniaturised sensors, one approach to developing an energy efficient network is to implement a scheduling or *Time Division Multiple Access* (TDMA) scheme for data transmission, such as the TD-DES protocol proposed by Cetintemel *et al* [76]. With TDMA, the power consumption can be optimised by switching on the radio only when it is required. Collision is also avoided with this scheme. As the timing information of the TDMA protocol is crucial for scheduling, in order to launch an attack on such a network, an attacker can simply corrupt the time synchronisation. One method of achieving this is to broadcast invalid synchronisation commands to the sensors, where a slight offset of the time could potentially lead to collisions. In addition, if dynamic timeslot allocation is enabled on the network, malicious sensor nodes can request an excessive amount of bandwidth and cause the scheduling to fail. Figure 10.21 illustrates an example time synchronisation attack where the corrupted time synchronisation message $t=7$ is sent to the sensor nodes when the actual time is only $t=5$.

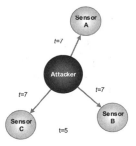

Figure 10.21 Time synchronisation corruption attack.

- *Worms*

Although very limited resources are available on a wireless sensor, a network worm attack is possible on a sensor node. Dynamic reprogramming of a sensor node is possible via recently developed software tools, such as Deluge [77]. Based on its distributed source code dissemination method, worms can be easily created and spread across the network based on the program distribution framework, thus causing severe damage to the system.

- *Trojan Horse*

  As with worms, Trojan horse programs can be transmitted to the sensor nodes to corrupt sensor data, override control of the sensor node, or damage the sensor network by using the compromised node.

- *Backdoor*

  Programs or routines can be uploaded to the sensor nodes by the attackers to open up a backdoor for enabling future access to the network and data.

- *Hoaxes*

  An attacker can compromise network security by sending false warning messages regarding security attacks, which can not only trigger energy consuming recovery or protection processes, but also reduce the ability of an adaptive protective system to prevent further virus attacks. As the system may disregard the hoax attacks after identifying them as being hoaxes, the system may fail to capture them when they become real attacks rather than hoaxes.

10.5.3 Secured Protocols

Unlike traditional computer systems, very limited resources are available for BSN nodes, and traditional cytological algorithms, encryption techniques, and secure protocols cannot be directly applied to WSNs and BSNs. Currently, there are a number of secured protocols that have been developed within the WSN community. One example of a secured protocol design for WSN is the *Security Protocols for Sensor Networks* (SPINS) introduced by Berkeley. It mainly consists of two components: µTESLA (*micro version of the Timed, Efficient, Streaming, Loss-tolerant Authentication Protocol*) and SNEP (*Secure Network Encryption Protocol*) [78] for unicast and broadcast messages. In addition, to cater for the *ad hoc* nature of sensor networks, different key distribution schemes, such as the pairwise key distribution method, are proposed.

SNEP

The SNEP protocol utilises the RC5 block cipher [79] to encrypt unicast messages. To fit the RC5 onto the severely constrained sensor node, SNEP implements only a subset of functions of RC5 [78]. To ensure the confidentiality of the data, a semantic security mechanism is imposed whereby a shared counter is used to encrypt the data with the block cipher. However, instead of transmitting the counter, each sensor of the node pairs keeps a monotonically increasing counter to minimise the overhead imposed. As shown in Figure 10.22, the block cipher is applied to the monotonically increasing counter which will then be XORed with the plaintext to generate the ciphertext. The same process is also applied to decrypt the message [78]. In this way, an eavesdropper will not be able to reconstruct the messages and the counter used can also guarantee the freshness of the messages. In addition, a separate master key is used in each sensor node, so that the authentication of the messages can be ensured. To authenticate the message, the *Cipher Block Chaining Message Authentication Code* (CBC-MAC) technique is adopted and the same block cipher is used to compute the *Message Authentication Code* (MAC).

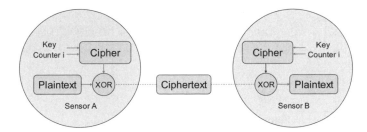

Figure 10.22 SNEP: Counter mode encryption and decryption.

µTESLA

Although SNEP provides secure communication between a pair of sensor nodes, SNEP does not support message broadcasting due to the use of different master keys in each sensor node. The µTESLA, which is a micro-version of the TESLA protocol [80], is proposed for secured data broadcast [78]. In µTESLA, the base station generates a chain of secret keys where the last key of the chain is picked randomly and all the other keys are then generated by applying a one-way function F, as shown in the following equations:

$$\mathrm{K} = \{K_0, K_1, K_2, ..., K_n\}$$
$$K_n = random \qquad\qquad\qquad (10.11)$$
$$K_i = F(K_{i+1}) \qquad where \quad i = 0, ..., n-1$$

As function F is a one-way function, any key from 0 to i-1 can be derived by the key K_i, but none of the other keys (K_i to K_n) can be determined. To securely broadcast messages, the µTESLA utilises a loose time synchronisation scheme where different keys are used to encrypt the packets as shown in Figure 10.23, where key K_i is used to encrypt the packets sent in time slot t_i. In addition, the initial key K_0 is first disclosed to the sensor nodes by using a secured link provided by SNEP. Subsequent key K_i is not disclosed until a certain interval after the time interval t_i. As shown in the figure, K_1 is disclosed at t_3, and once K_1 is disclosed, the receiver can then authenticate the data packet 1 and 2 by verifying that $K_0 = F(K_1)$.

As the initial key has to be distributed as a unicast message individually to each sensor node, this process can be energy inefficient. Liu *et al* proposed encoding the initial key K_0 onto the sensor nodes before deployment instead of distributing the key wirelessly [81]. In addition, Liu *et al* proposed a hierarchical organisation of the keys to reduce the memory required in the base station to store the key chain.

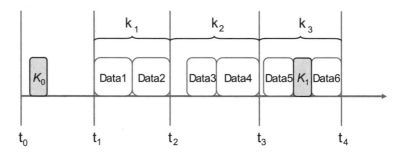

Figure 10.23 µTESLA data authentication.

Ad Hoc Network

The SPINS protocols described above are mainly designed for sensor networks with a static architecture. For BSN applications, however, sensors are often distributed in an *ad hoc* fashion where sensors may join or disconnect from sensor clusters dynamically. For instance, when a patient with on-body sensors is walking through a care home equipped with environmental sensors, the body sensors may attach to certain clusters of the care home network depending on the location of the patient. In addition, instead of routing all of the messages back to the server, messages could be requested by certain sensors in an *ad hoc* network, and sensors can also broadcast messages to other nodes. In the case of a patient in a homecare environment, environment sensor data can be requested by the on-body sensors to validate the findings of wearable sensors, *e.g.*, to confirm if the patient has had a fall. In such scenarios, SPINS-like approaches will not be able to provide the necessary secured *ad hoc* links.

Due to the limited resources of the sensor nodes, a symmetric key system is often adopted for *ad hoc* WSNs where a key is shared between the sensor nodes for data encryption and authentication. One efficient key distribution approach is the pairwise key management system, as proposed in Liu *et al* and Du *et al* [82-84]. In a pairwise key management system, a selection of keys are assigned to each sensor node initially [85]. To form secured links, sensor nodes announce and compare their keys, and a connection is established if the same key is found on both sensor nodes. Figure 10.23 illustrates how secured links are formed by using the pairwise key management scheme. As shown in the diagram, sensors A and B share the same key K_4. Therefore, a secured link is established between the sensor nodes. On the other hand, as no common key is found between sensors B and C, no direct connection can be established. However, since sensors A and C share the same key K_2, a secured link can be established between A and C. Once secured links are formed, new keys can be generated to connect disjointed nodes, such as nodes B and C in Figure 10.24.

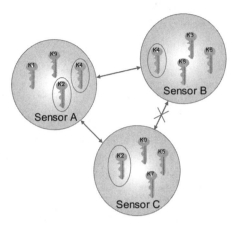

Figure 10.24 A schematic illustration of the pair-wise key management scheme.

With the above key sharing scheme, a subset of nodes can potentially be opened to security threats as each sensor node contains a subset of keys. To improve the resilience against attack on the subnet, an improved pairwise scheme is proposed by Chan *et al* [86]. Instead of connecting nodes if only one common key is found, the proposed method requires the nodes to share a certain number (q) of keys in order to form a direct link. Figure 10.25 illustrates the improved keying scheme with the q-composite key distribution scheme. In this case, $q=2$ and a secured link is formed between sensors A and C as they both share K_2 and K_4.

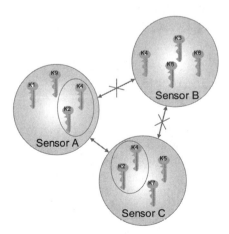

Figure 10.25 Q-composite key distribution scheme.

Although an asymmetric key scheme is often considered to be too expensive for miniaturised sensor nodes [87], it is argued that public key cryptographic key generation is necessary for WSNs [88]. In addition, Malan *et al* demonstrated the possibility of using asymmetric key distribution schemes for sensor networks [89], where the Elliptic Curve Cryptography key generation was implemented on a MICA-2 sensor node.

10.5.4 Self-Protection

As the sensor nodes becoming increasingly miniaturised and ubiquitous, it will be difficult to defend the BSN against security attacks with conventional means. To effectively protect BSNs from both virus and bacterial attacks, a proactive, preventive and autonomous approach must be taken. One possible approach to introducing self-protection to BSNs is to follow the general principles of the human immune system as illustrated in the concept of a bio-inspired *Artificial Immune System* (AIS) introduced recently [90, 91]. For example, Nishiyama *et al* proposed a network security system based on an immune system, where agents are developed for detecting and rejecting intrusion by means of cooperating with each other [92]. Harmer *et al* proposed an AIS-based agent system for computer security applications [93]. Based on the human immune system, AIS mainly implements three main protective mechanisms:

- *Recognising antigens*: The BIS recognises antigens by using the bio-receptors of the immunity cells, and it can recognise known antigens with only partial matches, meaning that it can detect marginally mutated antigens. In order to incorporate this very effective defence mechanism, AIS often implements a certain fuzziness in recognising viruses and only a certain short sequence of the virus is examined [90]. Various matching rules for virus identification are proposed by Harmer *et al* [93].

- *Eliminating antigens*: In the BIS, antibodies neutralise antigens by binding to the microorganisms, and T-cells kill infected host cells to prevent spreading of the virus. In AIS, once a known virus is detected, conventional virus recovery processes will be used to remove the infected entity from the system, such as destroying the infected file. To prevent self-replication, a "kill signal" mechanism for AIS was proposed by Kephart which isolates the infected host and thus prevents it from passing its infected message to its neighbours [90].

- *Adapting to new antigens*: Based on the training mechanism used by the BIS to train T-cells to recognise antigens, a negative selection mechanism was proposed by Forrest *et al* which enables the system to identify antigens while not attacking its own cells [91]. In addition, Kephart proposed the use of virtual environments and "decoy" programs to analyse the characteristics of the virus and develop antibodies accordingly [90].

Since the architecture of the BSN is much closer to the biological system than that of personal computers, the self-protection systems of BSNs could be modelled closer to the BIS. For instance, instead of the centralised approach in certain AIS methods, the distributed characteristics of the BIS can be adopted by the BSN. To explain the immune system concept for BSNs, the layered architecture of the BIS as shown in Figure 10.26 can be used. This includes:

- *Physical barrier*:

    - Sensor casing will provide physical protection against tampering, and for implantable sensors, biocompatible casing will be required to protect the sensor from the human immune system.

    - The short range communication design of the BSN will limit the spread of antigens and effectively lower the probability of being infected.

- *Physiological barrier*:

    - A secured network protocol will be able to identify and prevent certain service attacks. This can create an uninhabitable environment for antigens, like the physiological barrier of in the BIS.

    - The use of anonymity and transmitting raw sensor data could discourage eavesdroppers, because deriving the identity of the subject and the context of the data will require significant amounts of effort and time.

- *Innate immune system*:

    - To engulf an antigen, the neighbouring sensor nodes can form a guard to isolate the attacker. For instance, the sensor nodes can act as sinkholes to the antigen, so that malicious packets or programs cannot be distributed in the network

    - The BIS inflammation concept can be used in BSNs to slow down the spread of antigens.

- *Adaptive immune system*:

    - In order to recognise antigens, instead of keeping a record of all known antigens at a central storage, each sensor node could hold one or more sets of antigen information, similarly to the B-cells in the BIS. To investigate a suspicious packet or program entity, the signature of the packet or program (such as the checksum), could be broadcast to the B-cells to let them compare it with the known antigen records.

- In eliminating infected hosts, the infected node can be reset to a trusted program or even switched off upon receipt of the self destruct message from a T-cell, as there will be redundant nodes around that would serve its same function, similarly to biological cells.

- To adapt to new antigens, like the immune system proposed by Kephart [90] a virtual environment can be created by allocating a small group of sensors to extract the characteristics of the virus. In the virtual environment, a decoy sensor node (honeypot) can be assigned to lure the virus to infect the node, and then the characteristics of the virus can be extracted by monitoring the infected node's interaction with other nodes in the virtual environment.

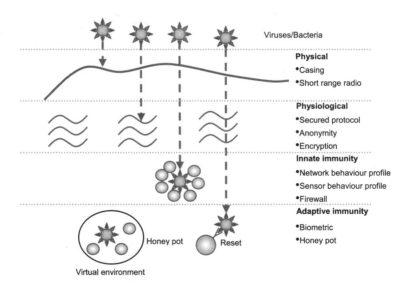

Figure 10.26 The architecture of a BSN immune system.

Although having an immune system for BSNs can provide protection against attacks, it must be noted that the nature of the immune system could cause adverse effects to the network itself in addition to the extra resources required for providing this function. Overreaction to certain stimuli, analogously to the case of human allergies, could bring certain parts or the whole BSN system into disarray. Nevertheless, these problems represent an interesting research issue for the BSN community in the coming years.

10.6 Conclusions

In this chapter, we have discussed the use of autonomic principles for self-healing, self-organisation, and self-protection in BSNs with effective fault tolerance and self-protection. Due to the inherent complexities involved in managing a large number of wireless sensors, bio-inspired sensing and networking is an important area of study and most of the work we discussed in this chapter only represents a tip of the iceberg.

One of the key principles derived from biological systems is the effective coordination that is possible through some very simple mechanisms in information exchange and message passing; and how this can be used to achieve a global behaviour that is adaptive and self-governing. In sensor networks, in addition to sensor noise, bias and node failures, uncertainties due to an imperfect understanding of the system to be monitored, as well as incomplete knowledge of the state of the environment at the time of the interaction are important factors to consider. For self-organisation, as well as fault detection and self-healing, belief propagation represents an attractive method for implementing some bio-inspired concepts in sensor networks. This is because the method has a compact representation, is distributed, and robustness to noise and network degradation. It has also been shown that belief propagation is highly effective for asynchronous communication and is suitable for heterogeneous networks.

In this chapter, we have outlined some of the basic principles of message passing in a belief network. The main benefits of probabilistic graphical representation to model sensor networks also include the ease of integrating heterogeneous data from different sensors, the possibility of continuously improving the accuracy of the system by learning from available data, and the advantage of reasoning under uncertainty, thus permitting the incorporation of high-level and domain specific knowledge into the distributed inferencing framework.

It is worth noting that the self-healing mechanism we discussed in relation to autonomic sensing is often referred to as the survivability of the system. One of the key emphases of self-healing is how the system can perform gracefully under deteriorating environmental conditions and system hardware. As mentioned in previous chapters, whilst the perpetual powering of the sensor nodes through energy scavenging remains an active research topic, our current focus should be directed at the effective processing and routing strategies that can maximise the overall power efficiency. For the practical deployment of BSNs, it is also important to consider a proactive approach towards fault tolerance, a strategy that is often relied upon by biological systems to improve their immunity to system failures.

As mentioned in the introduction to this chapter, the focus of our discussion has been mainly restricted to the illustration of some of the design principles of autonomic sensing based on the features derived from the ANS and BIS. Our aim here is not to reverse-engineer these biological systems but only to investigate some of the design principles so that plausible computational architectures suitable for the BSN can be developed. In this regard, the discussion about security and self-protection is only intended to outline the challenges, as well as the opportunities, faced by the BSN research community.

References

1. Beni G, Wang J. Swarm intelligence in cellular robotic systems. In: Proceedings of the NATO Advanced Workshop on Robots and Biological Systems 1989.
2. Wokoma I, Sacks L, Marshall IW. Biologically inspired models for sensor network design. In: Proceedings of London Communications Symposium 2002.
3. Wokoma I, Sacks L, Marshall I. Clustering in sensor networks using quorum sensing. In: Proceedings of the London Communications Symposium, University College London, 2003.
4. Kephart JO, Chess DM. The vision of autonomic computing. IEEE Computer Magazine, January 2003.
5. Venkatasubramanian V, Rengaswamy R, Yin K, Kavuri SN. A review of process fault detection and diagnosis I: quantitative model-based methods. Computers and Chemical Engineering 2003; 27(3):293-311.
6. Lazar AA, Wang W, Deng RH. Models and algorithms for network fault detection and identification: a review. In: Proceedings of Singapore International Conference on Communications/International Symposium on Information Theory and Its Applications 1992.
7. Kant L, Sethi AS, Steinder M. Fault localization and self-healing mechanisms for FCS networks. In: Proceedings of the Twenty-Third Army Science Conference, Orlando, Florida, 2002.
8. Kschischang FR, Frey BJ, Loeliger H-A. Factor graphs and the sum-product algorithm. IEEE Transactions on Information Theory, Special Issue on Codes on Graphs and Iterative Algorithms 2001; 47(2):498-519.
9. Frey BJ. Extending factor graphs so as to unify directed and undirected graphical models. In: Proceedings of the Nineteenth Conference on Uncertainty in Artificial Intelligence, Acapulco, Mexico, 2003.
10. Kim JH, Pearl J. A computational model for causal and diagnostic reasoning in inference engines. In: Proceedings of the Eighth International Joint Conference on Artificial Intelligence, Karlsruhe, West Germany, 1983; 190-193.
11. Pearl J. A constraint-propagation approach to probabilistic reasoning. In: Proceedings of the First Annual Conference on Uncertainty in Artificial Intelligence, Rome, New York, USA, 1985; 357-370.
12. Cooper GF. The computational complexity of probabilistic inferences. Artificial Intelligence 1990; 42:393-405.
13. Pearl J. Probabilistic reasoning in intelligent systems: networks of plausible inference. San Mateo, CA: Morgan Kaufmann, 1988.

14. Murphy K. A brief introduction to graphical models and Bayesian networks. http://www.cs.ubc.ca/~murphyk/Bayes/bayes_tutorial.pdf, 1998.
15. Chow CK, Liu CN. Approximating discrete probability distribution with dependence trees. IEEE Transactions on Information Theory 1968; IT-14:462-467.
16. Guo H, Hsu W. A survey of algorithms for real-time Bayesian network inference. In: Proceedings of Joint Workshop on Real-Time Decision Support and Diagnosis Systems, Edmonton, Canada, 2002.
17. Kwoh C-K, Gillies DF. Probabilistic reasoning and multiple-expert methodology for correlated objective data. Artificial Intelligence in Engineering 1998; 12:21-33.
18. Kwoh C-K, Gillies DF. Using hidden nodes in Bayesian network. Artificial Intelligence 1996; 88:1-38.
19. Thiemjarus S, Lo BPL, Yang GZ. A distributed Bayesian framework for body sensor networks. In: Proceedings of the Second International Workshop on Body Sensor Networks, Imperial College, London, 2005.
20. Thiemjarus S, Lo BPL, Yang GZ. A noise resilient distributed inference framework for body sensor networks. In: Adjunct Proceedings of the Third International Conference on Pervasive Computing, Munich, Germany, 2005; 13-18.
21. Shenoy PP, Shafer G. Propagating belief functions using local computations. IEEE Expert 1986; 1(3):43-52.
22. Shafer G, Shenoy PP. Probability propagation. Annals of Mathematics and Artificial Intelligence 1990; 2:327-352.
23. Shenoy PP, Shafer G. Axioms for probability and belief-function propagation. Readings in Uncertain Reasoning, San Francisco, CA: Morgan Kaufmann, 1990.
24. Jensen FV, Lauritzen SL, Olesen KG. Bayesian updating in causal probabilistic networks by local computation. Computational Statistics Quarterly 1990; 4:269-282.
25. Lauritzen S, Spiegelhalter D. Local computations with probabilities on graphical structures and their application to expert systems. Journal of the Royal Statistical Society B 1988; 157-224.
26. Dechter R. Bucket elimination: a unifying framework for several probabilistic inference algorithms. In: Proceedings of the Twelfth Conference on Uncertainty in Artificial Intelligence, Portland, Oregon, USA, 1996.
27. Cozman F. Generalizing variable elimination in Bayesian networks. In: Proceedings of Workshop on Probabilistic Reasoning in Artificial Intelligence, Atibaia, Brazil, 2000.
28. Shachter R. Intelligent probabilistic inference. In: Proceedings of the First Annual Conference on Uncertainty in Artificial Intelligence, UCLA, Los Angeles, CA, 1985.
29. Shachter R. Evidence absorption and propagation through evidence reversals. In: Proceedings of the Fifth Conference on Uncertainty in Artificial Intelligence, University of Windsor, Ontario, 1989.

30. Li Z, D'Ambrosio B. Efficient inference in Bayes Nets as a combinatorial optimization problem. International Journal of Approximate Reasoning 1994; 11(1):55-81.
31. Darwiche A. A differential approach to inference in Bayesian networks. In: Proceedings of the Sixteenth Conference on Uncertainty in Artificial Intelligence, Standford, Palo Alto, CA, 2000.
32. Shachter RD, Peot MA. Simulation approaches to general probabilistic inference on belief networks. In: Proceedings of the Fifth Conference on Uncertainty in Artificial Intelligence, University of Windsor, Ontario, 1989.
33. Geman S, Geman D. Stochastic relaxation, Gibbs distribution and the Bayesian restoration of images. IEEE Transactions on Pattern Analysis and Machine Intelligence 1984; 6(6):721-741.
34. MacKay D. Introduction to Monte Carlo methods. In: Jordan MI (eds) Learning in Graphical Models. MIT Press, 1998.
35. Horvitz HJS, and Cooper GF. Bounded conditioning: flexible inference for decisions under scarce resources. In: Proceedings of the Fifth Conference on Uncertainty in Artificial Intelligence, Windsor, Ontario, 1989.
36. Dechter R. Mini-buckets: a general scheme for generating approximations in automated reasoning in probabilistic inference. In: Proceedings of the Fifteenth International Joint Conference on Artificial Intelligence, Nagoya, Japan, 1997.
37. Murphy K, Weiss Y, Jordan MI. Loopy belief propagation for approximate inference: an empirical study. In: Proceedings of the Fifteenth Conference on Uncertainty in Artificial Intelligence 1999; 467-475.
38. Weiss Y. Correctness of belief propagation in Gaussian graphical models of arbitrary topology. Neural Computation 2001; 13(10).
39. Wainwrght MJ, Jordan MI. Graphical models, exponential families and variational inference. University of California, Berkeley, Technical Report, 649, 2003.
40. Chu M, Mitter SK, Zhao F. An information architecture for distributed inference on *ad hoc* sensor networks. In: Proceedings of the Forty-First Annual Allerton Conference on Communication, Control, and Computing, Monticello, IL, USA, 2003.
41. Alanyali M, Venkatesh S, Savas O, Aeron S. Distributed Bayesian hypothesis testing in sensor networks. In: Proceedings of the 2004 American Control Conference 2004; 6:5369-5374.
42. Ihler AT, Fisher JW, Moses RL, Willsky AS. Nonparametric belief propagation for sensor network self-calibration. IEEE Journal on Selected Areas in Communications 2005.
43. Crick C, Pfeffer A. Loopy belief propagation as a basis for communication in sensor networks. In: Proceedings of the Nineteenth Conference on Uncertainty in Artificial Intelligence, Acapulco, Mexico, 2003.
44. Paskin MA, Guestrin CE, McFadden J. A robust architecture for distributed inference in sensor networks. In: Proceedings of the Fourth International Symposium on Information Processing in Sensor Networks 2005.

45. Paskin MA, Guestrin CE. Robust probabilistic inference in distributed systems. In: Proceedings of the Twentieth ACM International Conference on Uncertainty in Artificial Intelligence, Banff, Canada, 2004; 436-445.

46. Akkaya K, Younis M. A survey on routing protocols for wireless sensor networks. Elsevier *Ad Hoc* Network Journal 2005.

47. Toh CK. Maximum battery life routing to support ubiquitous mobile computing in wireless *ad hoc* networks. In: Proceedings of IEEE Communications Magazine 2001; 138-147.

48. Singh S, Woo M, Raghavendra CS. Power aware routing in mobile *ad hoc* networks. In: Proceedings of The Fourth Annual ACM/IEEE International Conference on Mobile Computing and Networking, Dallas, Texas, 1998; 181-190.

49. Johnson DB, Maltz DA, Hu YC, Jetcheva JG. Dynamic source routing in *ad hoc* wireless networks. Mobile Computing 1996:153-181.

50. Jain R, Puri A, Sengupta R. Geographical routing for wireless *ad hoc* networks using partial information. IEEE Personal Communications 2001.

51. Van Dyck RE, Miller LE. Distributed sensor processing over an *ad hoc* wireless network: simulation framework and performance criteria. In: Proceedings of IEEE MILCOM, Washington, DC, 2001.

52. Liggins II ME, Chong C-Y, Kadar I, Alford MG, Vannicola V, Thomopoulos S. Distributed fusion architectures and algorithms for target tracking. Proceedings of the IEEE 1997; 85(1):95-107.

53. Ji X, Zha H. Sensor positioning in wireless *ad hoc* sensor networks using multidimensional scaling. In: Proceedings of the IEEE INFOCOM 2004.

54. Sammon JW. A nonlinear mapping for data structure analysis. IEEE Transactions on Computers 1969; C-18(5):401-409.

55. Heinzelman W, Chandrakasan A, Balakrishnan H. Energy-efficient communication protocol for wireless sensor networks. In: Proceedings, the Hawaii International Conference System Sciences, 2000.

56. Lindsey S, Raghavendra CS. PEGASIS: power efficient gathering in sensor information systems. In: Proceedings of the IEEE Aerospace Conference, Big Sky, Montana, 2002.

57. Shah R, Rabaey J. Energy aware routing for low energy *ad hoc* sensor networks. In: Proceedings of the IEEE Wireless Communications and Networking Conference, Orlando, FL, 2002.

58. Manjeshwar A, Agrawal DP. TEEN: a protocol for enhanced efficiency in wireless sensor networks. In: Proceedings of the First International Workshop on Parallel and Distributed Computing Issues in Wireless Networks and Mobile Computing, San Francisco, CA, 2001.

59. Manjeshwar A, Agrawal DP. APTEEN: a hybrid protocol for efficient routing and comprehensive information retrieval in wireless sensor networks. In: Proceedings of the Second International Workshop on Parallel and Distributed Computing Issues in Wireless Networks and Mobile Computing, Ft. Lauderdale, FL, 2002.

60. Subramanian L, Katz RH. An architecture for building self configurable systems. In: Proceedings of IEEE/ACM Workshop on Mobile *Ad Hoc* Networking and Computing, Boston, MA, 2000.

61. Yan R, Ball D, Deshmukh A, Gao RX. A Bayesian network approach to energy-aware distributed sensing. In: Proceedings of IEEE Sensors Conference, Vienna, Austria, 2004; 1:44-47.

62. Xiang Y, Poole D, Beddoes MP. Multiply sectioned Bayesian networks and junction forests for large knowledge based systems. Computational Intelligence 1993; 9:171-220.

63. Xiang Y, Lesser V. Justifying multiply sectioned Bayesian networks. In: Proceedings of the Fourth International Conference on Multi-Agent, Boston, 2000; 349-356.

64. De Castro LN, Timmis J. Artificial immune systems: a new computational intelligence approach. Springer Verlag, 2002.

65. Virus. Wikipedia.org, http://en.wikipedia.org/wiki/Virus, 2005.

66. Inman J. The antibody combining region: speculations on the hypothesis of general multispecificity. In: Bell G, Perelson A, Pimbley G (eds) Theoretical Immunology. Marcel Dekker, 1978; 234-278.

67. Rensberger B. In self-defense. In: Rensberger B (eds) Life Itself. Oxford University Press, 1996; 212-228.

68. Janeway CA, Travers P, Walport M, Capra JD. Immunobiology: the immune system in health and disease, 4th ed. Garland Publishing, 1999.

69. Hofmeyr SA, Forrest S. Architecture for an artificial immune system. Evolutionary Computation 2000; 7(1):45-68.

70. Immune System. Wikipedia.org, http://en.wikipedia.org/wiki/Immune_system, 2005.

71. Karl H, Willig A. Protocols and architectures for wireless sensor networks. Chichester, West Sussex: John Wiley and Sons, 2005.

72. Wood A, Stankovic J. A taxonomy for denial-of-service attacks in wireless sensor networks. In: Ilyas M, Mahgoub I (eds) Handbook of Sensor Networks. Boca Raton, Florida: CRC Press, 2005;32.1-32.20.

73. Karlof C, Wagner D. Secure routing in wireless sensor networks: attacks and countermeasures. In: Proceedings of the First IEEE International Workshop on Sensor Network Protocols Applications 2003.

74. Douceur JR. The Sybil attack. In: Proceedings of the First International Workshop on Peer-to-Peer Systems 2002.

75. Hu YC, Perrig A, Johnson DB. Wormhole detection in wireless *ad hoc* networks. Department of Computer Science, Rice University, Technical Report, TR01-384, 2002.

76. Cetintemel U, Flinders A, Sun Y. Power-efficient data dissemination in wireless sensor networks. In: Proceedings of the Third International ACM Workshop on Data Engineering for Wireless and Mobile Access, San Diego, California, 2003.

77. Hui JW, Culler D. The dynamic behavior of a data dissemination protocol for network programming at scale. In: Proceedings of the Second ACM Conference on Embedded Networked Sensor Systems, Baltimore, Maryland, USA, 2004.

78. Perrig A, Szewczyk R, Wen V, Culler S, Tygar JD. SPINS: security protocols for sensor networks. In: Proceedings of the Seventh Annual International Conference on Mobile Computing and Networking, Rome, Italy, 2001.

79. Rivest RL. The RC5 encryption algorithm. In: Proceedings of the Second Workshop on Fast Software Encryption 1995; 86-96.

80. Perrig A, Canetti R, Tygar J, Song DX. Efficient authentication and signing of multicast streams over lossy channel. In: Proceedings of IEEE Symposium on Security and Privacy 2000.

81. Liu D, Ning P. Efficient distribution of key chain commitments for broadcast authentication in distributed sensor networks. In: Proceedings of the Tenth Symposium of Network Distributed System, Security, Internet Society, Reston, VA, 2003.

82. Du W, Deng J, Han Y, Chen S, Varshney P. A key management scheme for wireless sensor networks using deployment knowledge. In: Proceedings of IEEE INFOCOM, Hong Kong, 2004.

83. Liu D, Ning P. Establishing pairwise keys in distributed sensor networks. In: Proceedings of the Tenth ACM Conference on Computer and Communications Security, Washington D.C., 2003.

84. Liu D, Ning P. Location-based pairwise key establishments for relatively static sensor networks. In: Proceedings of the 2003 ACM Workshop on Security of *Ad Hoc* and Sensor networks, George W. Johnson Center at George Mason University, Fairfax., V.A., USA, 2003.

85. Eschenauer G, Gligor D. A key management scheme for distributed sensor networks. In: Proceedings of the Ninth ACM Conference on Computer Communication Security, New York, USA, 2002.

86. Chan H, Perrig A, Song D. Random key predistribution schemes for sensor networks. In: Proceedings of IEEE Symposium of Security and Privacy, Los Alamitos, CA, 2003.

87. Slijepcevic S, Wong J, Potkonjak M. Security and privacy protection in wireless sensor networks. In: Ilyas M, Mahgoub I (eds) Handbook of Sensor Networks: Compact Wireless and Wired Sensing System. Florida, USA: CRC Press, 2004.

88. Arazi B, Elhanany I, Arazi O, Qi H. Revising public-key cryptography for wireless sensor networks. IEEE Computer 2005; 3(11):103-105.

89. Malan D, Welsh M, Smith MD. A public-key infrastructure for key distribution in TinyOS based on elliptic curve cryptography. In: Proceedings of the First Annual IEEE Communication Society Conference on Sensor and *Ad Hoc* Communications and Networks 2004; 71-80.

90. Kephart JO. Biologically inspired immune system for computers. In: Proceedings of the Fourth International Workshop on Synthesis and Simulation of Living Systems 1994; 130-139.

91. Forrest S, Perelson AS, Allen L, Cherukuri R. Self-nonself discrimination in a computer. In: Proceedings of IEEE Symposium on Research in Security and Privacy 1994.

92. Nishiyama H, Mizoguchi F. Design of security system based on immune system. In: Proceedings of the Tenth IEEE International Workshops on Enabling Technologies: Infrastructure for Collaborative Enterprises 2001.
93. Harmer PK, Williams PD, Gunsch GH, Lamont GB. An artificial immune system architecture for computer security applications. IEEE Transaction on Evolutionary Computation 2002; 6(3):252-280.

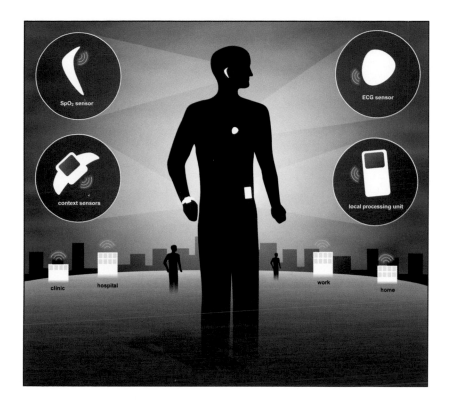

Figure 1.2 Diagrammatic representation of the BSN architecture with wirelessly linked context-aware "on body" (external) sensors and its seamless integration with home, working, and hospital environments.

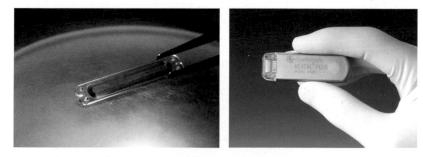

Figure 1.4 (Left) The CardioMEMS Endosure wireless aneurism pressure-sensing device (*courtesy of CardioMEMS Inc. and Professor Mark Allen, Georgia Institute of Technology*). (Right) Medtronic "Reveal Insertable Loop Recorder" (*courtesy of Medtronic Inc.*).

Figure 1.13 Conceptualisation of a MEMS robot attaching itself to a red blood cell (*copyright Coneyl Jay/Science photo library*).

Figure 1.14 Conceptualisation of a MEMS submarine injected into a blood vessel (*copyright microTEC, Germany*).

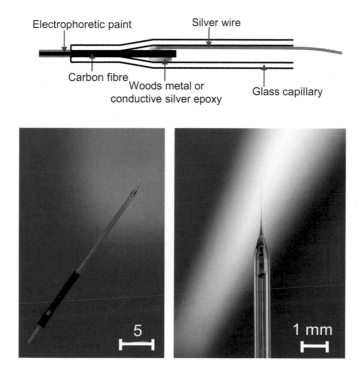

Figure 2.7 Schematic and photographs of serotonin sensors.

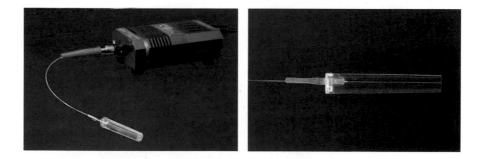

Figure 2.18 The MORE electrode complete with light source.

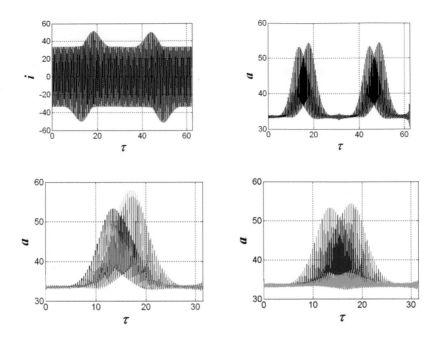

Figure 2.21 See Section 2.6 of Chapter 2 (page 78) for details.

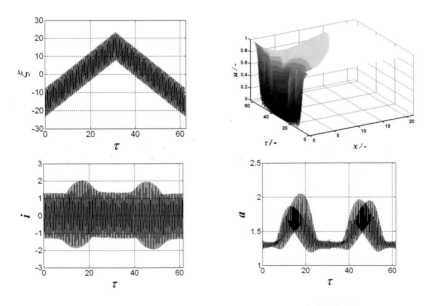

Figure 2.22 See Section 2.6 of Chapter 2 (page 79) for details.

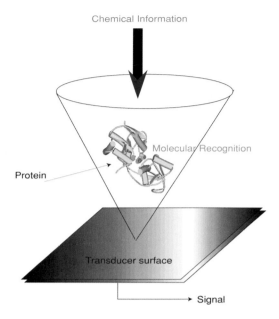

Figure 3.1 Molecular recognition lies at the heart of biosensor function.

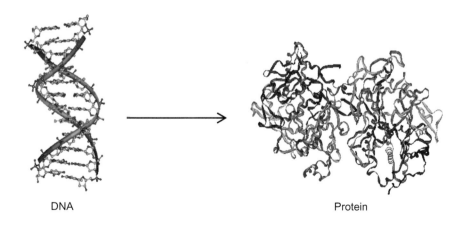

DNA   Protein

Figure 3.2 Protein engineering changes in the sequence of the DNA results in changes in protein sequence and hence protein properties.

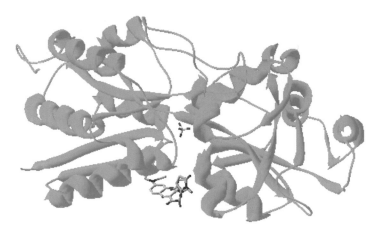

Figure 3.4 Structure of the *E.coli* phosphate binding protein showing the phosphate ligand and the coumarin fluorophore.

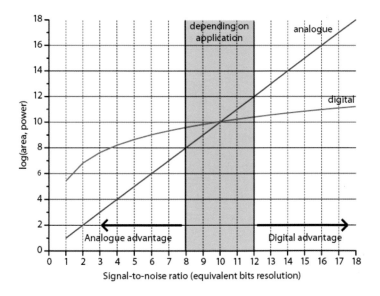

Figure 7.2 The relative cost of computation using analogue or digital signal processing. The crossover between analogue and digital having the advantage is between 50dB to 72dB SNR (8 to 12 bits resolution) depending on application and circuit topology.

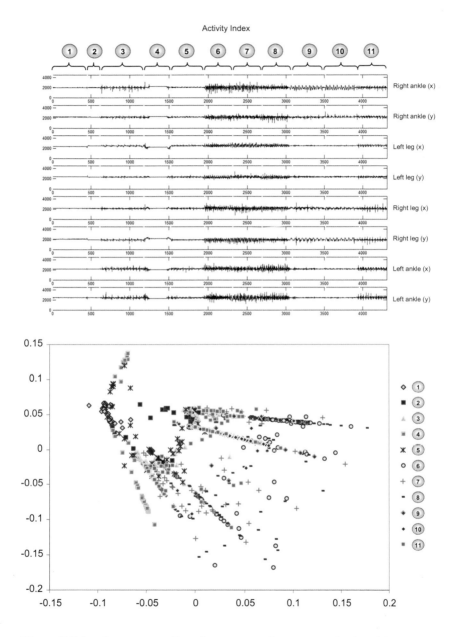

Figure 8.5 Accelerometer readings from an exercise sequence (top) and its corresponding Isomap embedding results (bottom). The residual variance of the embedded data decreases rapidly from 0.41 to 0.05, 0.04, 0.03 within the first four Isomap dimensions.

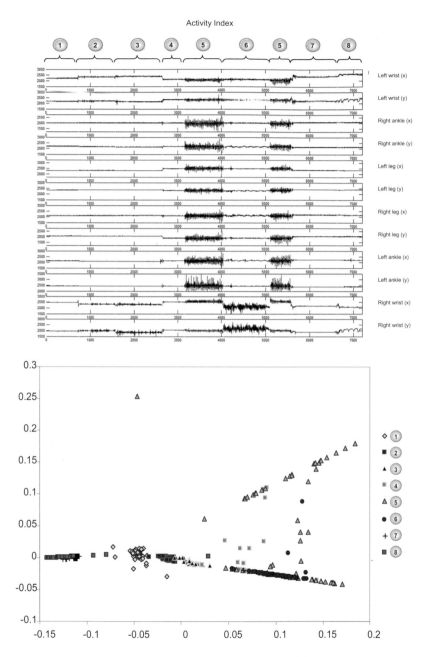

Figure 8.8 Accelerometer readings from an office activity sequence used for feature selection and the corresponding Isomap embedding result showing the separation of different activity classes.

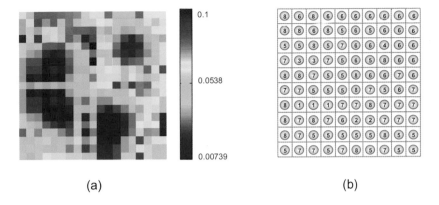

(a)   (b)

Figure 9.6 Two visualisation schemes for the standard SOM: (*a*) the U-matrix representation and (*b*) class label for each neuron.

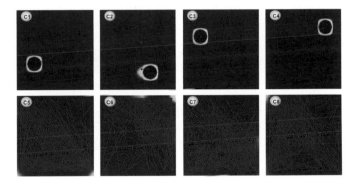

Figure 9.7 Class-specific activation plots of the static map output.

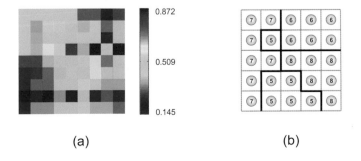

(a)   (b)

Figure 9.10 (*a*) The U-Matrix and (*b*) node labels of the dynamic map.

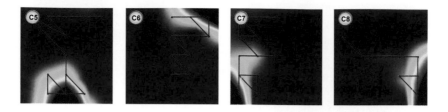

Figure 9.11 Class-specific activation plots of the dynamic map output.

Figure 9.14 A demonstration of errors due to overlaps between static classes.

Figure 9.16 Class separation for C2 and C3 of Figure 9.14 by increasing the map size from 16 to 25 neurons.

Figure 9.17 The activation plot of node expansion with sixteen neurons to achieve a clear class separation.

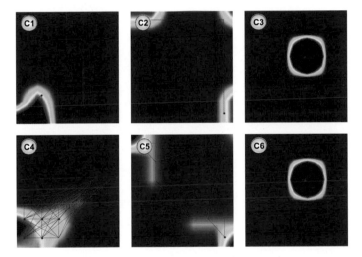

Figure 9.19 Illustration of three types of overlap in the static map with 36 neurons for the test data shown in Figure 9.18. The overlap occurs between static and dynamic classes (C1-C4), two dynamic classes (C2-C5) and two static classes (C3-C6), respectively.

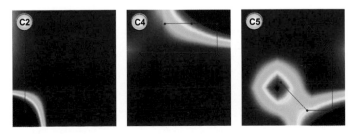

Figure 9.20 Class-specific activation plots for the dynamic map of the test data shown in Figure 9.18.

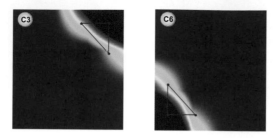

Figure 9.21 Class-specific activation plots after node expansion for C3 and C6 of Figure 9.19.

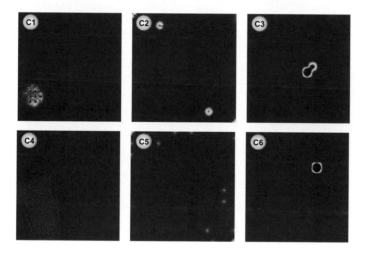

Figure 9.22 Class-specific activation plots of a standard SOM with 400 neurons for the synthetic dataset shown in Figure 9.18.

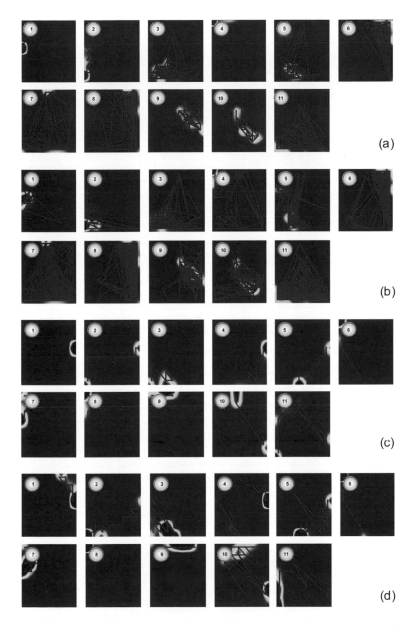

Figure 9.24 Class-specific activation plots of: (*a*) the static map with training data; (*b*) the static map with test data; (*c*) the dynamic map with training data; and (*d*) the dynamic map with test data.

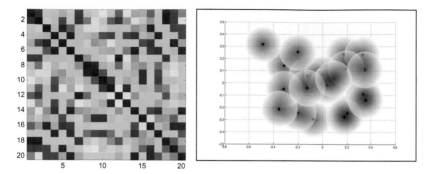

Figure 10.6 Result of nonlinear mapping based on the relative distance measures between the twenty sensors. (Left) The pairwise signal attenuation matrix. (Right) The reconstructed relative spatial configuration of the sensors represented in 2D.

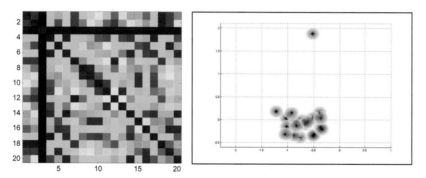

Figure 10.7 Result of nonlinear mapping based on the relative distance measures between the twenty sensors when one of the sensor nodes is faulty, illustrating the ability of the algorithm in singling out the defective node (node 3) while the relative geometrical configuration of the other sensors remains intact. (Left) Pair-wise signal attenuation matrix. (Right) the reconstructed relative spatial configuration of the sensors represented in 2D.

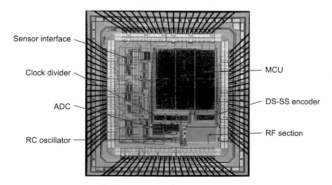

Figure 11.4 A photomicrograph of an integrated circuit providing nearly all the electronics for a capsule device.

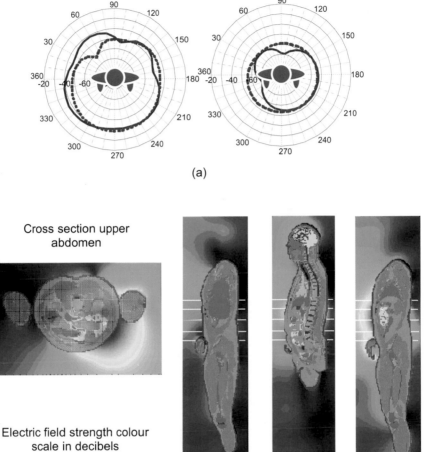

Cross section upper abdomen

Electric field strength colour scale in decibels

| 0 | -10 | -20 | -30 | -40 |

Centre   10 cm right   12 cm left

(b)

Figure 11.9 (*a*) Far-field radiation patterns from an ingested source at 150MHz (left) and 434MHz (right). The solid line is for E-field polarisation horizontal to the body, and the dashed line is for the vertical polarisation. (*b*) The near-field pattern showing the field strength around the body.

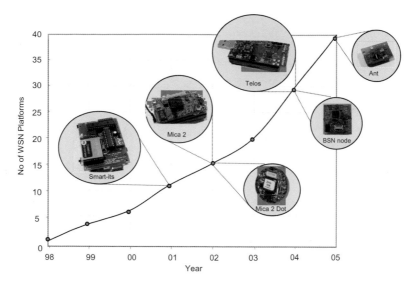

Figure A.1 Examples of WSN hardware platforms developed in recent years.

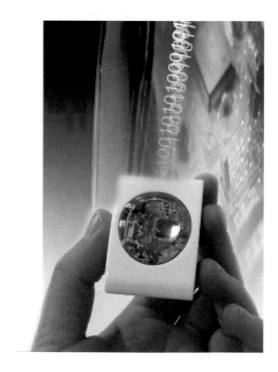

Figure B.1 BSN node.

11
Wireless Sensor Microsystem Design: A Practical Perspective

David R. S. Cumming, Paul A. Hammond, Lei Wang,
Jonathan M. Cooper, and Erik A. Johannessen

11.1 Introduction

The development of small sensor systems, often for use in distributed networks, has been actively pursued for more than 50 years. The stimulant to this activity, as with most modern technology, was the invention of the transistor that made miniaturization possible. The earliest wireless sensor devices were developed for use in a range of applications, including wireless animal tracking and medical instrumentation [1]. Indeed there was considerable activity in the field during the 1950s and '60s [2], but research activity appeared to recede in subsequent years. In the 1970s and '80s, the microelectronics industry rapidly developed after the invention of the first integrated microprocessor [3]. The focus then was on computing, but in the 1990s there was a rapid growth in consumer electronic products, exemplified by mobile communications and the Internet.

However, in the late 1990s researchers and practitioners began to realize the potential for personalized wireless systems incorporating location sensitive information and sensor technologies. In essence, these devices owe much to the early work of pioneers, but depend heavily on new technologies that have only recently become available, such as *System-on-Chip* (SoC) and mobile communications. The emerging wireless sensor systems can be carried, worn or implanted into the user and have found various expressions in wireless integrated microsystems [4, 5], "Picoradio" [6] and medical devices [7-9]. One of the most significant distinguishing aspects of these technologies was the integration of sensor functions including location (*e.g.* GPS), environmental sensors and body sensors.

The concept of building systems with many sensors that are closely integrated became prominent with the invention of the electronic nose [10]. Whilst not a wireless device, or even a networked one, the electronic nose relied upon the collection and interpretation of multisensor data. This concept lies at the core of many BSN systems where it is generally assumed that more data from more sources is a key requirement. The range of sensors that can be used in such multisensor systems is diverse and varied. The main sensor types are summarised as physical, chemical and biological. Physical applications include meteorological measurement [11], seismographic measurement [12], environmental sensing [13, 14], imaging [15], location [16], and so on. Chemical measurements rely on a range of techniques, and several integrated sensor technologies have been developed [17]. Biosensing has been driven by the laboratory-on-a-chip revolution. Many applications are found in DNA analysis [18], amongst others, but have yet to be fully implemented in wireless systems.

Microsensor devices are exposed to varied constraints that determine their size and capability. For example a body network device need not be especially small, but a medical implant often has rigorous size constraints that must be met. Furthermore, scaling can have a practical impact. A wireless system designed to operate in close proximity to the human body must not exceed regulated power limits, hence its range is compromised, especially if it is an implant. Wireless technology is also constrained by difficulties such as antenna design [19]. In another example, microfluidic systems allow analytical tools/sensors to complete assays more rapidly due to the relationship between size, diffusion and time [20].

A continuing theme in the execution of microsensor systems has been the use of *Application-Specific Integrated Circuits* (ASICs). Typically the ASICs that are used are less than 100,000 transistors and are therefore quite small by the standards of SoC designs. This is partly because the ASICs used in sensors are designed by research groups with relatively modest resources, but it is also because these designs are appropriate to the task that is required of them. Since wireless sensor microsystems are usually required to be small, it is often the case that functionality is stripped to a minimum, whereas in modern consumer electronics the trend is often in the opposite direction. Applications for this methodology have been found in medical implants [21] and electronic noses [22].

The application of IC and ASIC technologies has also been extended beyond the boundaries of straightforward electronic design. There are considerable advantages in being able to build the sensors on to the same substrate as the electronics. This has been achieved with many chemical sensors [17], and the technology has been used to build sophisticated gas sensors [23] and pH sensors [24]. Such technologies are quite expensive, but from the point of view of miniaturization they eliminated package interconnections and are therefore of particular advantage to sensor microsystems.

Wireless sensor microsystems offer very diverse functionality, and this brings about a range of technical design problems. Design skills include sensors, ASICs, wireless, low power, packaging, software, networking and power sources. These problems become more challenging the smaller the final device must be (Table 11.1). In the remainder of this chapter we will cover a range of design topics that are of relevance to wireless microsystem designers irrespective of their intended application. The material will be covered in the context of the ingestible laboratory-in-a-pill device that offers a particularly challenging case study containing many of the attributes one might expect to find in a wireless microsystem.

Table 11.1 Design challenges for wireless sensor systems.

Features	Technical Challenges
Size	Device required to work in constrained space
Power	Batteries are often quite big; power scavenging is still premature
Cost	Not mass market technology so products still very expensive
Lifetime	Devices need to operate over extended periods; difficult due to power and drift
Wireless	Must conform to standards; radio environment often complex; size constraints; tissue absorptions
Sensors	Size constraints; performance changes over time and environment
Electronics	Partitioning into system nodes; choice of analogue *vs* digital; hardware *vs* software
Packaging	Assists miniaturization; must conform to standards of applications (*e.g.* medical)

11.2 The Diagnostic Capsule

In order to diagnose a wide range of *GastroIntestinal* (GI) dysfunctions, it is extremely useful to be able to make measurements of the conditions inside a patient's gut. Conventional methods include noninvasive techniques such as radiography (X-ray, *Computed Axial Tomography* (CAT), *Positron Emission Tomography* (PET)), ultrasonography and *Magnetic Resonance Imaging* (MRI). Noninvasive methods cannot present any direct information on the biochemical environment within the GI tract, hence endoscopy, a relatively invasive technology, has gained clinical acceptance to view the GI tract and perform biopsies for later analysis [25]. Sedation or a general anaesthetic is often required for animal endoscopy, and the considerable inconvenience and irritation of this technique discourages patients from undergoing the procedure [26]. The technique is also unsuitable for monitoring GI dysfunction since it cannot measure the GI tract in real-time over an extended period [27]. As a consequence, there is growing interest in the application of wireless sensor microsystems for use in capsule or wireless endoscopy.

In 1957, the first two radiotelemetry capsules were developed independently in Stockholm [28] and New York [29]. They measured approximately 10mm in diameter and 30mm in length. Both were designed to measure pressure using a diaphragm to move an iron core inside a coil. The coil was the tuning element of a single-transistor oscillator circuit, the frequency of which therefore depended on the pressure. The circuit used by Mackay and Jacobson is shown in Figure 11.1 [28]. It produced bursts of oscillations in the 100kHz range; the frequency was a function of pressure, and the burst repetition rate a function of temperature. This ingenious circuit was capable of measuring both pressure and temperature, which were recorded using a standard radio receiver. Current suppliers of this technology include Given Imaging [15], Olympus, Medtronic, and Intellisite [30, 31]. Many research works still aim to advance the state of the art [21, 32-36]. A temperature monitoring pill has even been developed by NASA for use by astronauts [37].

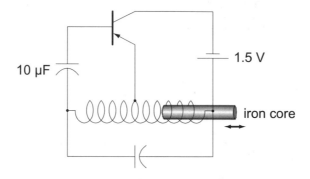

Figure 11.1 Circuit diagram of a pressure-sensitive single-transistor oscillator.

11.3 Applications for Wireless Capsule Devices

Whilst this chapter is aimed at providing a general review of some of the issues that concern the design of wireless microsystems, in practice, real designs are determined by the application for which they are intended. With this in mind, we provide a brief outline of the application domain of our exemplar microsystem.

11.3.1 Human Medicine

Medical devices must first satisfy the requirement for clinical efficacy. Because of this the capsule devices that have been developed to date have only a simple range of sensor capabilities due to the relative lack of medical data that would normally encourage the development of more sophisticated tools. At present the dominant measurement capabilities are image acquisition, temperature and pH, although devices capable of sample retrieval, pressure sensing and dissolved oxygen measurement, amongst others, have been explored.

pH is one of the most important parameters to measure in any biological system. In terms of pH measurement, capsule-based systems have been employed most successfully to diagnose *Gastro-Oesophageal Reflux Disease* (GERD) [38]. These systems require a tethered capsule to monitor whether stomach acid is refluxing back into the oesophagus and causing the burning sensation commonly known as heartburn. Measurements of pH in the GI tract using "flow-through" capsules have also been used to study *Inflammatory Bowel Diseases* (IBDs) such as Crohn's disease and ulcerative colitis [39, 40]. Knowledge of the pH profile along the GI tract has also led to the development of drug capsules that dissolve in alkaline environments, ensuring that the drug is only released beyond the acid environment of the stomach.

In 1959, Wolff [41] started to develop radiotelemetry capsules that could be mass produced, in order to reduce the cost and increase the quantity available for clinical trials. As well as a pressure-sensitive capsule, his laboratory developed capsules for measuring temperature and pH, all based on single-transistor oscillators. The temperature-measuring capsule used a coil wound on a core made from a nickel-iron alloy, which exhibited a large change in permeability with temperature. This changed the inductance of the tuning coil and shifted the frequency of transmission in a manner similar to the pressure sensor of Mackay [28]. The pH-measuring capsule used a glass electrode connected to a silicon diode, which operated as the tuning element for the oscillator. The potential of the electrode varied with pH and this voltage changed the capacitance of the diode. A reference electrode, needed to complete the pH circuit, was also included in the capsule, which is shown in Figure 11.2. A similar pH-sensitive capsule based on a glass electrode was described by Watson and Kay [42]. It was used in the first medical study to plot the pH profile along the entire length of the GI tract [43].

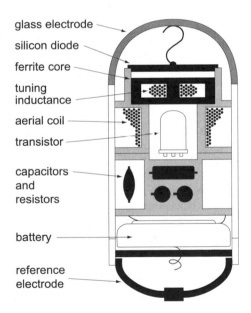

Figure 11.2 Diagram of the cross-section through a pH-sensitive radio-telemetry capsule.

These early capsules were prone to failure due to the ingress of moisture through the epoxy, which was used to seal the glass electrode in place. An improved design that housed the battery and electronics inside the glass electrode was developed by Colson [44]. The receiving antenna array was embedded in a cloth band worn around the waist. Data was collected on a portable solid-state recorder that allowed the patient to carry out their normal activities. This equipment was used in a much larger study of 66 subjects [45].

For conditions such as GERD, it is necessary to measure the pH at a fixed location, rather than measuring a flow-through profile. Early studies achieved this by "lowering" the capsule into position on a piece of thread, and fixing the free end to the subject's cheek when the capsule was in position. More recently, a capsule has been developed that is temporarily anchored to the wall of the GI tract using an endoscopic delivery system [38] that relatively invasive. A vacuum pump sucks tissue into a well in the capsule and a pin is pushed through the tissue holding it in place after the delivery system has been removed. This capsule is 6mm in diameter and 25mm long, and it uses an antimony pH electrode. It transmits to a pager-sized receiver, allowing patients to continue their normal activities without restriction of diet or exercise.

Commercial radiotelemetry capsules have been developed that have the potential to replace conventional fibre-optic endoscopy and colonoscopy. The M2A capsule from Given Imaging Ltd. contains a single-chip *Complementary Metal-Oxide-Semiconductor* (CMOS) image sensor, an ASIC for video transmission, and white *Light-Emitting Diodes* (LEDs) for illumination [15]. The data is transmitted to an array of eight antennae worn on a belt that also allow the capsule's position to be localised, it is claimed, to within 3.8cm. The system is particularly well suited to detection of bleeding and the software contains blood recognition algorithms to automatically highlight suspect areas. To date it has been used in numerous clinical trials and as a diagnostic tool [46].

11.3.2 Animal Applications

Data-logging telemetry capsules have been used to measure the pH inside the stomach of small animals [47] including penguins [48]. The same technology has been used in cattle where the capsule was located in the reticulum, which is the second stomach of a ruminant, to measure the effect of diet on subclinical acidosis [49]. In fact, livestock monitoring may well be the major market for capsule-based pH sensors. When combined with temperature, the data could be used by farmers to optimise feeding patterns, to detect illness, and to manage breeding. There is already a system available that combines temperature measurement with a *Radio-Frequency Identification* (RFID) chip that is unique to each animal. RFID tagging of livestock provides guaranteed information on the supply of meat from "farm-to-fork" and standards have been developed for the manufacture of such devices and systems [50].

11.4 Technology

11.4.1 Design Constraints

There are clearly tight constraints placed on the design and implementation of a capsule-based diagnostic system. The overall dimensions should be small enough to allow the device to pass through all the GI sphincters with relative ease, including the lower oesophageal sphincter and the pyloric sphincter. The capsule must also be cheap to make since it will only be used once. Low power consumption is a requirement to minimise battery (hence overall) size and increase operating time. A capsule might take a maximum of 8 hours to traverse the upper alimentary tract and the small intestine, while a complete passage through the GI tract might take up to 32 hours. Using readily available silver oxide battery technology, an energy storage density of 500mWh/mL can be achieved [51], thus a suitable source, such as two SR48 cells (110mWh each) could deliver enough energy to complete small intestinal measurements if the average power consumption was less than 20mW.

The data sampled in the GI tract by a capsule must be retrieved accurately and securely. This usually means that the data must be wirelessly transmitted and correctly received by a device worn by the patient. There are a number of radio communication standards encompassing several international *Industrial, Scientific and Medical* (ISM) telemetry bands (pan-European medical device frequency allocations [52], and the US Federal Communications Commission frequency allocations for biomedical telemetry and ISM devices – regulations S5.150, US209 and US350). The main bands of interest are at 418MHz, 434MHz, 868MHz and 915MHz.

As with all measuring devices, the user must be confident that the data retrieved is accurate. The problems of accuracy can be dealt with via the normal techniques of instrument design and calibration. However, an additional constraint for wireless devices is that the data must be secure. Since capsule devices operate in the unlicensed ISM frequency bands there is a severe risk of interference that could be particularly dangerous in the context of a medical device. Of necessity the sensors and signal acquisition electronics require analogue circuits. In the early devices the entire design was analogue, making the data transfer from the devices extremely insecure. However, modern electronic techniques permit designers to convert the analogue signal to the digital domain within the capsule, enabling the use of secure digital wireless techniques. These techniques ensure that data from any given capsule can be uniquely identified to avoid attributing diagnostic information to the wrong individual. Details of such designs, and others concerning wireless sensor systems, are discussed by Nikolaidis *et al* and Park *et al* [53, 54].

11.4.2 Microsystem Design

Whilst there is no single way to build a capsule system using current technology, many of the aspects of a complete solution are illustrated in Figure 11.3. In the capsule the sensors are the data gathering devices that are connected to the electronic instrumentation in order to acquire the signal. In the earlier devices all the data was managed by analogue electronics, but more recent devices convert the signals into a digital representation. In this way a common platform can be developed in which one basic controller design can be reused for successive products or different sensor modalities. This is an example of the SoC methodology, in which the majority of the components are connected together on a single chip. Commonplace examples of products containing these SoC devices are mobile telephones, digital television and radio receivers, and computer game consoles. The design of small SoCs is well suited to capsule design since the device requirements are both complex and unusual to the extent that a small enough device cannot readily be assembled from off-the-shelf components.

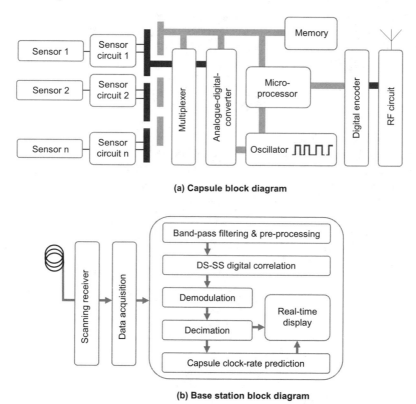

Figure 11.3 A typical block diagram of the key features of a capsule (a), and a receiver (b). Because the receiver is not constrained by power and size it can have any reasonable level of complexity [21].

For capsule devices the use of a digital architecture enables substantially more complex systems to be built that are capable of performing many measurements. Figure 11.4 shows an integrated circuit designed for use in a microcapsule system that contains all the electronics required. In this implementation, a small low-power transmitter has been integrated on to the same chip with a usable operating range of only 10–20cm. Because of the difficulty of building a suitable transmitter on to the same integrated circuit as the rest of the instrument, it is usual to have a separate RF section, usually made from commercially available parts. The majority of devices have only a one-way wireless link to enable data transmission to an external device. However, a device providing a two-way link has recently been demonstrated [55]. The advantages of a two-way wireless link are improved security of the wireless connection and external control of the capsule.

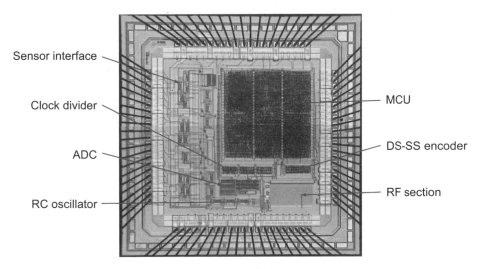

Figure 11.4 A photomicrograph of an integrated circuit providing nearly all the electronics for a capsule device. **(See colour insert.)**

Once all the measurements are combined, they are encoded and transmitted over a wireless link to a receiver outside the body. There are many possible ways of building the external system and for illustration purposes we show a system combining an RF section, a decoder and display or data storage unit. This latter unit, usually a wearable device, could simply record data on to storage media for subsequent analysis, or provide real-time display and analysis capabilities. Another possibility that has been investigated is to implement the external unit as a web server enabling clinicians to "look in" from potentially any networked device with a web browser [8].

11.4.3 Integrated Sensors

There are a wide variety of microsensor technologies now available, many of which can be applied to diagnostic capsule applications. A useful text describing many examples is given by Gardner [56]. Microsensors, and in particular, those sensors that can be integrated into a small format and sharing a common platform with the electronics, are very useful for size-constrained systems such as a diagnostic capsule.

11.4.3.1 Physical

One of the most significant examples has been the use of CMOS video chips by Given Imaging Ltd. In addition to the ability to integrate the electronics and the sensor on the same chip, the advantages of the CMOS video approach, as opposed to using a charge coupled device, are the relatively low cost and the ability of the device to operate at relatively low voltage.

The integration of CMOS image sensors with electronics is a result of the advance of consumer electronics. Other integrated sensors, targeted at industrial and medical applications, have also been developed that are well suited to capsule systems [17]. With the advent of *Micro Electro-Mechanical Systems* (MEMS), it is now possible to pattern complex 3D structures into CMOS chips. MEMS processes can be divided into either bulk or surface micromachining. In bulk micromachining, the silicon substrate is etched away from the back of the chip or wafer, using the oxide layer as an etch stop [57, 58]. This leaves a thin membrane containing the CMOS circuits, which has excellent thermal isolation and can be used for heat-based sensors. In surface micromachining of CMOS chips, the metal layers, or the intermetal dielectric layers, are etched away to leave freestanding structures [59]. Resonating beams for mass sensing or thin filaments for heat sensing can be made in this way. Several sensors have been fabricated using a combination of CMOS and MEMS technologies. For example, a recent capsule-type device for measuring intravascular pressure uses a MEMS capacitive pressure sensor integrated onto a CMOS chip [60, 61].

11.4.3.2 Chemical

As already discussed, pH sensors can be made using conventional glass electrode methods, but the arrival of chip-based sensors has allowed a more integrated approach to be adopted. Using this method it has been possible to implement more than one sensor on a single chip hence increasing functionality whilst contributing to the overall aim of reducing the capsule size. Figure 11.5 shows two sensor chips that have been developed for a laboratory-in-a-pill device [21]. The chips contain a diverse range of sensor technology, not least of which is a microfabricated Ag/AgCl reference electrode.

Chemical sensors have also been realised on CMOS chips. They may be classified as follows [17]:

- *Chemomechanical sensors* typically use a polymer-coated resonating beam whose fundamental frequency is changed by the mass of absorbed gas molecules.
- *Catalytic sensors* have an electrically heated suspended filament that causes local oxidation reactions, and measures the heat loss as a change in temperature.

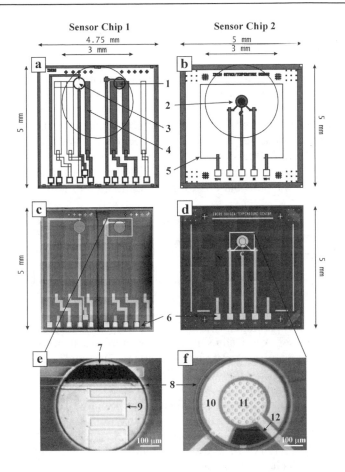

Figure 11.5 Two sensor chips developed for a laboratory-in-a-pill. *a*) Schematic diagram of *Chip 1*, measuring 4.75×5mm^2, comprising a pH based on an ISFET sensor (1), a dual electrode conductivity sensor (3) and a silicon diode temperature sensor (4); *b*) schematic diagram of *Chip 2*, measuring 5×5mm^2, comprising an electrochemical oxygen sensor (2) and a Pt resistance thermometer (5). Once integrated in the pill, the area exposed to the external environment is illustrated by the 3mm diameter circle; *c*) photomicrograph of sensor *Chip 1*; and *d*) sensor *Chip 2*. The bonding pads (6), which provide electrical contact to the external electronic control circuit, are shown; *e*) close up of the pH sensor consisting of the integrated 3×10^{-2}mm^2 Ag│AgCl reference electrode (7), a 500μm diameter and 50μm deep, 10nL, electrolyte chamber (8) defined in polyimide, and the 15×600μm floating gate (9) of the ISFET sensor; *f*) an oxygen sensor is likewise embedded in an electrolyte chamber (8). The three-electrode electrochemical cell comprises the 1×10^{-1}mm^2 counter electrode (10), a microelectrode array of 57×10μm diameter (4.5×10^{-3}mm^2) working electrodes (11) defined in 500nm thick PECVD Si$_3$N$_4$, and an integrated 1.5×10^{2}mm^2 Ag│AgCl reference electrode (12).

- *Thermoelectric sensors* use thermocouples to measure heat liberated or consumed by the interaction of a membrane with an analyte.
- *Optical sensors* use photodiodes to measure the light output from bioluminescent bacteria when they metabolise the target compound.
- *Voltammetric sensors* are miniaturised versions of the standard three-electrode cell to measure the electron exchange currents that occur in redox reactions.
- *Potentiometric sensors* use modified field-effect transistors to measure the potential due to the concentration of ions in a gas or liquid.
- *Conductometric sensors* use either resistors or capacitors coated with a sensitive material (polymers or metal oxides, for example) to measure changes in impedance on exposure to the analyte.

Most of these CMOS-compatible sensors produce analogue outputs and need to be connected to external equipment in order to make measurements. Recently, there have been several examples of CMOS chemical sensors that take full advantage of the 'system-on-chip' paradigm. The gas sensor chip described by Hagleitner [62] used a combination of chemically sensitive capacitors, resonant beams and thermocouples, as well as a temperature sensor, integrated on a single chip. All the control and sensing electronics, an *Analogue-to-Digital Converter* (ADC) and a digital interface were included on the chip. A commercial CMOS process was used, and both bulk and surface micromachining techniques were employed to define the sensing structures, after the chip had been fabricated.

In another example, a fully integrated pH measuring instrument was made using a standard CMOS foundry process with no modification by micromachining [24]. Figure 11.6 shows a photomicrograph of the instrument with the individual components labelled. At the heart of this device is a floating gate *Ion-Sensitive Field Effect Transistor* (ISFET) made by taking advantage of the foundries standard process materials and design rules.

11.4.3.3 Biological

Another example, this time of a 'partial SoC' CMOS chemical sensor, uses living cells as the transducer to detect the presence of a toxin [63]. It is not a complete SoC as it requires off-chip analogue electronics and a microcontroller to make measurements. A microfluidic chamber is clamped in place above the electrodes on the chip. Heart muscle cells are injected into the chamber and cultured there. The chip allows different electrode pairs to be addressed and the system automatically selects those giving the strongest action potential signals from the cells as they beat. The system was packaged into a battery-powered handheld unit complete with pumps for the microfluidics, allowing it to be used outside the laboratory.

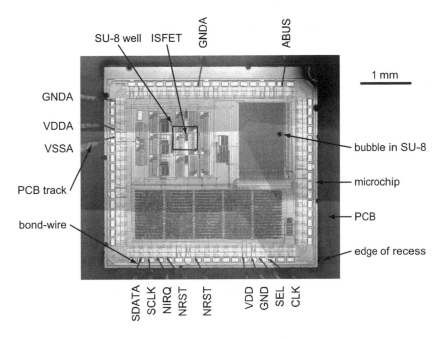

Figure 11.6 Photomicrograph of encapsulated SoC pH meter.

Living cells have also been used as bioluminescent 'bioreporters' with a CMOS SoC, to measure gas concentrations [64]. The cells used were luminescent in the presence of toluene. An integrated photodiode produced a current proportional to the light intensity, which was converted into a digital output by the on-chip processing circuitry. Depending on the length of integration time used, concentrations as low as 10 parts per billion of toluene were detected.

Clearly biologically based sensors as described above are not of immediate application to diagnostic capsule devices, but may have an application in the future as technology moves towards highly specific discriminatory techniques.

11.5 Electronics System Design

In addition to having all the required components for the implementation of a capsule device one must think about how the complete system will be designed to achieve the desired performance. As we have seen there is rapid progress away from benchtop instrumentation design to modern integrated circuit implementations. As a consequence it is appropriate to use silicon design methodologies. Such methodologies have emerged from the microelectronics industry as more complex designs have been required [65, 66]. We present a methodology here that is relatively simple by the standards of the industry, but encapsulates sufficient detail to enable accurate design of a sensor system.

11.5.1 Analogue Electronic Front-End Acquisition Design

The steps involved in designing an analogue circuit are illustrated in Figure 11.7. The main difference from digital design is that both the schematic and physical designs are created by hand. An analogue circuit starts off as a high-level model or simply a list of requirements that must be met. The first attempt at a circuit design is made using a schematic editor to draw a diagram of the components and their connections. The standard components available in a CMOS process are MOS-FETs, resistors and capacitors but others such as diodes, bipolar transistors and inductors can also be created. Parameterised models for all available component types, obtained by characterising fabricated devices, are provided by the foundry. The circuit is simulated by an analogue circuit simulator such as SPICE.

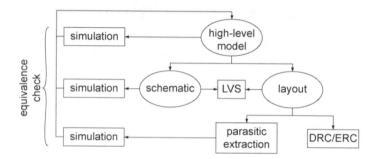

Figure 11.7 Flowchart for the computer-aided analogue circuit design process.

The circuit is unlikely to fulfil its requirements at the first attempt, so either the topology of the circuit or the parameters of its components are changed. Depending on the complexity of the circuit, several iterations may be required until the simulated response matches the desired response. When this is achieved, work can begin on the physical design (layout) of the circuit. A layout editor is used to draw areas of n-type and p-type silicon, polysilicon and metal that will form the components and connections. The task is usually made easier by the foundry that provides parameterised cell macros that generate the layout data for MOSFETs, resistors and capacitors. However, for low-noise, well-matched, or compact circuits it is often necessary to create these devices by hand. The arrangement of devices and the connections between them is also carried out by hand. Once complete, *Design Rule Checking* (DRC), *Electrical Rule Checking* (ERC) and *Layout Versus Schematic* (LVS) checks are performed to ensure that the final design is as intended. The design can be modified as required until a satisfactory conclusion is reached.

11.5.2 Digital System Design

A flow diagram of the steps involved in designing a digital circuit is shown in Figure 11.8. In contrast to the analogue design flow, the physical design can be generated using software. The digital circuit may start off as a high-level "behavioural" model written in a programming language such as C or Matlab. It is then re-coded into a *Hardware Description Language* (HDL) that allows the designer to describe digital circuits. The code is then compiled, simulated and debugged. Once the errors have been removed, simulation is required to ensure that the HDL code performs the functions described by the original high-level model.

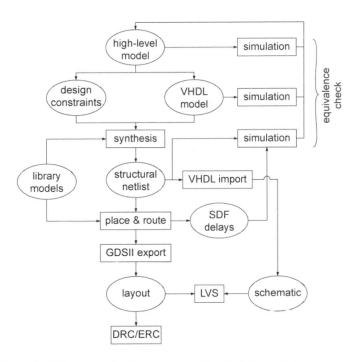

Figure 11.8 Flowchart for the computer-aided digital circuit design process.

If the HDL code uses only certain constructs that are allowed at a *Register Transfer Level* (RTL) (see [67] for a description of RTL), then the code may be synthesised. The synthesis process automatically generates the details of the gates and their interconnections to form a structural netlist. It attempts to optimise the netlist based on timing, area and power constraints that are set by the designer, and on the information contained in the library models provided by the foundry.

After synthesis, the netlist is converted into a physical layout by the automatic "place and route" tool. Delay information is extracted from this tool and used to annotate the structural netlist. If the simulation of this timing-accurate netlist fails to meet the specifications, then another iteration of the design loop is required. The next step in the process is to export the design, using the GDSII file format (GDSII is the standard file format for transferring/archiving 2D graphical design data) to describe the layout. The GDSII data and the HDL structural netlist are then imported into the layout editor (as used for the analogue design) to create the layout and schematic views respectively. As a final check, DRC, ERC and LVS checks are performed as for the analogue design process.

11.6 The Wireless Environment

The transmission of radio signals in and around the human body is of considerable importance to the success of a wireless capsule device. The behaviour of an electromagnetic field in the presence of a human body is influenced by the dielectric properties of human tissue. In addition, the dielectric function is frequency-dependent and the absorption of electromagnetic waves increases with increasing frequency. As a consequence reflection at boundaries, scattering, absorption and refraction of electromagnetic fields are frequency dependent. However, the radiation from electrically small sources in free space increases with frequency. In addition, the effect of the capacitive loading of the surrounding tissue on the source has a complicated frequency and spatial dependence.

Unsurprisingly, given the prevalence of mobile telephony, the majority of work that has been done to obtain a detailed understanding of radio transmission near the human body has focussed on the head and neck. Early work used relatively simple body models that assumed that human tissue was homogenous [68]. As work progressed research moved to more sophisticated models [69]. More recently there have been a number of studies looking at the abdominal region using detailed models for both female [70] and male bodies [19]. The main results of these latter simulations are shown in Figure 11.9. The simulations were carried out for an ingested transmitter at a number of possible locations and orientations and the data shown is therefore only representative.

Despite the fact that absorption of electromagnetic radiation increases with frequency it is found that, up to a point, increasing the frequency can improve the far-field signal strength from an ingested source (Figure 11.9(a)). The reason for this is that the size of the capsule device demands that an electrically small antenna be used, and that typically the antenna be very much smaller than $\lambda/2$ (the preferred size for the simplest radiating device), where λ is the wavelength. As a consequence, when the frequency is increased, the wavelength decreases towards the antenna dimensions, increasing the antenna's efficiency. It has been found that there is a competing effect between the increased efficiency of the antenna and the increasing absorption of the body tissue, and ultimately there is a trade-off in which an optimum frequency is found. Simulations have shown this to be in the region of 650MHz which does not correspond exactly with any of the available ISM bands around the world. Since it is comfortably between European and USA frequencies, most major markets can be supplied.

The near-field pattern data is of interest since in many applications it is anticipated that the receiver antennae will be in close proximity to the body, which is for the most part located in the near-field for the wavelengths concerned. From Figure 11.9(b) it can be seen that there is greater field strength to the left-hand anterior position of the abdomen due to the strongly absorbent nature of the liver on the right-

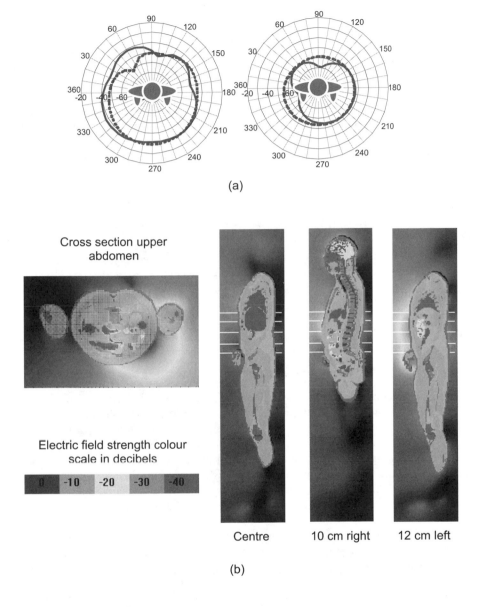

(a)

Cross section upper abdomen

Electric field strength colour scale in decibels

| 0 | -10 | -20 | -30 | -40 |

Centre   10 cm right   12 cm left

(b)

Figure 11.9 (*a*) Far-field radiation patterns from an ingested source at 150MHz (left) and 434MHz (right). The solid line is for E-field polarisation horizontal to the body, and the dashed line is for the vertical polarisation. (*b*) The near-field pattern showing the field strength around the body. (**See colour insert.**)

hand side. The results of simulations of this kind can be used directly to assist in the design of the antenna system.

An alternative to conventional propagating wireless systems is to communicate wirelessly using the inductive near-field [71]. Without dealing in detail with the electromagnetic problem here, it is possible to transmit wirelessly at low frequencies over distances that are very small compared to the propagating wavelength. In this evanescent regime designers can take advantage of the lower absorption of RF power at lower frequencies and replace the antenna with two coils (one internally and one externally) that effectively behave as the primary and secondary coils of a transformer respectively. Detailed design and experimentation have shown that such a system can communicate effectively over the required range consuming less electrical power than a more conventional radio system [21].

11.7 Power Sources

Powering capsule devices is perhaps one of the greatest challenges. There are many possible micropower sources currently being researched, a review of which has been written by Roundy [72]. Not all the available techniques, for example solar power, are useful in the context of an ingested device. More practical techniques include: a battery; electromagnetic induction; and electromechanical conversion. Other schemes, such as making direct use of gut mucosa as an electrolyte in an electrochemical cell arrangement, have been proposed but have not been explored in any serious way.

Although the use of batteries is by far the simplest power source it comes with certain restrictions. Not all types of cell are favourable to use in implants (*e.g.* ZnO_2), and achieving adequate power density from the safer choices available is difficult (*e.g.* AgO). However a potentially greater problem than integrated energy storage is peak current delivery, since even short periods of high demand, for example during signal transmission, can very rapidly deplete a battery. As a consequence, when designing a microtelemetry system it is important to complete a detailed power budget and make design decisions that will ultimately compromise the devices performance in order to ensure correct functionality during a complete gut transit.

Electromagnetic induction is an attractive option as it not only reduces the power constraint on the device but also removes the need for batteries would make the device smaller. The maximum power density permitted near the human body is in the region of 1 mW/cm^2 but varies from country to country [73]. This is a severe limitation given the power requirement and distance over which power must be transmitted to reach a device deeply embedded in the human abdomen. With the exception of the relatively simple RFID temperature sensing devices developed for animal use that we have already discussed there has not yet been any significant demonstration of this technology for the more sophisticated human medical devices.

11.8 Packaging

Having decided upon the internal apparatus of a laboratory-in-a-pill it must all be packaged into a capsule. The package must be mechanically strong, chemically inert and allow access between the sensors and their environment. For optical devices there is always the prospect of an obstruction blocking the lens, but the clear plastic dome structures that are used in current products, such as the M2A from Given Imaging, are relatively easy to manufacture and strong. It is significantly more complicated to construct packages that will permit fluid access onto to sensor devices, especially if these devices are integrated circuits or chips that will be adversely effected by current leakage due to liquids seeping into the encapsulating materials.

One of the main obstacles that has prevented the commercialisation of ISFET-based devices is the repeatability and reliability of the encapsulation procedure. It is normal for the encapsulant to be applied by hand, covering the chip and bond-wires but leaving a small opening above the sensing area. Epoxy is the most extensively used material although it is important to select a composition that is stable, a good electrical insulator and does not flow during encapsulation. Many commercially available epoxies have been assessed for their suitability by making measurements of their electrical impedance over time [74-77].

By using UV-curable polymers, it is possible to increase the automation of the packaging process using a standard mask aligner. A lift-off technique was developed using a sacrificial layer of photosensitive polyimide to protect the ISFET gates. Alumina-filled epoxy was applied by screen printing and partially cured, before the polyimide was etched away leaving a well in the epoxy [78]. After ten days in solution, leakage currents as high as 200nA were observed. Better results were achieved by direct photo-polymerisation of an epoxy-based encapsulant. ISFETs packaged using this method showed leakage currents of 35nA after three months in solution. To avoid polarising the reference electrode, common to such devices, a leakage current of less than 1nA is desirable [79]. This photolithographic patterning of the encapsulant was done at the wafer-level, to all the devices simultaneously. Subsequently the wafer was diced up and the individual chips were wire-bonded and coated with more encapsulant by hand.

At the chip-level, wire-bonded ISFET chips have been covered (again by hand) with a 0.5–1mm thick photosensitive, epoxy-based film, then exposed and developed [80]. After twenty days in solution, the devices retained low leakage currents. Some degree of automation was introduced by Sibbald [75] who used a dip-coating method to apply the polymers. The chip was mounted in a recess in a PCB and the wire-bond connections were made, before coating it with a layer of polyimide. Two layers of photoresist followed, before the underlying polyimide was etched away (Figure 11.10). The slight undercutting of the polyimide was reported to be useful in anchoring the CHEMFET membrane in place. The packaged devices showed less than 10pA leakage current after ten days in solution. However the encapsulation did exhibit electrical breakdown for applied bias voltages in excess of 1.5–2V. This was attributed to the high electric field in the thin layer of resist covering the bond-wires. More recently a single layer of an epoxy-based photoresist (SU-8) has been used to package a pH-sensing microchip [81]. In a separate study, photosensitive polyimide has also been used to create the wells that separate the ion-selective membranes on a multiple ISFET chip [82].

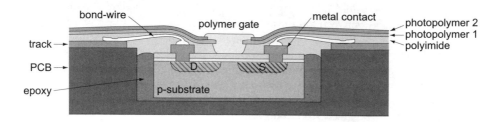

Figure 11.10 Diagram of the cross-section through a CHEMFET device in a recessed PCB, encapsulated using a layer of polyimide and two layers of photoresist [75].

It is interesting to note that although flip-chip bonding is a well established and robust packaging technique, it has not been applied to liquid-sensing ISFETs. In flip-chip bonding, solder bumps are patterned onto the bond-pads, allowing the chip to be directly connected to a PCB without the need for bond-wires. A gas sensor has been fabricated in this way, by bonding an ISFET to a ceramic substrate that had been coated with a suitable polymer [83]. It may be that the high cost of solder bumping, which is normally applied to a whole wafer of devices, has prevented wider use of flip-chip bonding in capsule packaging.

11.9 Conclusions

The development of microsystems for use in and around the body first came to the fore before the term microsystem had even been invented. It began with the invention of the transistor, and the end is not yet in sight. However the drivers have not significantly changed: the availability of cheap technology from more mainstream research and development has enabled sensor system designers to become more ambitious and hope to deliver tremendous technologies for many applications, especially in healthcare. In this chapter, we have reviewed the broad range of microsensor systems that have been explored. Some of the most exciting applications are in human medicine, and devices for use in the human gastrointestinal tract have received particular attention in recent years. In addition to reviewing these technologies we have provided a description of many of the design challenges that must be overcome to meet the demand requirements of these applications.

References

1. Mackay RS. Bio-medical telemetry – sensing and transmitting biological information from animals and man. New York: John Wiley and Sons, 1968.
2. Mackay RS. Radio telemetering from within the body. Science 1961; 134: 1196-1202.
3. Lewin MH. Integrated microprocessors. IEEE Transactions on Circuits and Systems 1975; 22(7): 577-585.
4. DeHennis D, Wise KD. A wireless microsystem for the remote sensing of pressure, temperature, and relative humidity. Journal of Microelectromechanical Systems 2005; 14(1): 12-22.
5. Wise KD, Anderson DJ, Hetke JF, Kipke DR, Najafi K. Wireless implantable microsystems: high-density electronic interfaces to the nervous system. Proceedings of the IEEE 2004; 92(1):76-97.
6. Rabaey JM, Ammer MJ, Silva da JL, Patel D, Roundy S. Picoradio supports ad hoc ultra-low power wireless networking. Computer 2000; 33(7):42-48.
7. Mokwa W, Schnakenberg U. Micro-transponder systems for medical applications. IEEE Transactions on Instrument and Measurement. 2001; 50(6):1551-1555.
8. Wang L, Johannessen EA, Cui L, Ramsey C, Tang TB, Ahmadian M, *et al*. Networked wireless microsystem for remote gastrointestinal monitoring. In: Digest of Technical Papers for the Twelfth International Conference on Solid-State Sensors, Actuators and Microsystems 2003; 1184-1187.
9. Cote GL, Lec RM, Pishko MV. Emerging biomedical sensing technologies and their applications. IEEE Sensors Journal 2003; 3(3):251-266.
10. Gardner JW, Bartlett PN. A brief history of electronic noses. Sensors and Actuators B 1994; 18(1-3):211-220.
11. Shams QA, Moniuszko M, Ingham JC. Applying MEMS technology to field, flight and space deployable systems. In: Proceedings of the Nineteenth International Congress on Instrumentation in Aerospace Simulation Facilities 2001; 246-255.
12. Seidl D, Hellweg M, Calvache M, Gomez D, Ortega A, Torres R, *et al*. The multiparameter station at Galeras Volcano (Colombia): concept and realization. Journal of Volcanology and Geothermal Research 2003; 125(1-2):1-12.
13. Shen LP, Mohri K, Uchiyama T, Honkura Y. Sensitive acceleration sensor using amorphous wire SI element combined with CMOS IC multivibrator for environmental sensing. IEEE Transactions on Magnetics 2000; 36(5):3667-3669.
14. Torfs T, Sanders S, Winters C, Brebels S, Hoof CV. Wireless network of autonomous environmental sensors. In: Proceedings of IEEE Sensors 2004; 923-926.
15. Iddan G, Meron G, Glukhovsky A, Swain P. Wireless capsule endoscopy. Nature 2000, 405:725-729.
16. Lucent-Medical-System. System and method to determine the location and orientation of an indwelling medical device. US patent #6,263,230. USA, 2001.
17. Hierlemann A, Baltes H. CMOS-based chemical microsensors. Analyst 2003; 128:15-28.

18. Auroux PA, Koc Y, deMello A, Manz A, Day PJR. Miniaturised nucleic acid analysis. Lab on a Chip 2004; 4(6):534-546.

19. Chirwa LC, Hammond PA, Roy S, Cumming DRS. Electromagnetic radiation from ingested sources in the human intestine between 150MHz and 1.2GHz. IEEE Transactions on Biomedical Engineering 2003; 50(4):484-492.

20. Madou MJ, Cubicciotti R. Scaling issues in chemical and biological sensors. In: Proceedings of the IEEE 2003; 91(6):830-838.

21. Wang L, Johannessen EA, Hammond PA, Cui L, Reid SWJ, Cooper JM, *et al.* A programmable microsystem using system-on-chip for real-time biotelemetry. IEEE Transactions on Biomedical Engineering 2005; 52(7):1251-1260.

22. Beeley JM, Mills C, Hammond PA, Glidle A, Cooper JM, Wang L, *et al.* All-digital interface ASIC for a QCM-based electronic nose. Sensors and Actuators B 2004; 103(1-2):31-36.

23. Graf M, Barrettino D, Zimmermann M, Hierlemann A, Baltes H, Hahn S, *et al.* CMOS monolithic metal-oxide sensor system comprising a microhotplate and associated circuitry. IEEE Sensors Journal 2004; 4(1):9-16.

24. Hammond PA, Ali D, Cumming DRS. Design of a single-chip pH sensor using a conventional 0.6μm CMOS process. IEEE Sensors Journal 2004; 4(6):706-712.

25. Cotton PB, Williams CB. Practical gastrointestinal endoscopy. Oxford: Blackwell Scientific, 1980.

26. Lee R. Manual of small animal diagnostic imaging. Gloucester: British Small Animal Veterinary Association, 1995.

27. Gladman LM, Gorard DA. General practitioner and hospital specialist attitudes to functional gastrointestinal disorders. Alimentary Pharmacology and Therapeutics 2003; 17(5):651-654.

28. Mackay RS, Jacobson B. Endoradiosonde. Nature 1957; 179:1239-1240.

29. Farrar JT, Zworykin VK, Baum J. Pressure-sensitive telemetering capsule for study of gastrointestinal motility. Science 1957; 126:975-976.

30. Casper RA. Medical capsule device actuated by radio-frequency (RF) signal. US patent #5,170,801. USA, 1992.

31. Clear NJ, Milton A, Humphrey M, Henry BT, Wulff M, Nichols DJ, *et al.* Evaluation of the Intelisite capsule to deliver theophyline and frusemide tablets to the small intestine and colon. European Journal of Pharmaceutical Sciences 2001; 13:375-384.

32. Johannessen EA, Wang L, Cui L, Tang TB, Ahmadian M, Astaras A, *et al.* Implementation of multichannel sensors for remote biomedical measurements in a microsystems format. IEEE Transactions on Biomedical Engineering 2004; 51(3):525-535.

33. Weitschies W, Karaus M, Cordini D, Trahms L, Breitkreutz J, Semmler W. Magnetic marker monitoring of disintegrating capsules. European Journal of Pharmaceutical Sciences 2001; 13:411-416.

34. Phee L, Accoto D, Menciassi A, Stefanini C, Carrozza MC, Dario P. Analysis and development of locomotion devices for the gastrointestinal tract. IEEE Transactions on Biomedical Engineering 2002; 49(6):613-616.

35. Guo S, Sugimoto K, Fukuda T, Oguro K. A new type of capsule medical micropump. In: Proceedings of the Nineteenth IEEE/ASME Conference on Advanced Intelligent Mechatronics 1999; 55-60.
36. Sendoh M, Ishiyama K, Arai KI. Fabrication of magnetic actuator for use in a capsule endoscope. IEEE Transactions on Magnetics 2003; 39(5):3232-3234.
37. Skidmore M. Mini transmitter saves babies. NASA Aerospace Technology Innovation 1999; 7(1):7-8.
38. Pandolfino JE, Ritcher JE, Ours T, Jason RN, Guardino M, Chapman J, *et al.* Ambulatory esophageal pH monitoring using a wireless system. American Journal of Gastroenterology 2003; 98(4):740-749.
39. Sasaki Y, Hada R, Nakajima H, Fukada S, Munakata A. Improved localizing method of radiopill in measurement of entire gastrointestinal pH profiles: colonic luminal pH in normal subjects and patients with Crohn's disease. American Journal of Gastroenterology 1997; 92(1):114-118.
40. Press AG, Hauptmann IA, Fuchs B, Fuchs M, Ewe K, Ramadori G. Gastrointestinal pH profiles in patients with inflammatory bowel disease. Alimentary Pharmacology and Therapeutics 1998; 12:673-678.
41. Wolff HS. The radio pill. New Scientist 1961; 261:419-421.
42. Watson BW, Kay AW. Radio-telemetering with special reference to the gastrointestinal track. In: Biomechanics and Related Bio-Engineering Topics 1965; 111-127.
43. Meldrum SJ, Watson BW, Riddle HC, Brown RL, Sladen GE. pH profile of gut as measured by radiotelemetry capsule. British Medical Journal 1972; 104-106.
44. Colson RH, Watson BW, Fairclough PD, Walker-Smith JA, Campbell CA, Bellamy D, *et al.* An accurate, long term pH sensitive radio pill for ingestion and implantation. Biotelemetry and Patient Monitoring. 1981; 8(4):213-227.
45. Evans DF, Pye G, Clark AG, Dyson TJ, Hardcastle JD. Measurement of gastrointestinal pH profiles in normal ambulant human subjects. Gut 1988; 29:1035-1041.
46. Swain P. Wireless capsule endoscopy. Gut 2003; 52(Supplement IV):48-50.
47. Kramer K, Kinter LB. Evaluation and applications of radiotelemetry in small laboratory animals. Physiological Genomics 2003; 13:197-205.
48. Peters G. A new device for monitoring gastric pH in free-ranging animals. American Journal of Physiology. 1997; 273(3):748-753.
49. Enemark JMD, Peters G, Jørgensen RJ. Continuous monitoring of rumen pH – a case study with cattle. Journal of Veterinary Medicine A 2003; 40:62-66.
50. ISO 11785 and ISO 3166.
51. Powers RA. Batteries for low power electronics. Proceedings of the IEEE 1995; 83(4):687-693.
52. Recommendation 70-30 relating to the use of short range devices (SRD). In: Proceedings of the European Conference of Postal and Telecommunications Administrations (CEPT), Tromso, Norway, CEPT/ERC/TR70-03, 1997.
53. Aydin N, Arslan T, Cumming DRS. A direct-sequence spread-spectrum communication system for integrated sensor microsystems. IEEE Transactions on Information Technology in Biomedicine 2005; 9(1):4-12.

54. Nikolaidis I, Barbeau M, Kranakis E. Ad-Hoc, Mobile, and Wireless Networks: Lecture Notes in Computer Science 3158. Heidelberg: Springer-Verlag, 2004.
55. Park HJ, Park IY, Lee JW, Song BS, Won CH, Cho JH. Design of miniaturized telemetry module for bi-directional wireless endoscopes. IEICE Transactions on Fundamentals of Electronics, Communications and Computer Sciences 2003; E86-A(6):1487-1491.
56. Gardner JW. Microsensors – principles and applications. Chichester: John Wiley and Sons, 1994.
57. Muller T, Brandl M, Brand O, Baltes H. An industrial CMOS process family adapted for the fabrication of smart silicon sensors. Sensors and Actuators A: Physical 2000, 84(1-2):126-133.
58. Tea NH, Milanovic V, Zincke CA, Suehle JS, Gaitan M, Zaghloul ME, *et al.* Hybrid postprocessing etching for CMOS-compatible MEMS. Journal of Microelectromechanical Systems 1997, 6(4):363-372.
59. Guillou DF, Santhanam S, Carley LR. Laminated, sacrificial-poly MEMS technology in standard CMOS. Sensors and Actuators A: Physical 2000; 85(1-3):346-355.
60. Krüger C, Pfeffer JG, Mokwa W, vom Bögel G, Günther R, Schmitz-Rode T, *et al.* Intravascular pressure monitoring system. In: Proceedings of the European Conference on Solid-State Transducers 2002; M3C1.
61. Dudaicevs H, Kandler M, Manoli Y, Mokwa W, Speigel E. Surface micromachined pressure sensors with integrated CMOS read-out electronics. Sensors and Actuators A: Physical 1994; 43(1-3):157-163.
62. Hagleitner C, Hierlemann A, Lange D, Kummer A, Kerness N, Brand O, *et al.* Smart single-chip gas sensor microsystem. Nature 2001; 414:293-296.
63. DeBusschere BD, Kovacs GTA. Portable cell-based biosensor system using integrated CMOS cell-cartridges. Biosensors and Bioelectronics. 2001; 16:543-556.
64. Simpson ML, Sayler GS, Applegate BM, Ripp S, Nivens DE, Paulus MJ, *et al.* Bioluminescent-bioreporter integrated circuits form novel whole-cell biosensors. Trends in Biotechnology 1998; 16:332-338.
65. Zhang Y, Ma KK, Yao Q. A software/hardware co-design methodology for embedded microprocessor core design. IEEE Transactions on Consumer Electronics 1999; 45(4):1241-1246.
66. Kundert K, Chang H, Jefferies D, Lamant G, Malavasi E, Sendig F. Design of mixed-signal systems-on-a-chip. IEEE Transactions on Computer Aided Design of Integrated Circuits and Systems 2000; 19(12):1561-1571.
67. Sjoholm S, Lindh L. VHDL for designers. Prentice Hall, 1997.
68. Toftgard J, Hornsleth SN, Andersen J. Effects on portable antennas of the presence of a person. IEEE Transactions on Antennas and Propagation 1993; 41(6):739-746.
69. Okoniewski M, Stuchly MA. A study of the handset antenna and human body interaction. IEEE Transactions on Microwave Theory and Techniques 1996; 44(10):1855-1864.
70. Scanlon WG, Evans NE. Radiowave propagation from a tissue-implanted source at 418MHz and 916.5MHz. IEEE Transactions on Biomedical Engineering 2000; 47(4):527-534.

71. Ahmadian M, Flynn BW, Murray AF, Cumming DRS. Data transmission for implantable microsystem using magnetic coupling. In: IEE Proceedings on Communications 2005; 152(2):247-250.
72. Roundy S, Steingart D, Frechette L, Wright P, Rabaey J. Power sources for wireless sensor networks 2004; LNCS 2920:1-17.
73. United Kingdom regulations for adults exposed to radiation in the band from 10MHz to 60MHz, http://www.who.int/docstore/peh-emf/EMFStandards/who-0102/Worldmap5.htm
74. Chovelon JM, Jaffrezic-Renault N, Cros Y, Fombon JJ, Pedone D. Monitoring of ISFET aging by impedance measurements. Sensors and Actuators 1991; 3(1):43-50.
75. Sibbald A, Whalley PD, Covington AK. A miniature flow-through cell with a four-function CHEMFET integrated circuit for simultaneous measurements of potassium, hydrogen, calcium and sodium ions. Analytica Chimica Acta 1984; 159:47-62.
76. Grisel A, Francis C, Verney E, Mondin G. Packaging technologies for integrated electrochemical sensors. Sensors and Actuators B 1989; 17:285-295.
77. Gràcia I, Cané C, Lora-Tamayo E. Electrical characterisation of the aging of sealing materials for ISFET chemical sensors. Sensors and Actuators B 1995; 24(1-3):206-210.
78. Münoz J, Bratov A, Mas R, Abramova N, Domínguez C, Bartrolí J. Planar compatible polymer technology for packaging of chemical microsensors. Journal of the Electrochemical Society 1996; 143(6):2020-2025.
79. Matsuo T, Esashi M. Methods of ISFET fabrication. Sensors and Actuators 1981; 1:77-96.
80. Bratov A, Münoz J, Dominguez C, Bartrolí J. Photocurable polymers applied as encapsulating materials for ISFET production. Sensors and Actuators B 1995; 24:823-825.
81. Hammond PA, Cumming DRS. Encapsulation of a liquid-sensing microchip using SU-8 photoresist. Microelectronic Engineering 2004; 73-74:893-897.
82. Tsukada K, Sebata M, Miyahara Y, Miyagi H. Long-life multiple-ISFETs with polymeric gates. Sensors and Actuators 1989; 18:329-336.
83. Fleischer M, Ostrick B, Pohle R, Simon E, Meixner H, Bilger C, *et al.* Low-power gas sensors based on work-function measurement in low-cost hybrid flipchip technology. Sensors and Actuators B 2001; 80:169-173.

12

Conclusions and Future Outlook

Guang-Zhong Yang

With demographic changes associated with the aging population and the increasing number of people living alone, the social and economic structure of our society is changing rapidly. Older adults of 65 and above already constitute one-fifth of the total population, and it is expected this will continue to grow to over 750 million by 2025. In almost all countries, longevity has given rise to expensive age-related disabilities and diseases. With the steady decline of the ratio of workers to retirees, a fundamental change to the way that we care for the aging population is inevitable. In the UK, for example, there are around 400,000 places in residential care homes and another 180,000 beds in nursing care homes. On top of this, more than 400,000 households receive home care, of which 30% require more than ten hours and/or six visits per week. The cost of such long-term care was around £11.1 billion in 1995 and it is projected to rise by 30% by 2010, and a further 35% by 2021, driven by the 20% increase in demand for residential care over the next twenty years and the shift towards more intensive support.

In a population consisting of several vulnerable groups, such as those with chronic disease and the elderly, the need for effective individualised health monitoring and delivery is the primary motivation for the development of *Body Sensor Networks* (BSNs). The concept of the BSN is an important ingredient for the future development of pervasive healthcare because technological developments in sensing and monitoring devices will not only change chronic disease management in a home or community setting, but also reshape the general practice of clinical medicine.

Although extensive measurement of biomechanical and biochemical information is available in almost all hospitals, this diagnostic and monitoring utility is generally limited to brief time intervals and perhaps unrepresentative physiological states such as being supine and sedated, or via artificially introduced exercise tests. Transient abnormalities, in this case, cannot always be captured. For example, many cardiac diseases are associated with episodic rather than continuous abnormalities such as transient surges in blood pressure, paroxysmal arrhythmias or induced or spontaneous episodes of myocardial ischaemia. These abnormalities are important but their timing cannot be predicted and much time and effort is wasted in trying to capture an "episode" with controlled monitoring. Important and even life threatening disorders can go undetected because they occur only infrequently and may never be recorded objectively.

High risk patients, such as those with end-stage ischaemic heart disease or end-stage myocardial failure, often develop life threatening episodes of myocardial ischaemia or ventricular arrhythmia. These episodes, if reliably detected, would lead to better targeting of potentially life-saving but expensive therapies. With the emergence of miniaturised mechanical, electrical, biochemical and genetic sensors, there is likely to be a rapid expansion of biosensor applications over the next decade with a corresponding significant reduction in size and cost. This will facilitate continuous wireless monitoring, initially of at-risk patients but eventually screening an increasing proportion of the population for abnormal conditions.

The ultimate aim of the BSN is to provide a truly personalised monitoring platform that is pervasive, intelligent, context-aware, and invisible to the patient, thereby avoiding activity restriction or behaviour modification. It is expected that the concept of BSNs will attract a range of applications, from monitoring of patients with chronic disease and care for the elderly, to general well-being monitoring and performance evaluation in sports. To promote its widespread use, there are a number of technical challenges that need to be tackled. These include the need for better sensor design, MEMS integration, biocompatibility, power source miniaturisation, low power wireless transmission, context awareness, secure data transfer, and integration with therapeutic systems.

In the last two decades, we have seen rapid advances in both chemical and biosensor development which have resulted in an improved understanding of microelectrode and ultramicroelectrode behaviour at micrometre and submicrometre spatial resolutions, as well as gaining us further insight into the electrode reaction mechanism and kinetics. They have permitted new techniques in protein engineering and molecular biology that allow the production of new mutant enzymes with improved stability, higher activity and controlled protein immobilisation. The emergence of new biological sensing elements such as catalytic antibodies and aptamers represents a new paradigm in biosensor design that has offered unprecedented selectivity. For the practical deployment of BSNs, recent developments in microfluidics, especially in microneedle array technology, hold out great potential for wearable, minimally invasive sampling of extracellular fluid. These developments are likely to fundamentally alter the way we apply biomeasurements in future.

In terms of implantable sensing, many of the issues associated with the extension of biosensor technology from *in vitro* to *in vivo* applications have long been appreciated, and a number of practical solutions are starting to emerge. Whether the vision of a long-term implantable sensor will ever be realised will depend on advances across a range of disciplines, many of which are discussed in this book. These include the development of perpetual powering of BSN devices through effective energy scavenging. Body-powered applications, however, remain a great challenge because of the low specific power levels at low frequencies, therefore substantial progress will be required in reducing power requirements before such solutions become feasible, particularly for wireless data transmission. As discussed, the need for integrated power conditioning circuits with energy scavenging also encourages a trend towards intelligent energy modules, possible incorporating several forms of scavenging as well as storage, power conditioning, and power management electronics.

The search for an effective power source for powering the BSN node is intimately related to the future hardware design of the BSN. In a BSN with limited bandwidth and power constraints, the conventional method of data acquisition and analogue-to-digital data conversion with signal processing taking place after transmission is no longer optimal. BSNs are a prime candidate for bio-inspired local processing to take place at the sensor front-end before transmission. This processing could include spatial and temporal averaging for drift and failure tolerance. The key principle of bio-inspired engineering in this application area is that biology does not often deal in absolute values, but in relative changes from a given norm.

From a sensor data processing and inferencing point of view, the development of the BSN has introduced a whole range of challenging research issues in pattern recognition and machine learning. The pursuit of low power, miniaturised, distributed sensing whilst the patient is under natural physiological conditions has also imposed significant challenges on integrating information from what is often heterogeneous, incomplete, and error-prone sensor data. In practice, it is therefore desirable to rely on sensors with redundant or complementary data to maximise the information content and reduce both systematic and random errors.

One important aspect of the book is the introduction of bio-inspired concepts both for hardware design and for developing software components that possess the *self-** properties of autonomic sensing. We have discussed the use of artificial neural networks for performing context-aware sensing, and the use of autonomic principles of self-healing, self-organisation, and self-protection for developing BSNs with effective fault tolerance and self-protection. Due to the inherent complexities involved in managing a large number of wireless sensors, bio-inspired sensing and networking is an important area of study for future BSN research.

In academic research and development, it is difficult to find a field that is greatly diversified, and yet still brings many challenges and innovations to each of the disciplines involved. The development of BSNs, however, is a striking exception. As we have stated previously, there is little doubt that for the development of the BSN, a panoply of technologies will need to be combined in new and previously unsuspected ways. However, the rewards for success, in terms of the quality and duration of life in the case of many of those suffering from chronic conditions, will be substantial.

A
Wireless Sensor Development Platforms

Benny Lo and Guang-Zhong Yang

A.1 Introduction

The development of BSN has greatly benefited from the rapid advances in *Wireless Sensor Networks* (WSNs) in recent years. Since the introduction of the concept of WSN and ubiquitous computing, a large number of development platforms have been introduced [1, 2]. During 2004 and 2005, for example, more than twenty different WSN hardware platforms have been proposed. Figure A.1 demonstrates this trend since 1998 with some of the WSN hardware platforms illustrated. A more detailed list of some of the major WSN platforms is provided in Table A.2. It must be pointed out, however, that this table is by no means exhaustive and unintentional omission is likely. As stated in Chapter 1, the general design and requirements for BSNs can be different from typical WSN applications. However, many of the WSN development platforms can be modified to cater for general BSN applications. Thus far, most research in BSN is based on general WSN platforms, particularly for wireless communication, data fusion and inferencing. This appendix outlines the system architecture of common WSN platforms and provides an overview of some of the main hardware components involved.

A.2 System Architecture

The system architectures of all WSN development platforms are relatively similar, and they mainly consist of six major components as depicted in Figure A.2:

- *Processor* – The brain of the sensor node
- *Wireless Communication* – wireless link between sensor nodes
- *Memory* – External storage for sensor readings or program images
- *Sensor Interface* – Interface with sensors and other devices

- *Power Supply* – Power source of the sensor node
- *Operating System* – Software for managing the network and resources

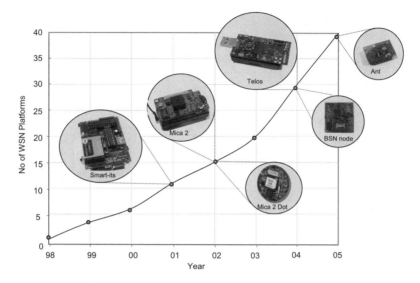

Figure A.1 Examples of WSN hardware platforms developed in recent years.
(**See colour insert**.)

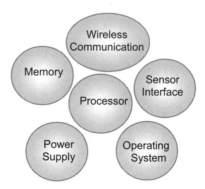

Figure A.2 The main components of common WSN nodes.

A.2.1 Processor

Most WSN platforms are based on COTS (*Commercial Off-The-Shelf*) components,
and the development of WSN depends extensively on the rapid advancement of microprocessors. For instance, the Mica2 node has about eight times the memory ca-

pacity and communication bandwidth as its predecessor, the Rene node developed in 1999, whilst maintaining the same power consumption and cost [3]. Unlike common *Personal Computing* (PC) applications, WSN requires much less processing power due to tight constraints on size and power consumption. For this reason, WSN platforms are mainly based on low power *Microcontroller Units* (MCUs) rather than using conventional PC-type processors. Depending on the amount of processing required, a number of WSN platforms are based on mobile computing MCUs, which are designed for *Personal Digital Assistants* (PDAs). Recently, significant effort has also been invested by a number of manufacturers in developing processors with integrated radio transceivers.

A.2.1.1 Low Power MCU

For many WSNs, node size and power consumption are often considered more important than the actual processing capacity because in most applications the amount of processing involved is relatively light. Among currently available MCUs, Atmel ATmega 128L and *Texas Instruments* (TI) MSP430 are the most popular processors used in WSN platforms due to their integrated low power design, multiple sensor interfaces, and widely available developing tools.

The Atmel ATmega 128L processor is an 8-bit microcontroller designed for embedded applications. With a 16MHz clock, the ATmega processor can deliver up to 16MIPS (*Million Instructions Per Second*) processing power [4]. Equipped with a relatively large programmable flash memory (128KB), 8-channels of 10-bit ADCs (*Analogue-to-Digital Converters*) and low operating voltage (2.7V), the ATmega processor has been widely used in many WSN platforms. They include the Mica motes [5], BTnode [6], Nymph [7], AquisGrain, DSYS25 [8], Ember [9] and Fleck [10]. Figure A.3 illustrates the Atmel processor used for the Mica2 mote.

Figure A.3 Atmel processor on a Mica2 mote.

The TI MSP430 processor is an ultra low power 16-bit RISC (*Reduced Instruction Set Computer*) processor [11]. Compared to the Atmel processor, which consumes 8mW in active mode and 75µW in sleep mode, the MSP430 requires much less power in both active (3mW) and sleep modes (15µW). It also has a much lower operating voltage of 1.8V [12]. With its wide range of interconnection functions, 12-bit ADCs and the serial programming interface, the MSP430 has been widely adopted in platforms such as Telos [5], Tmote sky [13], eyesIFXv2 [14], Ant [15], Pluto [16] and BSN node [17]. Figure A.4 illustrates the MSP430 processor used on the Telos node.

Figure A.4 MSP430 processor used on a Telos node.

A.2.1.2 Mobile Computing MCUs

For certain WSN applications, such as those for video based monitoring, relatively high processing power is required and typical MCUs will not be able to process the acquired sensor data in real-time [18]. To balance power consumption and processing performance, a few of the WSN platforms have used ARM processors designed for handheld devices such as the PDAs. For example, two of the early WSN platforms, AWAIRS 1 [19] and μAMPS [20], both used the Intel StrongARM SA-100 processor. This is a 32-bit RISC processor with operating frequency up to 206Mhz. The newly announced Sun Spot system also uses a 32-bit ARM processor, which is a new processor with lower power consumption and smaller size [62]. The recently proposed iMote2 [21] uses the new Intel PXA 271 processor operated at a frequency up to 416MHz. With its adjustable operating frequency function, the PXA processor can be configured for low power application as well as computationally demanding tasks. In addition, the PXA processor provides a wide range of connectivity including SD (*Secured Digital*), which allows iMote2 to use SD as an extended memory storage or existing SD-based wireless connections such as Bluetooth and Wireless LAN.

A.2.1.3 Integrated Processor with Radio Transceiver

Recently, *System-on-Chip* (SoC) Processors or integrated processors with radio transceivers are becoming popular due to their miniaturised size and simplicity in board design. One exemplar is the Berkeley Spec, which is a custom-made processor with an 8-bit RISC processor combined with a FSK (*Frequency-Shift Keying*) transceiver [3]. By integrating the radio transceiver, the size of the Spec is only 5mm^2. Since then, several commercial integrated MCUs have been introduced, and WSN platforms such as iMote1 [22], MITes [23], RFRAIN [24], RISE [25] and uPart0140ilmt [26] are designed with this type of MCU to facilitate size reduction. In addition to the radio transceiver, recent research has taken a further step to miniaturise the WSN node by integrating sensors and power supply onto the MCUs. One example of this is the SAND (*Small Autonomous Network Devices*) platform proposed by Philips research, which is a multiple stacked die SoC. It consists of sensors, signal processing, data storage, power management, low bit-rate wireless communication and a power source [27]. Similar 3D stacked sensor system has been proposed in IMEC's Human++ project and Match-X's VDMA system [28, 29].

A.2.2 Wireless Communication

Amongst all of the elements required, wireless communication is the most power-demanding component of WSNs. This often accounts for more than half the overall power consumption of a sensor node [30]. Parallel to the development of micro-power radio transceivers, such as the Pico radio [31], existing research in WSNs has been focused on developing energy-efficient protocols and routing strategies. The three main components of wireless communication are the radio transceiver, antenna, and communication protocols.

A.2.2.1 Radio Transceiver

Most of the early WSN platforms, such as WeC [32], Rene [33], Dot [5], SpotOn [34, 35] and CENS Medusa MK-2 [36], used RFM TR1000 as the radio transceiver due to its low power, small size, and hybrid design. Subsequent platforms, such as Mica2 [5] and Mica2Dot [5], are based on the Chipcon CC1000 chipset because it provides a more reliable FSK modulation, selectable modulating frequency, and low power architecture. Figure A.5 shows a Mica2Dot with a CC1000 transceiver. Other platforms, such as BTnode, iBadge [37] and iMote1, are based on Bluetooth radio transceivers in order to achieve high bandwidth data communication and ease of integration with other Bluetooth based mobile devices.

Figure A.5 Chipcon CC1000 on a Mica2Dot.

Since the introduction of the IEEE 802.15.4 standard for WSNs, most of the new platforms are using the Chipcon CC2420 wireless transceiver, which is one of the first IEEE 802.15.4 compatible chipsets. Although the power consumption of the CC2420 (19.7mA) is higher than the CC1000 (7.4mA), the CC2420 can deliver 250kbps, which is 6.5 times higher than its predecessor (38.4kpbs) [38, 39]. In addition, it also incorporates an AES-128 (*Advanced Encryption Standard*) hardware encryption engine and the IEEE 802.15.4 MAC (*Medium Access Control*) function, which enables it to act as a co-processor to handle all packet communications. Compared to the CC1000 and RFM TR1000, where the MCU has to handle all of the MAC layer communications, the CC2420 significantly reduces the computational demands on the MCU, thus leading to significant overall performance improvement on the sensor node. As such, most of the recent WSN platforms developed are based on the CC2420, such as Telos, Tmote sky, MicaZ, Pluto, iMote2, Sun Spot, and BSN node. Figure A.6 highlights the CC2420 on a Telos node.

Figure A.6 Chipcon CC2420 mounted on a Telos node.

A.2.2.2 Antenna

To achieve a balance between flexibility, miniaturisation and performance, four different types of antenna have been adopted in current WSN platforms.

PCB Antenna

To minimise the manufacturing cost and facilitate the modular design of sensor nodes, PCB (*Printed Circuit Board*) antennas have been widely used in embedded systems such as RFID (*Radio Frequency Identification*) applications. Telos and Tmote sky are designed with PCB antennas printed on the circuit board. Figure A.7 illustrates a prototype BSN node with a PCB antenna. Although printing the antenna onto the circuit board could reduce the manufacturing cost, the performance of PCB antenna is relatively poor due to the dielectric loss caused by poor circuit board material, and noise induced by coupling with other lossy components and circuit board traces [40]. For this reason, additional mounting points for external antennas are usually provided on these designs.

Figure A.7 A BSN node with PCB antenna.

Wire Antenna

An alternative to minimising the cost without losing the performance is to use a simple wire antenna. Wire antenna is often in loop, monopole or dipole forms. Since the wire antenna is located above the circuit board, it performs far better than the PCB antenna [40]. For BSN research, a wire antenna is preferred due to its simplicity and flexibility. Mica2, Mica2Dot and BSN nodes are all designed with wire antennas. Figure A.8 shows a BSN node with a $\lambda/2$-dipole antenna. However, as wire antennas require manual soldering, mass production in large quantities can be problematic.

Figure A.8 A BSN node with a dipole antenna.

Ceramic Antenna

To simplify manufacturing complexity and facilitate size reduction whilst maintaining the quality of wireless communication, ceramic antennas are often used in WSN platforms. Ceramic antennas are usually optimised for certain frequencies and they are much smaller in size than wire and PCB antennas. For example, ProSpeckz [41] and Ant are integrated with ceramic antennas designed for Bluetooth (or 2.4GHz) devices. Figure A.9 shows a BSN node with an alternative ceramic antenna configuration.

Figure A.9 A BSN node with a ceramic antenna.

External Antenna

To enhance the coverage of the sensor node, external antennas are also used in WSN platforms. As external antennas are often isolated from noise induced by the circuit board, a significantly higher performance can be achieved in practice [40]. Due to the size of the external antenna and its associated mounting, they are not practical for wearable applications. Figure A.10 demonstrates a prototype BSN node with an external antenna, illustrating the comparative size of the antenna and the BSN node itself.

Figure A.10 A prototype BSN node with an external antenna.

A.2.2.3 Communication Protocol

Depending on the hardware and the operating systems used, early WSN platforms are often developed with proprietary communication protocols. The introduction of the IEEE 802.15.4 standard enables the standardisation of communication between WSN platforms. Since then, most recent WSN platforms have adopted this standard as the basis for their wireless communication protocol, examples of which include Telos, Ember[9], MicaZ, Pluto, iMote2, Tmote sky, XYZ node[42], ProSpeckz, and BSN node.

Due to the broad range of WSN applications, the 802.15.4 standard defines only the two lower layers, *i.e.*, the MAC and physical layers of the communication protocol. This enables the design of application-specific protocols. For example, Zigbee is built to the 802.15.4 standard and is designed to ease the inter-operation between different devices. Zigbee specifies all the protocol layers required for forming a wireless network and it also provides an interface for application development. Although none of the existing platforms has fully adopted the Zigbee specification as yet due to its recent introduction, there has been strong interest in pursuing this both from the industrial and research communities. Further details on 802.15.4 and Zigbee can be found in Chapter 5.

A.2.3 Memory

Since limited *Random Access Memory* (RAM) is provided by MCUs, most WSN platforms are designed with an external flash memory or *Electrically Erasable Programmable Read-Only Memory* (EEPROM). Due to the non-volatile nature of the EEPROM, it is used in most embedded systems for storing configuration information because it does not require power to retain the stored data. It is also used as an immediate storage for sensor readings. For instance, in order to perform feature extraction or filtering of the sampled data, the EEPROM can be used as a processing buffer for these algorithms. Another use of the EEPROM is for storing program images. For example, Deluge, a TinyOS network-programming tool, uses the external flash memory to store the program image in order to enable dynamic reprogramming of the sensor nodes.

A.2.4 Sensor Interface

To enable practical application development, most WSN platforms offer analogue and digital sensor interfaces.

A.2.4.1 Analogue Interface

Sensors such as simple photo resistors and thermistors, or more complex gyroscope and condenser microphones, generally provide analogue readings. Most WSN platforms are equipped with ADC interfaces for data sampling and acquisition. For instance, the Atmel Atmega128L MCU has an eight-channel 10-bit ADC that can sample at a rate up to 15.4ksps (*kilo-samples per second*), whereas the TI MSP430 microcontroller has a 12-bit ADC which provides a higher precision reading than that of the Atmel processor. In addition to ADCs, some platforms are equipped with *Digital-to-Analogue Converter* (DAC) for controlling sensors or actuators.

A.2.4.2 Digital Interface

Since analogue readings are prone to voltage drift caused by the depletion of the battery power, sensors such as the 2-axis accelerometer ADXL202 [43] provide direct digital readings to maintain their precision. As sensor data is relatively small in size, serial communication is mainly used for interfacing with digital sensors, and the three most commonly used serial communication protocols are I^2C, SPI and UART.

Inter-Integrated Circuit Bus (I^2C)

I^2C is a patented interface protocol developed by Philips Semiconductors [44]. It is a half-duplex, synchronous, master-bus requiring only two signal wires for data (SDA) and clock (SCL), respectively [45]. With its master-slave design, I^2C allows a master device to communicate with multiple slaves by using a 7-bit or 10-bit address. Figure A.11 shows the basic configuration of an I^2C based master-slave system and Figure A.12 illustrates how the data is being transferred on the I²C bus. As can be seen from the timing diagram, the data is transferred with the *Most Signifi- cant Bit* (MSB) first, with a transfer sequence of address followed by data. The communication is controlled by the master, and the start and stop bit are sent by the master to initiate and terminate the data transmission. With the start and stop delim- iters, the I²C bus allows more than one byte of data to be transmitted after sending the address byte. Due to its simplicity and high-speed serial protocol, the I²C bus is widely used for interfacing between MCUs and other chipsets. For example, the humidity sensor SHT11 provided by Telos uses the I²C protocol as the communica- tion interface [46].

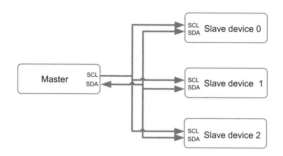

Figure A.11 Interface diagram of I²C.

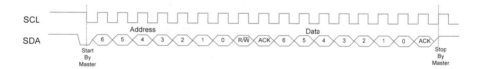

Figure A.12 The timing diagram of I²C.

Serial Peripheral Interface (SPI)

SPI is a synchronous serial bus developed by Motorola. Similar to the I²C bus, SPI is based on a multiple master/slave protocol. However, instead of using addresses to identify different devices, the master uses the chip select (CS) wire to establish the communication with a specific slave. In addition, SPI enables full duplex commu- nication up to 1Mbps with its three-wire interface, MOSI (*Master Out, Slave In*), MISO (*Master In, Slave Out*), and the *Serial Clock* (SCLK). Figure A.13 shows a sample connection diagram of a SPI-based system where the master device (usually a microcontroller) uses the CS signals to activate specific slave devices and the MOSI, MISO and SCLK signals for data transmission. Figure A.14 is the timing diagram of the SPI interface of a slave device and demonstrates how the commands and data are being transferred between the master and slave devices. As indicated in the timing diagram, data is shifted with the MSB first, and each bit is shifted out

(MISO) and sampled (MOSI) on the falling and rising edge of the SCLK signal respectively. Due to its high-speed full-duplex protocol, SPI is often used as the interface protocol between MCUs and radio transceivers. Although most sensors do not require full-duplex communications, for platforms that do not have built-in ADCs, an external ADC is required to interface with an analogue sensor. Most ADC chipsets, such as the AD7816 10-bit ADC [47], offer the SPI interface.

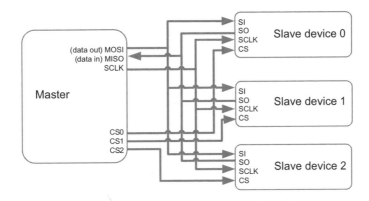

Figure A.13 SPI interface diagram.

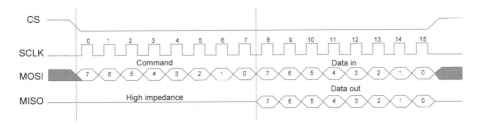

Figure A.14 SPI timing diagram.

Universal Asynchronous Receiver/Transmitter (UART)

UART, often known as the TTL (*Transistor-Transistor Logic*) version of the RS232[48], used to be the most commonly used interface between computers and peripherals before the introduction of *Universal Serial Bus* (USB). For embedded systems, however, it still remains the main communication mechanism. Unlike I^2C and SPI, UART is a peer-to-peer full-duplex network protocol, as shown in Figure A.15. Since UART is designed for asynchronous transmission, no clock signal is used and devices are expected to operate at the same frequency (*i.e.* baud rate). Figure A.16 illustrates the format of the UART protocol where start and stop bits are used to signal the beginning and end of the transmission. The data is shifted with the LSB (*Least Significant Bit*) first. UART is often used for device level communications and it allows long distance connections. For sensing applications, UART has been used for more advanced sensors such as SpO$_2$ sensors and vision-based sensors [18].

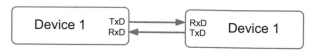

Figure A.15 UART interface.

Start
bit

Stop
bit

Figure A.16 UART data communication.

Table A.1 summarises the main features of the three protocols mentioned above. Most of the WSN platforms provide interfaces for all three protocols.

Table A.1 Serial interface protocol comparison.

Protocol	Bandwidth	Type	Duplex	Sync/Async
I^{2}C	3.4Mbps	Peer	Half	Sync
SPI	1Mbps	Multi-master	Full	Sync
UART (RS232)	115.2kbps	Multi-master	Full	Async

A.2.4.3 Integrated Sensors

To simplify application development, many WSN platforms have built-in sensors such as humidity, temperature, acceleration, and photo sensors. With integrated sensor board design, the hardware platform can be made more compact and immune to the noise induced by cables and connectors. However, integrating sensors on the hardware platforms can limit the general use of the platforms as different applications may have varying sensor requirements.

A.2.5 Power Supply

Currently, power supply is the main determining factor for the size and lifetime of the WSN hardware. Similarly to mobile phones, the battery or alternative power source is often the largest single component of WSN nodes. To miniaturise the sensor node, a number of alternatives have been proposed. For example, Berkeley's Golem Dust is designed to use an external laser beam to power up the sensor [49]. By relying on the external energy source, the size of the Golem Dust is only 11.7m^3, which is significantly smaller than typical WSN hardware. However, due to the line of sight constraint, this will be difficult to extrapolate to BSN applications.

Other power sources, such as the scavenging of power from temperature gradients or movement have been proposed. Due to the relatively high power requirement for radio transmission, batteries still remain the main source of power for current WSN platforms. Among different battery technologies, Li-ion battery is the most popular choice for WSN hardware because of its high power density. Although zinc-air batteries have a higher energy capacity than that of Li-ion batteries, the high rate of power drains from the current radio transceivers limits the direct use of zinc-air battery for WSN. This situation, however, is likely to change due to the emergence of new ultra-low power radio transceiver designs [50]. To simplify sensor deployment, most WSN platforms have integrated batteries. They include the Mica2Dot, Telos, MITes, BTNode, Smart-its [51], and SpotON. Primary batteries are often the preferred choice, due to their higher power densities. For BSN applications, however, rechargeable batteries may be preferable as the batteries can be enclosed in the sensor casing. As discussed in Chapter 6, the development of new power scavenging techniques coupled with ultra-low power BSN designs could provide significant improvements in BSN design in the next few years.

A.2.6 Operating System

As is currently the case with personal computers, the *Operating System* (OS) is one of the key elements for the development of WSNs and BSNs. According to Moore's law, transistor density on a die doubles every two years. This has contributed to the rapid growth in computer technologies and more powerful PCs are introduced almost every six months. Likewise, the WSN hardware is expected to evolve as rapidly as that of the PC.

Due to limited resources in WSN hardware, conventional embedded OS, such as Embedded Microsoft XP or Embedded Linux, are not suitable for WSN platforms. Thus far, a number of application-driven programming environments have been proposed. These include the Context Toolkit developed for the Smart-its project [52], the application development library for the RFRAIN platform, and μOS for μAMPs [53].

Another application-driven OS, Palos (*Power Aware Lightweight OS*) for iBadge and CENS Medusa MK-2, was designed originally for the Smart Kindergarten project in monitoring pupils [54]. Like a scaled down OS, Palos provides hardware abstraction and a light-weight pseudo-real-time multitasking. Other developments include a C-based *Multithreaded Operating System* (MOS) which was proposed in the MANTIS project [7], and a C-based operating system SOS proposed recently by UCLA for heterogeneous sensor deployments [55]. Contiki is another C-based OS which supports preemptive multithreading based on an event-driven kernel [63].

In addition to C-based systems, Java virtual machine has also been adopted for WSN. These include the MagnetOS [64], and "Squawk VM" proposed by Sun which is a small J2ME virtual machine designed for resource constrained wireless sensors [62].

Table A.2 Wireless sensor network development platforms.

Platforms	CPU	Clock (MHz)	RAM/Flash /EEPROM	Radio Transceiver	BW (kbps)	Freq. (MHz)	OS	Year	Organisation
WeC	Atmel AT90LS8535	4	512/8K/32K	RFM TR1000	10	916.5	TinyOS	1998	UC Berkeley
Rene 1	Atmel AT90LS8535	4	512/8K/32K	RFM TR1000	10	916.5	TinyOS	1999	UC Berkeley
AWAIRS 1	Intel StrongArm SA1100	59-206	1M/4M	Conexant RDSSS9M	100	900	MicroC/OS	1999	Rockwell
μAMPS	Intel StrongARM SA1100	59-206	1M/4M	National LMX3162	1000	2400	μOS	1999	MIT
Rene 2	Atmel Atmega 163	8	1K/16K/32K	RFM TR1000	10	916.5	TinyOS	2000	UC Berkeley
Dot	Atmel Atmega 163	8	1K/16K/32K	RFM TR1000	10	916.5	TinyOS	2000	UC Berkeley
Mica	Atmel Atmega 128L	4	4K/128K/512K	RFM TR1000	40	916.5	TinyOS	2001	UC Berkeley
BT node*	Atmel Atmega 128L	8	4K/128K/4K	ZV4002 BT/ CC1000	1000	2400	TinyOS	2001	ETH
SpotON	Dragonball EZ	16	2M/2M	RFM TR1000	10	916.5		2001	Intel
Smart-its (Lancaster)	PIC18F252	8	3K/48K/64K	Radiometrix	64	433	Smart-its	2001	Lancaster
Smart-its (Teco)[51]	ATMega 103L	4	4K/128K	Ericsson BT	1000	2400	Smart-its	2001	Teco
Mica2*	Atmel Atmega 128L	8	4K/128K/512K	Chipcon CC1000	38.4	900	TinyOS	2002	UC Berkeley/ Crossbow
Mica2Dot*	Atmel Atmega 128L	4	4K/128K/512K	Chipcon CC1000	38.4	900	TinyOS	2002	UC Berkeley/ Crossbow
iBadge	Atmel Atmega103L	6	4K/128K	Ericsson BT	1000	2400	Palos	2002	UCLA
CENS Medusa MK2	Atmel ATMega128L/ Atmel AT91FR4081	4/ 40	4K/32K 136K/1M	TR1000	10	916	Palos	2002	UCLA
iMote1	Zeevo ZV4002 (ARM)	12-48	64K/512K	Zeevo BT	720	2400	TinyOS	2003	Intel
U3 [60]	PIC18F452	0.031-8	1K/32K/256	CDC-TR-02B	100	315	Pavenet	2003	U Tokyo
Spec	8-bit AVR-like RISC core	4-8	3K	FSK Transmitter	100		TinyOS	2003	UC Berkeley
RFRAIN	CC1010 (8051)	3-24	2K/32K	Chipcon CC1010	76.8	0.3 -1000	RFRAIN Libraries	2003	MIT
Nymph	Atmel Atmega128L	4	4K/128K/512K	Chipcon CC1000	38.4	900	Mantis	2003	U Colorado

Platforms	CPU	Clock (MHz)	RAM/Flash /EEPROM	Radio Transceiver	BW (kbps)	Freq. (MHz)	OS	Year	Organisation
Telos*	TI MSP430F149	8	2K/60K/512K	Chipcon CC2420	250	2400	TinyOS	2004	UC Berkeley/Moteiv
MicaZ*	Atmel Atmega 128L	8	4K/128K	Chipcon CC2420	250	2400	TinyOS	2004	Crossbow
CIT Sensor Node [61]	PIC16F877	20	368/8K	Nordic nRF903	76.8	868	TinyOS	2004	Cork Institute of Technology
BSN node	TI MSP430F149	8	2K/60K/512K	Chipcon CC2420	250	2400	TinyOS	2004	Imperial College
MiTes	nRF24E1 (8051)	16	512/4K	Nordic nRF24E1	1000	2400	-	2004	MIT
AquisGrain	Atmel Atmega128L	4	4K/128K/512K	Chipcon CC2420	250	2400	-	2004	Philips Research
RISE	CC1010 EM (8051)	3-24	2K/32K	CC1010 EM	76.8	0.3-1000	TinyOS	2004	UCR
Particle2/29*[26]	PIC 18F6720	20	4K128K/512K	RFM TR1001	125	868.35	Smart-its	2004	Teco
Pluto	TI MSP430F149	8	4K/60K/512K	Chipcon CC2420	250	2400	TinyOS	2004	Harvard
DSYS25	Atmel Atmega 128	4	4K/128K	Nordic nRF2401	1000	2400	TinyOS	2004	UCC
EnOcean TCM120	PIC18F452	10	1.5K/32K/256	Infineon TDA 5200	120	868	TinyOS	2005	Helmut Schmidt University
eyesIFXv2	TI MSP430F1611	8	10K/48K	Infineon TDA5250	64	868	TinyOS	2005	TU Berlin
iMote2	Intel PXA 271	13-104	256K/32M	CC2420	250	2400	TinyOS	2005	Intel
uPart0140ilmt*	rfPIC16F675	4	64/1K	rfPIC16F675	19.2	868	Smart-it	2005	Teco
Tmote sky*	TI MSP430F1611	8	10K/48K/1M	Chipcon CC2420	250	2400	TinyOS	2005	UC Berkeley/Moteiv
Ember RF Module*	Atmel Atmega 128L	8	4K/128K	Ember 250	250	2400	EmberNet	2005	Ember
XYZ sensor node	OKI ML67Q500x (ARM/THUMB)	1.8-57.6	4K/256K/512K	Chipcon CC2420	250	2400	SOS	2005	Yale
Ant*	TI MSP430F1232	8	256/8K	Nordic nRF24AP1	1000	2400	Ant	2005	Dynastream Innovation Inc.
ProSpeckz	Cypress CY8C2764	12	256/16K	Chipcon CC2420	250	2400	Speckle net	2005	U Edinburgh
Fleck	Atmega128L	8	4K/128K/512K	Nordic 903	76.8	902-928	TinyOS	2005	CSIRO
Sun Spot	Atmel AT91FR40162S	75	256K/2M	CC2420	250	2400	Squawk VM (Java)	2005	Sun Labs

For most research-based OS developments, the open source approach is preferred so as to facilitate the development of WSN applications. However, commercial hardware platforms often use proprietary middleware, such as Ant, SmartMesh [56], SensiNet [57] and Agile-Link [58]. Thus far, the most widely adopted OS is the event-based TinyOS. With its open source initiative and ever growing TinyOS community, an increasing number of industrial- and research-based platforms are now supported by TinyOS. They include MicaZ, RISE, DSYS25, eyesIFXv2, EnOcean TCM120 [59], iMote2, Fleck and BSN node. A more detailed list is provided in Table A.2.

A.3 Conclusions

In this chapter, we have reviewed the common WSN development platforms that have emerged in recent years. As has been mentioned earlier, the hardware design of WSN nodes is a rapidly changing field and this appendix is only intended to outline some of the main efforts involved in this field. Although many of the WSN hardware platforms can be adapted for BSN applications, due to the specific requirements and constraints imposed by BSNs, a dedicated environment for BSN research and development is required. The platform will be expected to cater for both wearable and ambient sensing, with specific emphases on low-power design, context awareness, and high bandwidth wireless communication. As a development tool, the platform should also address the ease of integration of different sensor designs. In the next chapter, we will discuss the hardware and programming environment of the BSN development kit designed for this purpose.

References

1. WsLAN summary: WP1000 – state of the art. SINTEF, http://www.sintef.no/units/informatics/projects/wslan/WP1000-summary.pdf, 2004.
2. Weiser M. Hot topics: ubiquitous computing. Computer 1993; 26(10):71-72.
3. Hill J, Horton M, Kling R, Krishnamurthy L. The platforms enabling wireless sensor networks. Communications of the ACM 2004; 47(6):41-46.
4. Atmel 8-bit AVR microcontroller with 128K bytes in-system programmable flash. Atmel, http://www.atmel.com/dyn/products/product_card.asp?part_id=2018, 2004.
5. Polastre J, Szewczyk R, Sharp C, Culler D. The mote revolution: low power wireless sensor network devices. In: Proceedings of Hot Chips 16: A Symposium on High Performance Chips, Stanford University, 2004.
6. Beutel J. BTnodes – a distributed environment for prototyping *ad hoc* networks. ETH, http://www.btnode.ethz.ch, 2005.
7. Abrach H, Bhatti S, Carlson J, Dai H, Rose J, Sheth A, *et al*. MANTIS: system support for MultimodAl NeTworks of *In-situ* Sensors. In: Proceedings of the Second ACM International Conference on Wireless Sensor Networks and Applications, San Diego, CA, USA, 2003; 50-59.

8. Barroso A, Benson J, Murphy T, Roedig U, Sreenan C, Barton J, *et al.* The DSYS25 sensor platform. In: Proceedings of the ACM Conference on Embedded Networked Sensor Systems (Demo Abstract), Baltimore, Maryland, USA, 2004.

9. Ember JumpStart developer kit proof-of-concept prototype for embedded wireless applications. Ember Corporation, http://www.ember.com/downloads/pdfs/ember-jumpstart.pdf, 2005.

10. Corke P. Wireless sensor network devices. CSIRO, http://www.ict.csiro.au/page.php?cid=87, 2005.

11. MSP430x13x, MSP430x14x, MSP430x14x1 Mixed Signal Microcontroller. Texas Instruments, http://focus.ti.com/docs/prod/folders/print/msp430f149.html, 2004.

12. Polastre J, Szewczyk R, Culler D. Telos: enabling ultra-low power wireless research. In: Proceedings of the Fourth International Conference on Information Processing in Sensor Networks, Los Angeles, CA, 2005.

13. Tmote sky Ultra low power IEEE 802.15.4 compliant wireless sensor module. Moteiv, http://www.moteiv.com/products/docs/tmote-sky-datasheet.pdf, 2005.

14. Handzisk V, Lentsch T. The eyesIFX platform. http://www.tinyos.net/ttx-02-2005/platforms/ttx2005-eyesIFX.ppt, 2005.

15. The wireless personal area network. Dynastream Innovations Inc., http://www.thisisant.com, 2005.

16. Welsh M. CodeBlue: wireless sensor networks for medical care. Harvard University, http://www.eecs.harvard.edu/~mdw/proj/codeblue/, 2005.

17. Yang GZ, Lo B, Wang J, Rans M, Thiemjarus S, Ng J, *et al.* From sensor networks to behaviour profiling: a homecare perspective of intelligent building. In: Proceedings of the IEE Seminar for Intelligent Buildings, UK, 2004.

18. Lo B, Wang J, Yang GZ. From imaging networks to behavior profiling: ubiquitous sensing for managed homecare of the elderly. In: Proceedings of the Third International Conference on Pervasive Computing, Munich, 2005; 101-104.

19. Agre JR, Clare LP, Pottie GJ, Romanov NP. Development platform for self-organizing wireless sensor networks. In: Proceedings of SPIE AeroSense 1999.

20. μ-Adaptive multi-domain power aware sensors. Massachusetts Institute of Technology, http://www-mtl.mit.edu/researchgroups/icsystems/uamps/, 2004.

21. Nachman L. Imote2. http://www.tinyos.net/ttx-02-2005/platforms/ttx05-imote2.ppt, 2005.

22. Next-Generation Intel® Mote. Intel, http://www.intel.com/research/exploratory/motes.htm

23. Tapia EM, Marmasse N, Intille SS, Larson K. MITes: wireless portable sensors for studying behavior. In: Proceedings of Ubicomp 2004: Ubiquitous Computing, Nottingham, UK, 2004.

24. Laibowitz M. The RF random access integrated node. MIT Media Lab, http://www.media.mit.edu/resenv/rfrain/

25. Nodes project: a novel design for embedded sensor networks. Computer Science and Engineering Department, University of California Riverside, http://www.cs.ucr.edu/%7Esneema/nodes/rise.html

26. Selection of Smart-Its particle prototypes, sensor and add-on boards. Teco, http://particle.teco.edu/devices/devices.html

27. Wolf R, Viegers T, Roosmalen F. The key to ambient intelligence lies in the packaging. Philips Research, http://www.research.philips.com/password/archive/23/pw23_sip.html, 2005.

28. IMEC's Human++ Solutions. IMEC, http://www.imec.be/human, 2004.

29. Europe exploring new technology. Small Times Media, http://www.smalltimes.com/smallstage/images/ST_europe_Special_Section.pdf

30. Shnayder V, Hempstead M, Chen B, Allen GW, Welsh M. Simulating the power consumption of large-scale sensor network applications. In: Proceedings of the Second ACM Conference on Embedded Networked Sensor Systems, Baltimore, MD, 2004; 188-200.

31. Ammer MJ, Sheets M, Karalar T, Kuulusa M, Rabaey J. A low-energy chip-set for wireless intercom. In: Proceedings of the Annual ACM IEEE Design Automation Conference, Anaheim, CA, 2003; 916-919.

32. Welsh M, Malan D, Duncan B, Fulford-Jones T. Wireless sensor networks for emergency medical care. http://www.eecs.harvard.edu/~mdw/talks/ge-codeblue.pdf, 2004.

33. Hill JL. System architecture for wireless sensor networks. University of California, Berkeley, PhD Thesis, 2003.

34. Hightower J, Vakili C, Borriello G, Want R. Design and calibration of the SpotON *ad hoc* location sensing system. University of Washington, Seattle, WA, 2001.

35. Hightower J, Borriello G, Want R. SpotON: an indoor 3D location sensing technology based on RF signal strength. University of Washington, UW CSE 2000-02-02, 2000.

36. Sensor node platforms. Center for Embedded Networked Sensing, University of California Los Angeles, http://deerhound.ats.ucla.edu:7777/portal/page?_pageid=54,43973,54_43974:54_43977&_dad=portal&_schema=PORTAL&_calledfrom=2

37. Sung P, Locher I, Savvides A, Srivastava MB, Chen A, Muntz R, *et al.* Design of a wearable sensor badge for smart kindergarten. In: Proceedings of the Sixth International Symposium on Wearable Computers, Seattle, WA, 2002; 231-238.

38. CC1000 single chip very low power RF transceiver. Chipcon, CC1000 Datasheet, 2005.

39. CC2420 2.4 IEEE 802.15.4/ZigBee-ready RF transceiver. Chipcon, CC2420 Datasheet, 2005.

40. Callway EH. Wireless sensor networks architectures and protocol. Internet and Communications, Boca Raton: CRC Press LLC, 2004.

41. Arvind D, Bates CA. Counting and colouring in Specknets. In: Proceedings of the Second International Workshop on Body Sensor Networks, London, UK, 2005; 32-35.

42. Lymberopoulos D, Savvides A. XYZ: A motion-enabled, power aware sensor node platform for distributed sensor network applications. In: Proceedings of

the Fourth International Symposium on Information Processing in Sensor Networks, Los Angeles, CA, 2005.

43. Low-Cost ±2 g dual-axis accelerometer with duty cycle output. Analog Device, http://www.analog.com/en/prod/0,,764_800_ADXL202,00.html, 2000.

44. The I²C-BUS specification version 2.1. Philips Semiconductors, 9398 393 40011, 2000.

45. Patrick J. Serial protocols compared. http://www.embedded.com/showArticle .jhtml?articleID=9900637, 2002.

46. SHT1x humidity and temperature sensmitter. Sensirion, http://www.farnell.com/datasheets/29118.pdf, 2002.

47. Single and 4 channel, 9us, 10-Bit ADCs with on-chip temperature sensor. Analog Devices, http://www.analog.com/en/prod/0,,764814AD7816%2C00.html, 2004.

48. Interface between data terminal equipment and data circuit-terminating equipment employing serial binary data interchange. Electronics Industries Association Engineering Department, EIA232E, 1991.

49. Warneke B. Smart dust. http://www-bsac.eecs.berkeley.edu/archive/users/warneke-brett/SmartDust/index.html, 2004.

50. Best M, Burdett A, Castor-Perry K, Chan T, Dawkins M, McDonagh D, *et al.* An ultra-low power 1V wireless transceiver suitable for body sensor networks. In: Proceedings of the Second International Workshop on Wearable and Implantable Body Sensor Networks, London, 2005; 75-77.

51. Gellersen H, Kortuem G, Schmidt A, Beigl M. Physical prototyping with Smart-Its. IEEE Pervasive Computing 2004; 3(3):74-82.

52. Malm EJ, Kaartinen J, Vildjiounaite E, Alahuhta P. Smart-it context architecture. European Commission, E1SU00075, 2003.

53. Sinha A, Chandrakasan AP. Operating system and algorithm techniques for energy scalable wireless sensor networks. In: Proceedings of the Second International Conference on Mobile Data Management 2001.

54. Savvides A, Srivastava M. A distributed computation platform for wireless embedded sensing. In: Proceedings of the International Conference on Computer Design, Freiburg, Germany, 2002.

55. Han CC, Kumar R, Shea R, Kohler E, Srivastava M. A dynamic operating system for sensor networks. In: Proceedings of the Third International Conference on Mobile Systems, Applications, and Services, Seattle WA, 2005; 163-176.

56. SmartMesh. Dust Networks, http://www.dustnetworks.com/products/platform .shtml, 2005.

57. Sensinet mesh networking for wireless sensors. Sensicast Systems, Inc., http://www.sensicast.com/downloads/SensiNet%20Networking%20Protocol%20Brochure.pdf, 2005.

58. Software development kit for 900MHz Agile-Link. MicroStrain, http://www.microstrain.com/sdk.aspx, 2005.

59. Körber HJ, Wattar H, Scholl G, Heller W. Embedding a Microchip PIC18F452 based commercial platform into TinyOS. In: Proceedings of the Workshop on Real-World Wireless Sensor Networks, Stockholm, Sweden, 2005.

60. Kawahara Y, Minami M, Morikawa H, Aoyama T. Design and implementation of a sensor network node for ubiquitous computing environment. In: Proceedings of the IEEE Fifty-Eighth Vehicular Technology Conference, Orlando, USA, 2003; 5:3005-3009.
61. Lynch C, Reilly FO. PIC-based TinyOS implementation. In: Proceedings of the Workshop on Real-World Wireless Sensor Networks, Stockholm, Sweden, 2004.
62. A Sun Research Lab Project Sun Spot System: Turning Vision into Reality. http://research.sun.com/spotlight/SunSPOTSJune30.pdf, 2005.
63. Dunkels A, Gronvall B, Voigt T. Contiki - a Lightweight and Flexible Operating System for Tiny Networked Sensors. In: Proceedings of the First IEEE Workshop on Embedded Networked Sensors 2004 (IEEE EmNetS-I), Tempa, Flordia, USA, 2004.
64. Barr R, Bicket J, Dantas D, Du B, Kim T, Zhou B, Sirer E. On the need for system-level support for ad-hoc and sensor networks. SIGOPS Operating Systems Review, 36(2), 2002.

B

BSN Development Kit and Programming Guide

Benny Lo and Guang-Zhong Yang

B.1 Introduction

Although there are a number of context-aware sensing platforms currently available [5, 6], the incorporation of different physiological sensors often requires hardware modification. To facilitate research and development in BSNs, a general purpose BSN hardware platform, called the BSN node, has been designed at Imperial College London. Figure B.1 illustrates the basic design of the BSN node and its relative size. With its stackable design, different types of sensors can be easily incorporated. The BSN node follows the IEEE 802.15.4 standards and is suitable for most continuous, context-aware physiological monitoring applications. The BSN node is supported by TinyOS and can be seamlessly integrated with other networks that have TinyOS supported hardware. In this appendix, we will describe the software and hardware components of the BSN development kit so that interested readers can use this as the basis for putting together some example BSN applications.

B.2 BSN Architectural Design

For the design of the BSN node, several major criteria have been considered:

- Miniaturisation
- Low cost
- Low power consumption
- Wireless communication
- Secured and reliable protocol
- Intelligent
- Expandable

- Flexible
- Programmable
- Ease of sensor integration

Figure B.1 BSN node. (**See colour insert.**)

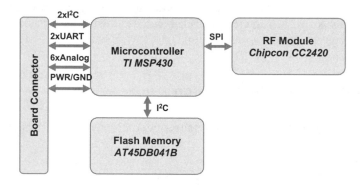

Figure B.2 The system architecture of the BSN node.

Instead of integrating all the components onto a single board, the BSN node is designed with only the processor, transceiver and memory on the main board and with other customisable components on stackable daughter boards. The basic structure of the BSN node is depicted in Figure B.2, illustrating the interconnection through the main board connector.

B.2.1 Microcontroller

The BSN node uses the *Texas Instrument* (TI) MSP430F149 16-bit ultra low power RISC processor with 60K+256B of flash memory and 2KB of RAM [7]. As mentioned in Appendix A, the TI *Microcontroller* (MCU) can operate with 280µA in active mode (1MHz 2.2V), 1.6µA in standby mode, and 0.1µA in off mode (RAM retention). To optimise the performance and power consumption of the MCU, the MSP430 provides different modes of operation and modular disabling/enabling controls. In addition, it provides an extensive number of interfaces for integrating with other devices. They include two USART (*Universal Synchronous/Asynchronous Receive/Transmit*) interfaces and 48 configurable I/Os. For interfacing with analogue devices, a fast 12-bit A/D converter is included in the MCU for handling up to eight different analogue signals. Figure B.3 schematically illustrates the functional blocks of the MSP430F149 processor.

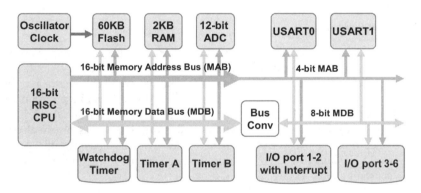

Figure B.3 The functional block diagram of MSP430F149.

B.2.1.1 RISC Processor

The CPU of the MSP430 has a 16-bit RISC architecture and sixteen registers are defined for reduced instruction execution. All operations (other than program flow instruction) are performed as register operations [8], and the MSP430 instruction set consists of 51 instructions with three formats (dual operands, single operands and relative jump) and seven address modes, and each instruction can operate on word or byte data.

To balance processing performance and power consumption, the MSP430 provides one active mode and five selectable low-power operation modes as indicated in Table B.1. In addition, the MSP430 provides three clock signals for different peripherals and the CPU, *i.e.*,

- ACLK: auxiliary clock; mainly used for peripheral modules.
- MCLK: master clock; the system clock used by the CPU.
- SMCLK: sub-main clock; used by peripheral modules.

Table B.1 MSP430 operation modes.

Modes	CPU	MCLK	SMCLK	DCO's DC generator	ACLK	Current draw (µA) at 3V, 1MHz
Active mode (AM)	1	1	1	1	1	340
Low-power mode 0 (LPM0)	0	0	1	1	1	70
Low-power mode 1 (LPM1)	0	0	1	1	1	70
Low-power mode 2 (LPM2)	0	0	0	0	1	17
Low-power mode 3 (LPM3)	0	0	0	0	1	2
Low-power mode 4 (LPM4)	0	0	0	0	0	0.1

1 : enabled, 0 : disabled

B.2.1.2 Flash Memory

The MSP430F149 has 60KB+256B of flash memory and the memory is partitioned into main and information sections, where the main memory has two or more 512B segments, and the information section has two 128B segments. The segments are further divided into 64B blocks. The MSP430 can be programmed by using the JTAG (*Joint Test Action Group*) port, the UART serial interface, and the *Bootstrap Loader* (BSL). In addition, the MSP430 processor can also be programmed directly via its CPU which enables dynamic updating of the program and the flash memory. To program the flash memory, the processor has to have a constant supply voltage of 2.7V or above.

B.2.1.3 Digital Input/Output (I/O)

The MSP430 processor provides six digital (I/O) ports, P1-P6, where each port has eight I/O pins, and each pin can be individually configured and set. In addition, ports P1 and P2 have interrupt capability, as indicated in Figure B.3. To reduce the power consumption, unused I/O pins should be configured as output ports and left unconnected on the circuit board.

B.2.1.4 Analogue to Digital Converter (ADC)

The MSP430 uses a 12-bit ADC module, called ADC12, which implements a 12-bit SAR (*Successive-Approximation-Register*) core, reference generators and a sixteen word conversion-and-control buffer. The conversion-and-control buffer allows up to sixteen independent ADC samples to be converted and stored without any CPU intervention. In addition, it contains two selectable voltage references (1.5V and 2.5V). The ADC12 converts the analogue signal with respect to the reference to digital values (N_{ADC}) ranging from 0 to 0FFFh based on the following formula:

$$N_{ADC} = 4095 \frac{V_{in} - V_{R-}}{V_{R+} - V_{R-}} \tag{B.1}$$

where V_{in} = analogue input, V_{R-}=GND, and V_{R+} = 1.5/2.5V. By setting the input multiplexer, eight external (A0 to A7) and four internal analogue signals (Ve_{REF+}, V_{REF+}/Ve_{REF}, temperature sensor, ($AV_{cc}-AV_{ss}$)/2) can be selected as the channels for conversion. The conversion function for the on-chip temperature sensor is as follows:

$$V_{TEMP} = 0.00355(TEMP_C) + 0.986 \tag{B.2}$$

where $TEMP_C$ represents the temperature in Celsius. The ADC12 is optimised for low power operation, and will be automatically disabled when no conversion is in process.

B.2.1.5 Timers

The MSP430 provides two 16-bit timers/counters, Timer_A and Timer_B, as shown in Figure B.3. Timer_A is an asynchronous timer/counter with four operating modes: Stop (timer is halt), Up (counts from 0 to a predefined limit), Continuous (counts from 0 to 0FFFFh) and Up/Down (counts from 0 to the predefined limit, then back down to 0). Similarly, Timer_B is also an asynchronous timer with four operating modes. However, the length of the Timer_B is programmable to be 8, 10, 12 or 16 bits

B.2.1.6 Universal Synchronous/Asynchronous Receive/Transmit (USART)

The MSP430F149 provides two USART ports, and each can be configured to either as an UART or a SPI (*Serial Peripheral Interface*).

- *UART Mode (SYNC bit is cleared)*
  In UART mode, two pins are used, UTXD (transmit) and URXD (receive), for transmitting and receiving data. It supports 7- or 8-bit data communication with even, odd, or non-parity. The baud rates can be set from 1200 to 115.2 kbps (*kilo-bits-per-second*).

- *SPI Mode (SYNC bit is set)*
  In SPI mode, three- or four-pin SPI mode is supported, where SIMO (*Slave-In, Master-Out*), SOMI (*Slave-Out, Master-In*), UCLK (*SPI clock*) and STE (*Slave Transmit Enable*) pins are used for data communication. It can be configured to 7- or 8-bit data size, and in either master or slave modes. The STE signal enables multiple slaves and masters on the bus, where it specifies which master/slave to gain control of the bus.

B.2.1.7 Hardware Multiplier

A hardware multiplier is provided by the MSP430. Instead of being integrated into the CPU, the hardware multiplier is designed to be a peripheral module where multiplications are performed independently without the processor's intervention. The multiplier supports signed/unsigned multiplication and accumulation, as well as 16×16, 16×8, 8×16 and 8×8 bit operations.

B.2.1.8 Watchdog Timer

A 16-bit watchdog timer is provided by the MSP430 for resetting the MCU when the application program fails. Based on the preset time interval, the MCU will be reset if the timer expires. In addition, the module can be used as an interval timer when the watchdog function is not required.

B.2.2 Radio Transceiver

To cater for the high bandwidth required for physiological sensors and ease the interface with other wireless sensors, the Chipcon CC2420 is used for the BSN node. As a IEEE 802.15.4 compliant chipset, the Chipcon CC2420 allows the BSN node to communicate with other wireless sensor networks.

B.2.2.1 Serial Interface

The CC2420 provides a 4-wire SPI interface (with pins SI, SO, SCLK and CSn) for interfacing with MCUs. It has been configured as a slave device which relies on the processor to initiate the communication. There are a total of 50 registers for setting and configuring the CC2420, and the internal RAM of the CC2420 can also be accessed through the SPI interface.

- *Register Access*
  Among the fifty registers, thirty-three registers are 16-bit configuration and status registers, fifteen are 16-bit command strobes, and two are 8-bit registers for accessing the transmit and receive FIFO buffers. Registers are addressed by a 6-bit address. Figure B.4 shows the format of the CC2420 SPI

command for accessing the registers where a read/write bit and a RAM/register bit are included in addition to the 6-bit address. After each SPI command, 2-bytes of data are transmitted, as illustrated in the timing diagram shown in Figure B.5.

Figure B.4 CC2420 Register access command.

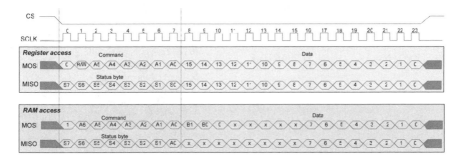

Figure B.5 Timing diagram of the CC2420 SPI interface.

- *Status Byte*
  As shown in Figure B.5, a status byte is returned on the MISO pin during the transfer of the register/RAM access command. The status byte indicates the status of the CC2420 and it consists of six status bits, as shown in Table B.2.

- *Command Strobes*
  Command strobes are single-byte instructions of CC2420, which enables the user to initiate and terminate functions of the chipset. Fifteen command strobes are provided by CC2420, and are listed in Table B.3.

- *RAM Access*
  The internal 368 byte RAM can be accessed through the SPI interface, as shown in Figure B.5. Unlike register access, in RAM access mode, data is read and written one byte at a time and a 9-bit address is used for accessing the RAM. As indicated in Figure B.5, apart from the 7-bit address (A0-A6) specified in the SPI command, 2-bits (B0-B1) of the second byte of the SPI data is used for accessing the RAM. As the

RAM is divided into three memory banks: TXFIFO (bank 0), RXFIFO (bank 1) and security (bank 2), the MSB (B0-B1) selects one of the three memory banks and the LSB (A0-A6) selects the address within the selected bank.

Table B.2 CC2420 status byte format.

Bit	Name	Description
7	-	Reserved
6	XOSC16M_STABLE	0: 16MHz crystal is not running 1: 16MHz crystal is running
5	TX_UNDERFLOW	0: No underflow 1: Underflow
4	ENC_BUSY	0: Encryption is idle 1: Encryption is busy
3	TX_ACTIVE	0: RF Transmission is idle 1: RF Transmission is active
2	LOCK	0: The PLL is out of lock 1: The PLL is in lock
1	RSSI_VALID	0: The RSSI value is not valid 1: The RSSI value is valid
0	-	Reserved

Table B.3 CC2420 command strobes.

Address	Register	Description
0x00	SNOP	No operation
0x01	SXOSCON	Turn on the crystal oscillator
0x02	STXCAL	Enable and calibrate frequency synthesizer for TX
0x03	SRXON	Enable RX
0x04	STXON	Enable TX after calibration
0x05	STXONCCA	If CCA indicates a clear channel: Enable calibration, then TX
0x06	SRFOFF	Disable RX/TX and frequency synthesizer
0x07	SXOSCOFF	Turn off the crystal oscillator and RF
0x08	SFLUSHRX	Flush the RX FIFO buffer and reset the demodulator
0x09	SFLUSHTX	Flush the TX FIFO buffer
0x0A	SACK	Send acknowledge frame with pending field cleared
0x0B	SACKPEND	Send acknowledge frame with pending field set
0x0C	SRXDEC	Start RXFIFO in-line decryption/authentication
0x0D	STXENC	Start TXFIFO in-line encryption/authentication without starting TX
0x0E	SAES	AES stand alone encryption strobe

- *FIFO Access*
  Like the RAM and registers, the built-in buffers, TXFIFO and RXFIFO, can also be accessed through the SPI interface. The TXFIFO is a write-only buffer, but data can be read back using RAM access. When data is written to the TXFIFO, the status byte will be returned which indicates if the buffer is underflow. On the other hand, the RXFIFO can be read and written; however, writing to RXFIFO should be restricted to debugging or security operations. As for RAM access, data is read and written one byte at a time.

B.2.2.2 IEEE802.15.4 Modulation Format

The IEEE 802.15.4 standard specifies the 2.4GHz *Direct Sequence Spread Spectrum* (DSSS) RF modulation. Figure B.6 shows the block diagram of the modulation and spreading function of the CC2420. Data is transmitted in the order of LSB first, except for security related fields where MSB is transmitted first. Each byte is divided into two symbols (4-bit each), and each symbol is then mapped to one of the sixteen predefined pseudo-random sequences (32 chips each). The chip sequence is transmitted at 2MChips/s with the order of least significant chip transmitting first. The *Offset-Quadrature Phase Shift Keying* (O-QPSK) modulation format is specified in the standard where each chip is shaped as a half-sine waveform, transmitted alternately in the I and Q channels with one half chip period first. Further details on different modulation formats can be found in [9] and [10].

Figure B.6 IEEE 802.15.4 modulation [9].

B.2.2.3 IEEE802.15.4 Frame Format

The IEEE 802.15.4 specifies the protocol for the physical and MAC layers for wireless sensor communication, and Figure B.7 details the frame format of the protocol used.

- *Synchronisation Header*
  The *Synchronisation Header* (SHR) consists of the preamble sequence and the *Start Frame Delimiter* (SFD). The preamble sequence is defined to be 4-bytes of 0x00 and the SFD has a value of 0xA7. In addition to the standard preamble length and SFD value, the CC2420 allows users to change the length and SFD for other non-IEEE compliant applications.

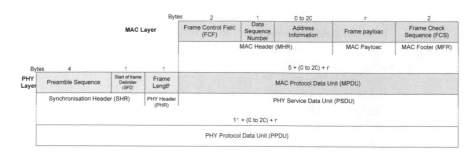

Figure B.7 IEEE 802.15.4 frame format [9].

- *Length Field*
  The 7-bit frame length indicates the number of bytes in the *MAC Protocol Data Unit* (MPDU), excluding the length of the field itself. It also includes the Message Integrity Code (MIC), if authentication is enabled.

- *MAC Protocol Data Unit*
  The MPDU consists of a *Frame Control Field* (FCF), data sequence number, address information, and frame payload and *Frame Check Sequence* (FCS), as shown in Figure B.7. The format of the FCF is illustrated in Figure B.8. As there is no hardware support for the data sequence number, the application software has to assign and verify the sequence number to the field.

Bits: 0-2	3	4	5	6	7-9	10-11	12-13	14-15
Frame type	Security Enabled	Frame Pending	Acknowledge request	Intra PAN	Reserved	Destination addressing mode	Reserved	Source addressing mode

Figure B.8 Format of the FCF [9].

- *Frame Check Sequence (FCS)*
  A 2-byte FCS is defined in the MAC footer to validate the packet. The FCS is calculated over the MPDU and is generated and verified automatically by hardware. The FCS polynomial is defined as follows [9]:

$$X^{16} + X^{12} + X^5 + 1 \tag{B.3}$$

As the FCS verification is handled by the hardware, the FCS will be attached to the packet automatically in transmit mode. In receive mode, the FCS will be verified by the hardware and will not be written to the RXFIFO.

B.2.2.4 RF Data Buffering

With the two FIFO, different transmit and receive modes are provided by the CC2420:

- Buffered transmit mode (TX_MODE 0)
- Buffered receive mode (RX_MODE 0)
- Unbuffered, serial mode

In buffered transmit mode, packets are buffered in the TXFIFO first before transmission. If too few bytes are written to the TXFIFO, the underflow alarm will be issued (the TX_UNDERFLOW status bit will be set) and the transmission will then be stopped automatically until the alarm is cleared (by issuing an SFLUSHTX command).

In buffered receive mode, received packets are first stored in the RXFIFO. If an overflow occurs, an alarm will be signalled (the FIFO pin will be low whilst the FIFOP pin is high) to the microcontroller, and the reception will be stopped immediately until the alarm is cleared (by issuing an SFLUSHRX command twice).

The unbuffered mode is designed for debugging and evaluation purposes. In unbuffered mode, a synchronised clock (250 kHz) is provided by the CC2420 through the FIFOP pin, and the FIFO pin is used as a data input/output channel. If the serial transmit mode is enabled (MDMCTRL1.TX_MODE=1), a synchronisation sequence is inserted at the beginning of each frame as in buffered mode. If serial receive mode is enabled (MDMCTRL1.RX_MODE=1), byte synchronisation is performed by setting the FIFOP clock to idle until a start of frame delimiter has been detected.

B.2.2.5 Address Recognition

The CC2420 provides a hardware address recognition function. If enabled, the address in the received packet will be checked against the following requirements:

- Frame type is valid
- If it is a beacon frame, the source PAN = macPANId, unless macPANId=0xFFFF
- If a destination PAN is included, the destination PAN = macPANId or 0xFFFF (broadcast)
- If a short destination address is included, it shall equal to macShortAddress or 0xFFFF(broadcast)
- If an extended destination address is included, it shall equal to the ExtendedAddress
- If only source addressing fields are included, the device has to be a PAN coordinator and the source PAN=macPANId

The CC2420 will disregard the frame if any of the requirements has not been met.

B.2.2.6 Acknowledge Frames

To comply with the IEEE 802.15.4 standard, the CC2420 provides a hardware acknowledgement function where, if enabled, an acknowledge frame is transmitted automatically whenever a valid packet is received (the address is recognised with the acknowledge request flag set and a valid CRC). Figure B.9 depicts the acknowledge frame format specified in the standard.

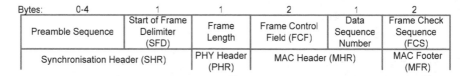

Bytes:	0-4	1	1	2	1	2
	Preamble Sequence	Start of Frame Delimiter (SFD)	Frame Length	Frame Control Field (FCF)	Data Sequence Number	Frame Check Sequence (FCS)
	Synchronisation Header (SHR)		PHY Header (PHR)	MAC Header (MHR)		MAC Footer (MFR)

Figure B.9 IEEE 802.15.4 acknowledge frame format [9].

For a beacon-based network, instead of sending the acknowledge frame immediately, the acknowledge frame will be sent after the first backoff slot boundary (~20 symbol periods), and the boundary is set by adjusting the SACK/SACKPEND register via the microcontroller. The timing diagrams for the packet acknowledgement of a beacon- and nonbeacon-based system are illustrated in Figure B.10.

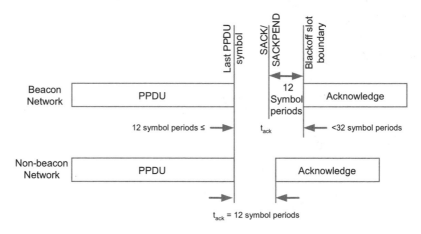

Figure B.10 IEEE 802.15.4 acknowledge frame timing [10].

B.2.2.7 MAC Security Operations (Encryption and Authentication)

The CC2420 encapsulated a hardware 128-bit AES-based encryption/decryption engine to provide the security operations required for IEEE 802.15.4 MAC [11].

To allow real-time secured MAC, the encryption/decryption processes are performed within the transmit and receive FIFO buffers on a frame basis.

Keys

The CC2420 provides two 128-bit security keys for encryption/decryption. Different keys can be selected for encryption and decryption. The keys are stored in the CC2420 RAM with the addresses 0x100 and 0x130.

Stand-Alone Encryption

Despite inline security operation, the CC2420 also provides standalone encryption with 128-bit plaintext and 128-bit keys. The plaintext is stored in a stand-alone buffer located in the RAM, and it will be overwritten by the cipher-text after encryption.

In-Line Security Operations

To provide a secured MAC, different modes of security functions are provided by the CC2420, which are CBC-MAC (*Cipher Block Chaining Message Authentication Code*), CTR (*Counter Mode Encryption*) and CCM (*Counter with CBC-MAC*). In the CBC-MAC mode, inline authentication is provided by the CC2420 hardware, where each message depends on the previous encrypted message and an MIC is attached to each message being transmitted. In the CTR mode, the CC2420 hardware encrypts a set of input blocks, called counters, which will be XORed with the plaintext. To handle real-time data transmission, the encryption and decryption are performed on FIFOs directly.

CCM is the combination of both CTR and CBC-MAC to provide encryption and authentication within an operation and with a single key. With the hardware encryption and decryption engine, the CC2420 can provide inline security operations on the MAC layer, and Table B.4 illustrates the time required for different security operations.

Table B.4 CC2420 security timing example [10].

Mode	Time (μs)
CCM	222
CTR	99
CBC-MAC	99
Stand-alone	14

B.2.2.8 RSSI/ Energy Detection

CC2420 has a built-in RSSI (*Received Signal Strength Indicator*) which indicates the strength of the RF power received. The RSSI Value (RSSI_VAL) is measured by averaging the signal reading over eight symbol periods (128μs), and it can be converted to RF power by using the following equation [10]:

$$P = RSSI\_VAL + RSSI\_OFFSET \quad [dBm] \tag{B.4}$$

where RSSI_OFFSET is approximately -45. In addition to testing radio coverage, the RSSI measurement can also be used for estimating the link quality to determine the quality of the received packet.

B.2.2.9 Clear Channel Assessment

To facilitate the implementation of the CSMA-CA function, the CC2420 provides a *Clear Channel Assessment* (CCA) signal which is based on thresholding the RSSI reading. If the channel is clear for at least eight symbol periods, the CCA signal will be triggered. The CC2420 can be set to transmit only when the channel is clear based on the CCA (by setting the STXONCCA register), in order to avoid collision.

B.2.2.10 Frequency and Channel Programming

The IEEE 802.15.4 specifies sixteen channels (11 to 26) within the 2.4GHz band, and the CC2420 can be programmed to any of these channels to avoid interference. The RF frequency of channel k is given by [9]:

$$Fc = 2405 + 5(k-11)MHz \quad k = 11,...,26 \tag{B.5}$$

To select to the specific channel k, the FSCTRL.FREQ register in the CC2420 should therefore be set to [10]:

$$FSCTRL.FREQ = 357 + 5(k-11) \tag{B.6}$$

B.2.2.11 Battery Monitor

As an internal voltage regulator is embedded in the CC2420, a battery monitor alarm is provided by the chip where a threshold can be set to trigger an alarm if the supply voltage is below the prescribed threshold. The battery status bit (BATTMON_OK) will be set to 0 (battery low) if the supply voltage is below the toggle voltage, which is obtained by [10]:

$$V_{toggle} = 1.25V \frac{72 - BATTMON\_VOLTAGE}{27} \tag{B.7}$$

where BATTMON_VOLTAGE is the 5-bit (0 to 31) control register for adjusting the alarm threshold.

B.2.2.12 Output Power Programming

The radio transmission power of the CC2420 can be programmed by adjusting the TXCTRL.PA_LEVEL register. Table B.5 lists the output power settings, the corresponding register value, and typical current consumption of the CC2420. Although the transmission power can be adjusted to lower the power consumption for short-range applications, the reception power (which usually consumes more power than data transmission) cannot be changed, which limits the usage of the power adjustment function.

Table B.5 CC2420 output power settings and typical current consumption [10].

PA_LEVEL	TXCTRL Register	Output Power (dBm)	Current Consumption (mA)
31	0xA0FF	0	17.4
27	0xA0FB	-1	16.5
23	0xA0F7	-3	15.2
19	0xA0F3	-5	13.9
15	0xA0EF	-7	12.5
11	0xA0EB	-10	11.2
7	0xA0E7	-15	9.9
3	0xA0E3	-25	8.5

B.2.2.13 Low Power Operation

In order to minimise the power consumption, the CC2420 should be powered down whenever wireless communication is not required. Further reduction can be achieved by disabling the internal voltage regulator; however, the interfacing circuit has to be redesigned, and registers and RAM configurations have to be reprogrammed.

B.2.3 Flash Memory

The BSN node is designed with an on-board flash memory for enabling high-speed sampling and dynamic program updates. For this purpose, a 4-megabit (or 512KB) Atmel AT45DB041B serial flash memory module is used [12]. The AT45DB041B is designed for low power operation, where it can operate at 2.7V and consumes only 4mA in typical read cycle and 2μA during standby mode. Although it requires relatively low power, the AT45DB041B can perform high speed read/write operations with a maximum clock speed of 20MHz, in conjunction with its two 264-bytes SRAM data buffers. In addition, the AT45DB041B provides an SPI interface for storing and retrieving the data. Figure B.11 illustrates the block diagram of the AT45DB041B chipset.

As shown in the diagram, the memory is organised as pages, and it consists of 2048 pages with 264 bytes in each page. As such, rather than byte operation, it supports page program operation, where memory is read and written in pages. To read/write a page from the flash memory, the MCU can choose to load the data onto the buffer first before accessing the memory or read/write from/to the flash memory directly. In addition to read/write operations, it also provides functions for erasing the memory, such as the page erase function for erasing a page and the block erase function for erasing a block of eight pages.

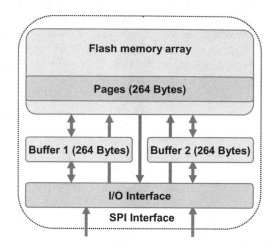

Figure B.11 AT45DB041B block diagram.

B.2.4 Board Connector

A stackable design is adopted for the BSN node; in other words, different sensor boards can be stacked on top of the node and different battery boards can be attached depending on the application requirements. To achieve this, two types of connectors are surface-mounted on each side of the board, and these are called the plug (female) and the socket (male), as shown in Figure B.12 (top). The plug is located on the top side of the board (where the LEDs are located), and the socket is on the other side of the node.

Based on the 20-pin surface mount connectors, various signal interfaces are provided by the BSN node. Figure B.12 (bottom) shows the schematic diagrams of the connectors with their pins labelled with associated signal interfaces. The descriptions of the pin labels are listed in Table B.6.

As shown in Figure B.12, the connectors are wired similarly to a bus where signals are designed to pass through from one side of the board to another, in order to provide the stackable functionality. To ensure the boards are properly connected, an arrow is printed next to each connector to indicate the direction of the board, and boards have to be connected with the arrows pointing in the same direction as shown in Figure B.13.

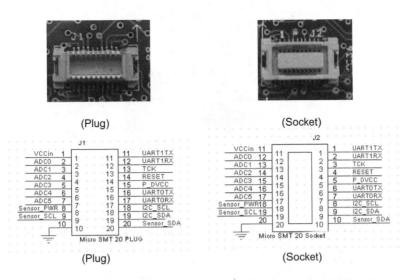

Figure B.12 BSN board connectors and the schematics: plug (left) and socket (right).

Table B.6 BSN board connector pin descriptions.

Pin	Description
VCCin	Power
ADC0	Analogue channel 0
ADC1	Analogue channel 1
ADC2	Analogue channel 2
ADC3	Analogue channel 3
ADC4	Analogue channel 4
ADC5	Analogue channel 5
Sensor_PWR	Power to sensors
Sensor_SCL	I^2C clock for sensors
Sensor_SDA	I^2C Data for sensors
GND	Ground
UART1TX	UART 1 transmit
UART1RX	UART 1 receive
TCK	Test clock for programming
RESET	Reset
P_DVCC	USB 3.3V power
UART0TX	UART 0 transmit
UART0RX	UART 0 receive
I2C_SCL	I^2C Clock
I2C_SDA	I^2C Data

Figure B.13 Stacking a sensor board onto a BSN node.

B.2.5 Antenna

Typical BSN applications require relatively short-range (2-3m) transmission. To enable different antenna design, the BSN node is designed with only the mounting holes (Ant and GND) for the user to try out different antenna designs. Even without an antenna, the BSN node can still transmit and receive data within a very short distance (~1m). For practical applications, dipole antenna would be preferred and this can easily be soldered onto the node through the mounting holes. Figure B.14 (left) shows a BSN node fitted with a dipole antenna. As a 2.4GHz transceiver is used, for a $\lambda/2$-dipole antenna, the length of the antenna should be 5.8cm (2.9cm on each arm), because L=14250/f where f is the modulation frequency in MHz and L is the length of the antenna (*i.e.* L=5.8 as f=2450MHz). For a $\lambda/4$-monopole antenna, the length of the antenna should be 2.9cm (*i.e.* L=7125/f). Alternatively, ceramic antennas can also be integrated onto the BSN node as shown in Figure B.14 (right).

Figure B.14 BSN nodes with a dipole antenna (left) and a ceramic antenna (right).

B.3 BSN Development Kit

To facilitate the development of BSNs, the BSN development kit is designed to simplify the prototyping of new biosensors and enable research and development in novel BSN applications. With the BSN development kit, users can program the sensors, experiment with different network configurations, test out different batteries, and build simple context aware sensing applications. The BSN development kit consists of five components, shown in Figure B.15.

- Two BSN nodes
- USB Programmer
- Sensor board
- Prototype board
- Battery board

Figure B.15 The BSN development kit.

B.3.1 BSN Nodes

With each BSN development kit, two BSN nodes are provided. The two BSN nodes are identical and can be programmed by using the USB programmer. To aid the debugging of the program, three programmable LEDs are incorporated in each node. It should be noted that by default, no antenna is fitted onto the nodes and it is down to the user to fit their preferred choice of antenna. As mentioned earlier, even without the antenna, the nodes can still communicate wirelessly within a short range of ~1m. Through the use of the other accessory boards provided, the two BSN nodes can form a basic peer-to-peer network for simple wireless sensing applications.

B.3.2 USB Programmer

The USB programmer is essential for programming the BSN nodes and interfacing with a host computer. The USB programmer consists of the following main components, and these are highlighted in Figure B.16:

- BSN board connectors
- USB interface chipset
- LEDs

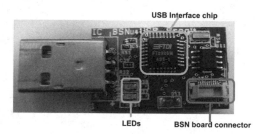

Figure B.16 USB programmer board.

The USB programmer is designed specifically with two BSN board connectors (one on each side of the board) to allow the stacking of sensors or BSN nodes on either side of the programmer. Instead of relying on battery power, the USB programmer draws power directly from the USB connection.

The USB interface chipset (FTDI FT232BM) enables communication between a PC and a BSN node via a serial connection. When connecting the USB programmer to the PC, it will be recognised as a USB serial port, and PC application programs can be in communication with the BSN node via a specific COM port. In addition, the USB serial port will also be used by the TI BSL for programming the BSN node.

B.3.3 Sensor Board

To assist in the development of BSN applications, a simple sensor board is provided with the development kit. The sensor board consists of the following main components:

- 2D accelerometer
- Temperature sensor
- BSN board connectors
- Extension slot

The components of the sensor board are highlighted in Figure B.17, where all the sensors are located on the top-side of the board. In addition, the board connectors are mounted on both sides of the board. Similarly to the BSN node and USB programmer, the board connectors' signal pins are connected like a bus, which enables the addition of other sensor boards. This also allows the sensor board to be stacked on top of or at the bottom of a BSN node.

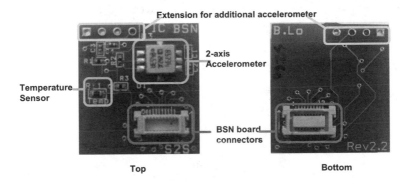

Figure B.17 Sensor board.

The accelerometer and the temperature sensors obtain power from the SENSOR_PWR pin of the BSN board connector, which allows the user program to activate/deactivate the sensors by setting/clearing the SENSOR_PWR pin. In this way, sensors can be switched on or off as required in order to save power.

B.3.3.1 Accelerometer

An Analogue Device ADXL202AE two-axis accelerometer is used in the sensor board. The analogue outputs of the two axes are connected to channels ADC2 (X axis) and ADC3 (Y axis). Figure B.18 shows a schematic diagram of the accelerometer designed for the sensor board.

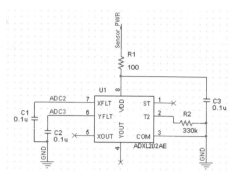

Figure B.18 Schematic of the two-axis accelerometer.

The accelerometer is a MEMS two-axis, +/-2G device, which is based on the force of gravity to determine the orientation and acceleration of the object in space. Figure B.19 illustrates the sensor's response towards changes in tilt [13]. The ADXL202AE is a low cost, low power accelerometer with power consumption of less than 0.6mA. It has a relatively high sensitivity of 2mg resolution at 60Hz. In addition to the analogue readings, the ADXL202AE also provide digital outputs for different applications.

Figure B.19 X and Y axis respond to the changes in tilt.

In addition to measuring acceleration, the accelerometer can also be used for measuring tilt, movement, and vibration. To convert the measurement to tilt angle, the following equations can be used [13]:

$$Pitch = \arcsin(Ax)$$
$$Roll = \arcsin(Ay)$$

(B.8)

where Ax and Ay are the normalised outputs of the two-axis accelerometer. To measure 360° of tilt, two accelerometers oriented perpendicular to each other are required.

B.3.3.2 Temperature Sensor

A Panasonic ERTJ1VR103J temperature sensor is integrated on the sensor board for measuring the ambient temperature. The sensor signal is connected to the channel ADC1 provided by the board connector. A schematic diagram of the temperature sensor is shown in Figure B.20.

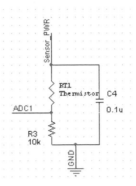

Figure B.20 Schematic of the temperature sensor.

The ERT1 VR103J is a negative temperature coefficient resistor where the resistance of the sensor changes as ambient temperature varies. The base resistance of the sensor is 10k Ohm at $25°C$ [14]. Figure B.21 illustrates the temperature sensor resistance at different temperature settings.

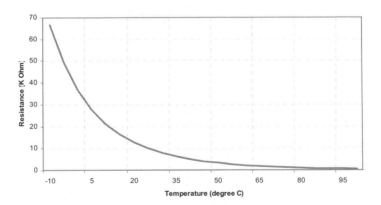

Figure B.21 Resistance to temperature conversion.

To convert the ADC reading to temperature, the following equations can be used:

$$R_0 = 10000$$
$$R_1 = 10000$$
$$T_0 = 298.15$$
$$B = 4250$$
$$V_i = 4095$$

$$R = \left(\frac{V_i - V_o}{V_o}\right) R_1$$

$$T = \left(\frac{T_0 B}{T_0 \ln\left(\dfrac{R}{R_0}\right) + B}\right) - 273.15\,^{\circ}C \qquad (B.9)$$

where V_o is the reading from the ADC and T is the resulting temperature in $^{\circ}C$.

B.3.3.3 Extension Slot

In order to introduce additional sensors to form a 3D accelerometer, four signal points have been designed on the sensor board, as highlighted in Figure B.22:

- Vcc – power for the sensor
- AccelX – for X axis accelerometer signal :ADC channel 0
- AccelY – for Y axis accelerometer signal: ADC channel 5
- GND – Ground

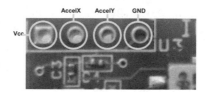

Figure B.22 Extension slot on the sensor board.

For capturing acceleration along the third axis, the additional accelerometer has to be mounted perpendicularly to the sensor board, as shown in Figure B.23. However, no support circuitry has been designed for the additional sensor and no power control is provided.

Figure B.23 Board configuration for three-axis accelerometer.

B.3.4 Battery Board

Since the power source is one of the main components of BSNs, the battery board in the BSN development kit is designed to be flexible in order to cater for different application requirements. The board consists of the following four main components as shown in Figure B.24:

- Power on/off switch
- Reset button
- Battery retainer
- BSN board connector

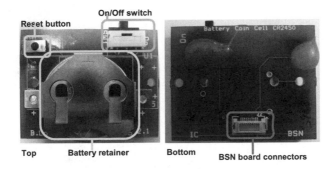

Figure B.24 The BSN battery board.

To simplify the testing and debugging of BSN nodes, the power switch and the reset button are provided in order to control and reset the BSN node. To connect to a BSN node, the BSN board connector is mounted on one side of the battery board. Although the BSN board connector can connect to up to 20 signals, the battery board only uses three signals for powering up and resetting the BSN node, as shown in Figure B.25. This figure illustrates the PCB layout, and Figure B.26 shows the schematic of the battery board.

To ease the testing of power usage and permit the use of different batteries, the battery board is designed to fit three different kinds of battery mountings

- CR123
- 1/2AA PCB mount batteries
- Coin cell batteries CR2430/CR2450

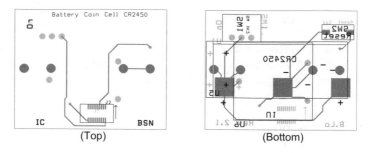

Figure B.25 The PCB layout of the BSN battery board.

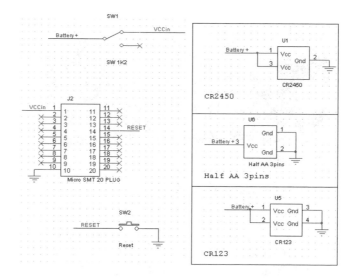

Figure B.26 Schematic diagram of the battery board.

B.3.4.1 Change to a Different Battery

The battery board is designed to enable the testing of different battery configurations such as the CR24350/CR2450, CR123, or ½ AA PCB mounted batteries. The battery board comes with a retainer for the CR2430/CR2450 battery, and readers can easily change this to a different battery type by simply replacing the retainer. To change to a different battery, you need first to unsolder the coin cell battery retainer, as shown in Figure B.27.

Figure B.27 Unsoldering the battery retainer.

In order to use a CR123 battery, the positive terminal of the retainer on the left side of the board has to be insulated with a piece of electric tape to avoid shorting, as highlighted in Figure B.28. Battery clips for the CR123 battery can then be soldered onto the board. For mounting a ½ AA PCB battery, the battery can be soldered directly onto the board.

Figure B.28 Soldering the mounting for CR123 batteries.

B.3.5 Prototype Board

A prototype board is included in the development kit for the evaluation of different sensors. The design of the prototype board is simple and it consists of just one pair of BSN board connectors (a plug and a socket) and a test point for each signal of the BSN board connector. As such, the board can also be used as a board adaptor, a hardware testing tool, or an interface to other processors. Figure B.29 shows the top and bottom sides of the prototype board with board connectors highlighted. The PCB layout and schematic diagram of the prototype board are shown in Figure B.30 and Figure B.31, respectively.

Figure B.29 BSN prototype board.

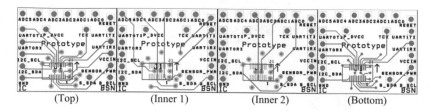

| (Top) | (Inner 1) | (Inner 2) | (Bottom) |

Figure B.30 PCB layout of the prototype board.

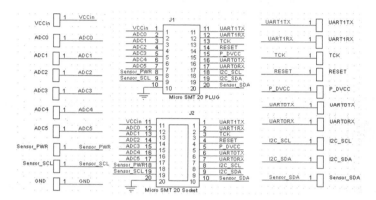

Figure B.31 Schematic of the BSN prototype board.

B.3.5.1 Sensor Board Design

Prototype board is designed to ease the integration, prototyping and testing of sensors. To this end, both digital and analogue channels are provided for interfacing with different sensors. They include:

- Analogue channels (ADC0-ADC5)
- I^2C (I2C_SCL, I2C_SDA)
- UART (UART0TX/UART1RX and UART1TX/UART1RX)

To integrate an analogue sensor to the BSN node, the following points need to be observed:

- The analogue sensor signal has to be within the range of 0-3V.
- The power (SENSOR_PWR) and ground (GND) must be connected to the sensor.
- The sensor output must be connected to one of the ADC channels (ADC0-ADC5).

Figure B.32 illustrates an example prototype with an accelerometer attached to the sensor board in order to provide measurements on all three axes.

Figure B.32 Integration of an analogue sensor using the prototype board.

To interface with an I²C digital sensor:

- Use the pins SENSOR_PWR and GND to power up the sensor
- Connect the sensor's I²C clock signal to the SENSOR_SCL pin and the data signal to the SENSOR_SDA pin

To interface with a sensor with an UART/RS232 interface, you need to observe the following:

- As the RS232 signal can operate up to ±15V, a RS232 line driver (such as the MAX3232) is required to interface with a RS232 based sensor.
- UART0TX/UART0RX or UART1TX/UART1RX pins can be used to interface with the sensors.

B.4 TinyOS

The BSN node uses TinyOS, by U.C. Berkeley, which is a small, open source, energy efficient sensor board operating system [15]. It provides a set of modular software building blocks, out of which designers can choose the components they require. The size of these files is typically as small as 200 bytes and thus the overall program size is kept to a minimum. The *Operating System* (OS) manages both the hardware and the wireless network by taking sensor measurements, making routing decisions, and controlling power dissipation.

Traditionally, proprietary programs are developed for embedded systems. To enable cross-platform software development and provide practical hardware abstractions, different operating systems have been introduced for embedded systems. These include Microsoft's Pocket PC, Java 2 Platform Micro Edition, and embedded Linux. However, due to the extensive overhead required for these operating systems, which offer multithreaded processing support and generic device interfacing, embedded operating systems are typically designed for relatively powerful processors rather than those suitable for WSNs.

Recently, a number of operating systems for wireless sensors have been introduced, and TinyOS is by far the most widely adopted OS mainly due to its open source paradigm and large community base. Because of resource constraints, a new programming language, called nesC, is proposed for the realisation of the structural design and reusable code concepts of TinyOS for miniaturised sensors. To facilitate the reusability of the source code and minimise the overhead of the program binary, TinyOS adopts a component-based architecture. In addition, to optimise power usage, TinyOS utilities an event-based execution model where programs are event-driven and the relevant resources are released once the handler completes.

To adapt to different hardware platforms, a flexible hardware abstraction layer within the core of TinyOS enables its support for a wide range of hardware platforms. As well as easing adaptation of different hardware platforms, the hardware abstraction layer greatly simplifies software development for WSNs. Furthermore, TinyOS also provides a set of development tools, namely TOSSIM [16], Deluge [17] and TinyDB [18], to aid in the research and development of WSN applications. Due to its efficient design, wide-ranging community support, and open source paradigm, TinyOS has become one of the most widely adopted OS for WSNs.

In the following sections, we will provide an introduction to the nesC programming language, followed by a description of TinyOS' execution model and hardware abstraction design. We will conclude with an overview of two TinyOS development tools, TOSSIM and Deluge, which are potentially applicable to BSN developments.

B.4.1 nesC

nesC is a programming language designed for low power, miniaturised wireless sensors with tight resource constraints. To enhance the usability of the language, nesC is based on a C-like syntax, and it adopts the code efficiency and simplified low-level features of the C language. It also introduces a structural design and addresses the issue of safe coding for microcontrollers [19].

In order to run programs on highly constrained hardware platforms, the nesC has a static configuration where no dynamic memory allocation is allowed. The programs are linked statically and optimised by linking only to the relevant components. nesC programs are built by connecting ("wiring") components together. To specify the connection, a set of interfaces are defined for each component which specifies the commands it provides and events it handles [20]. For the actual implementation of the components, it consists largely of two elements, configurations (header files) and modules (source files), in a similar programming paradigm to regular C programs.

B.4.1.1 Interface

Interfaces define the interaction between two components (the user and the provider). Interfaces are bidirectional, which means that a set of functions are declared that the provider must implement (*commands*), and another set of functions are declared that the users must implement (*events*) [20]. The basic

interface for components is the standard control interface which defines the
commands for initialising, starting, and stopping of the component.

```
interface StdControl {
  command result_t init ();
  command result_t start();
  command result_t stop ();
}
                                          StdControl.nc
```

As shown above, the standard control interface is mainly designed for controlling the component and it consists of a number of commands. For components
which return readings or issue events, event handlers will be required. As an example, the interface of the `Timer` component can be described as:

```
includes Timer; // make TIMER_x constants available
interface Timer {
  command result_t start(char type, uint32_t interval);
  command result_t stop();
  event result_t fired ();
}
                                          Timer.nc
```

where `start` and `stop` are the commands provided by this component and it
handles the `fired` event. As such, the user of this interface will be called
when the timer event triggers.

To handle concurrency, TinyOS is designed with no blocking operations.
For long latency operations, a split phase design is employed in which separate
functions are defined for requesting and signalling the completion of the operation. For example, sending a radio message could take a relatively long time,
and it is often handled by the radio transceiver. As in the case of BSN node, the
CC2420 handles the transmission of the message. Instead of waiting for the radio transceiver to complete the transmission task, a split phase design is used by
defining the `SendMsg` interface:

```
includes AM;
interface SendMsg {
  command result_t send(uint16_t address,
          uint8_t length, TOS_MsgPtr msg);
  event result_t sendDone(TOS_MsgPtr msg,
          result_t success);
}                                         SendMsg.nc
```

In this code snippet, separate functions are defined for sending the message
(`send`) and signalling the completion of the transmission (`sendDone`). By using the split-phase operation, the processor can be released to handle other
events and tasks.

B.4.1.2 Configuration

Configurations are components constructed by writing components together and specify the properties of the components. The following is an example configuration file for a component called MyLedC.

```
configuration MyLedsC { }
implementation {
  components Main,MyLedsM,TimerC,LedsC,SimulatedMsgC;
  Main.StdControl -> TimerC.StdControl;
  Main.StdControl -> MyLedsM.StdControl;
  Main.StdControl -> SimulatedMsgC.Control;
  MyLedsM.Timer   -> TimerC.Timer[unique("Timer")];
  MyLedsM.Leds   -> LedsC;
  MyLedsM.SendMsg -> SimulatedMsgC.Send;
}                                              MyLedC.nc
```

The MyLedsC is an application program that is implemented by wiring the Main, MyLedsM, TimerC, LedsC, SimulatedMsgC components together, as depicted in Figure B.33. As shown in the diagram, the Main component uses the StdControl interfaces provided by the TimerC, MyLedsM and SimulatedMsgC components. When any of the commands of the StdControl interface is called, the corresponding commands in all three wired components will be executed accordingly. Unlike other simple interfaces, the Timer interface is a parameterised interface which provides an array of interfaces. To identify an instance of an interface, an identifier has to be used, and in this case the function unique("Timer") is used to obtain an unique identifier for specifying the time instance. The unique function returns a different value every time the function is called with the same argument string [21].

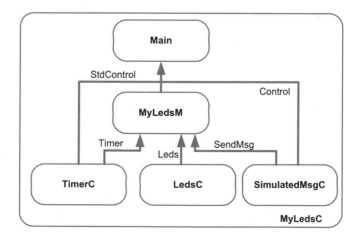

Figure B.33 Wiring diagram of MyLedsC.

For interconnection, the components must be compatible where interfaces wire to interfaces, commands to commands, and events to events. nesC specifies three types of wiring statements:

- $endpoint_1 = endpoint_2$
  Equal wires: any connection that involves an external element

- $endpoint_1 \rightarrow endpoint_2$
  Link wires: any connection that involves two internal elements

- $endpoint_1 \rightarrow endpoint_2$
  Equivalent to $endpoint_2 \rightarrow endpoint_1$

For example, in the following source configuration of the `SimulatedMsgC` component, the `Control` and `SimulatedMsgM.StdControl` are linked with an equal wire (as `Control` is an external interface), and the `SimulatedMsgM.Leds` and `LedsC` are linked with a link wire (as the `Leds` interface is linked internally). Figure B.34 illustrates the external and internal wiring of the `SimulatedMsgC` component.

```
configuration SimulatedMsgC {
  provides {
    interface StdControl as Control;
    interface SendMsg;
  }
}
implementation {
  components SimulatedMsgM, LedsC;
  Control = SimulatedMsgM.StdControl;
  SendMsg = SimulatedMsgM.Send;
  SimulatedMsgM.Leds -> LedsC;
}                                    SimulatedMsgC.nc
```

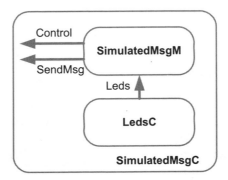

Figure B.34 Wiring diagram of SimulatedMsgC.

B.4.1.3 Modules

Similarly to the C/C++ source file, modules in nesC implement the functions in
C for the specific components. All of the commands (events) specified in the
component's configuration must be implemented in the module. As an example,
the module for the MyLeds component can be shown as follows:

```
module MyLedsM {
  provide interface StdControl;
  uses {
  interface Timer;
  interface Leds;
  interface SendMsg;
  }
}
implementation {
 uint16_t count;
  command result_t StdControl.init() {
    call Leds.init();
    count=0;
    return SUCCESS;
  }
  command result_t StdControl.start() {
    // Start a repeating timer that fires every 100ms
    return call Timer.start(TIMER_REPEAT, 100);
  }
  command result_t StdControl.stop() {
    return call Timer.stop();
  }
  event result_t Timer.fired() {
    call Leds.greenToggle();
    if (count == 30) {
    call SendMsg.send(0,0,0);//sending a null message
      count=0;
    }
    count++;
    return SUCCESS;
  }
  event result_t SendMsg.sendDone(TOS_MsgPtr msg,
                 result_t success) {
    call Leds.redOff();
  Return success;
  }
}                                              MyLedM.nc
```

As specified in the configuration file described in the previous subsection, the
MyLed component provides the StdControl interface and uses the Timer,
Leds, and SendMsg components. To provide the StdControl interface, the
init(), start() and stop() commands are implemented in the module
for initialising the Leds, and starting and stopping the Timer. In addition, the

`fired` and the `sendDone` functions are implemented for handling the events received from the `Timer` and `SendMsg` interfaces.

In addition to conventional C function calling scheme, nesC defines three additional function activation schemes for different types of functions:

- call (for commands)
- signal (for events)
- post (for tasks)

By explicitly defining function calling schemes for different types of functions, the activation schemes can assist the development of the software and ensure the safety of the programs. Different function calling schemes are demonstrated in the following source code for the `SimulatedMsg` module.

```
module SimulatedMsgM {
 provides {
   interface StdControl;
   interface SendMsg as Send;
   }
 uses interface Leds;
}
implementation {
 command result_t StdControl.init() {
  call Leds.init();
  return SUCCESS;
  }
 command result_t StdControl.start() {
   return SUCCESS;
  }
 command result_t StdControl.stop() {
   return SUCCESS;
  }
 // task for simulating as if the
 // processor is busy sending
 task void simulateSending() {
   uint16_t i;
   for (i=0;i<500;i++)  //wait for 500 ms
       TOSH_uwait(1000);//wait for 1000 micro-second
   signal Send.sendDone(0, FAIL);
  }
 command result_t Send.send(uint16_t address,
       uint8_t length, TOS_MsgPtr msg) {
   call Leds.redOn();
   post simulateSending();
   return SUCCESS;
  }
```

```
default event result_t Send.sendDone( TOS_Msg Ptrmsg,
      result_t success) {
return success;
  }
}                                              SimulatedMsgM.nc
```

As shown in the source code, the event `sendDone` is triggered by signalling the function. The task `simulateSending()` is initiated by posting the task onto the scheduler.

Since the `SimulateMsg` component provides the `SendMsg` interface, it implements the `send` and `sendDone` functions specified for the interface. As the `sendDone` is an event handler aiming to act as a call back function to signal other components that use the interface, the `sendDone` function is defined as a `default` function. Therefore, it can be signalled even if the `SendMsg` interface is not connected.

B.4.2 Execution Model

To optimise resource utilisation, TinyOS uses an event-based execution model where the program components are activated in response to events or hardware interrupts. In addition, TinyOS also provides an execution mechanism called tasks for handling operations with long-latency. As such, the TinyOS has two levels of scheduling. As events are designed for time-critical operations, they have higher priority than tasks, and can pre-empt tasks. On the other hand, tasks are designed for computationally intensive processes which can be run in the background. Figure B.35 shows an example of how tasks and events are scheduled in TinyOS.

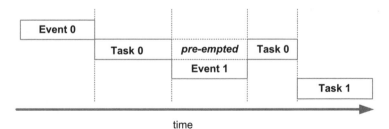

time

Figure B.35 TinyOS scheduling example.

B.4.2.1 Events

Events are time-critical processes for handling incoming events or hardware interrupts. As events are only activated when required, their use requires minimal resource utilisation and low power consumption. For this reason, TinyOS system modules are designed as events. An event is designed to run to completion without any interruption from tasks or other events. An example software event sendDone is shown in the following code segment of the SimulatedMsg module:

```
task void simulateSending() {
  uint16_t i;
  for (i=0;i<500;i++) //wait for 500 ms
    TOSH_uwait(1000);//wait for 1000 micro-second
  signal Send.sendDone(0, FAIL);
  }
default event result_t Send.sendDone(TOS_MsgPtr msg,
        result_t success) {
  return success;
}
```

B.4.2.2 Tasks

Tasks are designed for long-latency computations that can be run in the background. Unlike the tasks defined in PC-based operating systems, tasks are not pre-empted in TinyOS, and are designed to run to completion. To manage tasks, a simple FIFO-based scheduler is employed to decide the order of task activations. Although tasks cannot pre-empt tasks, tasks can be pre-empted by events in order to handle time-critical operations. An example of a task is shown in the following code segment of the SimulatedMsg module:

```
task void simulateSending() {
  uint16_t i;
  for (i=0;i<500;i++) //wait for 500 ms
    TOSH_uwait(1000);//wait for 1000 micro-second
  signal Send.sendDone(0, FAIL);
  }
command result_t Send.send(uint16_t address,
                  uint8_t length, TOS_MsgPtr msg) {
  call Leds.redOn();
  post simulateSending();
  return SUCCESS;
}
```

Here the SimulateSending task is designed to simulate the delay that occurs during message sending.

B.4.2.3 Atomic Statements

Atomic statements provide mutually exclusive operations where the section of code will be run to completion without interruption from other tasks, in order to avoid race conditions. The use of atomicity is illustrated in the following code segment:

```
task void simulateSending() {
  uint16_t i;
  atomic {
    for (i=0;i<500;i++) //wait for 500 ms
        TOSH_uwait(1000);//wait for 1000 micro-second
  }
  signal Send.sendDone(0, FAIL);
  }
```

The section of code highlighted as atomic will be guaranteed to run exclusively without interruption. To ensure atomicity, calling commands or signalling events are prohibited inside atomic statements.

B.4.3 Hardware Abstraction

Since hardware platforms are expected to evolve rapidly, TinyOS needs to be easily adaptable and extendable to different hardware platforms and components in order to sustain its role for WSN research and development. To this end, flexible hardware abstraction architecture has been incorporated into the TinyOS to simplify the adaptation of the OS to different platforms [22, 23]. To provide platform-independent interfaces, the hardware abstraction of TinyOS is designed as a three-layered architecture with high-level components, whilst at the same time maintaining the freedom to access the low-level mapping of hardware features. These three layers include:

- *Hardware Presentation Layer* (*HPL*)
  This is the lowest layer, which presents the capabilities of the specific hardware platform. This layer provides access to the hardware via memory mapping or I/O port setting, and it handles hardware interrupts or forwards the interrupts to higher layers.

- *Hardware Adaptation Layer* (*HAL*)
  The adaptation layer provides abstractions on the raw interfaces provided by the HPL layer and exports domain-specific interfaces, such as the ADC channels and EEPROM pages.

- *Hardware Interface Layer* (*HIL*)
  The interface layer ports the platform-specific interfaces provided by the HAL to platform-independent interfaces for cross-platform applications.

Figure B.36 illustrates the design of the three-layer hardware abstraction architecture. As an example, MicaZ, BSN Node and HW Platform X are shown in the diagram. For each platform, three layers of abstractions are required to support cross-platform applications. Because of this, in order to port TinyOS to a new platform, components have to be developed to provide the abstractions required. In addition, apart from abstracting the raw interfaces provided from HPL, HAL also enables the access of particular platform features for platform-specific applications, as shown in Figure B.36.

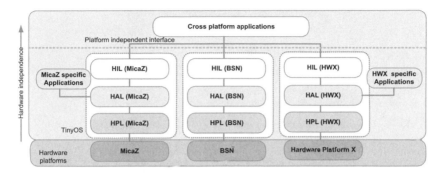

Figure B.36 TinyOS hardware abstraction architecture.

Figure B.37 gives an example of hardware abstraction for wireless communication via the CC2420 transceiver. As illustrated in the simplified diagram, the processor's registers are present in the HPL layer, whereas the SPI interface, I/O pins and interrupts are described in the HAL layer. As an SPI interface is a common accessory for hardware platforms, a generic HIL layer provides the cross-platform interface for SPI communication. As the CC2420 interfaces with the MCU through the SPI interface, although the registers of the CC2420 are low-level elements, the HPL layer of the CC2420 (which represents the CC2420 registers) is on top of the HIL SPI layer. The CC2420 functions are then represented by the CC2420RadioM and CC2420ControlM components. Based on the CC2420 functions, cross-platform high level components, such as Generic-Comm and RadioCRCPacket, can be built to provide high level wireless network functions.

B.4.4 TOSSIM

Since limited resources are available for wireless sensor hardware and virtually no user interface is provided for the sensors except for the LEDs, debugging programs with TinyOS is one of the most laborious tasks in embedded system development. To alleviate this problem, the TinyOS simulator, TOSSIM, has been introduced [24]. TOSSIM is a discrete event simulator for TinyOS which allows users to compile, debug and analyse their TinyOS applications on a PC rather than using the hardware [16].

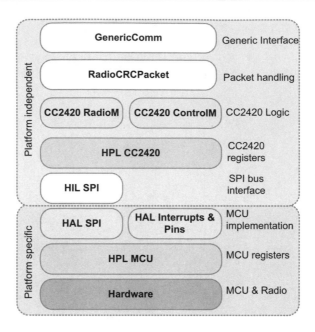

Figure B.37 The hardware abstraction for wireless communication.

To simulate the behaviour of sensors, the TOSSIM models the low level components of the sensor, which include the radio transceiver, ADC, and EEPROM. To enable a detailed study of wireless network behaviours, TOSSIM simulates the radio in bit-level, but at present it only implements the Mica's 40Kbit RFM [16] and Mica2's CC1000 radio [25]. The simulation model for the CC2420 radio has recently been developed, but it is still at the beta testing stage. However, extensive functions are provided for simulating different network configurations. In addition, in order to model sensor behaviour, ADC function is provided by TOSSIM for simulating random and manual alteration of ADC readings. To validate the sensor data storage, TOSSIM models the EEPROM, through mapping the memory to a file in which all data to be stored in the EEPROM is saved.

B.4.4.1 Running the Simulator

TOSSIM is built directly from the TinyOS source code. To simulate a sensor node, rather than running the program for a specific sensor platform, the tester runs the program for the PC platform. For example, to make the simulated program for the Blink application run the following code: (Note: details on how to compile and make TinyOS applications can be found in Section B.5 BSN Programming Guide)

```
>cd /tinyos-1.x/bsn/Blink
>make pc
```

After making the program, the TOSSIM executable, *main.exe*, is created and stored in the */build/pc* directory (*i.e.* for the blink program, the executable will be */tinyos-1.x/bsn/Blink/build/pc/main.exe*). The TOSSIM executable has the following usage[16]:

```
Usage: ./build/pc/main.exe [options] num_nodes
where[options] are:
```

Options	Descriptions
-h, --help	Display the help message
-gui	Pause simulation waiting for GUI to connect
-a=<model>	Specifies ADC model (generic or random)
-b=<sec>	Boot over first <sec> seconds
-ef=file	Use <file> for EEPROM
-l=<scale>	Run sim at <scale> times real time (fp constant)
-r=<model>	Specifies a radio model (simple, static or lossy)
-rf=<file>	Specifies file input for lossy model
-s=<num>	Only boot <num> nodes
-t=<sec>	Run simulation for <sec> virtual seconds
num_nodes	Number of nodes to simulate

For example, to simulate one node:

```
>./build/pc/main.exe 1
```

B.4.4.2 Debugger

TOSSIM provides runtime debugging by displaying chosen debug messages. For runtime debugging, debug messages have to be explicitly coded into the programs, for example:

```
dbg(DBG_BOOT, "Application initialised\n")
```

Each debug message is tagged "DBG_", which represents the mode of the message. In this case, the mode of the message is "boot" (i.e. DBG_BOOT). Table B.7 lists the defined modes for debugging. As well as identifying the mode of the debug message, the tag is also used to enable TOSSIM to identify and display specific debug messages. For example, to display the boot message, export the DBG=boot then run the simulator as follows:

```
>export DGB=boot
>./build/pc/main.exe 1
```

In addition to displaying real time messages, the TOSSIM executable, *main.exe*, can be debugged using GDB in which users can step through the programs.

- To use gdb:

```
>gdb build/pc/main.exe
```

- To insert a break point in the fired() function of the MyLedsM component described in the previous section:

```
(gdb) break *MyLedsM$Timer$fired
```

Note that '.' which identifies subordinate interfaces and functions of a component in nesC, are replaced by '$' which are required by GDB to identify a specific element. The '*' sign instructs the *gdb* command line parser to parse the function call properly.

- To start the executable (in debug mode):

```
(gdb) run 1
```

The number "1" identifies the number of instance of the executable to be run by the gdb. Once the executable is running, the gdb will stop at the predefined break points to allow the user to examine the value of the variables, and the executable will remain stopped until the user issues a *next*, *nexti*, *continue* or *finish*, *etc.* command to the gdb.

- To examine the value of a variable:

```
(gdb) print MyLedsM$count[0]
```

In the above example, the value of the variable count in the component MyLedsM of the node 0 will be displayed.

- To continue running the program:

```
(gdb) continue
```

- To step through the program:

```
(gdb) next
```

B.4.4.3 Graphical Visualisation Tool

To aid in the development of TinyOS applications with TOSSIM, a graphical visualisation tool, called TinyViz, has been developed by Berkeley[16]. In addition to displaying the simulated network layout in order for the user to visualise the configuration of the network, TinyViz also provides an intuitive user interface for developers to alter the parameters of their simulated programs. Figure B.38 demonstrates a screenshot of the TinyViz program, in which the left window displays the sensors in the virtual environment, and the right window provides the interfaces to a series of different plug-ins that enable the alteration of sensor and network behaviours.

Apart from being a user interface and visualisation tool for TOSSIM, Tiny-Viz is designed as a framework for plug-ins into which Java plug-ins can be added to extend the functionality of the simulator to cope with different scenarios. For instance, a plug-in called PowerTOSSIM has been added to simulate the power consumption of the individual sensor and the network as a whole[25].

Table B.7 TOSSIM debug modes[16].

Modes	Description
all	Enable all available messages
boot	Simulation boot and StdControl
clock	The hardware clock
task	Task enqueueing/dequeueing/running
sched	TinyOS scheduler
sensor	Sensor readings
led	LEDs
crypto	Cryptographic operations
route	Routing systems
am	Active messages transmission/reception
crc	CRC checks on active messages
packet	Packet-level transmission/reception
encode	Packet encoding/decoding
radio	Low-level radio operations: bits and bytes
logger	Non-volatile storage
adc	ADC
i2c	I^2C bus
uart	UART
prog	Network programming
sounder	Sounder
time	Timers
sim	TOSSIM internals
queue	TOSSIM event queue
simradio	TOSSIM radio models
hardware	TOSSIM hardware abstractions
simmem	TOSSIM memory allocation/de-allocation
usr1	User output mode 1
usr2	User output mode 2
usr3	User output mode 3
temp	For temporary use

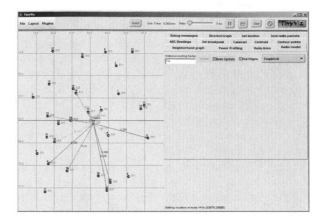

Figure B.38 TinyViz.

To use TinyViz, the user has to build the java program first:

```
>../tools//java/net/tinyos/sim/make
```

To use TinyViz to simulate a network of sensors:

```
>../../tools/java/net/tinyos/sim/tinyviz -run
 build/pc/main.exe 30
```

In the above example, the number *30* indicates thirty sensor nodes will be simulated by TOSSIM.

B.4.5 Deluge: TinyOS Network Programming

In order to facilitate the dissemination and maintenance of WSNs, Hui *et al* introduced a TinyOS tool called Deluge, which enables dynamic programming of the TinyOS hardware via the wireless network [17]. By utilising the external flash memory, Deluge allows up to three different program images to be stored in each sensor. To provide a reliable and efficient update of the programs, Deluge is based on an epidemic propagation protocol, where program images are first broken down into pages and packets, followed by their propagation to all of the sensor nodes in the network.

Deluge has been incorporated into the TinyOS (since version 1.11.14) at the point where a bootloader program, called TOSBoot, is preloaded into the first section of the microcontroller's flash memory in addition to the application program. Similarly to the booting program for a PC, the TOSBoot is executed whenever the senor node is reset (all three LEDs will flash when TOSBoot is called after reset). Depending on the previous received reprogramming instruction, the TOSBoot will load the desired program image from the external flash memory and program the microcontroller accordingly.

To enable Deluge, the external flash memory has to be formatted for storing program images and the Deluge component has to be incorporated into the application program. To set up the node for Deluge:

- Format the flash – compile and install the "Flash Format" Program [*tinyos-1.x\apps\TestDeluge\Flash-Format*]
- Install the DelugeBasic program to the node [*tinyos-1.x\apps\TestDeluge\DelugeBasic*]

The node ID (used in uploading the program to the sensor node) will be used as the address of the node. For adding Deluge support to your program, you need to take the following steps:

- Modify the configuration file of your program to add the DelugeC component

```
configuration Blink{ }
Implementation {
        Components Main,BlinkM,…,DelugeC;
        Main.StdControl->DelugeC;
        Main.StdControl->BlinkM.StdControl;………
}
```

To program the sensor nodes wirelessly using Deluge:

- Set the COM port

```
>Export MOTECOM=serial@COM2:telos
```

- Ping the node (in order to check that the program images have been installed on the node)

```
>java net.tinyos.tools.Deluge –ping
```

- Install a program image

```
>java net.tinyos.tools.Deluge –i
 –ti=tos_image.xml –in=0
```

Here *tos_image.xml* can be found in the *.\build\bsn* directory. The parameter "*-in=0*" identifies the program image [0-2], and in this case, the program image number 0 is being updated. While the program is being injected to the node, the program is also distributed to other nodes in the network. Up to three program images [0-2] can be stored in a sensor node, and Deluge allows the users to reboot the sensor node with any of the three program images.

- Reprogramming the node with program image "1"

```
>java net.tinyos.tools.Deluge -r -in=1
```

B.5 BSN Programming Guide

To facilitate BSN development, this section outlines the required software developing tools and provides a step-by-step programming guide for users to get familiar with the programming environment.

B.5.1 Programming Environment

To develop BSN applications, several software developing tools are needed:

- *Cygwin (http://www.cygwin.com)*
  Cygwin is a Linux-like environment for Windows which emulates Linux functions in a Windows operating system. A collection of Linux tools are provided by Cygwin to emulate the Linux environment, such as cp, rmdir, gcc, etc. As the TinyOS compiler, linker, *etc.* are Linux-based, Cygwin is required to build TinyOS applications.

- *TinyOS (http://www.tinyos.net/)*
  TinyOS consists of a number of components, example source code and documentation that can be of immense help in the the development of BSN application programs.

- *nesC (http://nesc.sourceforge.net)*
  In order to build TinyOS application programs, the nesC compiler is required. This converts TinyOS components into platform-specific C source code as required.

- *TI MSP gcc Compiler/Bootstrap Loader*
  (http://nesc.sourceforge.net)
  In order to build program binaries and upload those binaries into the TI processor on the BSN node, the TI MSP gcc compiler and the bootstrap loader are required. The TI gcc compiler converts the C source code generated by the nesC compiler into the TI-specific machine binary code, and the

bootstrap loader allows the user to upload the program binary into the TI processor through the serial port.

- *Java JDK (Java Development Kit)/Java COMM API (java.sun.com)*
  As TOSSIM and Deluge are Java-based programs, the Java JDK is required to run these programs, and as Deluge uses the Java COMM API to communicate to the node, the Java COMM API is required to run Deluge.

- *USB Programmer Driver (http://www.ftdichip.com/)*
  To use the USB programmer, the driver for the USB interface chipset has to be installed. This will emulate a USB serial port and thus enables serial communication to the BSN node.

- *Text Editor/IDE (Integrated Developing Environment)*
  To edit the source code, any text editor or IDE can be used.

B.5.2 Installation Instructions

All of the above software developing tools can be downloaded from the Internet, and detailed instructions are provided on the respective websites. To ensure compatibility and support for the latest software updates, the installation information is available on our web site: **http://www.bsn-web.info**.

B.5.3 BSN Node Programming

TinyOS provides a detailed tutorial with sample programs to demonstrate how to develop TinyOS applications. Instead of exhaustively detailing all of the elements of TinyOS, this subsection aims to provide a brief introduction to BSN programming by using two simple programs. For in-depth description of TinyOS, readers are suggested to go use the TinyOS tutorial, which can be found at http://www.tinyos.net/tinyos-1.x/doc/tutorial/.

B.5.3.1 Blink Program

Similarly to the "hello world" programs described in most software programming books, the "blink" program (which is similar to the "blink" program used in the TinyOS tutorial) is a very simple program and is an ideal exercise for the first time TinyOS programmer. The blink program simply toggles the red LED on a BSN node based on a timer. The source code for the blink program can be found in the `\tinyos-1.x\bsn\blink` directory. The configuration file and module for the blink component are shown below:

```
configuration Blink {}
implementation {
  components Main, BlinkM, TimerC, LedsC;
 Main.StdControl -> TimerC.StdControl;
 Main.StdControl -> BlinkM.StdControl;
 BlinkM.Timer -> TimerC.Timer[unique("Timer")];
 BlinkM.Leds -> LedsC;
 }
                                                  Blink.nc
```

```
module BlinkM {
   provides interface StdControl;
   uses {
      interface Timer;
      interface Leds;
   }
}
implementation {
  bool state;
 command result_t StdControl.init() {
    call Leds.init();
    call Leds.redOn();
   state=0;
   return SUCCESS;
   }
   command result_t StdControl.start() {
     call Timer.start(TIMER_REPEAT, 100);
     return SUCCESS;
   }
  command result_t StdControl.stop() {
    return call Timer.stop();
   }
   event result_t Timer.fired() {
     state = !state;
   if (state) call Leds.redOn();
   else call Leds.redOff();
   return SUCCESS;
   }
 }
                                                BlinkM.nc
```

Figure B.39 depicts the wiring diagram of the blink component. As shown in the diagram and in the configuration file, the Main component uses the StdControl interface provided by both BlinkM and TimerC. BlinkM uses the Timer interface from TimerC and Leds from LedsC. To provide the StdControl interface, BlinkM has to implement the init(), start() and stop() commands as shown in **BlinkM.nc**. In addition, the function fired() is included for handling the event from the Timer interface. By using the Timer and the Leds interfaces, the Blink program toggles the red LED on and off every 100ms based on a variable state.

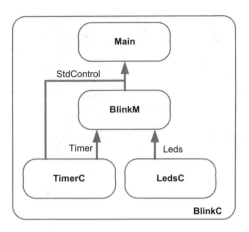

Figure B.39 Wiring diagram of the blink component.

B.5.3.2 Programming the BSN Node

To program the BSN node, you need to perform the following steps.

- Start "cygwin".

- Change to the TinyOS program directory.

```
>cd /opt/tinyos-1.x/bin/blink
```

- Compile the source code:

```
>make bsn
```

- If the program compiles successfully, no error message will be shown. The compiler will display the memory usage of the resulting program, as shown in Figure B.40.

Once the program is compiled, the program binary can be uploaded to the BSN node.

- To do this, plug the BSN node into the USB programmer and connect it to the PC, as shown in Figure B.41.

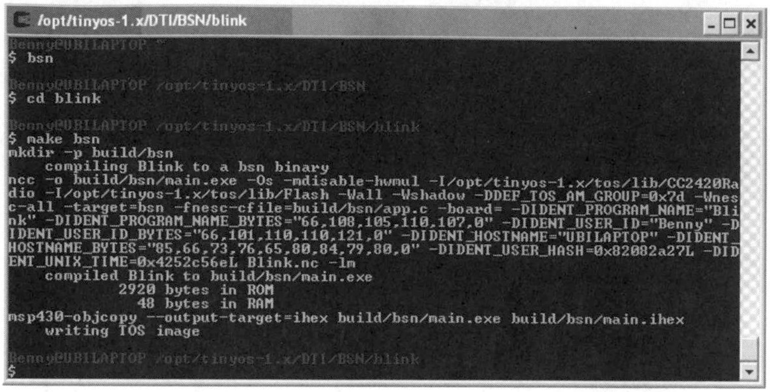

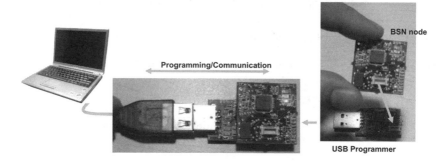

Figure B.40 A screen short of the nesC compiling result.

Figure B.41 Using the USB programmer to program a BSN node.

- Find out which COM port the USB programmer has been assigned to. (To do this, use the motelist program as shown below):

```
>motelist
```

Figure B.42 shows the result of running the motelist program, and it finds a BSN USB programmer connected to COM4.

Figure B.42 Motelist program result.

- To upload the program onto the BSN node:

```
>make bsn reinstall.xxx bsl,yyy
```

Here *xxx* is the unique identifier for the node, and *yyy* is the value of the COM port -1. For example, if COM4 is assigned to the programmer, the command would look like this:

```
>make bsn reinstall.1 bsl,3
```

As shown, the ID of the BSN node will be set to "1". Figure B.43 shows a screenshot of the result after uploading the program to a BSN node.

In addition to compiling and reinstalling the program to the BSN node separately, TinyOS also provides a command, called install, for compiling and uploading the program onto the BSN node in one statement:

```
>make bsn install.1 bsl,3
```

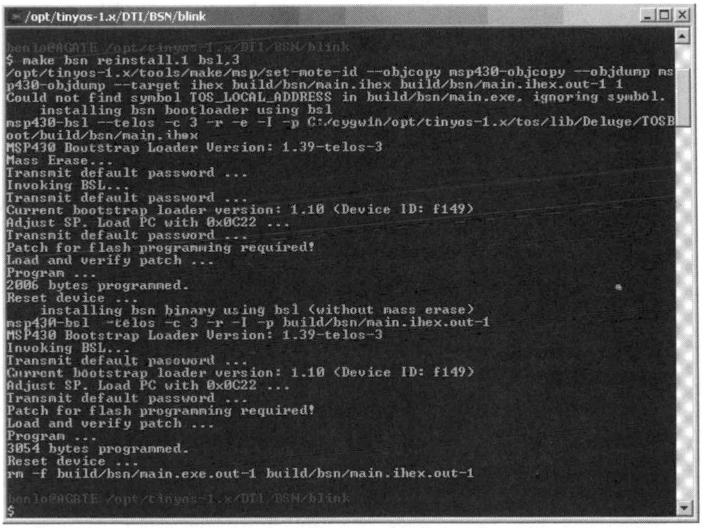

Figure B.43 Uploading a program binary onto a BSN node.

B.5.3.3 Radio Test Program

To demonstrate the wireless communication function of the BSN node, a simple RFTest program is designed. Two BSN nodes are required to test wireless communication between them. To do this, we require two different programs for the nodes, RFTestSend and RFTestRecv respectively. As shown in Figure

B.44, the `RFTestSend` is a transmitter program which sends the packets to the receiver, whereas the `RFTestRecv` program is designed to receive the packets.

RFTestSend   RFTestRecv

Figure B.44 Radio test programs.

The design of the program is relatively simple. The transmitter toggles its red LED and sends a packet to the receiver periodically (based on the time interval parameter `PACKET_INTERVAL`) and when the receiver gets the packet, it will blink the red LED at a lower frequency rate (half the frequency of the transmitter).

RFTestSend

In a similar manner to the blink program, `RFTestSend` uses the `Timer` and `Leds` interfaces to toggle the red LED and initiate the packet transmission. To send the packet to the receiver, the `GenericComm` component is used to handle the RF packet transmission. The `RFTestSend` program can be found in the `.\tinyos-1.x\bsn\Prg1\send` directory, and the configuration file and module of the program are as follows:

```
configuration RFTestSend{}
  implementation {
    components Main, RFTestSendM, GenericComm as Comm,
      TimerC, LedsC;
  Main.StdControl-> RFTestSendM;
  RFTestSendM.CommControl->Comm;
  RFTestSendM.CommSend->Comm.SendMsg[AM_MOTE_MSG];
  RFTestSendM.Timer-> TimerC.Timer[unique("Timer")];
  RFTestSendM.Leds-> LedsC;
  }                                              RFTestSend.nc
```

```
module RFTestSendM{
  provides interface StdControl;
  uses {
  interface StdControl as CommControl;
  interface SendMsg  as CommSend;
  interface Timer    as Timer;
  interface Leds;
  }
}
```

```
implementation {
  enum app{ PACKET_INTERVAL = 100, };//100 ms
  uint16_t  wSequenceNum;
    bool     fPending;
  TOS_MsgPtr pBuffer;
    TOS_Msg  Buffer;
  command result_t StdControl.init() {
    call CommControl.init();
    call Leds.init();
    wSequenceNum=0;
    fPending  = FALSE;
    pBuffer   =&Buffer;
    return SUCCESS;
  }
  command result_t StdControl.start() {
  call CommControl.start();
  call Timer.start(TIMER_REPEAT, PACKET_INTERVAL);
  return SUCCESS;
  }
  command result_t StdControl.stop() {
    call CommControl.stop();
    call Timer.stop();
  return SUCCESS;
  }
  event result_t Timer.fired() {
    uint16_t *wPtr;
    if(!fPending) {
      call Leds.redToggle();
      wPtr=(uint16_t *)(pBuffer->data);
      *wPtr=wSequenceNum++;
      fPending = TRUE;
    if(call CommSend.send(TOS_BCAST_ADDR,2,pBuffer))
     return SUCCESS;
      fPending = FALSE;
    }
    return FAIL;
  }
  event result_t CommSend.sendDone(TOS_MsgPtr pMsg,
      result_t success) {
    if(fPending && pMsg==pBuffer) fPending=FALSE;
    return SUCCESS;
  }
}                                      RFTestSendM.nc
```

As shown in the RFTestSendM module, the timer is set to trigger every
100ms, and when the timer is fired, the program will toggle the red LED and
send the packet, which consists of the sequence number (wSequenceNum), to
the receiver.

RFTestRecv

Similarly to the RFTestSend component, the RFTestRecv program uses the GenericComm to handle the RF packet communication and Leds for controlling the LEDs. However, as the RFTestRecv is designed to handle the packet received by the RFTestSend program, no timer is required. The source code for the RFTestRecv can be found in the *.\tinyos-1.x\bsn\Prg1\recv* directory, and is listed as follows:

```
configuration RFTestRecv{}
implementation {
  components Main, RFTestRecvM, GenericComm as Comm,
            LedsC;
 Main.StdControl->RFTestRecvM;
 RFTestRecvM.CommControl->Comm;
 RFTestRecvM.CommRecv-> Comm.ReceiveMsg[AM_MOTE_MSG];
 RFTestRecvM.Leds-> LedsC;
}                                         RFTestRecvC.nc
```

```
module RFTestRecvM{
 provides interface StdControl;
 uses{
   interface StdControl as CommControl;
   interface ReceiveMsg as CommRecv;
   interface Leds;
   }
}
implementation {
  enum{ CHECK_MASK = 0x0001, };
  command result_t StdControl.init() {
    call CommControl.init();
    call Leds.init();
    return SUCCESS;
  }
  command result_t StdControl.start() {
    call CommControl.start();
  return SUCCESS;
  }
  command result_t StdControl.stop() {
  call CommControl.stop();
  return SUCCESS;
  }
  event TOS_MsgPtr CommRecv.receive(TOS_MsgPtr pMsg) {
    uint16_t *wPtr;
    uint16_t wSequenceNum;
  wPtr=(uint16_t *)(pMsg->data);
  wSequenceNum=*wPtr;
  if( (wSequenceNum & CHECK_MASK) == CHECK_MASK)
```

```
    call Leds.redToggle();
  return pMsg;
  }
}                                              RFTestRecvM.nc
```

As shown in the `RFTestRecv` module, whenever a packet is received, the received `wSequenceNum` will be checked against the mask (in order to blink the LED in half of the frequency of the transmitter) and the red LED will be toggled accordingly.

Compiling and Uploading to BSN

To program the BSN nodes, you need to follow the instructions described in section B.5.3.2. However, different ID have to be set for each BSN node:

- For `RFTestSend`, set the node ID to 1

```
>make bsn install,1 bsl,yyy
```

- For `RFTestRecv`, set the node ID to 2

```
>make bsn install,2 bsl,yyy
```

B.5.3.4 Packet Address

As shown in the previous programs, a few addresses are predefined for packet transmission. Three constants are defined:

- TOS_BCAST_ADDR: address for radio broadcasting (0xffff).
- TOS_UART_ADDR: address for the USB (0x7e).
- TOS_LOCAL_ADDRESS: denotes the local address (*i.e.* the BSN node address), which is assigned when uploading the program to the node. For instance, if we use the following command to upload a program to a BSN node:

```
>make bsn install,2 bsl,3
```

The address of the node will be set to 2, *i.e.* TOS_LOCAL_ADDRESS=2 for this node.

B.5.3.5 Frequency and Channel Programming

The IEEE 802.15.4 standard specifies sixteen channels within the 2.4GHz band numbered 11-26, and the CC2420 enables user programs to choose different channels for communication, as described in section B.2.2.10. In addition,

TinyOS provides a high-level abstraction on the channel setting and allows compile time channel changes by setting the parameter "DCC242_DEF_CHANNEL" in the makefile to the specific channel (11-26) as shown in the following example (makefile for the RFTestSend program):

```
COMPONENT=RFTestSend
DEFAULT_LOCAL_GROUP := 0x44
PFLAGS += -DCC2420_DEF_CHANNEL=12
include ../../Makerules
                                        makefile
```

B.6 Conclusions

In this appendix, we have provided detailed information about the BSN development kit and its programming guide. With its miniaturised and stackable design, the BSN development kit provides a rapid prototyping platform for BSN research and development. Due to the current pace of both hardware and software development in wireless sensing, the hardware specification and software programming environment will continue to evolve. For this reason, we have provided a dedicated web site **http://www.bsn-web.info** that accompanies the contents of this book. Interested readers can use this site to find out the latest updates and useful programming resources.

References

1. Polastre J, Szewczyk R, Sharp C, Culler D. The mote revolution: low power wireless sensor network devices. In: Proceedings of Hot Chips 16: A Symposium on High Performance Chips, Stanford University, 2004.
2. Beutel J. BTnodes – a distributed environment for prototyping ad hoc networks. ETH, http://www.btnode.ethz.ch, 2005.
3. Nachman L. Imote2. http://www.tinyos.net/ttx-02-2005/platforms/ttx05-imote2.ppt, 2005.
4. Barroso A, Benson J, Murphy T, Roedig U, Sreenan C, Barton J, *et al.* The DSYS25 sensor platform. In: Proceedings of the ACM Conference on Embedded Networked Sensor Systems (Demo Abstract), Baltimore, Maryland, USA, 2004.
5. Malm EJ, Kaartinen J, Vildjiounaite E, Alahuhta P. Smart-it context architecture. European Commission, 2003.
6. Tapia EM, Marmasse N, Intille SS, Larson K. MITes: wireless portable sensors for studying behavior. In: Proceedings of the Sixth International Conference on Ubiquitous Computing, Nottingham, UK, 2004.

7. MSP430x13x, MSP430x14x, MSP430x14x1 mixed signal microcontroller. Texas Instruments, http://focus.ti.com/docs/prod/folders/print/msp430f149 .html, 2004.

8. MSP430x1xx family user's guide. Texas Instruments, http://focus.ti.com/ docs/prod/folders/print/msp430f149.html, 2004.

9. Wireless medium access control and physical layer specifications for low rate wireless personal area networks. IEEE 802.15.4, 2003.

10. CC2420 2.4GHz IEEE802.15.4/ZigBee-ready RF transceiver. Chipcon, http://www.chipcon.com/index.cfm?kat_id=2&subkat_id=12&dok_id=115, 2004.

11. Advanced encryption standard. Federal Information Processing Standards Publication 197, Department of Commerce/NIST, NIST FIPS Pub 197, 2001.

12. Atmel AT45DB041B : 4-megabit 2.5-volt or 2.7-volt data flash. Atmel, http://www.atmel.com/dyn/products/product_card.asp?family_id=616&fam ily_name=DataFlash%AE&part_id=2469, 2005.

13. Low cost 2g dual-axis accelerometer with duty cycle output ADXL202E. Analogue Devices, http://www.analogue.com/en/prod/0%2C2877%2CAD XL 202%2C00.html, 2000.

14. Multilayer chip NTC thermistors (ERTJ). Panasonic, http://rocky.digikey. com/WebLib/Panasonic/Web%20data/ERTJ%20Series.pdf, 2004.

15. Hill JL. System architecture for wireless sensor networks. University of California Berkeley, PhD Thesis, 2003.

16. Levis P, Lee N. TOSSIM: A simulator for TinyOS networks. University of California Berkeley, User Manual, 2003.

17. Hui JW, Culler D. The dynamic behavior of a data dissemination protocol for network programming at scale. In: Proceedings of the ACM Conference on Sensors and Systems, Baltimore, Maryland, USA, 2004.

18. Madden S, Hellerstein J, Hong W. TinyDB: in-network query processing in TinyOS. http://telegraph.cs.berkeley.edu/tinydb, 2003.

19. Gay D, Levis P, von Behren R, Welsh M, Brewer E, Culler D. The nesC language: a holistic approach to networked embedded systems. In: Proceedings of the ACM Conference on Programming Language Design and Implementation, San Diego, California, USA, 2003.

20. Gay D, Levis P, Culler D, Brewer E. nesC 1.1 language reference manual. http://nescc.sourceforge.net, 2003.

21. Gay D, Levis P, Culler D. Software design patterns for TinyOS. In: Proceedings of the ACM SIGPLAN/SIGBED Conference on Languages, Compilers, and Tools for Embedded Systems, Chicago, Illinois, USA, 2005.

22. Handziski V, Polastre J, Hauer J, Sharp C, Wolisz A, Culler D. The hardware abstraction architecture of TinyOS 2.x. http://www.tinyos.net/ttx-02-2005, 2005.

23. Handziski V, Polastre J, Hauer J-H, Sharp C, Wolisz A, Culler D. Flexible hardware abstraction for wireless sensor networks. In: Proceedings of the

Second European Workshop on Wireless Sensor Networks, Istanbul, Turkey, 2005.

24. Levis P, Lee N, Welsh M, Culler D. TOSSIM: accurate and scalable simulation of entire TinyOS applications. In: Proceedings of the ACM Conference on Embedded Networked Sensor Systems 2003.

25. Shnayder V, Hempstead M, Chen B-R, Allen GW, Welsh M. Simulating the power consumption of large-scale sensor network applications. In: Proceedings of the ACM Conference on Embedded Networked Sensor Systems, Baltimore, Maryland, USA, 2004.

Index